# Teacher Assessment and the Quest for Teacher Quality

## A Handbook

Edited by Mary M. Kennedy

Foreword by Marilyn Cochran-Smith

Published in Partnership with
The American Association of Colleges for Teacher Education

**JOSSEY-BASS**
A Wiley Imprint
www.josseybass.com

Published by Jossey-Bass
A Wiley Imprint
989 Market Street, San Francisco, CA 94103-1741—www.josseybass.com

Readers should be aware that Internet Web sites offered as citations and/or sources for further information may have changed or disappeared between the time this was written and when it is read.

Limit of Liability/Disclaimer of Warranty: While the publisher and author have used their best efforts in preparing this book, they make no representations or warranties with respect to the accuracy or completeness of the contents of this book and specifically disclaim any implied warranties of merchantability or fitness for a particular purpose. No warranty may be created or extended by sales representatives or written sales materials. The advice and strategies contained herein may not be suitable for your situation. You should consult with a professional where appropriate. Neither the publisher nor author shall be liable for any loss of profit or any other commercial damages, including but not limited to special, incidental, consequential, or other damages.

Jossey-Bass books and products are available through most bookstores. To contact Jossey-Bass directly call our Customer Care Department within the U.S. at 800-956-7739, outside the U.S. at 317-572-3986, or fax 317-572-4002.

Jossey-Bass also publishes its books in a variety of electronic formats. Some content that appears in print may not be available in electronic books.

**Library of Congress Cataloging-in-Publication Data**

Teacher assessment and the quest for teacher quality : a handbook / edited by Mary M. Kennedy ; foreword by Marilyn Cochran-Smith.—1st ed.
p. cm.
"Published in Partnership with The American Association of Colleges for Teacher Education."
Includes bibliographical references and index.
ISBN 978-0-470-38833-4 (cloth)
1. Teachers—Rating of—United States. 2. Prediction of teacher success—United States. 3. Effective teaching—United States. I. Kennedy, Mary M. II. American Association of Colleges for Teacher Education.
LB2838.T386 2010
371.14'4—dc22

2009041056

Printed in the United States of America
FIRST EDITION

*HB Printing*                                        10 9 8 7 6 5 4 3 2 1

# CONTENTS

The Authors   v

Foreword   xiii
   *Marilyn Cochran-Smith*

Introduction: The Uncertain Relationship Between Teacher Assessment and
   Teacher Quality   1
   *Mary M. Kennedy*

PART ONE: ASSESSMENT OF TEACHER CANDIDATES   7

1  The Use of Portfolios in Preservice Teacher Education: A Critical
   Appraisal   9
   *Ginette Delandshere, Anthony R. Petrosky*

2  Disposition Assessment: The Science and Psychology of Teacher
   Selection   43
   *Laurie Moses Hines*

**PART TWO: ASSESSMENT FOR TRANSITION INTO TEACHING**  67

3  Assessment for Learning in Preservice Teacher Education: Performance-Based Assessments  69
*Ruth Chung Wei, Raymond L. Pecheone*

4  Licensure Tests: Their Use and Value for Increasing Teacher Quality  133
*Dan Goldhaber*

5  Hiring Decisions  149
*Dane A. Delli*

**PART THREE: ASSESSMENT OF PRACTICING TEACHERS**  163

6  The Role of Formative Assessments in New Teacher Induction  165
*Peter Youngs, Ben Pogodzinski, Mark Low*

7  Assessing for Teacher Tenure  201
*Gary Sykes, Sarah Winchell*

8  Approaches to Annual Performance Assessment  225
*Mary M. Kennedy*

9  Value-Added: Assessing Teachers' Contributions to Student Achievement  251
*Douglas N. Harris, Daniel F. McCaffrey*

10  The National Board for Professional Teaching Standards: An Investment for the Future?  283
*Jillian P. Reese*

11  Judging Teachers: The Law of Teacher Dismissals  297
*Diana Pullin*

**PART FOUR: BROADER ASSESSMENT ISSUES**  335

12  Setting Standards for Teacher Evaluation  337
*Barbara B. Howard, Arlen R. Gullickson*

13  Thinking Systemically About Assessment Practice  355
*Pamela A. Moss*

14  Teacher Quality: An American Educational Dilemma  375
*David K. Cohen*

Discussion Questions  403

Index  405

# THE AUTHORS

*Marilyn Cochran-Smith* is John E. Cawthorne Professor of Education and director of the doctoral program in curriculum and instruction at the Lynch School of Education, Boston College. She is a member of the National Academy of Education and a former president of the American Educational Research Association. Her eighth book, *Inquiry as Stance: Practitioner Research for the Next Generation* (with Susan L. Lytle), was published in 2009. Cochran-Smith is coeditor (with Ken Zeichner) of *Studying Teacher Education: The Report of the AERA Panel on Research and Teacher Education,* coeditor (with Sharon Feiman Nemser, John McIntyre, and Kelly Demers) of the *Third Handbook of Research on Teacher Education,* and editor of the *Journal of Teacher Education* from 2000 to 2006. She is on the National Research Council's committee on teacher preparation in the United States, and she was the C. J. Koh Chair at the National Institute of Education in Singapore. She writes and speaks frequently about teacher education research practice and policy, as well as practitioner research, teacher learning, and social justice.

*David K. Cohen* is John Dewey Collegiate Professor of Education and professor of public policy at the University of Michigan. He received his doctorate from the University of Rochester in European intellectual history in 1960. He worked in the civil rights movement in the 1960s and led a study of northern school segregation at the U.S. Commission on Civil Rights in 1966–1967. He held professorships at the Harvard Graduate School of Education and Michigan State University College of Education. He joined the University of Michigan in 1993. His work includes studies of efforts to reform schools and teaching, the relations between policy and instruction, the nature of teaching practice, the evaluation of educational experiments, the relations between research and policy, and the effects of school improvement interventions. His books include *Learning Policy* (with Heather Hill); *Usable Knowledge: Social Science and Social Problem Solving* (with Charles E. Lindblom); and *The Shopping Mall High School* (with Arthur G. Powell and Eleanor Farrar). His most recent book (with Susan L. Moffitt) is *The Ordeal of Equality: Can Federal Regulation Fix the Schools?* (2009).

*Ginette Delandshere* is a professor in the School of Education at Indiana University in Bloomington, Indiana. She directs the inquiry methodology graduate program and teaches courses in research methodology, measurement and assessment, and statistics applied to social science research. Her research interests include the study of social science research methodology, as well as the study of the assumptions underlying educational measurement and assessment theories and practices.

*Dane A. Delli* is superintendent of River Trails School District 26 in Mount Prospect, Illinois, and has worked previously as a classroom teacher, high school principal, assistant superintendent for human resources, and university professor. He received his Ph.D. in educational policy and leadership from the Ohio State University and served on the faculty at Loyola University Chicago. He has published research in *Educational Administration Quarterly* and the *Journal of Personnel Evaluation in Education*. His most recent study, "Community Member Perceptions of Teacher Candidates During Panel Employment Interviews: Does Personality Mean More Than Competence?" appears in the *Journal of School Public Relations*. Delli's research interests focus on teacher hiring practices, including commercially designed employment interviews and psychological influences on face-to-face employment interviews. Currently he is investigating the extent to which school administrators regret making hiring decisions of classroom teachers.

*Dan Goldhaber* is a professor of public affairs at the University of Washington, an affiliated scholar at the Urban Institute, and editor of *Education Finance and Policy*. He served as an elected member of the Alexandria City School Board from 1997 to 2002. His work focuses on issues of educational productivity and reform at the K–12 level, and the relationship between teacher labor markets and teacher quality. Goldhaber's current research addresses teacher labor markets and the role that teacher pay structure plays in teacher recruitment and retention; the relationship between teacher licensure test performance and student achievement; the stability of teacher effectiveness measures over time; the influence of human resource practices on teacher turnover and quality; and the role of community colleges in higher education. Goldhaber holds degrees from the University of Vermont (B.A. in economics) and Cornell University (M.S. and Ph.D. in labor economics).

*Arlen R. Gullickson* is professor emeritus at Western Michigan University. He served as the Evaluation Center director from 2002 to 2007 and as its chief of staff from 1991 to 2002. Gullickson chaired the Joint Committee on Standards for Educational Evaluation from 1998 to 2008 during the time that the committee developed *The Student Evaluation Standards* (2003), revised *The Personnel Evaluation Standards* (2009), and made major strides in revising *The Program Evaluation Standards*, Second Edition (1994) for the forthcoming third edition. He currently directs three projects. One focuses on research related to assessment for learning, and a second provides evaluation support services for the National Science Foundation's Advanced Technological Education Program focusing on improvement in technology education. The third is developing and disseminating a tool kit to support teachers' efforts to improve their student evaluation practices.

*Douglas N. Harris* is an economist and associate professor of educational policy studies at the University of Wisconsin at Madison. His research combines advanced economic analysis with practical understanding of schools to develop positive directions for school reforms in areas like teacher quality, teacher labor markets, standards, and accountability. In his current work, with Eric Camburn, he is estimating the value-added of school principals as well as how successful different types of principals are in attracting and retaining high-value-added teachers. He also recently chaired the National Conferences on Value-Added with events in Madison and Washington, D.C. He presents his work regularly to educators and policymakers and consults with a wide variety of state and federal education agencies, think tanks, and education associations. Previously he was a school board member of the Florida State University School, a K–12 charter school in Tallahassee.

*Laurie Moses Hines* is an assistant professor of education at Kent State University-Trumbull, where she teaches cultural foundations of education to teacher education majors and U.S. and world history to undergraduate students. Her research focuses on the history and policy of teacher education, higher education, and teacher professionalization. She has served as assistant editor for the *History of Education Quarterly* and has published in that journal, as well as in *Education Next* and a number of edited volumes. She currently serves as first vice president of Pi Lambda Theta, an honorary and professional organization for teachers. Hines earned her Ph.D. in history of education and American studies from Indiana University-Bloomington.

*Barbara B. Howard* is an assistant professor and school administration program coordinator in the Department of Leadership and Educational Studies at Appalachian State University in Boone, North Carolina. She has been a teacher, assistant principal, principal, and central office executive director. As project director for SERVE Regional Education Lab, she developed and researched models of teacher evaluation that stressed standards-based accountability and guidance for professional growth. She served as the task-force chair for the development of the *Personnel Evaluation Standards*, Second Edition, issued by the Joint Committee on Standards for Educational Evaluation. Her research interests are grounded in personnel evaluation with its natural connection to leadership, teacher quality, and teacher development. She has presented at numerous national conferences and published both articles and book chapters on her work.

*Mary M. Kennedy* is a professor of education at Michigan State University. Her scholarship focuses on defining teacher quality and identifying the factors that most influence teacher quality. She has examined the influences of teacher education, research knowledge, attitudes and beliefs, credentials, and school context. From 1986 to 1994, she directed the National Center for Research on Teacher Learning. She has published three books addressing the relationship between knowledge and teaching and has won five awards for her work, most recently the prestigious Margaret B. Lindsey Award For Outstanding Research in Teacher Education. Her book *Inside Teaching: How Classroom Life Undermines Reform* (2005) addresses the influence of school context on the quality of teaching practices and shows how local circumstances make it difficult for teachers to live up to reform expectations. Kennedy has consulted with four ministries of education, the World Bank, and a host of national organizations and has published numerous articles on teaching, research, and policy.

*Mark Low* is a doctoral candidate in the teaching, curriculum, and education policy program at Michigan State University; he is also a research associate for Policy Studies Associates in Washington, D.C. His dissertation draws on theories of person-organization fit and uses social network analyses to understand the commitment levels of early-career teachers in public and Catholic high schools. His research interests include the development of human capital in schools and the ways in which education policies promote or interfere with that development.

*Daniel F. McCaffrey* is a senior statistician at the Rand Corporation. His research interests are in accountability and assessment; substance use and adolescent substance abuse treatment; and value-added modeling. His most recent projects at Rand include studies of causal effects estimates using value-added assessment: studying the effects of value-added assessments on educators' practices and studying student outcomes using data from the Pennsylvania Value-Added Assessment System. He is also working on methods for improving value-added estimation and developing statistical methods for estimating teacher effects using longitudinal student achievement data. He earned his Ph.D. in statistics from North Carolina State University.

*Pamela A. Moss* is a professor of education at the University of Michigan School of Education. Her research agenda focuses on validity theory in educational assessment, assessment as a social practice, and the assessment of teaching. Her approach to the study of assessment engages the critical potential of dialogue across research discourses—educational measurement, hermeneutics and critical theory, and sociocultural studies—sometimes to complement, sometimes to challenge established theory and practice in assessment. Her research has been funded by the Spencer Foundation, the Institute for Education Sciences, and the National Science Foundation. She was a member of the joint committee revising the 1999 AERA, APA, and NCME *Standards for Educational and Psychological Testing,* of the National Research Council's Committee on Assessment and Teacher Quality, and chair of AERA's task force on *Standards for Reporting on Empirical Social Science Research in AERA Publications.* She is cofounder and coeditor of the journal *Measurement: Interdisciplinary Research and Perspectives;* editor of the 2007 Yearbook for the National Society for the Study of Education, *Evidence and Decision Making;* and senior coeditor of the 2008 volume *Assessment, Equity, and Opportunity to Learn,* published by Cambridge University Press. She received her Ph.D. in educational research methods from the University of Pittsburgh.

*Raymond L. Pecheone* is the co–executive director of the Stanford School Redesign Network LEADS and the director of the Performance Assessment for California Teachers (PACT) program. PACT is a consortium of thirty-two California universities that have joined together to develop a reliable and valid preservice measure of teaching. Formerly he was the Connecticut bureau chief for curriculum, research, and assessment and developed the first performance-based licensure and induction system for beginning teachers in the nation. In addition, he cofounded the Interstate New Teacher Assessment and Support Consortium, and codirected the first assessment development laboratory for the National Board for Professional Teaching Standards. Pecheone has led the development of the redesign of the New York State's Regents Examinations, as well as served as a consultant to the Council of Chief State School Officers and Educational Testing Service for the development and validation of a performance-based assessment for school administrators.

*Anthony R. Petrosky*, associate dean of the School of Education at the University of Pittsburgh, holds a joint appointment as a professor in the School of Education and the English Department. Along with Stephanie McConachie, he codirects the English Language Arts Disciplinary Literacy Project in the Institute for Learning at the Learning Research Development Center. With her, he is the coeditor of *Content Matters: A Disciplinary Literacy Approach to Improving Student Learning*. He was the principal investigator and codirector of the Early Adolescence English Language Arts Assessment Development Lab for the National Board for Professional Teaching Standards. His first collection of poetry, *Jurgis Petraskas*, published by Louisiana State University Press, received the Walt Whitman Award from the Academy of American Poets and a Notable Book Award from the American Library Association. Along with David Bartholomae, he is the coauthor and coeditor of four books, including *Ways of Reading*.

*Ben Pogodzinski* is a postdoctoral fellow in the Curry School of Education at the University of Virginia. His research interests focus on state and district policy related to teacher quality. In particular, he studies how such policies, school-level social networks, and teacher unions influence teachers' instructional practices, commitment levels, and labor market decisions.

*Diana Pullin*, an attorney and an educator, is a professor in the Lynch School of Education and an affiliate professor of law at Boston College. She has served as legal counsel for students, teachers, and school systems in education law and testing disputes. She has published numerous books, chapters, and articles on education law and public policy, educational and employment testing, and individuals with disabilities. She serves on the Board on Testing and Assessment of the National Research Council of the National Academy of Sciences and is associate editor of the interdisciplinary journal *Educational Policy*.

∽

*Jillian P. Reese* is the coordinator of the principal and superintendent preparation programs at Penn State University, where she earned her Ph.D. from the educational leadership program. Under the mentorship of the late William Boyd, Reese studied education vouchers and other school choice issues. Her dissertation was a finalist for the Outstanding Dissertation Award for the Politics of Education Association. Reese has written and presented on a variety of other policy issues, including the National Board, the National Council for Accreditation of Teacher Education, No Child Left Behind, and state standards for leadership preparation. She previously served as the associate director of the Pennsylvania School Study Council and the book review editor for the *American Journal of Education*. Prior to her work in higher education, she taught at the elementary level in Colorado.

∽

*Gary Sykes* is a professor in the Department of Teacher Education, College of Education, Michigan State University. He teaches in the teacher preparation program and conducts policy-related research around issues of teachers and teaching, teacher education, and school staffing. His most recent publications are (coedited with Barbara Schneider and David Plank) *Handbook of Education Policy Research* (2009); and (with Kenne Dibner) "Fifty Years of Federal Teacher Policy: An Appraisal" (2009), a paper for the Center on Education Policy.

∽

*Ruth Chung Wei* is director of assessment research and development at the Stanford University School Redesign Network, where she leads performance-based assessment initiatives in high schools with the goal of promoting more balanced, multiple-measures assessment practices and policies in public schools. In the past, she has been a research associate for the Performance Assessment for California Teachers (PACT), supporting design work as well as conducting validity and reliability studies for PACT. Her research interests also include teachers' professional learning, teacher quality policy, and educative assessment practices. A former secondary school teacher in the New York City public schools, she completed her doctorate in education at Stanford University.

∽

*Sarah Winchell* is a doctoral student in education policy at Michigan State University. Previously she was a middle school language arts teacher in Brooklyn, New York, and the coordinator of a high school enrichment program. She has contributed to research on the effects of school racial composition and stability on students' civic outcomes, and she has worked with NAEP data to analyze how teachers' roles in accountability and professional development are related to student math performance. Her research interests also include teacher evaluation, teacher performance pay, and the unintended consequences of using single measures to evaluate work in complex organizations.

∽

*Peter Youngs* is an assistant professor of educational policy at Michigan State University. His research interests focus on education policy effects on teaching and learning in the core academic subjects. In particular, his work concentrates on state and district policy related to teacher preparation, induction, and professional development in the United States and their effects on teachers' instructional practices, commitment to teaching, and retention in the teaching profession. He is currently serving as principal investigator for a Carnegie Corporation–funded study of new teachers in Michigan and Indiana school districts. This study employs social network analysis and the experience sampling method data to better understand how teacher characteristics and school context affect beginning teacher commitment, retention, and effectiveness. His recent publications have appeared in *Teachers College Record, Educational Administration Quarterly, Journal of Education Policy,* and *Studying Teacher Education: The Report of the AERA Panel on Research and Teacher Education.*

# FOREWORD

At least as far as education goes, we live in an age of accountability. It is now commonplace for nearly every aspect of the education enterprise to be assessed and regulated through tests and other instruments, quality control procedures, and even entire accountability systems. Nowhere is this more evident than in teaching and teacher education where terms like *outcomes, results, consequences, effectiveness, impact, bottom lines, what works, empirical research base,* and *evidence* have been stitched so seamlessly into the logic of the discourse that they are now unremarkable. As the chapters in this handbook make clear, there are assessments for gauging the quality of virtually every aspect of teaching: recruitment, preparation, certification, induction, licensure, classroom performance, beliefs and dispositions, professional development, and school and curricular change. It is worth noting, of course, as many of the chapters in this handbook do, that accountability and assessment are not new to either the teaching profession or education more generally. Various kinds of teacher tests, for example, have been used since the mid-nineteenth century (Wilson & Youngs, 2005), and as Cuban (2004) pointed out a few years ago, contrary to the then-popular belief that accountability was a relatively new development in education, public education has never been unaccountable. What has changed—and essentially what makes this the age of accountability—are the prevailing conceptions of accountability, which have shifted over the past fifty years from the prudent use of resources to the effective production of desired results, as well as new ideas about the presumed link between assessment and quality.

This handbook addresses and sorts out many of the complex issues related to teacher assessment and teacher quality, and the connections between the two. This is no small task, given the numerous ways and time points at which teacher quality is assessed, the multitude of stakeholders with a vested interest in assessment processes and assessment products, the competing policy and political agendas to which various assessments of teachers and teaching are attached, and ongoing controversies about what *teacher quality* means and why it is important. One of the strengths of this handbook is that it does not shy away from or attempt to reduce the messiness of these issues by offering a simplified notion of assessment and quality. Rather, both the chapters in the book and the framework according to which they are juxtaposed are intended to focus on and make sense of the complexities and disagreements about teacher quality and assessment, including conceptual and methodological dilemmas, theoretical and practical questions, and systemic issues.

The broad and expansive notion of teacher assessment that is used to organize the chapters in this handbook is, in and of itself, a contribution to the field that many readers will find useful. Here teacher assessment is characterized in terms of three dimensions: (1) the time point during the process of teacher development at which an assessment is made (for example, during or at the end of the initial preparation period, once a teacher is on the job as the teacher of record, or following a period of substantial experience as a teacher); (2) the dimension of teacher quality that is assessed (for example, teachers' beliefs and values, their ability to reason and learn from teaching in an ongoing way, or the results of teaching in terms of students' measured learning); and (3) the type of assessment that is used (for example, teacher licensure or certification tests, portfolios representing teacher candidates' or teachers' work, or value-added assessments of teacher quality based on students' test score gains).

In addition to these three dimensions, the chapters take into account the differing purposes behind various teacher assessments and their short- and long-term consequences, such as assessments of teacher candidates' or students' learning that are used to make judgments about teacher preparation programs; assessments completed as part of the process of hiring, firing, or tenuring teachers; and assessments that are used to recommend policy and practice regarding the overall enterprise of teacher education or the larger teaching profession. Further complicating all of this is the fact that underlying the multiple dimensions and various purposes of teacher assessment are differing conceptions of the purposes of teaching and of education writ large, as well as different conceptions of the meanings of teachers' work as social and cultural activity. If this volume made no other contribution to the field than its multifaceted and insightful framework for sorting out the myriad approaches to assessing teacher quality, it would have done its job and earned the appreciation of many readers. But this handbook does much more.

Taking on complex and ambitious agendas related to teaching and teacher education is not a new pursuit for Mary Kennedy, the editor of this lengthy volume. Several of her previous analyses have undertaken similar tasks. For example, nearly fifteen years ago—and before it was a popular issue in teacher education—Kennedy (1995) suggested that in order to draw conclusions from research about whether teacher education made a difference, differing research genres had to be identified and sorted out. Based on the idea that these genres varied according to the way the question of effectiveness was framed in the first place and then how particular research methods were used to explore that question, Kennedy identified five research genres for assessing the effectiveness of teacher education. There have been many developments in assessments of teaching and teacher education over the past decade and a half, including rich new data sources, more powerful analytical techniques, and increasingly sophisticated researchers. But the contribution of Kennedy's earlier framework is not outdated, and I suspect that the new framework she offers in this book will also endure. These frameworks have longevity because of their capacity to sort out highly complex issues related to assessment.

As the chapters in this handbook make clear, one of the most important complexities involved in understanding teacher quality and assessment is the fact that there are multiple, but often unspecified and unexamined, definitions of *teacher quality*. Kennedy makes this point in the Introduction, noting that in spite of widespread agreement that teacher quality matters, there is no common definition. Policymakers and educational leaders with different interests, such as teacher recruitment or the equitable distribution of well-qualified teachers across student populations, also have widely varying notions about what they mean by teacher quality.

In addition to the chapters in this volume, there are many other examples of the lack of consensus about how to define teacher quality. My own favorite examples represent what are perhaps the extreme ends of a continuum (Cochran-Smith, 2005). At one extreme is Eric Hanushek's (2002) definition of *teacher quality* based on two decades of research on the impact of school inputs on students' achievement: "In simplest terms, if the objective is to improve student performance, student performance should be the focal point of policy.... I use a simple definition of teacher quality: good teachers are ones who get large gains in student achievement for their classes; bad teachers are just the opposite" (pp. 2–3). Here Hanushek defined and operationalized teacher quality solely and fully in terms of pupil performance. From this perspective, the point is to identify major differences in student achievement gains that are linked to teachers and then suggest implications regarding incentives programs, school accountability systems, and policies regarding the placement of teachers and students. Although he referred to complex econometric analyses, Hanushek's point throughout the chapter from which this quotation is drawn was straightforward and simple: teacher quality is test score gains; to improve gain scores, assessments and public policy should be geared to test scores, not school inputs.

In contrast, and probably at the other extreme, the definition of *teacher quality* posited by philosopher Gary Fenstermacher and teacher educator Virginia Richardson (Fenstermacher & Richardson, 2005) is not at all straightforward. They defined teacher quality as both good and successful teaching:

> By *good* teaching, we mean that the content taught accords with disciplinary standards of adequacy and completeness, and that the methods employed are age appropriate, morally defensible, and undertaken with the intention of enhancing the learner's competence with respect to the content studied.... By *successful* teaching we mean that the learner actually acquires, to some reasonable and acceptable level of proficiency, what the teacher is engaged in teaching.... Learning is more likely to occur when good teaching is joined with the other three conditions (willingness and effort, social surround, and opportunity).... When [the additional three conditions for learning are in place], then all conditions for quality teaching have been met [p. 191].

Obviously Fenstermacher and Richardson's definition of teacher quality, which is abbreviated here, is considerably longer than Hanushek's. Drawing on an array of conceptual and empirical work, they raised questions, pointed to differences in definitions of learning, and sorted out the psychological, logical, and moral aspects of teaching. No one would ever describe their definition of quality teaching as simple or straightforward.

Although the first definition of *teacher quality* is simple, linear, and causal and the second is complex, nuanced, and contingent, the major point is that neither of these is the right one, as this handbook confirms. Although both definitions of *teacher quality* are contemporary, they represent dramatically different agendas and purposes, and they vary enormously in terms of whether and how much of the complexity of teaching they attempt to capture. In this handbook, Chapter Nine by Harris and McCaffrey on value-added assessments of teachers' contributions to students' achievement and Chapter Four by Goldhaber on teacher licensure tests are closer to Hanushek's work in terms of the definition of teacher quality they use, while Chapter One by Delandshere and Petrosky on teacher portfolios in preservice teacher education and Chapter Ten by Reese on National Board certification are closer to the definition elaborated by Fenstermacher and Richardson. As Kennedy reminds us in the Introduction to the handbook, in light of the many dimensions of teacher quality that contemporary assessments are intended to measure, it might be wise for the education community to begin to talk about teacher *qualities* rather than to proceed as if the singular term, *teacher quality,* means one thing that is straightforward and clear in terms of measurement and policy implications.

Taken together, the chapters in this handbook present a useful and thoughtful analysis of a wide array of teacher quality assessments. Some of these approaches to assessment will be familiar to readers, such as Chapter One by Delandshere and Petrosky on teacher portfolios, or Chapter Ten on the National Board for Professional Teaching Standards. Others will be less familiar, such as Pullin's Chapter Eleven on teacher performance assessments that are currently used in legal proceedings to dismiss teachers, or Delli's Chapter Five on commercially designed teacher selection and hiring interviews. Some of the teacher assessments described in the handbook are now more or less accepted as the norm in teaching and teacher preparation, such as teacher assessments related to tenure decisions, explored by Sykes and Winchell in Chapter Seven; others, such as assessments of teacher candidates that are both formative and high stakes, as Chung Wei and Pecheone address in Chapter Three, and the assessment of teachers' dispositions, that Hines describes in Chapter Two, represent, respectively, new or controversial territory. Some chapters describe relatively new practices, such as Chapter Six on induction, while others describe practices that have existed for decades, such as Chapter Eight on annual performance reviews. The three closing chapters provide useful frames for viewing the preceding chapters by placing them in the context of personnel standards, measurement standards, and policy dilemmas, respectively.

Wisely, most of the chapters begin with an analysis of the political, historical, and social contexts within which a particular kind of assessment emerged. These discussions are especially valuable since they make the point that most contemporary assessments have roots that are much deeper than is often assumed. Many of the tensions that drive debates about teaching and the teaching profession—such as the tension between the technical and liberal aspects of teaching or the tension between teaching's role in the reproduction or reconstruction of the larger social structure—emerge, fade, and reemerge periodically. New incarnations of perennial issues may or may not appear on the surface to be different from previous incarnations, and in fact, their historically iterative dimensions are often unacknowledged. Nevertheless, as this handbook shows, the tensions underlying assessments of teacher quality are both old and new. They are new in that they are woven into the tapestry of changed and changing political, social, and economic times and thus have a different set of implications each time they reemerge in prominence. But they are also old in that they represent enduring and deep disagreements in society about the purposes of schooling, the value of teaching, and the education of teachers.

Each of the assessments or assessment systems reviewed in this handbook is intended to improve teacher quality and assumed to have the capacity to do so. Most of the chapters in this volume consider the operating assumptions about how things in schools work that are implicit in the particular assessment. In doing so, they get at what Argyris and Schön (1978) first called the theories of action that underlie change, or the assumed logic behind educational leaders' and policymakers' intended changes and the flow of processes assumed to function as the mechanisms and levers by which particular educational changes are enacted in context. Like their varying definitions of teacher quality, the theories of action underlying the approaches to assessment that are explored in the many chapters here are quite different from one another. They represent dramatically different views about not simply what the most important aspects of teacher quality are, but also how assessment can improve teacher quality systematically. Many of the chapters also make the argument that despite the research that is available about each type of teacher quality assessment, there is a lack of empirical evidence about systematic links between the assessment and teacher effectiveness. Most of the chapters examine why this is so and provide promising directions for continued research and analysis.

There is no question that this book will become a valuable reference for the education and policy communities. Readers will find it valuable in terms of the expansive array of conceptual and empirical research each chapter reviews and in terms of how the chapters are arranged to talk to each other regarding the many existing controversies about teacher quality and assessment.

MARILYN COCHRAN-SMITH
*John E. Cawthorne Professor of Education and Director of the Doctoral*
*Program in Curriculum and Instruction*
*Lynch School of Education*
*Boston College*

# REFERENCES

Argyris, C., & Schön, D. (1978). *Organizational learning: A theory of action perspective.* Reading, MA: Addison-Wesley.

Cochran-Smith, M. (2005). The politics of teacher education and the curse of complexity. *Journal of Teacher Education, 56*(3), 181–185.

Cuban, L. (2004). Looking through the rearview mirror at school accountability. In K. Sirotnik (Ed.), *Holding accountability accountable* (pp. 18–34). New York: Teachers College Press.

Fenstermacher, G., & Richardson, V. (2005). On making determinations of quality in teaching. *Teachers College Record, 107*(1), 186–213.

Hanushek, E. (2002). Teacher quality. In L. Izumi & W. Evers (Eds.), *Teacher quality* (pp. 1–12). Palo Alto, CA: Hoover Institution.

Kennedy, M. M. (1995). Research genres in teacher education. In F. Murray (Ed.), *Knowledge base in teacher education* (pp. 120–152). New York: McGraw-Hill.

Wilson, S., & Youngs, P. (2005). Research on accountability processes in teacher education. In M. Cochran-Smith & K. Zeichner (Eds.), *Studying teacher education: The report of the AERA panel on research and teacher education* (pp. 591–644). Mahwah, NJ: Erlbaum.

# American Association of Colleges for Teacher Education

*Serving Learners*

The American Association of Colleges for Teacher Education (AACTE) is a national alliance of educator preparation programs dedicated to the highest quality professional development of teachers and school leaders in order to enhance PK–12 student learning. The eight hundred institutions holding AACTE membership represent public and private colleges and universities in every state, the District of Columbia, the Virgin Islands, Puerto Rico, and Guam. AACTE's reach and influence fuel its mission of serving learners by providing all school personnel with superior training and continuing education.

# The Uncertain Relationship Between Teacher Assessment and Teacher Quality

Mary M. Kennedy

*Michigan State University*

Probably no other profession is subjected to more assessments with less effect than is the teaching profession. College students who aspire to teach are assessed when they apply for admission to college and assessed again when they enroll in teacher education programs. They are assessed throughout their course work and during their student teaching experience. Programs of teacher education use their assessments of their candidates to evaluate themselves. Once candidates are graduated, they must take licensure tests. When they apply for jobs, their prospective employers use interviews to evaluate their dispositions and values. Once hired, they may be assessed during an induction period, as part of a tenure-granting process, or as part of an annual review process. These assessments may focus on direct observation of classroom lessons, professional activities or participation in professional development, or how much their students actually learn. If teachers seek advanced certification from the National Board for Professional Teaching Standards they are assessed again, and if they are dismissed from their jobs, some form of assessment is likely involved in that process as well.

One cannot help but ask whether, and to what extent, these various assessments are contributing to improvements in the quality of any individual teachers or to the quality of the workforce as a whole. Despite the number and variety of assessments at our disposal, many observers remain dissatisfied with the quality of the nation's teaching workforce. Ironically, whenever new

1

problems with teachers are identified, one of the solutions frequently proposed is to introduce a new assessment.

How can an enterprise with so many quality control devices continue to dissatisfy so many observers? Without a better understanding of the relationship between our assessments and vision of teacher quality, we will not resolve this dilemma. At issue is the question of whether these assessments are capable of measuring relevant teacher qualities or providing evidence that can be used to improve or reward the qualities we value.

Two problems make the quest for teacher quality especially difficult. One is that teacher assessments routinely overlook the role that students play in their own learning. This issue became strikingly clear to me last year when a Chinese graduate student raised a question about teachers' daily routines. Further discussion revealed that in China, teachers can leave their students alone in the classroom at any time, knowing that the students will study during the teacher's absence because they understand that it is in their interests to do so. This is not the case in the United States, and teachers spend a great deal of intellectual and emotional energy searching for ways to entice students into curricular content.

The second problem is related to the first, in the sense that the task of teaching is not well understood. For some, it is simply a matter of imparting knowledge, so tests of knowledge are the best indicator of preparedness to teach. For others, it is a matter of motivating students or engaging students with content. For still others, it is a matter of skillful behaviors. We argue about whether the qualities that lead to successful teaching lie in teachers' knowledge, actions, character traits, or beliefs and values, and the reason we argue about this is that we really do not know how these different qualities influence student learning and consequently are not sure which qualities should be assessed.

The aim of this book is to examine these various ideas about teaching and their associated assessments, both individually and collectively, for their potential to improve teacher quality. The book is designed to examine the entire system, following the sequence of assessments that teachers undergo as they move through their own education and into the workforce. In Part One, we examine assessments that occur when teacher candidates are still students in college. In Part Two, we examine assessments that occur during the transition from college student to employed teacher. Part Three discusses assessments that occur after teachers are employed, beginning with their induction experiences and moving through to momentous decisions such as professional recognition or, on the other side, dismissal. In Part Four, authors address broader questions about the relationship between teacher assessment and teacher quality. Chapter Twelve examines teacher assessment from the standpoint of personnel evaluation standards, Chapter Thirteen from the standpoint of measurement, and Chapter Fourteen from the standpoint of the American education policy system more broadly.

With respect to the problem of definition, the term *teacher quality* has itself become so widely used that it lacks a clear meaning. How can we know whether teacher assessments are helping if we do not have a clear sense of what constitutes teacher quality? As researchers and policy analysts enter into debates about teacher quality, they use the phrase to refer to very different things. For example, people interested in recruitment often use *teacher quality* to refer to tested ability (Gitomer & Latham, 2000; Weaver, 1983; Corcoran, Evans, & Schwab, 2004). These authors want us to design recruitment practices that entice people with higher test scores to become teachers. Meanwhile, people interested in the equitable distribution of teachers across student populations often use the phrase *teacher quality* to refer to credentials (Ingersoll, 2006; Peske & Haycock, 2006). These authors want to ensure that all students have access to teachers who have obtained comparable licenses and certificates. For them, certificates and teaching experience are indicators of teacher quality. Within teacher education, we often find faculty who hope to produce teachers who can reason about their work and learn from their own experiences (Hiebert, Morris, Berk, & Jansen, 2007; Rosaen, Lundeberg, Cooper, Fritzen, & Terpstra, 2008). Their hope is to produce novices who can continue to grow over time.

Still other people use the phrase *teacher quality* to refer to the quality of teachers' classroom practices (Desimone, Smith, & Ueno, 2006; Smith, Desimone, & Ueno, 2005). These authors want to improve the things teachers actually do inside their classrooms when teaching students. For them, specific teaching practices are indicators of teacher quality. Then there are people who think about the most productive use of expenditures and often use the phrase *teacher quality* to refer to teachers' effectiveness at raising student achievement (Krieg, 2006; Hedges, Laine, & Greenwald, 1994). For them, student achievement gains are indicators of teacher quality. And there are always people who want teachers to subscribe to particular beliefs and values, for in their mind, these values are the chief indicator of teacher quality (Osguthorpe, 2008; Olafson & Schraw, 2006).

These are not the only definitions of *teacher quality* available, nor are their associated indicators—test scores, credentials, observed performance, and so forth—the only available indicators of teacher quality. But the list points to the different dimensions of teacher quality and suggests that perhaps we need to start talking about teacher *qualities* rather than teacher *quality*. This slight change in language reminds us that we need to be clear about the particular kind of qualities we want. True understanding of teacher quality requires a recognition that these many facets are distinct, not always overlapping, and not always related to each other.

Such variations in meanings should not be surprising, for there are indeed numerous qualities that are important to teaching, each of which may be important for different reasons to different people. And once we acknowledge the multiple qualities important to teaching, the number and variety of teacher assessments may seem more sensible, for these various assessments tend to focus on different qualities. For example, we use college course assignments to assess reasoning, licensure tests to evaluate knowledge, hiring interviews to assess dispositions and values, performance assessments to evaluate their classroom behavior, and so forth. Viewed in this way, the system makes sense.

The sequence of chapters in this book reflects the sequence of experiences teachers are likely to have, but readers interested in particular types of assessment or in particular teacher qualities may need to look across the entire book to find relevant material. Table I.1 provides a rough index to where chapters addressing these different qualities are located.

If we had a theory of how teachers learn to teach, perhaps we could devise a sequence of assessments that would reflect the learning process itself—one that could check that nascent teachers had cleared each known hurdle on their

### Table I.1. Guide to the Chapters

| Dimension of Teacher Quality | Type of Assessment | Chapters and Authors |
|---|---|---|
| Tested ability | Licensure tests | Chapter Four (Goldhaber) |
| Beliefs and values | Value inventories, class projects | Chapter Two (Hines) |
|  | Hiring interviews | Chapter Five (Delli) |
| Learning to learn, reasoning about teaching | Portfolios | Chapter One (Delandshere and Petrosky) |
|  |  | Chapter Three (Wei and Pecheone) |
|  |  | Chapter Ten (Reese) |
| Classroom practices | Performance assessments | Chapter Six (Youngs, Pogodzinski, and Low) |
|  |  | Chapter Eight (Kennedy) |
| Student learning | Value-added assessments | Chapter Nine (Harris and McCaffrey) |
| Global decisions | Tenure decisions | Chapter Seven (Sykes and Winchell) |
|  | Dismissal decisions | Chapter Eleven (Pullin) |
| Fitting assessments into a larger framework |  | Chapter Twelve (Howard and Gullickson) |
|  |  | Chapter Thirteen (Moss) |
|  |  | Chapter Fourteen (Cohen) |

way to teaching. But we do not. In fact, the sequence of assessments examined in this book more likely reflects the concerns of different actors involved in the formation of teachers than a well-defined theory of teacher development. Teacher educators care more about reasoning, values, and dispositions. They care about these things in part because their charges are not yet actually teaching. In the absence of concrete experience, learning must focus on their students' visions of themselves as teachers. States care more about teachers' knowledge than about their reasoning or values and often limit their assessments to that alone. And employers care both about teachers' ability to fit into the local community and the culture of the schools and their ability to foster student learning. They use hiring interviews to assess the first and typically use direct observations or student achievement data to assess the second. Hence, we have a system in which different actors assess different qualities not because these have a developmental relationship to one another but because these are the things they are capable of assessing.

Yet another problem faces teacher assessments: we lack strong evidence that any of our desired qualities actually matter to students—to either their well-being or their learning. While it is easy to envision ways in which all of these qualities would be relevant to students' experiences in school, we cannot say with certainty that any particular quality is more important than any other or that any particular intensity of quality is essential.

Yet teachers themselves do make a difference, and evidence that variations among teachers lead to variations in student learning is well established (Nye, Konstantopoulos, & Hedges, 2004). So we are in an unusual spot: we know that teachers make a difference, we have numerous hypotheses as to what aspects of teacher quality are most relevant, and we have numerous tools for assessing these various aspects of teaching. Yet we continue to feel that our collection of assessments has not ultimately improved the quality of teaching or of student learning.

Hence this book. None of the assessments reviewed here yields clear and unambiguous information about teacher quality, and the chapter authors offer some hints as to why. Certainly part of the problem is technical, for any assessment of human capacity or behavior will necessarily fall short of its intended aims. We simply lack the means for linking specific knowledge or behaviors that are measured in one situation to events that occur in other situations. Another part of the problem is conceptual, and many of these authors critique the conceptual rationales and underpinnings of the assessments they describe. Yet another part of the problem is systemic. That is, assessments often do not justify any particular decisions about teachers or teacher candidates. Some chapter authors raised questions about whether or how well assessment results guided teacher educators, teachers themselves, and school administrators.

Readers concerned about teaching and teacher quality will benefit from these chapters. The examinations are both thoughtful and meaty. Individually and collectively, they offer a variety of new insights regarding the uncertain relationship between teacher assessment and teacher quality. University teachers and students will also benefit from them, and to facilitate their value to university classrooms, the book includes some discussion questions at the end.

# REFERENCES

Corcoran, S. P., Evans, W. N., & Schwab, R. S. (2004). Changing labor market opportunities for women and the quality of teachers, 1957–2000. *American Economic Review*, *94*(2), 230–235.

Desimone, L. M., Smith, T., & Ueno, K. (2006). Are teachers who need sustained, content-focused professional development getting it? An administrator's dilemma. *Educational Administration Quarterly*, *42*(2), 179–215.

Gitomer, D. H., & Latham, A. S. (2000). Generalizations in teacher education: Seductive and misleading. *Journal of Teacher Education*, *51*(3), 215–220.

Hedges, L. V., Laine, R. D., & Greenwald, R. (1994). Does money matter? A meta-analysis of studies of the effects of differential school inputs on student outcomes. *Educational Researcher*, *3*(3), 5–14.

Hiebert, J., Morris, A. K., Berk, D., & Jansen, A. (2007). Preparing teachers to learn from teaching. *Journal of Teacher Education*, *58*(1), 47–61.

Ingersoll, R. M. (2006). Understanding supply and demand among mathematics and science teachers. In J. Rhoton & P. Shane (Eds.), *Teaching science in the 21st century* (pp. 197–211). Arlington, VA: NSTA Press.

Krieg, J. M. (2006). Teacher quality and attrition. *Economics of Education Review*, *25*, 13–27.

Nye, B., Konstantopoulos, S., & Hedges, L. V. (2004). How large are teacher effects? *Education Evaluation and Policy Analysis*, *26*(3), 237–257.

Olafson, L., & Schraw, G. (2006). Teachers' beliefs and practices within and across domains. *International Journal of Educational Research*, *45*, 71–84.

Osguthorpe, R. D. (2008). On the reasons we want teachers of good disposition and moral character. *Journal of Teacher Education*, *59*(4), 288–299.

Peske, H. G., & Haycock, K. (2006). *Teaching inequality: How poor and minority students are shortchanged on teacher quality*. Washington, DC: Education Trust.

Rosaen, C., Lundeberg, M., Cooper, M., Fritzen, A., & Terpstra, M. (2008). Noticing noticing: How does investigating video records change how teachers reflect on their experiences? *Journal of Teacher Education*, *59*(4), 347–360.

Smith, T. M., Desimone, L. M., & Ueno, K. (2005). "Highly qualified" to do what? The relationship between NCLB teacher quality mandates and the use of reform-oriented instruction in middle school mathematics. *Educational Evaluation and Policy Analysis*, *27*(1), 75–109.

Weaver, W. T. (1983). *America's teacher quality problem*. New York: Praeger.

# PART ONE

# ASSESSMENT OF TEACHER CANDIDATES

**Chapter One:** The Use of Portfolios in Preservice Teacher Education: A Critical Appraisal

*Ginette Delandshere, Anthony R. Petrosky*

**Chapter Two:** Disposition Assessment: The Science and Psychology of Teacher Selection

*Laurie Moses Hines*

# The Use of Portfolios in Preservice Teacher Education

## *A Critical Appraisal*

Ginette Delandshere, Anthony R. Petrosky

*Indiana University;*
*University of Pittsburgh*

P ortfolios are now extensively used throughout the education system from elementary schools to institutions of higher education. They are used to document and assess students' learning, teachers' teaching, and the working of schools and programs. They are part of the process of making decisions on licensure, certification, hiring, promotion and tenure, and program accreditation. Other than the dossiers compiled by higher education faculty members for promotion and tenure or by the few teachers nominated for an award, the use of portfolios in education is a fairly recent phenomenon. In this chapter, we focus exclusively on portfolios in preservice teacher education programs. To understand how and why they are used in this context, however, as well as their meanings and purposes, we first retrace the history of portfolio in education and analyze the first teaching portfolios developed for the purpose of assessing practicing teachers. Following a review of the portfolio literature to clarify differences in portfolio practices and the claims that have been made regarding their use, we raise a number of issues related to whether practicing teacher assessment portfolios constitute a useful model for preservice teacher education programs. We then present and contrast two cases purposefully selected to highlight differences in teacher education use of portfolios. Finally, we comment on how portfolios might be ideally envisioned in preservice teacher education.

# RETROSPECTIVE ON TEACHING PORTFOLIOS

Although almost every decade in the history of public education in the United States can be characterized as such, the 1980s represented yet another moment of intense questioning and great concern about the nation's schools, colleges, and universities, including the quality of teaching, learning, and the curriculum at the different education levels. *A Nation at Risk,* a report from the National Commission on Excellence in Education submitted to the U.S. secretary of education in 1983, called for educational reforms of school curriculum, teacher education curriculum, and university curriculum in general. Higher and more rigorous standards of performance for both students and prospective teachers were emphasized, among other things, along with accountability recommendations, including nationwide standardized testing of students' achievement at key transition points of the educational system. At the same time, educators were generally leery of additional testing requirements and became preoccupied with finding alternative forms of assessment.

To tackle the report's issues related to teacher education and the professionalization of teaching, the Carnegie Forum on Education and the Economy commissioned Lee Shulman and Gary Sykes to write a paper for consideration by the Carnegie Foundation's Task Force in Teaching as a Profession. In this paper, Shulman and Sykes (l986) outlined what they perceived to be the knowledge base of teaching, devised prototype assessments of this knowledge, and made recommendations for the creation and implementation of a national board for teaching standards. After receiving this position paper, the Task Force on Teaching as a Profession issued a report, *A Nation Prepared: Teachers for the 21st Century* (Carnegie, Foundation Task Force on Teaching as a Profession, 1986) and funded the Teacher Assessment Project (TAP) at Stanford University under Shulman's direction. The TAP's work from 1986 to 1990 consisted of imagining and developing new forms of teacher assessment in order to assist the National Board for Professional Teaching Standards (NBPTS), created soon after in 1987, with the development of professional standards for teachers and the implementation of an assessment system for the purpose of awarding national certification to accomplished elementary and secondary school teachers. The traditional mode of teacher assessment (the National Teachers Examination and later the PRAXIS examinations) had been generally recognized as inadequate, or at least insufficient, to capture the complexity and contextualization of teaching and teacher knowledge — hence the impetus for developing new forms of teacher assessment.

For the first two years, TAP researchers developed and tried out assessment center simulation exercises of teaching, such as developing and teaching a lesson and evaluating student work, for elementary mathematics and high school history. In the next two years, recognizing the importance of documenting teaching over time and in the context of the teachers' own classrooms, the TAP team turned its attention to the development of portfolios for documenting and evaluating teaching in elementary literacy and high school biology (Wolf, 1991). The focus on portfolios to document and represent teaching can partly be explained by how they have been used in other occupations (for example, architects, artists, professional writers), although early on, Bird (1990) warned the field about adopting them wholesale without carefully considering their purposes in the context of teaching.

The attention to the portfolio as a method of documentation and assessment of teaching by the Stanford researchers nevertheless played a pivotal role in their proliferation at all educational levels. Although some university faculty members had experimented with student portfolios in the teaching of freshman reading and writing in the late 1970s and early 1980s (Elbow & Belanoff, 1991), their use was minimal compared to what we would witness in the 1990s and thereafter.

Other initiatives also converged with the TAP work to create the momentum for the portfolio proliferation that would ensue. In 1987, funded by a grant from the National Governors' Association, the state of Connecticut formed a consortium with the state of California in collaboration with Stanford University to overhaul their standards and procedures for teacher licensure. As a part of this effort, they began to study the new assessments developed by the Stanford team and, in some modified forms, their viability for evaluating beginning teachers. This consortium quickly led to the creation of the Interstate New Teacher Assessment and Support Consortium (INTASC), an organization that now includes more than thirty states and was highly influential in the development of standards and assessments for beginning teachers across states. Meanwhile based on the initial efforts of the TAP, the NBPTS had begun its work and in 1990 released the first request for proposal for development of the first assessment for experienced English language arts teachers to be used for the purpose of awarding national certification. The University of Pittsburgh, in collaboration with the Connecticut State Department of Education, received the award for the Early Adolescent/English Language Arts Assessment Development Laboratory (ADL) and began its work in 1991, drawing in important ways on the TAP's work on assessment center exercises and portfolios. The assessment developed for the first ADL included a portfolio and became a model followed by recipients of subsequent ADL awards in other certification areas. To date, more than sixty-four thousand teachers nationwide have been awarded national certification.

Given the advocacy for the use of portfolios for assessment in the process of licensing beginning teachers and their use for awarding national certification to accomplished experienced teachers, as well as a strong call for performance-based assessment and alignment of standards and assessment at all levels, teacher education programs felt pressure to prepare their students for the initial licensing process and its assessment. By the late 1990s, many teacher education programs had adopted or were in the process of adopting a system of portfolio assessment aligned with state, professional, and INTASC teaching standards. In addition, the National Council for Accreditation of Teacher Education (NCATE) also contributed to the development of teaching portfolios through its program review requirements for accreditation. These program reviews are now typically conducted by professional organizations in the content area under review. And since some of these organizations also use the language of the teaching portfolio in the criteria that they consider important for an effective assessment and evaluation system for student-teachers (see, for example, National Council of Teachers of English, 2006), they exercise pressure on teacher education programs to include portfolios as a requirement for course or program completion or both.

To understand how portfolios are currently used in teacher education programs, it is important to analyze the context in which these portfolios were first developed, how they were defined, their form and content, and the purpose of their use. The first teaching portfolios (TAP, NBPTS) were developed exclusively for summative assessment purposes. They were designed to document various aspects of a teacher's best work on which a certification decision could be made. Portfolios were defined ''as a container for storing and displaying evidence of a teacher's knowledge and skills ... [that] embodies an attitude that assessment is dynamic and that the richest portrayals of teacher (and student) performance are based on multiple sources of evidence collected over time in authentic settings'' (Wolf, 1991, p. 130).

The first NBPTS portfolios were designed to capture experienced and accomplished teaching around core propositions and standards defined by the NBPTS and greatly influenced by Shulman's definition of the knowledge base for teaching (Shulman, 1987). They were, and still are, highly structured around specific teaching tasks (for example, conducting and evaluating an interpretive discussion with students, collecting and responding to students' work over a three-month period) and included multiple sources of evidence: curriculum material, unit and lesson plans, student work, videotape of teaching, and teachers' commentaries on their work and the work of their students, for example. The tasks are independent of each other, and, given the relatively high-stakes certification decision for which portfolios are used, comparability and standardization are important to ensure fairness and require providing detailed instructions for teachers to follow in constructing their portfolios. The NBPTS portfolio has more than two hundred pages of directions on how to proceed with their development. The teaching performances reflected in these portfolios are evaluated using a system of scoring rubrics directly linked to the NBPTS standards. Portfolio entries are judged independently by different assessors, and weighted scores for each portfolio entry are aggregated with other parts of the assessment (assessment center exercises and documented accomplishments entry) to yield a total weighted scaled score for which a passing score has been established.

Almost simultaneously with the efforts of the NBPTS, there was an attempt to develop similar assessment portfolios to be used in the context of state licensure. With the assistance of INTASC, some states, including Connecticut, that had been instrumental in the development of the first NBPTS portfolio took the lead in developing portfolio assessments for teachers seeking a teaching license after a period of induction. Given the call for alignment and the fact that some of the same people were involved in their development, the NBPTS and the INTASC portfolio prototypes were quite similar in form and content. Initially a group of fifteen states participated in the design of these portfolios, and several states experimented with them. By 2003 INTASC had developed three portfolio prototypes in mathematics, English language arts, and science. Like the NBPTS portfolios, these also require teachers to collect evidence of their teaching during their induction years over a period of weeks and according to very specific directions for specific tasks linked to the INTASC standards and principles. The plan was for these portfolios to be evaluated by trained teachers who used rubrics linked to the INTASC standards and principles and rating scales based on which licensure decisions could be made. Some states also experimented with pass/fail decisions (Indiana was one of them).

As of 2004 and after ten years of development, however, only three states (and one additional state where portfolios are optional) had adopted a portfolio assessment system as a requirement of their teacher induction program leading to the award of an initial teaching license (Council of Chief School State Officers, 2004). The current pressure on states' budgets and the high cost of establishing and maintaining such an assessment system may partly explain why more states have not adopted this type of assessment. Although only a few states are now using portfolios with beginning teachers, the rhetoric of performance-based assessment by professional organizations, their mandates by state agencies, and the message of preparing student teachers for future performance-based assessment led to a proliferation of portfolios in teacher education programs that seems to have developed a life of its own.

## LEARNING FROM THE PORTFOLIO LITERATURE

Following the dissemination of the TAP and NBPTS work, literature on portfolios emerged in the early 1990s. Barton and Collins (1993) reported finding over two hundred articles on the use of portfolios, mainly for the purpose of instruction and student assessment in reading, art, the performing arts, and science. Our own literature search on teaching and teacher portfolios returned approximately 175 articles and books published between 1990 and 2008. Of these, approximately a third specifically address the use of portfolios in preservice teacher education, with the rest equally divided between their use for evaluating teaching in higher education and in K–12 schools.

Here we focus most exclusively on the recent literature related to preservice teacher education and draw from elsewhere only to strengthen specific arguments. The majority of articles in this area consist primarily of narrative descriptions of portfolio use in specific programs or courses (Barton & Collins, 1993; Darling Farr, 2001; Hartmann, 2004; Hallman, 2007) and analyses of the ways teaching portfolios have been implemented or ways to conceptualize their use (Wolf & Dietz, 1998; Zeichner & Wray, 2001; Habib & Wittek, 2007). In addition, responding to the great anticipation that portfolios would be required for teacher licensure by many states, a number of books were published to promote the use of portfolios and offer procedural guidelines for constructing them (for example, Campbell, Cignetti, Melenyzer, Nettles, & Wyman, 1997; Anderson, Du Mez, & Peter, 1998; Wyatt & Looper, 1999; Campbell, Melenyzer, Nettles, & Wyman, 2000; Cole, Ryan, Kick, & Mathies, 2000; Bullock & Hawk, 2001). The few studies that have been conducted in this area mainly focus on student teachers' perception of the process of constructing a teaching portfolio and their perceived impact on their own learning, development, and reflection about teaching and rely primarily on self-report data using questionnaires, or essays, and interviews (Loughran & Corrigan, 1995; Wade & Yarbrough, 1996; Borko, Michalec, Timmons, & Siddle, 1997; Lyons, 1998; Meyer & Tusin, 1999; Darling Farr, 2001; Donnelly, 2005; Orland-Barak, 2005; Mansvelder-Longayroux, Beijaard, Verloop, & Vermunt, 2007; Wray, 2007). A few other studies have focused on the criteria used in evaluating portfolios and the reliability and validity of the ratings they generate (Smith & Tillema, 2007; Tillema & Smith, 2007; Derham & Diperna, 2007), the difference between notebooks or three-ring binders and electronic portfolios (Milman, 2005; Capraro, 2006; Hallman, 2007), the use of information and communication technology in constructing portfolios and their impact on professional learning (Hauge, 2006), and the perspectives of school administrators on using teaching portfolios for hiring decisions (Pardieck, 2002; Sullivan, 2004).

Most of these studies, however, do not specifically examine the portfolios themselves; the nature of the conversations, interactions, reflections, or learning that went on during portfolio development; or the representations of teaching that evolve during this process. In one study, Delandshere and Arens (2003) purposefully analyzed the nature of the evidence in the portfolios in the conversations about the portfolio between faculty and students and in their own conversations with them, as well as in the representations of teaching implied in these activities. But such studies are scarce, and there is unanimous agreement throughout the portfolio literature that although many claims have been made with regard to the benefits of teaching portfolios in teacher education, these claims have not been investigated through systematic inquiry and lack supporting evidence. Research studies of the use of portfolios with preservice teachers are few and are conducted in specific contexts, generally on a small number of cases, and they rely mostly on self-report data. As a result, it does not seem possible yet to make general claims about their impact on student teachers' learning, development, or reflection. We will, however, review and analyze the main characteristics on which teaching portfolios and their uses have been differentiated in the literature and the related claims that have been made about their use.

## Differences in Portfolio Practices

Several definitions and conceptions of teaching portfolios have been provided by researchers and professional organizations (Bird, 1990; Wolf, 1991; Wolf & Dietz, 1998; National Board for Professional Teaching Standards, 2006; National Council for Accreditation of Teacher Education, 2008). Definitions range from broadly encompassing to narrowly focusing on a particular use. The following examples are illustrative:

> The term *portfolio* is used to cover a wide range of pedagogical practices. It is used not only to describe the physical artifact that students build up either for their own sake or for the purpose of formative or summative assessment but also to refer to the various working patterns that arise when taking such tools into use, as well as the ways various types of users think and talk about the artifacts [Habib & Wittek, 2007, p. 268].

∽

> [A portfolio is an] accumulation of evidence about individual proficiencies, especially in relation to explicit standards and rubrics, used in evaluation of competency as a teacher or other school professional. Contents might include end-of-course evaluations and tasks used for instructional or clinical experience purposes such as projects, journals, and observations by faculty, videos, comments by cooperating teachers or internship supervisors, and samples of student work [National Council for Accreditation of Teacher Education, 2008, p. 89].

Such differences in how portfolios are conceived and why they are used make it difficult to work from a single definition. The main differences identified in the literature relate to their purpose; their structure and content, and how prespecified these are; the process by which they are constructed, including the level of interactions, collaboration, and feedback; and whether and how they are evaluated (Wolf & Dietz, 1998; Zeichner & Wray, 2001). Although these distinctions have been made in the literature, the connections between them are not always explicit. For example, how do differences in purpose affect the structure of portfolios and the process followed for their development? In our analysis, it did not seem possible to consider these differences independent of each other; therefore, we attempt to make the connections between them explicit.

Three broad portfolio purposes are generally recognized: learning, assessment, and employment portfolios. Learning portfolios are presumably used to engage student teachers in inquiry about their own learning and teaching and to document this process of learning, development, and reflection. Although the focus is on inquiry about teaching here, in most instances where learning portfolios appear to be used, it is unclear what students are actually learning about inquiry in developing their portfolios. Assessment portfolios (or credentials portfolios) are used to document proficiency on some prespecified criteria or teaching standards, such as state professional teaching standards or INTASC principles. Some teacher education programs also use credential portfolios as supporting evidence in the accreditation process. Finally, employment portfolios are used in the search for teaching positions and presumably include student teachers' best work.

Others (Loughran & Corrigan, 1995; Meyer & Tusin, 1999; Orland-Barak, 2005) have made a distinction between process and product portfolios, although this distinction does not directly address the issue of purpose and seems to be more a question of emphasis than of distinct alternatives. Student teachers' perceptions of purpose are not always consistent with those of the faculty. Loughran and Corrigan (1995), who used what appears to be a learning portfolio (open-ended and ungraded), report that 35 percent of the respondents in their study did not see a clear purpose for the portfolio, another 30 percent perceived it as an assessment assignment and ''a hurdle to pass the year'' (p. 570), and the other 35 percent viewed it as a job interview tool. In addition, although the portfolio was introduced early in the school year, half of the respondents did not start until later in the year, mainly because the due date was approaching—a practice that does not seem compatible with viewing the portfolio as a learning tool. Similarly Wade and Yarbrough (1996), studying the use of an open-ended learning and development portfolio in a social studies methods course, report that student teachers perceived different purposes and uses, with only 23 percent acknowledging that the portfolio helped them learn through reflection about teaching. In their conclusion, they emphasize the importance of students' understanding of the portfolio purpose and process for learning and reflection.

The structure, content, and prespecification of portfolios are not unrelated to their purpose, although in some instances, this relationship seems to be overlooked, particularly when purposes are confounded. Broadly speaking, portfolios can range from being highly structured to being more open ended. Highly structured portfolios are often organized by a set of required tasks (for example, planning a three-week unit) or prespecified rating criteria or standards (for example, attention to student learning and diversity) and may vary based on the content selected by the student teachers to perform the task or illustrate a particular standard. We did not find examples where the specific content of the task, say, teaching a lesson on ratio and proportion, was specified, although this could presumably occur in the context of course portfolios, where the focus is on particular disciplinary concepts, as in a course on mathematics methods.

Portfolios can also be more or less structured around program themes or principles. In more open-ended portfolios, the structure and organization are left up to the student teachers. They are often guided by a set of guiding questions or considerations provided by the faculty or negotiated with the students, or they are defined by the students themselves—that is, by students working on their own questions about teaching and learning (Grant & Huebner, 1998). Barton and Collins (1993) found that combining prescribed and elective tasks and documentations yielded the richest portfolios.

In the studies we reviewed, student teachers have generally acknowledged their lack of familiarity with portfolios, being very confused, lost, and overwhelmed at the beginning of the process and not clearly understanding the purpose. This would seem to indicate a need for some structure or support. Yet when guidelines are provided about what to include in the portfolio (for example, teaching philosophy, planning and teaching entries, or reflection), and even when allowances are made for self-selected entries, Borko et al. (1997) found students complaining about the overly prescriptive nature of the guidelines regarding content and structure and how they perceived these as being in conflict with developing portfolios that represent their own values and commitments.

The issue raised by the content, structure, and organization of portfolios, as they relate to purpose of the portfolios, seems to be a double-edged sword. On the one hand, if portfolios are used to promote learning, development, and reflection, imposing a particular structure, organization, or content may interfere with individuals' learning and development. It could discourage student teachers from formulating their own questions and gathering the data necessary to address these questions. In a sense, given the inquiry focus of learning portfolios, it would be akin to imposing a particular research methodology on all researchers regardless of their research questions or focuses. The absence of an externally imposed structure would seem workable only if a high level of individual support is in place for all student teachers—a level of support comparable to the mentoring of doctoral students working on their dissertation. This further highlights the interconnections between purpose, structure, and process or level of support, guidance, and feedback available to students.

The process by which portfolios are constructed, including the level and nature of interactions, collaborations, and the types of feedback provided, is another area that has not been well documented or studied. The time span allocated to portfolio development varies from one semester (Borko et al., 1997) to several semesters (Darling Farr, 2001), and from the culmination of a program of study, integrating experience in course work and student teaching, to focusing on a single course or on the student teaching experience only. Even when several semesters are allocated to portfolio development, it appears that in some cases, students wait until the due date is fast approaching to put it together.

The level of guidance for student teachers during this process varies from their working mostly independently, to providing detailed directions or some sample questions and regular assignments with feedback to help focus their efforts; discussions about the process during classes or seminars or regular workshops; meetings with faculty supervisors, school mentors, and other students to clarify problematic issues and provide feedback; public conversations with critical friends about teaching and learning to providing models of portfolios; or some combination of these. The frequency, intensity, and nature of these interactions are not documented in any of the studies that we reviewed. Yet this process would seem to be where learning, development, and reflection take place and are the most visible. Again, the nature of this process has some direct connection to the portfolio purpose, structure, and content, as well as to the way it is evaluated.

A learning portfolio would seem to call for a more open-ended structure to accommodate students' own questions and inquiry, and this would require a high level of support and guidance in the process of development. An assessment portfolio may require more prespecified structure, depending on how it will be evaluated at the end. When a particular structure and organization is externally imposed—recall the NBPTS portfolios with more than two hundred pages of directions on how to proceed—then the process of development becomes an exercise in following directions, and the support needed serves to ensure that the final product will meet the specifications. In other words, a highly structured and standardized portfolio limits the conversation about teaching and learning to what is required by the externally defined tasks and rating criteria and is not conducive to further inquiry about teaching. Snyder, Lippincott, and Bower (1998) observed this mechanistic understanding of teaching when they were studying whether it was possible to use one portfolio as both "a tool for inquiry into personal practice in the professional development of pre-service teachers and as a means of evaluation in their licensure" (p. 46). Their observation led to their decision to use two different portfolios. This is why we believe that for preservice teachers, a more open-ended structure would be important to allow students to engage in their own inquiry about issues relevant to their learning.

Intertwined in the purpose, structure, and process is whether and how the portfolios are evaluated. Predetermined and externally defined assessment criteria call for a more highly structured portfolio—a structure often imposed externally or self-imposed by the student teachers to ensure that documentation will be included for all rating criteria. Structuring one's own thinking is a great part of learning, however, and an externally imposed structure in a sense takes away individual responsibility or opportunity to learn. Richert (1990) also found that self-determination of portfolio content and structure was an important feature for student teachers and one that capitalized on how they normally collect material about their teaching and does not interfere with typical practice. Moreover, prestructured portfolios, externally imposed or self-imposed because of particular rating criteria, would not seem very conducive to inquiry, experimentation, or critical reflection.

For these reasons, we argue that, ideally, learning portfolios should have only a broad or loose structure externally imposed to serve as a guide or as general principles rather than as an organizational blueprint. In addition, assessment criteria can indirectly impose a particular structure. We observed that when the INTASC principles were used as scoring criteria, student teachers automatically organized their portfolios by these principles, with every entry labeled in reference to these principles (Delandshere & Arens, 2003). This seems to have prevented them from thinking about teaching in any terms other than these principles. This, to us, is greatly problematic because it essentially prevents them from considering multiple ways to learn about teaching.

Ideally, learning portfolios should not be scored, rated, or graded other than perhaps in terms of engagement, participation, and completion. Student teachers have expressed their fear of judgment and their need for a safe and nonevaluative environment where they can experiment, make mistakes, and be supported (Richert, 1990)—in other words, where they can learn. Of course, evaluative judgments are made during conversations, interactions, and feedback during portfolio construction, but these are tailored responses to the work of individual students and in support of their learning; they are not based on a set of criteria applied to all students regardless of the content of their work and on which they receive a failing or passing grade. Analysis of these conversations and feedback would be informative for understanding learning and reflection about teaching. In our review of the literature, it was not always clear whether and how learning portfolios are evaluated. In some cases (Loughran & Corrigan, 1995), these portfolios are required for program completion, but they are ungraded. Borko et al. (1997) report that the portfolio used in their program was intended mainly to support students' learning and reflection but also contributed to the grades in a professional seminar. In other cases (Darling Farr, 2001), the product is evaluated using broad, agreed-on criteria (for example, coherence, comprehensiveness, clarity) and often contributes to course grades, but the process of development does not appear to be evaluated other than in the weekly interactions and feedback among students and with the instructors. There is, however, no systematic study of the nature of interactions, dialogues, and feedback and how these contribute to furthering students' understandings.

An evaluative function is inherent in the assessment and employment portfolios. Most assessment portfolios appear to be rated or scored according to a predetermined set of criteria, standards, themes, or principles for which a passing score or rating has been determined. Others are evaluated as pass or fail. As we have observed, certain rating criteria tend to be used with student teachers to impose a particular structure and organization on the portfolio. Teacher educators have typically addressed the reliability of ratings issued by using multiple readers and reaching consensus on portfolio grades, scores, or ratings. Employment portfolios are not explicitly evaluated, and at this point, it is unclear what role they play in hiring decisions. Other than a few studies of school administrators' perception of the value of portfolios, we do not know how they are used in the application process. When all three purposes are explicitly folded into one portfolio development (Delandshere & Arens, 2003), the assessment purpose—hence the structure, process, and evaluation—appears to supersede all others, and the learning function in essence disappears, as we will see in a case example of current practice later in this chapter.

This situation has created many dilemmas and tensions for students and faculty and led some programs to require different portfolios for different purposes (Snyder et al., 1998). At this point, however, there are no comprehensive data on whether, why, and how teacher education programs across the states use portfolios for these different purposes. One of the reasons for using portfolios most often cited by teacher educators, at least in the United States, has been the anticipation that the states would require them for induction programs and licensure or program accreditation (Borko et al., 1997; Delandshere & Arens, 2003). This externally imposed reason has also often been justified by the claim that portfolios are best suited to represent teaching in context, over time, and from multiple sources of evidence.

## Claims Made About Portfolios

Most claims made about teaching portfolios relate to their potential rather than to their current use. Most claims are also about single elements, such as reflection, but without careful consideration of the conditions that would be necessary to realize and support these elements. One of the initial claims was that compared to traditional forms of assessment, portfolios made it possible to represent the context and complexity of teaching by using many sources and forms of representations (Shulman, 1987; Wolf, 1991; Darling-Hammond & Snyder, 2000). It is undeniable that compared to a multiple-choice test, a portfolio allows the documentation of many different aspects of teaching over a period of time and in different contexts. Just because this potential exists, however, does not warrant that teaching will always be represented in meaningful and complex ways when portfolios are used. A scrapbook of uninterpreted teaching artifacts, even if varied and sampled over time, is not very useful for the assessment or understanding of someone's teaching.

Perhaps the most universal claim made about portfolios, and mentioned in practically all writings on them, is that they provide student teachers with opportunities to engage in deep thinking and reflection about teaching and learning and, in turn, contribute to professional growth and development. An exploration of the concept of reflection is beyond the scope of this chapter. Reflection has been variously defined (Dewey, 1933; Schön, 1987; Zeichner & Liston, 1987) and is considered a critical aspect of one's teaching practice and a condition for learning and development. We have no doubt that it is possible to use a portfolio as a reflective tool, but simply introducing portfolios cannot be expected to yield greater reflection unless other conditions are met.

Reflection and self-reflection are difficult and do not occur naturally or automatically. To optimize the chance of meaningful reflection, student teachers have to be engaged in tasks, activities, or experiences conducive to reflection, and they need to be guided, encouraged, and supported in their efforts to be reflective. In addition, theoretical knowledge about learning and pedagogy, as well as understandings of the social, political, and historical foundations of education, also appear indispensable to reflection on teaching experiences (Yost, Sentner, & Forienza-Bailey, 2000). Without these understandings, there would be no framework within which to construct or reconstruct their meaning. The point is that reflection and its contribution to learning and understanding is the focus here, not the portfolio itself. If student teachers have never been asked to reflect on their learning, reason from evidence over time and in different contexts, or deliberate about the nature of evidence, it is unlikely that the portfolio alone will make that happen. In other words, we do not see reflection as a consequence of portfolio use. The portfolio is neither necessary nor sufficient for reflection; it is simply a place and a means to represent it if and when it happens.

The evidence that supports the link between reflection, learning, and portfolio construction is mixed and is primarily based on self-report data. Some respondents perceived that they learned a great deal through reflection when working on their portfolios, while others regarded it as just another hurdle (Wade & Yarbrough, 1996; Borko et al., 1997; Darling, 2001). We wonder how much these findings can be explained by the fact that portfolios in the programs studied were introduced to the students as a reflective tool. Could it be that some students simply repeat what they were told about the purpose of the portfolios or the program's theme? Darling (2001) noticed this happening in her own study. Whether student teachers are indeed as reflective about their learning and teaching as they say they are and the nature of their reflections are issues that have not been sufficiently investigated. Delandshere and Arens (2003) analyzed portfolios and their process of development, along with how they were evaluated by the faculty in three different teacher education programs; they found very little evidence of student teachers' reflection, even though many of them claimed that working on their portfolios forced them to reflect on their own teaching and "who they were as teachers." Yet when attempting to explain why they had selected particular artifacts to include in their portfolios or how these reflected their understanding of teaching or learning, many students could make only descriptive or declarative statements.

Lyons (1998) reports similar findings based on her pilot studies of reflection with interns and undergraduate student teachers engaged in constructing portfolios. Snyder et al. (1998) report finding evidence of reflection in both the portfolios and what student teachers said about the process. This study was conducted in a small master's of education program where they experimented with a learning portfolio and where the emphasis was on reflection, growth over time, and explanation of artifacts. The purpose was to support learning and reflection around student teachers' own questions and concerns with ongoing guidance and support from a collaborative network of critical friends within a safe environment, where students were allowed to fail and encouraged to analyze these failures. From what we have read elsewhere, this is an unusual level of support, with ongoing conversations and deliberations about the big ideas of teaching. Although we would want to see a more extensive analysis of reflection and learning in the portfolios and conversations related to their development, it is not surprising to find deeper reflection in this context given the purpose, the open-ended structure, and the highly collaborative and supportive process of development. We contrast this case with what appears to be a more typical portfolio development in the next section on current practices.

A related claim is that portfolios allow collaboration, dialogue, and feedback that promote learning (Lyons, 1998). Sociocultural learning theory does indeed emphasize the importance of participation, dialogue, deliberation, the intentional engagement with "knowing others" (Gill, 1993), and people's relational dependency (Lave & Wenger, 1991) to develop new understandings of the world and transform it. Except for a few references to the idea that portfolios support a constructivist view of learning, the portfolio literature has not explicitly articulated the claim about collaboration, dialogue, and feedback on theoretical grounds. From a sociocultural conception of learning, it would be possible to view portfolios as containing the cultural artifacts used in the process of learning, so this kind of engagement with others and with cultural artifacts of teaching is possible in the process of portfolio development, but, again, portfolios are not necessary or sufficient to create such engagement. Collaboration, dialogue, and feedback require a great deal of time and commitment from participants, commitment to their own learning, and commitment to the learning of the other. Dialogue and feedback from knowledgeable others and the intellectual, social, and emotional tools and dispositions that these imply are key conditions to furthering one's learning. There is scant evidence, however, about the nature of collaboration, dialogue, and feedback in the portfolio literature. In studying the nature of reflection of student teachers working in partnership (with and without portfolios), Richert (1990) reports that the most important elements of partnerships as perceived by student teachers were (1) time to reflect, (2) safety or nonevaluative environment, (3) a partner's observation of one's teaching so that they have a common basis for conversation, (4) knowledgeable partner, and (5) opportunity for deep reflective conversations. Although this study is based on students' self-report data and not on an actual observation and analysis of partnership, it constitutes a rare attempt to understand collaboration and dialogue in preservice teacher education. Also in a study based on self-report data, Wade and Yarbrough (1996) found significant differences in the reported experience and satisfaction of constructing a portfolio between student teachers working with different supervisors. We can only speculate at this point that the quality of dialogue and feedback and nature of collaborative engagement with the task may have contributed to some of the differences they found.

Other claims made are that by constructing portfolios, student teachers can bridge theory and practice and develop self-confidence and identity through reflection on what they do or how they think about teaching (Richert, 1990; Barton & Collins, 1993; Darling-Hammond & Snyder, 2000), but no supporting evidence could be found to substantiate these claims. A portfolio practice has also been presented as something that preservice teachers could take with them and continue through their years of teaching—a practice that would presumably result in improved teaching and student learning (Barton & Collins, 1993). Except for a few anecdotal cases (Lyons, 1998), there is no evidence that preservice teachers actually continue their portfolio practice after graduating. Teaching load and school organization are typically not conducive to such reflective and collaborative practice. Finally, to date, the impact of preservice portfolio development on teaching and learning has not been systematically investigated.

Conspicuously missing from the portfolio literature is any substantive discussion or theoretical elaboration on the meaning or nature of teaching, learning, or learning to teach. It seems peculiar to us that a means by which to represent teaching and learning would be promoted without fully addressing the meaning of these representations, and whether the forms of representation are consistent with the theoretical perspectives taken. Is it the case that we all understand teaching and learning in the same way? Is it the case that portfolios are a universal form of representation regardless of differing perspectives on learning and teaching? Later we illustrate how preservice teachers' portfolios can be used for quite different purposes, in quite different ways, and not always successfully. Yet we get a sense from the field and from the literature that portfolios are generally "good." But preservice teacher portfolios, which often have been modeled on licensure or certification portfolios, not only have not been studied in practice, they also do not appear to have been theoretically conceptualized as a form of engagement and for their potential to enhance or limit our understandings of teaching, learning, and learning about teaching. Let us then consider the models of teaching represented in the portfolios used for licensure and certification and the impact that these had on the use of portfolios in preservice teacher education programs.

## PORTFOLIO ASSESSMENTS OF EXPERIENCED TEACHERS AS MODELS FOR PRESERVICE TEACHERS

The concept of a portfolio was transplanted to teaching from other occupations. Judging by current practices, though, portfolios appear to have lost some of their potential due to overstandardization and the prescriptive process of their development for summative assessment purposes. Architects' portfolios, for example, are used to represent and promote one's work to other firms or potential clients, so in that sense, they are evaluated by people with varied conceptions and expectations of architecture. These portfolios are extremely visual—a characteristic not very suitable to representing teaching since much of it is intangible—and communicate quite effectively the elements of design, form, aesthetics, materials, and so on, and the values that are important to an architect or architectural firm. Portfolios here are also highly personalized; they include different pieces of work as examples of what each architect does best. Architects are not required to include in their portfolios samples of accomplishment on the same set of tasks (for example, a house, a bridge, and a bathroom). In other words, there are many ways to represent architectural accomplishments, not just those centered on specific projects that would have been predetermined by some board of architects. This is a critical point and one that differs greatly from many current uses of teaching portfolios. The open, evolving, ongoing, and creative process of developing portfolios in other occupations appears to have been lost when teaching borrowed this concept for the assessment of accomplished teachers, as the process became closed-ended and much more standardized and prescriptive—a process that was then passed down to beginning teachers and then quickly to preservice teachers in teacher education programs.

At this juncture, the first question we need to ask is whether it is appropriate to require of beginning teachers the same types of performances and similar tasks as those expected from accomplished teachers. Why not, one might ask, given that beginning and experienced teachers have the same responsibilities? This is of course a plausible question, and the fact that the INTASC principles, standards, and portfolio prototypes are so similar to those of the NBPTS indicates that the developmental nature of teaching—one that would require a much more open process of representation—was not carefully considered in the development of these standards and portfolio assessments. There are likely different paths to becoming an accomplished teacher, and assuming that beginning teachers are doing the same things and thinking in the same way as accomplished teachers, only in less sophisticated ways, seems overly simplistic and linear. But more specifically to our purpose here, the INTASC principles developed for beginning teachers and aligned on the NBPTS standards were then adopted by many states to guide their own standards development for teacher licensure and to frame the accreditation process of preservice teacher education programs. So core ideas developed in the context of accomplished teaching have been imposed not only on beginning teachers but now also on student teachers, that is, students learning about teaching, who in many cases have just a few months of actual teaching experience by the time they graduate from their programs.

It seems to us that there is a fundamental difference between experienced teaching and learning about teaching and that the principles of learning and the ways to document such learning, even for assessment purposes, should also be fundamentally different. Experts and novices are often compared in the research literature with the implicit assumption that if we could just teach novices to act and think like experts, the problem of education would be solved. What we do not know much about, however, is how experts become experts in the first place. Furthermore, in a fast-changing world, tomorrow's experts might be quite different from today's, and for novices to simply emulate them might not be the most useful learning strategy. Ignoring these critical issues, many teacher education programs and syllabi, as well as professional and state teaching standards (also modeled on the INTASC principles), have been rewritten in the language of INTASC principles that now define many program curricula and the framework within which portfolios are used in preservice teacher education programs across the states.

Another issue that raises concerns about the adequacy of a summative assessment portfolio as a model for preservice teacher education programs concerns the static, fragmented, and prescriptive nature of the representations of teaching contained in portfolios such as those developed for the NBPTS. These do not exactly constitute the dynamic assessment—something evolving and unfolding over time—that Wolf (1991) envisioned, unless the assessment offers an opportunity for teachers to engage in meaningful discussions about teaching with colleagues or unless it significantly improves their teaching. There is, however, scant evidence—other than anecdotal accounts and self-reports—that such meaningful discussions occur or that the assessment has a beneficial effect on teaching. In addition, these portfolios are constructed by sampling different teaching performances from different classes, different units, and different students and teachers. Teachers are not asked to look across these different performances or to analyze them for continuity or coherence. Similarly, different assessors rate the performances on the different portfolio tasks independently. Requiring the same tasks from all teachers and judging performances on these tasks independently with predetermined criteria represent teaching in a particular and rather fragmented way. It is only one way to represent teaching, because the standards on which the assessment is constructed view teaching as a set of skills, knowledge, and dispositions and not, for example, as a form of civic and social engagement. And it is a fragmented view because the standards are written as lists of these skills, knowledge, and dispositions that do not explicitly articulate the theoretical perspective that underlies the standards or makes connection between them.

Given the purpose of the portfolio as the basis for awarding national certification, we understand the standardization issue, the sampling framework on which these portfolios were conceived, and the related concern for the independence of ratings (a fundamental classical measurement assumption); however, this approach portrays the whole of teaching as the sum of some of its parts and leaves virtually no opportunity for the construction of understandings and representations of the whole of teaching or for reflection on these. The whole of teaching resides in "an articulated social and political ideal or theory of teaching, the role of teachers, and the purpose of schooling and education in general" (Delandshere & Arens, 2001, p. 557). But since such an overarching conceptualization of teaching is not an explicit part of teaching standards, it is not surprising to find it absent from the portfolio process. Yet we must wonder how one makes meaningful decisions about teaching without references to such an ideal. A related and equally serious issue for the education of future teachers is that such a prescriptive and deterministic representation of teaching is not at all conducive to thinking critically about teaching. How to think about teaching is predetermined by the standards and criteria used to judge the performances. Yet since these constitute only one possible interpretation of teaching, it may prevent future teachers from inquiring about other interpretations and representations.

A final consideration regarding how and whether practicing teacher assessment portfolios serve as a model to be used in preservice teacher education relates to the very term *portfolio*. As we have described them so far, practicing teacher portfolios used for assessment in the context of teacher licensure or certification are basically a means to package a set of performance tasks compiled by teachers at one point in time. The absence of connections among the entries makes these portfolios little more than containers documenting teaching. Except for the fact that the performances are documented in the context of teachers' classrooms, the portfolio entries are not very different from other performance exercises (for example, the NBPTS assessment center exercises). There is no whole to the portfolios in their conception or in the way they are read and evaluated. Separate folders could easily serve the same purpose. Moreover, they do not appear to be revisited, except for teachers who fail their first attempt to pass the assessment. There is no evidence that portfolios are used as an ongoing means to inquire into one's teaching or that they are kept by teachers as a running documentation or for reflection on their practice. If that is the case, these portfolios have not become a working tool for teachers or a way to study and revisit their practice over time. This limited use of portfolios has to some extent been replicated in many teacher education programs. We now examine two cases of preservice teacher portfolios to highlight existing and potential differences in their use.

# CASE EXAMPLES OF PORTFOLIO PRACTICE

In this section we analyze two cases of portfolio use with preservice teachers purposefully selected to illustrate quite different practices in the field. The first case is reconstructed from a study Delandshere and Arens (2003) conducted in three different teacher education programs to understand how teaching was represented, the quality of the evidence constructed, and the inferences drawn from the evidence. Based on the abundant feedback they received and are still receiving about this study, we believe that this is a typical use of portfolios in a number of teacher education programs across the country. The second case represents the use of a learning portfolio that is an integral part of a master of arts of teaching (M.A.T.) program designed to focus on teaching as a process of inquiry. These two cases are not directly comparable for a number of reasons, but they do provide an opportunity to understand the problems, dilemmas, tensions, and possibilities associated with using portfolios in preservice teacher education programs.

## Case 1: A Typical Mixed-Purposes Portfolio

This first case, we believe, is typical of undergraduate programs in states with a strong emphasis on teaching standards (state or INTASC standards and principles) and uses these as the basis for awarding teaching licenses and accrediting programs. The teacher education program faculty in this case view their use of portfolios as a response to the call for performance assessment in the accreditation process and anticipated state mandates to require portfolio for licensure. Not wanting to simply satisfy a mandate, they also considered portfolios useful to evaluate the program, develop and evaluate students' understandings of teaching according to the standards and their ability to exhibit these in the classroom, and prepare students for job interviews. All purposes here are expected to be served by a single portfolio that students are asked to develop over a period of time as a culmination of their program of study and student teaching.

This confounding of purposes is problematic for students in the program, with most of them focusing on the most utilitarian function of the portfolio and believing that the primary purpose was to showcase their best teaching qualities and prepare them for employment. Although some students mentioned that developing a portfolio made them think critically about their teaching, most of them did not regard the development of their understanding of teaching as a primary purpose. Students are introduced to this culminating portfolio during a workshop at the beginning of their final year, although they may already have prepared a course portfolio in the previous year. The workshop provides the students with a copy of the standards and emphasizes that portfolios should provide evidence that the students have "met the standards." Model portfolios from previous years are made available to students, and faculty suggest acceptable artifacts for the different standards. Rating criteria (some reformulation of the standards and program themes) used for the assessment of the portfolios, along with accompanying rubrics, are also provided to guide the selection of artifacts. Other than the fact that the portfolios have to provide evidence that the standards have been met, no particular structure or content is explicitly required to organize the portfolios, and this is apparently left up to each student. Throughout the year, the students discuss artifacts that they are considering for inclusion in their portfolios with the program faculty during seminars, course work, and individual meetings. They also consult with their student teaching supervisor. Discussions focus on some aspects of the standards and how the artifacts can be used to illustrate how students are "meeting the standards."

The faculty report that this process takes an enormous amount of time during course work and seminars to ensure that all students include sufficient evidence for all standards. At the end, the students present their portfolios to a team of faculty and supervisors. Portfolios are then rated using the rubrics on the basis of which a pass/fail decision is made or additional work is requested until they can receive a passing grade. No particular structure is imposed, but students tend to organize their portfolios according to the rating criteria or standards. The final product is a collection of artifacts (pictures, diagrams, brief lessons or unit descriptions, assessment beliefs, and students' work arranged by standards) with brief descriptive captions in the language of the standards (for example, ''This classroom diagram demonstrates INTASC principle no. 5; it displays my ability to create a cooperative learning environment''). Most entries remain unexplained, and the arguments that would turn the artifacts into supporting evidence of their understandings about teaching are not articulated. At times, the match between captions, standards, and artifacts appeared random, and when we asked students why they had selected a particular artifact to address a particular standard, they acknowledged that they really did not have a good explanation.

Teaching is represented in these portfolios as an eclectic set of discrete and generic skills, beliefs, and activities, with no explicit underlying conceptual structure and no connections among the different sections of the portfolios that at times appear inconsistent. Declarative statements of beliefs about various aspects of teaching and learning written in the language of the standards are presented as philosophy statements. Yet when students were interviewed about these statements, some were hard pressed to remember their own teaching philosophy. It is difficult for outside readers to make sense of these portfolios, given the absence of explanations and reflective statements. Nevertheless, most students in this case received high grades for their portfolios, and a few were given additional time to complete the requirement.

In reading and evaluating the portfolios, teacher educators call on an extensive repertoire of information (about the students, the program, their colleagues, the accountability requirements) that goes well beyond the portfolios. The inferences they draw are only partially based on the portfolios—which they recognize lack evidence of students' understanding about teaching—and consist of literal interpretations about their content (for example, a psychology paper written about a developmental theory is interpreted as understanding how students learn and develop) and how artifacts match to the standards. A lot of guesses and assumptions are made in the process. They rely heavily on what they already know about the students and the experiences they have had with them during course work and supervision. They deplore the lack of explanation and reflection in the portfolios, but generally resist making judgments about students' understanding or critically analyzing the work. They want to be supportive of students and ''get them through the program.'' They also acknowledge that it is difficult to evaluate the students' performance based on the INTASC standards, given that they have very little teaching experience. At the end, both students and faculty appear overwhelmed by the process.

## Case 2: A Single-Purpose Learning Portfolio

In this case, the portfolio is a centerpiece of a four-semester M.A.T program of studies that focuses on inquiry teaching and learning in its methods courses and field experience. Before beginning their portfolio, students study theory and action research cases to learn about the uses of various kinds of artifacts as evidence—units and lessons, students' work samples, classroom routines and rituals, physical configurations of classrooms, assessments, tests, classroom talk, students' performances, and so on—and the kinds of claims they can support when they are annotated, explained, or interpreted for their uses as evidence. Their studies and readings of action research cases and theory help students understand the ways artifacts, including classroom talk, can be used as evidence and the kinds and levels of explanation it takes to make a strong case based on compelling evidence. Students learn to annotate and interpret artifacts in writing for their use as evidence and explain how the evidence supports their claims.

Students then work on their portfolios in a discipline-specific capstone course (mathematics, English, and so on), taken during their student teaching, specifically designed to study their own teaching and their students' learning. The portfolio is designed to organize students' learning in the course and is not used by the program in any other way. Although program faculty once considered rating the portfolios against a common rubric, they decided against it after a small pilot project with two capstone courses. The mere fact of the portfolio being used in this way—that is, against a rubric—dramatically affected students' perceptions of and work on the portfolio. Their attention shifted to completing the entries in terms of the rubric rather than in thinking of the entries as open-ended problems or invitations to explore issues in their terms with the help of action research.

Given that learning was the primary focus of the course, students had time and many opportunities to present their work to peers and faculty for discussion and critique. When students took their capstone course, they were already familiar with cases, claims, artifacts, and uses and explanations of evidence. In their methods courses, they had studied examples of teaching from multiple cases in the professional literature, so that in their sequence of four mathematics methods courses, for example, they would have studied at least two cases of mathematics teaching in each course. Once in the capstone course, they continued their work with cases by formally studying action research. This meant that they thought about cases both practically and theoretically from examples of action research theory and practice. The tasks and the activities in which students engaged in developing their portfolio are presented as inquiry, in the language used and with the examples of cases that they study and analyze together. Each portfolio entry is conceived of as a type of action research. A student in the English capstone course, for example, would study his or her use of questions with literary selections by taping twenty minutes of a class discussion based on those questions for the portfolio entry on questioning and discussion. The student teacher would then transcribe the discussion and study it to understand how the questions affected the students' participation: for instance, who talks, the types of responses, the range of youngsters responding, the influence of the classroom configuration, and the nature of the ensuing discussion—whether a recitation or a discussion where students talk with each other. By engaging in this work, student teachers gain access to a set of tools and strategies that they can use in their careers to study their teaching and inquire into problems or issues that arise in their teaching.

Students create their portfolios in response to discipline-specific questions or tasks that allow them to design and choose the units and lessons for which they design action research projects or from which they draw their examples and artifacts to make claims about their teaching and their students' learning. The individual entries or tasks generally mesh with their studies of teaching and learning in their methods courses by highlighting critical tasks and approaches for thinking about teaching in the cases that they study in these methods courses. Their work on the portfolio is broadly structured by a set of tasks—referred to as spaces within which they work—that focus them on (1) changes they have made to their teaching, (2) experiments they have conducted with their pedagogy, (3) their uses of different pedagogies or modes of instruction, (4) the ways they adjust their instruction for diverse students or English language learners, and (5) their design and use of informal assessments.

Instructors generally write the individual entries to fit their specific disciplines, so, for example, English students study their uses of questioning and discussion in the third space, while mathematics students study their uses of students' errors as pedagogical scaffolds for students' learning. The main goal is for students to work in these spaces with studies and examples in their own disciplines rather than in any generic way. In that sense, students approach their questions through their own units and lessons of instruction rather than through standards or predesigned exercises focused on specific content. Students understand their work on the portfolio tasks as the action research thread in their inquiry preparation. The course encourages experimentation and risks, and students are expected to try different pedagogical approaches to such practices as questioning and discussions and with different lessons. As a part of this work, students are drawn into arguing in talk and writing about what they learn from different sources of evidence, so that they learn to explain the connections between artifacts and their abstract claims for the learning and performances of their students. Students are expected to tape their students and transcribe fifteen to twenty minutes of their tapes so that they can "get close to the student talk" and learn to argue from it about the kinds of learning represented. Talk and writing are the visible currencies of intellectual activity in classrooms, and they are extremely valuable windows into their students' thinking in response to teachers' questions and tasks. Students are expected to use classroom talk as primary sources of evidence for their claims and arguments—an expectation already emphasized in their methods courses.

More specifically, for example, students design a sequence of lessons on a particular historical topic in American history, in a unit designed to study World War II with specific attention to the historical contexts in which the United States first used the atomic bomb. They design and study the effects of different kinds of questions with their students. As an example, one lesson focuses on recitation questions with correct answers. Another focuses on inquiry questions for which students use primary source documents. Another might focus on analytical questions students answer from different perspectives or positions on a topic. Students might be asked how Truman's personal letters, for instance, could be used as evidence to support the positions that he did or did not want to use the bomb.

In many cases, student teachers design their portfolio tasks as experiments, so that they compare, for instance, the results of two or three different approaches to formative assessment. They use student talk and student work samples as data, and they have to structure their teaching to reveal the differences in their approaches to formative assessments. The student teachers then present their experiments to their instructor and peers, so that larger conversations can inform their studies. Student teachers in such situations learn to study their students' talk as indicators of the types of thinking and learning occurring in their lessons, so they could take this approach to studying changes they make in lessons over time, their students' engagement with the discussions over time, and their students' discussions in pairs or small groups. To engage in this kind of experimentation, they have to be able to structure lessons that reveal differences in talk as the outcome of differences in such things as questioning, engagement, room arrangement, and group size.

Finally, students produce each portfolio task as a case in a thick ring binder, and each student is also responsible for formally presenting two or three twenty-minute cases that highlight the claims being made, the artifacts used for evidence, and the arguments that link the evidence to the claims.

At the end, students reported in exit surveys that they noticed their growing sophistication over the design and explanation of the cases. Portfolios or individual entries are not graded, but students receive ongoing and elaborate feedback from each other and from the faculty in conversations as well as written responses to the various aspects of their entries. This kind of disciplined and principled inquiry—working on the portfolio tasks and commenting meaningfully on other people's work—requires considerable engagement on the part of both students and faculty. Students receive a grade in the course based on their level of engagement with the entries, their completion of all the entries, their uses of artifacts as evidence, their annotations and interpretation of evidence, the presentations of their entries to their colleagues, and their engagement in discussions of their peers' presentations. Program faculties in the different disciplines readily volunteer to teach this capstone course.

To provide additional context for the case, we also need to add that as students progress through their program of studies, they also complete an electronic compliance portfolio required by the state to ensure that they meet the state teaching standards for being recommended for initial licensure. To do so, they use some of the artifacts from their leaning portfolios as well as some other attestations to fit the categories set by the state. They are assisted in this task by their university supervisor, who is also responsible for evaluating this compliance portfolio.

## Learning from the Cases

We are not presenting the second case as the only alternative to the first. Case 2 has a particular orientation to learning about inquiry into teaching, and we recognize that other orientations are possible. We also acknowledge that a study of this case (and others) similar to the one conducted for case 1 would be greatly beneficial to shed additional light on the nature of the differences between them. Nevertheless, contrasting the cases at this point is quite informative.

The most striking difference between the two cases relates to their purpose and is likely the source of the resulting differences in portfolio practices. The confounded and conflicted purposes in the first case inevitably turn faculty and student attention to the more pressing concerns for survival: accountability, licensure, and, to some extent, employment. When the first priority is to meet externally imposed criteria, attention to learning is diverted and in this case seems to be replaced by a process of mechanically matching artifacts and criteria. As we noted, this mechanical matching also happens in the second case, but the compliance portfolio is completely separate from the learning portfolio. The multiple purposes are also conflicting because they focus attention in different directions. In the first case, for instance, the faculty explicitly discouraged students from writing long explanations of their portfolio entries because they did not think that school administrators would be interested in reading them. This is in direct contrast to the second case, where the aim is for students to be able to write lengthy and sophisticated explanations of their work. In this second case, not only is the purpose clearly and singularly on learning, but also the portfolio is integrated in and contributes to the inquiry theme of the program. In other words, the portfolio is not an add-on, not something that is done because of the need to use performance assessment; rather, it is used as a means and a space to engage in and organize inquiry into teaching and learning, organize the curriculum, and give a coherent purpose to the overall program.

Another crucial difference lies in the process of portfolio development. In the first case, this process consists of on-demand, unstructured portfolio discussions occurring in the context of other courses and seminars that otherwise have their own focus and purpose, while the second case illustrates a planned and structured teaching of inquiry that is woven throughout the program. How the time spent on portfolio work is allocated and structured is, we believe, a crucial issue that has not received much attention in the literature. Although it is generally recognized that reflection takes time, what is done during that time is equally important. So, for example, in the first case, students are generally encouraged to include a teaching philosophy statement for one of the standards. Yet nowhere in their course work are they taught what constitutes a teaching philosophy, why it might be important, and how this would relate to the many teaching decisions they have to make in the classroom. They seem to simply be expected to be able to write such a statement. So it is not surprising that most of the philosophy statements included in the portfolios are lists of beliefs about teaching that have been written using key words taken from the standards. These beliefs, however, were rarely reflected in other sections of the portfolios. If we consider portfolios as a place and means to inquire about one's teaching, the requirement to provide evidence that the students are meeting particular standards or criteria appears misguided, at least from an inquiry or research standpoint. It is generally understood that conducting research is not a process of rallying evidence to prove a point but rather a genuine investigation focusing on a question, an issue, or a problem in search of answers. Asking students to engage in this investigation either presumes that they already know how to conduct such inquiry or requires that they learn to do so. This is not a trivial endeavor, and from experience, we know how long and tedious the process of educating researchers is. Yet in the first case we presented, there is no evidence that student teachers are taught how to investigate their own teaching; they appear to simply be expected to do so by participating in discussions and receiving feedback about particular artifacts. What questions or problems they are trying to address is, however, rather unclear.

Learning to teach is overwhelming, and learning to examine one's teaching is even more so. Videotapes of class sessions along with lesson plans, student work, and so on raise many questions and many issues to think about, reflect on, and understand. How do student teachers make sense of these experiences? Moving from abstract questions or problems or standards to concrete artifacts and experiences, and vice versa, entails sophisticated reasoning and explanations based on systematic observations that do not happen automatically simply because they are requested. Reconstructing these experiences requires intense cognitive and metacognitive engagement, as well as theoretical perspectives within which to anchor explanations and interpretations. When students write statements in which they claim that particular artifacts or experiences show that they have met the standard, as they do in the first case, they are telling us that they really have not done the hard work of explaining how to connect generic standard statements with the concrete artifacts that they present as self-evident. So, for example, when a student writes that she understands how students develop because she has observed Piaget's stages of development during her student teaching, the nature of her observations and her interpretation of them are completely invisible, making it impossible to evaluate her claim and what it means in the context of her teaching. Students have to learn how to articulate questions or problems in the context of their experiences and how to gather and explain relevant information or data to address these questions. They also need to understand the rules of evidence, the role of artifacts and observations, and how to analyze and interpret these to warrant the claims they make. To do so, they have to be guided and provided the space to think about and work on their teaching, and to try out these new understandings as the second case describes. The portfolio in that case allows them to document performance over time, along with records of analyses of these performances. The portfolio space is broadly structured to focus students' attention on general tasks and problems and to give them a way into thinking about and studying their teaching. Within that space, they experiment and research how they teach and how their students learn.

This intense and substantive level of support and guidance is rare, we believe, but critical for portfolios to yield the kind of learning and reflection envisioned in the literature and to make these visible and understandable to others in writing. Structured opportunities that give students adequate time and safe environments to complete and reflect their portfolio work are important, as are structured conversations with others in different roles, such as peers, faculty, supervisors, and mentor teachers.

What is evaluated and how is another important difference between the two cases. Issues of evaluation and purposes are of course related. In the first case, since the primary emphasis is on assessment, program accountability, and employment, it is the product that gets evaluated using predetermined rating criteria (and standards). As described in the first case, this assessment system encourages students to focus their development effort on the product of the portfolio rather than on what is learned in the process. Portfolio discussions are about what to include and how, and although students collect artifacts throughout the year, the actual construction of the portfolio typically occurs at the end of student teaching and a few weeks before it is presented to the team of faculty and supervisors. What they learn over time or as a result of this process of portfolio construction is not visible or explicated, but some of this learning could actually be problematic, as Delandshere and Arens (2003) have explained:

> Given the time involved, what concerns us most is the learning that results from participating in these portfolio development activities that seem to be the main focus of the program. When a list of disjointed beliefs stands for a philosophy, when declarative statements in the language of the standards stand for explanations, interpretation and reflection, and when artifacts are confounded with evidence, there is a great danger for the changes resulting from these activities to be aimless and devoid of meaning. But also, as portfolios have been sanctioned and validated by the faculty, these distorted views of what constitutes a philosophy, an explanation, or a reflection, for example, have also been validated. If student teachers are led to believe that a two-sentence declarative statement about their work constitutes an explanation, they are likely to be able to justify anything they do, but moreover, their search for further explanation or understanding may be curtailed [p. 71].

In the second case where learning about teaching is the main emphasis, assessment and feedback are ongoing and integral to the conversations, presentations, and deliberations that make up the course work sessions. And in contrast to the first case, grades here focus on the students' level of engagement with the portfolio cases; their completion of all the entries; their appropriate use of data, observations, and artifacts to build evidence; the nature of their explanations and interpretations; the quality of their presentations to peers and faculty; and their level of engagement in the class discussions. In other words, assessment does not simply focus on the physical artifacts but on how they are used, studied, debated, and so on. There is a striking contrast here between evaluating a product based on a priori criteria and evaluating a process of engagement and the resulting development of conceptual and analytical tools that, it is hoped, will endure beyond the program of study. What is valued is also communicated through the assessment process. So, for example, when the portfolio product is evaluated, students will avoid questioning their choices, intending only to represent their best performance, whereas questioning and deliberating about the meaning of one's choice is an intended part of the learning portfolio. This contrast illustrates how portfolios can be conceived of as an end in themselves, which we do not believe is advisable for working with student teachers, to using portfolios as just a means, among others, to develop important learning about the study of teaching.

## FUTURE OF PORTFOLIOS IN PRESERVICE TEACHER EDUCATION

Many contributors to the portfolio literature appear to be proponents of portfolios and frequently make claims about their benefits. Portfolios, however, are neither essential, nor necessary, nor sufficient for student teachers to learn about teaching. And clearly the proliferation of portfolio use in preservice teacher education programs is primarily the result of political mandates (or their anticipation) related to licensure or accreditation requirements. This has led to many implementations similar to that described in case 1 where assessment and accountability are the primary concerns and the stakes are relatively high for students. Although these are important concerns for teacher education programs, they should not take precedence over or shortcut the main function of these programs, which is to educate preservice teachers. Based on our study of portfolios and our reading of the related literature, we hope that the future of portfolio use in preservice teacher education will emphasize learning—learning about teaching and about the study of teaching and student learning.

As we mentioned at the beginning of this chapter, there is a big difference between portfolios that are conceived of as assessment tools for practicing teachers to document what they do in their classrooms, how and why they do it, how they respond to student learning, and so on, and portfolios conceived as a structured space in which students are guided in inquiry about their own learning and understanding of teaching. The latter is unquestionably the kind of portfolio that we believe should be used in teacher education.

Having said this, portfolios should be adopted only if:

- They have been conceptualized as an integral part of a program of study where students prepare throughout their course work to engage in rigorous inquiry about their learning to teach. In other words, portfolio work should be an integral part of what students are already doing.

- Sufficient time has been allocated to this inquiry.

- The time and activities allocated to portfolio work have been purposefully and broadly structured to support and guide this inquiry.

- Both students and faculty are intellectually ready and committed to engage in this endeavor.

- There is evidence that portfolios contribute to developing important and new understandings.

Anything short of this will result in either a mechanical compilation of documents that will remain unanalyzed or aimless discussions about what to include. Students will feel that they are just meeting a requirement, faculty will feel overburdened by what they perceive as an add-on activity, and the time for these activities will be robbed from other courses and seminars that have otherwise their own purposes. Granted, the ideal situation we describe does not necessarily require portfolios. Case studies and problem-based inquiries, for example, are other means by which learning about teaching can be documented and evaluated (Darling-Hammond & Snyder, 2000). But portfolios, which can also include case studies and other forms of inquiry, may have a particular value because they create that space into which one can return over time.

Almost twenty years ago, in a study of reflection among student teachers, Richert (1990) observed that the use of portfolios seemed to result in more reflection focused on content and pedagogy than when they were not used because they helped students remember classroom events and experiences. So portfolios can be seen as an ethnographer's database, containing not only the raw data and artifacts collected over time, but the notes, commentaries, and preliminary reflections and interpretations that can be revisited time and time again to gain perspectives on one's learning and to explore particular aspects of teaching further. Just imagine what it would be like to try writing an ethnography without being able to refer to this corpus of work. In constructing this kind of portfolio, students socially engage with others in dialogue and deliberations about their work and in so doing develop the intellectual tools and habits of mind to reason and make decisions from evidence, question their beliefs and assumptions, gather and analyze data, formulate explanations and interpretations, and develop points of view while realizing that others are possible.

We realize that this conception of a portfolio is grounded in a particular inquiry view of learning and teaching, a view in which learning arises from people's experiences and their reconstruction of those experiences through conversations and dialogue with knowing others to develop new understandings and construct practical knowledge of teaching (Mansvelder-Longayroux et al., 2007). It is an open view of learning and teaching, not a closed-ended view where what is to be learned is already known—one that does not encourage searching for new understandings. Working on their own questions in the context of their own experience is presumably what gives students ownership of their own learning, an issue that has been highlighted as important in the portfolio literature (Barton & Collins, 1993; Wolf & Dietz, 1998; Mansvelder-Longayroux et al., ). Another way to think about this is in terms of appropriation of the portfolio concept. Working from James Wertsch's concept of mastery and appropriation, Habib and Wittek (2007) distinguish between students who master the portfolio assessment techniques during their studies because it is required, but they say, "If they fail to appropriate the concept of the portfolio, it is unlikely that portfolio thinking will become a part of their working culture after graduation" (p. 275). This is an important distinction and one that is particularly relevant to the distinction that has been made between the assessment and the learning portfolio. It seems to us that an assessment portfolio that emphasizes summative ratings of a product may lead students to successfully master the tasks at hand, whatever they may be, but that lasting appropriation of the portfolio concepts, the inquiry process, could occur only in the context of a learning portfolio where the primary emphasis is on learning to inquire about teaching.

We made the point previously that if portfolios are to be used within teacher education programs, learning portfolios are the most appropriate for working with student teachers. This does not rule out the possibility of constructing assessment or accountability portfolios, but we believe that in preservice teacher education programs, assessment portfolios could be constructed only from learning portfolios that precede them. Once students begin to think in terms of external criteria for the assessment of a product, they no longer think about teaching and learning in ways different from what these criteria imply. Their understandings become mechanical and basically prevent their continued learning.

We can imagine an assessment or accountability portfolio composed of selected pieces from the learning portfolio to represent one's best performance, reflection, explanation, and so on, as Snyder et al. (1998) proposed in the context of a study where it became apparent that external assessment purposes and internal needs to support learning and development could not be met simultaneously. But we are hard pressed at this point to imagine an assessment portfolio that would be beneficial—one that would not impose particular experiences on students and a particular structure on a program—without the understandings developed during the construction of a learning portfolio. This, however, remains an open question since such cases have not been documented and carefully studied. Another open question is whether portfolios endure beyond graduation. The outcome will greatly depend on the culture and organization of the schools, which we know have not been conducive to this kind of endeavor. The intellectual tools, concepts, and understandings developed in the process of developing a learning portfolio might endure, but that also is an open question.

# REFERENCES

Anderson, J. A., Du Mez, J., & Peter, M. G. (1998). Portfolio presentations in teacher education: Rites of passage for the emerging professional. In M. McLaughlin M. E. Vogt, J. A. Anderson, J. DuMez, M. G. Peter, & A. Hunter (Eds.), *Portfolio models: Reflections across the teaching profession*. Norwood, MA: Christopher-Gordon.

Barton, J., & Collins, A. (1993). Portfolios in teacher education. *Journal of Teacher Education*, *44*, 200–210.

Bird, T. (1990). The school teacher's portfolio: An essay on possibilities. In J. Millman & L. Darling-Hammond (Eds.), *The new handbook of teacher evaluation: Assessing elementary and secondary teachers* (2nd ed., pp. 241–256). Thousand Oaks, CA: Sage.

Borko, H., Michalec, P., Timmons, M., & Siddle, J. (1997). Student teaching portfolios: A tool for promoting reflective practice. *Journal of Teacher Education*, *48*(5), 345–357.

Bullock, A. A., & Hawk, P. P. (2001). *Developing a teaching portfolio: A guide for preservice and practicing teachers*. Upper Saddle River, NJ: Merrill Prentice Hall.

Campbell, D. M., Cignetti, P. B., Melenyzer, B. J., Nettles, D. H., & Wyman, R. M. (1997). *How to develop a professional portfolio: A manual for teachers*. Needham Heights, MA: Allyn & Bacon.

Campbell, D. M., Melenyzer, B. J., Nettles, D. H., & Wyman, R. M. (2000). *Portfolio and performance assessment in teacher education*. Needham Heights, MA: Allyn & Bacon.

Capraro, M. M. (2006). Electronic teaching portfolio + Portfolio development: Do they = Powerful pre-service teachers? *Teacher Education and Practice, 19*(3), 380–390.

Carnegie Foundation Task Force on Teaching as a Profession. (1986). *A nation prepared: Teachers for the 21st century*. New York: Carnegie Forum on Education and the Economy.

Cole, D. J., Ryan, C. W., Kick, F., & Mathies, B. K. (2000). *Portfolios across the curriculum and beyond* (2nd ed.). Thousand Oaks, CA: Corwin.

Council of Chief School State Officers. (2004). *Key state education policy on pk–12 education*. Washington, DC: Author.

Darling Farr, L. (2001). Portfolio as practice: The narratives of emerging teachers. *Teaching and Teacher Education, 17*, 107–121.

Darling-Hammond, L., & Snyder, J. (2000). Authentic assessment of teaching in context. *Teaching and Teacher Education, 16*, 523–545.

Delandshere, G., & Arens, S. (2001). Representations of teaching in standards-based reform: Are we closing the debate about teacher education? *Teaching and Teacher Education, 17*, 547–566.

Delandshere, G., & Arens, S. (2003). Examining the quality of the evidence in pre-service teacher portfolios. *Journal of Teacher Education, 54*(1), 57–73.

Derham, C., & Diperna, J. (2007). Digital professional portfolios of pre-service teaching: An initial study of score reliability and validity. *Journal of Technology and Teacher Education, 15*(3) 363–381.

Dewey, J. (1933). *How we think: A restatement of the relations of reflective thinking to the educative process* (2nd ed.). Boston: Heath.

Donnelly, A. M. (2005). Let me show you my portfolio: Demonstrating competence through peer interviews. *Action in Teacher Education, 27*(3), 55–63.

Elbow, P., & Belanoff, P. (1991). State University of New York at Stony Brook portfolio-based evaluation program. In P. Belanoff & M. Dickson (Eds.), *Portfolios process and product*. Portsmouth, NH: Boynton/Cook.

Gill, J. H. (1993). *Learning to learn: Toward a philosophy of education*. Atlantic Highlands, NJ: Humanities Press.

Grant, G., & Huebner, T. (1998). The portfolio question: A powerful synthesis of the personal and professional. *Teacher Education Quarterly, 25*(1), 33–43.

Habib, L., & Wittek, L. (2007). The portfolio as artifact and actor. *Mind, Culture, and Activity, 14*(4), 266–282.

Hallman, H. L. (2007). Negotiating teacher identity: Exploring the use of teaching electronic portfolios with pre-service English teachers. *Journal of Adolescent and Adult Literacy, 50*(6), 474–485.

Hartmann, C. (2004). Using teacher portfolios to enrich the methods course experiences of prospective mathematics teachers. *School Science and Mathematics, 104*(8), 392–407.

Hauge, T. E. (2006). Portfolios and ICT as means of professional learning in teacher education. *Studies in Educational Evaluation, 32*(1), 23–36.

Lave, J., & Wenger, E. (1991). *Situated learning: Legitimate peripheral participation*. Cambridge: Cambridge University Press.

Loughran, J., & Corrigan, D. (1995). Teaching portfolios: A strategy for developing learning and teaching in preservice education. *Teaching and Teacher Education, 11*(6), 565–577.

Lyons, N. (1998). Reflection in teaching: Can it be developmental? A portfolio perspective. *Teacher Education Quarterly, 25*, 115–127.

Mansvelder-Longayroux, D., Beijaard, D., Verloop, N., & Vermunt, J. (2007). Functions of the learning portfolios in student teachers' learning process. *Teachers College Record, 109*(1), 126–159.

Meyer, D. K., & Tusin, L. F. (1999). Preservice teachers' perceptions of portfolios: Process versus product. *Journal of Teacher Education, 50*(2), 131–139.

Milman, N. B. (2005). Web-based digital teaching portfolios: Fostering reflection and technology competence in pre-service teacher education students. *Journal of Technology and Teacher Education, 13*(3), 373–396.

National Board for Professional Teaching Standards. (2006). *Portfolio instructions*. Retrieved July 10, 2008, from http://www.nbpts.org/for_candidates/the_portfolio-?ID=6&x=17&y=10.

National Commission on Excellence in Education. (1983). *A nation at risk: The imperative for educational reform*. Washington, DC: U.S. Government Printing Office.

National Council for Accreditation of Teacher Education. (2008). *Professional Standards for the Accreditation of Teacher Preparation Institutions*. Retrieved July 10, 2008, from http://www.ncate.org/documents/standards/NCATE%20Standards%202008.pdf.

National Council of Teachers of English. (2006). *Guidelines for the preparation of teachers of English language arts*. Retrieved May 15, 2008, from http://www.ncte.org/store/books/middle/126639.htm?source=gs&source=gs.

Orland-Barak, L. (2005). Portfolios as evidence of reflective practice: What remains "untold." *Educational Researcher, 47*(1), 25–44.

Pardieck, S. C. (2002). Development of job search teaching portfolios for pre-service teachers. *Journal of Reading Education, 27*(2), 24–30.

Richert, A. E. (1990). Teaching teachers to reflect: A consideration of programme structure. *Journal of Curriculum Studies, 22*(6), 509–527.

Schön, D. A. (1987). *Educating the reflective practitioner*. San Francisco: Jossey-Bass.

Shulman, L. S. (1987). Knowledge and teaching: Foundations of the new reform. *Harvard Educational Review, 57*(1), 1–22.

Shulman, L. S., & Sykes, G. (1986). *A national board for teaching? In search of a bold standard*. Paper prepared for the Task Force on Teaching as a Profession, Carnegie Forum on Education and the Economy.

Smith, K., & Tillema, H. (2007). Use of criteria in assessing teaching portfolios: Judgmental practices in summative evaluation. *Scandinavian Journal of Educational Research*, *51*(1), 103–117.

Snyder, J., Lippincott, A., & Bower, D. (1998). The inherent tensions in the multiple uses of portfolios in teacher education. *Teacher Education Quarterly*, *25*, 45–60.

Sullivan, J. H. (2004). Identifying the best foreign language teachers: Teacher standards and professional portfolio. *Modern Language Journal*, *88*(3), 390–402.

Tillema, H., & Smith, K. (2007). Portfolio appraisal: In search of criteria. *Teaching and Teacher Education*, *23*, 442–456.

Wade, R. C., & Yarbrough, D. B. (1996). Portfolios: A tool for reflective thinking in teacher education? *Teaching and Teacher Education*, *12*(1), 63–79.

Wolf, K. (1991). The schoolteacher's portfolio: Issues in design, implementation, and evaluation. *Phi Delta Kappan*, *73*(2), 129–136.

Wolf, K., & Dietz, M. (1998). Teaching portfolios: Purposes and possibilities. *Teacher Education Quarterly*, *25*, 9–22.

Wray, S. (2007). Teaching portfolios, community, and pre-service teachers: Professional development. *Teaching and Teacher Education: An International Journal of Research and Studies*, *23*(7), 1139–1152.

Wyatt, R. L., & Looper, S. (1999). *So you have to have a portfolio: A teachers' guide to preparation and presentation.* Thousand Oaks, CA: Sage.

Yost, D. S., Sentner, S., & Forienza-Bailey, A. (2000). An examination of the construct of critical reflection: Implications for teacher education programming in the 21st century. *Journal of Teacher Education*, *51*(1), 39–49.

Zeichner, K. M., & Liston, D. P. (1987). Teaching student teachers to reflect. *Harvard Educational Review*, *57*, 23–48.

Zeichner, K., & Wray, S. (2001). The teaching portfolio in US teacher education programs: What we know and what we need to know. *Teaching and Teacher Education*, *17*, 613–621.

# CHAPTER TWO

# Disposition Assessment

*The Science and Psychology of Teacher Selection*

Laurie Moses Hines

*Kent State University*

Today the teacher education community believes that teacher attitude—more specifically, that a certain attitude or disposition—is critical to ensure that all children learn. Some people want teacher candidates to recognize latent racism, some want to ensure that they will be fair to all students, and others that they should be able to reflect on how their own actions affect their classrooms. This is driven by a moral concern and is translated into certain behaviors presumed to be indicative of appropriate attitude or disposition (Helm, 2007; Rike & Sharp, 2008; Burant, Chubbuck, & Whipp, 2007; Villegas, 2007). We must see these as distinct from concerns over acquisition of content knowledge or specific teaching (pedagogical) skills. Thus, teacher educators believe that they have a moral imperative to assess dispositions, as well as a procedural one, given that the National Council for Accreditation of Teacher Education demands that teacher preparation institutions evaluate all things they are to teach: the triumvirate of knowledge, skills, and, yes, dispositions (Helm, 2006).

This is not the first time that teacher educators have been motivated by a moral imperative or the first time that teachers' attitudes, dispositions, or personality have been seen as critical to good teaching. Between 1940 and 1960, many in teacher education focused on the mental health of teachers, and there are parallels between that foray into teacher psychology and today's. Then, as currently, teacher educators were concerned that those without the proper disposition would gain access to classrooms and that their own mental hygiene would adversely affect the development of those under their tutelage. They propounded on what was considered "good" personality and its relationship to "good" teaching, and they devised an array of scientific assessments to evaluate teacher candidates' personalities. They added personality, or mental hygiene, to teacher education—including psychoanalysis—as a way to improve teacher quality, and they attempted to include personality as part of the selection process to ensure that only mentally adjusted candidates made it to classrooms. Today dispositions assessments are part of many teacher education programs; candidates who fail such assessments are either ejected from teacher preparation programs or are mandated to undergo remedial education, usually some form of additional training (Hines, 2007).

The history of the science and psychology of personality, however, should give us pause to consider other aspects about the relationship between teacher education and dispositions or personality assessment. As teacher education attempted to assert control over personality—through defining what was good, scientific assessments, changes in teacher preparation to improve teaching effectiveness, and efforts at selecting teachers based on appropriate personality—alternative conceptions of good teaching and the ideas, desires, and customs of noneducators lost legitimacy as they were labeled provincial, nonscientific, hostile, or even hazardous to the mental health of the school and its teachers and students. Motivated by a moral imperative and empowered by their belief in a science of education, teacher educators concerned with mental hygiene wanted to inject the educational expert into the teacher's psychological life: her attitude, values, beliefs, and behaviors. Doing so would place educational experts, often distanced from local schools and communities, in a position of authority. With each step, professional educators encountered criticisms, which they often ignored, and their efforts at making personality assessment and adjustment scientific did not produce better teachers. After all their effort, almost all things remained as before: teacher personality was an amorphous concept, teachers had difficulty adjusting to the classroom, and local communities hired teachers who comported with the values they wanted.

## DEFINING "GOOD" DISPOSITIONS

Since the common school movement of the nineteenth century, educators have asserted that "good" teachers have certain character attributes or dispositions. Reformers such as Catherine Beecher and Horace Mann, who advocated preparation for female teachers, emphasized women's natural nurturing and their ability at moral persuasion as ideal qualities for pedagogues (Sklar, 1973; Hoffman, 1981). Public opinion about women supported this view, and public culture reflected this. Ichabod Crane cut a "ridiculous figure" with little courage, while Johnann Pestalozzi's Gertrude, from his *How Gertrude Teaches*

*Her Children* (1781), exemplified the ideal of the nurturing, affectionate teacher, implicitly affirming that women, with their qualities, were model teachers (Clifford, 1989). The desire for kindness in teachers by reformers and the middle class of the nineteenth century, however, did not disqualify those with more authoritarian styles of teaching. In rural America, in particular, hiring committees wanted assurance that a teacher could handle the bigger boys, and corporal punishment was not abhorred.

While common school reformers like Beecher and Mann saw teachers as custodians of virtue, local school boards selected teachers whose behaviors comported with community values. Often teachers were held to the strictest of codes of conduct for middle-class women: they could not smoke or drink; they could not socialize with men when unchaperoned; and they were to dress conservatively, attend church, and not engage in behavior considered deviant, such as homosexuality. Additional strictures forbade female teachers from marrying, at least until the teacher shortage brought on by the post–World War II baby boom. Communities also scrutinized teachers' political views. During World War I, the superintendent of public instruction of the Cleveland public schools suggested firing teachers sympathetic to Germany, and antiwar teachers lost their jobs in New York City. In the 1920s and 1930s, more than a dozen states, typically those in which there were anticommunist crusades, required teachers to take loyalty oaths (Blount, 2005; Ravitch, 2000).

Throughout the nineteenth century and the first few decades of the twentieth century, local communities determined the acceptable and unacceptable character, behaviors, and even political views of their teachers, and they hired and fired accordingly. This assessment of character occurred typically through the social network, in which people vouched for or maligned the dispositions of teachers. In rural schools, for instance, a hiring committee or representative from the board of education would perhaps quiz a teacher candidate on her subject matter knowledge and then rely on community members' opinion to judge her character—something that could work for or against the candidate (Kaestle, 1983; Tyack, 1974). Such informal means of attesting fitness to teach allowed widespread nepotism and was not standardized, so that throughout the second half of the nineteenth century, state-level reformers attempted to curb what they saw as an "excess of democracy," according to historian Michael Sedlak (1989), by instituting qualifications for teachers and creating the position of county superintendent as a way to standardize the teaching force.

By the early twentieth century, new trends emerged that enlarged educators' role in relation to local communities in determining teacher character and its assessment. The rise of psychology and its application in the mental hygiene movement brought the study of teacher character into the orbit of professional concern. Educational historian Sol Cohen uses the term *medicalization of education* to indicate the "infiltration of psychiatric norms, concepts, and categories of discourse'' (1983, p. 124) into American education during the first half of the twentieth century. This mental hygienist point of view replaced older notions of schooling and child rearing that emphasized academic subject matter and orderly behavior and discipline with the progressive concept of developing the child's personality (Cohen, 1983, 1999). Progressive educators focused on the development of the whole child—the social, emotional, physical, and vocational, along with the intellectual. G. Stanley Hall's 1904 publication of *Adolescence* expedited this shift toward psychology in education, and John Dewey's works, such as *The Child and the Curriculum,* gave it philosophical weight. This change required an adjustment in teacher behavior and attitude as educators began to value different characteristics and dispositions. Schools and teachers were to emphasize their quasi-parental and therapeutic role rather than that of academician or disciplinarian, and they were to tolerate aggressive classroom behavior in attending to the child's whole development. In addition, because of the psychological assumption that the actions and attitudes of adults toward children influenced personality development and mental health, attention turned toward the teacher's mental hygiene by the 1930s. The teacher was to ''demonstrate in her own personality adjustment sound mental health and emotional maturity'' because, as one educator considered, ''how can insecure, frustrated, deprived, emotionally immature, and maladjusted teachers bring about wholesome emotional growth in children?'' (Spencer, 1938).

Teachers therefore came under harsh scrutiny from the profession as their own personalities, maladjustments, behaviors, and dispositions were seen as influential on the child's development and as reflective of their abilities to discipline themselves along a professional ideal. Growing social concern that a maladjusted teacher could endanger a child's mental health—in other words, that the ''unhappy or worried or insecure teacher 'hurts' the children'' (Robinson, 1954, p. 22)—sanctioned the adjustment of teacher personality and dispositions and gave it a moral purpose: to save children from mental health endangerment.

Many different kinds of maladjusted personality traits of the teacher emerged and were considered ''potential sources of infection to the children'' (Zorbaugh, 1932, p. 332). Fussy, domineering, worried, depressed, or embittered teachers saw ''children as natural enemies'' and were ''a menace to the welfare of children who should grow up with sane and wholesome attitudes toward life'' (Andress, 1936, p. 263). Shy, nervous, timid, easily excitable, disorganized, irresponsible, introverted, sexually repressed, or hot-tempered teachers were not mentally adjusted. Teachers who worked too much and did not have a life outside school or, conversely, who worked too little had symptoms of mental maladjustment. Other views of teachers were no less or no more kind but simply paraded a gamut of personality and behavior traits that supposedly indicated maladjustment, neurosis, or some flaw in the teacher. Identifying the appropriate personality traits that indicated not only adjustment but good teaching became important.

Survey research beginning in the 1930s often polled students, parents, or even teachers to find personality attributes most effective, most liked, or most helpful in the classroom. These would yield lists of attributes: helpful, kind, honest, flexible, fair, cooperative, humorous, patient, warm, interested in children, pleasing of appearance (Leipold, 1949; Witty, 1947, 1955). By the mid- to late 1940s, some educators criticized this survey technique of determining appropriate qualities and dispositions. Some of this criticism reflected a bias against nonscientific, lay determination of what was considered good teacher characteristics; after all, this perspective asked, "Do children know who are the best teachers?" (Wilson, 1948). Other critics disagreed with the assumption that the teacher should change her personality to accommodate students, thus creating in the teacher a "chameleonic personality" (Rogers, 1950) and discouraging children from learning to adapt. Two critics, however, stand out for their macroview of the debate over which attributes teachers should possess.

University of Chicago professors of education Jacob Warren Getzels and P. W. Jackson contextualized the fruitless search for an effective teacher personality that yielded "recurring null results" by 1960. They noted that earlier images and conceptions of good teachers would not apply to the standards of the day. They reminded educators that the militaristic and authoritarian style considered "good" at the end of the nineteenth century gave way to the personal style brought in vogue with progressive education and that "the image of the teacher has undergone significant change so that many images of the 'good' teacher exist today" (Getzels & Jackson, 1960, p. 460). Getzels and Jackson recognized that the dispositions considered good were reflective of social values that changed and were valued differently by various people. For instance, conservatives, such as Catholics in the post–World War II years, favored authoritarian teaching rather than the progressive approach (de Forest, 2006).

The fruits of these explorations and surveys about good teacher personality and character between the 1930s and 1960 yielded little other than endless lists of attributes that reflected the researcher's assumptions and perspectives about good teaching at any given time. Educators, however, framed the debates and discussion over teacher personality and specific dispositions in both scientific and moral terms: scientific because supposedly objective research was used to identify good teacher personality, and moral because of the threat to children's mental health and development that those with the wrong disposition posed. Moral concerns about teacher character, as we have seen, were present from the nineteenth century; however, psychology and mental hygiene gave a scientific imprimatur to the study of teacher character and values.

# SCIENTIFICALLY ASSESSING TEACHER DISPOSITIONS AND PERSONALITY

Progressive educators generally embraced science and began a century-long search for a science of education with the turn of the century, as historian Ellen Condliffe Lagemann has shown (2000). The science of psychology and the imperative of child saving converged in the study of teacher personality and adjustment, endowing it with both a moral and a scientific dimension. Progressive educators attentive to teacher dispositions threw themselves into the task of surveying and researching teacher personality. Initially the surveys of children, parents, and teachers were in line with this science of teacher dispositions.

By the 1940s, the research on personality development became experimental and statistical, replacing the surveys of children and parents and the anecdotes about maladjusted teachers that were in the popular press. Much of this research attempted to predict personality traits best suited for effective teaching, thus enabling a better selection of teacher candidates and the identification of attitudes to be taught during teacher preparation. Researchers also sought a reliable, scientific instrument to assess teacher personality, thereby enabling experts and administrators to test teachers and predict effectiveness, recruit and select teachers based on their predicted effectiveness, and promote teachers with the desired traits once in a school system (see Barr, 1960). The *Journal of Experimental Education* and the *Journal of Educational Research* published much of the experimental research that exploded into the literature.

Many of the studies employed psychological or personality indexes to determine scientifically the relationship between good teaching and personality. Researchers developed their own tests and also used existing tests: the Rorschach test, James Cattell's 16 Factor Personality test, the Guilford-Zimmerman Temperament Survey, the Minnesota Teacher Attitude Inventory, the Minnesota Multi-Phasic Personality Inventory, the Strong Vocational Interest Blank, the Thurstone Temperament Schedule, and a whole host of other batteries designed to explore the teacher's behavior, personality, and attitude. The aspects of personality these instruments measured were varied. Indexes rated items as assorted as vocal projection, poise, emotional stability, and classroom climate; other instruments used psychological constructs such as impulsiveness, submissiveness, shyness, or sociability. Some assessments were self-reporting questionnaires; for others, administrators, psychologists, or teacher educators were to observe the teacher and make the dispositions assessment.

The results of the research were as diverse as the assessment instruments used. Some found certain qualities of good teachers. These teachers were more gregarious, adventuresome, frivolous, artistic, polished, cheerful, kind, and interested in the opposite sex than teachers rated more poorly. Others found good teachers to be those whose attitudes were positive toward children and administrators. Researchers informed by the mental hygiene movement found that teachers who had a mental hygiene perspective had a better-adjusted attitude. As one concluded, "Knowledge of principles of educational psychology, child development, and child behavior are significantly related to teacher attitudes" (LaBue, 1959, p. 434; see also Gowan, 1950, 1957; Lamke, 1951; Jones, 1956).

Neither personality researchers nor teacher educators could recognize how their assumptions, especially their progressive educational ideals, biased their research designs and testing instruments. Jennifer de Forest's case of the use of personality tests in New York City from 1947 to 1953 exposes, among other things, that the progressive educators created a test that "would reflect the values of the designers" and "would reward applicants who adhered to the ideals of progressive education and mental hygiene," even as they dismissed others' concerns or values (de Forest, 2006, pp. 727, 730). As historian Diane Ravitch (2000) notes, progressive educators had this habit: they would ignore those who disagreed with them. Researchers in teacher personality, perhaps blinded by their faith in science, their own expertise, and the moral righteousness of their endeavors to save children from mentally maladjusted teachers, ignored or dismissed considerations of others, in particular noneducators, who may not have agreed with the values they advanced.

Not all educators accepted such research blindly, and some questioned the underlying assumptions or the research designs of the growing body of scientific literature on teacher personality. J. T. Hunt (1956) of the University of North Carolina noted that "efforts to identify personality differences between superior and inferior school personnel, to isolate a 'teacher personality,' or to predict either competence or effectiveness of student teachers by means of psychometric or projective instruments led to limited results" (p. 507). Hunt recognized that personality was not a monolithic attribute; there were many kinds and types of teacher personalities, behaviors, roles, and effectiveness. He saw in the research he reviewed "a failure to recognize" these differences—that researchers on teacher personality entertained the idea that only one personality type (typically the progressive educators' ideal) was effective. Could not others be effective, just in differing ways? inquired Hunt.

While the progressive educators who advocated mental hygiene believed there was a consensus about teachers' personality qualities, critics disagreed. According to Fred Tyler (1960), professor of education at the University of California at Berkeley, no consensus existed as to what was considered good teaching, and moreover the idea of measuring it was problematic, as were the measurement instruments themselves. To Tyler, the entire design of research on teacher personality was flawed. Getzels and Jackson (1960), who had reminded researchers of the changing social value attached to various teacher traits, also criticized the mindless nature of much of the research on teacher personality. They believed that the lack of clear results was indicative of poorly conceived research and of researchers whose conception of good teaching and the good teacher were alienated from practitioner understanding: "These criteria [informing most test instruments] are largely irrelevant to the teaching situation" and there was "frequently little or no relation between the researchers' conception of effective teaching and the conception of effectiveness held by those who establish his criterion group" (pp. 457–458). In other words, researchers had one idea of effectiveness and the teacher attributes necessary for it, and teachers had another.

These critical and significant charges spoke not just to the underlying science of teacher personality, questioning its objectivity and validity. Such criticisms also exposed the lack of consensus on appropriate teacher attitudes and dispositions. The differing values of the progressive educators of New York City and the local community that de Forest documented, Hunt's commonsense appeal that researchers too narrowly conceived of good teacher behavior at the exclusion of other conceptions of effectiveness, the lack of consensus Tyler warned about, and the gulf between researchers' and teachers' conceptions of effectiveness identified by Getzels and Jackson indicate a difference in values between teacher educators advancing mental hygiene and practicing teachers and their communities.

Researchers (mostly teacher educators) and communities (practitioners and citizens) valued different traits, making it impossible to identify correct and effective attitudes. However, many teacher educators believed, in the name of scientifically assessing good teaching and saving the child from mental health endangerment, that teacher education should certify the intimate details of a candidate's personality. As has been documented in the historical literature on reforming school governance, on the curriculum, and on educational research, a paternalistic attitude existed among some members of the professional education community during the first half of the twentieth century, in which distinctions between experts and laypeople created a new hierarchy of authority based on science and professionalism (Tyack, 1974; Tyack & Cuban, 1995; Ravitch, 1983; Lagemann, 2000), although grassroots efforts to resist such changes existed (Reese, 2002). When faced with resistance from parents and teachers in the 1920s regarding, for instance, the shift from an academic to a child-centered curriculum, progressive educators "confidently told one another that implementation of their reforms would be delayed by a cultural time lag, until they had...trained a new generation of teachers and administrators" (Ravitch, 2000, p. 163). Perhaps the aura of research objectivity in education or the moral imperative to the scientific study of teacher character, or both, were powerful enough so that institutions of teacher education embarked on programs of teacher selection and counseling that utilized these personality measurement instruments, even given the criticism of them.

# PERSONALITY, TEACHER PREPARATION, AND IMPROVING TEACHER QUALITY

Teacher education institutions embarked on programs of dispositions assessment and counseling that used personality measurement instruments, if not for outright selection of teacher candidates, then for identification of personality problems so as to prescribe remedial education and psychotherapy to remedy the candidate before she graduated and entered her own classroom. The idea was that with personality assessment and remedial education, teacher dispositions and therefore quality would improve.

Personality and its assessment became increasingly important for teacher recruitment and selection during the preparation program from the late 1930s through at least the mid-1950s. However, the studies of selection practices among teacher education programs report different results. According to some reviews of the research, teacher education institutions believed personality was important, but few rejected teacher candidates on "character-personality bases" (Eliassen and Martin, 1948; Haskew, 1952). A comprehensive study of admissions practices at 785 accredited teacher education institutions by Ruth A. Stout (1957), director of field programs at Kansas State Teachers Association and later professor of education at Teachers College, Columbia University, found that 45 percent of institutions rejected teacher candidates (although a very small percentage of candidates, under 6 percent) based on academic qualifications or personality. Rejections based on academic qualifications alone could account for only 20 percent of this total, Stout approximated; beyond that, "some factors other than academic grades are operating" (p. 304). Thus, multiple institutions used personality tests but to what degree and for what purposes are unclear, even though those who were concerned with teacher assessment, like William Tanner (1954) of the Educational Testing Service, wanted a more "refined use" of these tests by colleges of education than were currently being employed (see also Archer, 1949; Downie & Bell, 1953; Gladstone, 1952).

Despite widespread interest in the role of dispositions, there were also pressures against their use. Market pressures on teacher education institutions and policies encouraging large enrollment eased entry for teachers into the field, especially after World War II (Lortie, 1975). Teacher education needed to prepare an adequate number of candidates to meet the high demand and therefore accepted all comers (Labaree, 1997), making selection during teacher preparation not very selective. Even before the teacher shortage, publicly supported teachers' colleges did not have selective admissions requirements and had to accept all applicants "where laws and regulations of state administering bodies curb attempts at selection and development of the student body on anything other than a scholastic basis" (Schellhammer, 1939, p. 64). There was resignation on the part of some teacher education administrators who recognized that the consideration of teachers' personality traits was caught between the realities of enrollment and the hiring practices of "school boards who do not demand highest standards" (Schellhammer, 1939, p. 64). In addition, teacher education institutions had no incentive to become more selective in their admissions requirements when their state funding allotment was tied to enrollment figures, as was the case. Institutions therefore admitted many and dealt with those who had personality problems through remedial education or psychotherapy.

Psychiatrists and some educators recommended offering psychoanalysis to teachers, either individually or in group therapy, as did Margaret Naumberg at her Walden School. Psychoanalysis for educators attracted the attention of teacher educators at Clark University and Columbia University, and the experimental use of psychoanalysis in teacher education received funding from the National Institute of Mental Health. Bank Street College of Education in New York, San Francisco State College, the University of Texas, and the University of Wisconsin incorporated lectures on mental health with "psychiatrically supervised individual guidance" of preservice teachers (Zimiles, 1962, p. 486; see also Hale, 1995; Herrick & Corey, 1944; Corey & Herrick, 1944; Watson, 1957; Symonds, 1954). Such psychoanalysis focused candidates' awareness on how their own childhood and adolescent experiences shaped teachers' performance in the classroom. As such, mental hygienists' concern with teacher adjustment and psychoanalysis helped to shift attention in teacher education from knowledge acquisition to personality. As Percival Symonds, professor at Teachers College, Columbia University, asserted: "Methods and procedures learned during college preparation may influence teaching superficially but they do not determine the nature of the relationship of a teacher to his pupil or the teacher's basic attitude toward teaching." An ardent mental hygienist, Symonds believed that "teaching is primarily a function of the teacher's personality," and thus "the selection of those who are to teach, and...the direction and modification of personality during the period of preparation" should be emphasized (Symonds, 1954, p. 79; see also Stewart, 1944).

Efforts at guidance and personality adjustment during teacher preparation may have had effects on teachers and teacher candidates, but not in ways they were designed to. More often, personality and psychological constructs found their way into teacher education through the curriculum, often at a cost to the academic side of teacher preparation, as critics claimed. Some teacher educators wanted to align their teacher preparation curriculum with the concepts measured in at least one of the assessment instruments (Kearney & Rocchio, 1956), but more simply incorporated psychological concepts and analysis into the curriculum rather than formally align them with any testing device. Educational psychology courses had become standard curricular fare for preservice teachers in the 1920s, and by 1946, as historian Stephen Petrina concludes, "mental hygiene . . . dominated the space of textbooks in educational psychology." Teacher candidates were getting heavy doses of behaviorism and personal psychoanalysis in their preparation (Petrina, 2004, p. 550).

By the late 1940s, the "psychological adjustment of educators themselves [had] received increasing attention in educational psychology" (Freeman, 1949, p. 259). The goals of educational psychology courses included changing the attitudes of teacher candidates, as well as providing content knowledge about child development, behavior, and learning (Raths, 1947), but there was little standardization of the courses. In remedy, the executive committee of the National Society of College Teachers of Education formed a subcommittee to more clearly define what the discipline could do for teacher education. While those participating may have had slightly different emphases, all agreed that child development, learning, and personality and adjustment, including that of the teacher, should be part of educational psychology (Freeman, 1949; Anderson, 1949; Trow, 1949; Blair, 1949). In addition, because teacher attitude toward topics such as child development—not just the knowledge acquisition of the content—was important, teacher educators agreed that exposure to these topics should occur in professional education courses offered by colleges of education, which were deemed better at preparing the teacher to have a correct attitude than were liberal arts programs (Krugman & Krugman, 1958; Scates, 1956).

For mental hygienists, personality and its adjustment became as important as academic and technical preparation for the classroom, and they recommended, as did Symonds, "a change in emphasis in teacher-training from intellectual courses to experiences for the better personal adjustment of teachers" (Mones, 1955, p. 144). For years, Symonds psychoanalyzed the teacher candidates in his classes and treated them as experimental subjects by having them write personal histories as part of their course assignments. He "first gained the pupil's confidence to a point where they would feel free enough to drag all the family skeletons out of the closet," then determined that "in every instance the teachers' classroom actions were tied directly to their own childhood experiences." In other words, he found maladjustment everywhere ("Analyzing the School Marm," 1943, p. 78). Setting aside a discussion of classroom ethics in regard to Symonds's use of psychoanalysis, we need to recognize that he and others openly advocated that the emotional life of the teacher candidate become the focus of teacher preparation, since "it is the teacher's personality that is the tool with which he works rather than the content in which he gives instruction" (Mones, 1955, p. 143). Personality was ascendant in considerations about teachers; the New York City school committee responsible for a project to test the personality of teacher applicants even dismissed the practice of testing for content knowledge in favor of testing dispositions (de Forest, 2006). In 1955, Harry Rivlin made the distinction between the teacher as "technician" and as "personality" in the *Yearbook of the National Society for the Study of Education,* simply articulating what others in the volume and in education widely thought as both cutting-edge educational theory and well-accepted perspective.

While Symonds, Rivlin, and others were enlarging the importance of psychology, mental hygiene, and personality in teacher education, others, such as Albert Bestor, professor of history variously at Oxford, Yale, and the University of Washington, criticized teacher education for its deemphasis of academics and its disassociation from traditional arts and sciences disciplines. Bestor's popular book *Educational Wastelands* (1953) was joined by others, such as James Conant's *The Education of American Teachers* (1963) and *The Miseducation of American Teachers* by James Koerner (1963). Clearly not everyone was pleased with the lack of attention to solidly academic disciplines, as Bestor and his fellow critics desired teacher preparation richer in subject matter content than psychology. These critics all believed in increased academic training as a way to improve teacher preparation (Johnson, 1989).

Throughout the mid-1950s, various programs emerged to invest arts and sciences faculty in—and to divest the stranglehold of teacher educators on—teacher preparation. The College Board, the National Science Foundation, and other private agencies supported the master of arts in teaching (M.A.T.) programs at many universities, such as the University of Chicago and Stanford and Harvard universities because of its emphasis on and direction by the arts and sciences. The Ford Foundation's Fund for the Advancement of Education developed "breakthrough programs" "to involve academic faculty in teacher education," according to historians Clifford and Guthrie (1988). Among many academicians associated with these programs, teacher preparation had a reputation for low standards. According to Teachers College professor Thomas Briggs, who sat on and then resigned from the Ford Foundation's advisory council and worked with some arts and sciences professors on these joint projects, the arts and science faculty members were condescending to or even outright hostile toward teacher educators (Clifford & Guthrie, 1988).

The criticisms from noneducators that teacher education had low academic standards and that the way to improve teaching was to focus on the acquisition of academic content, however, did not deter teacher educators, most of whom believed that professional education, with its educational psychology and efforts to adjust teacher personality, would improve teaching. Confident in their belief in progressive education and mental hygiene for teachers, the deans of the college of education at both Northwestern University and the University of Texas at Austin asserted that "criticism" of progressive education by laypeople "can impair seriously the mental health of teachers" (McSwain & Haskew, 1955, p. 340). Not only does this indicate the propensity to disregard criticism, but by labeling any challenge to educators' notions as hazardous, it delegitimized alternative conceptions of good teaching and, by implication, those who advanced other ideas.

Even aside from the concern that personality or any other nonacademic subjects crowded out academics in teacher preparation, the value of these courses and the psychoanalysis provided were in dispute. Symonds (1942; Symonds & Haggerty, 1942) reported that courses in mental hygiene led to minor changes in students' attitudes. Students felt less insecure and were better able to discuss personal issues, yet this did not necessarily transfer into a greater ability for them to display appropriate teacher dispositions. Other research indicated that teachers who took these courses had a better attitude toward children's behavioral and emotional problems and that they were more personally adjusted (Baruch, 1945; DiMichael, 1944). Students, some educators claimed, found courses in mental hygiene to be "their most valuable educative experiences," but their optimal value in ensuring the teacher's mental health "depend[ed] . . . upon the student's possessing the objectivity, integration, and fortitude needed to face his personal inadequacies, to see the need of treatment, and to carry through persistent effort toward self-help" (Spencer, 1938, p. 48).

Still, psychiatrists reported that teachers, especially novices, did not know how to handle their negative feelings toward children. I. N. Berlin (1958), professor of psychiatry at the University of California School of Medicine and psychiatric consultant to the San Francisco, San Joaquin County, and Stockton, California, school districts, captured the emotional dilemma of teachers and the bind in which their training put them:

> [Beginning teachers] seem to have absorbed from their professors, as a goal of successful teaching, love for their students. . . . These teachers were therefore dismayed to find how difficult it was to "love" certain students and they reported how frightened and secretive they were about the kinds of feelings they discovered within themselves. This emphasis on how good teachers "ought" to feel in contrast to the human feelings discovered within one's self in the process of classroom teaching . . . seemed to me to be a major factor in the teacher's difficulties in the classroom . . . . The attitudes the teacher has about himself and how he should feel are conditioned largely by the attitudes of his professors. He thus comes to believe that to have angry, thwarted, hateful feelings is pathological and means that there is something wrong with him as a person [p. 10].

According to Berlin, feelings and fear of mental pathology were causal factors in teacher maladjustment, and, unfortunately, these were exacerbated, not alleviated, by teacher education. Teacher educators, in Berlin's account, told candidates how to feel toward children, and when their emotions differed, teachers believed they had a psychological problem. Some psychiatrists believed that putting psychological experts in control of candidate education and adjustment would solve this problem, as teacher educators did not have deep understanding of psychology and as the courses were "isolated" and "may prove useless" (Rubenstein, 1959; Bernard, 1958; Pearson, 1958). Approximately fifteen years later, sociologist Dan Lortie found a similar dynamic: unlike psychologists or social workers trained to take an analytical approach to their personality, teachers were "moralistic" and "self-accusing" and did not know how to cope with their own feelings (Lortie, 1975, pp. 69, 159).

# SELECTING TEACHERS BASED ON PERSONALITY

The science of teacher personality and disposition assessment and the infusion of psychological principles into teacher education as a way to ensure that teachers had appropriate and healthy personalities were intricately connected to a process of regulating teacher labor by professional means alone that minimized the control noneducators had over teacher selection. In the name of child saving and objectivity, some teacher educators wished to exchange the oversight and discretion of local communities for that of teacher education. Much to their frustration, however, teacher educators found that even as states mandated professional training in four-year degree programs for certification, the selection of teachers lay in the hands of local school administrators and school boards. Teacher selection, then, became critical, especially if it was not done scientifically by experts with the greater good of proper child development in mind. Making this process scientific became part of the project on teacher mental hygiene.

Local school boards and schoolmen made the decisions about hiring a teacher, and often the desired dispositions reflected community norms. The process used a community's social network. The labor market also played a role in teacher selection and mental hygiene. During times of labor surplus, as during the 1930s, schoolmen could turn away those deemed unsuitable for the classroom because other candidates were available. A decade later, beginning in the 1940s during the wartime shortage and continuing through the baby boom of the 1950s, school districts were not in the same position. Replying to a questionnaire about selection practices, one administrator stated, "'If they are warm, we take them'" (Ryans, 1949a, p. 67). In addition, newly enacted tenure laws made it more difficult for school systems to rid themselves of teachers considered poor—in any sense of the word—once the teacher entered the classroom (Lynch, 1940; Williams, 1940; Kirk, 1949). Selection of teachers therefore became significant; however, most mental hygiene experts criticized local hiring processes as unscientific and political.

Mental hygienists and educational experts considered teacher selection methods used by school boards as "primitive" rather than scientific. [*Editor's note:* See Chapter Five for a discussion of how local school districts assess teachers' dispositions.] While administrators wanted "to have school boards free from politics" (Symonds, 1946, pp. 23, 33), experts perceived that favoritism abounded in the hiring process. Those valuing scientific selection claimed that school boards wanted to hire local women as teachers, promised jobs to relatives, made arbitrary hiring decisions, and generally allowed political favoritism to determine teacher selection. The community and teachers were seen as complicit in keeping teacher selection unscientific and biased, as communities found ways to hire whom they wanted regardless of professional concerns about dispositions and mental adjustment (Symonds, 1946; Hayden, 1948; Culp, 1940; Archer, 1946; Carey, 1959; Tyack, 1974; Fuller, 1982; Sedlak, 1989).

School superintendents and administrators were not immune to criticisms about their hiring practices. Critics claimed that superintendents were "still relying on snap judgments," "informal personal interviews," and "inadequate testimonials" rather than evaluations by trained psychologists to determine the personality of prospective teachers (Symonds, 1946, pp. 21–22). Critics also charged administrators with being won over by the personal appearance of the applicant and of having undue confidence in their ability to "spot a good teacher by talking with him for five minutes over coffee" (McIntyre, 1958, p. 250; see also Haskew, 1952; Reynolds, 1951). Especially egregious to the scientific crowd was not working with the placement office of teacher education institutions or not contacting the education department to inquire about the recent graduate's personal traits and abilities. Those castigating school officials questioned their ability to remain objective in the judgment of teachers. David G. Ryans, professor of education at the University of California at Los Angeles and the associate director of the National Committee on Teacher Examinations of the American Council on Education, wrote frequently advocating the scientific selection of teachers and warned that "subjectivity can be very dangerous in teacher selection" (Ryans, 1949b, pp. 45–46). He suggested rating scales, tests, and other means to objectively select teachers, even for personality, rather than using administrator preference or opinion (Ryans, 1946, 1949b). After all, as another advocate asserted, an administrator could "slant the results . . . in the direction he thinks personally desired" (Gowan, 1956, p. 663). The 1951 text, *Principles and Procedures for Teacher Selection* by the American Association of Examiners and Administrators of Educational Personnel, included application procedures and sample forms, rating scales, and regulations for selecting teachers to help administrators make the selection process more objective.

The editors of *School Executive,* the journal for administrators and boards of education, hoped that educating administrators to use statistical methods and data collection in assessing the "mental poise of a candidate" would take "selection out of the realm of guesswork or personal prejudices and place it in the sphere of science" (p. 14). They wanted to inform boards of education, citizens, and parent-teacher organizations about proper teacher selection and printed a bulletin, available "in quantities of ten or more," to advance the scientific approach (Dixon, 1948). However, by advocating scientific selection of teachers, educational experts argued to assume more control over a process historically controlled by local people.

Some educators suggested making personality assessment for hiring purposes scientific and controlled by experts through such means as personality tests, extensive interviews conducted by trained psychiatrists, personal histories analyzed by experts, stress tests, or even a "mental health certification" for each student (Patry, 1951). Certainly a growing chorus of educators called for teacher selection to be based on mental health, first and foremost, and many saw this process as occurring throughout the teacher education process. Teacher educators may have recommended their graduates to hiring boards "first as a personality . . . and only secondarily as the master of a subject matter," as happened at the Newark Normal School in the 1930s (Zorbaugh, 1932, p. 333), but in actuality, those in higher education could exert little control over who entered the classroom. Therefore, teacher educators focused their attention on the selection and guidance of teachers before the point of hiring, as teacher candidates progressed through their training period (Williams, 1940; Liggitt, 1954; Bernard, 1952). However, as we saw before, the testing, guidance, and education of teacher candidates along mental hygienic lines did not guarantee improved teacher quality.

The advocacy of a greater role for teacher educators in weeding out potential candidates based on personality—in other words, for teacher education to be concerned not just with knowledge and skill acquisition but the assessment of appropriate dispositions—cannot be separated from the view that many in teacher education held regarding local communities and their hiring practices. This should not be viewed simply as the inability of educators to build the necessary public support for their effort or simply as an attempt to assist communities in their recruitment and hiring of teachers. As in earlier decades, professional educators used the rhetoric of science and expertise to delegitimize community participation in local educational decision making (Tyack, 1974). Educational leaders in universities, note historians David Tyack and Larry Cuban (1995), "tended to dismiss their opponents as ignorant or self-interested," whether those opponents were urban school boards composed of neighborhood politicians, rural schoolmen, or teachers (p. 21). These university educators, most of whom were progressive educators concerned with social efficiency, social meliorism, or the child-centered curriculum, "gained a disproportionate authority over educational reform" between 1900 and 1950, claim Tyack and Cuban. However, for all the efforts of teacher educators to make selection of teachers scientific and reflective of mental hygienic principles, such decisions ultimately remained the purview of local communities, even if they were provincial, unscientific, or biased.

## DISCUSSION

Teacher education's use of personality tests and education to improve the mental health of teachers and ultimately to ensure quality teaching was misplaced for a variety of reasons. First, those advocating the search for certain attributes failed to recognize the socially constructed nature of teacher characteristics and that not all people adhered to their progressive philosophy. Thus, a search for the best attributes and dispositions could never yield any definitive list, and there is little doubt that no consensus would emerge among both laypeople and educators. Second, the research on teacher personality itself had multiple flaws, not the least of which was that any construct was not objective and scientific but laden with the researcher's assumptions. In addition, there was the question of value differences between those being judged (teacher candidates who may have held the values of their local communities) and the judges (professional educators). Third, attempts to inject personality into teacher education and selection failed. Education programs had pressures to be less than selective, and critics of teacher education saw the infusion of psychology into the curriculum, especially the emphasis on psychological self-help that personality became, as crowding out academic learning—the very thing these critics thought necessary to improve the quality of teaching in public schools. People across the board—mental hygienists in support of personality in teacher education and psychiatrists—questioned the effectiveness of courses in psychology and mental hygiene in either changing teacher behavior or helping teachers to mentally adjust. Thus, that dispositions assessment improved the quality of the teaching force was questionable. Finally, scientific selection of teachers based on dispositions or personality advanced a larger role for experts and teacher educators and prescribed that of local communities. As Paul Woodring, a professor of education who was critical of progressive education, noted in his 1953 book, *Let's Talk Sense About Our Schools,* professionals had "preempted the responsibility for policy making to such an extent that interested citizens, even members of elected boards of education, feel that they no longer have an adequate part in the establishment of basic educational policies" (quoted by Ravitch, 1983, pp. 76–77). Mental hygienic selection of teachers attempted to exchange one overseer—the local community leaders, with their diversity of values and even their political ways—for that of progressive-minded educators who believed that their expertise and moral concerns for the mental health of school children overrode local control of schooling.

By the mid-1960s, teacher educators became preoccupied with the socioeconomic lives of children rather than their inner psychological lives, perhaps due to the availability of federal funding directed toward education and children by Lyndon Johnson's Great Society programs, to the popular and academic attention on race and class spawned by the civil rights movement, and to the political ascendance of equal educational opportunity policies. The whole child and his psychological health did not vanish, however; it remained institutionalized in educational psychology courses and permeated the ethos of teacher education, but explicit focus on teacher personality faded. One historian has suggested that the emergence of teacher-proof curricula during this time reflects attempts of the educational community to "improve classroom instruction without necessarily improving teachers" (Johnson, 1989, p. 240). Personality assessment and education was about improving the very private aspect of the teacher's inner life; this no longer compelled teacher educators after 1960.

Once again, though, teacher education has turned its attention to dispositions assessment. Very little has changed, except for the particular personality attributes valued. Instead of the moral concern for the mental health of children, teacher educators are concerned about social justice and the attitudes that teacher candidates have toward urban school children—typically those from various socioeconomic, racial/ethnic, or cultural backgrounds. Aside from teacher educators' proclamations that certain teaching methods or classroom climates better serve these populations, there is no broad public consensus on the correct attitude or classroom approach for teachers other than a sense of equal treatment and opportunity. And even in the research, there is no evidence to suggest that teacher candidates' exploration of personal beliefs is linked to teacher efficacy or that any statements they make are anything more than "their ability to read their professors' expectations and supply the answer most likely desired" (Burant et al., 2007, p. 400). This has not stopped teacher educators, yet again, from using research (science) and morality to claim that their perspective on teacher dispositions is correct and that people in local communities, including teacher candidates before undergoing professional socialization, cannot be trusted with decisions about teacher dispositions because they may have "unexamined beliefs ... [that] tend to remain latent" but resurface or become "stumbling blocks or barriers to learning" (Villegas, 2007, pp. 373–374).

Clearly a teacher's dispositions are important, but research on personality, assessment of teacher candidates, the provision of remediation or socialization, and other attempts to carve a larger role for teacher education in the certification of dispositions, as this history suggests, may simply be a domain that teacher education cannot control unless it wishes to recreate the relationships of the first half of the twentieth century in which morally motivated experts attempted to delegitimize democratic control of schooling in favor of science and psychology.

# REFERENCES

American Association of Examiners and Administrators of Educational Personnel. (1951). *Principles and Procedures of Teacher Selection*. Philadelphia: Author.

Anderson, G. L. (1949). Educational psychology and teacher education. *Journal of Educational Psychology, 40*, 275–284.

Andress, J. M. (1936). Am I as a teacher a well adjusted person? *Hygeia, 14*, 267.

Archer, C. P. (1946). Local selection, placement, and administrative practices. *Review of Educational Research, 16*, 228–232.

Archer, C. P. (1949). Recruitment, institutional selection, and guidance of teachers. *Review of Educational Research, 19*, 191–200.

Barr, A. S. (1960). The assessment of the teacher's personality. *School Review, 68*, 400–408.

Baruch, D. W. (1945). Procedures in training teachers to prevent and reduce mental hygiene. *Pedagogical Seminary and Journal of Genetic Psychology, 67*, 143–178.

Berlin, I. N. (1958). Emotional factors in the teacher education process. *California Journal of Secondary Education, 33*, 7–12.

Bernard, H. (1952). *Mental hygiene for the classroom teacher*. New York: McGraw-Hill.

Bernard, V. W. (1958). Teacher education in mental health, From the point of view of the psychiatrist. In M. Krugman (Ed.), *Orthopsychiatry and the School*. New York: American Orthopsychiatry Association.

Bestor, A. (1953). *Educational wastelands: The retreat from learning in our public schools*. Urbana: University of Illinois Press.

Blair, G. M. (1949). The content of educational psychology. *Journal of Educational Psychology, 40*, 267–274.

Blount, J. M. (2005). Fit to teach: Same-sex desire, gender, and school work in the twentieth century. Albany, NY: SUNY Press.

Burant, T. J., Chubbuck, S. M., & Whipp, J. L. (2007). Reclaiming the moral in the dispositions debate. *Journal of Teacher Education, 58*, 397–411.

Carey, R. D. (1959). How to select and place teachers. *American School Board Journal, 139*, 17–19.

Clifford, G. J. (1989). Man/woman/teacher: Gender, family and career in American educational history. In D. Warren (Ed.), *American teachers: Histories of a profession at work*. New York: Macmillan.

Clifford, G. J., & Guthrie, J. W. (1988). *Ed school: A brief for professional education*. Chicago: University of Chicago Press.

Cohen, S. (1983). The mental hygiene movement, the development of personality and the school: The medicalization of American education. *History of Education Quarterly, 23*(2), 123–140.

Cohen, S. (1999). *Challenging orthodoxies: Toward a new cultural history of education*. New York: Peter Lang.

Conant, J. B. (1963). *The education of American teachers*. New York: McGraw-Hill.

Corey, S. M., & Herrick, V. E. (1944). Adjustment counseling with teachers. *Educational Administration and Supervision, 30*, 87–96.

Culp, V. H. (1940). Only "personal" applications considered. *American School Board Journal, 100*, 51–52.

Cussler, M. T. (1939). Emotional maturity for teachers. *Clearinghouse, 14*, 15–18.

de Forest, J. (2006). New York City's failed teacher selection project: Political reality trumps educational research, 1947–1953. *Teachers College Record, 108*, 726–747.

DiMichael, S. G. (1944). Comparative changes in teachers' attitudes resulting from courses in mental hygiene and educational guidance. *Journal of Educational Research, 37*, 656–669.

Dixon, M. (1948). Our schools: Selecting teachers for a school system. *School Executive, 67*, 11–14.

Downie, N. M., & Bell, C. R. (1953). The Minnesota Teacher Attitude Inventory as an aid in the selection of teachers. *Journal of Educational Research, 46*, 699–704.

Eliassen, R. H., & Martin, L. M. (1948). Teacher recruitment and selection during the period 1944 through 1947. *Journal of Educational Research, 41*, 641–655.

Freeman, F. S. (1949). The need to define and re-orient educational psychology. *Journal of Educational Psychology, 40*, 257–260.

Fuller, W. E. (1982). *The old country school: The story of rural education in the Middle West*. Chicago: University of Chicago Press.

Getzels, J. W., & Jackson, P. W. (1960). Research on the variable teacher. Some comments. *School Review, 65*, 450–462.

Gladstone, R. (1952). A note on certain test score relationships and their implication for research in teacher selection. *Journal of Educational Psychology, 43*, 116–118.

Gowan, J. C. (1956). The use of the adjective check list in screening teaching candidates. *Journal of Educational Research, 49*, 663–672.

Gowan, W. N. (1950). The measure of a successful teacher. *American School Board Journal, 121*, 17–19.

Gowan, W. N. (1957). Summary of the intensive study of twenty highly selected elementary women teachers. *Journal of Experimental Education, 26*, 115–124.

Hale, N. (1995). *The rise and crisis of psychoanalysis in the United States: Freud and the Americans, 1917–1985*. New York: Oxford University Press.

Haskew, L. D. (1952). Public school employment policies that affect teacher education. *Journal of Teacher Education, 3*, 3–6.

Hayden, F. S. (1948). The art of selecting good teachers. *California Journal of Secondary Education, 23*, 182–184.

Helm, C. M. (2006). The assessment of teacher dispositions. *Clearing House, 79*, 237–239.

Helm, C. (2007). Teacher dispositions affecting self-esteem and student performance. *Clearing House, 80*, 109–110.

Herrick, V. E, & Corey, S. M. (1944). Group counseling with teachers. *Educational Administration and Supervision, 30*, 321–330.

Hines, L. M. (2007). The return of the thought police? The history of teacher attitude adjustment. *Education Next, 7*, 58–65.

Hoffman, N. J. (1981). *Woman's true profession: Voices from the history of teaching*. Old Westbury, NY: Feminist Press.

Hunt, J. T. (1956). School personnel and mental health. *Review of Educational Research*, *26*, 482–487.

Johnson, W. R. (1989). Teachers and teacher training in the twentieth century. In D. Warren (Ed.), *American teachers: Histories of a profession at work*. New York: Macmillan.

Jones, M. L. (1956). Analysis of certain aspects of teaching ability. *Journal of Experimental Education*, *25*, 153–180.

Kaestle, C. F. (1983). *Pillars of the Republic: Common schools and American society, 1780–1860*. New York: Hill and Wang.

Kearney, N. C., & Rocchio, P. D. (1956). The effect of teacher education on the teacher's attitude. *Journal of Educational Research*, *49*, 703–708.

Kirk, P. L. (1949). Selection of teachers. *American School Board Journal*, *118*, 21–22.

Koerner, J. D. (1963). *The miseducation of American teachers*. Boston: Houghton Mifflin.

Krugman, M. (1958). Introduction. In M. Krugman (Ed.), *Orthopsychiatry and the school*. New York: American Orthopsychiatry Association.

Labaree, D. (1997). *How to succeed in school without really learning: The credentials race in American education*. New Haven, CT: Yale University Press.

LaBue, A. C. (1959). Teachers' classroom attitudes. *Journal of Teacher Education*, *10*, 433–434.

Lagemann, E. C. (2000). *An elusive science: The troubling history of education research*. Chicago: University of Chicago Press.

Lamke, T. A. (1951). Personality and teaching success. *Journal of Experimental Education*, *20*, 217–259.

Leipold, L. E. (1949). Teacher traits that pupils like or dislike. *Clearinghouse*, *24*, 164–166.

Liggitt, W. A. (1954). The personnel dean can help in the selection of teachers. *American School Board Journal*, *128*, 33–34.

Lortie, D. C. (1975). *Schoolteacher* (2nd ed.). Chicago: University of Chicago Press.

Lynch, J. M. (1940). The modern psychology of teacher selection. *American School Board Journal*, *101*, 31–32.

McIntyre, K. E. (1958). How to select teachers. *National Education Association Journal*, *47*, 250–251.

McSwain, E. T., & Haskew, L. D. (1955). Mental health through teacher education. In N. B. Henry (Ed.), *Mental health in modern education: The Fifty-Fourth Yearbook of the National Society for the Study of Education*. Chicago: University of Chicago Press.

Mones, L. (1955). Psychiatric insight into educational effort. *Education*, *76*, 139–150.

Patry, F. L. (1951). Mental hygiene is first need in the selection of teachers. *Nation's Schools*, *27*, 58.

Pearson, G.H.J. (1958). The most effective help a psychiatrist can give to the teacher. In M. Krugman (Ed.), *Orthopsychiatry and the school*. New York: American Orthopsychiatry Association.

Petrina, S. (2004). Luella Cole, Sidney Pressey, and educational psychoanalysis, 1921–1931. *History of Education Quarterly, 44*(4), 524–553.

Raths, L. (1947). Some recent research in helping teachers to understand children. *Journal of Educational Sociology, 21*, 205–211.

Ravitch, D. (1983). *The troubled crusade: American education, 1945–1980.* New York: Basic Books.

Ravitch, D. (2000). *Left back: A century of battles over schools reform.* New York: Simon and Schuster.

Reese, W. J. (2002). *Power and promise of school reform: Grassroots movements during the progressive era.* New York: Teachers College Press.

Reynolds, E. J. (1951). Common mistakes in hiring teachers. *School and Community, 37*, 155–156.

Rike, C. J., & Sharp, L. K. (2008). Assessing preservice teachers' dispositions: A critical dimension of professional preparation. *Childhood Education, 84*, 150–154.

Rivlin, H. (1955). The role of mental health in education. In N. B. Henry (Ed.), *Mental Health in Modern Education: The Fifty-Fourth Yearbook of the National Society for the Study of Education.* Chicago: University of Chicago Press.

Robinson, B. (1954). Emotional problems in the administration of educational personnel. *Education, 75*, 228–232.

Rogers, D. (1950). Implications of views concerning the "typical" school teacher. *Journal of Educational Sociology, 23*, 482–487.

Rubenstein, B. O. (1959). A comparison between cultural expectations regarding the role of the teacher and his actual role in the learning process. *Educational Administration and Supervision, 45*, 95–101.

Ryans, D. G. (1946). Notes on teacher selection: Sources of information about qualifications of the candidate. *Educational Administration and Supervision, 32*, 333–342.

Ryans, D. G. (1949a). Procedures employed in teacher selection. *Teachers College Journal, 20*, 58–59ff.

Ryans, D. G. (1949b). The interview in teacher selection can be improved and used successfully. *Nation's Schools, 43*, 45–46.

Scates, D. E. (1956). Significant factors in teachers' classroom attitudes. *Journal of Teacher Education, 7*, 274–279.

Schellhammer, F. M. (1939). It takes more than pedagogy. *Nation's Schools, 24*, 62–64.

Sedlak, M. (1989). "Let us go and buy a school master": Historical perspectives on the hiring of teachers in the United States, 1750–1980. In D. Warren (Ed.), *American teachers: Histories of a profession at work.* New York: Macmillan.

Sklar, K. K. (1973). *Catherine Beecher: A study in American domesticity.* New York: Norton.

Spencer, D. (1938). Mental hygiene for teachers. *Teachers College Record, 40*, 40–50.

Stewart, H. A. (1944). Maladjustment among teachers. *Teachers College Journal, 15*, 126–130.

Stout, R. A. (1957). Selective admissions and retention practices in teacher education. *Journal of Teacher Education, 8*, 299–317, 422–432.

Symonds, P. M. (1943). Dynamic factors contributing to personality formation in teachers. *Education, 63,* 616–626.

Symonds, P. M. (1946). Evaluation of teacher personality. *Teachers College Record, 48,* 21–33.

Symonds, P. M. (1954). Teaching as a function of the teacher's personality. *Journal of Teacher Education, 5,* 79–83.

Symonds, P. M., & Haggerty, H. R. (1942). The therapeutic value for teachers of the course in mental hygiene. *Journal of Educational Psychology, 33,* 561–583.

Tanner, W. C. (1954). Personality bases in teacher selection. *Phi Delta Kappan, 35,* 271–277.

Trow, W. C. (1949). Educational psychology charts a course. *Journal of Educational Psychology, 40,* 285–294.

Tyack, D. B. (1974). *The one best system: A history of American urban education.* Cambridge, MA: Harvard University Press.

Tyack, D., & Cuban, L. (1995). *Tinkering toward utopia: A century of public school reform.* Cambridge, MA: Harvard University Press.

Tyler, F. (1960). Teachers' personality and testing competencies. *School Review, 68,* 429–449.

Villegas, A. M. (2007). Dispositions in teacher education: A look at social justice. *Journal of Teacher Education, 58,* 370–380.

Watson, G. (1957). Psychoanalysis and the future of education. *Teachers College Record, 58,* 241–247.

Williams, C. O. (1940). Teacher selection assumes increased importance. *American School Board Journal, 101,* 21–22.

Wilson, L. A. (1948). Do children know who are the best teachers? *Educational Forum, 13,* 63–67.

Witty, P. (1947). An analysis of the personality traits of the effective teacher. *Review of Educational Research, 40,* 662–671.

Witty, P. (1955). The mental health of the teacher. In N. B. Henry (Ed.), *Mental health and modern education: The Fifty-Fourth Yearbook of the National Society for the Study of Education* (pp. 307–333). Chicago: University of Chicago Press.

Zimiles, H. (1962). Mental health and school personnel. *Review of Educational Research, 32,* 485–486.

Zorbaugh, H. (1932). Mental hygiene's challenge to education. *Journal of Educational Sociology, 5,* 325–533.

# PART TWO

# ASSESSMENT FOR TRANSITION INTO TEACHING

**Chapter Three:** Assessment for Learning in Preservice Teacher Education: Performance-Based Assessments

*Ruth Chung Wei, Raymond L. Pecheone*

**Chapter Four:** Licensure Tests: Their Use and Value for Increasing Teacher Quality

*Dan Goldhaber*

**Chapter Five:** Hiring Decisions

*Dane A. Delli*

# Assessment for Learning in Preservice Teacher Education

## Performance-Based Assessments

Ruth Chung Wei, Raymond L. Pecheone

*Stanford University*

Teacher education programs have long used a customized set of curriculum-embedded assessments to support teacher candidate learning. High-stakes summative assessments have been left up to the states, which have usually tested basic skills, content knowledge, and, increasingly, pedagogical knowledge. However, recent changes in national and state accreditation processes have put program outcomes under the microscope, and the policy environment increasingly demands that teacher education programs provide evidence that their graduates have learned to teach. The quest for more valid licensing examinations has led some states and teacher education programs to look toward the use of performance-based assessments that measure teachers' competencies with more authentic instruments as the basis for licensure and professional development.[1] Preservice teacher credential programs across the country have independently created and implemented their own assessment systems that include performance-based approaches, focusing not only on teaching knowledge but on the application of this knowledge in practice. (For descriptions of a wide variety of assessment approaches used in teacher education programs, see Castle & Shaklee, 2006; Wise, Ehrenberg, & Leibbrand, 2008; Coggshall, Max, & Bassett, 2008.)

The strength of university-based approaches to assessment is that they are often used in formative ways to support candidate learning, while current licensure examinations are only summative in nature and do not generate detailed information about specific strengths and weaknesses in candidate performance that can provide feedback to support candidate growth and program improvement. However, as accrediting agencies have moved toward outcome-based evidence of program effectiveness, the bar for meeting standards of reliability and validity has been raised. Even when local assessments are authentic, are thoughtfully implemented, and reflect program values, they may not have the psychometric properties that would allow policymakers to evaluate the validity or reliability of the information these assessments produce for the purpose of informing the licensure decision.

Several questions are raised by these seemingly competing (formative versus summative) approaches to teacher evaluation at the preservice level:

- Can curriculum-embedded performance tasks validly and reliably measure candidates' teaching knowledge and skill?
- Under what conditions can performance-based approaches support preservice teacher learning and professional development?
- Can a performance-based assessment be used to both inform summative licensure decisions for preservice teachers and support their professional learning and development?

To answer these questions, this chapter critiques the strengths and pitfalls of performance-based approaches to preservice teacher assessment, drawing on a review of research conducted to assess the technical quality and usefulness of these assessments for making high-stakes decisions and for supporting teacher learning. As part of this review, we highlight in greater detail a particular performance-based approach in preservice teacher assessment, the Performance Assessment for California Teachers (PACT), a project that has provided an innovative set of instruments to measure teaching effectiveness in a standardized and more reliable and valid way, and yet may also be used for formative purposes. The chapter describes this assessment system in some detail and summarizes the research documenting its validity and reliability and its formative function.

## WHY PERFORMANCE-BASED APPROACHES?

Over the past two decades, teaching performance assessments (TPAs) have found wide appeal in the context of teacher education programs and teacher licensing for their innovative ways of assessing teacher knowledge and skill, as well as their formative impact on teacher learning and instructional practice. Spurred by the shift of the National Council for Accreditation of Teacher Education (NCATE) from process-oriented accreditation to accreditation based on systematic performance assessment of teacher candidates, teacher education programs have been forced to grapple with the question of how to measure teacher competencies reliably and validly so that they can document the contributions of their programs to teacher quality.

Darling-Hammond, Wise, and Klein (1999) argue that more authentic assessments of teaching that simulate the complexities of teaching practice can improve the validity of licensing assessments and provide a valuable educational experience for teachers in the process of preparing for the assessment. Darling-Hammond and Snyder (2000) identify four characteristics of authentic assessments of teaching: (1) the assessments sample the actual knowledge, skills, and dispositions desired of teachers in real teaching and learning contexts; (2) the assessments integrate multiple facets of knowledge and skill used in teaching practice; (3) multiple sources of evidence are collected over time and in diverse contexts; and (4) assessment evidence is evaluated by individuals with relevant expertise against an agreed-on set of standards that matter for teaching performance. Darling-Hammond and Snyder highlight four assessment tools that meet these criteria: cases, exhibitions of performance, portfolios, and problem-based inquiries (or action research).

In their description of a variety of TPA formats, Long and Stansbury (1994) include portfolios that document a teacher's actual teaching experience over a specified period of time; semistructured interviews that ask teachers to answer a standardized set of questions designed to assess their knowledge and pedagogical skills in a particular content area, or to perform specific tasks such as designing a lesson unit, planning a lesson, and evaluating student performance; and semistructured simulation tasks that require teachers to respond in writing to a set of tasks in a classroom teaching scenario.

The performance assessments developed in the past two decades by the Interstate New Teacher Assessment and Support Consortium (INTASC) and the National Board for Professional Teaching Standards (NBPTS) represent the best-known national initiatives to develop alternative performance-based teacher assessments. These assessments are based on complex and holistic views of teaching and validated professional teaching standards, and represent authentic measurement tools that are context sensitive, longitudinal, and individualized (Darling-Hammond, 2001).

Researchers argue that in addition to being more authentic measures of teacher performance, innovative performance-based approaches to teacher assessment provide powerful professional development opportunities and stimulate teacher learning (Athanases, 1994; Anderson & DeMeulle, 1998; Darling-Hammond & Snyder, 2000; Davis & Honan, 1998; Haynes, 1995; Lyons, 1996, 1998a, 1998b, 1999; Rotberg, Futrell, & Lieberman, 1998; Tracz, Sienty, & Mata, 1994; Whitford, Ruscoe, & Fickel, 2000). However, not all TPAs are alike. They come in a variety of formats including case studies; tasks that ask teachers to analyze student work, evaluate textbooks, analyze a teaching video, or solve a teaching problem; lesson planning exercises; and portfolios.

There are a variety of tasks and activities that are called "performance assessments" and there is even variation in how portfolio assessments are defined. (See Chapter One, this volume.)

Because TPAs vary widely in format and content, it is important to distinguish among them and to evaluate their technical quality (validity, reliability), particularly if they are to be used for summative licensing decisions. In addition, it is important to investigate the conditions under which performance-based assessments can serve a formative purpose to support teacher learning and reflection.

# CURRENT STATE OF THE FIELD

A 2006 survey[2] conducted by the American Association for State Colleges and Universities (Wineburg, 2006) found that the four most common means of collecting evidence about the effectiveness of teacher preparation programs were (1) observation systems that included faculty-developed rubrics and program standards; (2) surveys of cooperating teachers, schools principals, and program graduates, both during the program and beyond; (3) work samples and portfolios of teacher candidates; and (4) state certification tests (for example, Praxis I and II). The study also indicated that while state colleges and universities were expending enormous energy and resources to assess preservice teachers and compiling data on their programs, most of the assessments lacked evidence of validity and reliability.

In this review, we evaluate curriculum-embedded performance-based approaches to assessment that are in current use in preservice teacher preparation programs. While exit and follow-up surveys or aggregated results of state certification tests may have some value as measures of program or teacher quality, we do not believe they provide sufficient information with enough rich detail about the qualities of individual teachers. In addition, neither of these types of instruments provides information that is formative for both individual teachers and programs.

In our review of the literature, we identified four primary types of curriculum-embedded performance-based assessments that are in wide use across preservice teacher credentialing programs:

- Observation-based instruments and systems
- On-demand performance tasks
- Child case studies
- Portfolio assessments and teacher work sampling

While there may be other types of performance-based assessments being used in some programs, these four types represent genres that are relatively well known, and the examples we use have been documented in research articles. This research review does not purport to account for every available research source or every example that merits review within each of these assessment genres.

In our analysis of the strengths and weaknesses of these different assessment approaches, we used three primary evaluative criteria:

1. How useful is the performance-based assessment for formative purposes?

   - Does the assessment promote teacher reflection and learning and lead to professional growth for individual teachers?
   - Does the assessment provide immediate and useful information for programs that can drive program faculty learning and inform revisions of program content and design?

2. How credible and defensible is the performance-based assessment for summative purposes?

   - Is there evidence that the assessment is based on valid constructs and aligned with validated teaching standards and professional expectations?
   - Is there evidence that the assessment can be scored reliably across scorers and sites and that there is a scoring moderation process for ensuring the fairness of summative decisions that depend on the scores?

3. How practical and feasible is the performance-based assessment (when there is information on this aspect of the assessment approach)?

   - What are the practical resources, such as time, human resources, and technology, required to implement the assessment?
   - What are the financial resources required to implement the assessment?

# OBSERVATION-BASED ASSESSMENT

Observations of teacher candidates within the context of their student teaching placements is one method of performance-based assessment that is likely to be used in all credentialing programs. Observation-based ratings instruments have a long history and have evolved over time. Throughout their history, observation forms and checklists have focused on specific behaviors that reflected the dominant view of effective teaching (Arends, 2006b). In the past, these instruments reflected a simplistic view of effective teaching as a set of discrete countable behaviors. In this age of accountability and state regulation, observation instruments and ratings systems often lift language straight out of the state teaching standards or national standards (for example, INTASC model standards), as though these standards statements represent valid constructs in themselves.

Observations of teaching, even if the sampling is infrequent and of short duration, are considered in teacher education to be indispensable to the evaluation of a candidate's readiness to teach. In some programs and circumstances, student teaching evaluations based on observations can trump all other evidence of candidates' proficiencies. For example, a candidate could be earning high marks in courses, but exhibit extremely negative behavior and lack of rapport with students. Such individuals are often counseled out of a program to minimize harm to students. While many teacher education programs place great faith in their observation protocols, the technical quality of the observation instruments and procedures in current use leaves much to be desired.

While research has found that assessors can be trained to reach a high level of interrater agreement on observation ratings instruments, most credential programs do not have the time or resources to provide sufficient training to supervisors and cooperating teachers to achieve an acceptable level of agreement. In addition, the quality of the scales used to score teaching performance varies. In some cases, teachers are scored as having "met" or "not met" the performance criteria, and in others, the scales may have four or five levels of performance, usually from novice to advanced or expert levels. The problem with many observation ratings instruments used to evaluate student teachers is that there are no descriptions of what performance would look like at these various levels. This means that evaluators (supervisors and cooperating teachers) are left to their professional judgment to decide what is considered proficient or passing performance. In more carefully constructed scales, rubrics describe in detail a developmental continuum of performance with clear indicators of expected performance at each score level (an example is the New Teacher Center's Continuum of Teacher Development). These descriptors not only bolster the ability of evaluators to score reliably, but also serve a formative purpose for student teachers by providing clear and concrete images of more advanced performance so that they have something to strive toward. Finally, while four- to five-point scales used to assess teaching performance appear to provide enough variation in scores so as to differentiate performance among beginning teachers, research and practice indicate little variance in the ratings candidates receive, with almost 100 percent of candidates who successfully complete a credential program receiving at least the minimum ratings required for passing student teaching.

## Observation-Based Teacher Education Tools

An entire chapter could be written on the strengths and weaknesses of observation-based evaluation instruments; however, we focus on a few examples of instruments for which documented evidence about their technical quality could be gathered to evaluate their merit as both summative assessments of teaching performance and instruments that can serve formative purposes.

**Washington Performance-Based Pedagogy Assessment.** Washington State is currently using an observation-based teacher assessment at the preservice teacher education level. The Washington Association of Colleges of Teacher Education worked with the Office of Superintendent of Public Instruction to develop the Performance-Based Pedagogy Assessment (PPA), designed to be used during student teaching to assess candidates' ability to:

- Set clear learning targets and assessment approaches
- Use empirically grounded instructional techniques
- Engage traditionally marginalized students
- Effectively manage classroom activities and students

The PPA also places a new focus on evidence of student learning. Candidates are required to design and implement an assessment that provides evidence of student learning. The instrument requires at least two observations, and prior to the observations, candidates provide assessors with a description of their class and student characteristics, their lesson plans and planned assessments, and a rationale for the plans (Wasley & McDiarmid, 2004).

The PPA evaluates preservice teachers across ten dimensions of teaching; five are scored based on the written "sources of evidence" provided prior to the observation, and five are scored based on the observations and evidence of student learning presented by the student teacher. Each of the dimensions has between four and nine analytical scoring criteria on which candidates are scored as having "met" or "not met" the criteria or the evidence is "not observed." (There are no level descriptors or indicators that specify what it means to have met or not met the criteria.) In order to pass the PPA, candidates must be scored as having met all fifty-seven criteria evaluated across ten dimensions, with evidence collected during two or more cycles of observation. (See Office of the Superintendent of Public Instruction, 2004, for specific directions to teacher candidates and the scoring rubrics.) Candidates are evaluated on the PPA by their university supervisor and the cooperating teacher.

*Technical Quality.* The validity of the Washington PPA rests on its alignment with validated standards for the teaching profession. The ten scoring dimensions of the rubrics are derived from the ten standards of the Washington Administrative Code (WAC): Effective Teaching Requirements for Teacher Preparation Program Approval. A validity study (Tisadondilok, 2006) examining the alignment of the Washington PPA against the INTASC model standards indicates that the INTASC standards are mostly aligned with the ten WAC standards, on which the PPA assessment rubrics are based. Tisadondilok also examined the construct and consequential validity of the PPA. She found that most faculty and supervisors at one university who had experience using the PPA instrument to evaluate teacher candidates' instruction felt confident that the PPA allowed student teachers to demonstrate their knowledge and skills. The percentage of faculty and supervisors expressing confidence in the construct validity of the PPA instrument and process ranged from 68 to 89 percent across the WAC standards. Interviews of these faculty and supervisors, however, indicated that they felt that there was also some construct irrelevance in the PPA, too many scoring criteria, and a redundancy in some of the criteria. In addition, faculty did not feel that the passing standard (meeting all fifty-seven of the criteria across the ten dimensions) was reasonable or fair.

There is no available information on the reliability of the Washington PPA instrument or the protocols for training supervisors and cooperating teachers to observe and score. However, given that the scale is a two-point scale (met or not met), and all candidates who are granted a license have to have met all of the scoring criteria, the ability to assess score reliability is severely threatened because there is little to no variation in scores. A two-point pass/fail scale also makes the rubrics less educative for teachers and program faculty. It provides neither detailed diagnostic information about candidates' performance nor detailed images of highly effective performance to guide candidate or program learning.

*Impact on Candidate Learning and Program Improvement.* In terms of consequential validity, Tisadondilok's (2006) interviews with faculty and supervisors at one university suggest that implementing the PPA resulted in a common understanding within and across universities in the state about what constitutes effective teaching, that the instrument and the WAC standards helped teacher candidates gain a clearer understanding of what is expected of their teaching performance, and that it may have prompted supervisors to pay greater attention to evidence of student engagement and learning, in contrast to the previous focus on student teacher behaviors. In addition, some supervisors reported that the PPA had made their observations and evaluation of student teachers more systematic and formal. But some supervisors expressed resentment about a substantially increased amount of paperwork during observations that led them to pay less attention to the teaching itself. Finally, the faculty and supervisors were asked to discuss the impact of the PPA on teacher candidates. Most of the discussion focused on candidates who failed the PPA and subsequently were denied a license or were counseled out of the program and efforts to support teacher candidates who failed the first time by helping them to meet the scoring criteria on the PPA.

Absent from these discussions was evidence that the university was using results of the PPA to inform program review and revision or that faculty used the results to support teachers in improving their teaching skills (beyond helping them pass the assessment). Yet a portion of the PPA is inherently formative: candidates are required to submit their written materials (characteristics of their classes and students, a lesson plan, planned assessments, and a lesson plan rationale) to their supervisors and cooperating teachers prior to the observation to receive feedback. Candidates then revise their written materials and resubmit them to be scored on the PPA rubrics. In addition, because candidates may take as many tries as is necessary to pass the PPA and are evaluated on the PPA instrument by their cooperating teacher and university supervisor (rather than an external evaluator), results of the PPA evaluation may inform the mentoring received from their cooperating teachers and supervisors to respond to identified weaknesses in their instruction.

**Teacher Work Sample Methodology: Observation Component.** Another observation instrument that was developed by a teacher education program and is used in the context of student teaching is the observation component of the Teacher Work Sample Methodology (TWSM), developed originally by Del Schalock and colleagues at Western Oregon University. (See the section on structured portfolios later in this chapter for a detailed description and summary of the TWSM as a whole.) Rather than requiring teachers to record their instruction on videotape, the cooperating teacher and university supervisor are responsible for observing and evaluating teacher candidates' teaching during the two- or three-week unit documented in the TWSM. One version of the scale (Rating Teaching Strategy Decisions Made During TWS Implementation) can be found in Girod (2002).

Instruction is evaluated along two major dimensions: "Establishing a classroom climate conducive to learning," which has eleven separate evaluative criteria, and "Engaging pupils in planned learning activities," which has six separate evaluative criteria. Similar to the Washington PPA, the TWSM observation instrument is scored on pass/fail basis: met and not met (this evolved from met, partially met, and unknown). In a more recent publication (Girod & Girod, 2006), the lesson observation scale used to assess teachers' instruction of a lesson that falls within the TWSM unit seems to have been revised to be scored on a five-point scale (1 = not observed, 2 = emergent, 3 = developing,

4 = competent, 5 = proficient). However, there are no descriptors for these levels of performance that would indicate specific indicators of performance.

***Technical Quality.*** In a journal publication documenting the technical quality of the TWSM, McConney, Schalock, and Schalock (1998) reported that the observation instrument is aligned with the proficiencies required by the Oregon Teacher Standards and Practices Commission. In addition, they reported that the agreement between cooperating teacher and supervisor ratings was between 81 and 98 percent across the evaluative criteria. These agreement figures are based on a three-point scale: met, partially met, and unknown. No interrater agreement data have been reported for the revised five-point scale.

***Impact on Candidate Learning.*** There are no published research reports about the formative opportunities of the observation-based portion of the TWSM in isolation from the TWSM assessment experience as a whole. However, given that the observations are conducted by the cooperating teacher and supervisor, who have an ongoing opportunity to provide feedback to candidates, the instrument may support the mentoring process.

**Praxis III—Educational Testing Service.** One observation-based assessment that has been developed for teacher licensure but is not implemented by teacher education programs is the Educational Testing Service's (ETS) Praxis III. The evaluation of teaching in the Praxis III is based on a classroom observation of one lesson, documentation of lesson plans and teaching materials, and a semistructured interview. The summative decision is made after a teacher has completed two or more assessment cycles, completed by two or more assessors. Teacher performance is assessed on nineteen criteria across four domains:

- Organizing content knowledge for student learning
- Creating an environment for student learning
- Teaching for student learning
- Teacher professionalism

Teachers are assessed on analytical rubrics that are scored on a scale of 1 to 3.5, with descriptors or indicators of performance along three points (1, 2, 3). (See Dwyer, 1998, for an example of one of the score scales.)

Praxis III is now used in at least two states (Ohio, Arkansas) to convert a preliminary license to a standard five-year license. In the 2007 fiscal year, Ohio spent about $4.2 million for Praxis III administration, including hiring and training regional coordinators who train assessors (about thirteen hundred statewide) and assigning them to administer the assessment for each entry-year teacher (between five thousand and six thousand each year in the state). Each assessor is paid four hundred dollars per assessment (Ohio Legislative Service Commission, 2007).

***Technical Quality.*** A lengthy development process, including job analyses, research studies, and field trials, was used to develop the assessment (documented in Dwyer, 1994, and briefly described in Dwyer, 1998), to ensure its construct validity. Development began in 1987, and the assessment underwent many revisions before its first operational use in 1993. The careful and iterative process used to develop the Praxis series exams was necessitated by the use for high-stakes licensing decisions, which require that assessments meet the highest standards of technical and legal defensibility. Assessors undergo a five-day training and must pass an assessor proficiency test to ensure their ability to score accurately and produce a satisfactory record of evidence.

Results from the 1992 pilot test indicate that across the nineteen scoring criteria, pairs of assessor ratings were within one-half point of each other for an average 85 percent of candidates assessed (Dwyer, 1998). While this level of interrater agreement is satisfactory for making high-stakes decisions, the fact that it depends on five days of training and a test of calibration suggests that comparable levels of agreement may not be possible among supervisors and cooperating teachers in preservice teacher education without a comparable investment in time and resources to train these assessors.

***Impact on Teacher Learning.*** Danielson and Dwyer (1995) suggest that the analytical rubrics used to score beginning teachers' performance based on observation could provide feedback to those being assessed and subsequently support teachers' professional learning, guide the design of individual professional plans, or, when aggregated for all teachers in a school or district, be used to inform the design and provision of professional development. However, there is little published evidence to date that supports formative learning outcomes for teachers being assessed on the Praxis III. In addition, in order to inform the design of professional development plans, individual teachers must voluntarily release their Praxis scores to districts, employers, or mentors (because licensing test scores are considered private information and only pass/fail outcomes are reported). There is little published evidence that the Praxis III scores have been used in this way for formative purposes.

## Observation-Based Research Tools

A number of other observation-based instruments have been developed for research purposes and can be used with high levels of reliability.

**Classroom Assessment Scoring System.** The Classroom Assessment Scoring System (CLASS) is an observational instrument developed by Pianta and colleagues at the University of Virginia to assess classroom quality in preschool through third-grade classrooms (Pianta, 2003). The focus of this observation instrument is on the interactions between and among teachers and students, and CLASS's three evaluative dimensions (Emotional Support, Classroom Organization, and Instructional Support) are based on developmental theory and research. The three dimensions are derived from constructs that have been validated in child care and elementary school research studies, literature on effective teaching practices, focus groups, and extensive piloting (CLASS, n.d.).

*Technical Quality.* The CLASS has been used and validated in more than three thousand classrooms from preschool to fifth grade (CLASS, n.d.). The overall level of reliability (agreement within one point on a seven-point scale) was 87.1 percent. Training for using the observation instrument takes two days, training to use the instrument for professional development takes two or three days, and training for the certification of trainers takes five days. CLASS ratings of classroom quality have been linked to the development of children's academic performance and language and social skills at the end of preschool and gains in their performance during the preschool years (Howes et al., 2008; Mashburn et al., 2008). This evidence of predictive validity is remarkable because it has been historically difficult to conduct the kind of research that could provide this kind of validity evidence about a performance assessment instrument.

*Impact on Teacher Learning.* While the CLASS instrument has been used in research to assess the effects of teacher education by following graduates of a teacher education program into their first years of employment (see Teachers for a New Era grant proposal by La Paro & Pianta, 2003), it is unclear that the instrument has ever been used in the context of preservice teacher education to evaluate the teaching practice of student teachers or support their professional learning. However, the CLASS instrument has been used as a protocol for an Internet-based professional development program for in-service pre-K teachers called MyTeachingPartner (MTP).

The MTP program has two components: on-demand access to video examples of high-quality teacher-child interactions that are sampled to represent specific dimensions of the CLASS observation instrument, and a Web-based consultation service in which teachers make and upload to the Internet video recordings of their own teaching, which are analyzed for the purpose of providing targeted feedback to teachers along the CLASS dimensions of teachers' emotional, organizational, and instructional interactions with students. The content of the Web-mediated consultation includes identifying positive and negative examples of teachers' interactions with students, problem solving to identify and implement alternative approaches, and a supportive relationship with a more expert consultant. In a controlled evaluation study, Pianta, Mashburn, Downer, Hamre, and Justice (2008) used the CLASS instrument to assess whether there were any differences in the classroom interactions and behaviors of teachers who had on-demand access to video exemplars as well as opportunities for online consultation, versus that of teachers who had access to the video exemplars only. They found that teachers who received the online consultation had significantly greater improvements in their classroom interactions with students than did teachers with video access only, especially in classrooms with higher proportions of students in poverty. While effect sizes were small and the ability to draw conclusions about causal relationships is limited, the findings support the idea that online coaching, focused on specific qualities of teaching through the lens of the CLASS instrument, can provide supportive learning experiences that lead to improved instruction.

**Instructional Quality Assessment.** Another classroom performance ratings instrument that was developed primarily for research purposes is the Instructional Quality Assessment (IQA), developed and piloted by the National Center for Research on Evaluation, Standards, and Student Testing (CRESST). (See Junker et al., 2006, for an overview of the IQA.) The IQA relies not only on observations of teaching practice but on structured interviews with teachers and students and a collection of teacher assignments. It assesses this body of evidence along four dimensions and twenty separate criteria: Academic Rigor, Clear Expectations, Self-Management of Learning, and Accountability. The design of the IQA was shaped by the Principles of Learning, a set of guidelines for instructional practice (Resnick & Hall, 2001; Institute for Learning, 2002) that integrates strong pedagogical knowledge with deep and rigorous subject matter knowledge (Junker et al., 2006).

*Technical Quality.*  In addition to reflecting research-based principles of learning and effective teaching, the instrument has been piloted in several different contexts to assess the ability of external assessors to score reliably with a standard training protocol (encompassing two and a half days). Reliability estimates from a 2003 pilot test indicate an overall 96 percent level of agreement (exact matches or within one point) in ratings (the Spearman $R$ statistic was less robust, at .58). While the level of interrater agreement on individual scoring criteria calls for some improvement in the design of the rubric and training protocol, the researchers conclude that the overall level of agreement is satisfactory, depending on the purpose of the evaluation.

In more recent research on middle school teachers and the quality of their instruction in reading comprehension and mathematics, the quality of teaching measured by the IQA was found to be a significant predictor of student achievement on the Stanford Achievement Test (Matsumura et al., 2006; Matsumura, Garnier, Slater, & Boston, 2008). Matsumara and colleagues found that it took at least two observations and four samples of assignments to yield stable measures of teaching quality. In addition, the observation tool had high levels of reliability (86.4 percent exact agreement for English language arts and 81.8 percent in mathematics), while the assignment tool had moderately high levels of reliability (71.3 percent in English language arts and 76.3 percent in mathematics). This validity and reliability evidence builds a strong case for the usefulness of the IQA as a summative measure of teaching performance.

***Impact on Candidate Learning.*** There is little published research to date that describes how the IQA has been used as a professional development tool. However, one of the strengths of the IQA is that each score level (1–4) of the rubrics has an associated descriptor intended to precisely and explicitly capture the expectations of performance at each level. (Copies of the rubrics can be found in Junker et al., 2006.) Not only does the design of the rubrics reduce the need for extensive rater training and a reliance on the professional knowledge and judgment of raters, but it also makes possible the opportunity to share results of the assessment with teachers in ways that could support their ongoing learning and development. In addition, by focusing on the technical core of teaching, that is, the interaction of teacher, student, and content, the IQA provides "a vision of the elements of teaching that matter most," based on a "coherent, research-based model of how high-quality instruction unfolds in classrooms" (Stein & Matsumura, 2008, p. 197).

## Discussion of Observation-Based Assessments

High-stakes decisions about student teachers are routinely based on the observations made by their supervisors and cooperating teachers. Yet the technical quality of the instruments used in preservice programs rarely meets the demands of a high-stakes instrument. In some ways, it appears that the usefulness of these instruments is tied to their ability to support collaborative examination of instruction, student teacher reflection, and formative discussions with supervisors and cooperating teachers that are grounded in a common set of teaching expectations or standards. The way that instruments are used in teacher education raises questions about how the observation data are used in combination with other information to make judgments about a prospective teacher's competence in the classroom. Given that the pass rates in student teaching are extraordinarily high (often approaching 100 percent), it appears that the assessment of student teaching using ratings instruments is treated more as a rite of passage than an objective evaluation of teaching.

If programs are committed to using observation-based evidence as the basis for passing or failing student teaching, then attention to the technical quality of these instruments and the processes used to train and calibrate assessors is sorely needed. Observation-based ratings instruments that have been developed carefully to ensure content and construct validity and to reflect the research base on effective teaching (for example, Praxis III, CLASS, and ITQ) show that it is possible to develop credible and reliable evaluation instruments and processes, with a heavy investment in the development of a valid instrument and a modest investment in the training of assessors—about two days of training (for CLASS and ITQ). One question about reliability that arises in practice is whether it is possible for evaluators to score reliably when they know the student teacher personally (those who directly supervise and mentor them and are invested in their success), even if they have undergone extensive training and calibration. This question arises for any curriculum-embedded performance assessment that is scored internally by course instructors, supervisors, and cooperating teachers who know the candidates. We have found in our own research on the Performance Assessment for California Teachers that raters who know the candidate in some capacity score marginally but significantly higher (0.2 point higher on a four-point scale) than raters who do not know the candidate. This is a practical measurement problem that needs further exploration.

Although there is limited evidence that the technically robust instruments we describe can also support teacher learning and development, they have the potential to be harnessed by programs to support and mentor student teachers when used by university supervisors and cooperating teachers. The observation instruments that are more reliable and credible (Praxis III, CLASS, and ITQ) are also designed to provide more diagnostic and specific indicators of performance at each score level. This design feature is an important one to consider as a way to bolster the quality of an observation instrument, both to improve scoring reliability and improve its use as a formative tool for teacher and program learning. Developing high-quality scales of this type, which also have predictive validity, is extremely difficult, and most programs are unlikely to have the resources or capacity to engage in the necessary development and research work. Drawing on or adapting existing scales and training systems looks to be a smart investment. State governments, national organizations, and consortia of universities should also be involved in procuring the resources and harnessing external expertise to get smarter about doing this kind of development work.

## ON-DEMAND PERFORMANCE TASKS

On-demand performance tasks are similar to traditional sit-down exams in that they present to the teacher candidates a standardized set of prompts, administered in a standardized way. What makes on-demand performance tasks different from traditional exams is that they present candidates with problem-based scenarios or simulations that mimic authentic teaching situations and do not necessarily have one correct answer (Arends, 2006b). For example, teachers may be given a topic and a description of students in a class, and then they are prompted to describe their plans for a lesson and explain how their plans reflect the strengths and needs of students in the class. A wide range of responses could satisfactorily meet the evaluative criteria for the task. Other tasks may prompt teachers to evaluate a student work sample and describe what kind of feedback they would provide to the student or describe how they would handle a challenging classroom situation.

Well-designed on-demand performance tasks prompt candidates to explain their thinking and decision making so as to make their content knowledge, pedagogical knowledge, and pedagogical content knowledge transparent to the assessor (Arends, 2006b). The teacher licensing tests used in some states include on-demand performance tasks designed to measure teachers' pedagogical knowledge and skills. The content pedagogy Praxis exam administered by ETS, for example, is a one-hour on-demand performance task that can include case studies or other types of open-response essays. Although the Praxis series exams are not embedded in teacher education programs, they present an example of an on-demand performance task that has sufficient technical quality to inform high-stakes decisions: adequate levels of interrater agreement and validation of the assessments based on job analyses. Nevertheless, these types of tasks are clearly less authentic than performance tasks that involve real classrooms and students whom teachers know well that require teachers to implement their plans and evaluate work samples completed by their students.

Another well-known example of an on-demand performance task is the NBPTS Assessment Center tasks, which assess candidates' content knowledge for teaching. Another example is the INTASC on-demand assessment Test of Teacher Knowledge (TTK), which measures "beginning teacher's professional knowledge in areas such as theories of teaching and learning, cognitive, social and physical development, diagnostic and evaluative assessments, language acquisition, the role of student background in the learning process, and other foundational knowledge and skills essential to the profession of teaching" (INTASC, 2009a). INTASC has created two secure forms of the TTK, which is still under development, and field-testing has provided validity and reliability analyses. INTASC plans to continue developing items for the TTK and administer the test for states interested in using it.

## Central Connecticut State University's Mid-Point Assessment Task

One example of an on-demand performance task that is implemented within a teacher education program is Central Connecticut State University's Mid-Point

Assessment Task (MAT), a two-hour essay exam administered in the semester prior to student teaching. While the assessment was intended originally as a gatekeeping device for admission to student teaching, it now serves primarily as a tool for advising students and for program evaluation (N. Hoffman, personal communication, April 29, 2009). The MAT requires that teacher candidates plan a lesson for a hypothetical group of students, describe how they would differentiate instruction for two focus students, and design assessments to measure student learning of the learning objectives. The information given to candidates about the teaching situation includes contextual information about the school and the unit of study, a lesson plan taught the previous day by a hypothetical teacher, information about class achievement of objectives in the previous day's lesson, and specific profiles of two focus students (one who struggles academically and the other a high-achieving student), along with samples of the focus students' work from the previous day's lesson. Candidates complete their reflective essays by responding to a series of questions presented on computer in a group setting (Arends, 2006b).

**Technical Quality.**  Candidates' responses are scored using a rubric (with eight dimensions) aligned with the program's conceptual framework and modified INTASC standards. The tasks also mirror, to some extent, the tasks in the Connecticut BEST portfolio assessment (see more on the BEST portfolio below). All candidate responses are double-scored by faculty members and triple-scored if there is a conflict in the scores. Interrater reliability levels of 0.85 have been reported (Arends, 2006b). The program stopped using the tool for high-stakes purposes for two reasons: not all program faculty were able to score reliably, even with training, and a sufficient number of candidates who did not meet the passing standard but performed well in student teaching (false-negatives) caused concern about the validity and fairness of the assessment. In addition, some students commented on the need for access to resources outside the testing situation and a desire for unlimited time to plan for the next lesson (N. Hoffman, personal communication, April 30, 2009). This suggests there are some validity issues to consider when using on-demand tasks with formats that are less authentic to instructional practice.

**Impact on Candidate Learning.**  When the MAT was piloted as a high-stakes assessment for entry into student teaching, candidates who received a failing score were offered special workshops to help prepare them for a second try. Candidates who failed the second time had to wait another semester before taking the assessment again (Arends, 2006b). Since the program has chosen to focus on using the tool primarily for advising students and as a program evaluation tool, the results of the assessment are now used to guide students in developing a diagnostic self-improvement plan in collaboration with a faculty member. In addition, MAT scores for all students and the improvement plans for students who failed the task are sent to the student teaching supervisors to ensure that areas of weakness identified by the MAT are immediately addressed and remediated. Finally, the program has found that engaging all faculty in the process of scoring the MAT has supported a culture of using evidence of candidate performance for program revision and articulation. Score data from the MAT are also used to guide program improvement (N. Hoffman, personal communication, April 30, 2009).

## Western Oregon University's Cook School District Simulation

On-demand performance tasks have the potential to become more innovative and authentic when computer technology is harnessed. The Cook School District Simulation was developed by Western Oregon University to simulate the experience of the Teacher Work Sample Methodology (TWSM; see details on this methodology in the section on structured portfolios below). The simulation tool has been piloted extensively with undergraduates, graduate students, and practicing teachers and is in use at three universities in their teacher education programs.

The simulation was designed to be used as a Web-based practice space for teacher candidates to practice the skills needed to make instructional decisions based on an analysis of student learning outcomes. A bank of two hundred students, whose characteristics and simulated academic behaviors were constructed based on teachers' descriptions of real students they had taught, are used to populate the class selected for the particular grade level and content area selected by the user. The user is directed to analyze the public profile of each student in the class to design instruction for learning objectives selected by the user. The user selects from a range of instructional strategies that (in the private profile of each student) are associated with varying levels of student engagement and student learning. In addition, users select from a range of assessment types that are also associated with varying levels of success for individual students. An algorithm uses both the public and private profiles of students, along with information about the selected learning objectives, instructional strategies, and assessment types, to produce the student outcomes (level of engagement and performance on the assessments). Feedback from formative assessments and the simulated student on-task behaviors may be used by users to make adjustments to instruction (Girod & Girod, 2006).

Girod (2008) suggests that the simulation can also be used to measure candidates' skills before and after the formative test in a number of areas:

- Analyzing the school and classroom context of teaching
- Identifying learning objectives appropriate to the school and classroom context

- Designing instruction toward meeting those selected learning objectives
- Adapting and differentiating instruction depending on the context
- Designing assessments to measure student learning
- Evaluating the effectiveness of instruction by analyzing student work
- Planning instruction based on the analysis of student work.

**Impacts on Candidate Learning.** Girod and Girod (2006) report that teacher candidates who practiced the skills required for the TWSM on the Cook School District simulation for six hours, in comparison with a control group, demonstrated significantly higher levels of skill in creating a classroom climate conducive to learning, adapting instruction to align with student needs; and using a broad array of instructional strategies in their student teaching experiences. (These comparisons were based on TWSM portfolio scores, self-ratings, and lesson observations.) In addition, interviews with users highlight other important impacts on candidate learning: clearer and deeper understanding of the importance of alignment; understanding the importance and challenges of individualizing instruction; understanding the role of assessment in supporting, scaffolding, and judging learning and progress; and understanding the importance of data-driven decision making, analysis, and systematic reflection (Girod, 2008). It seems likely that these impacts on candidate learning are associated with the use of the simulation as a professional learning tool (a practice space) rather than its use as an assessment. This characteristic distinguishes the Cook School District Simulation from other forms of on-demand performance tasks that are designed to serve an assessment function only.

**Technical Quality.** The technical quality of the simulation as an assessment instrument currently rests on the reliability and validity of the TWSM. Given the limited information about the technical quality of the Cook School District Simulation to date, it seems premature to use the simulation as a high-stakes assessment. Although the simulation leads candidates through tasks that are similar to that of the TWSM, there is a difference between authentic contexts and real contact with real students. The validity of the instrument changes when the evidence base on which candidates' performance is evaluated changes. The student outcomes produced by the simulation algorithms may be true to the students' profiles, but different teachers are differentially effective in producing student learning even when using the same instructional strategies and the same assessments to teach the same learning objectives. Thus, the ability of the simulation to assess the true instructional effectiveness of candidates is called into question.

## Discussion of On-Demand Performance Tasks

Of the four types of performance-based teacher evaluation assessments reviewed in this chapter, on-demand tasks seem to be the least intrusive into the curriculum of teacher education, provided that they are designed to be aligned with existing curriculum and do not require extensive time beyond what is normally taught to prepare candidates for the assessment. On-demand formats are also the easiest to implement as they are completed within a given amount of time under standardized conditions. Depending on the nature of the scoring rubrics and procedures, scoring these assessments could be either more efficient with respect to training and scoring time or as demanding and time intensive as the scoring process used for the other three types of performance-based assessment. Thus, it is difficult to assess whether on-demand assessments are more or less labor intensive to implement.

Although the technical quality of some on-demand tasks is robust (for example, Praxis, NBPTS Assessment Center tests, INTASC's TTK), it is unclear how useful they are in terms of their ability to provide formative opportunities that support teacher learning. When on-demand tasks are used exclusively for high-stakes summative purposes such as licensing tests and there are no opportunities for candidates to receive a detailed evidentiary record of why they were successful or why the performance fell short, there does not appear to be much opportunity to learn from the assessment. While it is possible to build an on-demand task into the context of a teacher education program in such a way that there are opportunities for feedback, revision, and learning, as the Cook School District simulation is used to provide practice with the TWSM and Central Connecticut State University's MAT is used for candidate advising and program evaluation, the less authentic nature of on-demand tasks may limit their formative function. For teachers to truly learn about how to improve the execution of their plans, for example, they must have opportunities to implement their plans and learn from what worked and what did not. This is not an experience that a simulation or a reflective essay on a teaching scenario can easily duplicate.

# CHILD CASE STUDIES

Child case studies have a long tradition in teacher education and are most often found in elementary-level credential programs, although some middle-level and secondary programs also assign adolescent case studies. In their survey of American Association for Colleges of Teacher Education (AACTE) programs, Salzman, Denner, and Harris (2002) found that 46 percent of respondents (representing 50 percent of teacher education program units) reported the use of case studies as one measure of candidate outcomes. Case studies are narrative reports that are usually focused on building a child's developmental profile, including physical, social, emotional, and academic and cognitive development, through interviews and observations of the child in a variety of contexts. The ultimate purpose of building this profile is usually for the candidate to draw some implications about the most appropriate ways to work with the child or to design instruction or an intervention focused on meeting the child's educational needs.

## Bank Street College Child Study

A well-known example of a teacher education program that requires all candidates to complete child case studies is the Bank Street College of Education, which prepares teachers for early childhood, elementary, and middle school levels. The child case study is an assignment embedded within a single course, The Study of Children in Diverse and Inclusive Settings Through Observation and Recording, and is usually completed during one of the two semesters in which they are enrolled in student teaching. This course has been offered since the college's inception in 1931. During the first half of the semester, candidates observe and take field notes on their observations (using running records, a form of continuous narrative that documents everything the child does as it is done) of a focus student in a variety of situations at school. During this period, candidates are required to submit weekly observation assignments and receive feedback from the instructor. During the second half of the semester, candidates use two methods for analyzing their field notes: an age-level study in which they analyze the child's development across a number of dimensions (social/emotional, physical, cognitive) and a study of patterns in the child's behavior and exceptions to those patterns. Results from these analyses are synthesized into a narrative report in which candidates make inferences about the reasons for the child's patterns in behavior, make links to theories of development learned in the program, consider the educational needs of the child, and pose strategies for working with the child effectively in an educational setting (Gropper, 2008).

**Technical Quality.** While it appears that a standard set of prompts is used for the case study assignment (with some tweaking of the assignment permitted across faculty teaching the course), there is little evidence that there are standard ways of evaluating or scoring the case studies, or that there is any effort to calibrate the course instructors who score these assignments. In addition, it is unclear whether there is a basis for establishing the validity of the assessment as a measure of teaching competency, although the process of observing and recording children's behavior is closely aligned with assessment practices used by the National Association for the Education of Young Children (Gropper, 2008).

**Impact on Candidate Learning.** In course evaluations, teacher candidates and graduates of the program have cited the course in which they complete this case study as being one of the most valuable courses they have taken at Bank Street, suggesting that this assignment provides a powerful formative assessment experience (Gropper, 2008):

> They learn to notice children's behavior in detail that eluded them before taking the course: they learn to think about the meaning of the behavior without judging it and to generate strategies for working more effectively with the child in the academic/cognitive, social/emotional, and physical realms. They learn to use observation notes for a range of assessment purposes which include curriculum planning, parent conferences, and referrals for evaluation [Gropper, 2008, p. 194].

## Wheelock College's Focus Child Assessment Project

A variant of Bank Street College's child study used by Wheelock College emphasizes the collection and analysis of assessment data in addition to formal and informal observations and running records, with the purpose of designing plans for improving instruction. This case study is assigned in the undergraduate elementary program in Meeting the Diverse Learning Needs of Elementary Students, a course required of all undergraduate student teachers at the college. The assessment is completed over one semester and is composed of the following:

- Informal and formal observations with documentation
- A series of formal neurodevelopmental assessments
- A review and evaluation of the focus child's academic performance (class work, state test results)
- Use of assessment results to inform the development or adaptation of instructional plans for the focus child
- Student work samples, reflection on findings, and analysis and revision of instructional materials to support the child's learning
- A final report that documents all components of the project

Similar to the Bank Street College case study, there are weekly assignments and opportunities to receive feedback on the components of the final report (McKibbens, Shainker, & Banks-Santilli, 2008).

**Technical Quality.** The assessment criteria and ten scoring rubrics used to evaluate the case study are aligned with the Association for Childhood Education International standards, Wheelock College Education Standards, student learning content standards (Massachusetts), and the Massachusetts Professional Standards for Teachers. The construct validity of the child assessment project is also reviewed by Wheelock faculty members with expertise in assessment and instruction. Interrater agreement is evaluated once a year by double-scoring a 20 to 25 percent subsample of the completed projects (McKibbens et al., 2008). However, there is no published record of the levels of interrater agreement achieved by the two faculty who have been primarily responsible for developing, administering, and scoring the assignment.

**Impact on Candidate Learning.** The reaction of candidates to this assignment is that the project is quite challenging. One of the challenges reported with the use of this extensive semester-long project is the ability of teacher candidates to keep up with the pace of weekly assignments so that they receive immediate faculty feedback. Nonetheless, many candidates report that it is a "pivotal assignment that changes the way they view themselves as teachers and are viewed by others. The point at which the candidates analyze student work and revise their teaching strategies based on those findings is typically noted by their P-12 students and cooperating practitioners as a significant point of progress in their ability to demonstrate competency and independence in the classroom" (McKibbens et al., 2008, p. 207).

## George Mason University's Reading, Writing, Spelling Analysis Task

Another variant of the child study is the literacy or mathematics learning assessment case studies that are used in a number of elementary credential programs. With a growing emphasis on testing literacy and math skills associated with No Child Left Behind accountability requirements, many programs have bolstered their preparation of teachers in the instruction and assessment of literacy and mathematics. George Mason University's Elementary Education Program uses the Reading, Writing, Spelling Analysis Task (RWS) to support its candidates in applying theories of literacy development and pedagogical strategies through an in-depth analysis of one child's literacy learning. The RWS also requires that a candidate design an instructional intervention aimed at supporting the student's literacy development.

Candidates collect information about the case study student by listening to the child reading and documenting the child's reading performance using anecdotal records, running records, miscue analysis, interviews, discussion, reading inventories, developmental reading assessments, or another research-based approach. The candidates also collect three writing samples that represent different writing genres, and using those writing samples, they assess the student's spelling level and word study strategies. The evaluative criteria for scoring the task are based on the diversity of assessments the teacher candidate uses, the accuracy of the developmental levels assigned, and the appropriateness of instructional plans connected with theories of learning and literacy development learned in the course. Teacher candidates complete the RWS task twice, during each of the literacy courses taken in the elementary credential program. Each of the twelve components of the RWS task is scored on four-point rubrics (Castle, Groth, Moyer, & Burns, 2006). In other programs, candidates are asked to take this task a step further by implementing and evaluating the planned literacy or math intervention.

**Technical Quality.** The content validity of the RWS task is based on its alignment with INTASC, the International Reading Association, and program standards, as well as course outcomes. Its construct validity depends on a review of one external consultant and surveys of experienced teachers on the instrument's authenticity and fit with real work expectations for practicing teachers. Reliability estimates for rubric scores in the second pilot year indicate 85 to 95 percent agreement in scores, depending on the course section (Castle et al., 2006). Groth (2006) also reports that candidates' scores range from 1.5 to 5.0 (on a five-point scale), with a mean score of 4.5, and that scores on the RWS are consistent with candidates' course grades. Unlike the previous two examples of child case studies, the systematic way in which George Mason's teacher education program scores the student case studies on a common set of scoring criteria and evaluates interrater reliability demonstrates that a case study project could meet standards of psychometric quality for a high-stakes assessment.

**Impact on Candidate Learning.** George Mason has collected feedback from teacher candidates on their experiences with the RWS task over three years, and although students list the RWS as one of the most difficult assignments of their two literacy courses, 89 percent agree that it is a highly valuable assignment ''because we could witness student growth and also see theories discussed in class, in practice'' (Groth, 2006, p. 9), and that it is ''extremely helpful for planning and assessment and helps apply philosophy and techniques learned in class'' (Castle et al., 2006, p. 77).

## Discussion of Child Case Studies

At face value, the activity of systematically observing one student in different settings; collecting detailed information about one student's prior achievement; learning about one student's social, emotional, and physical development; administering psychological or literacy assessments to one student; and writing up a lengthy and highly analytical case study for one student may seem to be a somewhat unrealistic academic exercise because teachers in real-world settings do not have the time to conduct such an intensive assessment (especially secondary school teachers, who can be responsible for as many as 150 to 180 students). However, the high marks that teacher candidates give these kinds of assignments as being one of the most powerful assignments for learning how to design and plan instruction suggests that the kind of thinking and learning that child case studies can provoke are strongly related to teaching and learning. While it is possible that a child case study task (such as the one designed and used by George Mason University) could be designed and evaluated in such a way as to produce credible and reliable information about teachers' competencies, it appears that its value as a formative learning opportunity overshadows its summative evaluative purposes in many teacher education programs. This is not to imply that teacher education programs should ignore issues of technical quality in their implementation of child case studies, especially if they are used for high-stakes purposes, but that the strength of the assignment may be its powerful formative potential.

# PORTFOLIOS

Portfolio assessments are widely used in preservice credential programs, most often as a form of capstone or culminating assessment (St. Maurice & Shaw, 2004). A survey study conducted by Salzman et al. (2002) on behalf of the AACTE found that 88 percent of respondents (representing a 50 percent response rate of 750 AACTE member institutions) reported the use of portfolios as one measure of candidate outcomes. Nearly 40 percent of those programs reported the portfolio as being required for receiving a license to teach. In most cases (95 percent), the portfolios were designed within the programs, but a small percentage (5 percent) reported that the portfolios were designed by the state.

Danielson and McGreal (2000) describe four common features of teacher portfolios currently in use for teacher evaluation (though not specifically in teacher preparation programs):

- Alignment with professional teaching standards as well as individual and school goals
- Selected examples of both student and teacher work
- Captions and commentaries that explain and reflect
- Mentored or coached experiences including conversations with colleagues and supervisors [p. 94]

When evaluating the usefulness of portfolios as a form of teacher evaluation, it is important to note the wide array of portfolio purposes and formats that are currently in use (see Zeichner & Wray, 2001, for a detailed analysis of variations in portfolios used at the preservice level). Tucker, Stronge, Gareis, and Beers (2003) describe the differences in portfolios based on their purpose:

These subtle differences in purposes tend to fall on a continuum that can be described as low stakes to high stakes. The continuum ranges from an informal, less structured, and improvement-oriented process (e.g., self-assessment, formative performance reviews) to a more formal, structured, and accountability-oriented process (e.g., initial hiring decisions, promotion and awards, pay-for performance plans, summative evaluation).... Some definitions emphasize processes of teaching, whereas others emphasize products such as evidence of student achievement [pp. 574–575].

While this dichotomy of low-stakes/high-stakes purposes seems valid, we do not subscribe to the notion of a strict dichotomy of low-stakes/formative versus high-stakes/summative or that a portfolio used for summative purposes cannot provide opportunities for teacher learning and improvement. This issue is discussed further below in our description of the Performance Assessment for California Teachers.

In our examination of portfolios, we distinguish structured and unstructured portfolios. Structured portfolios require candidates to submit specific artifacts of teaching with standardized prompts that require direct responses. These artifacts and responses are then scored in a standardized way by trained raters using a common evaluation tool, usually a rubric. The National Board for Professional Teaching Standards portfolio is an example of a highly structured portfolio. In unstructured portfolios, what and how artifacts are selected depend on the purpose of the portfolios. In showcase portfolios used to accompany applications for employment, teachers select artifacts that represent their best work. In portfolios that are meant to be used as a tool for professional learning or for the evaluation of their teaching, candidates may be required to include specific artifacts, such as a statement of teaching philosophy, a videotape of their teaching, lesson plans or units, or original curriculum materials they have developed, with accompanying reflections. In unstructured portfolios, candidates often have more choice in what is selected for inclusion in the portfolio as evidence for evaluation. Sometimes the required elements of the portfolio are meant to provide evidence of meeting state, national, or program teaching standards. However, unstructured portfolios often lack clearly defined evaluative criteria, or the grading of these portfolios may be conducted in less standardized ways (with little training or calibration of faculty scoring the portfolios).

Danielson and McGreal (2000) define several criteria for the summative use of portfolios that are often difficult for local programs and school organizations to meet because of a lack of capacity: "[A teacher's portfolio] can be used as a summative evaluation tool, but to do so requires a much more structured process and a complex set of assessment strategies. The assessment component requires clear criteria, an established set of reliable and valid scoring rubrics, and extensive training for the evaluators in order to ensure fairness and reliability. These considerations can all be met, but they are often beyond the capacity or the will of a local district" (pp. 94–95).

Wilkerson and Lang (2003) detail the legal and psychometric issues in using teacher portfolios as a teacher certification assessment, and they warn institutions of the myriad legal challenges they may face if the portfolio assessment system used for determining a teacher candidate's eligibility for state licensure does not meet accepted guidelines for the technical and psychometric quality of licensing tests (the Standards for Educational and Psychological Testing, APA/NCME/AERA, 1999).

Due to the lack of capacity within most teacher education programs to achieve the technical quality of their portfolio assessments, most teaching portfolios currently in use at the preservice level are of the unstructured variety. However, even unstructured portfolios have been perceived as useful tools for summative teacher evaluation. In one study evaluating the usefulness of a districtwide unstructured portfolio as an instrument for teacher evaluation (Tucker et al., 2003), administrators rated highly the fairness and accuracy of portfolios in assessing teacher performance, and focus group interviews revealed that some administrators felt that portfolios provided a more comprehensive view of teachers' instructional practice than even a series of observations could provide. While both teachers and administrators had less positive ratings of the usefulness and feasibility of the portfolios because of the workload and time involved in constructing the portfolios (a common complaint about portfolios), they also had high ratings of the usefulness of the portfolio for promoting teachers' self-reflection and identifying strengths and weaknesses, and the practicality of the portfolio for aiding them in carrying out their professional responsibilities and their evaluation review conferences. The formative function of portfolios for promoting teacher learning and reflection is explored in more depth below.

## Unstructured Portfolios and Formative Assessment

The use of unstructured portfolios as evidence of teacher candidates' learning over the duration of a teacher credential program has gained popularity over the last two decades. (See Chapter One, this volume, for a discussion of their use.) A survey study of teacher education programs conducted over a decade ago (Anderson & DeMeulle, 1998) had found that twenty-four programs had been using portfolios for a range of 6 months to 17 years, with an average of 4.75 years. Ninety-six percent of those programs reported that the purpose of portfolios was to promote student learning and development and 92 percent to encourage student self-assessment and reflection. Studies on the use of portfolio assessment in teacher education programs in Maine (Lyons, 1999) and California (Snyder, Lippincott, & Bower, 1998) have used the reflections of teacher candidates and evidence collected in their portfolios to make inferences about what they have learned through the process of developing their portfolios. Such studies, including an early study by Richert (1987), and a number of other studies on the use of portfolios in preservice teacher education (Anderson & DeMeulle, 1998; Darling-Hammond & Macdonald, 2000; Darling-Hammond & Snyder, 2000; Davis & Honan, 1998; Shulman, 1998; Stone, 1998; Whitford et al., 2000), have found that portfolios can facilitate teachers' reflections about the content of their lessons and their pedagogical strategies.

The secondary teaching program at the University of Southern Maine (USM) has been using unstructured portfolio assessment since 1994. Teacher candidates complete their professional portfolios during their student teaching intern placements in connection with a student teaching seminar; they present evidence of their having met the teacher certification standards in a final exhibition, which is framed more as an opportunity to "celebrate and share accomplishment" than as a high-stakes assessment event (University of Southern Maine, 2008, p. 16). The portfolio assessment requires candidates to select evidence that will serve as the basis for a final judgment about certification, made by a panel of school-based and university faculty following the portfolio exhibition. However, the body of evidence on which the certification decision is made includes informal and formal observations by the university supervisor and mentor teacher, standards review conferences at the middle and end of each placement, videotaped teaching and reflections, lesson and unit plans, evidence lists, and the professional teaching portfolio and exhibition. Thus, completing and presenting the portfolio is less of a high-stakes endeavor because of the inclusion of multiple sources of evidence.

Based on the reflections of teacher candidates and evidence collected in their portfolios, Lyons (1999) found that through the portfolio development process, intern teachers developed habits of mind that helped them define good practice, reflect on their own teaching and learning, and support the reflection of their students. In a three-year longitudinal study of ten preservice teachers at USM's Extended Teacher Education Program, including undergraduates preparing to enter the program, preservice teachers in the postbaccalaureate program taking part in a year-long intensive internship, and graduates of the program in their first or second year of teaching, Lyons (1998a) examined the meaning teacher candidates gave to the portfolio assessment process through case studies involving analysis of their portfolios and open-ended interviews. Cross-sectional and longitudinal analyses of the data yielded several emergent themes:

- Initial efforts at reflection are simple and become elaborated over time.
- Critical conversations interrogating portfolio entries provide a scaffold that fosters teacher consciousness of their own knowledge of practice.
- Significant aspects of teaching practice, such as teaching philosophy, are identified and emerge.
- The sometimes painful process of public, collaborative inquiry results in teachers' learning about themselves and the values they hold for teaching and learning.

Another study, examining the use of portfolio assessment in the fifth-year postbaccalaureate teacher education program at the University of California at Santa Barbara (Snyder et al., 1998), explored the tension between the use of performance assessment for new teacher support and development and as an assessment tool for accountability purposes. At that time, the UCSB program required that all teacher candidates construct a portfolio documenting successful attainment of the California standards for teacher credentialing (the credential portfolio), as well as a second portfolio for candidates working toward a master's of education degree (the M.Ed. portfolio). The collection of artifacts for the credential portfolio was left to the discretion of teacher candidates but had to be selected to show evidence of meeting each of the ten California teaching credential standards. The artifacts could be test or testlike events, such as class papers, unit plans designed for a course, or standardized test scores; observation-based evaluations; or performance tasks or other work samples such as lesson plans, videotapes of teaching, or student work samples. Over the course of the year, candidates had weekly opportunities during their student teaching seminars and in three-way conferences with their university supervisor and cooperating teacher to share the emerging contents of the portfolio and reflect on their work over time. In the last three-way conference in June, the teacher candidate, cooperating teacher, and university supervisor sign off on an official form that the portfolio artifacts as a whole provided evidence that the student had met all of the state's teaching standards.

The M.Ed. portfolio was designed to allow candidates freedom from externally imposed standards in order to encourage reflection on individual practice with a focus on supporting a candidate's ability to "learn from teaching" (Snyder et al., 1998, pp. 46–47). This portfolio could be considered a type of inquiry project, built around an issue of the candidate's choosing. Candidates start by collecting three artifacts to identify an issue and examine their instruction in relation to these three artifacts and educational theories learned in the program. Students form self-selected support groups with a university- or school-based facilitator, meet regularly to share and receive feedback on their portfolio artifacts and their reflection on the selected issue, and complete their portfolios in the summer following their full-time student teaching experience. Two checkpoints are required for successful completion: approval by every member of the candidate's support group and a public conversation in which feedback is received from five "critical friends" (two school-based educators, two university faculty, and a community member).

Snyder and colleagues followed two cohorts of student teachers (eighteen candidates) over the course of two years through their professional preparation year into their first year of teaching. They found that although the nature of the artifacts selected for the two types of portfolios differed, because the M.Ed. portfolios started with a personal issue and credential portfolios began with the state standards, both summative and formative portfolios can elicit reflection in student teachers when the assessments provide opportunities for the collection of multiple sources of evidence over time. However, it is unclear whether it is possible for teachers to have the same kinds of learning benefits when one portfolio is used for both formative and summative purposes. It is also unclear whether preservice teachers would have learned as much from their credential portfolios had there been no opportunity to develop a M.Ed. portfolio (Snyder et al., 1998).

## Discussion of Unstructured Portfolios

Although these examples of unstructured portfolios appear to serve important formative assessment purposes by promoting teacher reflection and teacher learning, it is clear that such instruments are insufficient for making high-stakes summative decisions about whether preservice teachers should be granted a license to teach. Without clear evaluative criteria and instruments such as scoring rubrics, evidence regarding the reliability and validity of these unstructured portfolio assessments, a system for training and calibrating scorers, and a process for the moderation of scores and eliminating bias, basing high-stakes decisions on such assessments is questionable. In addition, while a great deal of time and effort goes into the construction of these portfolios (on the part of the teacher candidates) and into the evaluation of the work (on the part of the program faculty), the time invested serves a primarily formative purpose. It then becomes a question of whether programs deem the formative purposes of the portfolio worth the effort, time, and resources. The programs that have continued to incorporate them into their programs seem to believe that it is worth the investment.

## Structured Portfolios

There are several national and state-level examples of structured portfolios that have been developed for the purpose of assessing the teaching performance of preservice or beginning teachers. Four of the best-known examples are the INTASC Teacher Portfolio; Teacher Work Sampling (Western Oregon University; Renaissance Group); the California Teaching Performance Assessment (developed by the California Commission on Teaching Credentialing in concert with the Educational Testing Service); and the Performance Assessment for California Teachers, developed by a consortium of California preservice credential programs. Although there are likely to be other examples of structured portfolio assessments in current use at the preservice level, these four examples have the most documentation regarding their reliability and validity, systems for the training and calibration of scorers, and moderation processes for ensuring that high-stakes consequences are warranted.

**INTASC Teaching Portfolio.** A project begun in 1987 (in the same year as the National Board for Professional Teaching Standards) by the Council of Chief State School Officers, the Interstate New Teacher Assessment and Support Consortium (INTASC) was commissioned to encourage collaboration among states to rethink teacher assessment for professional licensure. The ten INTASC principles, or model core standards, for new teachers were based on the National Board's five propositions about effective teaching (Arends, 2006a).

The INTASC Teacher Portfolio was designed to be used for evaluating teachers who have already received a preliminary license, not to evaluate preservice teachers. However, we include a brief description here because it laid the foundation for the preservice portfolio assessment systems described next. In 1995, the INTASC principles were incorporated into the NCATE standards. In 1998, NCATE decided to shift from an input-based model of accreditation to an emphasis on the assessment of teaching performance as evidence of program effectiveness. As a consequence, the INTASC principles and Teacher Portfolio had ripple effects on the standards and assessments used for preservice teachers.

The earliest versions of the INTASC Teacher Portfolio in English language arts, mathematics, and science were created and field-tested by the Performance Assessment Development Project (a joint effort of fifteen states) from 1994 to 2000 and were modeled after the National Board portfolio as well as prototypes of a portfolio assessment that were being developed by the Connecticut Department of Education for the advanced certification of beginning teachers (Arends, 2006a; INTASC, 2009b). The INTASC Teacher Portfolio requires that teachers submit

- Materials used in instruction
- Examples of student work
- Videotapes of teaching and learning in a candidate's classroom
- Written records of activities and assessments in a candidate's classroom
- Written commentaries that explain a candidate's thinking about teaching and learning

The portfolios are scored using a set of validated rubrics by trained scorers, and the reliability of the scores is checked through double-scoring of portfolios. (For a description of the INTASC scorer training and scoring process, see Moss, Schutz, & Collins, 1998.)

As of 2008, several states had incorporated the use of a teacher portfolio similar to the INTASC Teacher Portfolio into their licensure process for beginning teachers (among them are Connecticut, Indiana, California, and North Carolina) or master teachers (Wisconsin is one of them) (Coggshall et al., 2008). However, few states have required a portfolio assessment for initial certification (administered at the preservice level). California's efforts to implement its new teaching performance assessment requirement through preservice credential programs are described in more detail below.

*Technical Quality.* The content validity of the INTASC teacher portfolio and its evaluative criteria rests on its coherence with the INTASC general and content-specific standards, research on teaching knowledge and practice, and self-reported practices of teachers (Moss et al., 1998). Moss and colleagues describe and evaluate the scoring method that was under development, a collaborative evaluation by two raters, as a "dialogic and integrative" (p. 141) way of reading and interpreting teacher portfolios. They then argue for a more hermeneutic approach to construct a coherent interpretation that is challenged and revised as more and more available evidence is accounted for (in contrast to a psychometric approach that calls for independent readings of isolated performances). While the INTASC scoring approach is holistic, it is based on "a series of explicit steps involving data reduction and integration guided by questions from a detailed evaluation framework. At each stage, the steps of data reduction and integration are recorded for consideration at the next stage. By the time they are ready to reach consensus on an overall conclusion, readers have produced a written record of steps" (Moss, 1998, p. 209). While Moss and colleagues have articulated a validity research agenda, no additional information on validity or score reliability has been reported by INTASC to date.

In one recent study of the predictive validity of the Connecticut BEST portfolios in relation to the achievement of students taught by teachers with varying scores on the portfolios (Wilson, Hallam, Pecheone, & Moss, in press), there appeared to be a small but significant relationship between teachers' scores on the BEST portfolio and their students' achievement scores (there were no significant relationships between teachers' scores on Praxis I and II and student achievement scores). More large-scale studies that examine the predictive validity of large-scale portfolio assessments are needed to provide additional evidence of the validity of portfolio assessments.

*Impact on Teacher Learning.* Little research has been published on the impact of the INTASC Teacher Portfolios on teachers' professional learning. (For state case studies on Indiana, North Carolina, and Connecticut, see Kimball, 2002; White, 2002; Kellor, 2002; and Wilson, Darling-Hammond, & Berry, 2001.) The little research that has been published indicates that the process of constructing these structured portfolios, sometimes to meet high-stakes licensing requirements, also served a formative function by promoting teacher reflection and learning. In surveys of beginning teachers who completed the portfolio requirement in Connecticut as part of the Beginning Educator Support and Training program, 72 percent of respondents reported that the portfolio construction process had improved their ability to reflect, 60 percent reported that the process had helped them focus on important aspects of teaching, and 50 percent reported that the portfolio had improved their teaching practice (Wilson, et al., 2001). In another unpublished paper (Lomask, Seroussi, & Budzinsky, 1997), teachers who participated in a pilot science portfolio assessment provided written feedback indicating that most teachers found the process of portfolio development and the program's support seminars as an opportunity for reflection and professional growth.

*Practicality and Feasibility.*  Implementation of the Connecticut BEST program has required significant resources ($3.5 million per year) (Kellor, 2002), suggesting that statewide teacher certification by portfolio could be cost-intensive for most states. In fact, recent state budget cuts and legal challenges have forced Connecticut to revise the BEST program to rethink the portfolio requirement. In Indiana, the cost of training scorers was $58,000 per training session and the cost of scoring each portfolio was $120 (Kimball, 2002). In North Carolina, the total state cost of administering the teacher portfolio assessment for the 2000–2001 academic year was $500,000 and the cost of scoring each portfolio was estimated at $168 (White, 2002). The cost-benefit ratio regarding the use of portfolio methodology to support teacher learning and to assess teacher quality needs further study.

**Teacher Work Sampling.** In their survey study for AACTE, Salzman et al. (2002) found that 66 percent of respondents reported the use of teacher work sampling and 28 percent reported the use of measures of P–12 pupil learning as one measure of candidate outcomes. Teacher work sampling is a specific form of structured portfolio that is similar in format to the INTASC portfolios in that it requires teacher candidates to collect and submit specific artifacts that represent their teaching practice and respond to prompts that are aimed to help teachers elucidate the thinking behind their instructional decisions. Del Schalock and his colleagues at Western Oregon University are usually cited as the originators of the Teacher Work Sample Methodology (TWSM) (see Schalock, Schalock, & Girod, 1997). The TWSM used at Western Oregon University requires teacher candidates to develop a three- to five-week instructional unit that they implement during their student teaching placements. The evidence on which teachers are evaluated includes the following (McConney et al., 1998):

- A description of the teaching and learning outcomes to be accomplished
- A description of the teaching and learning context
- Instructional plans
- Pre- and postassessments developed and used to measure student progress

- Evidence of student learning gains
- Interpretation of and reflection on the success of the teaching-learning unit, including progress made by students in their learning and significance for the teacher's future practice and professional development

Each of these artifacts is assessed by supervising and research faculty on ratings instruments, and the teacher candidate's implementation of the instructional plans is observed and rated by university and school supervisors on an observation instrument. What is unique about this structured portfolio assessment is the requirement that teachers use pre- and postassessments to measure student progress during the course of the unit and that evidence of students' learning gains is used to evaluate teachers' ability to improve student learning. What is unclear from publications on the TWSM is the technical quality and comparability of the student pre- and postassessments that are designed and implemented by preservice teachers. While the quality, variety, and range of teachers' assessments and their alignment with stated learning objectives are evaluative criteria in the TWSM rubrics (see McConney & Ayers, 1998), how this relates to the validity of the teacher-designed pre- and postmeasures as evidence of student learning raises questions about the validity of judgments about a teacher's ability to impact student learning.

This series of assessments becomes part of a teacher profile that is used both formatively to provide feedback to teacher candidates and summatively to inform the credential decision. In the Western Oregon University program, candidates completed two TWSM cycles, the second with greater independence. But both were completed with ongoing feedback from supervising faculty. Evidence from interviews and focus groups with graduates of the program strongly supports the idea that a performance assessment that is a capstone assessment can also be formative by prompting teachers to articulate the rationale of their instructional decisions, learn how to plan for instruction and adapt their instruction based on their preassessments of students, and reflect on their instruction in light of student learning (Schalock, 1998; Girod & Schalock, 2002).

***Technical Quality.*** McConney et al. (1998) argued that the TWS instrument met criteria for authenticity and content and for face validity (based on alignment with program and state standards for teaching competency), but they acknowledged that the instrument's ability to meet psychometric standards for reliability and freedom from bias was mixed. While there were high levels of agreement in the observation ratings of school and college supervisors (between 81 and 98 percent agreement), interrater reliability for the other measures in the TWS could not be reported. The validity of the pre- and postassessment measures of student learning developed by teachers themselves was found to be strongly related to other measures of teaching quality in the TWS. To date, we know of no updates to information about the interrater reliability of the ratings instruments used for evaluating preservice teachers on the TWSM used by Western Oregon University. However, there is more published research on the technical quality of the teacher work sampling approach adapted, piloted, researched, and validated by the Renaissance Partnership for Improving Teacher Quality.

**Renaissance Teacher Work Sample.** The Renaissance Teacher Work Sample (RTWS) instrument was developed between 1999 and 2005 by a partnership of eleven members of the Renaissance Group, a consortium of colleges and universities committed to improving teacher education within their institutions. Funded in part by a Title II Teacher Quality Enhancement Grant, Western Kentucky University was the grantee and leading institution in the project. An adaptation of the Western Oregon University TWSM, the RTWS instrument assesses preservice teachers along seven teaching dimensions (Pankratz, 2008):

- Use of the student learning context to design instruction
- Development of clear instructional unit goals aligned with state and national content standards
- Design of an assessment plan to include pre-, post-, and formative assessments that guide and measure student learning
- Use of formative assessment to make sound instructional decisions
- Measurement and analysis of student learning that resulted from a unit of instruction (individual students, subgroups, and total class)
- Reflection on and evaluation of teaching and learning with respect to the unit of instruction

*Technical Quality.* During the period of the portfolio assessment's development and piloting, the Renaissance Partnership used specific processes to train scorers to score accurately and without bias. Pankratz (2008) reports that the RTWS had dependability coefficients of 0.80 or better with three scorers and 0.60 or better with two scorers based on Shavelson and Webb's (1991) test of generalizabilty.[3] The validity of the RTWS rests on high levels of face validity, based on Crocker's (1997) criteria for validity: criticality of tasks, frequency of task performance, realism, alignment with state and national standards, and representativeness. The RTWS was designed to align with INTASC's Model Standards for Beginning Teacher Licensing, Assessment and Development (Pankratz, 2008). Evidence on scorer dependability and validity was published in Denner, Salzman, and Bangert (2002) on a modified TWS instrument with modified holistic scoring procedures used at Idaho State University. Denner and colleagues found acceptable dependability coefficients ranging from 0.75 to 0.86 for two raters. This study, replicated with RTWS work samples from across nine of the eleven institutions (Denner, Norman, Salzman, & Pankratz, 2003), found that dependability coefficients of 0.77 to 0.82 could be achieved with three raters. Denner, Norman, and Lin (2009) also investigated the fairness and consequential validity of the TWS instrument using score and demographic data from two of the Renaissance Group institutions by examining whether the instrument had a disparate impact on candidates based on gender, age, or race/ethnicity. They did not find any disparate impact or adverse consequences based on these demographic backgrounds. The authors also investigated the relationship between candidates' TWS scores and their satisfaction of college entry requirements, Praxis I scores, and grade point average (GPA). They found that the GPA for the education core courses, the cumulative GPA, and Praxis I writing scores were significant predictors of the total TWS scores.

***Impact on Candidate Learning.*** When the Renaissance Partnership project ended in 2005, more than six thousand teacher work samples had been produced across the eleven partner institutions, and nine of those institutions have required the completion of the RTWS for graduation. While the initial reactions of most teacher candidates to the RTWS were that it required too much paperwork, that they did not have enough time in their student teaching placements to produce a high-quality TWS, and that they were overwhelmed by the high standards of performance on the RTWS, these negative attitudes tended to dissipate as the candidates completed their units and saw evidence of student learning outcomes in their classes. Some appreciated the realization that they were able to make a difference with their students and that the process helped them feel like professionals (Pankratz, 2008).

One of the questions that often arises in relation to the practicality of portfolio assessment is how long it takes to score this body of work, with the implication that the time required would make this form of assessment less feasible on practical grounds. The RTWS directs candidates to write some twenty or more pages of narrative, plus the artifacts of their teaching of an instructional unit. Denner, Salzman, & Harris (2002) reported that the average time it took to complete their modified TWS scoring protocol at Idaho State University was 13.5 minutes for each TWS. Another study reported an average scoring time of 24 minutes for teacher work samples that were not considered benchmarks (those representative of specific scoring levels) (Denner, Salzman, & Harris, 2002).

Another question, mentioned in the description of the Western Oregon University TWSM, was whether the evaluation of teacher quality based on the TWS pre- and poststudent learning measures (designed, implemented, and analyzed by teachers) is dependent on the quality of the student assessments themselves. Denner et al. (2003) analyzed the relationship between the quality of the student assessments and the overall evaluation of a TWS. They found significant positive correlations between independent evaluations of assessment quality and the teachers' RTWS scores, suggesting that the RTWS rubrics are able to distinguish the quality of the pre- and postassessments and that teachers are not given credit for showing improvements in student learning when the quality of the assessments is poor. Denner and Lin (2008) found a significant relationship between teachers' RTWS scores and the reported percentage gains in student achievement on the pre- and postassessments of student learning that comprise one required component of the RTWS. They also found greater gains in student achievement for candidates in the second intern-teaching experience than for the same candidates who constructed a RTWS during their pre-intern-teaching experience. The authors conclude that the RTWS provides evidence of the impact of teacher candidates' instruction on student learning and that "teacher preparation programs make a difference to the teaching abilities of their teacher candidates" (p. 16). (Additional research on the TWSM can be found at http://edtech.wku.edu/rtwsc.)

**California Teaching Performance Assessment.** In 1998, the California legislature passed Senate Bill 2042 with the goal of transforming the teacher licensing system in the state and reforming teacher preparation. One of the new requirements for the initial teaching credential introduced by SB 2042 was a teaching performance assessment (TPA) that would be completed during preservice preparation. Programs were given the option to administer the TPA developed by the state (through a contract with the ETS) or to design and administer their own TPA, provided that it meets the state's standards for psychometric quality. The TPA designed by the California Commission on Teacher Credentialing (CCTC), in partnership with ETS, was designed to measure the state teaching standards for beginning teachers.

The Cal TPA, a hybrid performance assessment that includes responses to classroom scenarios and portfolio components (in which teachers plan and teach lessons and collect student work samples), is designed to be administered during teacher education course work throughout the duration of the program.[4] It has four tasks:

- *Subject-specific pedagogy:* Candidates are given four case studies of specific classes and learners (specified for each credential—for example, elementary or secondary) and are prompted to develop teaching methods and lesson plans focused on the content, analyze and adapt assessment plans focused on the content, adapt lessons for English learners, and adapt lessons for students with special needs.

- *Designing instruction:* Candidates plan a lesson for an actual class of K–12 students, including adaptations for English-language learners and students presenting other instructional challenges.

- *Assessing learning:* Candidates plan an assessment based on learning goals, administer the student assessments, adapt the assessments for English learners and for students with other instructional challenges, and analyze and use the assessment results to plan instruction.

- *Culminating teaching experience:* This task integrates the three previous tasks by having candidates learn about their students, plan a lesson and assessment, adapt instruction and assessment for English learners and students with other instructional challenges, teach the lesson and administer the assessments, and analyze the lesson and assessment results to plan further instruction.

In addition, candidates reflect on what was learned in completing the task at the end of each task. As each task in the series is completed, it is scored holistically on a four-point rubric by the program faculty or other trained and qualified assessors. (The CCTC offers a one-day orientation training for scorers and a two-day training for scoring each of the four performance tasks. The commission also offers lead assessor training to provide local turnkey training sessions.) Candidates must earn a combined total of twelve points across the four tasks and must have a minimum score of 2 on any one task. Candidates are permitted to resubmit the tasks as many times as is necessary to earn the minimum number of points (California Commission on Teacher Credentialing, n.d.).

***Technical Quality.*** The Cal TPA was designed to measure the California TPEs for beginning teachers, which was created based on a job analysis for beginning teachers and validated by a committee of educators and stakeholders across the state. Thus, the content validity of the assessment rests on its alignment with these TPEs, as well as with the two regional focus review groups that were used to support the development, pilot testing, and review of the TPA prototype. Once the TPA prototype was finalized, it underwent an ETS sensitivity and fairness review process and was pilot-tested and scored in spring 2002. The purpose of the session (scoring a subsample of candidates' responses) was to collect information about the tasks, reactions to the tasks, and recommendations for modifying the tasks (California Commission on Teacher Credentialing, 2003a).

Following the pilot test, a larger field review of the four tasks was completed from October 2002 to April 2003. Forty-two assessors were convened centrally for training and calibration in June 2003 and scored the tasks. Based on score data from 104 teacher candidate performances with all four tasks scored, assessor agreement was calculated to range from 91 to 98 percent across the four tasks (exact agreement plus differences of one point on the score scale), and assessor reliability (using the Spearman Brown prophecy reliability statistic) was reported as ranging between 0.63 to 0.83 across the four tasks and 0.87 overall (California Commission on Teacher Credentialing, 2003b). These results indicate acceptable levels of interrater reliability when raters are trained and scoring is conducted centrally (raters are trained and score under direct supervision of the CCTC and ETS). Programs have the option of participating in centralized training of raters or using a trainer of trainers model for local scorer training. Local trainers receive specialized training from the CCTC's lead trainers before they may train local raters. There have been no additional official reports of rater consistency or reliability under this decentralized model of training and scoring.

*Costs of Implementing a Statewide Teaching Performance Assessment.* While approximately $10 million was appropriated by the state legislature for the development and validation of the Cal TPA, it is unclear what the total annual costs of implementing this performance-based assessment system for preservice teacher credential programs across the state would be. Some estimates have ranged from two hundred to four hundred dollars per teacher candidate (depending on whether the costs associated with implementing the assessment system include costs beyond payments to trainers and assessors for scoring). For large programs in the California State University system, which produce hundreds of teaching credentials per year, the pressure on program budgets is tremendous. There are divergent views about the responsibility of higher education institutions and other credentialing agencies for engaging in the assessment of candidates for beginning licensure. There are strong sentiments in the state legislature that assessment of graduates from credential-granting programs for purposes of quality control is inherent in the role of higher education programs and that the associated costs should be built into program budgets. The implication is that all program faculty, including supervisors, and other nontenured instructors would be required to support teacher candidates completing the TPA as well as participate in scoring the TPA as part of their job responsibilities (with no additional compensation). Given the current state budget crises and cuts to the state's education spending, few resources were appropriated for the purpose of funding the state's TPA mandate (as it went into effect in July 2008). Programs are struggling but making do with the few resources they were allocated, and they continue to lobby the state for additional funds on the grounds that the current mandate is unfunded.

*Tensions in the Formative and Summative Purposes of the TPA.* The Cal TPA model is designed to be implemented and scored in the context of teacher education course work. Teachers are to be prepared for and complete each of the four tasks as part of their course requirements and receive formative feedback and support on their tasks from course instructors. While on one level it seems more supportive of candidate learning and success to embed the tasks in the context of their teacher education course work, one of the complaints commonly raised about this model is that it "colonizes" the curriculum of teacher education. Many program faculty members across the state have objected to the increasing encroachment by state regulation on their academic freedom and being forced to teach to the test. Thus, while it appears that the integration of the Cal TPA into program course work is likely to improve its usefulness as a formative assessment, this integration is in tension with the assessment's high-stakes function as one gatekeeper to the initial credential. The high-stakes nature of the assessment and its integration into course work force program faculty to teach to the test. If higher education faculty members are required to adopt and integrate a TPA into their courses to this extent, it is imperative that research about the predictive validity of the TPA and its value as both a summative and formative assessment be documented.

**Performance Assessment for California Teachers.** The Performance Assessment for California Teachers (PACT), another form of a structured portfolio assessment, is currently used in thirty-two preservice credential programs in California and was recently adapted for use in Washington State as part of its initial teaching licensure requirement.[5] After California elected to require teacher preparation programs to use standardized performance assessments in making credentialing decisions (along with other measures), it contracted with the ETS to develop such an instrument, but gave teacher education institutions the option of using a different instrument if it met the CCTC's Assessment Quality Standards.

A coalition of California institutions of higher education formed PACT to develop such an alternative assessment method. The PACT Consortium was initially composed of twelve universities: University of California (UC) Berkeley, UCLA, UC San Diego, UC Santa Cruz, UC Santa Barbara, UC Riverside, UC Davis, UC Irvine, San Jose State University, San Diego State University, Stanford University, and Mills College. The consortium has since grown to include thirty-two preservice credential programs (including one district intern program). Based on the latest available data from the CCTC for 2005–2006, PACT institutions produced 3,877 or 31.6 percent of multiple subject (elementary), 2,544 or 35.1 percent of single subject (secondary), and 6,421 or 32.9 percent overall of the candidates receiving preliminary California teaching credentials. From 2002–2003 up to 2007–2008, the PACT Teaching Event was piloted across the consortium; 2008–2009 is the first year of full enactment of the law (performance on the TPA now counts for teacher licensure).

The development of and research on the PACT was funded by grants from the University of California Office of the President, the Flora and Sally Hewlett Family Foundation, the Hewlett Foundation, and the Morgan Family

Foundation.[6] A key motivation for the PACT Consortium was to develop an integrated set of rigorous, transparent, subject-specific, standards-based certification assessment instruments that would be consistent with the curricular and professional commitments of the member institutions. The goal of the PACT Consortium has been to strengthen the quality of teacher preparation by using curriculum-embedded assessment instruments developed by each member institution in combination with a standardized teaching performance assessment to recommend licensure for prospective teachers.

*PACT Assessment Design.* The PACT assessment system consists of two interconnected components: a standardized portfolio assessment, the Teaching Event (TE), and locally developed Embedded Signature Assessments (ESAs). The Teaching Event is an evidence-based system that uses multiple sources of data: teacher plans, teacher artifacts, student work samples, video clips of teaching, and personal reflections and commentaries. The TEs are subject-specific assessments integrated across four tasks—planning, instruction, assessment, and reflection—with a focus on the use of academic language embedded across the tasks.[7] To meet the needs of the range of credential programs offered by PACT campuses, there are six versions of the multiple-subject Teaching Event (including two for bilingual emphasis candidates and two for candidates concurrently earning a special education credential) and eighteen single-subject TEs. For each Teaching Event, candidates must plan and teach a learning segment of thee to five hours of instruction (an instructional unit or part of a unit), videotape and analyze their instruction, analyze student learning, and reflect on their practice. The Teaching Events are designed to measure and promote candidates' abilities to integrate their knowledge of content, students, and instructional context in making instructional decisions and reflecting on practice.

Individual PACT credential programs have also developed and administered ESAs, customized assessments to measure additional teaching competencies that are central to their program mission and goals. PACT is still tackling the technical challenge of combining scores from varied locally designed and customized assessments with scores from the Teaching Event, which serves as a standardized anchor assessment. The ultimate goal is to use both sources of evidence to contribute to the final pass/fail decision for the PACT teaching performance assessment. Until the measurement challenges have been resolved, the ESAs will be part of required course work and used formatively to build the teaching capacity of prospective teachers and for program evaluation or accreditation purposes.

*PACT Scoring System.* The proposed scoring system for the PACT Teaching Event by itself includes both a local and centralized scoring model. In most years, scoring is conducted at each local campus by a group of subject-specific trainers who are trained centrally each year. These trainers train, calibrate, and monitor scorers and oversee the local scoring process, including implementation of a plan for double-scoring selected TEs. All failing and borderline TEs are double-scored and checked by the lead trainer to confirm the decision. An additional random 10 percent sample stratified across passing score levels is double-scored by local scorers. The consistency of local scoring is managed through a centralized audit of 10 percent of local scores, with intervention aimed at campuses that are identified as producing unreliable scores. Every third year, a central standardized scoring model will be used to provide another check on the consistency of training and the scoring process and the reliability and validity of scores. It takes between two and four hours to score a single TE, depending on the experience of the rater. Scores from the pilot indicate that candidates across all subject areas tended to perform at a higher level on the planning and instruction tasks than on the assessment and reflection tasks. In addition, candidates tended to perform at a lower level of performance on the academic language–related rubrics.

***Technical Quality.*** To meet the assessment quality standards of the California Commission on Teacher Credentialing, which unanimously approved the PACT for use in meeting the requirements of the statute, the PACT Consortium spent considerable resources to collect evidence on and document the validity and reliability of the instrument. To document content validity, teacher educators who participated in the development and design of the assessments, as well as teacher educators not involved in the design of the assessment and who scored the portfolios, were asked to judge the extent to which the content of the TEs was an authentic representation of important dimensions of teaching. Another study examined the alignment of the Teaching Event tasks to the California teaching performance expectations (TPEs). Overall, the findings across all content validity activities suggest a strong linkage of the TPE standards, the Teaching Event tasks, and the skills and abilities needed for safe and competent professional practice (Pecheone & Chung, 2007).

***Bias Reviews and Analysis.*** Bias reviews, following guidelines put forth by the Educational Testing Service (2002) for conducting bias/sensitivity reviews of assessments, were conducted to examine the TE handbooks and rubrics used in each certification area to evaluate the text for offensive or potentially offensive language and to identify any areas of bias due to race, gender, ethnicity, or cultural-linguistic backgrounds. The findings from this process were used to flag areas of potential bias, which informed subsequent revisions of the TE handbooks, rubrics, and scoring process. Second, the performance of candidates on the PACT assessment was examined to determine if candidates performed differentially with respect to specific demographic characteristics.

For the 2003–2004 pilot, there were no significant differences in scores by race/ethnicity of candidates, percentage of English language learner students in candidates' classrooms, grade level taught (elementary versus secondary), academic achievement level of a candidate's students, and months of previous paid teaching experience. There were statistically significant differences between male and female candidates (with females scoring higher) and between candidates teaching in schools in different socioeconomic contexts (with candidates in suburban schools scoring slightly higher than those in urban or inner-city schools). The PACT Consortium plans to continue to monitor and reexamine the scorer training process, the design of the Teaching Event assessments, and differences in candidate scores based on demographic differences to uncover any potential sources of bias due to varying socioeconomic contexts (Pecheone & Chung, 2007).

Finally, score consistency and reliability were examined. Analysis of the consistency between 2003–2004 local campus scores and audit scores (in which a sample of locally scored TEs was rescored at a central scoring session) provided evidence about consistency across pairs of scores by computing consensus estimates within each subject area. Across content areas, 91 percent of score pairs were exact matches or within one point. Interrater reliability was also calculated using the Spearman Brown prophecy reliability statistic. For the 2003–2004 pilot year, the overall interrater reliability for all rubrics across tasks was 0.88 (Pecheone & Chung, 2007).

***High Stakes and Formative.*** The formative potential of the PACT Teaching Event for teacher candidates, individual faculty members, and programs as a whole is in large part related to the analytical nature of the rubrics and the specific information that the rubric scores provide about the strengths and weaknesses of preservice teachers' instructional practice. The design of the rubrics and the way in which they are written allow some transparency in interpreting the score results by providing concrete images of beginning teacher practice at various levels. This is supportive of program faculty who want to provide formative feedback to candidates as they construct their Teaching Events, as well as to programs engaging in an analysis of aggregate scores for the purpose of program review and revision.

Several research studies have been conducted that examine the impact of completing the PACT on the learning experiences of preservice teachers who have completed the PACT Teaching Event. Chung (2005, 2008), one of the authors of this chapter, collected both quantitative and qualitative evidence (surveys, ratings of teaching, interviews, observations) to examine whether preservice teachers who completed the PACT Teaching Event reported learning from their experiences with the portfolio assessment and whether there was any evidence of changes in their teaching practice consistent with their reports of learning. In a study conducted during the first pilot year (2002–2003) at a large urban university participating in the PACT Consortium, Chung (2008) interviewed and observed the classroom instruction of preservice teachers before, during, and after completion of the Teaching Event. She found that engaging in the process of planning, teaching, and documenting a unit of instruction for the Teaching Event afforded a number of important learning experiences related to the novelty of some of these experiences for the two case study teachers. For example, the teachers cited learning from the opportunity to formally investigate the characteristics and learning needs of their students, independently plan lessons (rather than implement lessons designed by their cooperating teachers), attend to the needs of English learners, analyze their students' learning and use that information to make adjustments to subsequent lessons, and reflect on their teaching effectiveness. In addition, some of the changes that teachers reported in their teaching practices were observed in their subsequent classroom instructional practice.

In another comparison group study of teacher candidates in another large urban university conducted during the second pilot year (2003–2004), Chung (2005) compared the learning experiences of those who had completed the Teaching Event and those who had not. She found that preservice teachers in cohorts that had completed the Teaching Event began with significantly lower average self-ratings and lower supervisor ratings of their teaching knowledge and skills than teachers in cohorts that had not completed the Teaching Event, but by the end of the program, they had closed the gap in their self-ratings and supervisor ratings. Through case studies of teachers in the piloting and nonpiloting cohorts, Chung analyzed more closely the learning gains of teachers in both groups and was able to disentangle to some extent the learning gained from experiences with the Teaching Event and program experiences overall. Teachers in the piloting cohorts were more likely to report improving their ability to reflect on their teaching decisions and assess student learning. However, candidates' reports of learning were moderated by the quality of implementation at the university during the second pilot year, which led many of the piloting teachers to feel that the requirements of the Teaching Event were too burdensome. These constraints detracted from their abilities to learn from their planning and teaching experiences.

In the first and second pilot years of the PACT, the Teaching Event at most universities in the PACT Consortium was not completed as a high-stakes assessment with scores counting toward the credential decision. However, in most cases, piloting teachers were required to complete the assessment as part of a course or program requirement and contributed in some way to the credential decision. During the first two pilot years, the PACT Consortium administered a survey to all candidates completing Teaching Events across the consortium. They found that approximately 90 percent felt that the Teaching Event validly measured important elements of their teaching knowledge and skill, and two-thirds felt that they had learned important skills through their experiences with the Teaching Event. In particular, survey respondents reported that they had learned the importance of using student work analysis to guide their instructional decisions and reflect more carefully about their teaching. In addition, preservice teachers have reported that the experience of investigating their students' backgrounds for the instructional context task of the Teaching Event has prompted them to pay greater attention to their students' specific learning needs in designing instruction, as this comment from a California State University teacher candidate illustrates:

> So, you know, at the beginning, the PACT lesson has you analyze: What's the context? Who are the kids? What needs do they have? Do you have English language learners?...What kind of English language learner are they and how much, where are they on the spectrum? Are they beginning language learners? Are they advanced language learners? And then, to take that information about all the kids in your class, and then think about teaching to every single one of them. That was kind of a new experience for me. It was actually the first time in my teaching experience that everything came together from beginning to end, and made sense. It made sense.

In more recent years, many of the piloting programs have required a passing score on the Teaching Event for successful completion of the credential program. Nonetheless, the reports of preservice teachers have been no less positive regarding the learning gained from their experiences with the Teaching Event. One California State University teacher candidate who had gone back to graduate school to earn a public school credential after having taught for ten years in a private school setting recently commented on her experience with PACT:

> It made a huge change in the way that I assessed. And that was kind of a surprise for me when I got to the end of the PACT.... When I went to assess, I kind of floundered for a second. I'm kind of looking at the kid's work in front of me, and I'm kind of spinning my wheels for a second. What am I assessing? What am I assessing? And it kind of took me an hour or two to figure out, wait a second, I need to go back to my big idea to be up front. And that's the first time I—and I've been teaching for ten years—I ever thought of assessment in that sense. And when I pulled out the big idea, it allowed me to assess not only the students, but to assess my own teaching, and that was kind of a new experience for me too. I never used objectives or the big idea to assess my own teaching to particular students. And it just kind of opened up a whole new world that made more sense to me as to what my role was in the classroom, what my role is as a teacher to these students, and a tool that allowed me to analyze my own teaching over three lessons to see if I was really effective in teaching a big idea. It allowed a focus—before there was so much data coming at me, there were multiple objectives, it was too much—and this way, it kind of gave me a focus to say, this big idea, did I teach this well? Did the students know this, and if not, why not?

Using survey data from candidates completing the PACT, the PACT Consortium has found that the more teachers reported being supported in their completion of the assessment, the better prepared they felt by their course work and field placements, and the more likely they were to report having learned from the Teaching Event. Higher ratings of program supports and preparation and higher levels of reported learning have been associated with higher scores on the PACT Teaching Event (Chung, 2007; Chung & Whittaker, 2007). (See Tables 3.1 to 3.4.)

These findings suggest that even in a high-stakes environment, preservice teachers can have positive learning experiences associated with a summative evaluation of their teaching when their programs are able to provide the supports for candidate learning and their prior program experiences are supportive of success on the Teaching Event.

Bunch, Aguirre, and Tellez (2008) emphasize the formative value of preservice assessments that explicitly prompt preservice teachers to attend to the academic language development of their students. Their analysis of the Teaching Events of eight teacher candidates, focused on teachers' understanding of

Table 3.1. Association Between Candidate Ratings of Support for Completing the TE and Their Perceptions of Learning from the TE, 2003–2004

| Total Support Score[a] | Number | Mean Agreement Level on Learning | Standard Deviation | Standard Error | 95 Percent Confidence Interval | |
|---|---|---|---|---|---|---|
| | | | | | Lower Bound | Upper Bound |
| Group 1: 1–6 | 25 | 2.04 | .889 | .178 | 1.673 | 2.407 |
| Group 2: 6–12 | 156 | 2.37 | .924 | .074 | 2.226 | 2.518 |
| Group 3: 13–18 | 220 | 2.58 | .843 | .057 | 2.465 | 2.689 |
| Group 4: 19–24 | 136 | 2.84 | .762 | .065 | 2.709 | 2.968 |
| Group 5: 25–30 | 34 | 3.03 | .870 | .149 | 2.726 | 3.333 |

Note: The mean differences between groups 1 and 4, groups 1 and 5, groups 2 and 4, groups 2 and 5, and groups 3 and 4 are statistically significant at the .05 level. Dependent variable: "I learned important skills from the process of constructing the Teaching Event" (1 = strongly disagree, 2 = disagree, 3 = agree, 4 = strongly agree).

[a]The total support score is a composite score (the sum) of six items on which candidates rated various potential sources of support for completing the Teaching Event on a scale of 1 (not very helpful) to 5 (very helpful), including other credential candidates, university supervisor, cooperating or master teacher, school site administrator, university instructors and professors, and the teacher education program director.

**Table 3.2.** Association Between Candidate Ratings of Course Work Preparation for Completing the Teaching Event and Their Perceptions of Learning from the Teaching Event, 2003–2004

| Course Work Preparation for Teaching Event | Number | Mean Agreement Level on Learning | Standard Deviation | Standard Error | 95 Percent Confidence Interval | |
|---|---|---|---|---|---|---|
| | | | | | Lower Bound | Upper Bound |
| 1) Strongly disagree | 25 | 1.80 | .913 | .183 | 1.423 | 2.177 |
| 2) Disagree | 65 | 2.05 | .856 | .106 | 1.834 | 2.258 |
| 3) Agree | 331 | 2.57 | .792 | .044 | 2.488 | 2.660 |
| 4) Strongly agree | 161 | 2.93 | .891 | .070 | 2.787 | 3.064 |

*Note:* The mean differences between groups 1 and 3, groups 1 and 4, groups 2 and 3, groups 2 and 4, and groups 3 and 4 are significant at the .01 level.

**Table 3.3.** Association Between Candidate Ratings of Course Work Preparation for Completing the Teaching Event and Their Scores on the Teaching Event, 2003–2004

| Course Work Preparation for Teaching Event | Number | Mean Teaching Event Scores | Standard Deviation | Standard Error | 95 Percent Confidence Interval | |
|---|---|---|---|---|---|---|
| | | | | | Lower Bound | Upper Bound |
| 1) Strongly disagree | 15 | 2.469 | .765 | .198 | 2.045 | 2.893 |
| 2) Disagree | 26 | 2.395 | .572 | .112 | 2.164 | 2.626 |
| 3) Agree | 169 | 2.533 | .584 | .045 | 2.444 | 2.622 |
| 4) Strongly agree | 76 | 2.768 | .606 | .070 | 2.629 | 2.906 |

*Note:* The mean difference between groups 2 and 4 and groups 3 and 4 are significant at the .01 level.

academic language and its role in the teaching of mathematics to elementary students, found that candidates responded in a range of ways and exhibited varying levels of sophistication in their understanding of how academic language and mathematics content understandings are interrelated. They suggest that even high-stakes performance assessments like the PACT that have an explicit focus on academic language can formatively support candidate learning in this area and could provide useful information to programs about their candidates' understandings of academic language and its role in the teaching of content.

Table 3.4. Association Between Candidate Perceptions of Learning from the Teaching Event and Their Scores on the Teaching Event, 2003–2004

| "I learned important skills from completing the Teaching Event" | Number | Mean Teaching Event Score | Standard Deviation | Standard Error | 95 Percent Confidence Interval | |
|---|---|---|---|---|---|---|
| | | | | | Lower Bound | Upper Bound |
| 1) Strongly disagree | 47 | 2.44 | .668 | .098 | 2.248 | 2.641 |
| 2) Disagree | 84 | 2.56 | .598 | .065 | 2.429 | 2.689 |
| 3) Agree | 175 | 2.58 | .587 | .044 | 2.491 | 2.666 |
| 4) Strongly agree | 45 | 2.75 | .686 | .102 | 2.541 | 2.952 |

Note: The mean difference between groups 1 and 4 is significant at the .05 level.

In another study that examined preservice teacher learning, Nagle (2006) described the use of the PACT Teaching Event artifacts as the prompts for preservice teachers' inquiry into their own practice through guided collaborative discussions in a small seminar for science credential candidates:

> Through this study it is evident that state mandated assessments like the Teaching Event can afford learning opportunities for preservice teachers to examine their practice in an in-depth and collaborative manner. The tasks of the Teaching Event provide a structure or scaffold to investigate the primary areas of teaching—planning, instruction, assessment and analysis. As this study illustrates the tasks of the Teaching Event complement the learning goals of the teacher education program. The Teaching Event affords direction for the preservice teachers to investigate their teaching practice, but the specific issues that the preservice teachers eventually investigated were influenced primarily through the theoretical foundations of the teacher education program. Two-thirds of the issues investigated and presented by the preservice teachers in the Student Teaching Seminar involved student learning, one of the primary goals of the teacher education program [p. 15].

Nagle points out that the Teaching Event in itself is insufficient to ensure successful in-depth collaborative examination of practice and that structured, theory-guided discussions, as well as a culture of trust and community that was previously built during the program, are needed to facilitate honest examination of practice that leads to learning in practice.

The positive association that the PACT Consortium found between teachers' ratings of their program supports and preparation and their scores on the Teaching Event also suggests that the aggregated results of the scores from the PACT Teaching Events from each campus could serve as an important indicator of program quality. But more important, surveys of program leaders and faculty have found that the results of PACT Teaching Event scores have been used in some campuses to formatively guide program review and revision (Pecheone & Chung, 2006). There is evidence from programs that the PACT scores have helped to guide program review and revision by making more clearly visible the strengths and common weaknesses of candidate performance in particular areas of teaching, such as assessment and the instruction of English learners. Perceived weaknesses in the ability of teacher candidates to design and analyze assessments of student learning have led to a greater focus on assessment literacy in preservice program courses across the PACT Consortium. Likewise, historically lower scores on the rubric dimension Academic Language, which focuses on teachers' understanding of the language demands of their lessons and their strategies to support English learners' acquisition of academic language and content, have led many programs to work toward a common understanding of academic language among program faculty members, and to attend to teacher candidates' weaknesses in this area. One California State University program director said:

> We've always gone out into the classrooms and observed and we've always assessed their work inside the classroom. Now this is asking them to write and think about, in one assessment, in an official culminating assessment process, what they're actually thinking about as they're teaching. What's important about that is that the rubrics are sufficiently detailed enough so that when we analyze the data, it gives us important information about the strengths of our program. And in terms of what students know, what do we think we're teaching, yet the students aren't getting? In other words, where are the holes in our program? And that has been really valuable for us.... One of the areas that we've found we need to work on is: What do student teachers do next? Once they've analyzed the student work in the assessment of student work [task], what do they need to do next to actually improve on the student learning in their classroom? And I know, because of the consortium, that's actually a weakness in many of the student teacher programs.

Another California State University faculty member and program coordinator explained:

> A major change in our program has been a stronger emphasis on academic language. It's always been a goal for the program, but I think there has been historically a conception that "Oh well, that course will handle it and the students will remember what they learned in that one course and it will carry forward." But we've been doing a lot of professional development with our supervisors, in particular around academic language, to have them think about what linguistic demands are embedded in their candidates' lessons and to help the candidates

understand that they need to think about academic language development while they're planning, not after they've done a plan and then modify the plan, that it is a consideration from the very beginning of their lessons. And when they look at student work, they want to ask, "To what extent does the student performance reflect an academic language issue, in addition to a content learning issue?"

Peck, Gallucci, Sloan, and Lippincott (2008) describe the inquiry process used by the Teacher Education Program at the University of California-Santa Barbara to engage faculty in collaborative examination of candidate portfolio work and to address gaps in teacher performance through innovations in program design. For this purpose, all of the UCSB program faculty (including administrators) score the PACT Teaching Events (whereas at many other campuses, supervisors or nonladder faculty score Teaching Events) because it allows them to examine together the evidence of student performance in a way that creates a common language and common understandings about what preservice teachers should know and be able to do by the time they graduate from the program. It also allows an evidence-based discussion around gaps in candidate knowledge or skills.

*PACT Embedded Signature Assessments (ESAs).* The introduction of the ESAs was based on the finding that almost all PACT institutions had designed and developed unique assessments of teaching to support course instruction or meet programmatic or state or national accreditation requirements. After much deliberation, PACT made a strategic and practical decision to build on rather than supplant existing assessment practices. In an examination of teaching assessments across programs, clear patterns emerged:

- Teacher education programs developed assessments that were purposefully aligned to the California TPEs and were emblematic of tasks that appeared to be representative of the universities' goals and mission.
- The teaching assessments were embedded in university courses and often contributed to course grades.
- The teaching assessments occurred throughout the program (from entry to completion).
- The teaching assessments were most often used formatively to enable both instructors and teacher candidates to identify areas of strengths and weaknesses, as well as to monitor individual progress toward meeting state teaching standards.

In sum, the embedded assessments used by colleges and universities were customized campus-specific records of practice (assignments), developed by instructors using standard criteria to track a candidate's growth over time.

The PACT development committee struggled with the question of how to take into account the assessment work in which universities were already engaged and bring some rigor to the developmental process. The ESA definition was developed to signify signature features of the customized assessments. The assessments that represented signature assessments were course-embedded assignments that all candidates in a particular course of study (for example, multiple subjects, science, special education) were administered, and reliability and validity evidence was systematically collected for these signature tasks. That is, not all teaching assignments are designated as ESAs. To be considered an ESA, evidence of reliability and validity needs to be gathered for each ESA teaching assignment within a specific course of study, and candidate scores can be aggregated to inform program evaluation or accreditation. Examples of ESAs could include case studies, lesson plans, observations, classroom management plans, and other assignments or activities that fulfill the selection criteria.

In summary, the PACT system is based on the synergistic alignment of evidence that occurs at two points: during student teaching as a capstone demonstration of teacher competence through the Teaching Event and formatively throughout the program by means of ESAs. Table 3.5 contrasts the key features that distinguish the two PACT components.

## Discussion of Structured Portfolios

Structured portfolio assessments provide promising examples of performance-based assessments that collect and assess multiple sources of evidence about student teacher performance that are based on valid constructs and can be scored reliably with a systematic process for training assessors to score and a moderation process to ensure that the scoring process is fair. In addition, some of these assessment systems (for example, the TWSM, RTWS, and PACT) have created scoring rubrics that describe in detail the indicators of performance at each level and across multiple scoring criteria. This increases the potential of these assessment instruments to provide detailed feedback to candidates and programs about the quality of the candidate performance on the portfolio assessment and contribute to the educative, formative purpose of the process. At least three of these cases (TWSM, RTWS, and PACT) offer substantial evidence of the formative benefits of the portfolio assessment process for candidate learning and development, and some evidence of the potential of the assessments to serve a formative purpose in the context of program self-study and revision. However, we also know that the quality of candidates' learning experiences in relation to a summative portfolio assessment is strongly shaped by the quality of program implementation of these assessments. Programs must provide multiple opportunities for candidates to practice and hone the kinds of skills measured by these assessments (for example, analyzing evidence of

**Table 3.5.  Key Features of the PACT Teaching Event and Embedded Signature Assessments**

| Key Feature | Teaching Event | Embedded Signature Assessment |
|---|---|---|
| Evaluation purpose | Summative. | Formative. |
| Timing | Capstone event usually during the student teaching placement. | Continuous; administered throughout program. |
| Records of practice | Common tasks focused on three to five days of instruction organized around planning, instruction (videotape), assessment (student work for whole class and two students), reflection, and academic language. | Customized university-based teaching assignments, linked to one or more teaching standards or specific to the program mission; for example, ESAs may include course assignments, fieldwork, case studies, observations. |
| Context | During student teaching, guided by detailed subject-specific handbooks and implementation guidelines for faculty and staff. | Embedded in university courses; includes a range of customized teaching activities aligned to standards or the mission or goals of the teacher preparation program. |
| Scoring system | Trained scorers within disciplines who meet calibration standards; benchmark Teaching Events within each discipline; standardized rubric within each discipline; failing TEs are judged by multiple raters; and overall there is a 10 percent program audit within each IHE. | Customized rubrics aligned to standards (TPEs) and matched to specific tasks; generally scored by faculty, instructors, clinical supervisors. |
| Stakes | High stakes for California preliminary credential. Requirement that all candidates meet or exceed a proficiency standard for the Teaching Event in order to be eligible for an initial teaching license. | Low to moderate stakes: formative feedback to monitor progress on the TPEs or is included in course grades and supports program evaluation. |

what students have learned in pre- and postassessments, supporting students' acquisition of academic language) by embedding these skills in their course work and fieldwork experiences and providing ongoing feedback to candidates on these skills.

The work and the costs associated with creating and validating a portfolio assessment, administering and scoring the assessment on a large scale, as well as the additional work it creates for teacher candidates and credential programs supporting candidates as they complete the assessment, need to be addressed. We cannot ignore the effort and resources that went into creating and validating the Cal TPA, as well as the PACT assessment system. This is why a state law and public funding of the work (in the case of the Cal TPA), and combining the resources and expertise across consortia (for example, the Renaissance Group and PACT Consortium), have been so indispensable to getting the work done well. It seems imperative that for assessment systems like those described here to be adopted, a targeted investment in both fiscal resources and the tools and technologies needed to streamline the work involved will be necessary.

# DISCUSSION

U.S. policy for developing a competitive, highly effective teaching force is rooted in state-by-state licensure requirements that generally focus on measuring basic core knowledge (reading, writing, and mathematics) and content knowledge. These are proxy measures of teacher quality that are designed to assess minimum competency to meet legal requirements for licensure assessment. Importantly, a few states have statutes that require teachers to demonstrate their teaching competence in the classroom. The importance of gathering evidence about classroom practice in making teacher certification decisions was highlighted in a report from the National Research Council (Mitchell, Robinson, Plake, & Knowles, 2001). The authors of the report concluded that "paper and pencil tests provide only some of the information needed to evaluate the competencies of teacher candidates" and called for "research and development of broad based indicators of teaching competence," including "assessments of teaching performance in the classroom" (p. 172). Thus, our investigation of curriculum-embedded assessments of teaching led us to identify broader university policies and practices that focus on how existing evidence-based embedded assessments of teaching were aligned, interconnected, and used to support candidate learning and program change. Because instruments to assess teaching differ widely across programs in quality and practice, it is difficult to identify particular reforms or innovative methodologies that can serve as a unifying model for raising the level and quality of teacher education programs.

Fostering change in teacher assessment within teacher education programs can be viewed from three perspectives that together provide a framework for understanding the evolution and current state of the art of assessment in teacher education: a design perspective, a sociocultural perspective, and a policy perspective. These are depicted in Figure 3.1.

The design perspective includes those educational aspects of the assessment of teaching that have been identified as key indicators of effective performance. In the case of this review, these include identifying those research-based teacher-preparation assessment practices that can stand alone or be combined to support valid judgments of a candidate's teaching performance. Promising practices that have been identified in this review include observation protocols (CLASS, ITQ), teacher work samples (Renaissance Group), and portfolio assessment (PACT). Of the three assessment types, both the teacher work sampling

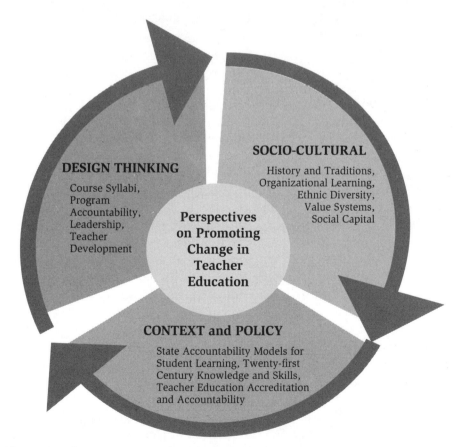

**Figure 3.1** Three Perspectives for Promoting Organizational Change in Teacher Education

methodology and PACT incorporate the use of multiple measures of teaching and learning to evaluate teacher competence. That is, both systems include the collection of similar records of practice: lesson plans, teacher assignments, videotapes or observations of teaching, and student work samples. However, the PACT assessment also provides universities additional opportunities to gather both formative (ESAs) and summative evidence (TE) to enable candidates and faculty to both monitor candidate progress and use this information for program improvement and initial licensure.

Other considerations in designing credible and defensible systems to assess teaching focus on decisions regarding whether to proceed with development using a generic or subject-specific framework for design, decisions about training and scoring, decisions about calibration and benchmarking, decisions about feedback and support, and decisions about standard setting. These decisions around assessment design and development are essential because they provide a window into the thinking behind what a program values regarding their views of effective teaching and learning. Therefore, the assessment of classroom practice can serve either to reinforce the value, respect, complexity, and challenges presented in teaching or, if conceptualized too narrowly, to deconstruct teaching in ways that marginalize and trivialize teaching and learning. Choosing the right path is embedded in the values, norms, and conversations within universities around their philosophy and definition of effective teaching.

The sociocultural perspective addresses in part the social, cultural, and historical features of teacher education programs. The implicit theory underlying current assessment policies and practices in teacher education is that programs will improve when objective evidence of candidate outcomes becomes the basis for making judgments of teacher quality (Fallon, 2006; McDiarmid & Peck, 2007). But it is unclear whether teacher education programs will actually act on objective evidence of candidate performance when they have it. In fact, research on evidence-based decision making in other fields suggests the opposite effect (Estabrooks, 2007; Putnam, Twohig, Burge, Jackson, & Coix, 2002). What appears to be needed in teacher education is to investigate what changes in social practice, collaboration, and organizational learning should be put in place to support organizational innovation and change. Teacher education is a complex system in which multiple roles and practices are orchestrated and enacted across many stakeholders: tenure line faculty, adjunct faculty, clinical supervisors, cooperating teachers, and prospective teachers. Therefore, the organizational norms and structure of the work, including the protocols and tools used to inform practice, the unique ways it is carried out by individuals and programs, and the social capital that is needed to effectively use assessment data to inform change, are at best challenging and often not addressed in making assessment decisions. These organizational structures must be considered if evidence-based assessment is to become the policy lever used to drive changes in teacher education. Clearly we have a lot to learn about how teacher education programs will respond to high-stakes assessment initiatives (licensure and accreditation) and how these initiatives can be used to promote innovation and positive change.

The policy context perspective is situated in the national trend of adopting high-stakes accountability policies for students, schools, and districts (for example, No Child Left Behind). Success or failure of schools and teachers is now determined by standardized tests and external evaluations that often delimit educational outcomes to a small subset of content knowledge and skills, such as standardized state tests of literacy, mathematics, and science. Consequently, this laser-like focus on closing the gap in student achievement is closely tied to the processes of accrediting, promoting, rewarding, or punishing schools and teachers. It is in this policy context where the outcomes of assessment practice in teacher education are being discussed and evaluated. Research in teacher education appears to be following a similar accountability model that is being used to judge student performance and school performance with value-added statistical modeling. The use of value-added methodologies to evaluate teacher education programs is an emerging trend, fueled by Carnegie Foundation–funded grants from the Teachers for a New Era project that sponsored value-added studies to examine the relationship between teacher education program practices and student learning. While maintaining a focus on learning in teacher education is important, defining learning around basic knowledge and skills can lead to narrowing teaching to content and methods beneficial to attaining predefined results. The challenge ahead is to broaden our definition of teaching and learning to focus on raising standards for learning to better prepare all students for college and the workplace, giving significant attention to all aspects of a teacher's professional competencies: dispositions, cultural sensitivity, content knowledge, and teaching skills.

Assessment practices in teacher education do not occur in isolation; they are influenced and shaped by the sociocultural and policy demands on the system. In addition, the technical aspects of assessment design are essential tools in the development of a curriculum-embedded evidence-based system that promotes organizational learning and change as evidenced by improved educational outcomes for all children.

## Notes

1. According to Wiggins (1989), an authentic assessment is one that replicates the challenges and standards of performance that typically face actual practitioners. In addition, legitimate assessments are responsive to individuals and contexts. Accurate and equitable evaluation also entails dialogue with the person being assessed, allowing clarification of questions and explanations of answers.

2. The survey had a 65 percent response rate, representing 240 institutions and 65,000 education degrees awarded each year.

3. While generalizability coefficients depend on the relative standing or ranking of individual scores, dependability coefficients are used when making absolute decisions about the level of performance (as in pass/fail decisions) (Shavelson & Webb, 1991).

4. In California, there is a wide range of teacher credential program designs, including blended undergraduate programs, district intern programs, and two-year master's programs. However, most teacher credential programs in California are one-year postbaccalaureate programs, sometimes leading to a master's degree. Most preservice teachers are enrolled for two or three semesters or quarters of teacher education course work, with concurrent student teaching experiences.

5. Both authors of this chapter have participated in the development of the PACT assessment, and we devote more space to this than to the other assessments. As members of the technical development group leading the design and implementation of the PACT, we draw from the technical report and other published articles that we have written about the PACT assessment for this chapter. The PACT handbooks and the PACT technical report can by found online at http://www.pacttpa.org.

6. Even with funding, this work could not have been completed without the in-kind contributions (the sweat equity) put forth by volunteer faculty and staff of the consortium members, and the investment of member programs to provide the release time and cover travel costs so that faculty and staff could contribute thousands of hours of work to the project.

7. *Academic language* is defined as "the language needed by students to understand and communicate in the academic disciplines" (Pecheone & Chung, 2007, p. 9). It includes specialized vocabulary, conventional text structures within a field (for example, essays, lab reports), and other language-related activities typical of classrooms (for example, expressing disagreement, discussing an issue, asking for clarification). Academic language includes both productive and receptive modalities.

# REFERENCES

Anderson, R. S., & DeMeulle, L. (1998). Portfolio use in twenty-four teacher education programs. *Teacher Education Quarterly, 25*(1), 23–32.

APA/NCME/AERA (American Psychological Association, National Council on Measurement in Education, & American Educational Research Association). (1999). *Standards for educational and psychological testing 1999*. Washington, DC: Author.

Arends, R. I. (2006a). Performance assessment in perspective: History, opportunities, and challenges. In S. Castle & B. D. Shaklee (Eds.), *Assessing teacher performance: Performance-based assessment in teacher education* (pp. 3–22). Lanham, MD: Rowman and Littlefield.

Arends, R. I. (2006b). Summative performance assessments. In S. Castle & B. D. Shakle (Eds.), *Assessing teacher performance: Performance-based assessment in teacher education* (pp. 93–123). Lanham, MD: Rowman and Littlefield.

Athanases, S. Z. (1994). Teachers' reports of the effects of preparing portfolios of literacy instruction. *Elementary School Journal, 94*(4), 421–439.

Bunch, G. C., Aguirre, J. M., & Tellez, K. (2008, January 19). *Language, mathematics, and English learners: Pre-service teachers' responses on a high stakes performance assessment.* Paper presented at the Center for the Mathematics Education of Latinas and Latino Research Symposium, Santa Cruz, CA.

California Commission on Teacher Credentialing. (2003a, July). *California TPA field review report.* Sacramento: Author.

California Commission on Teacher Credentialing. (2003b, July). *Scoring analysis for the field review of the California TPA.* Sacramento: Author.

California Commission on Teacher Credentialing. (n.d.). *California Teaching Performance Assessment (CalTPA).* Retrieved March 10, 2009, from http://www.ctc.ca .gov/educator-prep/TPA-files/CalTPA-general-info.pdf.

Castle, S., Groth, L., Moyer, P. S., & Burns, S. (2006). Course-based performance assessments. In S. Castle & B. D. Shaklee (Eds.), *Assessing teacher performance: Performance-based assessment in teacher education* (pp. 49–92). Lanham, MD: Rowman and Littlefield.

Castle, S., & Shaklee, B. D. (Eds.). (2006). *Assessing teacher performance: Performance-based assessment in teacher education.* Lanham, MD: Rowman and Littlefield.

Chung, R. R. (2005). *The Performance Assessment for California Teachers and beginning teacher development: Can a performance assessment promote expert teaching?* Unpublished doctoral dissertation, Stanford University School of Education.

Chung, R. R. (2007, April). *Beyond the ZPD: When do beginning teachers learn from a high-stakes portfolio assessment?* Paper presented at the Annual Meeting of the American Educational Research Association, Chicago.

Chung, R. R. (2008). Beyond assessment: Performance assessments in teacher education. *Teacher Education Quarterly, 35*(1), 7–28.

Chung, R. R., & Whittaker, A. K. (2007, April). *Preservice candidates' readiness for portfolio assessment: The influence of formative features of implementation.* Paper presented at the Annual Meeting of the American Educational Research Association, Chicago.

CLASS (Classroom Assessment Scoring System). (n.d.). *Technical appendix.* Retrieved June 2, 2008, from http://www.brookespublishing.com/class2007/CLASS_ Pre-K.pdf.

Coggshall, J., Max, J., & Bassett, K. (2008, June). *Key issue: Using performance-based assessment to identify and support high-quality teachers.* Washington, DC: National Comprehensive Center for Teacher Quality. Retrieved June 13, 2008, from http://www.tqsource.org.

Crocker, L. (1997). Assessing content representativeness of performance assessment exercises. *Applied Measurement in Education, 10*, 83–95.

Danielson, C., & Dwyer, C. A. (1995). How Praxis III supports beginning teachers. *Educational Leadership, 53*(6), 66–67.

Danielson, C., & McGreal, T. (2000). *Teacher evaluation to enhance professional practice.* Alexandra, VA: Association for Supervision and Curriculum Development.

Darling-Hammond, L. (2001). Standard setting in teaching: Changes in licensing, certification, and assessment. In V. Richardson (Ed.), *Handbook of research on teaching* (4th ed., pp. 751–776). Washington, DC: American Educational Research Association.

Darling-Hammond, L., & Macdonald, M. B. (2000). Where there is learning, there is hope: Bank Street College of Education. In L. Darling-Hammond (Ed.), *Studies of excellence in teacher education: Preparation at the graduate level* (pp. 1–95). New York: National Commission on Teaching and America's Future; Washington, DC: American Association of Colleges for Teacher Education.

Darling-Hammond, L., & Snyder, J. (2000). Authentic assessment of teaching in context. *Teaching and Teacher Education, 16*(5–6), 523–545.

Darling-Hammond, L., Wise, A. E., & Klein, S. P. (1999). *A license to teach: Raising standards for teaching.* San Francisco: Jossey-Bass.

Davis, C. L., & Honan, E. (1998). Reflections on the use of teams to support the portfolio process. In N. Lyons (Ed.), *With portfolio in hand: Validating the new teacher professionalism* (pp. 90–102). New York: Teachers College Press.

Denner, P. R., & Lin, S. (2008). *Evidence for impact on student learning from the teacher work samples at Idaho State University.* Paper presented at the Annual Meeting of the American Association of Colleges for Teacher Education, New York.

Denner, P. R., Norman, A. D., & Lin, S. (2009). Fairness and consequential validity of teacher work samples. *Educational Assessment, Evaluation, and Accountability.* Retrieved May 1, 2009, from http://www.springerlink.com/content/g604442h281g0535/fulltext.pdf.

Denner, P. R., Norman, A. D., Salzman, S. A., & Pankratz, R. S. (2003, February 17). *Connecting teacher performance to student achievement: A generalizability and validity study of the Renaissance Teacher Work Sample Assessment.* Paper presented at the Annual Meeting of the Association for Teacher Educators, Jacksonville, FL.

Denner, P. R., Salzman, S. A., & Bangert, A. W. (2002). Linking teacher assessment to student assessment: A benchmarking, generalizability, and validity study of the use of teacher work samples. *Journal of Personnel Evaluation in Education, 15*(4), 287–307.

Denner, P. R., Salzman, S. A., & Harris, L. B. (2002, April). *Teacher work sample assessment: An accountability method that moves beyond teacher testing to the impact of teacher performance on student learning.* Paper presented at the Annual Meeting of the American Association of Colleges for Teacher Education, New York, February 2002. (ERIC Document Reproduction No. ED 463 285)

Dwyer, C. A. (1994). *Development of the knowledge base for the Praxis III: Classroom performance assessments assessment criteria.* Princeton, NJ: Educational Testing Service.

Dwyer, C. A. (1998). Psychometrics of Praxis III: Classroom performance assessments. *Journal of Personnel Evaluation in Education, 12*(2), 163–187.

Educational Testing Service. (2002). *ETS Standards for Quality and Fairness 2002.* Princeton, NJ: Author.

Estabrooks, C. (2007). A program of research on knowledge translation. *Nursing Research, 56*(4), 4–6.

Fallon, D. (2006). *Improving teacher education through a culture of evidence.* Paper presented at the Sixth Annual Meeting of the Teacher Education Accreditation Council, Washington, DC. Retrieved January 15, 2008, from http://www.teac.org/membership/meetings/Fallon remarks.pdf.

Girod, G. (Ed.). (2002). *Connecting teaching and learning: A handbook for teacher educators on teacher work sample methodology.* Washington, DC: AACTE Publications.

Girod, G. (2008). Western Oregon University: Cook School District simulation. In A. E. Wise, P. Ehrenberg, & J. Leibbrand (Eds.), *It's all about student learning: Assessing teacher candidates' ability to impact P-12 students* (pp. 213–215). Washington, DC: National Council for the Accreditation of Teacher Education.

Girod, M., & Girod, G. (2006). Exploring the efficacy of the Cook School District simulation. *Journal of Teacher Education, 57*(5), 481–497.

Girod, G., & Schalock, M. (2002). Does TWSM work? In G. Girod (Ed.), *Connecting teaching and learning: A handbook for teacher educators on teacher work sample methodology* (pp. 347–358). Washington, DC: AACTE Publications.

Gropper, N. (2008). Bank Street College of Education child study (for observation and recording, "O&R") In A. E. Wise, P. Ehrenberg, & J. Leibbrand (Eds.), *It's all about student learning: Assessing teacher candidates' ability to impact P-12 students* (pp. 191–202). Washington, DC: National Council for the Accreditation of Teacher Education.

Groth, L. A. (2006, October). *Performance based assessment in a preservice literacy class: The reading, writing, spelling analysis.* Paper presented at the Annual Meeting of the College Reading Association, Pittsburgh, PA.

Haynes, D. (1995). One teacher's experience with national board assessments. *Educational Leadership, 52*(8), 58–60.

Howes, C., Burchinal, M., Pianta, R., Bryant, D., Early, D., Clifford, R., et al. (2008). Ready to learn? Children's pre-academic achievement in pre-kindergarten programs. *Early Childhood Research Quarterly, 23*(1), 27–50.

Institute for Learning. (2002). *Principles of learning.* Pittsburgh, PA: Author.

Interstate New Teacher Assessment and Support Consortium (INTASC). (2009a). *Test of teaching knowledge.* Retrieved March 14, 2009, from http://www.ccsso.org/projects/interstate_new_teacher_assessment_and_support_consortium/Projects/Test_of_Teaching_Knowledge/.

Interstate New Teacher Assessment and Support Consortium (INTASC). (2009b). *INTASC portfolio development.* Retrieved January 15, 2009, from http://www.ccsso.org/Projects/interstate_new_teacher_assessment_and_support_consortium/projects/portfolio_development/792.cfm.

Junker, B., Weisberg, Y., Matsumara, L. C., Crosson, A., Kim Wolf, M., Levison, A., et al. (2006). *Overview of the instructional quality assessment.* Los Angeles: Center for the Study of Evaluation, National Center for Research on Evaluation, Standards, and Student Testing.

Kellor, E. M. (2002). *Performance-based teacher licensure in Connecticut.* Madison: Consortium for Policy Research in Education, University of Wisconsin-Madison. Retrieved June 2, 2008, from http://cpre.wceruw.org/tcomp/research/standards/licensure.php.

Kimball, S. (2002). *Performance-based teacher licensure in Indiana.* Madison: Consortium for Policy Research in Education, University of Wisconsin-Madison. Retrieved June 2, 2008, from http://cpre.wceruw.org/tcomp/research/standards/licensure.php.

La Paro, K. M., & Pianta, R. C. (2003). *Observational assessment of teaching practices.* Retrieved March 17, 2009, from http://www.virginia.edu/provost/tneuva/about.html#.

Lomask, M., Seroussi, M., & Budzinsky, F. (1997). *The validity of portfolio-based assessment of science teachers.* Paper presented at the Annual Meeting of the National Association of Research in Science Teaching, Chicago.

Long, C., & Stansbury, K. (1994). Performance assessments for beginning teachers: Options and lessons. *Phi Delta Kappan, 76*(4), 318–322.

Lyons, N. P. (1996). A grassroots experiment in performance assessment. *Educational Leadership, 53*(6), 64–67.

Lyons, N. P. (1998a). Reflection in teaching: Can it be developmental? A portfolio perspective. *Teacher Education Quarterly, 25*(1), 115–127.

Lyons, N. P. (1998b). Portfolio possibilities: Validating a new teacher professionalism. In N. P. Lyons (Ed.), *With portfolio in hand* (pp. 247–264). New York: Teachers College Press.

Lyons, N. P. (1999). How portfolios can shape emerging practice. *Educational Leadership, 56*(8), 63–65.

Mashburn, A. J., Pianta, R., Hamre, B. K., Downer, J. T., Barbarin, O., Bryant, D., et al. (2008). Measures of classroom quality in pre-kindergarten and children's development of academic, language and social skills. *Child Development, 79*(3), 732–749.

Matsumura, L. C., Garnier, H., Slater, S. C., & Boston, M. B. (2008). Measuring instructional interactions "at-scale." *Educational Assessment, 13*(4), 267–300.

Matsumura, L. C., Slater, S. C., Junker, B., Peterson, M., Boston, M., Steele, M., et al. (2006). *Measuring reading comprehension and mathematics instruction in urban middle schools: A pilot study of the Instructional Quality Assessment.* Los Angeles: University of California, National Center for Research on Evaluation, Standards, and Student Testing.

McConney, A. A., & Ayers, R. R. (1998). Assessing student teachers' assessments. *Journal of Teacher Education, 49*(2), 140–150.

McConney, A. A., Schalock, M. D., & Schalock, H. D. (1998). Focusing improvement and quality assurance: Work samples as authentic performance measures of prospective teachers' effectiveness. *Journal of Personnel Evaluation in Education, 11*, 343–363.

McDiarmid, B., & Peck, C. (2007, March). *Theories of action and program renewal in teacher education.* Paper presented at the Annual Meeting of the Northwest Association for Teacher Education. Seattle, WA.

McKibbens, D. E., Shainker, S., & Banks-Santilli, L. (2008). Focus child assessment project. In A. E. Wise, P. Ehrenberg, & J. Leibbrand (Eds.), *It's all about student learning: Assessing teacher candidates' ability to impact P-12 students* (pp. 203–212). Washington, DC: National Council for the Accreditation of Teacher Education.

Mitchell, K. J., Robinson, D. Z., Plake, B. S., & Knowles, K. T. (2001). *Testing teacher candidates: The role of licensure tests in improving teacher quality.* Washington, DC: National Academy Press.

Moss, P. A. (1998). Rethinking validity for the assessment of teaching. In N. Lyons (Ed.), *With portfolio in hand* (pp. 202–219). New York: Teachers College Press.

Moss, P. A., Schutz, A. M., & Collins, K. M. (1998). An integrative approach to portfolio evaluation for teacher licensure. *Journal of Personnel Evaluation in Education, 12*(2), 139–161.

Nagle, J. F. (2006, April). *Collaborative examination of practice: Using a state mandated assessment as part of teacher inquiry.* Paper presented at the Annual Conference of the American Educational Research Association, San Francisco.

Office of the Superintendent of Public Instruction. (2004). *Performance-based pedagogy assessment of teacher candidates.* Olympia, WA: Author. Retrieved March 15, 2009, from http://www.k12.wa.us/certification/profed/pubdocs/PerfBased-PedagogyAssessTchrCand6–2004SBE.pdf.

Ohio Legislative Service Commission. (2007, October). *HB 347 Fiscal note and local impact statement.* Retrieved March 15, 2009, from http://www.lbo.state.oh.us/fiscal/fiscalnotes/127ga/HB0347IN.htm.

Pankratz, R. (2008). Renaissance Partnership for improving teacher quality: Renaissance Teacher Work Sample. In A. E. Wise, P. Ehrenberg, & J. Leibbrand (Eds.), *It's all about student learning: Assessing teacher candidates' learning to impact P-12 students* (pp. 45–74). Washington, DC: NCATE.

Pecheone, R., & Chung, R. R. (2006). Evidence in teacher education: The Performance Assessment for California Teachers. *Journal of Teacher Education, 57*(1), 22–36.

Pecheone, R. L., & Chung, R. R. (2007). *The Performance Assessment for California Teachers (PACT) technical report.* Stanford, CA: PACT Consortium.

Peck, C., Gallucci, C., Sloan, T., & Lippincott, A. (2008). Organizational learning and program renewal in teacher education: A socio-cultural theory of learning, innovation and change. *Educational Research Review, 4*(1), 16–25.

Pianta, R. C. (2003). *Standardized classroom observations from pre-K to third grade: A mechanism for improving quality classroom experiences during the P-3 years.* Unpublished manuscript. Retrieved March 16, 2009, from http://www.fcd-us.org/usr_doc/StandardizedClassroomObservations.pdf.

Pianta, R., Mashburn, A. J., Downer, J. T., Hamre, B. K., & Justice, L. (2008). Effects of Web-mediated professional development resources on teacher-child interactions in pre-kindergarten classrooms. *Early Childhood Research Quarterly, 23*, 431–451.

Putnam, W., Twohig, P., Burge, F., Jackson, L., & Coix, J. (2002). A qualitative study of evidence in primary care: What practitioners are saying. *Canadian Medical Association Journal, 166*(12), 1525–1530.

Resnick, L. B., & Hall, M. W. (2001). *The principles of learning: Study tools for educators.* [CD-ROM, version 2.0]. Available at www.instituteforlearning.org.

Richert, A. E. (1987). *Reflex to reflection: Facilitating reflection in novice teachers.* Unpublished doctoral dissertation, Stanford University School of Education.

Rotberg, I. C., Futrell, M. H., & Lieberman, J. M. (1998). National Board certification: Increasing participation and assessing impacts. *Phi Delta Kappan, 79*(6), 462–466.

Salzman, S. A., Denner, P. R., & Harris, L. B. (2002, February). *Teacher education outcomes measures: Special study survey.* Paper presented at the Annual Conference of the American Association for Colleges of Teacher Education, New York. (ERIC Document Reproduction Service NO. ED465791)

Schalock, M. D. (1998). Accountability, student learning, and the preparation and licensure of teachers: Oregon's Teacher Work Sample Methodology. *Journal of Personnel Evaluation in Education, 12*(3), 269–285.

Schalock, H. D., Schalock, M., & Girod, G. (1997). Teacher work sample methodology as used at Western Oregon State College. In J. McMillan (Ed.), *Grading teachers, grading schools: Is student achievement a valid evaluation measure?* (pp. 15–45). Thousand Oaks, CA: Corwin Press.

Shavelson, R. J., & Webb, N. M. (1991). *Generalizability theory: A primer.* Thousand Oaks, CA: Sage.

Shulman, L. (1998). Teacher portfolios: A theoretical activity. In N. P. Lyons (Ed.), *With portfolio in hand* (pp. 23–37). New York: Teachers College Press.

Snyder, J., Lippincott, A., & Bower, D. (1998). The inherent tensions in the multiple uses of portfolios in teacher education. *Teacher Education Quarterly, 25*(1), 45–60.

Stein, M. K., & Matsumura, L. C. (2008). Measuring instruction for teacher learning. In D. Gitomer (Ed.), *Measurement issues and assessment for teacher quality* (pp. 179–205). Thousand Oaks, CA: Sage.

St. Maurice, H., & Shaw, P. (2004). Teacher portfolios come of age: A preliminary study. *NAASP Bulletin, 88*(639), 15–25. Retrieved November 2, 2009, from http://bul .sagepub.com/cgi/content/ abstract/88/639/15.

Stone, B. A. (1998). Problems, pitfalls, and benefits of portfolios. *Teacher Education Quarterly, 25*(1), 105–114.

Tisadondilok, S. (2006). *Investigating the validity of the Washington State performance-based pedagogy assessment process for teacher licensure.* Unpublished doctoral dissertation, Oregon State University. Retrieved February 1, 2009, from http://ir.library.oregonstate.edu/dspace/handle/1957/2232.

Tracz, S. M., Sienty, S., & Mata, S. (1994, February). *The self-reflection of teachers compiling portfolios for national certification: Work in progress.* Paper presented at the Annual Meeting of the American Association of Colleges for Teacher Education, Chicago.

Tucker, P. D., Stronge, J. H., Gareis, C. R., & Beers, C. S. (2003). The efficacy of teacher portfolios for teacher evaluation and professional development: Do they make a difference? *Educational Administration Quarterly, 39*, 572–602.

University of Southern Maine. (2008). *Teachers for Elementary and Middle Schools (TEAMS) Program: 2008–09 handbook.* Retrieved March 14, 2009, from http://www.usm.maine.edu/cehd/TED/pdfs/TEAMS percent20Handbook percent2008–09.pdf.

Wasley, P. A., & McDiarmid, G. W. (2004, June 28–30). *Connecting the assessment of new teachers to student learning and to teacher preparation.* Prepared for the National Commission on Teaching and America's Future, National Summit on High Quality Teacher Preparation, Austin, TX.

Wiggins, G. (1989). A true test: Toward more authentic and equitable assessment. *Phi Delta Kappan, 70*(9), 703–713.

White, B. (2002). *Performance-based teacher licensure in North Carolina.* Madison, WI: Consortium for Policy Research in Education, University of Wisconsin. Retrieved June 2, 2008, from http://cpre.wceruw.org/tcomp/research/standards/licensure.php.

Whitford, B. L., Ruscoe, G., & Fickel, L. (2000). Knitting it all together: Collaborative teacher education in southern Maine. In L. Darling-Hammond (Ed.), *Studies of excellence in teacher education: Preparation in the undergraduate years* (pp. 173–257). New York: National Commission on Teaching and America's Future; Washington, DC: American Association of Colleges for Teacher Education.

Wilkerson, J. R., & Lang, W. S. (2003, December 3). Portfolios, the pied piper of teacher certification assessments: Legal and psychometric issues. *Education Policy Analysis Archives, 11*(45). Retrieved August 30, 2008, from http://epaa.asu.edu/epaa/v11n45/.

Wilson, M., Hallam, P. J., Pecheone, R., & Moss, P. (in press). Using student achievement test scores as evidence of external validity for indicators of teacher quality: Connecticut's Beginning Educator Support and Training Program. *Education Evaluation and Policy Analysis.*

Wilson, S. W., Darling-Hammond, L., & Berry, B. (2001). *A case of successful teaching policy: Connecticut's long-term efforts to improve teaching and learning.* Seattle: University of Washington, Center for the Study of Teaching and Policy.

Wineburg, M. (2006). Evidence in teacher preparation: Establishing a framework for accountability. *Journal of Teacher Education, 57*(1), 51–64.

Wise, A. E., Ehrenberg, P., & Leibbrand, J. (Eds.). (2008). *It's all about student learning: Assessing teacher candidates' ability to impact P-12 students.* Washington, DC: National Council for the Accreditation of Teacher Education.

Zeichner, K., & Wray, S. (2001). The teaching portfolio in US teacher education programs: What we know and what we need to know. *Teaching and Teacher Education, 17*, 613–621.

# CHAPTER FOUR

# Licensure Tests

## *Their Use and Value for Increasing Teacher Quality*

Dan Goldhaber

*University of Washington*

A number of new research studies buttress the conventional wisdom that teacher quality is the key educational investment school systems can make to improve student achievement. Among schooling resources, it is the most influential factor explaining growth in students' standardized test scores (Aaronson, Barrow, & Sander, 2007; Rivkin, Hanushek, & Kain, 2005; Rockoff, 2004), and there is evidence that teacher quality varies considerably in the workforce. Thus, it is no surprise that states, which have a constitutional obligation to provide adequate schooling options, seek to regulate admission into the teacher labor market in order to guarantee a minimum level of teacher quality. In most state systems, a central component of this regulation of the teacher labor market, teacher licensure, is teacher testing.

The idea behind testing teachers is a simple one: "smarter" teachers are better teachers; therefore, testing is one possible way to guarantee a basic level of smartness in the teacher workforce. But for a variety of reasons, this simple idea does not necessarily mean that the testing of prospective teachers will lead to better student outcomes. First, although licensure tests place a lower bound on the measured knowledge individuals must have to teach, they do not guarantee that this knowledge is in fact linked to teacher effectiveness as measured by teachers' contributions toward student learning. There is some evidence that this link exists, but researchers have only recently begun to look at the relationship between teacher test performance and student outcomes in empirically convincing ways.

Second, even if teacher tests do tend to identify more effective teachers, we would need to know something about how testing requirements influence the potential pool of teachers. It is possible that prospective teachers, knowing they will have to demonstrate competency on a licensure test, work harder (in school, for instance) to obtain the knowledge needed to meet the state standard. As a consequence, the overall knowledge level of prospective teachers may be higher than in the absence of a licensure testing system. But testing requirements, along with any other requirements needed for licensure, impose costs on individuals, and these costs may dissuade some from pursuing a career as a teacher. Unfortunately, precious little empirical literature touches on the relationship between teacher testing requirements and the composition of the potential pool of teachers.

Finally, we would need to know how state testing systems affect who is hired in order to know their ultimate impact. Local hiring authorities weigh various factors when making decisions about which prospective teachers (for instance, those making it into the pool) they wish to extend job offers to. The performance of prospective teachers on licensure tests might provide information that could be used to make better hiring decisions. But it is also possible that this information is superfluous, in the sense that it may not add to the information that local authorities would gather about candidates on their own in the absence of a testing system. In this case, one could imagine licensure testing having no impact on who is hired whatsoever (if there were both no change in the pool of teacher applicants and no change in hiring decisions). It is also possible that testing could have a negative impact. For example, to the extent that local authorities have good knowledge about the quality of their teacher candidates, testing systems may preclude them from hiring some applicants who would have been effective in the classroom. In other words, even if there is a positive association between teacher test performance and student achievement, the absence of a state testing requirement could potentially result in a higher-quality teacher workforce, because individuals who do not test well but would make good teachers nonetheless would remain in the applicant pool; local authorities would then select these applicants over those who did well on the test but would be ineffective in the classroom.

In this chapter, I explore states' use of licensure tests, the empirical literature on the relationship between teacher performance on these tests and student achievement, and what we do and do not know about the impact that testing requirements have on who opts to teach. The chapter describes the history of teacher testing and the typical process of developing licensure tests and cut scores; reviews the empirical literature on the relationship between teacher performance on licensure tests and teacher effectiveness, as measured by student achievement; and focuses on the potential impact of licensure testing on the potential pool of teacher applicants.

# LICENSURE TESTING HISTORY AND CUT SCORE SETTING

State requirements for teachers to pass one or more standardized tests are not new; many states have been testing teachers as a condition of employment since the 1960s. Since then, teacher testing has become an increasingly common policy. As of 2008, all but three states require teachers to pass one or more licensure tests (NASDTEC Survey, 2009). This emphasis on teacher testing was strengthened by passage of the 2001 No Child Left Behind (NCLB) Act, which requires states to ensure that all teachers are "highly qualified," meaning that they have received state certification and demonstrated content knowledge of the material they teach. One of the ways that teachers can demonstrate subject matter knowledge is by passing a subject area exam.

Licensure tests vary in topic and substance, but the four basic types are generally basic skills, liberal arts general knowledge, subject matter knowledge, and pedagogical skills—with some tests covering various combinations of these areas. As of 2008, 70 percent of states require a basic skills exam either prior to entering a teacher education program or prior to certification; 78 percent require a subject matter exam; and 54 percent require a pedagogy exam. Fewer than 20 percent require a general knowledge exam (NASDTEC Survey, 2009). There are both multiple-choice and constructed-response essay tests, and some that include both types of questions, though the emphasis appears to be on multiple-choice questions.

States place differing levels of emphasis on testing teachers in terms of the number of tests that must be passed and the relative importance of passing tests compared to other licensure criteria that are used (for example, graduation from an approved teacher training program or completion of student teaching requirements). But regardless of the various levels of emphasis, most states' approach to determining the cut score that candidates must achieve to become teachers tends to be the same. This process generally relies on a panel of education experts who attempt to relate the knowledge they believe ought to be minimally required of beginning teachers to what is measured by the various licensure tests. For example, the Educational Testing Service, one of the main developers of teacher licensure tests, provides states with guidelines on assembling cut score panels. The recommended composition is for no fewer than ten members, each possessing more than one and less than eight years of experience, who are themselves certified in the content area of the test, with the entire panel accurately representing the geographical, gender, and ethnic distribution of teachers in the state (Hibpshman, 2004).

The appropriate cutoff is typically determined using an Angoff-type (1971) model. First, a panel of experts estimates the proportions of minimally qualified candidates who would answer each test question correctly. Second, the estimated proportions for each expert are summed to get what may be thought of as an individual panelist's cutoff score. Finally, the individual panelist's cut scores are averaged, and the resulting mean is taken as the consensus cut score (Mitchell, Robinson, Plake, & Knowles, 2001).

Since a subjective element is associated with setting the cut scores, it is not surprising that cut scores differ among states. National comparisons of these are difficult given the variation in the use of specific tests, but first-time pass rates for teaching are typically in the 70 to 90 percent range—far higher than licensure exams in professions such as law, accounting, or medicine (Boyd, Goldhaber, Lankford, & Wyckoff, 2007), with considerable state-to-state variation. Part of this variation may be due to differences in the samples of test takers, but comparisons of cut scores among states that use the same test illustrate that underlying differences in the cutoff standard itself are likely a much larger factor. In the late 1990s, for example, Connecticut and North Carolina required prospective elementary teachers to pass the same two tests to be eligible for full-state credentials. The two states, however, had established very different cut score standards, with Connecticut's exceeding those of North Carolina by about .6 standard deviation on one and about 1.75 standard deviations on the second (Goldhaber, 2007).

The degree of difference in cut scores is surprising if one believes that the demonstrated knowledge of what is required to be a teacher in one state should be roughly equivalent to what is required in another. The lack of consistency among states in the setting of licensure test cut score standards implies that minimum competency in one state is quite different from that in another. One possible reason for the lack of uniformity is that licensure test standards change over time, possibly as a result of political or labor market pressures. It is not surprising that these factors may have played an outsized role in establishing cut score standards. Until recently, there was shockingly little credible empirical evidence about the power of licensure tests to predict teacher effectiveness as measured by student learning.

## TEACHER TESTS AND STUDENT ACHIEVEMENT

The theory behind teacher testing is that states can use these tests as a screen for employment eligibility to prevent local hiring officials from making poor hiring decisions that would result in the employment of some very poor teachers. But the downside of using tests in this way (that is, an applicant is eligible to participate in the labor market only by achieving a state-determined standard) is that the tests invariably screen out some individuals who would have been effective teachers. This statement is true unless the tests are perfect predictors of teacher ability in the classroom, an impossible standard. Moreover, if the tests are imperfect, they will not screen out all those who would make ineffective teachers, meaning that localities still have an important role to play in the teacher selection process.

The imperfection of licensure tests in predicting teaching effectiveness means these tests cannot be used without a cost—state policy that screens out those who would be effective teachers—but the stronger the association is between licensure test performance and teacher effectiveness (here I assume this is some measure of teacher contribution toward student learning), the more this cost is reduced, a point that is graphically illustrated by Figure 4.1.

Figure 4.1 shows the hypothetical relationship between licensure test scores and some other measure of teaching quality, however one wants to judge it. The assumption is that both quality (measured on the x-axis) and teacher test performance (measured on the z-axis) have bell-shaped distributions; consequently, the joint distribution of the two will be a bell-shaped mound (the y-axis) that represents the number of individuals (who are not necessarily allowed into the teacher labor market) with particular combinations of test score and teacher quality.

It is essential to remember here that we can never directly observe teacher quality, and certainly not for those who are not yet teaching or never teach.

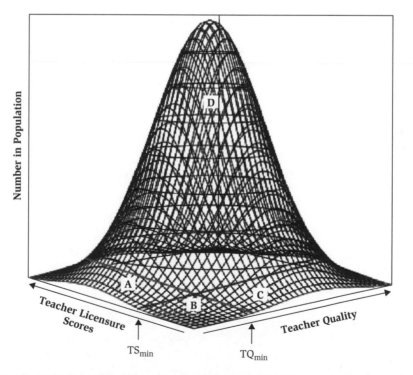

**Figure 4.1** Hypothetical Relationship Between Teacher Test Scores and Some Indicator of Teaching Quality

Thus, while policymakers might wish to exclude prospective teachers who fall below a set standard of quality (TQmin) from participating in the labor market, they have to use a proxy for quality, like a licensure test score. Setting a minimum cut score (TSmin) will result, then, in both false positives and false negatives. Individuals in quadrant A do well on the test but would be low-quality teachers, so they represent false positives in the sense that they are allowed by the state into the teacher labor market despite the fact that they would be unacceptably low-quality teachers. Individuals in quadrant C do poorly on the licensure test but would, if allowed to teach, meet a state's minimum quality criteria. These individuals, however, are prohibited from participating in the teacher labor market by their test performance. Finally, individuals in quadrants B and D represent true negatives and true positives, in the sense that they are correctly categorized, according to a state's teacher-quality standard, by their test performance.

The shape of the mound shows the number of individuals who will fall into the four quadrants and depends on the correlation between unobserved teacher quality and licensure test performance; the more closely the two are related, the fewer false positives and negatives. This is illustrated by Figure 4.2, which shows the mound as it would appear looking straight down from above, as on a topographical map, with the height of the mound represented by the ellipses in the diagram (the smaller ellipses represent higher points on the mound).

Figure 4.2A shows a relatively strong correlation between teacher test performance and teacher quality, and Figure 4.2B shows a much weaker relationship between the two. The quadrants in the panels of this figure

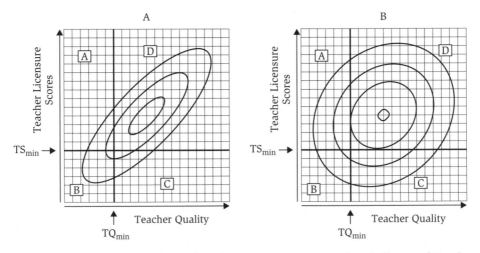

**Figure 4.2** Two Possible Relationships Between Test Scores and an Indicator of Teaching Quality

correspond with those in Figure 4.1 and depict once again that there are fewer false positives and false negatives in the case where a strong relationship exists between licensure test performance and teacher quality.

The strength of the relationship between licensure test scores and teacher quality is a key determinant of the value of using these tests as a screen for employment eligibility. Given this and the near-universal use of these tests, it is surprising how little empirical work focuses on this issue. A small and somewhat old literature shows consistent evidence that teacher tests, though not licensure tests alone, do serve as an indicator of teacher quality (Ehrenberg & Brewer, 1995; Ferguson, 1991; Ferguson & Ladd, 1996; Strauss & Sawyer, 1986; Summers & Wolfe, 1975). However, these findings should be viewed with some skepticism because they are mostly estimated at the aggregate level and generally fail to account for the potential nonrandom match between teachers and students. Research shows that both aggregation (Hanushek, Rivkin, & Taylor, 1996) and nonrandom matching (Clotfelter, Ladd, & Vigdor, 2007) tend to overstate the true association between teacher attributes and student achievement.

Several recent studies that use disaggregated data and attempt to account for confounding issues associated with student-teacher matches find a consistent though small positive relationship between teacher performance on licensure exams and student achievement. Clotfelter et al. (2007) and Goldhaber (2007) use data from North Carolina and find that licensure exams have a stronger relationship between student achievement in math than in reading, and the effect sizes (the estimated effect on student achievement of a 1 standard deviation change in a teacher's test performance) tend to be on the order of magnitude of .01 to .05. Boyd, Lankford, Loeb, Rockoff, and Wyckoff (2008) use data from New York City and estimate only a model using math scores. They find a substantially smaller coefficient on licensure scores but also include SAT scores, which are highly correlated with licensure scores, in their model. All of these effects are far smaller than the earlier research based on aggregated data, which were in the .10 to .25 range.

In thinking about the value of teacher tests in predicting teacher effectiveness, it is important to recall that the tests are designed to differentiate knowledge around a cut score. These cut scores, at least by design, delineate individuals who meet minimal quality standards from those who do not. Moreover, many of those who fail to achieve the cut standard (either those who actually do fail or those who would fail were they to take the exam) are not observed in the teacher labor market, so there is a restriction of the range of performance that we observe. For both reasons, we might expect teacher tests to perform less well as a proxy for skills and knowledge, and ultimately as a predictor of teacher effectiveness, as scores move away from the cut point. Cut scores, however, differ from state to state, and over time within states;

therefore, it is possible to assess the extent to which a minimum licensure test requirement from one state might affect the workforce of another (ignoring the implications for the population that opts to take the test), or how requirements imposed during one time period would affect the workforce in another period.

Goldhaber (2007) engages in these types of thought experiments by exploiting the fact that both North Carolina and Connecticut require the same tests of elementary-level teachers and that North Carolina changed testing requirements in the late 1990s. For example, Figure 4.3 shows the results of applying the (higher) Connecticut standard cut score on one of the Praxis tests to the population of teachers in North Carolina who also had to sit for this exam. This figure is an empirical representation that corresponds roughly with the theoretical relationship between teacher test performance and effectiveness described by Figure 4.2. Figure 4.3 is the scatter plot of estimated value-added teacher effects in mathematics plotted against the Praxis II Curriculum test performance (more heavily shaded circles represent a greater population concentration); the

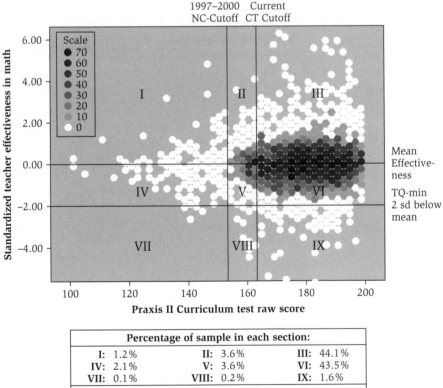

**Figure 4.3** Alternative Cutoff Scores on Praxis II and the Resulting Population of Teacher Candidates Admitted into Teaching

vertical lines are the North Carolina and Connecticut standards on the test, and the horizontal lines are the median and two-standard deviations below the median estimates of teacher effectiveness of teachers in the North Carolina workforce. Figure 4.3 shows the trade-offs inherent in imposing a minimum test requirement.

Under the North Carolina standard, there are a number of false positives, represented by the sum of areas VIII and IX (nearly 2 percent of the teacher workforce), and of false negatives, represented by the sum of areas I and IV (just over 3 percent of the teacher workforce). Were the testing standard to be raised to the higher one used in Connecticut, the number of false positives would fall in the area represented by VIII, with the trade-off that there would be an increase in the number of false negatives, represented by the sum of areas II and V (about 7 percent of the workforce). Whether this type of trade-off makes sense is clearly a value judgment, which would have to be weighed against labor market conditions, the potential harm that ineffective teachers might do to students, and the extent to which a test hurdle might dissuade talented individuals from attempting to become teachers. But regardless of the judgments, the trade-off is reduced with a stronger relationship between teacher licensure tests and student achievement. Given the scant research connecting these two in general, it is no surprise that almost no research is focused on the value of different kinds of tests (for example, those focused on pedagogy versus content knowledge) for predicting teacher effectiveness, though the Goldhaber (2007) study does suggest that different tests differentially predict teacher effectiveness, implying that the nature of the test is important in determining the number of false positives and negatives.

Perhaps even more important, there is, to my knowledge, no research that sheds light on how testing teachers might influence the hiring decisions made by local officials. It is not clear, for instance, that potential teachers screened out by a licensure test would be in the teacher workforce simply by virtue of being eligible to teach. Eligibility does not guarantee being hired, and individuals screened out of the potential teacher applicant pool by their failure to achieve a state's licensure test standard might not have been hired anyway. Moreover, only recently have researchers begun to examine whether the hurdles associated with licensure tests might have an effect on the number of people who opt to pursue a career in teaching.

## LICENSURE TESTS AND THE TEACHER WORKFORCE

The short-run labor economics of requiring prospective teachers to pass tests or any other employment-related hurdle for employment eligibility are simple: in theory and practice, testing increases the cost of labor market production by restricting the supply of eligible workers and thus increasing wages in an occupation (Kleiner, 2000). But the theoretical impact on the quality of the workforce is ambiguous. The test may have a screening value, but the imposition of a hurdle to eligibility will also discourage some individuals from opting to pursue that line of employment. In the longer term, the wage level or requirements, or both, may change the public's perception of the occupation (Kleiner, 2000). Were it perceived as more prestigious because of licensure requirements, conceivably these requirements could have a net positive impact on the quality of teacher applicant pools. But to the degree that testing (or other licensure policies) dissuades talented individuals from entering the profession, such policies could lead to a negative impact on the prestige of being a teacher and subsequent negative consequences.

On the surface, it seems likely that there is a relatively low direct cost to individuals associated with licensure testing (however, a very large cost may be associated with some other teacher licensure requirements, such as the forgone earnings associated with the time taken to obtain pedagogical training from an approved education program). Sitting for the tests themselves costs about $130 for the basic skills test and $80 for each subject test (Educational Testing Service, 2008). I am unaware of any work that quantifies the time that individuals typically invest in preparing to take licensure exams, but the great majority of test takers—nearly 90 percent for those taking a Praxis series test (Gitomer & Latham, 1999) pass the test the first time they take it. (In a recent study of Praxis candidates between 2002 and 2005, Gitomer, 2007, found that the passing rate decreased to 80.5 percent and attributes this precipitous decline to states' adoption of more rigorous licensing requirements rather than a decline in the quality of the applicant pool.) Despite this, the little available quantitative work on the relationship between teacher licensure test requirements and the teacher workforce suggests that these requirements have a negative impact on the likelihood of pursuing a career as a teacher (Hanushek & Pace, 1995) and little impact on the qualifications of the teacher work-force. (I distinguish qualifications from quality here, since the studies I discuss are related to teacher attributes such as degrees rather than direct value-added measures of teacher quality; see Angrist & Guryan, 2008.)

Hanushek and Pace (1995) analyze the flows in and out of teacher training using longitudinal data from the early and mid-1980s High School and Beyond Survey. Among the factors that they find influence the likelihood that individuals receive an education-focused bachelor's degree (conditional on receiving a bachelor's degree) is whether a state requires teachers to pass a licensure exam. Specifically they estimate that having such a requirement reduces the probability of prospective teachers (those who are enrolled in teacher training) from pursuing teacher preparation by about 4 percentage points.

A more recent study by Angrist and Guryan (2008) uses several waves of the Schools and Staffing Survey and focuses on the relationship between licensure testing and the qualifications of the teacher workforce. They examine whether testing is related to the selectivity of the college from which teachers graduate (based on the average SAT score of incoming freshmen and Carnegie classifications) and whether teachers had an undergraduate degree in the subject in which they taught. They do not find any statistically significant relationships between state testing requirements and the selectivity of the college from which teachers graduate, and although there are some statistically significant findings for the relationship between testing and undergraduate major (a positive relationship), these findings are not robust across model specifications. In particular, they conclude that "testing has acted more as a barrier to entry than a quality screen" (p. 500).

These findings are consistent with the notion that some individuals opt not to pursue a career in teaching because of the testing hurdle. But it is important to be quite cautious about this conclusion, since both of these studies are attempting to identify the impacts of testing requirements based on cross-state variation in those requirements. States that had licensure tests requirements at the time may also have had other licensure-related requirements that influenced the supply of individuals into the teaching profession (and were unobservable to the researchers). It is also conceivable that states impose licensure tests either because they are concerned about the low quality of their teachers (which may be due to any number of factors) or because there is a slack demand for teachers so they can afford to raise standards. In either case, the negative association between tests and the workforce may simply be a reflection of other factors that lead to test standards rather than the causal effect of the tests themselves. In addition, neither study accounts for the difficulty of passing the test, just whether states have testing requirements. Finally, both studies are focused on the contemporaneous effects of testing on the teacher workforce. It is conceivable, though perhaps not likely, that the longer-run impacts (such as through wage effects influencing the prestige of the occupation) of state testing requirements on the workforce are different.

# DISCUSSION

Three areas determine the total effect of licensure testing of teachers on student achievement: (1) the strength of the relationship between the performance of teachers on licensure tests and student achievement, (2) the impact that testing has on who opts to pursue a career as a teacher (the potential teacher pool), and (3) how testing affects local hiring decisions. Thus far, I have described literature that speaks to the first two areas. This research suggests that a significant, albeit small, positive association between some licensure tests and student achievement and the imposition of state tests and minimum cutoff scores appears to dissuade some prospective teachers and, on the whole, has little systematic impact on several indirect measures of the quality of the teacher workforce.

There is little quantitative evidence on the third determinant of the effects of licensure testing on students: how tests might affect local hiring decisions. Studies (Daugherty, DeAngelis, & Rossi, 1997; Daugherty & Rossi, 1996) about hiring criteria from the late 1980s and early 1990s (prior to the widespread use of licensure tests) suggest that localities were more likely to require credentials other than performance on licensure tests (for example, graduation from a state-approved teacher training institution) when making hiring decisions. In theory, these tests might provide local policymakers with more information about prospective teachers than would be garnered in their absence. But much of the information the tests could convey is lost if all that localities learn is whether a prospective applicant achieved a cutoff requirement rather than details on the full range of performance (that is, an individual's actual test score). Furthermore, there is very little evidence on whether school systems make good selections among teacher applicants. Some research suggests that applicants who attend more selective colleges are actually less likely to be hired than applicants who attend less selective institutions and that subject specialty and college grade point average have only small (relative to those in other occupations) effects on a prospective teacher's probability of being hired (Ballou, 1996). Other work finds that localities are sensitive to the academic qualifications of applicants and have a preference for those from more selective colleges and who score higher on licensure tests (Boyd, Lankford, Loeb, & Wyckoff, 2003). More recent case study work (DeArmond, Gross, & Goldhaber, 2008; Harris, Rutledge, Ingle, & Thompson, 2007) suggests that when principals are given discretion over hiring teachers, they are often more concerned with the attitudes of prospective teachers and how they would fit within a school culture than measures of cognitive ability.

In short, we know relatively little about how licensure testing affects the teacher workforce overall or the distribution of teacher quality across schools and districts. Given the prevalence of teacher testing as a policy tool, this gap in our knowledge is shocking. But the gap is beginning to be addressed with the availability of new longitudinal state data sets that not only included detailed information about teachers (specifically their performance on licensure exams) but also link them to performance and background information about the students in their classrooms.

In practice, state testing systems are likely to have very different impacts on different types of teachers, different localities, and ultimately different students. There is substantial evidence that minority teachers are less likely to perform well on licensure tests than white teachers (Gitomer & Latham, 2000; Gitomer, 2007; Goldhaber & Hansen, 2008). The disparate impact of these tests may in turn have achievement implications for the students these teachers might have taught. For example, evidence is growing that same-race matches between teachers and students may have positive student achievement benefits (Dee, 2004, 2005; Goldhaber & Hansen, 2008). Moreover, school districts themselves face very different labor markets and have differing capacities to discern teacher quality. Licensure testing is likely to have little impact on the applicant pools of affluent school districts that often have numerous applicants for any open teaching position. Difficult-to-staff schools and districts, however, often employ teachers who have not passed required tests, and stricter enforcement of the minimum cutoff requirements would surely have significant implications for teacher hiring in these localities.

# REFERENCES

Aaronson, D., Barrow, L., & Sander, W. (2007). Teachers and student achievement in the Chicago public high schools. *Journal of Labor Economics, 25*(1), 95–135.

Angoff, W. H. (1971). Scales, norms, and equivalent scores. In R. L. Thorndike (Ed.), *Educational measurement*. Washington, DC: American Council on Education.

Angrist, J. D., & Guryan, J. (2008). Does teacher testing raise teacher quality? Evidence from state certification requirements. *Economics of Education Review, 27*(5), 483–503.

Ballou, D. (1996). Do public schools hire the best applicants? *Quarterly Journal of Economics, 111*(1), 97–133.

Boyd, D., Goldhaber, D. D., Lankford, H., & Wyckoff, J. H. (2007). The effect of certification and preparation on teacher quality. *Future of Children, 17*(1), 45–68.

Boyd, D., Lankford, H., Loeb, S., Rockoff, J. E., & Wyckoff, J. (2008). *The narrowing gap in New York City teacher qualifications and its implications for student achievement in high-poverty schools* (Working paper 14021). Cambridge, MA: National Bureau of Economic Research.

Boyd, D. J., Lankford, H., Loeb, S., & Wyckoff, J. H. (2003). *Analyzing the determinants of the matching public school teachers to jobs: Estimating compensating differentials in imperfect labor markets* (Working paper 9878). Cambridge, MA: National Bureau of Economic Research.

Clotfelter, C. T., Ladd, H. F., & Vigdor, J. L. (2007). *How and why do teacher credentials matter for student achievement?* Washington, DC: National Center for Analysis of Longitudinal Data in Education Research.

Daugherty, S., DeAngelis, K., & Rossi, R. (1997). *Credential and tests in teacher hiring: What do districts require?* Washington, DC: U.S. Department of Education, Office of Educational Research and Improvement.

Daugherty, S., & Rossi, R. (1996). *What criteria are used in considering teacher applicants?* Washington, DC: U.S. Department of Education Office, Educational Research and Improvement.

DeArmond, M., Gross, B., & Goldhaber, D. (2008). *Is it better to be good or lucky? Decentralized teacher selection in 10 elementary schools* (Working paper 2008–3). Seattle: University of Washington Center for the Renewal of Public Education.

Dee, T. S. (2004). Teachers, race, and student achievement in a randomized experiment. *Review of Economics and Statistics, 86*(1), 195–210.

Dee, T. S. (2005). A teacher like me: Does race, ethnicity, or gender matter? *American Economic Review, 95*(2), 158–165.

Educational Testing Service. (2008). *Praxis I overview.* Retrieved July 28, 2008, from http://www.ets.org/portal/site/ets/menuitem.1488512ecfd5b8849a77b13bc3921 509/?vgnextoid=27832d3631df4010VgnVCM10000022f95190RCRD&vgnextchannel=6d315ee3d74f4010VgnVCM10000022f95190RCRD.

Ehrenberg, R. G., & Brewer, D. J. (1995). Did teachers' verbal ability and race matter in the 1960s? Coleman revisited. *Economics of Education Review, 14*(1), 1–21.

Ferguson, R. F. (1991). Paying for public-education: New evidence on how and why money matters. *Harvard Journal on Legislation, 28*(2), 465–498.

Ferguson, R. F., & Ladd, H. F. (1996). How and why money matters: An analysis of Alabama schools. In II. F. Ladd (Ed.), *Holding schools accountable: Performance-based reform in education.* Washington, DC: Brookings Institution.

Gitomer, D. H. (2007). *Teacher quality in a changing policy landscape: Improvements in the teacher pool.* Princeton, NJ: Educational Testing Services.

Gitomer, D. H., & Latham, A. S. (1999). *The academic quality of prospective teachers: The impact of admissions and licensure testing* (Rep. ETS RR-03–35). Princeton, NJ: Educational Testing Service.

Gitomer, D. H., & Latham, A. S. (2000). Generalizations in teacher education: Seductive and misleading. *Journal of Teacher Education, 51*(3), 215–220.

Goldhaber, D. (2007). Everyone's doing it, but what does teacher testing tell us about teacher effectiveness? *Journal of Human Resources, 42*(4), 765–794.

Goldhaber, D., & Hansen, M. (2008). *Race, gender, and teacher testing: How objective a tool is teacher licensure testing?* (Working paper 2008–2). Seattle: University of Washington Center for Reinventing Public Education.

Hanushek, E. A., & Pace, R. R. (1995). Who chooses to teach (and why)? *Economics of Education Review, 14*(2), 101–117.

Hanushek, E. A., Rivkin, S. G., & Taylor, L. L. (1996). Aggregation and the estimated effects of school resources. *Review of Economics and Statistics, 78*(4), 611–627.

Harris, D. N., Rutledge, S. A., Ingle, W. K., & Thompson, C. C. (2007). *Mix and match: What principals look for when hiring teachers and what this means for teacher quality policies.* Retrieved September 2009 from http://www.teacherqualityresearch.org/research.html.

Hibpshman, T. (2004). *Considerations related to setting cut scores for teacher tests.* Frankfort: Kentucky Education Professional Standards Board.

Kleiner, M. M. (2000). Occupational licensing. *Journal of Economic Perspectives, 14*(4), 189–202.

Mitchell, K., Robinson, D. Z., Plake, B. S., & Knowles, K. (Eds.). (2001). *Testing teacher candidates: The role of licensure tests in improving teacher quality.* Washington, DC: National Academy of Sciences Press.

NASDTEC Survey (National Association of State Directors of Teacher Education and Certification KnowledgeBase Portal). (2009). *Topical tables: B2 Degree and undergraduate general education requirements; B5 Evaluation of the student teacher; and G1 Required examinations: Sequence of test publisher.* Retrieved January 5, 2009, from http://www.nasdtec.info/.

Rivkin, S. G., Hanushek, E. A., & Kain, J. F. (2005). Teachers, schools and academic achievement. *Econometricarki, 73*(2), 417–458.

Rockoff, J. E. (2004). The impact of individual teachers on students' achievement: Evidence from panel data. *American Economic Review, 94*(2), 247–252.

Strauss, R. P., & Sawyer, E. A. (1986). Some new evidence on teacher and student competencies. *Economics of Education Review, 5*(1), 41–48.

Summers, A. A., & Wolfe, B. L. (1975). *Which school resources help learning? Efficiency and equality in Philadelphia public schools.* Philadelphia: Federal Reserve Bank of Philadelphia, Department of Research.

# CHAPTER FIVE

# Hiring Decisions

Dane A. Delli

*River Trails School District #26, Mount Prospect, Illinois*

The employment interview has been a topic of published research for over eighty years and remains a widely used method to select employees. Furthermore, the interview continues to surpass in frequency any other hiring practice (Delli & Vera, 2003). In the K–12 education setting, interviews are a required component of the selection process and represent the most used predictor for hiring teachers (Young, 2007).

Given a research base replete with studies on the employment interview in general and on the teacher selection interview specifically, one might expect that most substantive issues related to teacher selection have been resolved. A substantial void exists, however, in our understanding of the theoretical linkages and practical application of how teachers are selected for employment. Specifically, a noticeable vacancy exists with respect to the relationship between preemployment hiring decisions about applicants and postemployment job performance (Young & Delli, 2003).

Typically teacher applicants have been first reviewed as "paper people": that is, their résumés, transcripts, or other documents are reviewed first, and only later are they interviewed face-to-face at either the school district or school building level, with widespread variance in both interview structure and interview format. The advent of commercially designed teacher employment interviews began to change the dynamics of the teacher selection process in the 1980s. The popularity of structured interview protocols produced by private companies grew largely in response to the most common employment interview research finding: structured interviews yield higher reliability and validity than unstructured interviews (Campion, Palmer, & Brown, 1997).

Structured interviews are intended to improve these psychometric properties of the interview by increasing standardization and assisting the interviewer in determining what questions to ask and how to evaluate responses. Furthermore, standardization allows the interviewer rather than the interviewee to control the interview process. It is only through a standardized or structured protocol that the impact of the interview can be evaluated in terms of reliability, validity, and interviewer reaction (for example, perceived fairness of the interview). Unstructured interviews, conversely, consist of the interviewer exploring particular themes in an open-ended and conversational style. Although this type of interview may yield interesting information about a candidate from a qualitative perspective, it lacks measurable reliability because different candidates engage in different conversations. In other words, there is no reliable way to determine the interview performance of one candidate over another candidate when different criteria are being applied.

This chapter on commercial hiring interviews provides a historical overview of teacher selection research and hiring practices; an overview of commercially designed teacher selection interviews, with emphasis on the Teacher Perceiver Interview (TPI); and recommendations for considering the use of commercial interview protocols.

# RESEARCH ON TEACHER SELECTION AND HIRING PRACTICES

For decades, researchers have examined characteristics of successful teaching (Becker, Kennedy, & Hundersmarck, 2003; Darling-Hammond & Youngs, 2003; Murphy, Delli, & Edwards, 2004), teacher behaviors (Gage, 1978), and principles of good teaching (Brophy, 1986; Evertson, 1979). This body of research has identified competencies associated with good teaching (for example, organized, task driven, structured) as well as personality and behavioral characteristics associated with good teaching (for example, enthusiastic, empathetic).

Overlooked throughout most of this is how such factors should influence the evaluations of prospective teachers during a face-to-face employment interview. It might be assumed that teacher competence and preparation would be the main criteria assessed when hiring teachers. However, recent scholarship has suggested that psychological and contextual factors may be equally influential, if not more so, in real-world hiring decisions. For instance, Delli and Vera (2008) examined the primary factors that influenced community members' preferences for teacher candidates during a simulated employment interview. Results from this study indicate that personality characteristics were nearly two times more likely to be cited by the interviewers as selection factors than were indicators of competency such as experience and qualifications. Furthermore, personality characteristics were more frequently cited by female interviewers than by male interviewers, 73 percent and 27 percent, respectively.

The employment interview represents one component of a much broader staffing process. The overall process consists of a recruitment phase, when applicant pools are identified; a selection phase, when résumés are reviewed and a subset of candidates is interviewed; and an employment phase, when an employment offer is made to the desired finalist (Delli, 2001). Although there exists a literature base replete with research in each of these staffing phases, the purpose here is to focus specifically on the employment interview.

The majority of organizational research on employment interviews, spanning more than eighty years, has underscored the importance of structuring interviews to maximize their reliability as a decision-making tool (see Arvey & Campion, 1982; Harris, 1989; Mayfield, 1964; Schmitt, 1976; Ulrich & Trumbo, 1965; Wagner, 1949; Wright, 1969). Researchers in educational administration have sought to apply this widely accepted conclusion to selection practices for classroom teachers from both organizational and individual perspectives. From an organizational perspective, researchers have sought to determine how school administrators make decisions specific to delimiting an applicant pool. In contrast, studies focusing on applicant perspective have addressed how teacher applicants are influenced by the selection process as they choose specific jobs in specific school districts (Miller-Smith, 2001).

The teacher selection research base is built largely on survey methodology, using hypothetical job candidates whose paper applications can be used to manipulate variables such as sex, age, focal position, quantity and quality of information (for example, applicant background), professional work experience, interviewer-interviewee similarities, or interviewer-interviewee differences. This "paper people" paradigm was explained by Gorman, Clover, and Doherty (1978) as a research framework where research subjects (interviewers) are presented with sheets of paper (résumés) that are supposed to represent real people. Subjects are then asked to evaluate the paper representations and make employment decisions. In other words, the phrase *paper people* is used to refer to hypothetical candidates who appear only in their résumés.

Findings from this research, however, do not readily generalize to the more dynamic face-to-face interview most commonly used in teacher selection practices (Delli & Vera, 2003). In an attempt to move beyond résumé study methodology, several investigations focused on simulated interviews. Two notable studies, conducted by Young (1983) and Young and Pounder (1985), examined interviewing decisions made by school administrators using simulated role playing and video-recording techniques, respectively. Role-playing techniques have been used to represent interpersonal interactions and simulate the intricacies of an actual interview, while video-recording has been used to capture the performance of interviewees and help control for unwarranted variance associated with an actual interview.

In the first study, Young (1983) investigated the interview context by simulating a dyad selection interview, which consisted of one administrator playing the part of the interviewer and one teacher playing the part of the teacher candidate, while the simulated panel selection interview consisted of three administrators role-playing the interviewer and one teacher role-playing the teacher candidate. Young discovered that administrators were more likely to recommend the employment of teachers in dyad interviews than equally qualified candidates in panel interviews. Interestingly, though, he also found virtually no difference in how administrators perceived teaching ability between the two interview contexts.

In the second study, Young and Pounder (1985) sought to determine if age discrimination occurred during the interview stage of teacher selection and if this adverse impact could be moderated by the quality of applicant stimuli. These researchers conducted two separate experiments to test their hypothesis: using videotaped interviews and simulated role-playing interviews. Results of the two experiments indicated that older candidates received equitable treatment during both the simulated role-playing interview experiment and the videotaped interview experiment. Young and Pounder concluded that while the résumé criteria employed in the simulated interview study correlated strongly with administrators' perceptions of offering candidates employment, the employment perceptions of administrators failed to correlate with the chronological age of teacher candidates.

Research addressing the preemployment decisions of school administrators also lacks a common framework. Some studies differentiate preemployment decisions of school administrators as either screening decisions or interviewing decisions, other studies use person perception theories to provide a contextual framework for explaining preemployment decisions of school administrators, and still other studies follow a policy-capturing perspective for exploring the preemployment decisions of school administrators. Complicating the review of existing teacher selection research is the fact that studies addressing the pre-employment decisions of school administrators are commingled among these different frameworks (Young & Delli, 2003). Differentiating among preemployment decisions, screening decisions, and interviewing decisions is nontrivial within the selection literature. Studies from the private sector (Gorman et al., 1978), as well as studies from the public sector (Young & Pounder 1985), show that decisions made within the selection process are moderated by the type of candidate stimuli on which the assessments are based. Candidate stimuli for screening decisions consist of paper credentials submitted by the job candidate, while candidate stimuli for interviewing perceptions are based on interpersonal interactions between the interviewer and the applicant (Delli &

Vera, 2008). Furthermore, preinterviewing perceptions are used to delimit the initial applicant pool of candidates, and interviewing perceptions are used to extend or defer a job offer.

Reasons for differentiating between screening decisions and interviewing decisions according to some investigators is that "the prescreening process is fundamental to employee selection because it precludes many applicants from further consideration and it establishes interviewers' initial perceptions of job applicants" (Cable & Gilovich, 1998, p. 501). To assess prescreening decisions of school administrators, researchers rely almost exclusively on employment applications, résumés, letters of recommendation, and placement files. In contrast, studies of interview decisions require at least two people for each unit of data (interviewer and interviewee). As a result of these experimental inefficiencies, only three studies are found within the educational literature addressing teacher selection through interviews: Bolton (1969) explores masking certain information about teacher candidates in the selection interview; Young (1983) compares dyad and panel interviews; and Delli and Vera (2003) investigate the interplay between interviewer and interviewee during face-to-face interviews.

Although knowledge about the selection of teachers has increased considerably within the past two decades, most of this knowledge pertains to selection processes rather than selection outcomes. Omitted almost entirely from these research streams is information concerning how preemployment decisions about teacher applicants relate to postemployment job performance of these teachers. Because the ultimate measure of effectiveness for selection (predictive validity) is determined by the relationship between preemployment predictors and postemployment outcomes, Young and Delli (2003) conducted the first known field study to assess this relationship. They assessed the relationship between preemployment responses of teacher candidates to a structured interview protocol and postemployment job performance exhibited by these teacher candidates once they were teaching.

The preemployment structured interview protocol examined by Young and Delli (2003) was the Teacher Perceiver Interview Protocol (TPI). The TPI is sponsored by the Gallup Organization (1997) and is used by approximately two thousand public school districts across the United States. The postemployment outcomes that Young and Delli used were principals' ratings of teachers and work attendance of teachers as provided by public school administrators.

## COMMERCIALLY DESIGNED TEACHER SELECTION INTERVIEWS

The advent of commercially designed teacher employment interviews began to change the dynamics of the teacher selection process in the 1980s. The emergence of interview protocol produced by private companies was spawned largely in response to the most common employment interview research finding: structured interviews yield higher reliability and validity than non-structured interviews (Campion et al., 1997). Commercially designed interview assessments are marketed to school districts as a means to screen and hire teacher candidates who demonstrate particular traits or qualities. "Over the past two decades, scholars have explored the field of teachers' beliefs, attitudes, and values and tried to define these difficult, ambiguous concepts" (Metzger & Wu, 2008, p. 923).

The use of the structured interview coincided with the idea that a specific and universal set of beliefs or values held by a candidate may indicate the potential success of that candidate. At the same time, private companies created structured interview guides to aid in strengthening the reliability and validity of the employment interview. Emerging from these trends and the work of private corporations is the increased use of commercially designed interview systems for teacher selection. *Editor's note:* See Chapter Two for a review of how noncognitive qualities have been treated in teacher education programs.

According to Kuzniewski (2008), the perception of interview objectivity may be one reason that school districts are attracted to commercial interview products. School administrators have become much more accountable to boards of education and school communities for their hiring decisions. Using an interview protocol designed by a third party might bring a sense of perceived fairness and objectivity to a process that might otherwise be prone to favoritism.

Another attractive feature of these interviews is that they bring some measure of consistency to the hiring process, which increases the fidelity of the selection system. Most private companies that publish interview instruments require that interviewers be trained for high levels of interrater reliability. Furthermore, these commercial instruments allow school districts to assert that teacher candidates, independent of who interviews them and regardless of grade-level position of building assignment, will be asked the same questions, in the same order, and within the same general time frame.

Yet another attractive feature of commercial interview protocols is the convenience of having a preestablished bank of structured interview questions available for use. This ready-made feature provides school administrators the ability to conduct employment interviews without much preparation time. The school administrators interviewed by Kuzniewski (2008) said that school districts lack the necessary time and expertise to develop meaningful interview questions that can be used in a consistent fashion across their respective school districts.

I use *commercial teacher selection interviews* here to refer to protocols as the TPI, TeacherInsight, Automated Teacher Screener, Urban Teacher Selection Interview, Omaha Teacher Interview, Cardinal Selection Interview, the Haberman Star Teacher Selection Interview Tool, and Ventures for Excellence. However, the bulk of research on interviewing has concentrated on the oldest of these, the Teacher Perceiver Interview, described in the following section.

# THE TEACHER PERCEIVER INTERVIEW: HISTORICAL BACKGROUND AND RESEARCH

The most widely used commercial teacher selection instrument, the TPI, is employed in over twelve hundred school districts (Young & Delli, 2003). The TPI was produced in the 1970s by Selection Research (SRI), which later acquired the Gallup Organization and adopted its corporate name. The TPI is a face-to-face interview in which the administrator asks the applicant to respond to sixty open-ended prompts directly related to the TPI's overarching themes. Gallup purports that twelve themes are drawn from research identifying the characteristics of teachers most successful at educating students. Metzger and Wu (2008, p. 923) summarize the themes in this way:

> *Mission*: The teacher's goal is to make a significant contribution to student growth.
> *Empathy:* The teacher responds to the individual student's feelings and thoughts.
> *Rapport Drive*: The teacher likes students and promotes warm, accepting relationships.
> *Individualized Perception*: The teacher considers the interests and needs of each student.
> *Listening:* The teacher listens to students' feelings with responsiveness and acceptance.
> *Investment*: Teacher satisfaction comes from the learner's response, not teacher performance.
> *Input Drive*: The teacher searches for new ideas and experiences to share with students.
> *Activation:* The teacher motivates students to think, respond, and feel in order to learn.
> *Innovation:* The teacher is determined to implement creative new ideas and techniques.
> *Gestalt:* The teacher tends toward perfectionism, but works from individual to structure.
> *Objectivity:* The teacher responds to the total situation rather than reacting impulsively.
> *Focus:* The teacher has models and goals and selects activities in terms of these goals.

Gallup requires that administrators be trained to score the applicant's responses based on "listen-fors"—specific phrases or concepts that reflect the TPI's themes. Administrators are certified to use the TPI only if they have received over a hundred hours of initial training at Gallup's national headquarters and can demonstrate at least 85 percent interrater reliability in item-by-item scoring with Gallup trainers. The face-to-face interview takes up to two hours to administer, so trainers recommend that the administrator keep a running tally of the applicant's score and stop the interview after the first or second third of the questions if the score is under a certain point total.

Subsequent validation studies produced in the mid-1970s reported significant correlation between the TPI and student and administrator ratings of teachers. Also, school districts in several areas of the country have conducted local validation studies and these studies indicate that the Teacher Perceiver Process correlates with other evaluations of teachers. Some studies, however, reported positive, but not significant results with regard to the Teacher Perceiver process (Simmons, 1976).

The Gallup Organization (1990) conducted a validity study of the TPI process on a sample of 162 teachers from public and private school systems across the United States. In this unpublished study, the TPI was administered to each teacher in the sample, and each teacher was subsequently evaluated independently by school administrators. Each teacher was then placed, based on overall teaching proficiency, in one of four quartiles, as determined by the teacher's evaluating administrator. The results of the Gallup (1990) study indicated that teachers included in the top quartile based on independent evaluations had an average of 26.55 raw score points on the TPI; teachers placed in the second quartile had an average of 24.80 raw score points on the TPI; teachers placed in the third quartile had an average of 22.08 raw score points on the TPI; and teachers perceived to be in the bottom quartile achieved an average raw score of 16.71 on the TPI. Researchers reported a correlation of .38, at the .05 level of probability, between high scores on the TPI and high ratings of overall teaching performance by school administrators. Specifically, "teachers who received higher scores on the TPI tended to be rated higher by administrators in terms of overall teaching proficiency" (Gallup Organization, 1997, p. 5).

Since 1990, Gallup has conducted two additional studies examining the validity of the TPI. Its 1994 study used a sample of 211 teachers from urban, suburban, and rural school districts and reported again a significant correlation between the TPI score of a teacher and the ranking received by the evaluating administrator. In the second study, ratings of over twenty thousand students, in grades 4 through 12, were correlated with quartile rankings made by principals, and these researchers found a .42 correlation.

It was not until 2003, when Young and Delli contributed the first published article in a refereed journal, that the relationship of preemployment TPI scores and postemployment performance was examined in a systematic fashion. These researchers examined the individual preemployment TPI theme scores of 196 classroom teachers and their subsequent teaching performance as reported by principal ratings. Investigating the individual theme scores rather than just the composite scores allowed the researchers to test the predictive validity of each theme separately.

Young and Delli (2003) found that with respect to internal consistency, Cronbach alphas were less than .30 for five of the twelve TPI themes and that only one theme (Investment) had an alpha above .60. With respect to predictive validity, these researchers failed to find any theme score with a correlation of .20 or higher with performance ratings of teachers by principals. Four of these themes revealed weak positive relationships of .05 or less, and one relationship with Individualized Perception yielded a −.03.

Moreover, individual theme ratings often correlated more strongly with principal ratings for different themes. For example, questions purporting to measure Individualized Perception correlated more strongly with principals' ratings of Empathy ($r = .25$) than with principals' ratings of Individualized Perception itself ($r = -.03$). Anomalies such as these raise questions about the reliability, and therefore the validity, of the TPI selection system.

One unpublished meta analysis of Perceiver-style interviews across a variety of occupations was conducted by Schmidt (1993).This meta analysis, which included only twelve studies that involved 380 teacher interviews, revealed a correlation of .37 for the predictive validity of the Perceiver process in general. Schmidt, purporting that the validity of the TPI interview was generalizable across organizational settings, stated, "These findings show that the Perceiver Interview is a valid predictor of job performance ratings and sales success across a variety of jobs. The magnitude of the validity may vary with a particular type of job, but in the studies included in this meta-analysis the validity was fairly large and generalizable across situations, organizations, jobs, employers, etc." (Schmidt, quoted in Gallup Organization, 1997, p.6).

In the most recent meta analysis of the TPI, Metzger and Wu (2008) examined sixteen dissertations, one journal article, and seven TPI validity reports from the Gallup Organization. These investigators reported a moderate average relationship ($r = .28$) between the TPI and other measures of teaching quality. Although they acknowledge that their findings are consistent with relationships found in other research on hiring decisions, they remain skeptical as to the extent to which universal TPI themes relate to teacher effectiveness, which most would argue is context-specific to elementary students, middle school students, and high school students as teacher selection decisions are being made.

In 2002, Gallup introduced TeacherInsight, an Internet-based selection system that asks applicants to respond to a series of statements using a five-point Likert scale; a range of multiple-choice questions that reveal their attitudes, beliefs, and behaviors; and a number of open-ended questions. TeacherInsight takes approximately forty minutes to complete and nearly immediately reports to the school the applicant's percentile ranking of predicted potential for teaching success based on how well the responses fit with Gallup's themes. Gallup markets TeacherInsight as a "solution" to help schools "hire the best teachers . . . fast." Potential client districts are informed that the system can help them attract a larger pool of candidates who are similar to their best teachers, using a centralized approach that requires less staff time. According to Metzger and Wu (2008), the TPI appears to have a continuing role in this next-generation product: Gallup recommends the Teacher FIT (Further Insight Into Talent) interview as a "supplemental set of questions" that administrators can use with applicants face-to-face. Because Gallup purports that "the TeacherInsight System is based on more than thirty years of Gallup research into selecting and developing teachers," there must be direct continuity between the TeacherInsight assessment, Teacher FIT, and the long-standing themes underlying the TPI. Gallup's system is likely to remain the most widely employed mechanism for selecting teachers on the basis of their educational beliefs, attitudes, and values.

# RECOMMENDATIONS TO DISTRICTS

Because the ultimate responsibility for teacher hiring decisions continues to rest largely with school administrators and because time continues to be cited as one of the greatest constraints facing administrators in completing this important administrative task, commercial interview products will likely continue to garner the attention of both educational human resource professionals and educational administration researchers.

Delli (2001) outlines several criteria for school districts wishing to adopt commercially designed teacher interviews. To better assist local boards of education and school administrators and evaluate the appropriateness of these types of interview protocol Delli suggests that districts develop a rationale, review published research, examine methodology and instrumentation, review legal considerations, and review cost implications.

## Develop a Rationale

From a school policy perspective, the development of an employee selection system rationale provides a guiding principle for administrative implementation. Because boards of education, teacher unions, and community members expect employment recommendations from school administrators using a variety of sources, administrators must demonstrate that these recommendations are unbiased and supported by data from multiple sources. From a school administrator's perspective, clear articulation is needed as to why a commercially designed interview protocol is being used and how the use of such a product will result in better hiring decisions than other more traditional predictors of performance.

## Review Published Research

The U.S. Equal Employment Opportunity Commission (1978) Uniform Guidelines on Employee Selection Procedures states, "Under no circumstance will the general reputation of a test or other selection procedure, its authors or publisher, or casual reports of its validity be accepted in lieu of evidence of validity" (sec. 1607.9, A). Therefore, promotional literature, personal endorsements, and reports made in the popular press are insufficient for making informed decisions as to the credibility of a commercially designed interview system. Furthermore, unpublished doctoral dissertations, unpublished reports by private companies, studies that combine private and public sector data, or articles that have not otherwise met the scrutiny of a refereeing process generally fail to meet the acceptable boundary conditions described above. School districts must therefore insist that validity data be provided by commercial entities as instrument adoption is being considered.

## Examine Methodology and Instrumentation

The training of interviewers is fundamental when considering interrater reliability. Although the TPI and other commercial instruments require training of interviewers to ensure a high level of scoring agreement, this level of agreement must complement a preestablished level of internal consistency. Because reliability sets the upper limit for validity, a thoughtful item analysis must be provided by the testing company. Other factor-confounding results from commercial interview protocols include interviewee prior test exposure (for example, interviewing in several different school districts that all employ the same interview), interview exposure and experience through teacher education programs or seminars in interviewing strategies, and level of prior teaching experience.

## Address Legal Considerations

The identification of an appropriate performance criterion for validating an interview system is critical because mandated federal employment procedures exist to ensure fairness when examining relationships between two employment variables. The Uniform Guidelines on Employee Selection Procedures (U.S. Equal Employment Opportunity Commission, 1978) outlined specific validation standards, which included, "Evidence of the validity of a test or other selection procedure by a criterion-related validity study should consist of empirical data demonstrating that the selection procedure is predictive of or significantly correlated with important elements of job performance" (sec. 1607.5, A).

## Consider the Cost Implications

The costs associated with implementing a commercial interview system need to be measured in time as well as in dollars. In terms of cost associated with time, these interviews often require well over an hour to administer, not to mention time needed to train interviewers. If an audio or video copy of the interview is recorded, reviewing such a recording creates an additional investment of time. In terms of cost associated with dollars, the purchase price for an instrument like the TPI typically runs in the thousands of dollars, with subsequent training and retraining adding hundreds of dollars per interviewer to the total cost.

# DISCUSSION

For school districts insisting on using a commercial instrument like the TPI and after having considered the suggestions outlined in this chapter, several recommendations are made to aid in the employment decision-making process for classroom teachers by school administrators. First, these interview protocols should be used in conjunction with other predictive sources of relevant employment information based on a valid job description. Second, validity assessments should be conducted in-district rather than relying on single-source information from test makers. Third, a cost-benefit analysis should be conducted to determine the relative worth of using such a system. Fourth, interview adoption criteria should be developed that all relevant stakeholders in the selection process understand and support. Finally, school districts should encourage colleges and universities to incorporate the advantages and disadvantages of these forms of assessments into course work for aspiring administrators.

For decades, researchers and educational administrators have sought to find a silver bullet that will address the important need to hire only the most highly qualified classroom teachers. Unfortunately, a single best method to ensure good hiring does not exist, and efforts to commercialize this important administrative task have failed to add noticeable improvements in how teachers are selected for employment. As H. L. Mencken stated, ''For every complex problem, there exists a solution that is clear, simple, and wrong.''

# REFERENCES

Arvey, R., & Campion, J. (1982). The employment interview: A summary of recent research. *Personnel Psychology, 35,* 281–322.

Becker, B. J., Kennedy, M. M., & Hundersmarck, S. (2003, April). *Communities of scholars, research, and debates about teacher quality.* Paper presented at the meeting of the American Educational Research Association, Chicago.

Bolton, D. L. (1969). The effects of various information formats on teacher selection decisions. *American Educational Research Journal, 6*(3), 329–347.

Brophy, J. (1986). Teacher influences on student achievement. *American Psychologist, 41*, 69–77.

Cable, D. M., & Gilovich, T. (1998). Looked over or overlooked? Prescreening decisions and postinterview evaluations. *Journal of Applied Psychology, 83*, 501–508.

Campion, M., Palmer, D., & Brown, B. (1997). A review of structure in the selection interview. *Personnel Psychology, 50*, 655–702.

Darling-Hammond, L., & Youngs, P. (2003). Defining "highly qualified teachers": What does "scientifically-based research" actually tell us? *Educational Researcher, 31*(9), 13–25.

Delli, D. A. (2001). Criteria for adopting commercial instruments for teacher selection. *AASA Professor, 25*(1), 30–34.

Delli, D. A., & Vera, E. M. (2003). Psychological and contextual influences on the teacher selection interview: A model for future research. *Journal of Personnel Evaluation in Education, 17*(2), 137–155.

Delli, D. A., & Vera, E. M. (2008). Community members' perceptions of teacher candidates during panel employment interviews: Does personality mean more than competence? *Journal of School Public Relations, 29*(3), 319–344.

Evertson, C. (1979). *Teacher behavior, student achievement and student attitudes: Descriptions of selected classrooms, correlates of effective teaching*. Austin, TX: Research and Development Center for Teacher Education.

Gage, N. L. (1978). The yield of research on teaching. *Phi Delta Kappan, 60*, 229–235.

Gallup Organization. (1990). *Teacher Perceiver: Concurrent validity study*. Unpublished report. Lincoln, NE: Author.

Gallup Organization. (1997). *The teacher perceiver: Overview, background, and research*. Lincoln, NE: Author.

Gorman, C. D., Clover, W. H., & Doherty, M. E. (1978). Can we learn anything about interviewing real people from "interviews" of paper people? Two studies of the external validity paradigm. *Journal of Organizational Behavior and Human Performance, 22*, 165–192.

Harris, M. (1989). Reconsidering the employment interview: A review of recent literature and suggestion for future research. *Personnel Psychology, 42*, 691–726.

Kuzniewski, M. L. (2008). *Investigating a commercially designed interview tool for teacher selection*. Unpublished doctoral dissertation, National Louis University.

Mayfield, E. C. (1964). The selection interview: A reevaluation of published research. *Personnel Psychology, 17*, 239–260.

Metzger, S. A., & Wu, M.-J. (2008). Commercial teacher selection instruments: The validity of selecting teachers through beliefs, attitudes and values. *Review of Educational Research, 78*(4), 921–940.

Miller-Smith, K. (2001). *An investigation of factors in résumés that influence the selection of teachers*. Unpublished doctoral dissertation, Ohio State University.

Murphy, P. K., Delli, L. M., & Edwards, M. N. (2004). The good teacher and good teaching: Comparing beliefs of second-grade students, preservice teachers, and inservice teachers. *Journal of Experimental Education, 72*(2), 69–92.

Schmidt, W. D. (1993). *The teacher perceiver interview as a predictor of teacher performance.* Unpublished doctoral dissertation, University of Missouri.

Schmitt, N. (1976). Social and situational determinants of interview decisions: Implications for the employment interview. *Personnel Psychology, 29,* 79–100.

Selection Research Incorporated. (1990). *The teacher perceiver interview.* Lincoln, NE: Author.

Simmons, J. E. (1976). *A study to test the teacher perceiver interview as an instrument that would select vocational agriculture instructors that develop positive rapport with their students.* Unpublished doctoral dissertation, University of Nebraska.

Ulrich, L., & Trumbo, D. (1965). The selection interview since 1949. *Psychological Bulletin, 63,* 100–116.

U.S. Equal Employment Opportunity Commission. (1978). *Uniform guidelines on employee selection procedures.* Washington, DC: U.S. Government Printing Office.

Wagner, R. (1949). The employment interview: A critical review. *Personnel Psychology, 2,* 17–46.

Wright, O. (1969). Summary of research on the selection interview since 1964. *Personnel Psychology, 22,* 391–413.

Young, I. P. (1983). Administrators' perceptions of teacher candidates in dyad and panel interviews. *Educational Administration Quarterly, 19*(2), 46–63.

Young, I. P. (2007). *The human resource function in educational administration* (8th ed.). Upper Saddle River, NJ: Prentice Hall.

Young, I. P., & Delli, D. A. (2003). The validity of the teacher perceiver interview for predicting performance of classroom teachers. *Educational Administration Quarterly, 38*(5), 586–612.

Young, I. P., & Pounder, D. G. (1985). Salient factors affecting decision-making in simulated teacher selection interviews. *Journal of Educational Equity and Leadership, 5*(3), 216–233.

# PART THREE

# ASSESSMENT OF PRACTICING TEACHERS

**Chapter Six:** The Role of Formative Assessments in New Teacher Induction

*Peter Youngs, Ben Pogodzinski, Mark Low*

**Chapter Seven:** Assessing for Teacher Tenure

*Gary Sykes, Sarah Winchell*

**Chapter Eight:** Approaches to Annual Performance Assessment

*Mary M. Kennedy*

**Chapter Nine:** Value-Added: Assessing Teachers' Contributions to Student Achievement

*Douglas N. Harris, Daniel F. McCaffrey*

**Chapter Ten:** The National Board for Professional Teaching Standards: An Investment for the Future?

*Jillian P. Reese*

**Chapter Eleven:** Judging Teachers: The Law of Teacher Dismissals

*Diana Pullin*

# The Role of Formative Assessments in New Teacher Induction

Peter Youngs, Ben Pogodzinski, Mark Low

*Michigan State University*

Over the past decade, No Child Left Behind has led school districts and states across the United States to focus increasingly on induction support for and formative assessment of beginning teachers. Under strong pressure to staff their schools with "highly qualified" teachers and to make Adequate Yearly Progress, these jurisdictions have sought ways to augment new teachers' instructional competence, satisfaction levels, and retention rates. But districts and states face several important questions with regard to the use of formative assessments during induction.[1] In particular, they confront decisions related to (1) the purposes of beginning teacher assessments, (2) the teaching standards on which the assessments are based, (3) the nature of the assessments and the frequency and timing of their use, (4) the nature of the scoring rubrics associated with the assessments, and (5) support provider (formative assessor) selection and training. Furthermore, a jurisdiction's decision regarding any one of these issues will influence available options for addressing the remaining issues.

This chapter explicates the set of decisions that districts and states face in considering the use of formative assessments with beginning teachers; research findings on innovative, high-intensity formative assessments; and the challenges and potential difficulties that districts and states are likely to face in using them. The chapter begins with a brief history of the use of performance assessments with beginning teachers. We then elucidate the decisions jurisdictions face by analyzing the nature of promising, high-intensity formative assessment efforts in several districts and states.[2] (Table 6.1 presents an overview of the systems we look at.)

Finally, we offer a critique of current formative assessment practices during induction and identify challenges and potential pitfalls that districts and states may experience in using them.

# HISTORY OF AND CONCEPTIONS OF TEACHING UNDERLYING PERFORMANCE ASSESSMENTS DURING INDUCTION

In the 1980s, in part due to dissatisfaction with standardized, multiple-choice teacher certification tests, several states began to use performance assessments with beginning teachers for the first time. In these states, many in the South, candidates were granted an initial teaching certificate after they completed their course requirements and passed tests of basic skills, content knowledge, and pedagogical knowledge.[3] They did not receive a professional teaching certificate until they had attained a teaching position and passed an on-the-job performance assessment. Among the more prominent of these assessments were the Florida Performance Measurement System, the Georgia Teacher Performance Assessment Instruments, and the Texas Appraisal System (Porter, Youngs, & Odden, 2001).

Many educators, researchers, and policymakers viewed these assessments favorably in the 1980s because they were based on empirical research, particularly process and product research on teaching (Brophy & Good, 1986; Kuligowski, Holdzkom, & French, 1993). By drawing their assessment criteria from the same research base, Florida, Georgia, Texas, and other southern states were able to promote a common understanding of teaching across the region and to provide educators within and across states with a common language for discussing teaching practice (Kuligowski et al., 1993). Process and product research also influenced the data collection methods used in these assessment systems. In some states, low-inference systems were used; the Florida assessment, for example, focused on the frequency of different teaching behaviors. Other states, including Georgia and Texas, employed higher-inference or modified scripting procedures where assessors used five-point scales to measure the quality of teaching they observed (Pecheone & Stansbury, 1996).

While the Florida, Georgia, and Texas assessments and other similar performance assessments were fairly popular, they were criticized for reinforcing a narrow conception of teaching (Darling-Hammond, Wise, & Klein, 1995). By focusing on a uniform set of teaching behaviors and strategies, regardless of the content area or grade level being taught, assessments based on process and product research may have led teachers to follow a fixed set of prescriptions

Table 6.1. The Use of Formative Assessments in New Teacher Induction

| Type of Assessment | Purpose | Teaching Standards | Nature, Frequency, and Timing of Assessments | Rubrics | Formative Assessor-Selection and Training |
|---|---|---|---|---|---|
| California Formative Assessment and Support System (CFASST) | Formative purposes only; assessment data used to diagnose new teachers' strengths and weaknesses in areas of planning, instruction, student assessment, and reflection | Organized around six domains: instructional strategies, classroom environment, content knowledge, designing instruction, student assessment, and professional development; reflect developmental conception of teaching; each domain features several elements | Classroom observations and conferences occur twice a year; new teachers share student work at conferences; novices complete two six-week investigations of one element from each of three domains: class environment, designing instruction, and student assessment | Descriptions of Practice (the CFASST rubric) feature each of the six domains; each element in each domain is divided into four levels of performance; there is a specific and distinct definition of practice for each performance level | Candidates have to demonstrate teaching expertise and ability to work with other adults; three days of training |
| Pathwise/ Danielson Framework for Teaching | Primarily formative purposes; some districts have used the Danielson framework in making decisions related to performance-based pay | Twenty-two components across four domains: planning and preparation, class environment, instruction, and professional development | Classroom observations and conferences on monthly basis; at conferences, new teachers reflect on their lessons and discuss future plans to modify instruction | Each component is divided into four levels of performance; there is a specific and distinct definition of practice for each performance level | Candidates have to demonstrate five years of teaching experience, content knowledge, instructional expertise, and ability to work with other adults; three days of initial training and four days of follow-up |

*(continued)*

**Table 6.1. The Use of Formative Assessments in New Teacher Induction (continued)**

| Type of Assessment | Purpose | Teaching Standards | Nature, Frequency, and Timing of Assessments | Rubrics | Formative Assessor-Selection and Training |
|---|---|---|---|---|---|
| New Teacher Center's Formative Assessment System (FAS) | Formative purposes only (see CFASST description above) | Organized around six domains (see CFASST description above); reflects developmental conception of teaching; each domain features several elements | Assessment tools used on ongoing basis: novice's learning plan, collaborative assessment log, evidence of instruction; midyear review; end-of-year reflection | Each element in each domain is divided into four levels of performance; there is a specific and distinct definition of practice for each performance level | Candidates have to demonstrate five years of teaching experience, instructional expertise, and ability to work with other adults; ten days of training over course of school year |
| Peer assistance and review (PAR) programs in Toledo and Rosemont (a pseudonym) | Formative and summative purposes; assessment data used to diagnose new teachers' needs, help teachers improve their instruction, and help administrators make decisions regarding renewal or dismissal. | Toledo PAR: twenty-three criteria in four categories: teaching procedures, classroom management, content knowledge, and professional responsibility Rosemont PAR: Organized around six domains (see CFASST description above) | Classroom observations; lesson plans; instructional assistance | Each criterion is divided into three general levels of performance; there are only general (not specific nor distinct) definitions of performance for each level | Candidates must demonstrate five years of outstanding teaching and ability to work with other adults; two days of training; monthly meetings |

| Local assessment systems based on Connecticut Competency Instrument | Formative and summative purposes (see PAR programs description above) | Ten indicators of effective teaching including communicate lesson objectives, present information, engage students in learning, and lesson closure | Two to four assessment cycles per year; classroom observations; lesson plans | Each indicator is divided into two levels of performance; there are only general (not specific nor distinct) definitions of performance for each level | Candidates must demonstrate teaching expertise and ability to work with other adults; three days of mentor training; more extensive training for state CCI scorers |
| --- | --- | --- | --- | --- | --- |
| Local assessment systems based on Connecticut BEST portfolios | Formative and summative purposes (see PAR programs description above) | Revised teaching standards: pedagogical decisions based on knowledge of students, content, and context | Unit and lesson plans; videotapes of instruction; student assignments and work samples; written analyses | Each teaching standard is divided into four levels of performance; there is a specific and distinct definition of practice for each performance level | Candidates must demonstrate teaching expertise and ability to work with other adults; three days of mentor training; more extensive training for state BEST portfolio scorers |

(Porter et al., 2001). In the Florida assessment, for example, the "observers record[ed] the frequencies of specific behaviors in two columns—one for 'effective' behaviors, the other for 'ineffective'"—without taking account of contextual factors (Darling-Hammond et al., 1995, p. 64). Consequently, in this and similar systems, teachers were discouraged "from adapting their instruction to the particular subjects and students they [were] teaching" (Floden & Klinzing, 1990, p. 16). In the 1990s, California became the first state to go beyond the use of performance assessments for making certification decisions to employ them for formative purposes with novice teachers. In 1992, the California legislature initiated the Beginning Teacher Support and Assessment program. Jointly sponsored by the California Department of Education and the Commission on Teacher Credentialing, this program consisted of several local induction projects designed to provide new teachers with guidance and support as they entered the profession. For the first several years of the Beginning Teacher Support and Assessment program, local projects were "encouraged to 'subcontract' with any appropriate assessment entity or to develop their own assessments" (Bartell & Ownby, 1994, p. 16). Consequently, by 1996–1997, most of the local projects used either the California Teacher Portfolio or Pathwise, and the rest subcontracted with other organizations or developed their own assessments.

For the California Teacher Portfolio, each beginning teacher has to write a description of his or her teaching context and complete entries in six domains. Each entry consists of a four-step process known as plan-teach-reflect-act (WestEd, 1997). In this process, the teacher selects a content area and develops a series of lesson plans, teaches the lessons, and reflects on his or her teaching. Each entry has to include the lesson plans, examples of student work from the series of lessons, and the teacher's written reflection on the students' work. When the teacher has completed several entries, he or she critiques the domain evidence (for example, lesson plans, samples of student work, observation notes, and reflective writing), considering what the teacher learned about his or her students' needs and own professional growth (WestEd, 1997). The teacher then develops a research question, focused on one domain, that is based on his or her own findings. The teacher then uses the plan-teach-reflect-act cycle to investigate the research question, and his or her support provider helps the teacher to "collect evidence, critique it, and make changes in [his or her] practice to improve student performance" (WestEd, 1997, p. 7). The teacher is expected to seek professional development activities based on the findings.

The conception of teaching underlying the initial teacher performance assessments of the 1980s (the Florida, Georgia, and Texas assessments) differs considerably from the one that informs the California Teacher Portfolio. Based on process and product research, the former focuses on the same generic teaching behaviors (begin class on time, state the learning objectives for the lesson, present the content of the lesson, maintain time on task, address students' questions, and bring closure to the lesson, for example) regardless of the content area or schooling level that the teacher taught. In addition, this conception views teaching primarily as the transmission of knowledge, with some attention to helping students develop basic intellectual skills. While to some extent this conception addresses the teacher's ability to lead discussions and ask questions of students, it assumes that the teacher skills and behaviors associated with these activities would be uniform across different teaching contexts (Porter et al., 2001).

In contrast, the teaching standards underlying the California Teaching Portfolio are organized around six domains of teaching practice (California Department of Education and Commission on Teacher Credentialing, 1996).[4] According to these standards, new teachers need to demonstrate knowledge and skills in several areas in order to help students acquire procedural and foundational knowledge as well as higher-order skills. In particular, beginning teachers need to demonstrate knowledge of subject matter, the ability to make subject matter accessible to students, and the ability to reflect on and modify their teaching (California Department of Education & Commission on Teacher Credentialing, 1996). As compared to the teaching criteria underlying the Florida, Georgia, and Texas assessments, the conception of teaching that informs the California Teacher Portfolio focuses more on teachers' content knowledge, knowledge of students, and ability to reflect on the instruction (Porter et al., 2001).

In the next section, we describe several current and recent formative teacher assessments and the teaching standards or criteria on which they are based. Before doing so, we describe our notion of effective teaching by noting a few key aspects of instruction that are not fully addressed by the conceptions underlying the Florida, Georgia, and Texas assessments or the California Teaching Portfolio.

First, effective teaching includes the ability to promote student engagement and motivation (Fenstermacher & Richardson, 2005). Some theorists contend that teachers can foster motivation by engaging students in meaningful tasks at which they are likely to be successful (Brophy, 2004; Weinstein, 2007). Others address the roles of teacher legitimacy and student-teacher trust in facilitating learning (Erickson, 1987; Bryk & Schneider, 2002).

Second, effective teaching requires knowledge of formative student assessment and the ability to obtain and use information about students to plan and modify instruction. While research on human cognition has advanced significantly over the past several decades, new scientific understandings of how people learn are not yet reflected in schooling practices on a widespread basis (Shepard, 2000). Thus, it is important for conceptions of effective teaching to address teachers' ability to assess students' prior knowledge, employ clear evaluation criteria, and provide students with feedback.

Finally, it is important to take account of how teaching is influenced by contextual issues such as students' racial/ethnic backgrounds, socioeconomic status, level of English proficiency, and state and district accountability policies (Fenstermacher & Richardson, 2005). In order to inform the development of formative assessments for beginning teachers, it may be necessary for teaching standards (the conceptions of teaching on which assessments are based) to more fully account for how effective teaching is influenced by such contextual factors.

In sum, the conception of teaching on which the Florida, Georgia, and Texas assessments are based view teaching as the transmission of knowledge and focus on the same instructional behaviors regardless of subject area or grade level taught. In contrast, the conception underlying the California Teacher Portfolio focuses more on teachers' content knowledge, knowledge of students, and ability to engage in reflective practice. Our notion of effective teaching builds on that of the California Teacher Portfolio by emphasizing teachers' ability to promote student engagement, teachers' knowledge of student assessment, and the social contexts in which teachers work.

In the next section, we discuss the conceptions of teaching underlying several teacher assessments and consider the extent to which these conceptions address teachers' ability to promote student engagement and motivation, teachers' knowledge and skills related to student assessment, and the social contexts in which teachers work.

# DECISIONS ASSOCIATED WITH THE USE OF FORMATIVE ASSESSMENTS IN INDUCTION

In the 1990s, several states, districts, and national organizations created or implemented new approaches to teacher assessment in order to better measure complex teaching performance (Porter et al., 2001). These approaches featured a range of assessment strategies, including classroom observations, structured interviews, videotapes of instruction, unit and lesson plans, student assignments and tests, student and teacher work samples, and written reflections on practice. At the level of early-career teachers, the Educational Testing Service and the Interstate New Teacher Assessment and Support Consortium (INTASC) developed performance assessments for summative purposes, and by 2008, several states were using these assessments in making licensure decisions.[5] With regard to experienced teachers, the National Board for Professional Teaching Standards created assessments in more than thirty subject areas and school levels for use in identifying highly accomplished teachers and awarding them advanced certification.

Alongside efforts by the Educational Testing Service, INTASC, the National Board, and several states to devise performance assessments or enact them for summative purposes, a number of previously inchoate attempts to use formative assessments with novice teachers took hold during the 1990s and grew significantly in the first decade of the new millennium. These included the California Formative Assessment and Support System (CFASST); the Path-wise/Danielson Framework for Teaching, developed by the Educational Testing Service; the New Teacher Center's Formative Assessment System (FAS); peer assistance and review (PAR) programs[6]; and local teacher evaluation systems in Connecticut based on the Connecticut Competency Instrument (CCI) and BEST portfolios. Both CFASST and the New Teacher Center FAS were attempts to expand and improve upon the California Teacher Portfolio. Furthermore, almost all of these assessments were intended to measure beginning teachers' ability to promote student engagement and their knowledge of student assessment. But these assessments varied significantly in the extent to which they took account of new teachers' social contexts.

In this section, we describe several of these assessments in order to elucidate the numerous decisions that districts and states confront in considering the use of formative assessments during induction. In particular, we compare and contrast them with regard to the purposes of the assessments, the teaching standards on which they are based, the nature of the assessments and the frequency and timing of their use, the nature of the scoring rubrics associated with the assessments, and support provider (formative assessor) selection and training.

## Purposes of New Teacher Assessments

All of the assessment systems reviewed in this chapter are designed to improve the quality of beginning teachers' instructional practices and thereby have a positive impact on student learning. In addition, each system is or was part of a district or state induction program that also features mentoring and other forms of structured assistance for novice teachers; thus, each is also intended to improve teacher retention. Despite these common characteristics across systems, they differed from each other in one important respect: some are designed for formative purposes, and others are intended for both formative and summative purposes. Formative teacher assessments are used to diagnose teachers' relative strengths and weaknesses and to identify areas of teacher knowledge and practice in need of improvement. Summative teacher assessments are employed in making high-stakes decisions, such as those regarding professional certification, contract renewal, and salary increases.

Two of the assessment systems reviewed here, CFASST and the New Teacher Center FAS, use data from teacher performance assessments for formative purposes only. In jurisdictions that used these systems, assessment data were employed to diagnose beginning teachers' strengths and weaknesses in the areas of planning, instruction, student assessment, and reflection; identify professional development or other sources of support if necessary; and help novices improve or refine their practices in each of these areas. In contrast, in the PAR programs and the local Connecticut evaluation systems, teacher assessments are used to diagnose novices' needs, help them improve their instruction, and make decisions regarding contract renewal or dismissal; in other words, districts use these approaches for both formative and summative purposes. Finally, although the Pathwise/Danielson Framework was originally designed for formative use, some districts have used it for making decisions related to performance-based pay (Kimball, White, Milanowksi, & Borman, 2004; Milanowski, 2004). *Editor's note*: See Chapter Eight for more on how the Danielson Framework functions in posttenure teacher evaluations.

The distinction between formative and summative purposes is important in the area of new teacher assessment. When assessments are used for formative purposes, there may be less pressure placed on beginning teachers, more opportunities for support providers to promote new teacher development, and less need for districts or states to provide evidence of assessment validity and reliability. At the same time, while summative assessments may place greater pressure on novices and may require jurisdictions to provide evidence of validity and reliability, beginning teachers and support providers may take such assessments more seriously and therefore may be more likely to fully complete them (Porter et al., 2001).

## Teaching Standards

Teaching standards, formative assessments, and rubrics should aid schools and districts in providing instructional guidelines or expectations for all teachers, identifying poorly performing teachers, and supporting the efforts of all teachers to improve their practice. Therefore, in analyzing standards and rubrics associated with formative assessments, it is important to consider the conceptions of teaching on which they are based, their levels of specificity, and how rubrics based on the standards discriminate among varying levels of performance (Kaboolian & Sutherland, 2005; Porter et al., 2001). In this section, we briefly describe the standards on which CFASST, the Pathwise/Danielson Framework, the New Teacher Center FAS, two examples of PAR programs, and the Connecticut local evaluation systems were based; we then analyze them based on the first of these criteria.[7] Since teaching standards and the ways they are used influence and are influenced by teacher assessments, rubrics, and assessor training, decisions with regard to standards can have important implications for the implementation of formative assessments during induction and their impact on teachers.

CFASST and the New Teacher Center FAS are based on the California Standards for the Teaching Profession, which in turn are organized around six domains: instructional strategies, classroom environment, subject matter knowledge, designing instructional experiences, assessing student learning, and professional development and community outreach (California Department of Education & Commission on Teacher Credentialing, 1996). Each domain features several elements. The domain of subject matter knowledge, for example, has five elements.[8] The California Teaching Standards reflect a developmental conception of teaching, according to which "teachers' knowledge, skills, and abilities develop throughout their professional careers" (California Department of Education & Commission on Teacher Credentialing, 1996, p. 6). For these capacities to grow over time, the California Teaching Standards assert that "teachers must become reflective practitioners who actively work to strengthen and augment their knowledge and skills throughout their careers" (p. 6).

The conception of effective teaching underlying the California Teaching Standards also emphasizes that effective teachers use their knowledge of subject matter, instruction, and student assessment, and the relationships among them, to inform their instructional practices. Furthermore, this conception posits that individual teachers enter the profession at varied levels of experience and ability and develop at different rates in different areas of teaching (California Department of Education & Commission on Teacher Credentialing, 1996). While CFASST and the New Teacher Center FAS are based on the same conception of teaching on which the California Teacher Portfolio is based (the California Standards for the Teaching Profession), the actual CFASST and New Teacher Center FAS assessments focus much more on novices' ability to promote student engagement and on their knowledge of student assessment than does the California Teacher Portfolio. Furthermore, the conception underlying CFASST and the New Teacher Center FAS also addresses teachers' social contexts.

The conception of teaching underlying Pathwise was initially reflected in the Praxis III criteria and later articulated by Charlotte Danielson in what became known as the Danielson Framework (Danielson, 1996; Danielson & McGreal, 2000).[9] This framework features twenty-two components across four domains of teaching[10]—planning and preparation, classroom environment, instruction, and professional responsibilities (Danielson, 1996)—and it shares many similarities with the conception of teaching underlying CFASST and the New Teacher Center FAS. Like the California Teaching Standards, the Danielson Framework reflects a developmental conception of teaching and emphasizes the need for teachers to engage in reflective practice (Danielson, 1996). In addition, both conceptions stress the need for teachers to be knowledgeable about their students and the subjects they teach; to create an environment that promotes student learning; to engage students in active, in-depth learning; to employ assessment strategies aligned with learning goals; and to apply pedagogical content knowledge (California Department of Education & Commission on Teacher Credentialing, 1996; Danielson & McGreal, 2000). Furthermore, the Danielson Framework also posits that effective teachers use their knowledge of content, pedagogy, and assessment, and the relationships among them, in making instructional decisions. Like the California Teaching Standards, the Danielson Framework also addresses teachers' social contexts.

As of 2004–2005, the PAR program in Toledo was based on twenty-three criteria in four categories: teaching procedures, classroom management, knowledge of subject, and personal characteristics and professional responsibility. Although these criteria are consistent with research on effective teaching from the 1980s, Kaboolian and Sutherland noted that they "may not have taken into account shifts in research or evolving views" about effective instruction (2005, p. 44). In particular, they place less emphasis on cognitive learning theory, pedagogical content knowledge, and the relationship among content, pedagogy, and assessment than the California Teaching Standards or the Danielson Framework. With regard to the PAR program in Rosemont that Goldstein studied, it is aligned to the California Teaching Standards (Goldstein, 2004).[11]

Finally, by the end of the 1990s, virtually all districts in Connecticut had adopted or modified the Connecticut Competency Instrument (CCI) for use in local district evaluation (Baron, 1999; Youngs & Bell, in press). Furthermore, a number of Connecticut districts implemented components of the BEST portfolios for use in local evaluation during the first decade of the 2000s. The conception of teaching underlying the CCI is similar in many ways to those underlying CFASST and the New Teacher Center FAS. The CCI conception states that effective teachers "have a complete understanding of the structures of [their] subject matter, its basic concepts, principles, and procedures" (Armour-Thomas & Szczesiul, n.d., p. 3). According to this conception, effective teachers have high academic expectations for all of their students and engage all of them in active learning. Furthermore, such teachers reflect on each of their lessons, making decisions before, during, and after the act of teaching (Armour-Thomas & Szczesiul, n.d.).

Similar to the Florida, Georgia, and Texas assessments, the CCI in Connecticut was designed to measure generic teaching competencies and is based on a conception of teaching as involving the same actions regardless of subject matter or context: communicating lesson objectives, presenting information, engaging students in learning activities, and bringing closure to the lesson. Assessors use ten indicators of effective teaching behavior to assess first-year teachers' performance on the CCI. These indicators are based on a set of fifteen teaching standards known as the Connecticut Teaching Competencies that the state adopted in 1984. In 1999, the Connecticut State Department of Education revised the state's teaching standards, which became known as the Common Core of Teaching. The revised teaching standards are explicitly based on Connecticut's ambitious learning standards and describe the knowledge and skills teachers should have in order to help students meet the learning standards. Compared to the state's previous teaching standards, the Common Core of Teaching represents a significant advance in that it reflects the complex, discipline-based nature of teaching. In particular, the revised teaching standards focus more on using knowledge of students, content, and context as a basis for pedagogical decisions. Furthermore, these standards are based on the principles that teaching should be evaluated in relation to student learning rather than on the basis of teaching behaviors alone and that teacher assessments should be content-specific as opposed to applying to all subject areas.

In sum, the teaching standards on which teacher assessments are based can play a key role in the design of an effective formative assessment system. Districts and states can send weak or misguided policy signals to teachers and support providers when they fail to adopt or revise teaching standards so that they are consistent with current research on how children and adults learn.

## Nature, Frequency, and Timing of Assessments

Some key decisions regarding formative teacher assessments that jurisdictions must make are to determine the nature of the assessments that they will employ and the frequency and timing of their use. As noted, this chapter focuses on CFASST, the Pathwise/Danielson Framework, the New Teacher Center FAS, the PAR programs in Toledo and Rosemont, and local Connecticut evaluation systems. While many of these assessments share at least some common features, there is a range of strategies that districts and states can choose from, and even otherwise similar instruments differ in notable ways with regard to assessment content, as well as the frequency and timing of their use. Furthermore, jurisdictions face decisions regarding the number and specificity of their teaching standards, the number and specificity of their rubrics, and assessor training; all of these decisions can shape the implementation and outcomes of formative assessments.

According to Thompson, Goe, Paek, and Ponte (2004), "CFASST is a structured professional development program for first- and second-year teachers that is used as part of the statewide Beginning Teacher Support and Assessment program" (p. 2).[12] In 2002–2003, more than 130 of the 142 local Beginning Teacher Support and Assessment programs in the state used CFASST as the primary formative assessment component. At that time, novices participating in CFASST worked on a series of twelve assessment events[13] over two years (six during their first year of teaching and six during their second year).[14] In CFASST, each novice is matched with an experienced teacher trained as a support provider. Based on the California Standards for the Teaching Profession, the CFASST Descriptions of Practice are used by novices and support providers to describe the new teachers' social contexts, establish goals for their growth, acquire information about effective instruction, plan units and lessons, and receive feedback based on classroom observations (Thompson, Goe, et al., 2004). Observations and postobservation conferences generally occur twice over the course of each school year, and during conferences, beginning teachers are asked to share and analyze examples of student work with their support providers. With regard to inquiries, each new teacher has to complete two six-week investigations of one element from each of the following standards: classroom environment, designing instructional experiences, and assessing student learning.

In research on the state Beginning Teacher Support and Assessment program,[15] Mitchell et al. (2007) found that "participating teachers report meeting with their support providers more than twice a month, but less than weekly" (p. 74). In addition, participants indicated that on average, their meetings with their support providers were more than thirty minutes in length. Furthermore, participants reported frequent opportunities to reflect on their teaching through their local Beginning Teacher Support and Assessment program, analyze student work, and be observed by their support providers, and they placed high value on these activities (Mitchell et al., 2007). In another study that focused on CFASST, Thompson, Paek, Goe, and Ponte (2004) reported that about half of their research participants completed all twelve assessment events over a two-year period and that about 25 percent completed two or fewer events each year (out of six). Approximately half of the beginning teachers in their study indicated that their meetings with their support providers usually lasted from thirty minutes to an hour, and about 33 percent reported that these meetings typically lasted more than an hour. At the same time, the authors noted that these meetings primarily addressed emotional support, as well as instructional support, and student behavior issues (Thompson, Goe, et al., 2004).

In describing the Pathwise/Danielson Framework assessment activities, Glazerman, Senesky, Sefotr, and Johnson (2006) wrote that the new teachers and their mentors were expected to focus on seven monthly events: "The Teaching Environment Profile, Classroom Environment Action Research, Profile of Practice and Individual Growth Plan I, Focus on Engaged Learning Action Research, Profile of Practice and Individual Growth Plan II, Analyzing Student Work/Assessment Action Research, and Assessment and Summary of Professional Growth" (p. 8). For the Profiles of Practice in Pathwise, similar to the CFASST Descriptions of Practice, the beginning teacher would complete an instruction profile and then be observed and interviewed by an assessor.[16] In "the instruction profile, the teachers have to describe their goal for the lesson with regard to student learning and how the content of the lesson is related to what students had learned previously and what they will be learning in the future" (Porter et al., 2001, p. 269). Furthermore, the novices have to provide information about the teaching methods, learning activities, and instructional materials they plan to use and how these are related to their goals for the lesson.

During the observations, the assessor records key aspects of what the beginning teacher and students said and did that were related to the components. The postobservation interview also serves as a source of evidence for several components of the Danielson Framework. During this interview, novices are asked to reflect on how the lesson went and if they departed from their lesson plan to explain why. In addition, the assessor inquires whether teachers would do anything differently if they were to teach the lesson to the same class again. After the postobservation interview is complete, the assessor reviews all of the notes taken during the observation and interview along with the information from the instruction profile. The assessor then determines what evidence, positive or negative, exists for each of the components and writes a summary statement about the four domains, but not necessarily for each component (Porter et al., 2001).

While in the early 2000s almost all local Beginning Teacher Support and Assessment programs in California employed CFASST, the New Teacher Center at the University of California Santa Cruz has taken a leadership role in developing a widely respected alternative known as the New Teacher Center Formative Assessment System (FAS). As of 2002–2003, the New Teacher Center FAS was being used by several districts in California and in other states. Furthermore, it was selected in 2005 as one of two formative teacher assessments (along with the Pathwise/Danielson Framework) to be featured in a national experimental design study funded by the Institute of Education Sciences and conducted by Mathematica Policy Research on the effects of high-intensity induction programs on new teacher retention and effectiveness (Glazerman et al., 2006).

Comparable to CFASST and the Pathwise/Danielson Framework, the New Teacher Center FAS uses a series of interactions between a new teacher and his or her mentor that address student learning. Several tools are "used to structure the mentor-beginning teacher interactions and support each beginning teacher's development in relation to professional teaching standards. The focus, process, and pacing of the New Teacher Center FAS tools are determined collaboratively by the mentor and beginning teacher in light of the teacher's individual needs" (New Teacher Center, n.d.). The New Teacher Center FAS tools feature activities and protocols employed by the mentor to provide guidance and, in collaboration with the novice, document their teaching context and their work. In particular, tools include an individual learning plan, a collaborative assessment log,[17] evidence of instructional practice, a self-assessment summary, a midyear review, and "reflections on one's professional growth — an end-of-the-year process through which mentors assess novices' practice while identifying successes and key decisions affecting student achievement by analyzing standards-based evidence of student learning'' (Glazerman et al., 2006, pp. 7–8).

Similar to most other PAR programs, the PAR program in Toledo features classroom observations as the main source of assessment data. In particular, mentor teachers (known as consulting teachers) have responsibility for providing assistance to new teachers (referred to as interns) and observing them at least seven times during their first year. According to the program guidelines, the first observation of the intern by the consulting teacher must be held at a mutually convenient time and be preceded by a preobservation conference. Later observations should be unannounced, and all are to last at least twenty minutes, although many last forty-five minutes to an hour. An intern who is doing well would be observed at least five times in the first semester and at least twice in the second semester. And an intern who is struggling could be observed six to ten times in the first semester alone. In addition to the observations, principals compiled data about interns' performance with regard to attendance, compliance with district and state policy, and cooperation with others (Kaboolian & Sutherland, 2005).

It is important to note some key differences between Toledo's program (and other PAR programs), on the one hand, and CFASST, the Pathwise/Danielson Framework, and the New Teacher Center FAS, on the other. First, the Toledo PAR program combines formative and summative assessment, while the assessment systems concentrate exclusively on formative assessment. For a given intern, the consulting teacher's observations and the principal's reports are shared in a summary report for Toledo's Intern Board of Review, which makes the final decision regarding contract renewal. Second, compared to CFASST, the New Teacher Center FAS, and the Pathwise/Danielson Framework, the assessment data in the Toledo PAR program are limited because they are almost exclusively based on lesson plans and classroom observations. In contrast, the other assessment systems feature analyses of student learning, teacher research projects, and self-assessments by the novices. Third, the Toledo PAR program focuses on only first-year teachers.[18] At the same time, Toledo's program features a greater number of classroom observations than the other programs. Furthermore, after the first observation, the remaining visits are unannounced, which reduces the likelihood that interns would plan special lessons or activities for these occasions.

The PAR program in Rosemont, the California district that Goldstein (2004, 2007) studied, is similar to the Toledo PAR program in that it focuses on first-year teachers, uses lesson plans and classroom observations as the primary sources of assessment data, and has consulting teachers observing and interacting with new teachers on a frequent basis. In particular, Goldstein reported that all consulting teachers in the Rosemont PAR program ''were expected to visit their [first-year teachers] an average of one time per week, to make some unannounced visits, and to conduct three formal observation cycles during the year" (2007, p. 485). Of the thirty-six consulting teachers, principals, and novices interviewed in her study, Goldstein reported that thirty-four (94 percent) "cited the feedback and suggestions on instructional strategies given by consulting teachers to [beginning teachers], making it the most frequently named element of PAR in the research" (2007, p. 489).

Goldstein also found that most consulting teachers in the Rosemont PAR program were very knowledgeable about the teaching standards and that conversations between consulting teachers and novices were typically grounded in the language of the CSTP (2004). When asked about PAR's impact on the use of teaching standards in Rosemont, the mean responses of principals, panel members, and consulting teachers (thirty-four in all) was 4.60 ($SD = 0.63$) on a 1-to-5 scale, with 5 being "a very positive effect" (Goldstein, 2004). As in Toledo, consulting teachers in Rosemont share their evaluation data with principals and the district's PAR panel, and the PAR panel makes the ultimate decision regarding beginning teachers' contract renewal.

The CCI was pilot-tested in the late 1980s and used with first-year teachers across Connecticut to make provisional certification decisions from 1989 to 2000. By the end of the 1990s, almost all districts in the state had adopted or modified the CCI for use in observing and evaluating nontenured teachers, and such teachers were usually observed three or four times per year (Baron, 1999; R. L. Pecheone, personal communication, July 20, 2001). Like some observation instruments used in other states in the 1990s, district versions of the CCI were designed to measure generic teaching competencies in the areas of instruction, assessment, and classroom management. In particular, teachers were required to demonstrate proficiency with regard to ten indicators of effective teaching behavior during a series of observations and interviews conducted by principals and district administrators.

For each assessment cycle, the school or district administrator would observe a lesson, take notes on teacher and student behavior, sort evidence by indicator, and determine whether evidence represented a satisfactory or unsatisfactory performance (Pecheone & Stansbury, 1996). Although mentors in Connecticut trained in the CCI provided support to new teachers on an ongoing basis, they did not play a role in formally evaluating them. Also, similar to the PAR programs in Toledo and Rosemont, Connecticut districts employed the CCI for both formative and summative purposes.[19]

Between 1995 and 2001 under the leadership of Raymond Pecheone, the Connecticut State Department of Education developed and implemented a set of content-specific performance assessments, known as the Beginning Educator Support and Training (BEST) portfolios, in ten certification areas (Pecheone & Stansbury, 1996). As of 2005–2006, teachers in virtually all content areas in the state had to go through the BEST portfolio process in their second year of teaching. For the portfolio, teachers are required to describe their teaching context and complete several entries integrated around one or two units of instruction.[20] By 2005, several Connecticut districts had begun to use components of the BEST portfolios in their local evaluation systems, including unit and lesson plans, videotapes of instruction, samples of student work, and written reflections. As with the CCI, these components are used for both formative and summative purposes. Data from these assessments reveal information about the logic and coherence of the teacher's curriculum, the appropriateness of her or his instructional decisions for students, and the range of pedagogical strategies used. The portfolios also provided rich data about the quality of the teachers' assignments, their skill in assessing student learning, and their ability to modify their teaching based on evidence of student learning (Wilson, Darling-Hammond, & Berry, 2001).

The formative assessment PAR programs in Toledo and Rosemont and local Connecticut systems based on the CCI rely on a combination of lesson plans and observations. In contrast, CFASST, the Pathwise/Danielson Framework, the New Teacher Center FAS, and local Connecticut systems based on the BEST portfolios generally produce richer, more comprehensive data on new teacher growth and performance because they involve analyses of student work and more explicit attention to novices' social contexts. While the inclusion of student work and attention to social context in these systems provided valuable data about teacher performance in relation to key standards, it also increased the demands on new teachers and support providers and threatened fidelity of implementation.

## Rubrics

Most of the teaching standards and accompanying rubrics for these formative assessments are characterized by detailed levels of specificity and clear distinctions among different levels of performance; consequently, most of them provide new teachers and their support providers with a common vocabulary with which to discuss and critique instruction. The California Teaching Standards are organized around six domains, or categories, of teaching practice, with each domain featuring numerous elements. Each of the six domains is featured on the CFASST Descriptions of Practice, and each (and each element) is divided into four levels of performance: practice not consistent with standard expectations, developing beginning practice, maturing beginning practice, and experienced practice that exemplifies the standard. Each element in each domain has detailed and unique definitions that describe practice at each of the four performance levels. Novices work with their support providers to determine their performance levels with respect to the various elements and, when necessary, identify professional learning opportunities to help them improve their practice.

The rubric that mentors use as part of the New Teacher Center FAS is comparable to the CFASST Descriptions of Practice in that it divides each of the six domains in the California Teaching Standards into four levels of performance and clearly distinguishes among various levels of performance. Similarly, each of the twenty-two components in the Danielson Framework delineates a distinct aspect within its domain. According to the framework, beginning teachers are expected to work with mentors to improve their instruction according to a continuum of effective practice "based on four levels of performance: unsatisfactory, basic, proficient, and distinguished" (Glazerman et al., 2006, p. 8). Similar to the CFASST Descriptions of Practice and the New Teacher Center FAS rubric, there are specific and distinct definitions of practice for each component at each of the performance levels.

As of 2004–2005, the Toledo PAR program articulated twenty-three teaching criteria across four domains. Compared to the CFASST Descriptions of Practice and the Danielson Framework, though, the rubric used in Toledo's program is much more general. In particular, the Toledo rubric is characterized by fairly unspecified definitions for three levels of performance: satisfactory, unsatisfactory, and outstanding.[21] Consulting teachers in Toledo are expected to use these broad definitions to evaluate novices' practices across all twenty-three criteria. Kaboolian and Sutherland observed, "Without further guidance, these definitions alone are not likely sufficient to ensure that consulting teachers selected levels for each criterion based on the same rules" (2005, p. 15). At the same time, the level of specificity in the Toledo rubric may be due to the fact that the PAR program in Toledo focuses on both formative and summative evaluation. Furthermore, since the program was a negotiated agreement between the teacher association and district, it may have been difficult for both sides to agree on a more detailed rubric. In contrast to the Toledo PAR program, though, the PAR program in Rosemont uses the CFASST Descriptions of Practice, and offers clear distinctions among different levels of performance (Goldstein, 2004).

Local district evaluation systems in Connecticut based on the CCI focus on teachers' performance with regard to ten indicators of effective practice in the areas of instruction, assessment, and classroom management. Somewhat similar to the Toledo PAR program rubric, most district rubrics in Connecticut distinguish between only two levels of performance: satisfactory and unsatisfactory. They also employ broad, fairly unspecified definitions for these terms and apply the same definitions across all ten indicators. In contrast, the state and district rubrics associated with the BEST portfolios (and local evaluation systems that employed components of these portfolios) closely approximate those used in CFASST, the Pathwise/Danielson Framework, and the New Teacher Center FAS. In particular, the rubrics linked to the BEST portfolios clearly distinguish among four performance levels and feature detailed definitions that articulate practice at each of the performance levels.

In sum, rubrics can potentially provide important guidance to novices and support providers in terms of how to work toward meeting instructional expectations (that is, standards). But rubrics are unlikely to meet this goal when they do not clearly discriminate among varying levels of performance or are not written with sufficient specificity. The demands on new teachers and those who work with them are heightened when jurisdictions employ highly developed rubrics (with detailed levels of specificity and distinct demarcations among performance levels). At the same time, such rubrics are key to providing novices and support providers with a common language regarding instruction, diagnosing beginning teachers' needs, and determining ways to support them and promote their professional growth.

## Selection and Training of Assessors and Support Providers

While the use of formative assessments with beginning teachers at the district or state level is strongly influenced by the standards and rubrics that accompany them, it is also affected by jurisdictions' decisions regarding the selection of and training for support providers and assessors. Some of the assessment systems analyzed in this chapter focus exclusively on formative assessment, but the PAR programs in Toledo and Rosemont and the Connecticut local evaluation systems use performance assessments for both formative and summative decisions. In either case, it is crucial for districts and states to ensure that support providers have high levels of teaching expertise and strong abilities to mentor or coach other teachers and are well trained to use teaching standards, assessment components, and rubrics in their regular interactions with beginning teachers. In this section, we examine selection and training practices in each of the assessment systems in order to explicate some additional questions facing jurisdictions.

Local Beginning Teacher Support and Assessment programs, including those that use CFASST, develop their own criteria for selecting support providers. They generally require candidates to demonstrate teaching expertise and the ability to work with other adults (Porter et al., 2001). In the early 2000s, Mitchell et al. (2007) conducted a statewide evaluation of California's statewide Beginning Teacher Support and Assessment program. At the time, more than 90 percent of local Beginning Teacher Support and Assessment programs were using CFASST. The researchers reported that many support providers believed that "the adequacy of their role preparation matched with their ability to provide adequate and timely support are key factors in the emergence of a Beginning Teacher Support and Assessment program that embodies a strong assessment system and is helpful overall in facilitating the professional growth of teachers'' (Mitchell et al., 2007, p. 89).

According to the Educational Testing Service, mentor candidates in jurisdictions employing the Pathwise/Danielson Framework are required to have at least five years of teaching experience, including at least two years in their current district, strong subject matter knowledge, acknowledged expertise in teaching, the ability to collaborate with other adults, and experience with or commitment to promoting new teacher learning. After mentors are chosen, they attend three days of training prior to the beginning of the school year and two two-day sessions during the year. In the initial session, mentors address ''what quality induction looks like, the teaching practices in the Pathwise Framework for Teaching, and how to implement the initial [events] that constitute[d] the curriculum for their work with beginning teachers'' (Glazerman et al., 2006, p. 8). In the second and third sessions, participants go over strategies for enacting the rest of the curriculum. Additional support is provided to mentors through monthly meetings and regular conference calls with designated Educational Testing Service staff members. Finally, in some districts, monthly study groups for novices and mentors enabled them to discuss past or upcoming Pathwise events.

Selection criteria for mentors in districts that use the New Teacher Center FAS include ''a current teaching credential, at least five years of recent teaching experience, recognized expertise in standards-based instruction and subject matter knowledge, good interpersonal skills, and a demonstrated commitment to professional growth for teachers'' (Glazerman et al., 2006, p. 6). After mentors are selected, they participate in ten days of training during four sessions over the course of a school year.[22] The first training session addresses strategies for communicating effectively, building trust, assessing new teachers' performance, and diagnosing their needs. In the second session, participants discuss how to collect and analyze classroom data, how to make use of teaching standards, and how to provide feedback to novices. The third session features ways to help new teachers identify students' needs, differentiate instruction, and link their instruction to student learning. Finally, in the fourth session, participants go over the end-of-year review process for novices and reflect on their own experiences as mentors (Glazerman et al., 2006). Along with the four training sessions, new and continuing mentors also attend weekly coaching forums facilitated by a New Teacher Center staff member designated to work with their district. In these meetings, mentors address issues related to program implementation and how to promote collaboration among novices and themselves.

In Toledo, selection criteria for consulting teachers include five years of outstanding service, a favorable reference from the principal at the teacher's school, and favorable references from three teachers who also work at the candidate's school (Kaboolian & Sutherland, 2005). Dal Lawrence (2003), former president of the Toledo Federation of Teachers, wrote of other important characteristics for potential consulting teachers to demonstrate, including the ability to communicate effectively and work well with adults, being respected as a teacher and a leader, being committed to the teaching career, and being willing to not renew a teacher contract. Once teachers are initially selected for this role, they attend a few intern board of review meetings and shadow an experienced consulting teacher to gain familiarity with the process. During the summer, new consulting teachers attend two days of formal training, in which they are further introduced to the program and procedures and spend three to four hours on strategies for observation, evaluation, and conferences. Once they start working with new teachers, new consulting teachers are paired with a veteran who has already served in this role, and all of them participate in monthly meetings. In the words of Kaboolian and Sutherland, "through all of these mechanisms, consulting teachers continually share knowledge and learn from each other" (2005, p. 26).

In the Rosemont PAR program that Goldstein (2007) studied, potential consulting teachers have to be considered master teachers; they are also required to demonstrate prior success mentoring a peer, submit a letter of recommendation from a previous mentee, and be observed during classroom instruction by two PAR panel members. With regard to training for consulting teachers, Goldstein (2007) noted that many participated in professional development on coaching and spent several hours learning how to use teaching standards in their work with beginning teachers. In her words, "While consulting teachers were not experts in performance standards for teaching at the time they were hired, they poured many professional development hours into becoming experts, and then into becoming calibrated among themselves in their use of the standards for evaluating to a rubric" (p. 489). At the same time, it is important to note that Goldstein studied the Rosemont PAR program in its first year of implementation. Consequently, there was some variation among the ten consulting teachers in her study with regard to their understanding and use of the assessment data and rubrics (Goldstein, 2007).

In the 1990s and first decade of the 2000s, teacher assessments in Connecticut were used at the district and state levels for both formative and summative purposes. Almost all districts adopted or modified the CCI for use in local teacher evaluation, and in the 1990s, the state required first-year teachers to complete the CCI in order to maintain their teaching certificates. By requiring all first-year teachers to be assigned to state-trained mentors and by involving experienced teachers and principals in CCI scoring, the state increased the likelihood that veterans and administrators would use the CCI for diagnostic purposes in their work with new teachers. When the Connecticut State Department of Education later implemented portfolios for use in making certification decisions, the mentor training process was revised, portfolio scorer training and scoring sessions were initiated, and several districts subsequently adapted components of the portfolio for local teacher evaluation.

As of 2001–2002, mentors in Connecticut were required by the state to participate in three days (twenty-four hours) of BEST support teacher training; two and a half days were provided in August, prior to the start of the school year. This training addresses a range of topics related to mentoring, including the needs of beginning teachers, the Connecticut teaching standards, and the BEST portfolio requirements. Participants discuss strategies for establishing trust, instructional coaching, promoting reflective inquiry, relating instructional practice to the teaching standards, and providing portfolio-related support. Training is provided at several regional Educational Service Centers and in a number of districts around Connecticut and facilitated by experienced mentors, teacher educators, or BEST regional field staff.[23] In the fall, mentors complete their twenty-four hours of training by attending half-day content-specific sessions provided by the regional centers that focused on the teaching standards and portfolio requirements in their particular content areas.

The selection of mentors across districts in Connecticut is fairly similar. In New Britain and Bristol in 2000–2001, for example, committees of teachers and administrators reviewed applications. In both districts, candidates had to demonstrate evidence of expertise in teaching, based on principal evaluations, and the ability to collaborate with other adults in roles such as cooperating teachers or instructional coaches (Youngs, 2002). While mentors play important roles in helping first- and second-year teachers understand the state's teaching standards and portfolio requirements, teachers and administrators who have been trained as portfolio scorers are well prepared to diagnose novices' needs and draw on components of the portfolio process to help them improve their practice. With regard to portfolio scorer training, each year in the spring, first-year assessors attend two days of training that address the teaching standards, portfolio requirements, and evaluation framework for the particular subject area in which the assessors teach. The new assessors also practice collecting evidence from sample lesson plans, videotaped lessons, student performances, and written reflections. In the summer, new and experienced assessors then spend ten to twelve days reviewing sample portfolios, participating in proficiency scoring, and scoring portfolios (Youngs, 2002).

In sum, all of the assessment systems reviewed here require support providers (mentors) to demonstrate teaching expertise and the ability to work with other adults. At the same time, these systems vary in the nature and length of support provider training that is required. CFASST and the Connecticut systems require support providers to participate in three days of training, while the Pathwise/Danielson Framework, the New Teacher Center FAS, and the PAR programs require seven to ten days of initial or ongoing training. Furthermore, support providers in Connecticut who also serve as CCI or BEST portfolio scorers have several additional days of training on teaching standards and the use of evidence in making scoring decisions. Glazerman et al. (2008) found that intensive training for support providers (and intensive mentoring) had little effect on first-year teachers in a large-scale study in seventeen districts (when compared to support provided by those with substantially less training). But it is unclear from the research whether intensive training for support providers has an impact on beginning teachers after two or three years of teaching.

# POTENTIAL IMPACTS ON TEACHER QUALITY

In the current climate of high-stakes accountability, districts and states that consider the use of formative assessments with beginning teachers will be interested in their effects on teacher outcomes and student learning. In this section, we review research on whether and how CFASST, the Pathwise/Danielson Framework, the New Teacher Center FAS, PAR programs in Toledo and Rosemont, and the CCI and BEST portfolios are related to teacher commitment, teacher retention, and student learning.

## CFASST

Mitchell et al. (2007) conducted a major research study on the California Beginning Teacher Support and Assessment program in the early 2000s that featured three components: a population study, case studies of twenty-seven local programs that were undergoing review in 2007, and intensive case studies of ten local programs. The population study used data from the 28,264 teachers across California who participated in local Beginning Teacher Support and Assessment programs in 2006–2007. (These data were obtained from the California Department of Education and the Commission on Teacher Credentialing.) For the twenty-seven case study sites, the researchers conducted interviews with the local program directors and analyzed documents regarding program designs and budgets. Of the ten programs that were the focus of the intensive case studies, six were using CFASST in 2006–2007, two were using the New Teacher Center FAS, and two were using locally developed formative teacher assessments. While Mitchell et al.'s study focused on all local Beginning Teacher Support and Assessment programs in the state (not just those using CFASST), their findings pertain to CFASST because more than 90 percent of local programs were using this assessment system at the time data were collected.

Of those surveyed, more than 80 percent of Beginning Teacher Support and Assessment program participants reported feeling "either satisfied or very satisfied" with teaching in their current district, teaching at their current school, and their current teaching assignment. Furthermore, over 80 percent of respondents indicated that they felt "confident or very confident (about) staying in the teaching profession in 5 years" (Mitchell et al., 2007, p. 79). Additional analyses revealed that satisfaction and commitment seemed related to the enactment of CFASST (and the formative assessment systems in the other local projects). According to the authors, when the formative assessment system was carefully implemented, it not only facilitated "a strong and positive relationship between participating teachers and support providers, but [it] also impact[ed] [beginning teachers'] overall satisfaction with and commitment to the teaching profession" (Mitchell et al., 2007, p. 84). In contrast, Mitchell and colleagues (2007) found that when novices experienced the assessment system as confusing or obstructive, they were likely to find teaching less satisfying and to express lower levels of commitment. The researchers also investigated the relationship between Beginning Teacher Support and Assessment program participation and continuation in the teaching profession. Of the first-year participants in all local programs in 2003–2004, 92 percent were still teaching in 2004–2005 and 84 percent were teaching in 2005–2006 (Mitchell et al., 2007).

In a second major research study, researchers at the Educational Testing Service surveyed teachers who had participated in local Beginning Teacher Support and Assessment programs that used CFASST. For each study participant, the researchers created a measure of engagement with CFASST based on support for CFASST in the local program, the beginning teacher's level of access to their support provider, the level of rapport between them and their support provider, and the degree to which the beginning teacher, the support provider, and their use of CFASST addressed substantive teaching and learning issues. The researchers found that "teachers with higher CFASST engagement levels tended to report teaching for a longer period of time" (Thompson, Goe, et al., 2004, p. 16). The generalizability of this finding was limited, though, by the low survey response rate in this study; only 287 out of 1,125 third-year teachers completed surveys (a response rate of 26 percent). Of the 287 survey respondents, the researchers obtained student testing data for 144 of them. Across all six subtests,[24] the researchers found that "the students of teachers who had a high level of engagement with CFASST outscored the students of teachers with a low level of engagement with the assessment system, after controlling for" the Academic Performance Index of each teacher's school (Thompson, Paek, Goe, & Ponte, 2004, p. iv). Again, these results had limited generalizability because of the low survey response rates.

## Pathwise/Danielson Framework and New Teacher Center FAS

Glazerman and colleagues' (2008) recent study investigated the effects of the Pathwise/Danielson Framework and the New Teacher Center FAS on beginning teachers. The researchers employed random assignment to compare a group of new elementary school teachers who experienced comprehensive induction with an equivalent group exposed to their districts' conventional induction activities.[25] The novice teachers in the treatment group participated in comprehensive induction featuring either the Pathwise/Danielson Framework or the New Teacher Center FAS. Seventeen districts in thirteen states participated in the study, each of which had more than 50 percent of its students eligible for free or reduced-price lunch. In each district, elementary schools were assigned to either the control group or one of two treatments (selected by the district). "The final sample sizes included 418 schools: 100 treatment schools and 103 control schools in the 9 ETS districts and 110 treatment and 105 control schools in the 8 NTC districts" (Glazerman et al., 2008, p. ix). In their analyses, Glazerman and colleagues considered the teachers who received comprehensive induction through the Pathwise/Danielson or the New Teacher Center FAS systems to be part of one treatment group.[26]

Based on the first year of data collection (2005–2006) and analysis, Glazerman and colleagues (2008) reported "no statistically significant differences between treatment and control group teachers' performance on any of the three domains of classroom practices" on which they focused: lesson implementation, lesson content, and classroom culture. With regard to the effects of comprehensive induction on teacher effectiveness, "the average impacts across all grades were not significantly different from zero for math or reading." Finally, they reported that "comprehensive teacher induction had no statistically significant impact on teacher retention" (Glazerman et al., 2008, pp. xv, xvi). The researchers did note, though, that analyses based on the second year of their data collection (when complete) may indicate some statistically significant long-term effects of comprehensive induction programs.

In sum, the analyses by Glazerman et al. (2008) based on their first year of data raise questions about the impact of comprehensive induction programs on first-year teachers in urban, high-poverty districts. It is important to note, though, that Glazerman and colleagues conducted additional analyses in which they grouped the treatment and control teachers together and examined correlations between induction support and outcomes, regardless of treatment status. In these analyses, "eight of the relationships between the induction variables and retention measures were positive and statistically significant" (Glazerman et al., 2008, p. xxi). At the same time, because these analyses did not control for preexisting differences among teachers, the researchers caution that these results should not be used to draw causal inferences.

## PAR Programs

It is difficult to determine the effect that PAR programs have on the retention rate of teachers. As in any other profession, there will be a certain level of teacher attrition for extraneous reasons such as relocation of a spouse or other family issues. It also may be that PAR programs increase teacher attrition by better identifying subpar teachers, which leads to termination or nonrenewal of their contracts. Or PAR programs may improve teacher retention because they provide interventions that help teachers become successful, which is likely to keep them in the profession. Overall, though, there is a lack of quality data to help answer this question.

In their study, Kaboolian and Sutherland (2005) compared the retention rates of teachers who began teaching in Toledo in 1995–1996 (a year in which the PAR program was temporarily suspended) with those who started working in the district in 1994–1995 and 1996–1997 (when the program was in operation). The authors asserted that "the retention rate after 3 years and 5 years [was] significantly lower for those in the 1995–96 cohort" (p. 37). But they did not provide any data in support of this claim. In another study of the Toledo PAR program, Kerchner, Koppich, and Weeres (1997) reported that of the 1,141 teachers who had completed the program as of 1994–1995, 6.4 percent resigned, were not renewed, or were terminated. It is not clear how this compares to other districts, or whether these results could be attributed solely to the PAR program in Toledo. These studies did not examine the relationship between participating in the Toledo PAR program and student achievement.

In her study of the PAR program in Rosemont, Goldstein (2004, 2007) did not examine the effect of the program on teacher retention or student learning.

## Local Evaluation Systems Based on CCI or BEST Portfolios

With regard to local teacher evaluation systems in Connecticut based on the CCI or BEST portfolios, there has been little research on how such evaluation systems affect beginning teacher retention or student learning.

# DISCUSSION

The research suggests that formative assessments for new teachers have become more prevalent in the United States. Furthermore, the use of such assessments seems to have the potential to increase teacher commitment and retention, influence the quality of novices' instruction, and have an impact on student learning. At the same time, jurisdictions face several challenges and possible difficulties in implementing or continuing to use such assessments over time. In this section, we discuss four such challenges and address why some districts and states have been reluctant to employ performance assessments with new teachers for formative purposes.

One challenge that districts and states confront is the need to recruit, select, and train experienced teachers to serve as formal mentors (support providers) to beginning teachers, use formative assessments to diagnose new teachers' strengths and weaknesses, and support novices' instructional growth. It can be time-consuming for veteran teachers to participate in mentor training and acquire expertise in teaching standards and performance assessments.

In addition, it can be intellectually and emotionally demanding for them to work closely with new teachers on a regular basis. Districts and states have employed a variety of incentives to interest experienced teachers in serving as mentors: annual stipends, professional development (continuing education) credits, and release time from teaching. In addition, many districts have negotiated with teacher associations to include such incentives for mentors in collective bargaining agreements (Pogodzinski & Youngs, 2009). Without attention to and financial support for such incentives, though, jurisdictions are unlikely to interest sufficient numbers of veterans in serving as mentors.

Once experienced teachers are selected to serve as mentors, it is critical that jurisdictions train them in a variety of coaching skills and in how to use performance assessments with beginning teachers. In particular, mentors "need significant training in such skills as observation and analysis of instruction, peer coaching, adult learning theory, trust building, reflective conversations, diagnosis of instructional practices, conflict management, teacher legal rights, and obligations" (Mitchell et al. 2007, p. xxvi). In addition, mentor training should familiarize participants with assessment components and the standards on which they are based; feature examples of teacher performances that meet, exceed, and fail to meet standards; and include practice scoring of performances.

In addition to understanding assessment procedures, it is also very important to train mentors how to use formative teacher assessment data to identify and interpret novices' strengths and weaknesses and assist them in acquiring new knowledge and skills and, when necessary, in modifying their instruction (K. Stansbury, personal communication, June 19, 2008). For example, as part of the New Teacher Center mentor training, participants addressed how to collect and analyze assessment data, how to make use of teaching standards, and how to provide feedback to beginning teachers (Glazerman et al., 2006). One of the main reasons that formative assessment systems sometimes come up short and have little effect on beginning teachers is that jurisdictions often have not set up strong mentor training programs, and therefore the mentors in such programs are not prepared to use assessments with novices.

A second challenge that districts and states face pertains to the level of complexity of the various performance assessments described in this chapter. In brief, the greater the degree of complexity, the less likely it is that new teachers and mentors will maintain the fidelity of the instrument unless they have clear incentives to complete it. For example, half of the respondents in Thompson, Goe, et al. (2004) reported completing fewer than all twelve assessment events over a two-year period, and 25 percent indicated that they completed two or fewer assessment events (out of six) per year. In the PAR programs in Toledo and Rosemont, in some districts that used the Pathwise/Danielson Framework and in Connecticut districts that employed the CCI, assessments were used for both formative and summative purposes; in such jurisdictions, participants were likely to maintain the fidelity of the assessments. But when assessments were used only for formative purposes, especially in the case of CFASST and the New Teacher Center FAS, the possibility was greater that beginning teachers and mentors would not complete them.

Districts can take a number of steps to increase the likelihood that novices and mentors will complete formative assessments. First, it can be helpful when both parties have common release time, which can be used for meetings, classroom observations, and working on components of a given formative assessment. Second, financial incentives for mentors can prompt them to take their mentoring roles seriously, ensure that new teachers complete the assessments, and use data from the assessments to coach novices and help them improve their practice. Third, CFASST, the New Teacher Center FAS, the Pathwise/Danielson Framework, and the local Connecticut systems based on the BEST portfolios call for beginning teachers to analyze student work samples or videotape and analyze their instruction. In order to support new teachers and mentors in these activities, schools and districts can build norms that call for all teachers to engage in them.

A third challenge involves using performance assessments with beginning teachers for both formative and summative purposes. While doing so can increase the fidelity of the use of the instrument, it can also raise potentially complicated situations for mentors and principals (Yusko & Feiman-Nemser, 2008). In particular, research on mentoring suggests that it can be important for new teachers to view their interactions with their mentors as confidential places where they can admit mistakes, share difficulties, and potentially work through some of the emotional difficulties that many novices experience (Gold, 1992, 1996; Veenman, 1984).

When, for summative purposes, mentors are expected to share information from their interactions with and assessments of their mentees with administrators, this can threaten the trust that is an integral part of mentor-mentee relationships (Yusko & Feiman-Nemser, 2008). Some assessment systems (for example, CFASST, New Teacher Center FAS) have addressed this issue by clearly separating the results of formative assessments from decisions regarding contract renewal or tenure for early-career teachers. But several other systems have successfully employed performance assessments for both formative and summative purposes (the PAR programs; districts that use the Pathwise/Danielson framework as part of performance-based pay systems; and Connecticut districts that employ the CCI or components of the BEST portfolio in local teacher evaluation systems). More research is needed to determine whether and how mentors are able to maintain productive working relationships with novices in jurisdictions that use performance assessments for both formative and summative purposes.

# Notes

1. Formative teacher assessments are used to diagnose teachers' relative strengths and weaknesses and to identify areas of teacher knowledge and practice in need of improvement. They can be distinguished from summative assessments—those used in making high-stakes decisions such as decisions regarding professional certification, contract renewal, and salary increases.

2. We chose to focus on these assessments for three main reasons. First, all were used widely in many school districts in the United States in the 1990s or the first decade of the 2000s. Second, these instruments had all been documented in reports or assessment materials, and many had been studied by researchers, including CFASST, the Pathwise/Danielson Framework, the New Teacher Center FAS, Peer Assistance and Review programs, and local evaluation systems in Connecticut. Third, these assessments, and the programs of which they were a part were characterized by strong assessment content and rubrics, close links to teaching standards, assessor training, and other features that are a main focus of this chapter.

3. In this chapter, initial certification requirements are those that teaching candidates must meet in order to begin working as classroom teachers in public schools: university course work, student teaching, tests of basic skills, subject matter knowledge, and professional knowledge. Professional certification requirements are those that practicing teachers must meet in order to continue teaching in public schools: professional development credits and performance assessments.

4. The California Teacher Portfolio was based on a set of teaching standards known as the *California Standards for the Teaching Profession* (California Department of Education & Commission on Teacher Credentialing, 1996).

5. Summative teacher assessments are used in making high-stakes decisions regarding professional certification, contract renewal, and salary increases. They can also be used for formative purposes to diagnose teachers' relative strengths and weaknesses and identify areas of teacher knowledge and practice in need of improvement.

6. In selecting a few peer assistance and review (PAR) programs on which to focus in this chapter, we believed it was important to include two PAR programs from two different states, one of which had been in place for a much longer period than the other. In addition, we were interested in including PAR programs that had been recently been studied by researchers. Based on these criteria, we elected to include the PAR program in Toledo, studied by Kaboolian and Sutherland (2005), and the PAR program in Rosemont (a pseudonym), a California district studied by Goldstein (2004, 2007). Readers interested in literature on PAR programs are encouraged to see Anderson and Pellicer (2001); Bloom and Goldstein (2000); Gallagher, Lanier, and Kerchner (1993); Koppich, Asher, and Kerchner (2002); and Stroot et al. (1999).

7. See the "Rubrics" section for discussion of the levels of specificity in the standards and rubrics associated with each of these assessments and whether the various rubrics distinguished different levels of performance.

8. The five elements in the domain of subject matter knowledge are (1) demonstrating knowledge of subject matter, (2) organizing curriculum to support

student understanding of subject matter, (3) integrating ideas and information, (4) demonstrating student understanding of subject matter through instructional strategies, and (5) using materials, resources, and technologies to make subject matter accessible to students (California Department of Education & Commission on Teacher Credentialing, 1996).

9. Praxis III was an observation-based instrument developed by the Educational Testing Service for use with first-year teachers in making state-level certification decision. See Porter et al. (2001) for more information about Praxis III.

10. For example, the domain of planning and preparation included the following elements: demonstrating knowledge of content and pedagogy, demonstrating knowledge of students, setting instructional outcomes, demonstrating knowledge of resources, designing coherent instruction, and designing student assessments (Danielson, 1996).

11. Goldstein used a pseudonym, Rosemont, to refer to the district she studied.

12. In the first decade of the 2000s, most beginning teachers in California participated in local Beginning Teacher Support and Assessment programs, with the exception of those with emergency teaching credentials.

13. CFASST included a class-school-community profile, Descriptions of Practice, inquiries, a summary statement, a colloquium, and an individual induction plan.

14. While earlier versions of CFASST covered the same topics, they had previously been organized into ten events in year 1 and seven events in year 2 (Thompson, Goe, et al., 2004).

15. More than 130 of the 142 local Beginning Teacher Support and Assessment programs in 2002–2003 used CFASST.

16. For the Pathwise/Danielson Framework, the assessor was often the new teacher's mentor.

17. According to the New Teacher Center FAS materials, the Collaborative Assessment Log was the primary tool of the New Teacher Center FAS process and provided a framework for regular interactions between novice and mentor. At the time of "each meeting and classroom visit, the Collaborative Assessment Log reminds [the novice] to celebrate classroom successes, identify and prioritize challenges, and commit to specific next steps. The Log not only guides the interaction, but also serves to document" professional growth (New Teacher Center, n.d.).

18. In Toledo, teachers in their first two years of teaching participated in the PAR program, but principals were responsible for evaluating second-year teachers (as opposed to consulting teachers who evaluated first-year teachers). In addition, tenured teachers who received unsatisfactory ratings also participated in the program, but this was uncommon.

19. By state law, districts in Connecticut in 2000–2001 had to decide whether to award tenure by the end of the teacher's fourth year of teaching in public schools.

20. These entries included a description of the teaching context, a set of lesson plans, a videotape of instruction during the units, samples of student work, and written

reflections on the teacher's planning, instruction, and assessment of student progress.

21. For example, "satisfactory" in the Toledo PAR program was defined as "should be the point of departure. A check there should indicate that the teacher is showing the degree of professional qualities and growth to be expected and desired as a beginning teacher" (Kaboolian & Sutherland, 2005, p. 14).

22. Mentors in the New Teacher Center FAS programs received full-time release from teaching while they were serving as mentors.

23. The regional Educational Service Centers were intermediate units designed to bridge the gap between the Connecticut State Department of Education and local school districts.

24. The six subtests were CAT-6 math, reading, language arts, and spelling; and the California Standards Tests in Math and English Language Arts (Thompson, Paek, et al., 2004).

25. Comprehensive induction is defined in this study as including the following: "carefully selected and trained full-time mentors; a curriculum of intensive and structured support for beginning teachers that includes an orientation, professional development opportunities, and weekly meetings with mentors; a focus on instruction, with opportunities for novice teachers to observe experienced teachers; formative assessment tools that permit evaluation of practice on an ongoing basis and require observations and constructive feedback; and outreach to district and school-based administrators to educate them about program goals and to garner their systemic support for the program" (Glazerman et al., 2006).

26. The researchers also conducted separate analyses by induction program type (Pathwise/Danielson Framework or New Teacher Center FAS) to ensure that their findings were not specific to one of the two induction providers.

# REFERENCES

Anderson, L., & Pellicer, L. (2001). *Teacher peer assistance and review: A practical guide for teachers and administrators*. Thousand Oaks, CA: Corwin Press.

Armour-Thomas, E., & Szczesiul, E. (n.d.). *A review of the knowledge base of the Connecticut Competency Instrument*. Hartford: Connecticut State Department of Education.

Baron, J. B. (1999). *Exploring high and improving reading achievement in Connecticut*. Washington, DC: National Educational Goals Panel.

Bartell, C. A., & Ownby, L. (1994). *Report on implementation of the Beginning Teacher Support and Assessment program (1992–94)*. Sacramento: Commission on Teacher Credentialing and California Department of Education.

Bloom, G., & Goldstein, J. (Eds.). (2000). *The peer assistance and review reader*. Santa Cruz: New Teacher Center, University of California, Santa Cruz.

Brophy, J. (2004). *Motivating students to learn* (2nd ed.). Mahwah, NJ: Erlbaum.

Brophy, J., & Good, T. (1986). Teacher behavior and student achievement. In M. C. Wittrock (Ed.), *Handbook of research on teaching* (3rd ed., pp. 328–375). New York: Macmillan.

Bryk, A. S., & Schneider, B. (2002). *Trust in schools: A core resource for improvement*. New York: Russell Sage Foundation.

California Department of Education & Commission on Teacher Credentialing. (1996). *California standards for the teaching profession*. Sacramento, CA: Authors.

Danielson, C. (1996). *Enhancing professional practice: A framework for teaching*. Alexandria, VA: Association for Supervision and Curriculum Development.

Danielson, C., & McGreal, T. (2000). *Teacher evaluation to enhance professional practice*. Alexandria, VA: Association for Supervision and Curriculum Development.

Darling-Hammond, L., Wise, A. E., & Klein, S. P. (1995). *A license to teach: Building a profession for 21st-century schools*. Boulder, CO: Westview Press.

Erickson, F. (1987). Transformation and school success: The politics and culture of educational achievement. *Anthropology and Education Quarterly*, *18*(4), 335–356.

Fenstermacher, G. D., & Richardson, V. (2005). On making determinants of quality in teaching. *Teachers College Record*, *107*(1), 186–213.

Floden, R. E., & Klinzing, H. G. (1990). What can research on teacher thinking contribute to teacher preparation? A second opinion. *Educational Researcher*, *19*(5), 15–20.

Gallagher, J. J., Lanier, P., & Kerchner, C. T. (1993). Toledo and Poway: Practicing peer review. In C. T. Kerchner & J. E. Koppich (Eds.), *A union of professionals: Labor relations and educational reform* (pp. 158–176). New York: Teachers College Press.

Glazerman, S., Dolfin, S., Bleeker, M., Johnson, A., Isenberg, E., Hugo-Gil, J., et al. (2008). *Impacts of comprehensive teacher induction: Results from the first year of a randomized controlled study*. Washington, DC: U.S. Department of Education, Institute of Education Sciences.

Glazerman, S., Senesky, S., Sefotr, N., & Johnson, A. (2006). *Design of an impact evaluation of teacher induction programs*. Washington, DC: Mathematica Policy Research, Inc.

Gold, Y. (1992). Psychological support for mentors and beginning teachers: A critical dimension. In T. M. Bey & C. T. Holmes (Eds.), *Mentoring: Contemporary principles and issues* (pp. 25–34). Reston, VA: Association of Teacher Educators.

Gold, Y. (1996). Beginning teacher support: Attrition, mentoring, and induction. In J. Sikula (Ed.), *Handbook of research on teacher education* (2nd ed., pp. 548–594). Washington, DC: Association of Teacher Educators.

Goldstein, J. (2004). Making sense of distributed leadership: The case of peer assistance and review. *Educational Evaluation and Policy Analysis*, *26*(2), 173–197.

Goldstein, J. (2007). Easy to dance to: Solving the problems of teacher evaluation with peer assistance and review. *American Journal of Education*, *113*, 479–508.

Kaboolian, L., & Sutherland, P. (2005). *Evaluation of Toledo Public School District Peer Assistance and Review Plan*. Cambridge, MA: Harvard University, John F. Kennedy School of Government.

Kerchner, C. T., Koppich, J. E., & Weeres, J. G. (1997). *United mind workers: Unions and teaching in the knowledge society*. San Francisco: Jossey-Bass.

Kimball, S. M., White, B., Milanowski, A. T., & Borman, G. (2004). Examining the relationship between teacher evaluation and student assessment results in Washoe County. *Peabody Journal of Education, 79*(4), 54–78.

Koppich, J., Asher, C., & Kerchner, C. (2002). *Developing careers, building a profession: The Rochester Career in Teaching Plan*. New York: National Commission on Teaching and America's Future.

Kuligowski, B., Holdzkom, D., & French, R. (1993). Teacher performance evaluation in the southeastern states: Forms and functions. *Journal of Personnel Evaluation in Education, 1*, 335–358.

Lawrence, D. (2003). *The Toledo Plan: Practical advice for beginners*. Toledo, OH: Toledo Public Schools and Toledo Federation of Teachers.

Milanowski, A. T. (2004). The relationship between teacher performance evaluation scores and student achievement: Evidence from Cincinnati. *Peabody Journal of Education, 79*(4), 33–53.

Mitchell, D. E., Scott-Hendrick, L., Parrish, T., Crowley, J., Karam, R., Boyns, D., et al. (2007). *California Beginning Teacher Support and Assessment and Intern Alternative Certification Evaluation Study* (Tech. Rep.). Riverside: University of California-Riverside.

New Teacher Center. (n.d.). *New Teacher Center Formative Assessment System*. Santa Cruz: University of California Santa Cruz New Teacher Center.

Pecheone, R. L., & Stansbury, K. (1996). Connecting teacher assessment and school reform. *Elementary School Journal, 97*(2), 163–177.

Pogodzinski, B., & Youngs, P. (2009). *How labor-management relations influence the commitment of new teachers*. Manuscript submitted for publication.

Porter, A. C., Youngs, P., & Odden, A. (2001). Advances in teacher assessment and their uses. In V. Richardson (Ed.), *Handbook of research on teaching* (4th ed., pp. 259–297). New York: Macmillan.

Shepard, L. A. (2000). The role of assessment in a learning culture. *Educational Researcher, 29*(7), 4–14.

Stroot, S., Fowlkes, J., Langholz, J., Paxton, S., Stedman, P., Steffes, L., et al. (1999). Impact of a collaborative peer assistance and review model on entry-year teachers in a large urban school setting. *Journal of Teacher Education, 50*(1), 27–41.

Thompson, M., Goe, L., Paek, P., & Ponte, E. (2004). *Study of the impact of the California Formative Assessment and Support System for Teachers: Report 1, Beginning teachers' engagement with BTSA/CFASST* (CFASST Rep. No. 1, ETS RR-04-30). Princeton, NJ: Educational Testing Service.

Thompson, M., Paek, P., Goe, L., & Ponte, E. (2004). *Study of the impact of the California Formative Assessment and Support System for Teachers: Report 3, Relationship of BTSA/CFASST engagement and student achievement* (CFASST Rep. No. 3, ETS RR-04-32). Princeton, NJ: Educational Testing Service.

Veenman, S. (1984). Perceived problems of beginning teachers. *Review of Educational Research, 54*(2), 143–178.

Weinstein, C. (2007). *Secondary classroom management* (3rd ed.). New York: McGraw-Hill.

WestEd. (1997). *California teacher portfolio*. San Francisco: Author.

Wilson, S. M., Darling-Hammond, L., & Berry, B. (2001). *A case of successful teaching policy: Connecticut's long-term efforts to improve teaching and learning*. Seattle: Center for the Study of Teaching and Policy, University of Washington.

Youngs, P. (2002). *State and district policy related to mentoring and new teacher induction in Connecticut*. New York: National Commission on Teaching and America's Future.

Youngs, P., & Bell, C. (in press). When policy instruments combine to promote coherence: An analysis of Connecticut's policies related to teacher quality. *Journal of Educational Policy*.

Yusko, B., & Feiman-Nemser, S. (2008). Embracing contraries: Combining assistance and assessment in new teacher induction. *Teachers College Record*, *110*(5), 923–953.

# CHAPTER SEVEN

# Assessing for Teacher Tenure

Gary Sykes, Sarah Winchell

*Michigan State University*

This chapter takes up issues concerning assessment for teacher tenure. Interest in this topic has increased in recent years following from evidence that teaching effectiveness is a significant school-related factor in student achievement; that having a grade-to-grade succession of effective teachers can boost student achievement markedly; and that there is great variability among teachers in their effectiveness (Ehrenberg & Brewer, 1994; Kane, Rockoff, & Staiger, 2008; Rivkin, Hanushek, & Kain, 2005; Sanders & Rivers, 1996).[1] Some analysts now argue that if school systems were better able to identify and dismiss, or "deselect," those teachers unlikely to be or to become effective, this would have a major impact on student learning. Other analysts raise a variety of objections to the use of student outcomes in teacher assessment for tenure and propose other alternatives for tenure reform.

To assess these prospects, this chapter begins with a brief history of teacher tenure and then appraises its current status, presents a framework for evaluating tenure, and concludes with recommendations for the future of assessment for tenure. We argue that assessment for tenure must involve a collaboration that ideally includes state policy, district-union agreements, and administrator-teacher involvement. We also argue that multiple lines of evidence regarding both the practice of teaching and its results in student learning be used in making determinations of teacher effectiveness and, ultimately, to make the tenure decision.

# A BRIEF HISTORY OF TEACHER TENURE

Tenure for teachers has become an institution in American education. It is deeply embedded in legislation and law, custom and tradition, the local practices of districts and schools, and the expectations of teachers. It has become a stable feature of the system of education, achieving a legitimacy that only recently has come under serious challenge.

When New Jersey legislators passed the first state teacher tenure legislation in 1909, they did so in order to protect teachers from unjustifiable dismissals, stabilize the teaching force, orient incentives around a more careful teacher hiring process, and establish high standards for veteran teachers (Holmstedt, 1932). Interestingly, the reasons for adopting tenure policies varied somewhat across districts and states. In his study of New Jersey's tenure legislation, Holmstedt (1932) found that of 1,239 teachers surveyed, half cited "protection" as the greatest feature of the tenure law, and of these, "30 percent emphasized security against political attacks" (p. 86). These fears underscore an oft-cited reason for tenure in higher education: intellectual freedom. Earlier, however, Chicago teachers had lobbied the Illinois state legislature to grant them pensions at the end of their careers. Once these were secured in 1895, they recognized the need for job security and petitioned the legislature for tenure. As Urban (1982) writes, "Tenure for Chicago's teachers thus reflected a pension-related interest in job protection rather than recognition of their right to academic freedom" (p. 69). In addition, a number of state tenure laws arose out of civil service reforms that aimed to end patronage and other abuses. Conceived as civil servants, teachers were "entitled to protection similar to that afforded recognized members of the civil service" (Scott, 1934, p. 9).

Despite these varying motivations for securing tenure, states gradually adopted a common model that includes a brief probationary period before tenure can be awarded; annual principal evaluations culminating at the end of the probationary period to determine if a teacher should receive tenure; and an extended postprobationary period, during which continuing evaluation is an administrative responsibility, and a teacher can be dismissed only with substantial evidence that he or she is unfit or derelict in her duties. Today thirty-three states, a majority, require three years of teaching before the award of tenure. Missouri and Indiana have five-year probationary periods and Wisconsin has no state law on tenure (Miller & Chait, 2008). These investigators note that

> several states have tinkered with their tenure statutes. Connecticut, Michigan, and South Dakota have increased the length of their probationary periods and streamlined due process procedures. In North Carolina, reforms in 1998 shortened dismissal timelines and allowed principals in low-performing schools to recommend that specific teachers be evaluated. Florida, Idaho, Mississippi, Texas, and

Utah eliminated tenure by instituting renewable contracts for specified periods of time. Yet veteran teachers in these states still have de facto tenure by way of due process protections similar to those provided by tenure in other states [p. 17].

While teacher tenure has been established as a key feature of the occupation, criticisms about incompetent teachers have a long history that predates the 1909 New Jersey tenure law. For example, in 1893, the physician Joseph Rice published his famous muckraking account of the schools, based on a six-month study tour of thirty-six cities. Among his criticisms, he noted: "There is absolutely no incentive to teach well.... In New York City teachers are very rarely discharged, even for the grossest negligence and incompetency" (Rice, 1893, p. 44). He went on to claim:

> The power to appoint the teachers is vested in the Board of Trustees, while the appointment of superintendents and principals lies in the hands of the Board of Education.... The superintendents should naturally be held responsible for poor teaching, but justly they cannot be so held for the reason that it is almost impossible for them to have incompetents discharged. Indeed, the superintendent has said that he has given up, as a hopeless task, attempting to have incompetent principals and teachers discharged. Therefore the supervisors can justly lay the blame of poor teaching on the members of the Board of Education, while the Board of Education can justly throw this responsibility on the shoulders of those whose duty it is to secure proper teaching. So things have always been, and so they will remain until a radical change is effected [pp. 48–49].

Bridges (1990) updates the story in characterizing the tenure system as "complaint driven." As he describes it, once teachers achieve tenure, evaluations routinely elicit favorable ratings from principals until complaints mount from parents and students. Then principals seek "escape hatches" to avoid continuing and future complaints (see also Levin, Mulhern, & Schunck, 2005). Common escape hatches include transferring teachers to other schools, assigning teaching of electives, or converting classroom teachers into roving substitutes. Bridges further notes that these processes have tended to disadvantage poor schools serving poor and minority students, where parents and students are less vocal. Principals, he notes, "spared themselves the unpleasantness involved in communicating negative feedback and avoided the need to spend countless hours with the teacher in order to improve his or her performance" (p. 148). He continues: "Given the principal's broad range of responsibilities and large span-of-control (i.e., number of employees to supervise), these tolerant responses were understandable, even if not acceptable" (p. 148).

These accounts are reflected in a more recent study (Weisberg, Sexton, Mulhern, & Keeling, 2009) that has coined the term *widget effect* to refer to the manner in which school districts treat all teachers as though they were alike, that is, as interchangeable widgets. The study revealed that in the twelve districts studied, well over 90 percent of teachers routinely receive satisfactory ratings annually and that the districts make almost no use of teacher performance information for personnel decisions. The image rising out of this influential study is of a disconnect between the management of human resources in education and teachers' performance on the job.

The tenure system also provokes unease among many teachers. In one recent survey, for example, teachers reported dissatisfaction with assessment for tenure:

> The most obvious technique used to assess teacher quality—the formal obser- vation and evaluation—is not doing the job. In fact, only 26 percent of teachers report that their own most recent formal evaluation was "useful and effective." The plurality—41 percent—say it was "just a formality," while another 32 percent say at best it was "well-intentioned but not particularly helpful" to their teaching practice. Almost seven in 10 teachers (69 percent) say that when they hear a teacher at their school has been awarded tenure, they think that it's "just a formality—it has very little to do with whether a teacher is good or not" [Duffett, Farkas, Rothertham, & Silva, 2008, p. 3].

## THE CURRENT STATUS OF TEACHER TENURE

Despite the perceptions that schools harbor many incompetent teachers who should be dismissed, there are few data on how the current system filters teachers across multiple points in the process of becoming a teacher. An older generation of studies found a negative relationship between teacher qualifications and selection: at every point in the process, from the initial choice of major in teacher education through attrition in the early years, teachers with higher academic qualifications were more likely to leave teaching (Murnane, Singer, Willett, Kemple, & Olsen, 1991; Schlechty & Vance, 1981, 1983); difficult-to-staff schools were even more likely to lose highly credentialed teachers with strong qualifications (Boyd, Lankford, Loeb, & Wyckoff, 2005).[2] Recent studies, though, look not at qualifications but at value-added measures of teacher effects on student achievement. These studies find that the least effective teachers are more likely to leave teaching in the early years.[3] In this case, what might be termed "natural (de)selection" rids the profession of incompetent teachers because these teachers are counseled out, depart because they are dissatisfied or are not having success, or exit the profession because they are not committed to teaching. However, if incompetent teachers are simply moving to other schools rather than leaving teaching altogether, the problem of incompetent teachers persists.

Several studies have explored the relationship between teacher leavers or movers and teacher effectiveness (Boyd, Grossman, Lankford, Loeb, &

Wyckoff, 2007; Goldhaber, Gross, & Player, 2007; Hanushek & Rivkin, 2008). These studies all indicate that the most effective teachers, as measured by their contribution to student achievement on standardized tests, are more likely to stay in their schools than less effective teachers. Boyd et al. (2007) found that New York State teachers who left their schools were about as likely to transfer to another school in the state or district as they were to leave teaching altogether. Since less effective teachers tend to be those who leave their schools, it seems likely that some of these teachers have been pressed to transfer because of poor performance, as Bridges (1990) suggested. Evidence from this study further indicates that less effective teachers are more likely to leave both high-achieving and low-achieving schools. All three studies found that highly effective teachers are more likely to stay at the most challenging schools than less effective teachers. This helps to buttress the claim that natural deselection, retention policies, and informal norms already may play a role in securing higher-quality teachers, especially for low-performing schools.

Hanushek and Rivkin's (2008) study in a single Texas district also found that teachers who left the profession completely were less effective than those who stayed in their schools, and this held when compared to teachers in the same district and those in the same school and year. Unfortunately, they also found that teachers who moved within the same district were significantly less effective than those who stayed at their schools, again supporting Bridges's (1990) general description. Still, what remains unknown in this research is whether a teacher who is ineffective in one school is also ineffective in the school to which she or he transfers. If effectiveness depends not simply on teacher characteristics but also on the match with features of particular schools, then teacher self-sorting through voluntary transfers could result in overall efficiencies in the system.

These recent findings provide some evidence that natural deselection already works to some extent to weed out ineffective teachers. What are admittedly imprecise national estimates indicate that only between 0.1 and 1.0 percent of teachers are dismissed each year (Miller & Chait, 2008). When teachers are surveyed, they report that significant numbers of their colleagues are not high-quality teachers. In a report from the American Federation of Teachers (AFT) and the National Education Association (NEA) (1998), teachers say that about 5 percent of their colleagues are "poor teachers and should not remain in the classroom," and 21 percent of respondents "say that tenure is sometimes awarded to teachers who do not meet professional standards" (p. 8). Other studies confirm the 5 percent incompetent estimate, with some indicating that up to 10 percent of teachers may be marginal performers (Lavely, 1992; Menuey, 2005; Peterson, 2000; Tucker, 1997). Fifty-five percent of teachers surveyed in the Education Sector report say they know at least one teacher in their building who is ineffective (Duffett et al., 2008). While it is impossible to know what criteria these respondents use to judge competence, these numbers intimate that a sizable fraction of the teacher workforce may not meet standards of performance and effectiveness.[4] Although teachers, along with most other people, may have an intuitive sense of a normal distribution of quality and view about 3 percent of the population as at least two standard deviations below the mean, it is still incumbent on policymakers to help schools understand which teachers are falling well below the mean and why, so that personnel decisions and professional development can be targeted meaningfully. A distribution of teachers may be inevitable, but it is not inevitable that we will be unable to determine how and why teachers perform the way they do and use this information to guide personnel decisions, including assessment for tenure.

## A FRAMEWORK FOR THE APPRAISAL OF TEACHER TENURE

We organize our appraisal of prospects for tenure reform around Table 7.1. This framework proposes three perspectives on tenure: (1) in the formation of a teaching profession, (2) as an organizational process and capacity within schools and districts, and (3) as an administrative, quality-control function in staffing schools. These perspectives stand in some tension with one another yet partially share orientations to three key questions about teacher tenure: What is the purpose? Who should be involved, and in what ways? And What should be assessed, and in what ways?

### Table 7.1. Three Perspectives on Tenure

| | Professional Formation | Organizational Process | Administrative Function |
|---|---|---|---|
| Who is involved? | Organized teachers; professional associations | Teachers, district, administrators, parents, students | Local administrators; state policymakers |
| What are the tools of assessment? | Professional standards; observations; surveys; student outcomes | Professional standards; peer assistance and review; multiple sources of evidence, including practice and its outcomes | Value-added evidence; principal ratings; observations |
| What are the purposes and stakes? | Formation of the teaching profession | Organizational and individual improvement | Deselection; quality control |

## Tenure and the Formation of a Teaching Profession

We begin with a conception of tenure as a critical aspect in the formation of teaching as a profession. Teachers have a strong stake in the competence of their colleagues for two reasons. First, competence is required if schools are to be successful in educating all students. Rather than assuming that students learn from one teacher at a time, a professional perspective argues that students are the shared responsibility of a school staff functioning as a community. Teachers then have a stake in the competence of their colleagues because this affects their ability to be effective. Second, profession-wide competence supplies legitimacy to the profession as a whole, serving as an influence on the general public's perceptions of teachers. A perception of widespread incompetence undercuts the status and standing of the teaching profession and impedes its collective advancement.

A dual ambiguity surrounds tenure and the professional status of teachers. First, McDonnell (1991) identified a critical dilemma of teacher policy:

> The inability to measure teacher performance reliably and to collect relevant data cost-effectively remains one of the most serious problems associated with teacher policy. In fact, the greatest obstacle to states in their struggle to balance democratic control and professionalism may be the inability to resolve the questions of who should evaluate teachers and how they should be evaluated [p. 252].

Teaching is a state-sanctioned public profession with jurisdiction over the mandated attendance of students through which important public goals such as civic education for life in a democracy are pursued (Labaree, 1997). Consequently authority over teaching must involve public oversight and management. At the same time, a central ideological claim of professionalism in its historic development in the United States has been that complex work requires peer evaluation because relevant expertise is needed to make judgments about quality. Advocates who seek to develop professionalism in teaching insist that teachers must play a central role in standard setting and evaluation. Historically professional guilds have claimed jurisdiction over their membership, even if the historical record does not fully support the contention that guilds are genuinely self-policing. In teaching, however, control over the membership must balance public and professional aims, and the nature of this balance remains ambiguous and contested, as is the case today in most professional fields.

Education features a second ambiguity with respect to professional aspirations among teachers. The organization that represents teachers has become the union rather than the guild. Within the framework of labor law and labor-management relations, employee evaluation is the responsibility of management, not of labor. With the rise of teacher unionism beginning in the late 1950s, labor relations have placed responsibility for teacher evaluation squarely with administrators; this has become a sticking point in the efforts launched in the 1980s to create what has been termed the "new unionism" or "professional unionism" (Kerchner & Koppich, 1993; Kerchner, Koppich, & Weeres, 1997). Among the features of this development, organized teachers in some locales have begun to bargain for greater teacher involvement in evaluation. The initial foray of this kind emerged in Toledo, Ohio, in 1982, and continues to this day (Marshall, 2008). We describe this development in greater detail below, but here we note that the tension between unionism and professionalism is particularly sharp around the issue of teacher evaluation. Who shall evaluate teachers is a point of contention between administrators and teachers, unions and management. Both the NEA and the AFT support aspirations toward professionalism in teaching, but in many locales, the history of labor-management relations has ceded jurisdiction over tenure to administrators.

In the face of these ambiguities, vanguard teacher unions across the country have formed the Teacher Union Reform Network (TURN), which currently includes thirty-one districts representing over 40 percent of central city students (Marshall, 2008, p. 18). Many of these districts have followed the lead of Toledo in developing peer assistance and review (PAR) programs. The approach involves releasing master teachers full or part time to conduct evaluations of pretenure teachers and tenured teachers who are having difficulty. A committee composed of administrators and teachers reviews the evidence gathered by the master teachers and principals in making decisions about assistance that teachers need, and ultimately about the award of tenure. From the professional perspective, teachers have a stake in the tenure process and its outcomes, so they must be involved in making decisions about their own membership. PAR programs have created the framework, as bargained with management, for such involvement.

Equally important, evaluation in the professions involves attention to both standards of good practice and the results or outcomes of practice. As Fenstermacher and Richardson (2005) have argued, a distinction must be made between the task (a teacher tries to bring about learning in students) and achievement (students learn as a result of teaching) senses of quality. They note a conceptual affinity between such task achievement pairs as "selling-buying," "racing-winning," and "teaching-learning." With respect to such activity, what they refer to as discernment naturally requires attention to both task and achievement aspects of such activity. They write, "Successful teaching is teaching that yields the intended learning. Good teaching is teaching that comports with morally defensible and rationally sound principles of instructional practice" (p. 189). They argue that both aspects must be included in making determinations of quality. Articulating, establishing, and implementing such standards and principles requires involvement of teachers as arbiters. In particular, teachers must be involved in deliberations that discern the qualities of good teaching, even as they also must be held to reasonable account for their students' learning.

A recent research synthesis (Goe, Bell, & Little, 2008) on effective teaching supplies one version of this general point. The investigators first argue that *effectiveness* is a value-oriented term that requires a normative definition to guide measurement and evaluation. Based on the literature, these authors supply a five-point definition, wherein effective teachers:

- Have high expectations for all students and help students learn, as measured by value-added or other test-based growth measures, or by alternative measures.

- Contribute to positive academic, attitudinal, and social outcomes for students such as regular attendance, on-time promotion to the next grade, on-time graduation, self-efficacy and cooperative behavior.

- Use diverse resources to plan and structure engaging learning opportunities; monitor student progress formatively, adapting instruction as needed; and evaluate learning using multiple sources of evidence.

- Contribute to the development of classrooms and schools that value diversity and civic-mindedness.

- Collaborate with other teachers, administrators, parents, and education professionals to ensure student success, especially the success of students with special needs and those at high risk of failure [p. 8].

This example illustrates how normative elements mix with technical requirements in defining *effectiveness*. It favors the values of diversity and civic-mindedness, among others. Other definitions are possible of course, but our point is simply that the starting point is not a measure but a conception that necessarily conveys certain values.

This definition includes attention to student learning but also to standards of good practice that pertain to teaching itself. The definition is quite broad in indicating the complex responsibilities and duties of teachers together with the multiple outcomes they seek to achieve with students. Goe et al. (2008) describe seven methods of assessment: classroom observations, principal evaluations, instructional artifacts (for example, lesson plans, assignments, and scoring rubrics), portfolios, surveys of teachers, student surveys, and value-added models. Many of these approaches are reviewed in other chapters in this book.

The perspective of professional formation, then, reckons that the tenure decision has important implications for the development of the teaching profession. It argues that the tenure decision must include teachers in a central—but not sole or dominant—role and that teacher evaluation must employ a wide range of methods to discern qualities of teaching itself, as well as its multiple outcomes in student learning and development. If the public holds teachers responsible for teaching many different skills, beliefs, and behaviors, then it is necessary to measure teacher effectiveness using a broad range of outcomes that help us understand teachers' effectiveness in accomplishing all of their duties. For instance, a teacher may be excellent at instructing upper-elementary-school students in mathematics but be completely ineffective at cultivating principles of teamwork and respect for others. In this situation, her students may reach middle school knowing algebra, but they may get suspended for fighting with other students. Math knowledge and respect for others are both outcomes we expect to see in students, and both should be valued in the teacher assessment process.

## Tenure as an Organizational Process

A second perspective on tenure regards it not as an isolated personnel decision but as a complex organizational process, an important element in the overall management of human resources in districts and schools. Here, the focus is not on the profession but on the organization of work and the management of careers. From this vantage, the purpose of tenure is to improve the overall effectiveness of districts and schools in educating all students, as this includes effects on individuals and the organization itself. This perspective raises questions about the nature of management in education and the kind of organization that schools represent. While some management approaches favor command-and-control strategies that establish tenure as a managerial function, other approaches emphasize management's role in securing the commitment of workers to the organization and its ideals.

Schools may be conceived as bureaucratic organizations in which a managerial hierarchy prescribes, enacts, and enforces the rules, roles, and routines of school workers and students (Chubb & Moe, 1990). Or schools can be developed as professional organizations that manage the complexities of work through collegial interactions, workplace norms enforced by peer pressure, and many substitutes for leadership that support professional judgment, deprivatize practice, and work on the hard cases that practice presents (Weick & McDaniel, 1989). In this second conception, tenure is one element in clarifying organizational goals and in binding members to them.

Some might argue that the professional form of organization can be harmful to students, since inevitably some teachers will stay past their prime and drag down student achievement. In an effective teacher assessment system, however, teachers would be assessed throughout their tenured years by peers and administrators using a variety of methods intended to assess both the practice of teaching and its important outcomes. In conjunction with such organization-wide evaluations, teachers would have opportunities for professional development and additional training; in instances of continued subpar teaching, tenured teachers would be put on probation and then be dismissed if remediation efforts failed to improve his or her performance.

Tenure is an organizational process in several other ways. Conceived as a decision—a point in time—the aim is to reduce two types of error: admitting teachers who are or will become incompetent or dismissing teachers who are or may become competent. The larger issue, though, is how schools and districts organize processes that provide accurate feedback to teachers on where growth in teaching is needed and then supply the professional development that promotes such growth. A professional conception of tenure regards the process as part of a larger organizational campaign to develop human capital oriented around a mission, goals, and strategies for improvement. Teacher evaluation is an ongoing process that of necessity is linked to organizational processes that promote learning. Because many teachers locate careers in the classroom, teacher development over time is vital in improving the overall human capital available in districts and schools.

Tenure as an issue of organizational capacity raises equity concerns as well. Districts that offer advantages in salary and working conditions and have more efficient hiring practices can select the strongest candidates before other schools have the opportunity to do so. They are likely to have fewer problems with tenure than less-favored and less-well-organized districts. Recruitment, selection, placement, and support for new teachers interact with tenure processes to produce a qualified workforce in particular locales. Districts encountering difficulties in recruiting and selecting new teachers are likely to have more problematic tenure cases to contend with than more advantaged districts. In such cases, "tenure" misspecifies the problem whose origins may involve the relative lack of competitive wages, poor working and living conditions, or poor hiring practices. Sykes (1983) characterized the issue years ago as one of "screens and magnets." The absence of strong magnets and inefficient management practices contributes, along with weak screens, to limiting human capital and organizational capacity. If an underlying problem involves weak attractions for teaching in certain locales, then the solution requires improving incentives of various kinds—some combination of screens and magnets. Tenure reform then must be conceived in the broader context of human resource management and the systemic inequities that confer advantages on some districts while disadvantaging others. Such reform likely implicates state and federal policy along with local management practice and policy.

In their review of the teacher evaluation literature, Darling-Hammond, Wise, and Pease (1983) capture this perspective in identifying what they hypothesized are four minimal conditions for successful teacher evaluation:

- All actors in the system have a shared understanding of the criteria and processes for teacher evaluation.
- All actors understand how these criteria and processes relate to the dominant symbols of the organization, that is, there is a shared sense that they capture the

most important aspects of teaching, that the evaluation system is consonant with educational goals and conceptions of teaching work.

• Teachers perceive that the evaluation procedure enables and motivates them to improve their performance; and principals perceive that the procedure enables them to provide instructional leadership.

• All actors in the system perceive that the evaluation procedure allows them to strike a balance "between adaptation and adaptability, between stability to handle present demands and flexibility to handle unanticipated demands" (Weick, 1982, p. 674); that is, that the procedure achieves a balance between control and autonomy for the various actors in the system [p. 320].

Conceived as an organizational process or part of an overall strategy to build both individual and organizational capacity, tenure would employ multiple methods for evaluating teachers in order to represent a complex organization's processes and outcomes—that is, its means and ends. Such evaluation would involve all the major stakeholders in decision making in pursuit of a satisfactory balance in the tension between organizational control that administrators seek and the member commitment, development, and involvement that teachers seek.

## Tenure for Teacher Quality Control

A third perspective holds that tenure's primary purpose is to ensure quality control as a key managerial function. If the tenure process served to dismiss more teachers, student achievement would be positively affected (Gordon, Kane, & Staiger, 2006). For example, if estimates of incompetence in teaching range from 5 to 10 percent overall and if the current tenure process results in the dismissal of at most 1 percent of teachers, then there are many working teachers who may have negative effects on student achievement. Furthermore, if this gap is particularly large in districts serving concentrations of poor and minority students, then the equity argument for reforming tenure policy and practice is powerful.

Here, the emphasis is on developing procedures that result reliably in the dismissal of ineffective teachers. If such procedures are to be practical, they must not be costly, administratively complex and burdensome, or time-consuming. These considerations point strongly to making more central use of direct measures of a teacher's ability to produce student learning, in comparison with other teachers who have similar assignments (as related to such matters as class size, student characteristics, and other working conditions). In this reckoning, the primary purpose of tenure is quality control as it relates to the production of student achievement and other valued outcomes.

What has strengthened this perspective in recent years has been the development of new methods for attributing student growth in learning to individual teachers. One important class of such methods uses what are termed value-added models (VAM), which measure what value teachers add to student achievement from some entering baseline (see Chapter Nine for more information on these models). Gordon et al. (2006), among others, have made the case for this approach, and their analysis specifies how student test scores might be used to assess teachers in order to make personnel decisions. First, to address the recruitment problem, they recommend reducing barriers to entry based on certification status, arguing that measures of teacher qualifications bear little relationship to student achievement. Then they would use VAMs to identify teachers performing in the bottom quartile of student achievement over several years and base dismissal on this evidence. To retain some flexibility, principals might appeal such automatic decisions and seek waivers for teachers they deem worthy, but these teachers' low value-added scores would still be publicized. To bolster the process, state tenure laws would be revised to require dismissal if teachers did not demonstrate effectiveness in raising student achievement, as measured by VAM.

This argument goes on to recommend that a balance of subjective and objective measures be included in teacher evaluation, including principal ratings that have been shown to correlate broadly with teacher effectiveness (Jacob & Lefgren, 2008); that alternative and new evaluation methods be developed for teachers in nontested subjects and grade levels; that the state not control for gender, race, or class so that the same standards for all students might be maintained; that principals retain a strong role in evaluating teachers; and that comparisons among teachers be made not at the school level but rather at district or even state levels. Each of these proposals is intended to manage a range of practical difficulties in implementing a plan to orient tenure around teachers' contribution to student achievement.

While the proposal provides room for multiple measures and methods, including multiple evaluators, the critical element is the use of VAM in tested subjects to evaluate teachers. They propose that one-third to two-thirds of the weight in teacher evaluations be based on value-added estimates of effectiveness. Goldhaber and Hansen (2008) provide one explicit test of the value-added approach for teacher tenure, using comparisons of fifth-grade reading and math achievement among a small set of teachers in North Carolina. Their analysis suggests that the reliability of a teacher's scores from year to year over the first three years is relatively good for math but less so for reading. They also model a test for tenure by including either or both the math and reading scores, and find that this decision has a large impact on who receives tenure. If teachers fall into the lowest quintile in reading or math achievement, then 83 of 281 teachers (30 percent) in this sample would not receive tenure under the policy. If instead the tenure decision were based on teachers falling into the lowest quintile in both scores, then 31 of 281 teachers (11 percent) would be dismissed. These numbers simply suggest one of the many judgment calls needed in using VAMs for tenure decisions.

Ultimately they conclude that this small analysis provides comfort to both proponents and opponents of using value-added for tenure:

> Those opposed to the idea might point to the finding that the year-to-year correlations in teacher effects are modest, and that we cannot know the extent to which this reflects true fluctuations in performance or changes in class or school dynamics outside of a teacher's control [Goldhaber & Hansen, 2008, p. 10].

On the other hand, they also conclude:

> These inter-temporal estimates are very much in line with findings from other sectors of the economy that do use them for policy purposes. Perhaps more importantly, based simply on the percentage of teachers who move from the 4th to 5th year, it does not appear that schools are very selective in terms of which teachers receive tenure. Nevertheless, pre-tenure estimates of teacher job performance clearly do predict estimated post-tenure performance in both subjects, and would therefore seem to be a reasonable metric to use as a factor in making substantive teacher selection decisions [p. 10].

The emergence of new methods for assessing teacher effectiveness based on student achievement has given rise to a new policy proposal with respect to teacher tenure that would dismiss teachers in the first two to three years of teaching whose students fall in the bottom quartile or quintile of achievement. Such methods of evaluation would be established primarily by state policymakers and district administrators rather than through collaborative or negotiated processes that involve teachers more centrally. They would serve administrative purposes in gaining greater control over who is permitted to continue in teaching. Although VAMs would play a primary role, proponents could include other sources of evidence and even other models of evaluation for teachers not covered by tested subjects, among them, band teachers, vocational teachers, coaches, and special education teachers. In this manner, their proposal would stretch to cover the majority of teaching positions, maintain the role of judgment in the appraisal of teaching, and keep the system flexible to a degree. Still, this alternative might restrict organizational capacity by instituting a strong administrative control system around teaching rather than supporting greater professional controls and teacher involvement in the process.

## RECOMMENDATIONS FOR THE REFORM OF TEACHER TENURE

These contending perspectives on teacher tenure are represented in the APPLE criteria for standards of teacher effectiveness enunciated by James Kelly, founding executive director of the National Board for Professional Teaching

Standards. He argued that such standards must be **A**dministratively feasible, **P**rofessionally acceptable, **P**ublicly credible, **L**egally defensible, and **E**conomically affordable (Baratz-Snowden, 1991). These criteria imply that trade-offs are always necessary in pursuing standards for teaching. The perspectives identified in this chapter regarding the stakes, methods, and purposes of assessment for tenure help to illuminate the trade-offs. From the perspective of profession building, the tenure process must be acceptable to the profession and legally defensible. From the quality control perspective, the criteria associated with credibility, cost, and feasibility are paramount. On balance, we favor an approach that takes a broad view of the process in order to support professional formation and build organizational capacity.

Almost all arguments for tenure reform call for some kind of hybrid model that involves both the direct evaluation of teaching and the use of student learning outcomes. The differences are in the details—the relative emphasis placed on teaching (the task of teachers) or learning (student achievement outcomes). A judgment call is necessary here, and we favor more emphasis on the evaluation of teaching in its task sense than in its achievement sense. In part this judgment rests, as we have argued, on the importance of tenure to professional formation and organizational capacity rather than just on its administrative function in controlling quality. But this judgment also is based on an appraisal of VAMs for use in tenure, and here we must extend our argument.

A number of technical and practical problems confront the use of VAMs to measure teacher effectiveness. The technical complications of value-added modeling include selection bias, measurement error, missing data, and standard error problems (for greater detail, see Chapter Nine, this volume). For example, VAM does a poor job of accounting for students being placed in certain teachers' classrooms in a systematic way so that disproportionate numbers of high- or low-performing students end up in certain teachers' classes (J. Rothstein, 2008). Most student standardized tests were not developed to measure teacher effectiveness, and there is no evidence that the difference in questions on different grade-level tests equals the difference in achievement expected during that time period (Ballou, 2008). Other problems include student mobility between test administration points (Hanushek & Jorgenson, 1996), coteaching and other collaborations among teachers so that learning results are shared, models not accounting for student background and demographics (Tekwe et al., 2004), oversensitivity to class size of teachers, and a range of validity and reliability issues (Amrein-Beardsley, 2008).

Even if the technical issues are remedied, there are potentially serious unintended consequences that may come about in employing standardized test scores to determine teacher tenure, not least that teachers may begin to behave as if the tested subjects and tested material are all that they are responsible for. In a test-based assessment system, teachers may narrow the curriculum to specific subjects, such as reading and math. In turn, they may then focus on specific topics that are tested and further still on specific items that appear regularly on tests. Standardized tests can only assess a sample of the knowledge we want students to have, and using these tests as the foundation for teacher assessment for tenure might convince teachers that this sample encompasses the whole of what we want teachers to teach. Rather, public school teachers in America are charged with developing citizens, instilling work ethic and self-confidence, teaching tolerance and kindness, and teaching subjects that are rarely tested regularly, such as social studies, art, music, and health (see R. Rothstein, Jacobsen, & Wilder, 2008, for elaboration). And if we return to the definition of teacher effectiveness proposed by Goe et al. (2008), three of their five points are not included at all in a regime oriented largely around the production of student achievement and related measures. We concur with their argument that a normative definition of teacher effectiveness should guide measurement rather than let measurement determine the definition of effectiveness.

Already in the high-stakes testing environment shaped by No Child Left Behind, schools are trimming their courses of study, reducing or eliminating important subjects, and deemphasizing the less easily measured goals associated with citizenship and human development (Center on Education Policy, 2009). In addition, as Campbell's law predicts,[5] evidence suggests that teachers in a high-stakes testing context will begin to deform standards of learning through such practices as drilling students on how to answer questions in the ''right'' way, how to give formulaic answers that will meet the criteria used in the scoring rubrics (Koretz, 2002), and even cheating (by giving students hints, letting them see the test beforehand, or even changing students' answers before submitting their tests). We worry that if the accountability stakes are further increased to implicate employment and job security, such adverse consequences will increase, along with perverse incentives to avoid teaching students who present learning difficulties or other challenges. In such case, dismissal procedures could have grave consequences for equity by making it even more difficult to recruit and retain teachers in hard-to-staff schools.

Other analysts also have concerns about the effects of more stringent dismissal policies on long-term recruitment to teaching. Traditionally the occupation has relied on job security in its mix of recruitment inducements (Lortie, 1975). If job security is compromised by a higher dismissal rate, then recruitment might suffer, at least for those intending long stays in teaching. In their proposal, Gordon et al. (2006) couple reduced standards for entry with enhanced dismissal procedures that rely substantially on VAMs. They argue that in this manner, recruitment to teaching will not suffer. We argue, however, that reducing or eliminating standards for entry in order to boost recruitment looks to be dangerous and irresponsible. There is a standard of safe practice that must be established to protect the public. Although current state certification policy may not be functioning to meet this standard, the proper response is not to do away with certification but rather to strengthen and improve it. The other possible response to the problem would be to raise wages considerably to help offset the presumed adverse impact that stringent dismissal would have on recruitment, where "stringent" has been pegged to the bottom fourth (Gordon et al., 2006) or the bottom fifth (Goldhaber & Hansen, 2008) of the teacher effectiveness distribution. This would add substantially to the costs of education while yielding uncertain overall effects on recruitment when paired with a strict tenure policy. For all these reasons, we recommend caution coupled with active experimentation in the use of VAMs for making tenure decisions.

The evidence suggests a gap between the incidence of dismissal and of incompetence in the teacher workforce, and this serves as one target for the reform of tenure. One useful framework may be found in the analysis by Toch and Rothman (2008), who set forth some sound guiding principles for teacher evaluation: (1) the use of explicit standards; (2) multiple measures of teacher quality and effectiveness; (3) teamwork, where teachers are evaluated by multiple stakeholders that might include peers, administrators, parents, and students; and (4) connection to professional development and opportunities to make improvements in teaching. These principles suggest a systematic approach that emphasizes organizational capacity within which teacher career development is stressed.

Already, districts have available to them Praxis III teaching standards that are based on "teaching strategies and behaviors that research linked to student success," which were formulated for teacher evaluation by Charlotte Danielson (Toch & Rothman, 2008, p. 4). Connecticut and California have developed teaching standards for use in their licensure systems based on the pioneering work of the National Board for Professional Teaching Standards. The first principle then requires explicit standards of good teaching that reference the task conception of the practice, including its moral and civic dimensions. Without explicit standards, evaluation procedures are unlikely to serve their professional and capacity-building functions. With appropriate use, such standards can serve to direct and focus districtwide attention on what is valued most in teaching and on what commitments and competence are called for.

But there is a need for research and development in how to assemble multiple methods of teacher evaluation for use in tenure procedures. All parties agree that evidence of student learning is necessary in teacher evaluation; how to measure such evidence and weigh it relative to other kinds of evidence is the issue. Recently developed methods include teacher portfolios, as used, for example, in National Board Certification and in Connecticut's Beginner Educator Support and Training program; and new classroom observations systems. For example, Pianta and Hamre (2009) developed the Classroom Assessment Scoring System for use across the grade levels, which evaluates global classroom quality on three dimensions: emotional supports, classroom organization, and instructional supports. In addition, Danielson (1996) developed the Framework for Teaching Observation Survey, based on the Educational Testing Service's Praxis III exam, to measure effectiveness throughout teachers' careers. As with the process-product studies from a prior era (Brophy & Good, 1986) such instruction emphasizes general or generic features of effective classrooms. The more recent emphasis on content knowledge and "pedagogical content knowledge" (Shulman, 1987) suggests that other instruments and protocols might be needed to get at issues of how content is represented, but the larger point is that new evaluation systems that merge evidence about the quality of teaching together with evidence on a range of outcomes are needed in order to reflect the complexities of teaching in the face of multiple goals.

Toch and Rothman's (2008) third principle, concerning teamwork and improved opportunities for teacher learning, leads to a closer consideration of peer assistance and review. Here, an examination of the Toledo Plan, which has been in near-continuous operation since 1982, provides one assessment. As a rust belt city facing hard times, Toledo is a midsized urban district educating substantial numbers of poor children, and it can serve as an important case study. The details of the Toledo plan are well known. The reform came about through negotiations between the Toledo Federation of Teachers and the district. It involves selecting and training a cadre of veteran teachers who serve full time for three years as consultants, receiving an extra salary supplement. These consultants evaluate novice teachers in their first year based on a set of district standards, issuing ratings of outstanding, satisfactory, or unsatisfactory. Overall, the consulting teachers spend upwards of fifty to seventy hours annually observing and providing verbal and written feedback to new teachers. In the second year, principals rate the novice teachers as well, using the same standards and criteria, and these dual ratings are submitted to an interim review board composed of teachers and administrators who make tenure recommendations to the superintendent and ultimately the school board. Some evidence suggests that the Toledo system has not changed much since it was initiated, indicating that one component of a peer review system in a reform bargaining context might need to be regular evaluations of the system itself, perhaps making changes every five years or so based on what has worked and what has not (see Chapter Six, this volume, for more on the Toledo system).

PAR has not been subject to rigorous evaluation that establishes facts and pins down causal relations, but some details illustrate its promise (Marshall,

2008). Through 2003, 80 percent of all Toledo teachers had participated in the plan, and from its inception to 2004, some four hundred teachers were dismissed, including forty-nine veteran teachers. In the five years prior to the plan, the district had terminated one teacher. When the district suspended the reform over an unrelated contract dispute in 1995–1996, Toledo dismissed no teachers. The PAR system was subsequently reinstated, based on strong support from teachers and administrators. Toch and Rothman (2008) provide an estimate that ''about 10 percent of new teachers fail peer review and leave the school system, not a small percentage'' (p. 13), but the numbers of tenured teachers who are dismissed under PAR programs are still quite small. Missing are systematic evaluations of the effects of PAR programs that now exist in such locales as Rochester, New York; Columbus, Ohio, Minneapolis, Minnesota; and others. What does seem clear, though, is that pretenure dismissal rates tend to be higher under PAR programs than under traditional administrative procedures.

Koppich (2005) adds to a favorable review of PAR in her study, noting, ''After about a year with peer review, both teachers and administrators become enthusiasts. Teachers view the support they receive as crucial and administrators come to recognize that teacher peer reviewers are able to provide the colleagues with whom they work far more intensive and targeted assistance than principals can''(p. 23). A study conducted by the AFT and NEA (American Federation of Teachers/National Education Association, 1998) also found that teachers valued peer review and the support that it provided within the assessment process.

We favor PAR-oriented tenure reform based on the principles set forth by Toch and Rothman (2008). Explicit teaching standards are essential, coupled with multiple measures for evaluating teaching according to the standards. Evidence of student learning should be one component of the model. Such evidence might include VAM, but it should also incorporate other measures and indications of student learning, as well as evaluations from students and parents where practicable. We imagine that multiple models based on these principles might be developed and tested, serving as an important topic for research and development in the future. Gordon et al. (2006) call for federally funded pilot tests of their ideas in ten states, an acknowledgment that many details must be worked out and that no single best system exists at present. We agree with this recommendation but would place less emphasis on VAM and more on locally negotiated plans that involve peer assessment as a critical hallmark of professionalism. Several districts already have used standards-based systems to assess teachers, and some evidence indicates the promise. For example, Kimball, White, Milanowski, and Borman (2004) found that in one district where Danielson's (1996) Framework for Teaching was used to assess teachers, these measures were positively and significantly related to student achievement gains in four out of nine grade-test combinations.

New models might explore a variety of features, including the weight they place on VAM-derived student outcomes. Teachers and administrators in local districts should negotiate these programs in order to capitalize on the resources, needs, and goals of individual locales. In addition, teachers should be involved in the planning, implementation, and review of evaluation systems. We also recommend that experiments with tenure reform be evaluated not simply on dismissal rates but as part of larger human capital strategies that enhance the teaching profession while building organizational capacity. Teacher evaluation for tenure involves implicit, if not explicit, consequences for teacher morale, commitment, responsibility, and knowledge, making research into these results essential in the quest for models that work best.

In conclusion, we advocate models of assessment for tenure that attend to the full goals of education, acknowledge the complex nature of teaching, incorporate teachers into the evaluation process, and seek to improve, before dismissing them, teachers who may not yet meet professional standards or reliably produce student learning.

## Notes

1. The term *teacher effectiveness* has come to be associated with a teacher's capacity or ability to produce growth in student achievement or learning. Another term, *teacher quality*, has come to be associated with the qualifications a teacher possesses, such as a state teaching license, a master's degree, or National Board Certification. While considerable research has explored relationships among various kinds of qualifications and teacher effectiveness, more recent research using value-added methods has provided direct measures of a teacher's ability to promote growth in student learning. In this chapter, we use the first term to indicate a teacher's capacity to promote growth in student learning.

2. There is a distinction between academic credentials and academic ability. Credentials are not always the best measure of academic ability, which has been shown to be associated with student outcomes of certain kinds.

3. Such a finding might vary over time by teacher era, but the contemporary studies cannot confirm this possibility. It is worth noting that the more recent research measuring teacher effectiveness (rather than teacher academic ability or credentials) challenges the earlier account of natural selection by lack of academic ability.

4. It would be valuable to compare the incidence of incompetence between occupations that feature tenure protections and those that do not. The most relevant comparison would be with education sectors where teachers work on renewable term contracts that permit wider latitude for dismissal for cause. Such sectors include private schools, charter schools, and a considerable fraction of faculty in higher education. But we located no rigorous studies around such comparisons so did not pursue this question.

5. The research methodologist Donald Campbell made the prediction, in the form of a "law," that "the more any quantitative social indicator is used for social decision-making, the more subject it will be to corruption pressures, and the more apt it will be to distort and corrupt the social processes it was intended to monitor" (cited in Nichols and Berliner, 2007, pp. 26–27).

# REFERENCES

American Federation of Teachers/National Education Association. (1998). *Peer assistance and peer review: An AFT/NEA handbook.* Washington, DC: Author.

Amrein-Beardsley, A. (2008). Methodological concerns about the education value-added assessment system. *Educational Researcher, 37*(2), 65–75.

Ballou, D. (2008, April 22–24). *Test scaling and value-added measurement.* Paper presented at the National Conference on Value-Added Modeling, Madison, WI.

Baratz-Snowden, J. (1991). Performance assessments for identifying excellent teachers: The National Board for Professional Teaching Standards charts its research and development course. *Journal of Personnel Evaluation in Education, 5*(2), 133–145.

Boyd, D., Grossman, P., Lankford, H., Loeb, S., & Wyckoff, J. (2007). *Who leaves? Teacher attrition and student achievement.* Washington, DC: Urban Institute.

Boyd, D., Lankford, H., Loeb, S., & Wyckoff, J. (2005). Explaining the short careers of high-achieving teachers in schools with low-performing students. *American Economic Review, 95*(2), 166–171.

Bridges, E. (1990). Evaluation for tenure and dismissal. In J. Millman & L. Darling-Hammond (Eds.), *The new handbook of teacher evaluation: Assessing elementary and secondary teachers.* Thousand Oaks, CA: Sage.

Brophy, J., & Good, T. (1986). Teacher behavior and student achievement. In M. Wittrock (Ed.), *Handbook of research on teaching* (pp. 328–375). New York: Macmillan.

Center on Education Policy. (2009). *Lessons from the classroom level about federal and state accountability in Rhode Island and Illinois.* Washington, DC: Author.

Chubb, J., & Moe, T. (1990). *Politics, markets, and America's schools.* Washington, DC: Brookings Institution.

Danielson, C. (1996). *Enhancing professional practice: A framework for teaching.* Alexandria, VA: Association of Supervision and Curriculum Development.

Darling-Hammond, L., Wise, A. E., & Pease, S. R. (1983). Teacher evaluation in the organizational context: A review of the literature. *Review of Educational Research, 53*(3), 285–328.

Duffett, A., Farkas, S., Rotherham, A. J., & Silva, E. (2008). *Waiting to be won over: Teachers speak on the profession, unions, and reform.* Washington, DC: Education Sector.

Ehrenberg, R., & Brewer, D. (1994). Do school and teacher characteristics matter? *Economics of Education Review, 13*(1), 78–99.

Fenstermacher, G., & Richardson, V. (2005). On making determinations of quality in teaching. *Teachers College Record, 107*(1), 186–213.

Goe, L., Bell, C., & Little, O. (2008). *Approaches to evaluating teacher effectiveness: A research synthesis*. Chicago: National Comprehensive Center for Teacher Quality.

Goldhaber, D., Gross, B., & Player, D. (2007). *Are public schools really losing their "best"? Assessing the career transitions of teachers and their implications for the quality of the teacher workforce*. Washington, DC: Urban Institute.

Goldhaber, D., & Hansen, M. (2008). *Assessing the potential of using value-added estimates of teacher job performance for making tenure decisions*. Seattle: University of Washington.

Gordon, R., Kane, T. J., & Staiger, D. O. (2006). *Identifying effective teachers using performance on the job*. Washington, DC: Brookings Institution.

Hanushek, E. A., & Jorgenson, D. W. (1996). *Improving America's schools: The role of incentives*. Washington, DC: National Academies Press.

Hanushek, E. A., & Rivkin, S. G. (2008). *Do disadvantaged urban schools lose their best teachers?* Washington, DC: Urban Institute.

Holmstedt, R. (1932). *A study of the effects of the teacher tenure law in New Jersey*. New York: Teachers College.

Jacob, B. A., & Lefgren, L. (2008). Can principals identify effective teachers? Evidence on subjective performance evaluation in education. *Journal of Labor Economics, 26*(1), 101–136.

Kane, T. J., Rockoff, J. E., & Staiger, D. O. (2008). What does certification tell us about teacher effectiveness? Evidence from New York City. *Economics of Education Review, 27*(6), 615–631.

Kerchner, C. T., & Koppich, J. E. (1993). *A union of professionals: Labor relations and educational reform*. New York: Teachers College Press.

Kerchner, C. T., Koppich, J. E., & Weeres, J. G. (1997). *United mind workers: Unions and teaching in the knowledge society*. San Francisco: Jossey-Bass.

Kimball, S. M., White, B., Milanowski, A. T., & Borman, G. (2004). Examining the relationship between teacher evaluation and student assessment results in Washoe County. *Peabody Journal of Education, 79*(4), 54–78.

Koppich, J. E. (2005). Addressing teacher quality through induction, professional compensation, and evaluation: The effects on labor-management relations. *Educational Policy, 19*(1), 90–111.

Koretz, D. (2002). Limitations in the use of achievement tests as measures of educators' productivity. *Journal of Human Resources, 37*(4), 752–777.

Labaree, D. (1997). Public goods, private goods: The American struggle over educational goals. *American Education Research Journal, 34*(1), 39–81.

Lavely, C. (1992). Actual incidence of incompetent teachers. *Educational Research Quarterly, 15*(2), 11–14.

Levin, J. A., Mulhern, J., & Schunck, J. (2005). *Unintended consequences: The case for reforming the staffing rules in urban teachers union contracts*. New York: New Teacher Project.

Lortie, D. C. (1975). *Schoolteacher: A sociological study* (2nd ed.). Chicago: University of Chicago Press.

Marshall, R. (2008). *The case for collaborative school reform. The Toledo experience.* Washington, DC: Economic Policy Institute.

McDonnell, L. (1991). Ideas and values in implementation analysis: The case of teacher policy. In A. Odden (Ed.), *Education policy implementation* (pp. 241–258). Albany: State University of New York Press.

Menuey, B. P. (2005). Teachers' perceptions of professional incompetence and barriers to the dismissal process. *Journal of Personnel Evaluation in Education, 18,* 309–325.

Miller, R., & Chait, R. (2008). *Teacher turnover, tenure policies, and the distribution of teacher quality: Can high poverty schools catch a break?* Washington, DC: Center for American Progress.

Murnane, R. J., Singer, J. D., Willett, J. B., Kemple, J. J., & Olsen, R. J. (1991). *Who will teach? Policies that matter.* Cambridge, MA: Harvard University Press.

Nichols, S., & Berliner, D. (2007). *Collateral damage. How high-stakes testing corrupts America's schools.* Cambridge, MA: Harvard Education Press.

Pianta, R., & Hamre, B. (2009). Conceptualization, measurement, and improvement of classroom processes: Standardized observation can leverage capacity. *Educational Researcher, 38*(2), 109–119.

Peterson, K. D. (2000). *Teacher evaluation: A comprehensive guide to new directions and practices* (2nd ed.). Thousand Oaks, CA: Corwin Press.

Rice, J. M. (1893). *The public-school system of the United States.* New York: Century.

Rivkin, S. G., Hanushek, E. A., & Kain, J. F. (2005). Teachers, schools, and academic achievement. *Econometrica, 73*(2), 417–458.

Rothstein, J. (2008). *Student sorting and bias in value added estimation: Selection on observables and unobservables.* Princeton University and NBER.

Rothstein, R., Jacobsen, R., & Wilder, T. (2008). *Grading education: Getting accountability right.* New York: Teachers College Press.

Sanders, W. L., & Rivers, J. C. (1996). *Cumulative and residual effects of teachers on future student academic achievement.* Knoxville: University of Tennessee Value-Added Research and Assessment Center.

Schlechty, P. C., & Vance, V. S. (1981). Do academically able teachers leave education? The North Carolina case. *Phi Delta Kappan, 63*(2), 106–112.

Schlechty, P. C., & Vance, V. S. (1983). Recruitment, selection, and retention: The shape of the teaching force. *Elementary School Journal, 83*(4), 469–487.

Scott, C. W. (1934). *Indefinite teacher tenure: A critical study of the historical, legal, operative, and comparative aspects.* New York: Teachers College.

Shulman, L. (1987). Knowledge and teaching: Foundations of the new reform. *Harvard Educational Review, 57*(1), 1–22.

Sykes, G. (1983). Public policy and the problem of teacher quality: The need for screens and magnets. In L. Shulman & G. Sykes (Eds.), *Handbook of teaching and policy* (pp. 97–125). New York: Longman.

Tekwe, C. D., Carter, R. L., Ma, C. X., Algina, J., Lucas, M. E., Roth, J., et al. (2004). An empirical comparison of statistical models for value-added assessment of school performance. *Journal of Educational and Behavioral Statistics, 29*(1), 11.

Toch, T., & Rothman, R. (2008). *Rush to judgment: Teacher evaluation in public education.* Washington, DC: Education Sector.

Tucker, P. D. (1997). Lake Wobegon: Where all teachers are competent (or, have we come to terms with the problem of incompetent teachers?). *Journal of Personnel Evaluation in Education, 11*(2), 103–126.

Urban, W. J. (1982). *Why teachers organized.* Detroit: Wayne State University Press.

Weick, K. E. (1982). Administering education in loosely coupled schools. *Phi Delta Kappan, 63*(10), 673–676.

Weick, K. E., & McDaniel, R. (1989). How professional organizations work: Implications for school organization and management. In T. J. Sergiovanni & J. H. Moore (Eds.), *Schooling for tomorrow: Directing reforms to issues that count* (pp. 330–355). Needham Heights, MA: Allyn and Bacon.

Weisberg, D., Sexton, S., Mulhern, J., & Keeling, D. (2009). *The widget effect: Our national failure to acknowledge and act on differences in teacher effectiveness.* New York: New Teacher Project. Retrieved August 15, 2009, from http://widgeteffect.org/downloads/TheWidgetEffect.pdf.

# CHAPTER EIGHT

# Approaches to Annual Performance Assessment

Mary M. Kennedy

*Michigan State University*

T here used to be a popular expression about not knowing anything about art but knowing what you liked. The implication was that one needed no specialized knowledge to appreciate art. A similar claim could be made about teaching. Few people believe they need specialized training to tell good teaching from bad, and virtually every parent and every student has strong feelings about the quality of teaching they encounter as they or their children move through the school system. Everyone can recognize good teaching when they see it.

Everyone, that is, except school administrators, who have been struggling for an entire century to devise strategies for defining and measuring teaching practice and for discriminating between good teaching and bad. Throughout this century, they have tinkered with a variety of checklists, forms, rating scales, and measurements of all sorts and have yet to achieve a consensus on either definition or procedure. Even the language we have used to describe good teaching has changed over time. At the beginning of the twentieth century, when industrial efficiency was a new and fashionable concept, school administrators sought teachers who were efficient. Then they sought teachers who were virtuous. Then teachers who were not neurotic. Later in the century, they sought teachers who had specific competencies, and toward the end of it, they sought professionalism and expertise. Today we tend to want teachers who meet professional standards.

These changes in terminology illustrate the variety of ways people have thought about teaching over the century. But they reflect changes in fashion more than changes in the underlying concepts. For example, teachers evaluation forms ostensibly assessing efficiency often included virtues, and those assessing competencies included some items that look like contemporary standards. So while the century has seen many changes in terminology and methods of documentation, it has nearly always incorporated into these terms a wide variety of competing, and sometimes even contradictory, criteria for teaching quality.

We face two central problems. One is that we actually hold numerous public values, or criteria for defining teaching quality, and sometimes they contradict one another. As a society, we want our youngsters to learn particular content, but we also want them to be nurtured, to be developed into good citizens, and to be motivated to participate productively in society. We want teachers to be role models for moral and ethical behavior and to create positive climates for learning in their classrooms, but we also want them to be efficient and goal oriented. We want teachers to treat all children equally, but we also want them to respond to each child's unique needs. We want them to be caring and nurturing, but we also want them to be rigorous and demanding. We want them to cultivate cooperation in students, yet enable them to compete in later life. These different ideas wax and wane in their social popularity, and they strain the education system. When they get translated into formal assessment instruments, it should be no surprise that they lack coherence or consistency. This is the problem of accommodating public values.

The second problem is that as an enterprise, teaching events have meanings that are difficult to capture on a form. No matter which public value we choose to evaluate, we quickly discover that we cannot directly see it. It must be inferred from sequences and patterns of events. Gergen (1982) gives a useful example of this problem. He invites us to imagine ourselves at a party, and across the room, we see Ross touch Laura's hair. Gergen asks what action we have actually observed. We are not illuminated to know that Ross's hand moved at a particular velocity along a particular trajectory. We need to know what the action *means*, what its significance is. If Ross recently said he loved Laura, we might infer that his touch was an act of affection. If Ross and Laura had recently had an argument, perhaps the gesture was an act of derision. If they had just met, perhaps it was flirtatious. Or perhaps it was merely an effort to flick off a piece of lint. Gergen's point is that meaning derives from our knowledge of history and context. If we know these other things, we can interpret the gesture. And we continue to reconstruct the meaning of events as we gather more information. Does Laura brush his hand away or smile warmly at him? Each new piece of information we obtain about these two people adds new layers of meaning to this brief action.

Meaning by itself is not difficult to infer, but it is very difficult to infer if we want an objective evaluation, one that multiple observers would agree on. The problem is that while two observers could agree that a touch occurred, thus giving us interrater agreement, they would likely infer different meanings from the event, especially if they were privy to different subsets of historical or contextual information. The problem we face when evaluating teaching practices is that we need, on one side, to capture the meaning of events, yet at the same time, we need to ensure that our instruments meet standards of fairness, reliability, and objectivity. This is the problem of balancing meaning and objectivity. We seek an approach to evaluation that allows us to evaluate the meaning of events, but to do so reasonably objectively.

The combination of these two problems has made teacher assessment an especially perplexing problem. My aim in this chapter is to review our century-long history of efforts to solve these two problems: the problem of accommodating public values and the problem of balancing attention to objectivity with attention to meaning. This history reveals a persistent, century-long tendency to overlook the intellectual core of teaching itself. Our efforts to accommodate public values have focused on nearly every aspect of teaching except its intellectual purpose, and our efforts to generate reliable and objective instruments have similarly overlooked the intellectual work of teaching and learning.

This is not to say that we have made no progress, for we have. Our efforts to accommodate public values have progressed from an early focus on the personal qualities of teachers as individuals—their dress, friendliness, virtue, and so forth—to a focus on what they actually do. In regard to the second problem, we have progressed from highly judgmental, high-inference rating scales to our current reliance on performance rubrics. The two shifts, from personal qualities to practice and from rating scales to performance rubrics, are substantial, and they make it possible for us to now look at the intellectual work of teaching.

## ACCOMMODATING PUBLIC VALUES

During this past century, Americans have embraced several different conceptions of the Good Teacher, and teacher educators have tried to give clarity to these conceptions. One early attempt (Charters & Waples, 1929) came up with these twenty-five essential qualities: Adaptability, Attractiveness, Breadth of Interest, Carefulness, Consideration, Cooperation, Dependability, Enthusiasm, Fluency, Forcefulness, Good Judgment, Health, Honesty, Industry, Leadership, Magnetism, Neatness, Open-Mindedness, Originality, Progressiveness,

Promptness, Refinement, Scholarship, Self-Control, and Thrift. Teachers, in other words, had to do better than Boy Scouts.

This list is revealing for several reasons. One is that it is a list of qualities of teach*ers,* not qualities of teach*ing.* Another is that it is a very long list and represents a remarkable diversity of ideas. In fact, these ideals may be incompatible. Is it possible for one individual to be both dependable and adaptable, for instance, or might adaptability lead to some lapses in dependability? Is it possible to be both enthusiastic and also self-controlled, or might one's enthusiasm trigger lapses in self-control? Some of these qualities, such as neatness, good judgment, promptness, and self-control, suggest a great interest in propriety, something Waller (1932/1961) commented on in his early analysis of teachers. But other qualities, such as forcefulness, magnetism, and open-mindedness, suggest a personality that may occasionally be unconventional and even controversial. These early documents contain no discussion or even recognition of potential contradictions among valued qualities of teachers. In that sense, they represent public values, which are frequently contradictory, far more than they represent the kind of a rational, internally consistent model of teaching with explicit constructs that can be measured. And in fact, Charters and Waples's intention was to capture public values. Their list was generated from interviews with parents, teachers, administrators, and teacher educators. It was not intended to be a list of precise terms but rather a list of valued qualities.

A look at the teacher assessments in use during that early period reveals a shorter list of qualities, but also numerous variations on each themes, thus suggesting a lack of precision. Nearly all early evaluations took the form of rating scales — that is, teachers were rated as good, fair, poor, and so forth on a list of qualities. Some qualities consisted of character traits, like those listed by Charters and Waples, while others resided in teaching practice itself. As is the case today, each district created its own assessment form, and they were quite various. Occasionally someone would survey school districts to learn what criteria they were using. One such early survey (Boyce, 1915) found that the most frequently evaluated qualities were these, listed in order of the percentage of rating forms that included them:

37 percent discipline

23 percent instructional skill

23 percent cooperation and loyalty

22 percent scholarship and education (this refers to their educational background, not their personal inclinations)

Although this list looks relatively parsimonious, notice that none of these criteria appeared in even half the rating systems. Most appeared in fewer than a quarter of them, suggesting very little agreement about criteria for defining teaching quality. Boyce also found references to dozens of other criteria: planning and method, personality, professional interest, manner, voice, daily preparation, accuracy and promptness, attitude toward criticism, appearance, health, routine, attitude toward work, attitude toward pupils, character, tact, housekeeping, and more. The list, in both its variety of criteria and low rates of redundancy, reminds us again that there are numerous ways to recognize a good teacher and that our public values are tremendously multifaceted.

Boyce was not alone in trying to forge a consensus during the early twentieth century. There was far more attention to the question of what qualities we value than there was to how to measure them precisely. The problem of defining good teaching was not one of precision or reliability, but rather one of achieving consensus about which qualities were most important. Yet despite these efforts to forge a consensus, rating scales continued to be various, with occasional literature reviews and hand-wringing about what was being learned from them (see, for example, Butsch, 1931). Even by midcentury, authors despaired at their lack of knowledge about what really made for a good teacher. For example, Ryans (1949) lamented that school people routinely go through motions such as interviewing job candidates and evaluating teachers as if they could recognize a good teacher when they saw one, but in fact, they lacked real knowledge about how to recognize a good teacher.

Even by midcentury, the field had failed to achieve consensus. In 1945, Reavis and Cooper examined eighty-five local rating scales and tallied the number of items that fell into each of seven general categories of values. Their tallies looked like this:

- 329 items evaluating social relations (for example, appearance, tact, loyalty, relations with students, leadership, tolerance, courtesy, participation in community activities, cooperativeness)

- 298 items evaluating instructional skill (for example, presenting lessons, remedial instruction, questioning, evaluating, making assignments, preparing lessons)

- 229 items evaluating personal characteristics (for example, emotions, morality, appearance, attitude, judgment, honesty, humor, use of English)

- 217 items evaluating noninstructional school service (for example, clerical work, safeguarding supplies, extracurricular activities, discipline and guidance)

- 168 items evaluating professional qualifications (for example, level of education, philosophy of education, knowledge of subject, professional attitude)

- 152 items evaluating habits of work (for example, initiative, punctuality, resourcefulness, efficiency, dependability, originality, ability to plan and organize)

- 146 items evaluating pupil results (for example, pupil initiative, response, participation, habits, spirit, attention, participation in classroom control)

Most of these efforts to survey the field were intended to find common ground rather than to critique current practice. The first survey I found that critically examined the content of these instruments appeared in Wood and Pohland (1979). Their analysis focused not on whole instruments, but instead on the 1,928 discrete items contained in their sample of instruments, and they raised questions about the content they found. First, they noticed that only a relatively small fraction of items had to do specifically with teaching itself; most had to do with personal qualities, class management, citizenship within the school, or other relatively tangential qualities. Second, they pointed out that the particular personal qualities itemized tended to emphasize conformity with the status quo rather than striving for improvement. For example, the rating forms included criteria such as punctuality, dependability, and loyalty rather than criteria such as creativity, leadership, or initiative.

So for more than half of the twentieth century, local efforts to evaluate teachers could be characterized by these important features. First, they incorporated a wide range of valued qualities, most of which were very general qualities and not well defined. Second, they were remarkably various and remarkably idiosyncratic with respect to the particular qualities they included. Third, many, if not most, of the qualities referred to the teachers' personality or moral character rather than to teaching practices. And finally, the scoring systems relied heavily on subjective judgment. The heavy attention to teachers' decorum and moral character suggests that teachers were expected to convey proper behavior more than substantive ideas.

## BALANCING OBJECTIVITY AND MEANINGFULNESS

The second problem we confront in devising performance assessments is developing evaluation forms that are sufficiently objective that multiple observers would document the same thing when they watched the same teacher and yet sensitive enough to capture meaningful events in the classroom. The problem of objectively recognizing good teaching was also apparent relatively early in the twentieth century, almost as soon as evaluation systems were first developed. As researchers began to examine these local efforts, they found not only that district-based rating forms were quite various in their content (Boyce, 1915; King, 1925), but also that they were quite various in their ability to predict student achievement gains (Hill, 1921), and they suffered from very low interrater agreements (Barr, 1929). In effect, these rating scales formalized the kind of ad hoc recognizing that parents and others do when they meet or observe teachers. Supervisors believed they could recognize good teachers when they saw them, but different supervisors noticed and valued different things. Their rating sheets simply captured on paper their subjective and impressionistic judgments. In one early study, Barr (1924) asked teacher supervisors what they looked for when evaluating teachers and obtained 131 different qualities from about a hundred supervisors. Significantly, over half of these qualities were mentioned by only one person, suggesting that the ability to recognize good teaching was distinctly idiosyncratic.

Perhaps because early attention was focused on the problem of sorting out values and agreeing on a set of criteria for good teaching, attention to the measurement properties of teacher evaluation instruments was postponed until the second half of the twentieth century, when researchers began to suspect that the problem of teacher assessment lay in the instrumentation and scoring procedures rather than in the criteria themselves. They made a distinction between high-inference instruments, meaning those that required a high degree of subjective judgment on the part of the observer, and low-inference instruments, meaning items that used carefully worded prompts to reduce ambiguity and reduce the need for interpretation, and they began to develop new low-inference techniques for observing teaching. These instruments forced observers to check off or tally discrete behavioral events rather than rating global impressions, thus increasing the likelihood that two observers would agree about what they just saw. Use of these instruments greatly increases the likelihood that two observers would rate a given event in the same way. Exhibits 8.1 and 8.2 illustrate these two approaches to assessment. Each example is a small portion of an evaluation form.

Exhibit 8.1 comes from an early rating system used by the Oakland school system. The criteria themselves are very broad, and the rater is given substantial latitude in judging the teacher on each of these criteria. At that time, it was assumed that the qualities of good teaching were self-evident, so that anyone could fill out such a form without being trained. Anyone could recognize a good teacher when they saw one. Exhibit 8.2 comes from a system used by the state of Florida from the 1980s until the early 2000s. It focuses on very specific events that are expected to occur in any given classroom lesson. Observers have to be trained in the meaning of each coding category and on rules for counting or not counting particular types of events.

The movement toward low-inference measurements occurred in part because classroom instruction had become an object for research, in addition to being an object for administrative oversight. Researchers came to see classroom observation as a tool for learning more about the nature of

**Exhibit 8.1** Excerpt from an Early High-Inference Form: Oakland Public Schools, circa 1945

*Character*

| Possesses highest ideals | | Possesses good ideals | | Possesses low ideals |

*Personality*

| Winning | | Agreeable | | Unattractive |

*Disposition*

| Even, cheerful, pleasant, fine sense of humor | | Moderate amiability and balance | | Erratic, morose, unpleasant |

*Personal Appearance*

| Neat, clean, dressed tastefully and becomingly | | Reasonably well dressed | | Careless in cleanliness and dress |

*Mental Alertness*

| Outstanding initiative and imagination; keenly alert at all times | | Reasonable amount | | Passive |

**Exhibit 8.2** Excerpt from a Low-Inference Form: Florida Performance Measurement System, circa 1990

| Domain | | Tot Freq | Frequency | Frequency | Tot Freq | |
|---|---|---|---|---|---|---|
| 3.0 Instruction organization and development | 1. Begins instruction promptly | | | | | 1. Delays |
| | 2. Handles materials in an orderly manner | | | | | 2. Does not organize materials systematically |
| | 3. Orients students to class work/maintains academic focus | | | | | 3. Allows talk/activity unrelated to subject |
| | 4. Conducts beginning/ending review | | | | | 4. |
| | 5. Questions: Academic comprehension/lesson development | a. Single factual | | | | 5a. Allows unison response |
| | | b. Requires analysis/reasons | | | | 5b. Poses multiple questions asked as one |
| | | c. | | | | 5c. Poses nonacademic questions/nonacademic procedural questions |
| | 6. Recognizes response/amplifies/gives correct feedback | | | | | 6. Ignores student or response/expresses sarcasm, disgust, harshness |
| | 7. Gives specific academic praise | | | | | 7. Uses general, nonspecific praise |
| | 8. Provides for practice | | | | | 8. Extends discourse, changes topic with no practice |
| | 9. Gives directions/assigns/checks comprehension of homework, seatwork assignments/gives feedback | | | | | 9. Gives inadequate directions on homework/no feedback |
| | 10. Circulates and assists students | | | | | 10. Remains at desk/circulates inadequately |

instruction and the relationship between teaching practices and student responses. They became interested in specific instructional processes and began to abandon interest in teachers' personal qualities. Two themes guided much of this development. First, researchers hoped to learn more about the relationship between classroom practice and student learning, and second, they wanted to devise instruments that had greater precision.

Interest in low-inference measurement shifted attention away from what to measure and toward how to measure it. Presumably better methods could improve both precision and interrater agreement. Analysts evaluated the strategies used to document teaching, the coding systems, training procedures, interrater agreements, and procedural safeguards (for illustrative reviews of these issues, see Dwyer & Stufflebeam, 1996; Evertson & Green, 1986). The third American Educational Research Association (AERA) handbook of research on teaching included, for the first time, a chapter devoted entirely to observation as a form of data collection (Evertson & Green, 1986). It examines every aspect of observation systems, including how units of behavior are defined, how scales are developed, how raters are trained, and how data are stored and aggregated. It does not, however, address the question of what to measure.

But the problem of meaningfulness remained. Researchers still had to make decisions about what to document when they observed classrooms, and they subscribed to many different theories and hypotheses about what was most important in the classroom. A book edited by Biddle and Ellena (1964) illustrates this variety. Each chapter of the volume describes a prominent and substantial program of research on teaching, and the programs are almost completely unrelated to one another. One focused on teacher reasoning (Turner, 1964), another on classroom atmosphere (Ryans, 1964), another on content representations (Meux & Smith, 1964), and another on "restrictive" versus "inviting" comments from teachers (Flanders, 1964). By the late 1960s, research-oriented observation systems had became so various that a multivolume compilation was produced (Simon & Boyer, 1967a, 1967b, 1970, 1974) to catalogue all the available instruments. In a major literature review appearing around that time, Rosenshine and Furst (1973) expressed dismay at the variety and incomprehensibility of the tools that had been created. The instruments varied in their scoring techniques, substantive foci, and theoretical underpinnings.

Researchers had solved the problem of reliably ascertaining meaning by stipulating allowable meanings within each assessment instrument. Observers could be trained to see the particular meanings that researchers were interested in, so that there was interrater agreement within a research project even if different meanings were documented across research projects. Rosenshine and Furst (1973) demonstrate these differences in their contribution to the *Second Handbook of Research on Teaching.* They present a relatively common classroom event in which a teacher poses a question and a student offers an unusual or unexpected response. The teacher then says, "That's an interesting idea." Unexpected student ideas are common occurrences in classrooms and typically present dilemmas for teachers. Teachers' responses have been evaluated on many different observation forms, and Rosenshine and Furst show how this particular event would have been coded in a collection of different observation instruments. They take their sample of coding categories from instruments that were catalogued in Simon and Boyers's (1967b, 1969, 1970) anthology of classroom observation instruments. Here are the relevant coding categories offered by different instruments, along with a reference to the instrument number within the Simon and Boyer anthology and the theoretical basis for the instrument. Rosenshine and Furst argue that all of these coding categories are intended to capture the same event:

1. Teacher entertains even "wild" or far-fetched suggestions (from Brown, #36, based on Dewey)

2. Routine agreement (from Aschner and Gallagher, #3, based on Guildford)

3. Teacher accepts or uses ideas of students (from Flanders, #5, based on a theory of interpersonal relationships)

4. Sanctions-search (from Joyce, #11, based on miscellaneous sources in instructional theory)

5. Exits-approved (from Medley, #13, originated by the author)

6. Evaluate without public criteria (from Miller and Hughes, #14, based on Hughes' hypothesis about Group Processes) [Rosenshine & Furst, 1973, p. 146]

These different coding categories allow observers to document the fact that the teacher responded positively to an unexpected student idea, but each instrument gives a different meaning to the event. By training observers to see teaching in one particular way, each instrument achieves reliability.

By the mid-1980s, though, researchers began to believe that they had zeroed in on a set of teaching practices that improved student achievement. In the 1986 *Handbook of Research on Teaching*, Brophy and Good identified three broad categories of classroom practices that were by then known to be related to student achievement gains:

1. *Quantity and pacing of instruction.* Included in this aspect of teaching quality are things like the volume of content covered; the amount of time that students are academically engaged (which depends on the teacher's ability to keep things running smoothly, keep transitions brief, and so forth); ensuring that students are continuing to be successful as they move along; and actively teaching rather than assigning student seat work.

2. *Organizing the information that is presented.* This includes structuring lessons with advanced organizers, providing some redundancy, and being clear in explanations.

3. *Questioning the students.* This factor includes a variety of features of teachers' questioning practices, such as ensuring that questions vary in their difficulty but ensuring that most can be answered by most students; ensuring that the cognitive level of the questions is mixed; ensuring that questions are clear; and giving students time to formulate their answers and providing feedback.

The success of this body of research motivated many states and school districts to respond by embracing low-inference assessment systems that focused on these specific practices. They abandoned their rating scales and their interest in personality traits and adopted new low-inference techniques that focused on teaching practices rather than on the teachers' personal qualities. This new research gave districts a way to settle their long-standing disputes about criteria for good teaching and at the same time to create more objective assessment instruments. The move to research-based teacher evaluation (RBTE) seemed to solve both assessment problems.

## REPLACING PUBLIC VALUES WITH RESEARCH-BASED CRITERIA

The ideas from this body of research quickly migrated from the research community to school districts. There was a widespread sense that we had finally solved the problem of how to recognize good teaching, and the literature began to be populated by instrument developers describing, with pride, new administrative instruments that reflected research findings (Ellett, Capie, & Johnson, 1980; Peterson, Kromrey, Micerri, & Smith, 1986).

However, almost as quickly as RBTE became fashionable, it became the object of criticism. Critics pointed out that most of the research findings came from lower grade levels and would not necessarily apply when teachers were teaching older students and more advanced content; they noted that intellectual life in the classroom had been overlooked (though it was also overlooked in earlier high-inference rating schemes) and that student achievement test scores were not an adequate criterion for evaluating teaching practices because they captured only a narrow range of the outcomes we sought from students. There were concerns that the findings encouraged administrators to prescribe and regiment teaching practices in a way that overlooked teachers' need to adapt to variations in context and circumstances.

These problems with RBTE became especially evident when Greta Morine-Dershimer (1986), then AERA president, asked a group of scholars to write critiques of a particular lesson, each using his own approach to evaluation. The lesson was a high school history lesson given by William Bennett, U.S. secretary of education at that time. The lesson certainly did not represent typical teaching as it occurs in the United States. One difference was that Bennett was there for just a single lesson on a single day; someone else taught the students the day before, and someone else would teach them the day after. The demonstration also took place in an honors class and was videotaped by all the major news networks. The camera lighting was so hot that the secretary was visibly sweating throughout the lesson. Students no doubt had been prepared by their regular teacher on how to behave when the secretary came.

In the lesson, Bennett taught primarily through a recitation-type examination of Federalist Paper No. 10, which offers an argument about the role of government based on a set of observations about human nature. Bennett presented the argument, as well as the view of human nature, as central to the foundation of the United States. Bennett had an intense personality. He paced the room and, pounding one hand against the other, pressed students to think harder about the Federalist paper they had read. Students appeared to be generally passive, uncertain how to respond to him.

The fact that this lesson was taught by a politician also hinders our ability to interpret it purely as an instructional event. I have presented a videotape of this lesson on more than one occasion in graduate courses on research methods, asking students to observe and document what they saw. I found that my American graduate students, who tend politically to be liberal Democrats, mostly noticed flaws and weaknesses in this lesson offered by a conservative Republican politician. Students from other countries, however, nearly always mentioned how much they learned from the lesson.

Since the lesson was such a politically charged and self-conscious event, we might expect that the best strategy for evaluating it would be to use an RBTE instrument, for such an instrument would ensure reliable and objective measurement. And in fact one of the responses to Bennett's lesson (Peterson, Kromrey, Micerri, & Smith, 1986) applied the Florida Performance Measurement System illustrated in Exhibit 8.1. These authors offered an evaluation of the secretary's lesson that gave norm-referenced scores for each of the following items, arranged here according to the scores Bennett received.

Bennett was in the top 25 percent on:

- Analysis/reasoning
- Concept treatment
- Corrective feedback
- Body behavior shows interest
- Express enthusiasm/challenge

He was in the middle 50 percent on:

- Handles materials orderly
- Orients/maintains focus
- Beginning/ending review
- Single factual question
- Specific academic praise
- Discuss cause/effect
- Value judgment
- Emphasize important points

And he was in the lowest 25 percent on:

- Begins instruction promptly
- State/apply academic rule
- Provide for practice
- Homework/seatwork assign
- Circulates and assists
- Stops misconduct
- Maintain momentum

These scores do seem to present a factually accurate representation of the secretary's lesson. He was intense and focused on the central concepts in the essay, features that would lead to high scores on the enthusiasm and concept treatment. There was no time during the lesson when he stopped actively teaching in order to give students seat work exercises, so Bennett received low scores on variables associated with seat work.

Here, in a nutshell is the fundamental problem with the RBTE approach to teacher evaluation, for the items on which Bennett scored low were irrelevant to this particular lesson and there is no reason to believe that he should have given students repetitive practice in order to grasp the essence of the essay he was teaching. The authors concluded that the secretary of education had scored at the fiftieth percentile (presumably because he was high on the intellectual dimensions but low on the seat work exercise dimensions) and therefore would not be qualified to teach in the state of Florida. The rating was more impartial than those my doctoral students offered, but it still incorporated a bias toward a particular view of instruction.

Perhaps the most poignant response to Bennett's lesson was from Barak Rosenshine (1986), whose comments centered on the discrepancy between measurable behaviors and intellectual importance. Rosenshine pointed out that research on teaching had focused on the teaching of skills (teaching students to subtract double-digit numbers, for example) rather than on the teaching of content (the planetary orbits, the history of the United States, or mitosis and miosis). The kind of good teaching that had been revealed by low-inference observation instruments entailed presenting a skill, demonstrating it on the board, guiding students through some examples, giving them independent practice, and then circulating around to monitor their learning. But Bennett's lesson was not a lesson about how to do something; it was a lesson about an idea. Rosenshine volunteered the remarkable admission that we researchers had not found a way to characterize the content that teachers teach. "We have not developed a technology for practice in this type of lesson," Rosenshine admits, and then says, "Because there is relatively little research on the teaching of content, I find it inappropriate to critique this lesson" (p. 304). This is an astonishing concession and suggests that the preceding eighty or so years of efforts devoted to recognizing good teaching, in spite of the tremendous array of qualities it had examined, had nonetheless overlooked the most central aspect of teaching: helping students learn subject matter.

Research-based teacher evaluation, then, was unable to solve the century-long problem of establishing a set of agreed-on public values or of balancing objectivity with attention to the substantive meaning of classroom interactions. But criticisms of this approach laid the groundwork for attention to the intellectual work of teaching. From the ashes of low-inference, research-based teacher evaluation arose a new approach, often called a standards-based approach, which represents our current solution to the problem of accommodating public values and the problem of balancing objectivity with meaningfulness.

## THE STANDARDS SOLUTION

The most prominent approach to performance assessment today is the standards-based approach, best exemplified by the National Board for Professional Teaching Standards and the Interstate New Teacher Assessment and Support Consortium, which focus on expert teachers and new teachers, respectively. Both groups organize their assessment around five central principles:

- Teachers are committed to students and learning.
- Teachers know the subjects they teach and how to teach those subjects to students.
- Teachers are responsible for managing and monitoring student learning.
- Teachers think systematically about their practice and learn from experience.
- Teachers are members of learning communities.

The tenor of these propositions is a strong and clear contrast to RBTE and a clear return to public values as the source of our criteria for good teaching. Whereas RBTE focused on a specific list of empirically documented behaviors, standards-based approaches emphasize professional knowledge, commitment, and judgment. Notice that each sentence begins with the word *teachers*, not the word *teaching*. Whereas RBTE focused on observed practice, standards-based approaches look at a broader range of evidence that includes artifacts from practice and teachers' critiques of their own practice. Whereas RBTE offered a single set of behaviors for teachers in all grades and subjects, these standards-based systems are developing different assessments for different grades and subjects.

But the standards-based approach to measuring teaching quality did not abandon the concern with precise language and reliable measurement that characterized RBTE. The National Board's procedures represent a substantial leap from the judgmental ratings that school administrators used in the early part of the twentieth century (see, for instance, examinations by Bond, 2000; Bond, Smith, Baker, & Hattie, 2000) in its effort to accommodate public values and balance attention to the meaning of events with attention to objective and reliable scores. *Editor's note*: Chapter Ten provides more detail on the National Board assessment process and its rationale.

The National Board's assessments also move substantially beyond a simple observation of teaching practice itself by examining teachers' reasoning and rationales for their practices, attending to student learning as well as teaching practices, and giving explicit attention to the intellectual quality of teachers' lessons. There is a cost for this success, however. The board's assessment system is a lengthy and costly affair. Costs are prohibitive for many teachers, and critics have raised questions about the cost-benefit ratio. It is not intended to be, nor could it be, a system that school districts could feasibly incorporate into their annual performance evaluations of teachers. But it does appear to provide a reliable method of recognizing good teaching when we see it.

Districts prefer more cost-efficient approaches to standards-based assessments, and in the past decade, standards-based assessments of teaching have almost completely replaced RBTE throughout the education system. Probably the most widespread approach to standards-based teacher evaluation derives from Danielson (1996), who offers a framework that districts can adopt wholesale or use as a starting point for devising their own system. Danielson identifies four major domains: planning and preparation, classroom environment, instruction, and professional responsibilities, with each domain containing itemized lists of specific standards within it. Moreover, Danielson claims her system is based in research. So even if specific evaluation forms vary from district to district, the terms are not precise, and the reliability of ratings is unknown, we could consider her standards-based evaluations to be a research-based approach. *Editor's note*: See Chapter Six for how the Danielson Framework is incorporated into Induction programs.

However, the Danielson system includes a number of items that look more like statements of public values than like research-based findings: items such as "integrity and ethical conduct," "service to the school," and "relations with colleagues." In fact, this system tries to incorporate both fashionable ideas and enduring ideas into a coherent and practicable system. In that sense, it serves a purpose very much like Boyce's 1915 guidelines did: a consensus overview of things we care about. Moreover, the phrasing of these standards, and many other locally developed standards, is such that they require relatively higher inferences on the part of the evaluator, who needs to evaluate things like "quality of questions," "suitability" of learning goals for diverse learners, or "accuracy" of reflections on teaching. Still, Danielson's system offers a substantial improvement over earlier judgmental rating scales, and there is some evidence that district-level teacher assessments based on the Danielson framework are associated with student achievement gains (Gallagher, 2004; Kimball, White, Milanowski, & Borman, 2004; Milanowski, 2004).

The standards-based approach to teacher evaluation is an improvement over the early rating scale and an improvement over RBTE. Its focus on standards reintroduces public values and provides a language for helping districts sort out the values they care most about. Its reliance on performance rubrics increases the objectivity and reliability of scores. But the instruments currently in use by local districts are still remarkably various in the aspects of teaching they evaluate, and many still lack sufficient reliability as well. Next I examine the current state of teacher evaluations.

## Aspects of Teaching Currently Evaluated

Although we tend to speak of standards-based evaluations as if they represented a single approach, there is tremendous variety among the standards-based instruments used by school districts and by researchers. Recently I analyzed the contents of four illustrative teacher assessment instruments (Kennedy, 2007). Two were instruments used by school districts to evaluate their teachers, and the other two were used by researchers to study teaching. I sorted the items in these instruments into the following categories:

- Professionalism: teachers' planning, record keeping, out-of-classroom contributions to the school, interactions with parents and others
- Organization and ambience of classroom life
- Inclusiveness in discourse and classroom activities
- Clarity of communications within the classroom
- Thoughtfulness of classroom discussions
- Quality of the students; learning activities

These categories can be viewed as arrayed in a continuum from those most distant to those most immediately relevant to student learning. The first category, professionalism, includes teaching practices that are most distant from student learning: things teachers do when they are outside the classroom. The next two categories have to do with the general organization of the classroom and the treatment of students, things that are important but not directly related to student learning. The fourth category, clarity, is the first category in the list that we might expect to have a direct bearing on learning. The last two categories, those having to do with the kind of intellectual work students are doing, would presumably bear most directly on their learning. These are aspects of teaching that were largely absent from teacher evaluations in the early part of the twentieth century and in the RBTE instruments but that are now beginning to appear in standards-based instruments.

Figure 8.1 displays the percentage of evaluation items in each assessment system that addressed each of these six broad public values. The first two instruments came from school districts and the second two from researchers. Notice that just as we did a century ago, we still face substantial differences in how much attention we give to these different criteria. For example, the first instrument gives no attention to the nature of the learning activities students participate in, whereas the third and fourth give substantial attention to that. On the other side, the first and third give substantial attention to professionalism, while the fourth does not address this at all. These differences do not necessarily reflect a disparity between district and researcher either.

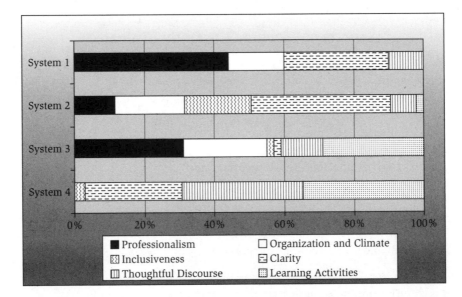

**Figure 8.1** Content Analysis of Four Teacher Assessment Instruments

Notice that inclusiveness, the third category, receives no attention in the first system but quite a bit of attention in the second. Thus, a given teacher would be evaluated against quite different criteria depending on which of these districts employed him or her.

The second important message from this figure is that the school district systems give the bulk of their attention to aspects of teaching that are relatively more distant from student learning. These two assessment systems were selected because they represent common approaches to school district teacher evaluations, but in fact, both lack attention to the very things that constitute the intellectual core of teaching: classroom discussions and learning activities. Even after a century of efforts to improve teacher evaluations, most district evaluations still overlook the intellectual work that occurs in classrooms. No doubt one reason for this omission is that these are difficult things to evaluate, and we are only now beginning to devise solutions. This observation brings us to the second problem, which still remains to be solved.

## Objectivity in Scoring

The two assessment samples shown in Exhibits 8.1 and 8.2 illustrate the difference between the high-inference, judgmental ratings used at the beginning of the previous century and the low-inference documentation of practice used for research-based teacher evaluations. Standards-based systems use a third approach, performance rubrics, which lie in between these other two approaches. Typically a performance rubric is based on a scale, like the rating scale shown in Exhibit 8.3, but instead of asking for a judgment about how far to the left or right a teacher is, the scale defines what an observer might see if the teacher were to be assigned a score of a "1" or a "2." Still, the phrasing of these items can vary substantially in how much judgment the observer is expected to draw on in establishing a rating. Exhibit 8.3 illustrates a handful of performance rubrics, all focused on classroom teaching practices. They are listed in order of their dependence on the observer's subjective interpretation of events. Those at the top are higher-inference items, those at the bottom lower. The first one, for instance, asks whether "instruction respects student knowledge." Deciding that a teacher's practice respects student knowledge is a highly interpretive act. In addition, the item gives only a general idea of how the points on the scale differ from one another, so judgment is required here as well. The second item is only slightly better. It offers descriptions of each point on the scale but still depends on the observer to evaluate the appropriateness of the teacher's strategies.

As we move down this list, item scores are defined more and more precisely, thus depending less and less on the judgments and interpretations of the observer. The last item asks about the proportion of students who participated in a discussion and gives relatively precise descriptors of the participation rates

**Exhibit 8.3** Illustrative Performance Rubrics

| Lowest precision | Instruction Respects Students' Prior Knowledge | | | |
|---|---|---|---|---|
| | 1. never | 2. sometimes | 3. often | 4. typically |
| Lowest precision | Instructional Strategies | | | |
| | 1. Are ineffective or inappropriate | 2. A limited range is effective and appropriate to the content | 3. Typically are effective and appropriate | 4. Broad range of effective and appropriate strategies |
| Low precision | Teacher Questions | | | |
| | 1. Generally poor quality | 2. Combination of low and high quality but rapidly given | 3. Most are adequate to high quality, and time is given for response | 4. Uniformly high quality, with adequate time for response |
| Medium precision | Learning Activities | | | |
| | 1. Students repeat or recall declarative knowledge | 2. Students apply a known procedure; may be asked to show their work | 3. Something in between 2 and 4 | 4. Students use complex reasoning or apply nonalgorithmic thinking |
| Higher precision | Response to Student Errors | | | |
| | 1. Does not correct student errors | 2. Corrects errors but without explanation | 3. Corrects with an explanation that clarifies the process or concept | 4. Corrects with an explanation that clarifies and also facilitates student self-correction |
| Highest precision | Classroom Participation | | | |
| | 1. Less than 25% of the students participated in the discussion | 2. Twenty-five to 50 percent of the students participated minimally in the discussion (they contributed only once) | 3. Twenty-five to 50 percent of the students participated consistently in the discussion OR over 50 percent of the students participated minimally | 4. Over 50 percent of students participated in classroom discussion |

required for each score. The one just above it asks whether or how teachers respond to student errors. Here, four scale scores are possible, and each is associated with a uniquely defined response.

These performance rubrics are a substantial improvement over the undefined rating scales of the previous century, and a substantial improvement over RBTE scales as well. They remove some of the judgment that early rating scales encouraged, but at the same time they acknowledge that teaching practices are meaningful events. But the variations shown in Exhibit 8.3 suggest that we still have far to go. One reason teacher evaluation scales have not improved more quickly is that the articulation of these distinctions requires a great deal of thought and observation. Distinguishing between better and worse approaches turns out not to be self-evident at all, and in fact requires close attention to, and analysis of, details.

# DISCUSSION

We have accumulated a century of experience trying to systematically recognize good teaching when we see it. Although most students and parents believe they can spot good teaching in an instant, education administrators and researchers have struggled to develop reliable procedures for distinguishing among teachers. One reason for the difficulty of this task is that we have faced serious technical problems in trying to translate our intuitive perceptions into precise terminology and reliable measurement scales. In fact, it has taken almost the entire century to distinguish the teacher from the teaching. Early instruments routinely evaluated the entire person and focused on such personal qualities as dress, comportment, loyalty, and efficiency. Even efforts to focus on classroom practices still tended to look at subjective qualities such as friendliness or orderliness. Our century has been filled with public hand-wringing by researchers and school administrators who struggle with the difficulty of obtaining fair, accurate, justified evaluations from observers with different personal or theoretical views about teachers and teaching.

Associated with this problem of translating intuitive perceptions into standardized protocols is the fact that until recently, assessments have not attended to the intellectual substance of teaching: to the content actually presented, how that content is represented, and whether or how students interact with it. This may seem like a surprising and glaring omission, especially since it has been pointed out more than once (Buchmann, 1982; Rosenshine, 1986; Shulman, 1986). But it is not surprising at all when we consider the difficulty of agreeing on the meaning to the events we see. And any assessment of the intellectual and substantive merits of teaching is entirely about its meaning. The central problem here has to do with the difficulty of developing reliable procedures that can capture the substantive meanings of events rather than just the events themselves, and yet do so in a way that is not idiosyncratic.

The most significant problem remaining in most state and district assessments of teaching, including those based on Danielson's *Enhancing Professional Practice: Framework for Teaching,* is that they still do not give sufficient attention to the substantive and intellectual merits of classroom lessons themselves. Evaluators may be asked to judge the clarity of lesson plans, the quality of classroom interactions, the physical arrangement of the classroom, or interactions with parents, but they rarely are asked to evaluate the accuracy, importance, coherence, or relevance of the content that is actually being taught or to rate the level of intellectual work students are asked to do. This absence of attention to content is especially puzzling in Danielson's *Framework* because Danielson cites many chapters from Wittrock's 1986 *Handbook of Research on Teaching* as the source for the elements in her framework. Yet it was a chapter in that very handbook (Shulman, 1986) that first brought to our attention the need for more attention to content in research on teaching.

Documenting the intellectual meaning of teaching events remains the elusive final frontier in performance assessment. Researchers are now moving in this direction and are exploring a variety of approaches to defining the substantive meaning and intellectual value of classroom lessons. They are finding ways to characterize the logic of whole lessons (Stigler, Gallimore, & Hiebert, 2000), the intellectual requirements entailed in student assignments (Newmann & Associates, 1996), and the content and thoughtfulness of classroom discourse (Resnick, Matsumura, & Junker, 2006). These new instruments are often limited to particular subjects and grade levels, and they require more observer training than school districts may be willing to embrace, but they offer districts a glimpse of their own likely future.

*Mary Kennedy appreciates financial support from the National Science Foundation (NSF). This book was motivated and influenced by NSF grant award no. 0554477. Any opinions, findings, and conclusions or recommendations expressed here are those of the various authors and do not necessarily reflect the views of the National Science Foundation.*

# REFERENCES

Barr, A. S. (1924). *Elementary school standards for the improvement of teaching.* Ann Arbor, MI: Edwards Bros.

Barr, A. S. (1929). *Characteristic differences in the teaching performance of good and poor teachers of social studies.* Bloomington, IL: Public School Publishing Company.

Biddle, B. J., & Ellena, W. J. (Eds.). (1964). *Contemporary research on teacher effectiveness*. New York: Holt.

Bond, L. (2000). *The measurement of teaching ability*. Washington, DC: National Academy of Sciences National Research Council.

Bond, L., Smith, T., Baker, W., & Hattie, J. A. (2000). *The certification system of the National Board of Professional Teaching Standards: A construct and consequential validity study*. Greensboro, NC: University of North Carolina, Greensboro.

Boyce, A. C. (1915). Methods for measuring teachers' efficiency. In *The Fourteenth Yearbook of the National Society for the Study of Education* (Part II, pp. 9–83). Bloomington, IL: Public Schools Publishing.

Brophy, J., & Good, T. L. (1986). Teacher behavior and student achievement. In M. C. Wittrock (Ed.), *Handbook of research on teaching* (3rd ed., pp. 328–375). New York: Macmillan.

Buchmann, M. (1982). The flight away from content in teacher education and teaching. *Journal of Curriculum Studies, 14*(1), 61–68.

Butsch, R.L.C. (1931). Teacher rating. *Review of Educational Research, 1*(2), 99–107.

Charters, W. W., & Waples, D. (1929). *Commonwealth teacher training study*. Chicago: University of Chicago Press.

Danielson, C. (1996). *Enhancing professional practice: A framework for teaching* (2nd ed.). Alexandria, VA: Association for Supervision and Curriculum Development.

Dwyer, C. A., & Stufflebeam, D. (1996). Teacher evaluation. In D. C. Berliner & R. Calfee (Eds.), *Handbook of educational psychology* (pp. 765–786). New York: Macmillan.

Ellett, C. D., Capie, W., & Johnson, C. E. (1980, December). Assessing teacher performance: Georgia's performance-based certification project combines assessing teachers' performance with assisting teachers' growth. *Educational Leadership*, 219–220.

Evertson, C., & Green, J. (1986). Observation as inquiry and method. In M. C. Wittrock (Ed.), *Handbook of research on teaching* (3rd ed., pp. 162–213). New York: Macmillan.

Flanders, N. A. (1964). Some relationships among teacher influence, pupil attitudes, and achievement. In B. J. Biddle & W. J. Ellena (Eds.), *Contemporary research on teacher effectiveness* (pp. 196–231). New York: Holt.

Gallagher, H. A. (2004). Vaughn Elementary's innovative teacher evaluation system: Are teacher evaluation scores related to growth in student achievement? *Peabody Journal of Education, 79*(4), 79–107.

Gergen, K. J. (1982). *Toward transformation in social knowledge*. New York: Springer.

Hill, C. W. (1921). The efficiency ratings of teachers. *Elementary School Journal, 21*, 438–443.

Kennedy, M. M. (2007, April). *Monitoring and assessing teacher quality*. Paper presented at the American Educational Research Association, Chicago.

Kimball, S. M., White, B., Milanowski, A. T., & Borman, G. (2004). Examining the relationship between teacher evaluation and student assessment results in Washoe County. *Peabody Journal of Education, 79*(4), 54–78.

King, L. A. (1925). The present status of teacher rating. *American School Board Journal,* *70,* 44–46.

Meux, M., & Smith, B. O. (1964). Logical dimensions of teaching behavior. In B. J. Biddle & W. J. Ellena (Eds.), *Contemporary research on teacher effectiveness* (pp. 127–164). New York: Holt.

Milanowski, A. (2004). The relationship between teacher performance evaluation scores and student achievement: Evidence from Cincinnati. *Peabody Journal of Education, 79*(4), 33–53.

Morine-Dershimer, G. (1986). Introduction: Perspectives on a teaching episode. *Teaching and Teacher Education, 2*(4), 299–300.

Newmann, F. M., & Associates. (Eds.). (1996). *Authentic achievement: Restructuring schools for intellectual quality.* San Francisco: Jossey-Bass.

Peterson, D., Kromrey, J., Micerri, T., & Smith, B. O. (1986). Evaluation of a teacher's performance using the Florida Performance Measurement System. *Teaching and Teacher Education, 2*(4), 309–314.

Reavis, W. C., & Cooper, D. H. (1945). *Evaluation of teacher merit in city school systems.* Chicago: University of Chicago.

Resnick, L., Matsumura, L. C., & Junker, B. (2006). *Measuring reading comprehension and mathematics instruction in urban middle schools: A pilot study of the instructional quality assessment.* Los Angeles: CRESST.

Rosenshine, B. (1986). Unsolved issues in teaching content: A critique of a lesson on Federalist Paper No. 10. *Teaching and Teacher Education, 2*(4), 301–308.

Rosenshine, B., & Furst, N. (1973). The use of direct observation to study teaching. In R.M.W. Travers (Ed.), *Second handbook of research on teaching* (pp. 122–183). Skokie, IL: Rand McNally.

Ryans, D. G. (1949). The criteria of teaching effectiveness. *Journal of Educational Research, 42,* 690–699.

Ryans, D. G. (1964). Research on teacher behavior in the context of the Teacher Characteristics Study. In B. J. Biddle & W. J. Ellena (Eds.), *Contemporary research on teacher effectiveness* (pp. 67–101). New York: Holt.

Shulman, L. S. (1986). Paradigms and research programs in the study of teaching: A contemporary perspective. In M. C. Wittrock (Ed.), *Handbook of research on teaching* (3rd ed., pp. 3–36). New York: Macmillan.

Simon, A., & Boyer, E. G. (1967a). Mirrors for behavior. In A. Simon & E. G. Boyer (Eds.), *Mirrors for behavior: An anthology of classroom observation instruments* (pp. 1–24). Philadelphia: Research for Better Schools and Temple University Center for the Study of Teaching.

Simon, A., & Boyer, E. G. (1967b). *Mirrors for behavior: An anthology of classroom observation instruments.* Philadelphia: Research for Better Schools. (ERIC Document Reproduction Service No. ED029833)

Simon, A., & Boyer, E. G. (1969). *Mirrors for behavior: An anthology of classroom observation instruments.* Philadelphia: Research for Better Schools. (ERIC Document Reproduction Service No. ED031613)

Simon, A., & Boyer, E. G. (1970). *Mirrors for behavior: An anthology of classroom observation instruments*. Philadelphia: Research for Better Schools. (ERIC Document Reproduction Service No. ED042937)

Simon, A., & Boyer, E. G. (1974). *Mirrors for behavior III: An anthology of classroom observation instruments*. Philadelphia: Research for Better Schools. (ERIC Document Reproduction Service No. ED170320)

Stigler, J. W., Gallimore, R., & Hiebert, J. (2000). Using video surveys to compare classrooms and teaching across cultures: Examples and lessons from the TIMSS video studies. *Educational Psychologist*, *35*(2), 87–100.

Turner, R. L. (1964). Teaching as problem solving behavior: A strategy. In B. J. Biddle & W. J. Ellena (Eds.), *Contemporary research on teacher effectiveness* (pp. 102–126). New York: Holt.

Waller, W. (1932/1961). *The sociology of teaching*. New York: Russell and Russell.

Wittrock, M. C. (Ed.). (1986). *Handbook of research on teaching* (3rd ed.). New York: Macmillan.

Wood, C. J., & Pohland, P. A. (1979). Teacher evaluation: The myth and realities. In W. R. Duckett (Ed.), *School evaluation: The politics and process* (pp. 73–82). Bloomington, IN: Phi Delta Kappan.

# CHAPTER NINE

# Value-Added

## Assessing Teachers' Contributions to Student Achievement

Douglas N. Harris, Daniel F. McCaffrey

*University of Wisconsin–Madison;*
*RAND Corporation*

State and federal governments have rapidly expanded their use of incentives for educators to raise student outcomes, especially student achievement scores, over the past decade. This "new accountability" (Fuhrman, 1999) is premised on the idea that students can and should reach certain academic standards, their progress toward standards can be measured with standardized tests, and—in the final key step—the test results can be used to draw conclusions about school performance and therefore serve as the basis for sanctions and rewards for school personnel. With the 2001 bipartisan reauthorization of the federal Elementary and Secondary School Act, commonly known as No Child Left Behind (NCLB), standardized and outcome-based incentives have become cemented as key levers in the cause of improved academic success for students.

By providing incentives at the school level, however, the law may suffer from a free-rider problem for individual educators within those schools. There may be pressure on the school as a whole, but this may not filter down to teachers and administrators, whose individual efforts have little influence on school-level outcomes. In addition, limited empirical evidence and much common wisdom suggest that teachers are the educational input with the greatest leverage on student learning. Consequently, targeting incentives directly at teachers may be the most efficient use of these resources to promote change. For these and other reasons, interest is growing in taking the new accountability logic a step further and shifting responsibility for outcomes from school to individual school personnel. The federal Teacher Incentive Fund program, for example, is providing resources to many school districts to institute teacher merit pay, and large school districts such as Denver, Houston, and Nashville and states such as Florida and Minnesota also are pursuing merit pay based on student test scores. Gordon, Kane, and Staiger (2006) proposed, and New York City briefly considered, a proposal to make teacher contributions to student achievement the primary basis for tenure decisions. These proposals all have one thing in common: they hold individual teachers accountable for the achievement of their own specific students.

These new teacher accountability policies are motivated partly by the belief that the other forms of assessments have provided inadequate incentives and more generally have fallen short of raising achievement to desired standards. Teachers who are certified and have a master's degree do not seem to generate achievement more than teachers who lack these credentials (Goldhaber & Brewer, 1997; Harris & Sass, 2007a, 2007b). Unlike these and other forms of assessment that focus on what goes into education—what teachers know and do—accountability focuses on what comes out. It is also arguably more objective and less prone to the personal views, biases, and dispositions of the people making the assessments, as when a school principal evaluates a teacher.

Outcome-based accountability has a significant disadvantage relative to other assessments, however. The teacher is far from the only factor influencing students' outcomes, and this means it is necessary to isolate the teacher's contribution from the contributions of factors such as the students' home environments, the effectiveness of previous teachers, and the contributions of administrators. This chapter describes methods that attempt to isolate teacher impacts on student achievement, known as teacher value-added (VA) measures or VA measures of teacher effects.[1] These measures are created by tracking the trajectory of each student's learning over time and calculating an average rate of growth for each student. This average serves to establish what each student should be expected to learn in any given year. Analysts can then look to see whether students taught by a targeted teacher tend to learn at a rate above that average. If so, then this teacher receives a high assessment in terms of value-added. As we discuss, teacher VA measures can be calculated in many ways and adjusted to account for a variety of other factors that may be important for student achievement but outside the control of teachers.

Following a brief background on this strategy, we discuss statistical models. We then consider empirical evidence about the validity of the assumptions and other evidence about the statistical properties of VA measures of teacher effects. We conclude by comparing the advantages and disadvantages of VA accountability to other forms of assessment and describing some future research directions.

# BACKGROUND ON VALUE-ADDED

Economic theory provides important insights about the decisions organizations make about inputs, outputs, and production. A key part of this theory is the available technology, or production function, that determines what outputs are possible for any given combination of inputs such as labor and capital. In the case of education, the organization is a school or school system, the inputs include factors such as teachers and textbooks, and the outputs are measured by student test scores, graduation rates, and other measures.

Because it facilitates understanding of the effects of education inputs on education outputs, the education production function (EPF) has been one of the central research tools of quantitative education researchers, especially economists of education, for many decades. The EPF is implicitly part of any research that attempts to establish a statistical relationship between education resources and measures of student outcomes.

The term *value-added* also comes from the economics literature and refers to the contribution of specific inputs to outputs (after accounting for prior inputs). In the education literature, VA refers to efforts to measure the effects on student achievement of students' current teachers and schools separate from other inputs. More broadly, the phrase is often used to describe any analysis using longitudinal student test score data to study the effects of educational inputs on achievement. When the input of interest is a program or broad input such as class size, it is called *value-added modeling for program evaluation* (VAM-P; Harris, 2008). Our interest in this chapter, however, is in using VA to assess individual teachers. This form of value-added modeling is called value-added for accountability (VAM-A). The models for VAM-P and VAM-A are often structured in similar ways, although the statistical problems that arise are arguably more challenging in VAM-A (Harris, forthcoming-a).

While the origins of VA teacher effects date back to the early EPF studies thirty years ago, interest in these methods among researchers, policymakers, and educators grew exponentially following the publication a technical report by William Sanders and June Rivers (1996) that found teacher VA measures estimated using student test score gains predict student outcomes at least two years into the future, suggesting that teachers have persistent effects on their students' achievement and the accumulation of these effects could be substantial. The following year, Sanders and his colleagues published another paper claiming that teachers are the most important source of variance in student achievement (Wright, Horn, & Sanders, 1997). Interest in VAM was further stoked by replication of the Sanders and Rivers results and several other papers finding that variability among teachers is large (Aaronson, Barrow, & Sander, 2007; Nye, Konstantopoulos, & Hedges, 2004; Rivkin, Hanushek, & Kain, 2005; Rowan et al., 2002) and that VA estimates of teacher effects predict teachers' future students' outcomes (Cantrell, Fullerton, Kane, & Staige, 2008; Mendro, Jordan, Gomez, Anderson, & Bembry, 1998). In the United States, the growing availability of student achievement data due to increased emphasis on test-based accountability and the passage of NCLB led to explosive growth in empirical research on the effects of teachers on student outcomes.

# VALUE-ADDED AND CAUSAL EFFECTS

Although often tacit, the goal of VA modeling is to make what quantitative researchers refer to as *causal inferences* or to estimate *causal effects*. The causal effect measures the change in outcomes caused by an intervention or other agent such as a teacher. In VA, the goal is to determine how students' learning and achievement differ having been in their assigned teacher's classroom rather then being taught by an alternative teacher.

The modern approach to causal modeling builds on approaches of Neyman, Iwaszkiewicz, and Kolodziejczyk (1935) and Roy (1951) and was formalized in the Neyman-Rubin causal model (Rubin, 1974; Holland, 1986). In this approach, a student's potential achievement with a given teacher is defined as his or her achievement if that teacher is assigned to his or her classroom, assuming that student classroom assignment could remain constant and teachers assigned to them could potentially differ. Potential outcomes exist for every teacher who could hypothetically be assigned to the student's classroom (even if such assignments would require significant changes such as teachers' switching schools). Causal effects are defined as differences in potential outcomes—for instance, the difference between the observed potential outcome for the student's actual teacher and the potential outcome for an alternative teacher teaching in the same school and grade. In most VA applications, the tacit causal effect of interest is the difference between the student's outcome with the teacher assigned to his or her classroom and the average of all of his or her potential outcomes across all potential teachers who might teach this class. The averages of the causal effects across all students in each classroom are then the causal effects of teachers whom VA models are trying to estimate. To aid in this estimation, assumptions are often made about the relationships between observed factors and the values of the potential outcomes. We can use the small set of observed potential outcomes (small because we observe only one of the many potential classroom assignments for each student) to extrapolate to what is unobserved and make causal estimates.

In social science, estimation of causal effects is challenging because people's outcomes are influenced by many factors, and the people receiving any program often choose to do so for reasons that are unknown. This may result in systematic differences among the people who do and do not receive an intervention or input. It therefore becomes difficult to separate the characteristics of the people who select into programs from the effect of the programs.

Such is true for education and assessing teachers' causal effects. Many factors determine which students are assigned to any particular teacher's classroom. These include family choices about where to live and where to send their children to school. They also involve factors used by principals, guidance counselors, teachers, and other school professionals when creating classes that they feel are best suited for each student's learning needs. We do not know what all these factors are and clearly do not measure them all, but we do know they result in classes that differ within and between schools in terms of the students' demographic and socioeconomic backgrounds and their prior achievement. Also the learning of students in a classroom is influenced not only by the teacher but also by other factors, including school resources, school personnel, neighborhood inputs, and the interactions of the other students.

This task of estimating teacher causal effects is all the harder because nonschool inputs are well known to have strong influences on student learning. The importance of nonschool inputs initially became evident with the publication of the Coleman Report (Coleman, 1966), which reported that the variation in education outcomes was explained primarily by the variation in family background rather than school inputs. While Coleman's methods were somewhat simplistic, the central importance of family background has been widely corroborated in more recent and sophisticated studies (see, for example, R. Rothstein, 2004, for a review). Research by Lee and Burkham (2002) suggests wide differences in education achievement between different racial groups when students enter kindergarten, and these are partly explained by observed differences in the home environment.

This complex setting, in which there are many conflated inputs that influence learning, creates a challenge. VA modeling is intended to meet that challenge by using longitudinal student achievement data and a relatively small number of other measured factors to determine the causal contributions of individual teachers to student learning.

## MODELS AND ASSUMPTIONS

Current approaches to VA modeling grew out of three distinct traditions: statistics, economics, and ad hoc methods. We discuss each approach with details on the statistical and economic models and careful consideration of the assumptions used by each tradition and what is known about the validity of those assumptions.

## Ad Hoc Methods

Ad hoc methods are typically developed by individual schools, school districts, or states for their particular needs. These measures might derive from the other traditions but also might include nonstandard analytical procedures or combine standard measures with other empirical evaluations. For example, one school district we are aware of is using average percentage gains in achievement to evaluate school performance and compensate principals because the measure places greater value on lower-performing students. Another district is measuring school performance by combining VA measures with the percentage of students who graduate from high school.

The use of ad hoc measures appears to be motivated by the desire to provide measures that offer strong signals to teachers about expected performance. Teachers may also accept these measures because they are comprehensible and believed to be trustworthy based on face validity (they appear to measure what they are supposed to measure). The statistical properties of these measures are rarely considered and may be extremely difficult to assess. Because these measures tend to be unique to their local applications, we do not discuss them further in this chapter.

## Statistical Methods

VA models, from the perspective of researchers trained in statistics, provide a description of students' achievement trajectories that captures the important statistical features of the data, such as average growth across students, variance around the average, and correlation among scores that share common features such as repeated scores from the same students or scores from different students who share or have shared a classroom or school.

The models describe the correlation among students who share or shared common classrooms by assuming that achievement test scores can be decomposed into additive random components associated with each classroom (current or prior) and residual terms that depend on the student and the year of testing. For example, $A_{it}$ denotes a student's achievement in a given subject area (say, mathematics) at time $t$. A simple representation of a statistical model is:

$$A_{it} = \mu_t + \theta_{tt} + \theta_{tt-1} + \ldots + \theta_{t1} + \epsilon_{it} \qquad (9.1)$$

where $\mu_t$ equals the mean or average for all students at this time, $\theta_{tt}$ equals a random variable that is common to all students who shared the student's classroom at time $t$, $\theta_{tt-1}$ equals a random variable that is common to all students who shared the student's classroom at time $t-1$, and so on, and $\varepsilon_{it}$ describes how the student's score in this year deviates from the average of all other students and all other students who share his or her history of classroom assignments. It also describes how the student's achievement this year deviates from his or her achievement in other years. For example, if $A_{it}$ equals student $i$'s mathematics achievement at the end of seventh grade, then $\mu_t$ equals the average mathematics achievement for all seventh graders, $\theta_{tt}$ describes how on average the achievement of students in student $i$'s seventh-grade mathematics class deviates from the overall mean of seventh-grade achievement, $\theta_{tt-1}$ describes how on average the achievement of students in student $i$'s *sixth*-grade mathematics class deviates from the overall mean of *seventh*-grade achievement, and so on. The model accounts for classroom membership in prior grades when modeling current achievement through the inclusion of the $\theta_{tt'}$ terms ($t' < t$). The current achievement of students who shared a classroom at some point in the past shares a common feature.

Analysts have taken multiple approaches to modeling these components for prior-year classroom membership ($\theta_{tt-1}$ to $\theta_{t1}$ in equation 9.1). Some analysts (Sanders, Saxton, & Horn, 1997; Raudenbush & Bryk, 2002) assume complete persistence, where these components do not change over time, so that the component for fourth-grade classroom membership on fourth-grade scores is the same as it is on fifth-, sixth-, seventh-, and all future grade scores. The fourth-grade classroom leaves an indelible mark on students that persists unchanged through the remaining years of testing. In the notation of equation 9.1, this complete persistence assumption can be specified by: let $\theta_{t't'}$ equal year $t$'s (for example, grade 4) classroom effect on student achievement in year $t'$, then the effect for this classroom on student achievement in all future years $t$ (for example, grades 5, 6, 7, and so on) is $\theta_{tt'} = \theta_{t't'}$.

McCaffrey, Lockwood, Koretz, Louis, and Hamilton (2004) and Lockwood, McCaffrey, Mariano, and Setodji (2007) suggested a "variable persistence" model that allows classroom effects to diminish over time by a constant that depends on the year of testing and the year of the classroom assignment but does not differ across students. For instance, a fourth-grade teacher's effect on a student's fifth-grade scores might be estimated to be 50 percent as large as his or her effect on the student's fourth-grade scores. In the notation of equation 9.1, these variable persistence models assume that $\theta_{tt'} = \alpha_{tt'}\theta_{t't'}$. Recently Mariano, McCaffrey, and Lockwood (2008) extended this model further to allow the components to be distinct but correlated random variables.

A key feature of the statistical models is the correlation among the $\varepsilon_{it}$ terms in equation 9.1 from repeated measures on the same student. That is, the model allows for a student who scores high in sixth grade after accounting for his or her current and prior classroom assignments to tend to score high in fifth, seventh, and eighth grades and so on. Some analysts (Sanders et al., 1997; McCaffrey et al., 2004; Lockwood & McCaffrey, 2007) make no assumptions about the correlation across years, so that the student's seventh- and eighth-grade scores are correlated, but the model does not assume a particular structure for the correlation. Other researchers (Raudenbush & Bryk, 2002) assume more structure among the residual errors by describing their growth as a direct function of time (for example, achievement grows linearly with time, and the intercept and slope are specific to the student and vary randomly across students). Regardless of the assumptions for the structure of the correlation, the correlation among these student-by-grade–specific terms is the feature of the statistical model that leads to an adjustment for students' prior achievement when estimating the current year teacher or classroom effect.

Analysts use these models to generate estimates from longitudinal test score databases of the random effects for classroom assignments (estimates of the $\theta_{tt}$'s) which are then commonly used as the teacher VA measures.

## Defining and Estimating Causal Effects in Statistical Models for VA

The key feature of the statistical models is that they describe the sources of variance and correlation among observed achievement scores for students who shared classroom assignments. The models make no explicit attempts to identify the sources of the correlation in scores. However, the goal of VA is to estimate the causal effect of the teacher, so the critical question is: Do the estimates of the random effects in statistical models that describe correlation among scores for students who shared a classroom actually provide accurate estimates of the causal effect of teachers? Of particular concern is the possibility that the estimated random effects might be capturing variation among classrooms in achievement due to both teacher effects and the common background characteristics of students assigned to the classroom that results in the nonrandom assignment of students to classrooms due to family choices or school policy and practice. Also of concern is what other schooling or nonschooling factors that apply to the classroom of students might be conflated with teachers' causal effects in the estimated random effects used as VA estimates of teacher effects.

Lockwood and McCaffrey (2007) establish conditions under which the estimates of the classroom components from statistical models will recover essentially unbiased estimates of the causal effects of the classroom that are not confounded by the individual student's background characteristics. The conditions require a large number of tests and that student-level factors associated with classroom assignment and achievement be fully described by a low-dimensional latent variable. For instance, suppose that students have a latent general level of achievement: some students generally score high every year, and other students score low every year. Furthermore, suppose that classroom assignment depends on this general level of achievement but not on other student-level factors. Then the assumptions of Lockwood and McCaffrey

(2007) would be met. If instead classroom assignment depends on this general level of achievement and other factors such as performance on any particular test or classroom behavior during the prior school year, then the assumptions of Lockwood and McCaffrey (2007) would not be met. Through simulations, Lockwood and McCaffrey (2007) show that with as few as five or so test scores per student, the statistical models could provide estimates of causal effects that have very limited bias due to student classroom assignments.

Even if the assumptions of Lockwood and McCaffrey (2007) are met, the causal effects of the classroom assignment are not necessarily a causal effect of the teacher. Many factors vary by classroom, and which of those contribute to student learning remains unknown. Some of these factors might be related to the context of the neighborhood and local involvement in the school and classroom. Others could be other schooling factors or complex interactions between the teacher and the context that may or may not be related to the causal effect of the teacher or the causal effect of interest. Suppose a teacher's causal effect would be strong and positive in a school where the principal is a strong instructional leader, but it would be smaller in a school where the principal is not. If the goal is to use VA to make a tenure decision, then such a decision should be made about a teacher in the likely context where she or he would be teaching. But any causal effect that can be estimated will fail to account for the role of the context.

## Assumption Tests

The most common method of studying the validity of making causal inferences on the basis of estimates from statistical models is to use simulation studies, like those described above, where the properties of the estimates are derived under differing assumptions about the data and their relationship to a causal model. Another common approach to studying the properties of the estimates is to compare estimated effects from alternative models and compare these estimates with student background characteristics aggregated to the classroom level.

These studies have tended to find mixed results. As noted above, Lockwood and McCaffrey (2007) created scenarios in which the estimated effects from the models fit to simulated data were similar to the true causal effects used in creating the simulated data. However, McCaffrey et al. (2004) created scenarios where this did not occur. In their scenarios, classrooms and students were stratified into disjoint groups such that students in any one group never shared a classroom with any of the students in any of the other groups. In these situations where classroom and student are stratified, the statistical models cannot recover causal effects if student growth differs on average by strata. Recent work by McCaffrey, Lockwood, Sass, and Mihaly (2009) found that stratification appeared to be a very limited problem in large urban school districts in Florida, so this source of bias might be inconsequential in practice.

Authors have found that estimated teacher (classroom) effects are sensitive to the specification of equation 9.1.[2] For example, Lockwood et al. (2007) find a correlation of about 0.8 between the estimated teacher effects from the complete persistence models (models that assume $\theta_{tt'} = \theta_{t't'}$ for $t > t'$) and the variable persistence model (models that assume $\theta_{tt'} = \alpha_{tt'}\theta_{t't'}$ for $t > t'$). In addition, authors have found somewhat mixed results in comparing estimates to aggregated student characteristics. Sanders and Wright report weak correlation between VA estimates of teacher effects and students' demographic characteristics. Using data from Nashville middle school students and their mathematics teachers, McCaffrey, Han, and Lockwood (2009) also found weak correlation between estimated teacher effects and classroom averages of demographic variables; however, through comparisons of estimated teacher effects across many alternative VA procedures (including the statistical methods described above and the econometric approaches described below), the authors found that VA estimates of teacher effects from the statistical approaches slightly favored teachers of classes with students who tended to be higher achieving prior to entering the teachers' classrooms.

The statistical models that have been used in practice have tended not to include student-level covariates such as race or socioeconomic status measures. One argument for excluding covariates from models is that including them might suggest to some people that there are different expectations for students of different sociodemographic or other groups.[3] However, there are also technical challenges to including these variables in the model. The decision to exclude the models has been criticized by researchers and practitioners, which resulted in an empirical investigation of the effects of including these variables in the models. That study (Ballou, Sanders, & Wright, 2004) developed a method for including student-level covariates in the models that avoided the technical problems and found that including student-level covariates had no appreciable effect on estimates of teacher effects.[4]

## Economic Models

Unlike the statistical models, which start with descriptive models for student achievement data and generally pay less attention to the assumptions and causal interpretations, models developed by economists start with an explicit model for students' potential outcomes given their current classroom assignment and establish a set of assumptions for that model so that standard estimation techniques will provide unbiased estimates of the model parameters and causal effects.

The basis for these economic models is the education production function (EPF), which involves a range of assumptions and mathematical terms. In the most generic terms, the EPF defines the education output for individual student $i$ at time $t$ as $A_{it}$ with school (including teacher) inputs of $S$ and family inputs $F$ from current and all previous time periods as a function $f(\cdot)$ of these inputs, a fixed student contribution $I_i$, and an error term, $\varepsilon_{it}$. This yields:

$$A_{it} = f(S_{it}, S_{it-1}, \ldots, F_{it}, F_{it-1}, \ldots, I_i, \varepsilon_{it}) \tag{9.2}$$

The fixed student contribution, $I_i$, is assumed to be determined by factors that cannot be observed by the data analyst and remain constant over time for each student, although they may vary across students. It is often called "innate ability" by economists and is akin to what psychologists consider general intelligence, or $g$. The more general term, *fixed student contribution,* is used here because it is virtually impossible with education data sets to estimate anything like innate ability. No data sets include measures of student abilities at birth or, in their absence, sufficiently measure family and other environmental factors well enough to distinguish innate from environmental differences.

Because the home environment contributes substantially to student outcomes, but in ways difficult to observe and measure, researchers increasingly emphasize the importance of accounting for "unobserved" differences among students, which are also represented in equation 9.2 by the fixed student component. Accounting for something that is unobserved may seem impossible, but it is possible when data are available on individual students over time so that each student can, in effect, serve as his or her own control group for the subsequent year. As noted earlier, the basic strategy in VA modeling is to look for deviations from each student's average rate of growth and then look to see whether students in particular classrooms—with particular teachers—are especially likely to learn faster than their usual rates. Hence, assuming that unobserved differences can be fully characterized by a single constant term for students provides a basis for estimating the parameters of the structural model. However, the appropriateness of this assumption has not been established.

Consider what would happen if the (unobserved) student contribution were not accounted for. Taking simple averages of student achievement gains by classroom, one would be concerned that students with higher scores come from families with higher incomes who, not coincidentally, send their children to local schools and their teachers teach students who differ from teachers teaching in schools located in lower-income neighborhoods. In this case, how is one to determine to what degree the simple correlation between school inputs and achievement gains reflects a causal effect of teacher inputs or a causal effect of family background? In an experiment, these unobserved differences would be addressed by randomly assigning students to control and treatment groups. In secondary data analysis, and specifically in equation 9.2, observed differences are captured by $F_i$ and unobserved differences are captured by $I_i$. This makes it reasonable to interpret the estimated relationships as causal effects of school inputs and, more generally, to call the EPF approach a quasi-experimental method.

The fact that equation 9.2 includes school inputs from previous periods ($t-1$ is shown and $t-2$, $t-3$, and so on are implied) is important and reflects the cumulative nature of education—that outcomes in each period are the result of the accumulation of all student experiences from birth up to the current time $t$.

With some additional assumptions, it is possible to make equation 9.2 more concrete. Boardman and Murnane (1979) were arguably the first to consider these assumptions in depth, and their work has been followed by more recent work by Todd and Wolpin (2003). The additional assumptions they discuss are:

1. *Age independence.* The cumulative EPF does not vary with age, so, for example, the effect of an input applied in second grade on third-grade student outcomes is the same as the effect of an input applied in third grade on fourth-grade student outcomes.

2. *Additive separability.* The EPF is additively separable, so that the effects of inputs do not interact with one another; for instance, the effects of schooling in grade 2 do not depend on the inputs to schooling in grade 3.

3. *Fixed family inputs.* All family inputs are fixed over time.

This last assumption implies further that the fixed family contribution can be combined with the fixed student contribution, so that the student contribution $I_i$ becomes the student-family contribution $\gamma_i$. This assumption, like many others, is mainly one of convenience and reflects the lack of data available on students' families and home environments. These assumptions yield the following more concrete EPF:

$$A_{it} = \varphi_1 S_{it} + \varphi_2 S_{it-1} + \ldots + \gamma_i + \varepsilon_{it} \tag{9.3}$$

where $\varphi$ represents the set of contributions given by current and previous school inputs.

Some additional simplification can be achieved by adding another assumption:

4. *Geometric decay.* Suppose the effects of all prior school inputs decline at an equal rate and decline geometrically with the time between the application of the input and the measurement of achievement so that $\varphi_2 = \lambda \varphi_1$, $\varphi_3 = \lambda \varphi_2 = \lambda^2 \varphi_1$, and so on, where $\lambda$ is some constant.

Intuitively, this formalizes the idea that the most recently received inputs have the greatest impact on current student achievement. For example, some studies estimate $\lambda = 0.8$, suggesting that a small increase in school inputs such as class size in the previous period $(t-1)$ would increase current achievement only 80 percent as much as the same increase in inputs in the current period $(t)$. If the geometric decay assumption is valid, then the achievement equation can then be reduced to:

$$A_{it} = \varphi_1 S_{it} + \lambda A_{it-1} + \gamma_i + \eta_{it} \tag{9.4}$$

It is important to note that not only have prior educational inputs been captured by the prior achievement measure, but the error term has also changed; in particular, it includes the error term from the prior year and a term involving the fixed student family contribution. Equation 9.4 and similar models that account for unobserved differences across students and families are sometimes referred to as the *value-added* EPF specification. Again, one reason for using this term is that accounting for unobserved student and family contributions makes it reasonably plausible that the estimated effects are causal.

Note that by making a judicious series of assumptions, we arrive at equation 9.4, which can be estimated by the newly available administrative data sets, unlike equations 9.2 and 9.3 which essentially never can be estimated. However, doing so is difficult even in the case of equation 9.4 and requires a number of assumptions in addition to those mentioned above regarding the derivation of the equation:

5. *Interval-scaled tests.* The student achievement test scores are "interval scaled" so that a one-unit change in score means the same thing on all parts of the scale.

6. *Uniform input effectiveness.* Each school input, including each teacher, is equally effective for all types of students.

7. *Student assignment is based on fixed characteristics.* Students are assigned to school (and nonschool) inputs in each period based on their fixed characteristics, not time-varying characteristics such as previous period achievement gains.

In summary, there are general EPF assumptions (for example, regarding the school and nonschool influences on student outcomes) as well as three assumptions necessary to derive a general cumulative EPF (age independence, additive separability, and fixed family inputs), and assumptions required to obtain the VA specification and allow causal interpretation of school input effects (geometric decay, interval scaled tests, equal teacher effectiveness, students assigned based on fixed characteristics). While these assumptions may be unrealistic, having explicated them, we now have a basis for estimating model parameters, including the supposed teacher causal effects, and then evaluating the assumptions required for making causal interpretations of the estimates.

## Value-Added for Teacher Accountability

The model we developed so far focused on the effects of school inputs, broadly defined. Here we are interested in the contributions to student learning made by individual teachers that could be used to hold educators accountable for their performance.

We can make the model depend on teachers by distinguishing among various school inputs. If we do this and assume that all school inputs decay at the same rate, we arrive at:

$$A_{it} = \omega T_{it} + \varphi_1 Z_{it} + \lambda A_{it-1} + \gamma_i + \eta_{it} \tag{9.5}$$

where $T_{it}$ denotes the input of the teacher at age $t$ and $Z_{it}$ denotes schooling inputs other than the teacher. When the teacher effect is being estimated, $\omega T_{it}$ is specified as a mean for the teacher's classroom and treated as an attribute of the teacher. However, this effect may be better characterized as a classroom effect since without further modeling, it corresponds to the average potential outcome for students when assigned to the teacher's classroom, and other factors associated with that classroom might be contributing to that mean. Causal effects are defined as differences in these teacher and classroom means.

Given all the necessary assumptions, the parameters of equation 9.5 can now be estimated without bias using standard linear regression techniques.[5] The teacher effects are obtained by including indicator variables for each teacher that equal 1 for students in the teacher's classroom and 0 otherwise into the data. This yields an estimated teacher effect that can be interpreted as the teacher's contribution to student learning (controlling, once again, for the student's contribution). This effect is identified from the movement of students across teachers from year to year. These moves allow the researcher to observe and compare each student's learning trajectory under multiple teachers.

It is possible to include variables in VAM-A other than the teacher indicators. For example, including teacher experience would change the model so that the VA measures essentially reflected comparisons of teachers with the same level of experience. Since the purpose of accountability is to measure performance and downplay the role of credentials and other qualifications, any measures of teacher credentials or other characteristics would generally be excluded.

Equation 9.5 lacks specificity about the other schooling inputs, such as class size and principal effectiveness, represented by $Z_{it}$, that are needed to fully specify the model. That is, it is necessary to account for school factors that influence student achievement but are outside the control of the teacher. Given that administrative data typically have limited measures of specific schooling inputs, it can be challenging to include all the necessary measures in the model when estimating teacher effects, and this misspecification could bias the estimated effects. One approach sometimes used to avoid underspecifying school inputs is to include school indicators in the estimation and school means (school effects) in the model. However, this creates an estimation problem since the average teacher mean at the school is now confounded with the school mean. Computationally this is solved in estimation by defining teacher causal effects as relative to the average effect for the school and estimating these effects by including both school and teacher indicator variables into the linear models used for estimation.

Although such a strategy allows estimation of a well-defined causal effect, making this change is not without consequences. Teacher VA measures in this case would now be based on direct comparisons with their colleagues in their school, and this is generally considered unacceptable for accountability. So while school effects help address the technical problem of the omission of school inputs, it is generally impractical for VAM-A. Rather, models drawing on available data on school inputs are used with known potential for bias from misspecification.[6] As we will see, this constraint on the estimation of VA models has significant consequences for the statistical validity of the models.

## Economic Versus Statistical Models

The two paradigms for estimating teacher VA measures are quite different. Economists start with models and make a series of assumptions to allow estimation of the parameters that equal causal teacher effects if the models' assumptions hold. They then test those assumptions empirically using various specification tests to determine if the estimates can be treated as unbiased causal effects or are potentially biased. The economic models include fixed effects for students (and, of course, teachers). The parameters are estimated by linear regression, often with gain scores as the dependent variable and indicator variables for teachers and students and other measures of educational inputs (peers and schooling) as the independent variables (Harris & Sass, 2007a, 2007b). In some applications, economic models use achievement level as the dependent variable and include prior-year test score as the independent variable.

Statistical models are descriptive models for repeated achievement scores for students. They include random effects to explain the correlation among the scores of students who shared a classroom in the current or prior years. Users treat these random effects as causal effects, though they pay less attention than economists to the assumptions necessary for this interpretation to be correct. Estimates of the current-year teacher (classroom) effect are adjusted for students' prior achievement because the complex estimation methods account for the correlation in residual error among repeated measures on the same student. The statistical models make fewer assumptions about the relationship between prior classroom inputs and current achievement than do economic models, but the resulting estimates are unbiased for causal effects only under untestable assumptions. Moreover, the statistical models, unlike the economics models, generally do not account for other educational inputs and conflate these with the teacher effect. Properties of the estimates from statistical models are generally studied by simulation studies, which have shown that under the right conditions with a modest number of years of testing, statistical models can yield nearly unbiased estimates of classroom effects.

## Assumption Tests

As interest in VA measures has grown, so has research about the assumptions and properties of these economics models. Are the assumptions described in the previous section valid? Do the patterns of teacher VA measures results make sense? These are the questions we address next as a way of establishing the degree of validity of VA estimates of teacher effects as measures of teachers' contributions to student learning.

We focus on evidence about assumptions 4 through 7 above. The other assumptions are difficult to test, and, in any event, we are not aware of any evidence that would allow comment on those assumptions.

**Geometric Decay (Assumption 4).** Education is a cumulative process. The educational resources students receive early in life affect their academic success later in life. But as a practical matter, it is impossible to explicitly measure the whole range of resources students receive at any given time, let alone in past years. To avoid this problem, we made explicit assumptions that inputs decay geometrically, so that when trying to explain why students reached achievement level $A$ at time $t$ $(A_t)$, we can account for past school resources by controlling for achievement in the previous time period $(A_{t-1})$. The effects of all school resources experienced up to time $t-1$ should be reflected in $A_{t-1}$. This assumption has not been directly explored empirically by, say, fitting models that include effects for current and prior teachers without including the geometric assumption and testing this against the more restrictive model.

Studies have explored the rate of decay ($\lambda$) given the assumed geometric decay. Kane and Staiger (2008b) show that the impacts of individual teachers decay by 50 percent or more per year. That is, the impact of having a good teacher does not seem to last. As J. Rothstein (2008) points out, this could be because the variation in VA estimates of teacher effects is driven by differences in instruction that have only ephemeral impacts, such as how much teachers teach to the test. Another possible explanation is that the content of achievement tests is somewhat independent across years. Psychometricians argue that constructs tested by most standardized tests change in response to changes in the content as a student matures across grades, and even tests of a supposedly single subject area measure different constructs for students of different ages (Martineau, 2006; Reckase, 2004; Schmidt, Houang, & McKnight, 2005; Hamilton, McCaffrey, & Koretz, 2006). If teachers affect only some constructs and these fade over time, their effects would also fade out of the achievement scores.[7] Whatever the explanation for the high rate of decay, Harris and Sass (2005) find that the impact of school resources is relatively insensitive to any decay assumption that might be imposed.

It might be surprising to some readers that prior scores are included in the model as a control for prior educational inputs, not for family, community, and student factors. In many social science applications and in ad hoc VA approaches, the primary motivation for adding prior scores as a variable in regression is to control for the student-specific inputs. The distinction is made because of assumptions about unobserved characteristics and how those are distributed across classrooms. In deriving equation 9.5, we allow that a student's potential outcomes can depend on time-invariant unobserved student characteristics *and* we make no assumptions about how these are associated with classroom assignments. Because of this generality of our model, controlling for prior achievement alone will not yield unbiased estimates of causal effects. For prior achievement to fully account for family and community factors, we must also assume that students are assigned to teachers based solely on their previous achievement (or in ways perfectly correlated with previous achievement), not on unobserved student characteristics that may also be related to students' subsequent achievement. This is implausible. For example, Feng (2005) finds that students are assigned to teachers partly based on students' discipline problems, which are generally unobserved in VA models. Also, Harris and Sass (2005) and McCaffrey, Sass, and Lockwood (2009) show that the findings regarding teacher effects are quite different when there is no attempt to control for unobserved student characteristics which might be related to classroom assignment.

**Interval-Scaled Tests (Assumption 5).** VA models are, at a basic level, models of student achievement. Therefore, it is unsurprising that they require strong assumptions about the measurement of student achievement. Specifically, it is assumed that a one-point change in the score is the same on every point on the test scale regardless of the students' initial level of achievement or the test year—that is, the test is interval-scaled within and across all years in the data. Even the psychometricians who are responsible for test scaling shy away from making this assumption in the strict sense (Schafer, 2006).

Ballou (2008) argues that the assumptions of traditional scaling techniques, based on item response theory (IRT), are inherently difficult to test. Furthermore, even the plausibility of the resulting test scales from these methods is questionable, and other reasonable approaches yield quite different measures of achievement gain. Ballou describes an alternative non-IRT method of measuring student progress, requiring less restrictive assumptions, in which students are ranked based on their achievement gains and then the teacher VA measures are calculated based on these rankings rather than the gains themselves.[8] He finds that the rankings of teachers on their VA measures often vary dramatically between the traditional approach using IRT-based scaled scores and the student rank-order approach, even though cases can be made for each. Briggs, Week, and Wiley (in press) also examine sensitivity to test scaling and find less sensitivity than Ballou, but this is likely due to the narrower range of assumptions that they consider (all fall within the IRT paradigm) and the fact that they focus on school VA rather than teacher VA. Given that the variation in true student gains is larger across teachers than across schools, VA estimates of teacher effects are almost necessarily more sensitive to the test scale than VA estimates of school effects. Thus, there remains considerable need for empirical research into the potential biases that might result from a lack of an interval scale—although this is considerable theoretical justification to question the validity of this assumption.

**Uniform Input Effectiveness (Assumption 6).** To achieve causal estimates, the model assumes that each teacher contributes the same additive amount to every student's learning regardless of level of achievement or other student attributes.[9] If this assumption is not true, then estimates are likely to be biased. To see the problem more clearly, suppose that some teachers were effective with low-achieving students and other teachers were effective with high-achieving students. Furthermore, suppose that all teachers were assigned only to students with whom they were most effective and that, in such a situation, all teachers appear equally effective in their VA measure. Now suppose instead that some teachers were "misassigned" to students with whom they were ineffective and their VA measures decrease as a result. These same teachers who had been judged effective will now appear ineffective simply because of the assignment process. This is problematic because teachers cannot control which students they are assigned to, and it would be difficult to argue that these misassigned teachers are really less effective than the others.

This example is an extreme case, intended to illustrate the potential problem created for VA if teachers are not equally effective with all students. Lockwood and McCaffrey (forthcoming) conclude that differential effects explain less than 10 percent of the variation in overall teacher effects. Therefore, what seems like a potential issue in theory may not be significant in practice.

**Student Assignment Is Based on Fixed Characteristics (Assumption 7).** It would be unrealistic to assume that students are assigned to teachers based on qualities available to the analysts. More likely, assignments depend on many factors, some observed and some not, and many that might be related to students' likely growth in achievement. To address this, we have included a fixed student-family contribution to the model and assumed that if classroom assignment depends on any unobservable characteristics of the student, those characteristics are accounted for by this static variable. For estimation, we account for this contribution to the structural model by including student-specific indicator variables or student fixed effects in the model. J. Rothstein (2008) describes this as the "static selection" assumption. This does not preclude changes over time in students' propensities to make learning gains, but it does mean that whatever factors are used in the classroom assignment process, any time-varying propensities to make learning gains are randomly distributed among teachers and are not associated with class assignments. Otherwise there is what J. Rothstein (2008) calls "dynamic selection," which may introduce bias into the teacher VA measures even when student fixed effects are included.

The static selection assumption with student fixed effects is almost certainly more realistic than the alternative, which would be that classroom assignment depends on only observed qualities (see assumption 2 and Harris & Sass, 2005), which explains why economists typically include student fixed effects in their models. But the matter is still not completely settled. j. Rothstein (2008) tests the dynamic selection assumption by considering whether the teacher assignment in any given year predicts past achievement growth. While we would expect the current teacher to affect current achievement, a current teacher cannot change what has already happened—or rewrite history—and will only appear to do so when students are nonrandomly assigned. Rothstein estimates VA models with student fixed effects and indeed finds that current teacher assignment does predict past student achievement. Moreover, these effects are not constant as he looks to earlier years, so that a fifth-grade teacher's effect on a student's fourth-grade scores does not equal the effect on this child's third-grade scores. This type of variation in effects on prior scores is contradictory to static selection and supports the hypothesis that classroom assignment is a dynamic selection process on factors related to student achievement.

It is worth considering how violations of the static selection assumption might arise in practice. Monk (1987) finds that most school principals randomly or evenly distribute students in elementary grades, apparently because principals want to even out the workload among teachers. But he also finds that some principals try to match students to teachers who have skills particularly well suited to students' needs, thus violating the static selection assumption, provided they are using the most recent information on students to make these assignments. This is consistent with Rothstein's results and particularly problematic for value-added estimation because all approaches (economic, statistics, and ad hoc) rely on assumptions that class assignment depends on at most a small number of mostly stable unobserved student factors (Lockwood & McCaffrey, 2007), or, even if not stable, they are fully captured in the prior achievement scores, but his findings suggest that in at least one setting, this does not appear to be true.[10] If this result is replicated in other studies, we might need to reconsider our interpretations of VA. But the full implication of the size of the potential bias that such violation of assumptions might create has not been studied, so this remains an area for further research before we make any extensive conclusions about VA estimation.

**Other Schooling Inputs.** We conclude the discussion of assumptions with one that was imposed at the end of the previous section: that the goal of accountability is to compare each teacher to all other teachers, not just those in the same school. This requires an additional assumption: school administration and teamwork among teachers do not have a significant impact on student achievement other than through any limited measures we have on these inputs. The data on school administration tend to be limited, even in very rich data sets, to factors such as principal tenure or years in the building. This leaves one of two options: invest in data collection to measure the quality of school administration directly (through surveys of teachers and parents, for example) and include these in the VA model, or assume that the impact of administration is small. Information from surveys is rarely, if ever, used in external accountability systems, which limits the practicality of the first option.

A similar problem arises with teacher teamwork. The purpose here is to measure how much each teacher contributes to student achievement, but it is possible, contrary to the assumptions of the VA models, that teachers contribute to the achievement of students of other teachers, for instance, by mentoring. The only rigorous evidence we are aware of on this point is Harris and Sass (2007b), who find that the number of National Board certified teachers in a school has no impact on the VA of other teachers within the same schools, but this is far from definitive. It is possible that neither administration nor teamwork plays a significant role; some researchers describe teaching as ''loosely coupled,'' meaning that teachers mainly work on their own in their classrooms, making it difficult for anyone else to have a significant impact on what they do or how well they do it.

**Summary of Assumptions.** The assumptions do not represent an exhaustive list of assumptions that apply to all VA models, though they are arguably the ones that are considered to be potentially most problematic.[11] Other assumptions vary depending on the model specification. Harris and Sass (2005) test a variety of these, finding, for example, that assumptions about rates of decay have relatively little impact on estimates of teacher value-added. It is also important to point out that these assumptions may be interrelated, so that violating one assumption might compound, or offset, the impact of violations in other assumptions. Research currently is mainly focused on testing individual assumptions, which is often quite complicated in itself.

## Statistical Properties of Value-Added Estimates of Individual Teacher Effects

It is possible that all of the assumptions of VA models are violated, but that the violations are not so severe that they have a practical impact on whether teachers would be rewarded or punished in an accountability system. Conversely, all of the assumptions might hold, but the models might still not have the statistical properties necessary for particular types of policy uses. This section explores other empirical findings regarding VA estimates of teacher effects that are relevant to understanding their usefulness for accountability.

VA estimates of teacher effects are positively correlated with other measures of teacher effectiveness. The estimates can be viewed as objective measures of teacher effectiveness in the sense that the method of calculating them is the same for all teachers and is not filtered through the subjective preferences and beliefs of a supervisor or other evaluator. A long history of research studies the relationships between subjective and objective measures of worker productivity, as well as the implications of this relationship for employment contracts. As Harris and Sass (2007c) and Jacob and Lefgren (2005) noted, this research suggests a positive, but arguably weak, relationship between subjective and objective measures. A limited amount of literature specifically addresses this issue for estimated teacher effects. These studies have examined the relationship between teachers' students' test scores and their principals' subjective assessments (Milanowski, 2004; Murnane, 1975). All of these studies find a positive and significant relationship despite differences in the degree to which the observations are used for high-stakes personnel decisions.

Some studies have used longitudinal data to estimate gain scores models that partly address the selection bias issues described earlier when comparing teachers' students' achievement to principals' evaluations of their performance (Medley & Coker, 1987; Peterson, 1987, 2000). Also, Jacob and Lefgren (2005) used VA models to study two hundred teachers in a midsized school district and reached two main conclusions: there is a 0.3 to 0.5 correlation between the subjective and objective measures, and this correlation holds even after controlling for teacher experience and education levels, which are currently the primary bases for determining teacher compensation. Harris and Sass (2007c) found similar results from an analysis of a midsized school district in Florida.[12] In addition to asking for their overall subjective assessments, they asked principals how well teachers contributed to student achievement so they could determine how much of their subjective assessments reflected teachers' contributions to outcomes other than achievement. With a simple correlation of 0.7 between principal overall evaluations of teachers and their evaluations of teachers' contributions to student test scores, the results suggest that achievement is probably the main objective of these principals, but also that other outcomes, such as willingness to contribute to school projects, serve on committees, and meet with parents, may partly explain the modest size of the correlation between the two measures.[13] For this reason, the comparison of principals' evaluations of teachers with teacher VA measures cannot be viewed as a validity check in itself, but it does suggest that VA measures provide useful information.

Education researchers and educators have typically measured teacher performance by measuring teacher inputs into education through observational assessments of what is defined on the basis of educational theory as "good teaching" (Fenstermacher & Richardson, 2005) or measures of teacher knowledge, training, credentials, or qualifications. There is limited study of the relationship between observational measures of inputs and VA. One study has found the Classroom Assessment Scoring System (CLASS) to be correlated with early learning gains among preschool students (Howes et al., 2008). Other researchers (Hill, Schilling, & Ball, 2004) have developed a test of teachers' knowledge for teaching mathematics and have found that these measures also correlate weakly with student growth and VA scores (Hill, Rowan, & Ball, 2005, McCaffrey, Han, and Lockwood, 2009).

Kane and Staiger (2008a; 2008b) report on an experiment involving seventy-eight classrooms in the Los Angeles School District. The researchers solicited school principals willing to randomly assign teachers to classrooms within their schools. The researchers then compared the VA measured before the experiment to those calculated on the basis for random assignment, which, so long as the random assignment was carried out with fidelity, cannot be driven by systematic assignment of students to teachers. Specifically, they regressed mean end-of-year test scores on previous VA. A coefficient of 1 on the VA variable would suggest that the previous VA estimates of these teacher effects are a perfect predictor of teacher contributions when random assignment is used. For some VA specifications, they did find coefficients close to 1, suggesting that the VA methods applied to the historic data with the natural classroom assignments were unbiased and did not differ systematically from the teachers' effects on randomly assigned classes. Conducting an experiment of this sort is inherently difficult, which makes Kane and Staiger's work especially impressive. However, some limitations make it difficult to view this as a validation of teacher VA measures. First, it is unclear how principals were assigning teachers before the experiment took place. If they were assigning teachers in effectively random ways, then the ''experiment'' is really no different from what was already happening, and their results could not be interpreted as evidence in support of VA measures.[14] If principals were tracking students and nonrandomly assigning students to different types of teachers, then the results here are significant and reinforce the potential of teacher VA measures. Although greater details on the nature of classroom assignment prior to the experiment are needed to determine the full implications of this study, it suggests that VA measures can line up with experimental measures in at least some cases and offer some support for optimism about VA measures. The study also provides a framework for additional studies of the properties of VA estimates of teacher effects.

Based on these findings—that VA estimates of teacher effects are correlated with principal evaluations and measures of teacher inputs, and it has been replicated in a random assignment experiment—the news on VA reinforces the potential use of VA measures for accountability. This is not the case with the following two findings.

Teacher value-added measures are imprecise. A prerequisite for any performance measure to be useful is that different teachers obtain different scores. Sanders and Horn (1998) and Rivkin et al. (2005), for example, find considerable differences between the most and least effective teachers based on VA results. However, it is important to consider to what degree this reflects variation in actual performance of the teachers rather than the idiosyncratic outcomes of the teachers' students in any given year (for example, the statistical error in the VA estimates of teacher effects).

Research has shown that VA estimates of teacher effects have large statistical errors, so the estimated VA effect of any teacher is likely to deviate substantially from the teacher's true effect due to chance coincidence of good or bad fortune of the sample of students in his or her class for a given year. By the usual standards of statistical significance, it is possible only to clearly distinguish very-low-VA teachers from very-high-VA teachers (Jacob & Lefgren, 2005; McCaffrey, Lockwood, Mariano, & Setodji, 2005). These large statistical errors in VA estimates of teacher effects are primarily the result of the high variability of student outcomes within classrooms after controlling for students' prior achievement and other terms in the model and the relatively modest number of students taught by each teacher. Large statistical errors in estimated effects is a problem for policies that intend to make high-stakes decisions based on the measures, except perhaps if those decisions pertain only to rewards for very high performers and punishments (for example, rejection of tenure) for very low performers. It is also a difficult problem to address because large variability among students' outcomes after controlling for other factors exists with all the proposed specifications of the VA models. Reduction of statistical errors cannot be achieved through model specification and would require more students per teacher per year, but increasing class size to improve estimation of teacher effects is clearly not feasible.[15]

As a result of these large sampling errors and potential variation in teacher effectiveness, VA estimates of individual teacher effects are unstable over time. For instance, Koedel and Betts (2007) found that only 35 percent of teachers ranked in the top fifth of teachers on the VA estimates of their effects from one year were still ranked in the top fifth in the subsequent year. Stability appears somewhat higher in studies by Aaronson et al. (2007) and Ballou (2005), but this may be due solely to the fact that in contrast to Koedel and Betts, who divided teachers into five groups, these other two studies divided teachers into only four groups, making it less likely that changes in groups would be observed. Overall these results are remarkably similar across studies.

McCaffrey, Lockwood, Sass, and Mihaly (2009) make an important contribution to this literature by showing that the vast majority of this instability stems from statistical error due to annual chance variation of student outcomes within classrooms rather than other sources. If sampling error in test score gains could be removed, then the degree of stability, as measured by the percentage of teachers staying within the same quartile from one year to the next, doubles or triples so that 50 to 90 percent of teachers would remain in the same performance group.

Like Koedel and Betts (2007), McCaffrey, Lockwood, Sass, and Mihaly (2009) also find that stability of effects is sensitive to model specification. For instance, estimates from models that include both student and school fixed effects were found by both studies to be less stable than estimates from alternative models. Different models and estimation methods make more or less efficient use of the available data, and this can result in estimates from some models having larger sampling errors than estimates from other models. Estimates with larger sampling errors will have greater instability since sampling errors are by definition unstable across time.[16]

The remaining instability may be due to genuine changes in teacher effectiveness over time, which VA measures are intended to capture, or to violations in the assumptions. For example, VA models assume that accounting for past achievement is sufficient to account for past resources. If instead, as J. Rothstein (2008) suggests, teachers are assigned based on unobserved time-varying student characteristics and these unobserved characteristics (or the process of nonrandom assignment) change over time, then this might generate false instability. Also, if each teacher's true effectiveness did vary considerably across student groups, then year-to-year changes in assignment of students to teachers, combined with differential impacts, would reflect true changes in teacher effects.

# DISCUSSION

Can value-added be used to bring the new accountability and better evaluations to teachers? Can it solve the free-rider problem or provide a way to efficiently use incentives where they are likely to have the most leverage without creating a host of new and perhaps greater problems?

The evidence in this chapter clearly shows that although some of the findings supporting VA measures are strong and positive, there are some serious technical challenges. VA models require a variety of restrictive assumptions (the nature of the assumptions varies with the statistics versus economics paradigms) that not only seem implausible but do not receive much support in empirical analysis. Also, the results are imprecise, which limits their practical utility. Nevertheless, VA estimates are correlated with other measures of teacher performance and have been apparently validated in a randomized trial.

But the case for teacher VA may be more about what it provides than whether it provides it perfectly. VA and other empirical studies find that teachers matter and are not all equally effective, and even very critical evaluations of the VA literature (McCaffrey et al., 2004) conclude that the VA studies support this claim. The traditional credential and qualification proxies for teacher effectiveness do not appear to provide good evidence about teachers' ability to produce student learning. The current evaluation system based on observations is broken (Wilson, 2009) and relies on practices that are highly subjective, burdensome, outdated, and unable to provide sound guidance about how to improve teaching practices or which teachers to tenure into the profession (Danielson & McGreal, 2000). Newer observations-based protocols also rely on ideas of "good teaching" based in educational theory, with only limited evidence that these measures can truly identify teachers who most (or least) effectively promote student learning. Given the existing system of standardized testing, the cost of creating VA measures is also quite low (Harris, 2008). VA may be imperfect, but so are evaluations not based on student outcomes, as well as other methods that consider outcomes in other ways.

For this reason, teacher VA measures may be quite valuable in guiding the right teachers to continue best practices or seek professional development. They might also be useful for developing incentives and accountability so that teacher compensation programs can reward the most effective teachers, respond to younger teachers' and young potential teachers' demands for being rewarded on the basis of their merits and inspire a broader range of professionals to enter the profession, and motivate teachers who are struggling to seek the advancement opportunities they require.

Other uses of student test scores suffer from all the same shortcomings of VA measures and more. For this reason, some researchers have called for switching federal Adequate Yearly Progress definitions, which focus on percentage proficient, to a VA approach (Toch & Harris, 2008). The same logic applies to individual teachers.

Simply calculating the VA measures is only a first step. Educators need to be trained in how to use VA measures and understand their limitations. Programs using these need to be piloted and evaluated through randomized experiments in which teachers whose performance is measured by VA are randomly assigned to the intervention, while their peers are assigned to control conditions, for example, such as the POINT experiment being carried out by the National Center on Performance Incentives in Nashville to study performance pay.

There also needs to be more development of methods for estimating unbiased effects with fewer assumptions and greater data collection so that data rather than assumptions are used to identify teacher effects. More studies like the inventive experiment of Cantrell et al. (2008) are also needed. All this research will be supported by greater use of VA in practice, so regardless of the many limitations of VA, it seems that greater rather than less use is the only way forward.

## Notes

1. We use the terms *teacher VA measures* and *VA measures of teacher effects* interchangeably throughout this chapter. We are following the convention in the literature to refer to the statistics created from student longitudinal data as measures of teacher effects. We do not mean to suggest that these measures accurately reflect attributes of individual teachers. Although this is the intended inference to be drawn from these measures, as we discuss in this chapter, the current research is mixed on the appropriate inferences to draw from these measures.

2. To be consistent with use in the literature and the intention of the estimation process, we will refer to the estimated classroom-level effects from the statistical models as *teacher effects* even though they might not be accurate estimates of the teacher's contribution to learning.

3. Heuristically, VA measures equal the classroom average of the differences between a student's predicted or expected score had he or she had the average teacher and his or her actual score. Including racial background measures into the model for VA might then be perceived as setting different expectations for different racial/ethnic groups. It also suggests that the lower achievement for minority students is a characteristic of the students rather than a result of schooling.

4. Ballou et al. (2004) did find some sensitivity to the inclusion of classroom-level variables, but this appeared to be due to limitations in the data (Ballou, 2005).

5. Formally the estimates are asymptotically unbiased and will have a bias that decays with the sample size.

6. A strong case can be made for comparing teachers within schools in VAM-P models so that the impact of school administration and the nonrandom assignment of

teachers to schools can be accounted for. In contrast to VAM-A, the results from VAM-P studies are used only to set broad policies rather than evaluate teachers in ways that might lead teachers to compete with one another in unproductive ways.

7. This statement refers to models in which lagged achievement is included as an independent variable. Value-added models that use the change in score as the dependent variable assume zero decay. When lagged achievement is included on the right-hand side for estimation, the rate of decay can be estimated directly or restricted to a specific value. The empirically estimated rate of decay depends on other aspects of the model specification. For example, the rate of decay in a model with student fixed effects is likely to be lower because, in the absence of student fixed effects, lagged achievement reflects both average achievement and the year-specific deviation. With student fixed effects, lagged achievement reflects only the latter.

8. The advantage of ordinal scales is that they require less restrictive assumptions, although they do throw out potentially useful information.

9. When we say the model assumes that a teacher contributes the same amount to every student, we mean that if we could compare every student's outcome when taught by this teacher to his or her outcome when taught by the average teacher, the difference in these two potential outcomes would be the same across students regardless of the student's characteristics. This assumption allows us to model the contributions of the teacher with a single additive factor $\omega T_{it}$ in equation 9.5 rather than separate factors depending on the student's attributes.

10. Rothstein, in discussing the issue of principal assignment decisions, wrote that "it requires in effect that principals decide on classroom assignments for the remainder of a child's career on the day that child begins kindergarten" (p. 10). In response, Harris (forthcoming-b) notes, "This statement unintentionally makes the assumption seem less realistic than it is." As noted above, the assumption of value-added models is satisfied under the "even distribution" assumption, even if the decisions about even distribution are made dynamically, such that principals take into account time-varying information about students. It would therefore be more accurate to say, in the context of within-school comparisons of teachers, that the models assume that some principals randomly assign students, and the remaining principals make decisions about each year's track based solely on the previous year's track, without making use of any new information. This still seems implausible, but a little less so than Rothstein's formulation. Also note that Rothstein's evidence seems to reject even the weaker assumption.

11. Another assumption is that student test data are missing at random. The data requirements for value-added are significant, and those data will be missing for a large portion of the students due to absenteeism, mobility across schools, and data processing errors. Missing data do not bias the results so long as they are missing at random, though missing data significantly diminish the reliability of the estimates. This is a strong assumption and is especially likely to be a problem in high-poverty schools where absenteeism and mobility are high and test-taking rates are lower. It is therefore a significant question whether valid value-added estimates can be made in schools with high mobility.

12. The correlations in Harris and Sass (2005) are somewhat lower, but apparently because they did not adjust for measurement error. Jacob and Lefgren (2005) show both adjusted and unadjusted measures, and the results in Harris and Sass are very similar to the former.

13. A related issue is that school principals in the study had some access to some of the same data as the researchers, and their assessments of teachers' contributions to student achievement might have been direct reflections of this. On the other hand, the principals had at most access to simple student achievement gains and not the value-added measures described here.

14. Their findings regarding value-added specifications would still be valid even if principals had been randomly assigning teachers and students to begin with. Each specification makes different assumptions, as the earlier discussion highlights, and the goal is to get as close to the experimental estimates as possible.

15. For earlier work on the imprecision of grade-level effects, as opposed to teacher effects, see Kane and Staiger (2001, 2002).

16. Alternatively, the stability of estimates can be inflated if estimated effects are confounded by other inputs that tend to be stable across time. For example, classroom average prior achievement tends to be relatively stable across years for many teachers' classes. Estimated effects that confound student inputs with the teacher effects could therefore tend to be very stable across time relative to methods that removed such confounds.

# REFERENCES

Aaronson, D., Barrow, L., & Sander, W. (2007). Teachers and student achievement in the Chicago public high schools. *Journal of Labor Economics*, *25*, 95–135.

Ballou, D. (2005). Value-added assessment: Lessons from Tennessee. In R. Lissetz (Ed.), *Value added models in education: Theory and applications*. Maple Grove, MN: JAM Press.

Ballou, D. (2008, April). *Test scaling and value-added measurement*. Paper presented at the Wisconsin Center for Educational Research National Conference of Value-Added Modeling, Madison.

Ballou, D., Sanders, W., & Wright, P. (2004). Controlling for student background in value-added assessment of teachers. *Journal of Educational and Behavioral Statistics*, *29*(1), 37–65.

Boardman, A. E., & Murnane, R. J. (1979). Using panel data to improve estimates of the determinants of educational achievement. *Sociology of Education*, *52*, 113–121.

Briggs, D., Week, J., & Wiley, E. (in press). The sensitivity of value-added modeling to the creation of a vertical score scale. *Education Finance and Policy*.

Cantrell, S., Fullerton, J., Kane, T. J., & Staiger, D. O. (2008). *National Board certification and teacher effectiveness: Evidence from a random assignment experiment*. Paper developed under a grant from the Spencer Foundation and the U.S. Department of

Education. Retrieved September 8, 2009, from http://harrisschool.uchicago.edu/Programs/beyond/workshops/ppepapers/fall07-kane.pdf.

Coleman, J. S. (1966). *Equality of educational opportunity*. Washington, DC: U.S. Department of Health, Education, and Welfare, Office of Education/National Center for Education Statistics.

Danielson, C., & McGreal, T. L. (2000). *Teacher evaluation to enhance professional practice*. Alexandria, VA: Association for Supervision and Curriculum Development.

Feng, L. (2005). *Hire today, gone tomorrow: The determinants of attrition among public school teachers*. Munich: University Library of Munich, Germany.

Fenstermacher, G., & Richardson, V. (2005). On making determinations of quality in teaching. *Teachers College Record, 107*(1), 186–213.

Fuhrman, S. (1999). *The new accountability*. Philadelphia: University of Pennsylvania.

Goldhaber, D. D., & Brewer, D. J. (1997). Why don't schools and teachers seem to matter? Assessing the impact of unobservables on educational productivity. *Journal of Human Resources, 32*(3), 505–523.

Gordon, R., Kane, T. J., & Staiger, D. O. (2006). *Identifying effective teachers using performance on the job* (Discussion Paper 2006–01). Washington, DC: Brookings Institution.

Hamilton, L., McCaffrey, D., & Koretz, D. (2006). Validating achievement gains in cohort-to-cohort and individual growth-based modeling contexts. In R. Lissitz (Ed.), *Longitudinal and value-added modeling of student performance* (pp. 407–435). Maple Grove, MN: JAM Press.

Harris, D. N. (2008). The policy uses and "policy validity" of value-added and other teacher quality measures. In D. H. Gitomer (Ed.), *Measurement issues and the assessment for teacher quality* (pp. 99–130). Thousand Oaks, CA: Sage Publications.

Harris, D. N. (forthcoming-a). Education production functions: Concepts. In B. McGaw, P. L. Peterson, & E. Baker (Eds.), *International encyclopedia of education*. Oxford: Elsevier.

Harris, D. N. (forthcoming-b). Would accountability based on teacher value-added be smart policy? Evidence on statistical properties and comparisons with policy alternatives. *Education Finance and Policy*.

Harris, D. N., & Sass, T. (2005). *Value-added models and the measurement of teacher quality*. Paper presented at the 2005 conference of the American Education Finance Association.

Harris, D. N., & Sass, T. (2007a). *Teacher training, teacher quality, and student achievement*. National Center for the Analysis of Longitudinal Data in Education Research (Working Paper no. 3). Washington, DC: Urban Institute.

Harris, D. N., & Sass, T. (2007b). *The effects of NBPTS-certified teachers on student achievement*. National Center for the Analysis of Longitudinal Data in Education Research (Working Paper no. 4). Washington, DC: Urban Institute.

Harris, D. N., & Sass, T. (2007c). *What makes a good teacher and who can tell?* Paper presented at the summer workshop of the National Bureau of Economic Research, Cambridge, MA.

Hill, H. C., Rowan, B., & Ball, D. L. (2005). Effects of teachers' mathematical knowledge for teaching on student achievement. *American Educational Research Journal*, *42*(2), 371–406.

Hill, H. C., Schilling, S. G., & Ball, D. L. (2004). Developing measures of teachers' mathematics knowledge for teaching. *Elementary School Journal*, *105*(1), 11–30.

Holland, P. W. (1986). Statistics and causal inference. *Journal of the American Statistical Association*, *81*(396), 945–960.

Howes, C., Burchinal, M., Pianta, R., Bryant, D., Early, D., Clifford, R., et al. (2008). Ready to learn? Children's pre-academic achievement in pre-kindergarten programs. *Early Childhood Research Quarterly*, *23*(1), 27–50.

Jacob, B. A., & Lefgren, L. (2005). *Principals as agents: Subjective performance measurement in education* (NBER Working Paper no. 11463). Cambridge, MA: National Bureau of Economic Research.

Kane, T. J., & Staiger, D. O. (2001). *Improving school accountability measures* (NBER Working Paper no. 8156). Cambridge, MA: National Bureau of Economic Research.

Kane, T. J., & Staiger, D. O. (2002). The promise and pitfalls of using imprecise school accountability measures. *Journal of Economic Perspectives*, *16*(4), 91–114.

Kane, T. J., & Staiger, D. O. (2008a, April). *Are teacher-level value-added estimates biased? An experimental validation of non-experimental estimates*. Paper presented at the National Conference on Value-Added Modeling, Madison, WI.

Kane, T. J., & Staiger, D. O. (2008b). *Estimating teacher impacts on student achievement: An experimental evaluation* (NBER Working Paper no. 14607). Cambridge, MA: National Bureau of Economic Research.

Koedel, C., & Betts, J. R. (2007). *Re-examining the role of teacher quality in the educational production function* (Working Paper no. 2007–03). Nashville, TN: National Center on Performance Initiatives.

Lee, V. E., & Burkham, D. T. (2002). *Inequality at the starting gate*. Washington, DC: Economic Policy Institute.

Lockwood, J. R., & McCaffrey, D. F. (2007). Controlling for individual heterogeneity in longitudinal models, with applications to student achievement. *Electronic Journal of Statistics*, *1*, 223–252. Retrieved from http://dx.doi.org/10.1214/07-EJS057.

Lockwood, J. R., & McCaffrey, D. F. (forthcoming). Exploring student-teacher interactions in longitudinal achievement data. *Journal of Education Finance and Policy*.

Lockwood, J. R., McCaffrey, D. F., Mariano, L. T., & Setodji, C. (2007). Bayesian methods for scalable multivariate value-added assessment. *Journal of Educational and Behavioral Statistics*, *32*(2), 125–150.

Mariano, L. T., McCaffrey, D. F., & Lockwood, J. R. (2008). A model for teacher effects from longitudinal data without assuming vertical scaling. Manuscript submitted for publication.

Martineau, J. (2006). Distorting value-added: The use of longitudinal, vertically scaled student achievement data for value-added accountability. *Journal of Educational and Behavioral Statistics*, *31*(1), 35–62.

McCaffrey, D. F., Han, B., & Lockwood, J. R. (2009). Turning student test scores into teacher compensation systems. In M. Springer (Ed.), *Performance incentives: Their growing impact on American K–12 education* (pp. 113–147). Washington, DC: Brookings Institution Press.

McCaffrey, D. F., Lockwood, J. R., Koretz, D., Louis, T., & Hamilton, L. (2004). Models for value-added modeling of teacher effects. *Journal of Educational and Behavioral Statistics, 29*(1), 67–101.

McCaffrey, D. F., Lockwood, J. R., Mariano, L. T., & Setodji, C. (2005). Challenges for value added assessment of teacher effects. In R. Lissitz (Ed.), *Value added models in education: Theory and practice* (pp. 272–297). Maple Grove, MN: JAM Press.

McCaffrey, D. F., Lockwood, J. R., Sass, T. R., & Mihaly, R. (2009). The inter-temporal variability of teacher effect estimates. *Education Finance and Policy, 4*(4), 572–606.

Medley, D. M., & Coker, H. (1987). The accuracy of principals' judgments of teacher performance. *Journal of Educational Research, 80*(4), 242–247.

Mendro, R. L., Jordan, H. R., Gomez, E., Anderson, M. C., & Bembry, K. L. (1998). *An application of multiple linear regression in determining longitudinal teacher effectiveness.* Paper presented at the 1998 Annual Meeting of the American Educational Research Association, San Diego, CA.

Milanowski, A. (2004). The relationship between teacher performance evaluation scores and student assessment: Evidence from Cincinnati. *Peabody Journal of Education, 79*(4), 33–53.

Monk, D. H. (1987). Assigning elementary pupils to their teachers. *Elementary School Journal, 88*(2), 166–187.

Murnane, R. J. (1975). *The impact of school resources on the learning of inner city children.* Cambridge, MA: Ballinger.

Neyman, J., Iwaszkiewicz, K., & Kolodziejczyk, S. (1935). Statistical problems in agricultural experimentation. *Journal of the Royal Statistical Society, 2,* 107–180.

Nye, B., Konstantopoulos, S., & Hedges, L. V. (2004). How large are teacher effects? *Educational Evaluation and Policy Analysis, 26*(3), 237–257.

Peterson, K. D. (1987). Teacher evaluation with multiple and variable lines of evidence. *American Educational Research Journal, 24*(2), 311–317.

Peterson, K. D. (2000). *Teacher evaluation: A comprehensive guide to new directions and practices* (2nd ed.). Thousand Oaks, CA: Corwin Press.

Raudenbush, S. W., & Bryk, A. S. (2002). *Hierarchical linear models: Applications and data analysis methods* (2nd ed.). Thousand Oaks, CA: Sage.

Reckase, M. (2004). The real world is more complicated than we would like. *Journal of Educational and Behavioral Statistics 29*(1), 117–120.

Rivkin, S. G., Hanushek, E., & Kain, J. F. (2005). Teachers, schools and academic achievement. *Econometrica, 73,* 417–458.

Rothstein, J. (2008). *Teacher quality in educational production: Tracking, decay, and student achievement* (Working Paper no. 14442). Cambridge, MA: National Bureau of Economic Research.

Rothstein, R. (2004). *Class and schools: Using social, economic, and educational reform to close the black-white achievement gap.* New York: Teachers College Press.

Rowan, B., Correnti, R., & Miller, R. J. (2002). What large-scale survey research tells us about teacher effects on student achievement: Insights from the Prospects study of elementary schools. *Teachers College Record, 104,* 1525–1567.

Roy, A. D. (1951). Some thoughts on the distribution of earnings. *Oxford Economic Papers, 3*(2), 135–146.

Rubin, D. B. (1974). Estimating causal effects of treatments in randomized and nonrandomized studies. *Journal of Educational Psychology, 66*(5), 688–701.

Sanders, W. L., & Horn, S. P. (1998). Research findings from the Tennessee Value-Added Assessment System (TVASS) database: Implications for educational evaluation and research. *Journal of Personnel Evaluation in Education, 12,* 247–256.

Sanders, W. L., & Rivers, J. C. (1996, November). *Cumulative and residual effects of teachers on future academic achievement.* Knoxville: University of Tennessee, Value-Added Research and Assessment Center.

Sanders, W., Saxton, A., & Horn, B. (1997). The Tennessee Value-Added Assessment System: A quantitative outcomes-based approach to educational assessment. In J. Millman (Ed.), *Grading teachers, grading schools: Is student achievement a valid evaluation measure?* (pp. 137–162). Thousand Oaks, CA: Corwin Press.

Schafer, W. D. (2006). Growth scales as an alternative to vertical scales. *Practical Assessment Research and Evaluation, 11*(4). Retrieved from http://pareonline.net/getvn.asp?v=11&n=4.

Schmidt, W. H., Houang, R. T., & McKnight, C. C. (2005). Value-added research: Right idea but wrong solution? In R. Lissitz (Ed.), *Value added models in education: Theory and practice* (pp. 272–297). Maple Grove, MN: JAM Press.

Toch, T., & Harris, D. (2008, October 1). Salvaging accountability. *Education Week,* pp. 30–31, 36.

Todd, P. E., & Wolpin, K. I. (2003). On the specification and estimation of the production function for cognitive achievement. *Economic Journal, 113,* F3–F33.

Wilson, S. (2009). Measuring teacher quality for professional entry. In D. H. Gitomer (Ed.), *Measurement issues and assessment for teaching quality.* Thousand Oaks, CA: Sage.

Wright, S. P., Horn, S. P., & Sanders, W. L. (1997). Teacher and classroom context effects on student achievement: Implications for teacher evaluation. *Journal of Personnel Evaluation in Education, 11,* 57–67.

# The National Board for Professional Teaching Standards

## *An Investment for the Future?*

### Jillian P. Reese

*In remembrance of William L. Boyd*

It has been over twenty years since the establishment of the National Board for Professional Teaching Standards (NBPTS), through which over fifty-five thousand teachers have earned recognition. While estimates of the dollars expended on the program vary from approximately $350 million to nearly $500 million, inarguably a significant amount of money has been spent on the development and implementation of this national certification process. According to a recent NBPTS (National Board for Professional Teaching Standards, 2007) report, the process raises the bar for improving teacher effectiveness. It has "set rigorous standards for teachers and developed a voluntary national certification system that recognizes, rewards, and helps retain highly accomplished teachers." At the same time, studies have found a scarcity of National Board Certified Teachers (NBCTs) in the classrooms where excellent teaching is needed the most. Also in question is the overall effectiveness of the process of identifying and promoting good teaching and how the education system is able to capitalize on the expertise of these teachers.

In an educational era defined by standards and accountability and a climate of doubt as to the effectiveness of American public schools, examining the

---

William L. Boyd was originally invited to author this chapter. Having recently been diagnosed with pancreatic cancer, he asked me to coauthor it. William Boyd lost his fight against cancer before this chapter was completed. However, his lasting mentorship guided me through the final revisions.

impact of this costly, high-profile venture in American public education is critical. With the board mission serving as a framework for analysis and with consideration of current research, interviews with key NBPTS participants both for and against the program, and analyses of alternatives to different aspects of the National Board process, this chapter explores where the board began, how it looks today, and where it is—or should be—going.

# THE BIRTH OF THE NATIONAL BOARD

The idea for the National Board was first articulated in a 1985 speech by American Federation of Teachers president Albert Shanker. Shanker's remarks were intended to advocate a system that would boost the professionalism of teachers as experts, who, by virtue of that expertise, would be permitted to operate fairly independently, as is done in other professions. Shanker's ideas were a centerpiece of the 1986 report of the Carnegie Forum on Education and the Economy's Task Force on Teaching as a Profession, *A Nation Prepared: Teachers for the 21st Century.* The report called for the creation of a national board for professional teaching standards "to establish high standards for what teachers need to know and should be able to do, and to certify teachers who meet that standard," to restructure schools "while holding them accountable for student progress," to "restructure the teaching force, and introduce a new category of Lead Teachers," and to "relate incentives for teachers to school-wide student performance" (p. 3).

The founding board of the NBPTS established the following year, consisted of sixty-three board members, including teachers, government officials, representatives from national teachers' associations, and individuals from business and other private sectors. The board was defined as "an independent, non-profit, nonpartisan, and non-governmental organization" whose "mission is to advance the quality of teaching and learning by maintaining high and rigorous standards for what accomplished teachers should know and be able to do, providing a national voluntary system certifying teachers who meet these standards, and advocating related education reforms to integrate National Board Certification in American education and to capitalize on the expertise of National Board Certified Teachers" (NBPTS, 2008)

At the outset, the founders of NBPTS had no idea how time-consuming and expensive the pursuit of its goals would be. Six years and $200 million later, the first group of teachers became National Board certified. To get to that point, the board had significant hurdles to clear (Hannaway & Bischoff, 2005). A certification process had to be defined absent the support of existing research on effective processes. Numerous problems associated with devising criteria, measurement items, and scoring strategies had to be addressed. In addition, there was no demand from policymakers or the public for the creation of a cadre of master teachers. Efforts to create rigorous standards for teachers, evaluate them against such standards, and offer differential or merit pay had always faced strong resistance from teacher unions. Finally, it was unclear why teachers would opt for this special certification given the prevalence of the single salary schedule.

The methods used to overcome these obstacles were exceptional even in the eyes of many critics. The National Board gained extraordinary support from foundation and government leaders through a powerful combination of astute leadership, political savvy, skillful lobbying, and an organizational structure and process that involved the key stakeholders. The board immediately gained legitimacy with educators by giving a majority of the places on the National Board to teachers—two-thirds of the sixty-three seats on the founding board. Representatives of both national teacher associations were also invited to participate in the launch of the National Board. Noted critic of the National Board Chester Finn suggested that the efforts to overcome these initial challenges were a "fascinating case study in getting millions of dollars" (personal communication, May 2005).

Indispensable and remarkably effective leadership was provided by North Carolina's governor, Jim Hunt, chair of the board of directors for the first ten years, and by James Kelly, who, in addition to being the original board president, was a veteran of years of work in education and social policy for the Ford Foundation. Over the first six years, Kelly, Hunt, and the other founding board members succeeded in convincing many states to join the effort and offer incentives to teachers who agreed to go through the rigorous certification process. The enthusiasm, commitment, and testimonies of these teachers often helped other school and government leaders see the value of supporting the National Board process.

While acceptance for the many facets of the National Board was critical to its initial growth, perhaps the greatest contribution of the founding board was the identification of a set of standards to be used as a basis for the certification process (Joe Aguerrebere, personal communication, May 3, 2005). Prior to the National Board, the field lacked consensus on what constituted good teaching. Finding agreement on standards for effective teaching and a way to measure this broke new ground for American public education. And using these standards to improve teaching and teacher training could ultimately lead to increased student achievement. As many of the early board-certified teachers agreed, the standards reassured them that there was a professional set of skills and practices and caused them to ponder how they could use these skills and practices to be successful with all students.

Standards were originally developed for just two content areas, but have been expanded across twenty-five certificate areas. All of the standards are based on the five core propositions of the NBPTS: (1) teachers are committed to students and their learning, (2) teachers know the subjects they teach and how to teach those subjects to students, (3) teachers are responsible for managing and monitoring student learning, (4) teachers think systematically about their practice and learn from experience, and (5) teachers are members of learning communities.

Another important aspect of the certification process has been the rigorous criterion it established and upholds in identifying excellent teachers. National Board assessments consist of two main parts: portfolio entries and assessment center exercises. Specific entries and exercises vary across content areas, but the major parts are consistent. The portfolios consist of videotapes, student products, teaching artifacts, and candidate analyses of their teaching practice. Assessments reflect specific knowledge of content areas and are meant to validate the content of the portfolios. According to the board, a candidate's efforts to achieve National Board certification likely takes the better part of a school year and represents two hundred to four hundred hours of work. The often painstaking process certifies only about 50 percent of candidates in their first effort at achieving national certification (Goldhaber, Perry, & Anthony, 2004). According to James Kelly (personal communication, April 2005), the process was intended to be challenging to help build the credibility of the venture with business and political leaders. The demanding nature of the process leads some applicants to describe it as a powerful transformative professional development experience (Joe Aguerrebere, personal communication, May 3, 2005).

# THE NATIONAL BOARD TODAY

A glimpse at the National Board today shows a widespread program with substantial support from educators and political leaders alike. Questions remain, however, about important aspects of the National Board process. Using the original mission of the NBPTS as a framework for analysis, this section looks at how well the National Board is advancing the quality of teaching and learning by maintaining high and rigorous standards for what accomplished teachers should know and be able to do, providing a national voluntary system certifying teachers who meet these standards, and advocating related education reforms to integrate National Board certification in American education and capitalize on the expertise of National Board Certified Teachers.

## Education Reform and National Voluntary Certification

All states now offer regulatory or legislative support for National Board certification, and a number of states and more than five hundred school districts offer financial incentives. Incentives vary significantly from the payment of the application costs of twenty-five hundred dollars to as high as a 12 percent increase in annual salary, as is the case in North Carolina. (As noted previously, James Hunt was the governor of North Carolina at the inception of the National Board. North Carolina currently employs more NBCTs than any other state.) With research suggesting that the impact of NBCTs is greater in the early grades of high-poverty schools (Goldhaber & Anthony, 2005), some states offer different incentives based on the school of employment. In Colorado, for example, teachers receive an additional thirty-two hundred dollars to the initial sixteen hundred dollars if they teach in a school that received a rating of low or unsatisfactory on the previous year's accountability report (National Board for Professional Teaching Standards, 2008). These differentiations in a pay scale traditionally based on years of experience and level of education demonstrate at least a minimal, if not significant, reform in American public education.

One telling indication of the success of the National Board program comes from those who have voluntarily undergone the arduous certification process. Growth of the National Board initially came from the lengthy testimonials these individuals gave to policymakers and other political leaders. Today there continues to be a perception that those who have gone through the process believe it greatly improved their teaching. Some say it was the most meaningful professional development experience of their career, and studies have found that "National Board Certification revitalizes teachers' interest and enthusiasm for teaching" (National Board for Professional Teaching Standards, 2007). With seventy-four thousand teachers already certified through the process, the national system has inarguably worked its way into the mainstream of education and continuing professional development for teachers.

## Advancing the Quality of Teaching and Learning

How, and how well, the NBPTS process is advancing the quality of teaching and learning is a much more controversial aspect of the program. Under the umbrella of teaching and learning, one must look at the impact the process is having on identifying and developing quality teachers, as well as the effect of these teachers on student learning and achievement. As the NBPTS (National Board for Professional Teaching Standards, 2007) itself declared, the core message and creed is, "Better Teaching, Better Learning."

In a penetrating discussion of quality teaching in the *Teachers College Record*, Fenstermacher and Richardson (2005) make clear that appraising teaching is not a simple matter. They differentiate between the task of teaching and the student achievement that is expected to follow. While it seems obvious that quality teaching requires strength in both content knowledge and pedagogical techniques, getting the right balance between these components remains controversial. Except where individuals are self-taught, learning is a jointly produced outcome, involving effort by both a teacher and a learner.

The pedagogical techniques help engage and communicate to the learner. Fenstermacher and Richardson stress, "We all know that learners are not passive receptors of information directed at them. Learning does not arise solely on the basis of teacher activity.... It follows that success at learning requires a combination of circumstances well beyond the actions of a teacher" (p. 191). Consequently, they conclude, it makes sense to appraise both the task dimension and the achievement dimension of teaching. If there is no recognition of this difference, then it is hard to recognize some of NBPTS's important virtues and easy to be impatient with it.

While assessing teacher quality is difficult, the NBPTS has endeavored to show the positive impact board-certified teachers have on student learning by commissioning numerous independent studies. At least three recent studies show a positive correlation between NBCTs and student learning. A study by Goldhaber et al. (2004) found that, on average, North Carolina students whose teachers were board certified scored higher on tests than students whose teachers attempted but failed to gain certification. The study also found that the impact was the greatest on younger students and those from low-income families. The North Carolina study looked at more than 600,000 student records and their state test scores over a three-year period.

Vandervoort, Amrein-Beardsley, and Berliner (2004) also found that board-certified teachers were doing a better job of raising student achievement. This study looked at the results of three different standardized tests given to third through sixth graders in fourteen Arizona districts. It showed a link between nationally certified teachers and an overall average one-month greater gain in their students' performance as compared to others in the same districts.

A third study (Cavalluzzo, 2004) looked at 108,000 Miami–Dade County, Florida, student records from the 1999–2000 and 2002–2003 school years. This study found that ninth and tenth graders in classrooms with NBCTs scored measurably higher than other students on a Florida mathematics exam. Similar to the Goldhaber study, the Miami–Dade County study showed that black and Hispanic students benefited most from having National Board Certified Teachers.

Bringing the validity of these studies into question, another study (Sanders, Ashton, & Wright, 2005) showed that students of NBCTs do not have significantly better rates of academic progress than students of other teachers. Similar to another report, "The Value-Added Achievement Gains of NBPTS-Certified Teachers in Tennessee" (Stone, 2002), this study looked at the relationship of student achievement and teacher effectiveness and questions why the National Board certification process focuses on what teachers know and should be able to do rather than on their effects on student learning.

In his book *Common Sense School Reform* (2004), Frederick Hess wrote, "In theory, [NBPTS] is an interesting idea," but "in execution, it is a disaster":

> The NBPTS approach undermines commonsense efforts to link teacher compensation or recognition to their effectiveness as a classroom teacher, faculty colleague, and member of the school community. Instead, it has constructed an exhausting, expensive process that wastes time and money while suggesting that the measure of teacher quality is not whether students learn but whether teachers write sufficiently passionate essays about their "commitment" and "reflectiveness" [p. 128].

Meanwhile, the 2002 report found that none of the sixteen board-certified teachers in Tennessee who taught grades 3 to 8 (the only grades for which value-added scores were available) met a standard for exceptional teaching set by an incentive program in Chattanooga. The author argued that the results provided reason to suspend public expenditures on NBPTS certification by casting serious doubt on the claims of the National Board. Prompted by the report, the Education Commission of the States commissioned an independent panel of four experts to review the validity of Stone's research. The panel acknowledged that the study addressed an important policy question and that the absence of studies of this type was due in part to the board's approach to identifying excellent teachers through examining practices rather than focusing on student achievement. While the review concluded that the study was badly flawed and its claims therefore were unsupported, Stone continued to assert that a good value-added assessment would more accurately identify excellence in teaching than what he referred to as the "costly and time consuming process" (Holland, 2004).

Stone's was not the last argument made for a need to place a stronger emphasis on estimates of the teachers' value-added to student achievement. One study on the relationship between National Board certification and teacher effectiveness (Cantrell, Fullerton, Kane, & Staiger, 2008) found that students assigned to teachers with high prior value-added estimates significantly outperformed those with low value-added scores. The study did offer the caveat that value-added techniques are still being refined, and more research is necessary in this area. *Editor's note*: For more on the merits of value-added assessments, see Chapter Nine.

## The ABCTE Alternative

Partially motivated by the argument for value-added assessment, an alternative to the NBPTS, the Distinguished Teacher (formerly called Master Teacher) identification of the American Board for Certification of Teacher Excellence (ABCTE) was proposed. Still in development, the ABCTE certification process is based on four elements defined as contributing to a Distinguished Teacher.

The first element is impact on learning gains: a Distinguished Teacher's students must, on average, make more than one year's worth of growth while in their class. As once noted on the Web site of the American Board (American Board for Certification of Teacher Excellence, 2008), "We use a statistical teacher impact model to control for students' characteristics. This process provides the most scientifically accurate and fair representation of a teacher's effectiveness. The impact model can accommodate all tested subject areas by using a yearly student growth scale."

The three remaining elements for a Distinguished Teacher are excellent teaching practice, distinguished professionalism and leadership, and subject matter expertise. These elements align closely with the goals of the NBPTS in terms of the focus on what teachers should know and be able to do and creating a cadre of expert teachers to help improve the broader teaching profession. It is the first element, focused on impact on learning gains, that distinguishes the ABCTE from its counterpart.

Although conversations about the Distinguished Teacher certification began as early as 1999, the ABCTE program has not gained nearly the support as did the NBPTS in its earlier years. Initial intentions were to provide an alternative master teacher option that was a "more cut to the chase" and less expensive approach than that of the National Board (Kathy Madigan, personal communication, May 6, 2008). The ABCTE also offers an alternative route to teaching that challenges state routes to certification and may have hindered the progress of gaining support for the master teacher program. If, and when, the program begins issuing Distinguished Teacher certification, analyses will undoubtedly examine its effectiveness in meeting its goals.

In concluding their study on teacher effectiveness, Cantrell et al. (2008), importantly noted:

> Practice-based approaches to assessing teacher performance, such as the NBPTS application process, have typically been portrayed as being at odds with the value-added approach. This is an unfortunate historical accident, driven more by the ideological pre-dispositions of the respective supporters, rather than any substantive reason. Our results imply that the combination of both the NPTS scores and the prior value-added estimates could be helpful in identifying those teachers most likely to produce exemplary student gains [p. 43].

This begs the obvious question: Why create another system of national certification rather than just improve on the one already in existence?

## Capitalizing on the Expertise of Board-Certified Teachers

Let us assume that the National Board process does lead to or contribute to quality teaching and that it also leads ultimately to increased student learning. Then in order for public education to capitalize on the expertise of board-certified teachers, as set forth in the mission, students who require greater increases in learning should benefit from the quality teaching of the NBCTs. However, a 2005 study by Humphrey, Koppich, and Hough highlighted an equity issue concerning the distribution of board-certified teachers in the schools that need them the most. They found that a disproportionate number of board-certified teachers were working in high-performing schools serving more advantaged students.

The generally uneven distribution of educational resources in the United States led to a harsh *New York Times* column (Kristof, 2009) declaring American education as a "national shame." Columnist Kristof declared, "One of the greatest injustices is that America's best teachers overwhelmingly teach America's most privileged students. In contrast, the most disadvantaged students invariably get the least effective teachers, year after year—until they drop out" (p. WK11). Kristof's solution to this and other educational woes was to scrap certification, use testing to better measure which teachers are effective, and then pay them significantly more, with special bonuses to those who teach in poorly performing schools. Similarly, in a 2005 commentary on National Board certification, Andrew Rotherham declared, "The dispersion of board certified teachers between high- and low-poverty schools is abysmal" (p. 48).

The National Board does recognize the need to provide better distribution of its teachers into low-performing schools. A board program, the Targeted High Need Initiative, was established to raise the number of minority NBCTs, certify more teachers from high-needs schools, and place more board-certified teachers in schools where they are needed the most.

Getting teachers into schools with great need is only part of the problem. Schools also need to capitalize on the expertise of these teachers once they have them. In passing knowledge and expertise along to other teachers, National Board Certified teachers can have a multiplier effect that makes this certification more than it is criticized as being: just recognition and reward for already highly effective teachers. Unfortunately, efforts to use NBCTs to mentor or provide professional development to other teachers are scattered at best—not surprising given the history of a relatively flat hierarchical structure in schools, with little experience in differentiating among teachers and deploying them differently. Furthermore, teachers often hesitate to take on leadership roles, whether due to resistance, lack of opportunities, lack of interest, or limited capacity.

NBPTS stakeholders are beginning to view the need to help schools learn how to better organize and use their nationally certified teachers as a priority. They realize this is a place where the NBPTS has the potential to make a valuable contribution to broader efforts to improve teacher quality and transform school performance.

# DISCUSSION

Reflecting on the mission set forth by the founding members of the National Board, it is clear that the system has made significant progress. Still, a great deal of money and effort has been spent on growing and sustaining the board. Recognizing its areas of weaknesses is critical to both its growth and development, as well as to the positive impact it can make on American public education. This analysis is not intended as a means to dismantle the program, but rather to serve as sustenance for its future.

One substantial influence it has made comes from its development of standards for what teachers should know and be able to do. Schools at the K–12 level have been influenced by these standards, with some now looking at conceptions of teaching, not just standards for learning, as other chapters in this handbook reveal. *Editor's note*: See specifically Chapter Six. University-based teacher preparation and master's programs have also shown an interest in standards.

The teaching profession in the United States has also been affected by the National Board through a reduced resistance to, and increased acceptance of, differential certification and pay for outstanding teachers. The ideas of identifying mentor teachers and merit pay remain at the forefront of many conversations about the American system of public education. Opening the door even partway on these issues has been a significant accomplishment of the National Board.

In terms of its impact on teaching and learning, the NBPTS is situated within a context of such strong demands for standards and accountability that education experts are diligently seeking a fail-proof method of ensuring student achievement. The National Board needs to recognize that the identification of standards for what teachers should know and be able to do was only the beginning. Finding ways to link teachers' expertise to its impact on the children in their classrooms is a critical next step. With a growing body of research on different approaches to value-added assessments, this is an area that board members should continue to consider for the growth of their program. It seems reasonable to believe that a system that has already expended so much energy on the development of standards in such a wide variety of content areas, as well as a rigorous process of assessing whether teachers meet these standards, can incorporate additional elements that consider the value-added effects of a teacher. Study after study shows that the most important factor to the progress of students is the quality of the teacher. Knowing that the National Board process both contributes to and assesses high-quality teaching would lend to the credibility of the program.

In some regard, it seems that the criticism of, and ultimate reaction to, the fact that a disproportionate number of NBCTs work in high-performing classrooms fails to recognize that the process of placing teachers is not in the hands of the National Board. However, if the board could offer a certification system that inarguably—at least for the most part—identifies high-quality teachers, then schools, districts, and states might consider NBCTs more often as they develop strategies for placing the best teachers with students who most need them. Lobbying for states to offer incentives to NBCTs who teach in low-performing schools, as is the case in Colorado, should continue to be a priority for members of the National Board.

The same argument could also be used for the underuse of board-certified teachers in leadership roles. Ultimately schools themselves are responsible to create opportunities for teachers to help mentor and guide other teachers—an area that the education system has not progressed with on a wide scale. Schools for the most part are still structured so that all teachers are at the same level. However, there is movement in this area: scattered districts are creating opportunities for leadership, and colleges and universities are developing programs aimed at teacher leadership. Differentiated roles for teachers, providing a network to share local and district efforts throughout a state, and creating forums of NBCTs to debate and speak on important policy issues are being explored and implemented around the country (Aguerrebere, personal communication, 2005; Southeast Center for Teaching Quality, 2002). The National Board could contribute to this effort by making teacher leadership an explicit expectation of individuals seeking the national recognition. Perhaps the new standards for school leaders that the board is currently exploring could be considered for both teachers and administrators (National Board Certification for accomplished educational leaders, 2009).

The National Board (National Board for Professional Teaching Standards, 2007) does recognize the importance of expanding the influence of its teachers. As it notes, ''From its inception, the National Board was designed not to create a niche or elitist group of teachers, but to strengthen the entire teaching profession in order to improve student learning, schools, and school districts'' (p. 13). Unfortunately, the board, like most other organizations within public education, does not emphasize enough the importance of building these skills in individuals. It is not enough to say that somebody will be a leader. That person has to know how to lead. The current certification process does not focus on building these skills.

The other argument is for the National Board Certified Teachers who have little, if any, interest in taking on a leadership role once they receive the certification. This is similar to the many teachers who earn administrative certificates with no intention of becoming an administrator. Although the National Board would be foolish to turn away candidates who say they do not want to be leaders—just as a university would be foolish for turning away students seeking their principal certification but do not want to be a principal—building leadership skills could become a part of the process. With an increased capacity, a nationally certified teacher may eventually seek leadership opportunities.

The mission of the National Board makes no reference to expenditures in terms of time or money. The board is looking at ways of lowering the financial costs of the program, including with the help of a seven-year grant from the U.S. Department of Education. However, it must consider the larger picture. Education budgets in this country are continuously in flux, with budgets rarely considered adequate. The promise of a system to deliver highly qualified teachers was well received in the aftermath of enactment of No Child Left Behind, when schools were scrambling to promote the competencies of teachers. However, as schools learn to navigate the demands of the regulations on their own and without significant proof of their impact on student learning, national certification programs will hold less interest to school administrators looking to make the most of the money they have. It is possible that even with more convincing evidence on the impact of national certification on student achievement, incentives may vanish as districts focus on what they perceive to be more important budgetary items.

From a time-consumption perspective, the public accountability demands on teachers' time make voluntary efforts that are extensive and complex difficult to justify. A quicker, less costly alternative could lure even the best teachers away. While the expectation that not everyone can, and should, be able to achieve National Board recognition is critical to its legitimacy, the rigor of the program should not be tested and measured through a process that has been shown to place such high demands on teachers that student achievement may actually decrease during a teacher's certification attempt. This contradicts the mission of the National Board to advance the quality of teaching and learning in American public education. A more streamlined process that maintains the strengths of the program could eliminate this factor from analysis.

The National Board for Professional Teaching Standards is dedicated to its mission of improving American public education. It is looking to develop standards for school administrators in addition to those for teachers (National Board Certification for accomplished educational leaders, 2009). Although some may suggest eliminating this certification, the National Board is using it as a tool to identify high quality (Kristof, 2009). The dilemma is making sure that the tool measures what it is intended to measure.

It is not enough for teachers to meet high standards. They must also show a positive impact on student learning. This is how they will advance the quality of teaching and learning as set forth in the mission of the National Board. High-quality teachers should also take responsibility for sharing their knowledge and expertise with other teachers. Capitalizing on the expertise of its teachers would allow the board to contribute to educational reform that penetrates beyond the individuals who seek certification. Continued progress toward these goals could also foster a greater respect for teachers and for their contribution to American education.

# REFERENCES

American Board for Certification of Teacher Excellence. (2008, August 29) Research. http://www.abcte.org/research.

Cantrell, S., Fullerton, J., Kane, T., & Staiger, D. (2008, December). *National Board certification and teacher effectiveness: Evidence from a random assignment experiment.* Cambridge, MA: National Bureau of Economic Research.

Carnegie Forum on Education and the Economy. (1986, May). *A nation prepared: Teachers for the 21st century.* New York: Carnegie Corporation.

Cavalluzzo, L. (2004). *Do teachers with National Board certification improve students' outcomes?* Alexandria, VA: CNA Corporation.

Fenstermacher, V., & Richardson, V. (2005, January). Teachers' college record: On making determinations of quality in teaching. *Teachers College Record, 107*(1), 186–213.

Goldhaber, D., & Anthony, E. (2005). *Can teacher quality be effectively assessed? National Board certification as a signal of effectiveness.* Washington, DC: Urban Institute.

Goldhaber, D., Perry, D., & Anthony, E. (2004). That National Board for Professional Teaching Standards (NBPTS) process: Who applies and what factors are associated with NBPTS certification? *Educational Evaluation and Policy Analysis, 6*(4), 259–280.

Hannaway, J., & Bischoff, K. (2005). Philanthropy and labor market reform in education. The case of the National Board for professional teaching standards and Teach for America. In F. M. Hess (Ed.), *With the best of intentions: How philanthropy is reshaping K-12 education* (pp. 157–176). Cambridge, MA: Harvard Education Publishing Group.

Hess, F. (2004). *Common sense school reform.* New York: Palgrave Macmillan.

Holland, R. (2004, May). New study first to affirm value of national teacher certification. *School Reform News.* Retrieved from http://www.heartland.org/publications/school%20reform/article/14800/New_Study_First to Affirm Value of National Teacher Certification.html.

Humphrey, D. C., Koppich, J. E., & Hough, H. J. (2005, March 3). Sharing the wealth: National Board Certified Teachers and the students who need them the most. *Education Policy Analysis Archives, 13*(18). Retrieved September 8, 2008, from http://epaa.asu.edu/epaa/v13n18/v13n18.pdf.

Kristof, N. D. (2009, February 17). Education: Our greatest national shame. *New York Times,* p. WK11.

National Board Certification for accomplished educational leaders. (2009, Winter). *UCEA Review.*

National Board for Professional Teaching Standards. (2007). *55,000 reasons to believe: The impact of the National Board certification on teacher quality in America.* Arlington, VA: Author.

National Board for Professional Teaching Standards. (2008). http://www.nbpts.org.

Rotherham, A. J. (2005, March 30). Credit where it's due: Putting nationally certified teachers into the classrooms that need them most. *Education Week, 24*(29), 34, 48.

Sanders, W., Ashton, J., & Wright, S. P. (2005, March 7). *Comparison of the effects of NBPTS certified teachers with other teachers on the rate of student academic progress* (Tech. Rep.). Middleton, MA: SAS Institute.

Shanker, A. (1985). In support of teachers: The making of a profession. *NASSP Bulletin, 69*, 93–99.

Southeast Center for Teaching Quality. (2002, April). *Teacher leadership: An untapped resource for improving student achievement.* Hillsboro, NC: Author.

Stone, J. E. (2002, May). *The value-added achievement gains of NBPTS-Certified Teachers in Tennessee* (Policymaker Briefing). Johnson City, TN: East Tennessee State University, College of Education.

Vandervoort, L., Amrein-Beardsley, A., & Berliner, D. (2004). National Board Certified Teachers and their students' achievement. *Education Policy Analysis Archive, 12*(46). Retrieved May 15, 2005, from http://epaa.asu.edu/epaa/v12n46/.

# CHAPTER ELEVEN

# Judging Teachers

## *The Law of Teacher Dismissals*

Diana Pullin

*Boston College*

Most policymakers, and most parents, believe that teachers hold the key to improving educational achievement. Recent public policy discussions and legal initiatives have focused on teacher content knowledge, teacher certification or licensure requirements, and teacher education. There is now increasing interest in the use of teacher performance assessments or job evaluations and the use of student results from large-scale tests to make judgments about teacher quality. The public accountability requirements of the No Child Left Behind Act (2001) and many state education reform laws mean that there is more information, more readily available, about school performance. Local school officials have begun to pay attention to the need to more vigorously enforce quality standards among the teaching force (Honawar, 2007) and to implement more approaches based on pay-for-performance models. At the same time, more attention to such initiatives as educator collaboration, distributed leadership within schools, and educator learning communities has perhaps begun to contribute to transparency and break down the traditional autonomy of individual classroom practice.

In response to concerns about primarily subjective and localized approaches to pursuing teacher quality, recent legal initiatives have focused on efforts to define and enhance teacher quality and promote accountability for teaching effectiveness. The federal government has implemented new teacher quality requirements as part of its regulation of both higher education and elementary and secondary education (Pullin, 2004). In addition, states and local school districts are beginning to implement systematic teacher performance assessments, as well as the use of scores from standardized student tests, to make determinations about the quality of teachers (Braun, 2005; Odden & Kelley, 2002; Ballou & Podgursky, 1997). As a result of these changes, more evidence, and perhaps more transparent evidence, about individual teacher performance is available, and more attention may potentially be paid to the dismissal of low-performing teachers.

This chapter addresses the legal frameworks in which teacher dismissals occur and the role of assessment or evaluations in termination decisions. It discusses the role of judges and arbitrators in dismissals and describes the constitutional and statutory requirements governing teacher termination, as well as the impact of collective bargaining agreements. It focuses on the procedural protections for teachers as well as the grounds for establishing that there is sufficient cause to end a teacher's employment. The use of performance evidence in teacher dismissals is considered in light of both the legal requirements for the processes to be followed in teacher dismissals and the criteria for evidence sufficient to constitute a basis for termination. The primary focus is on individual teacher performance in school, but there is also consideration of dismissals based on student test scores as well as dismissals arising from teacher activities outside the classroom or the school.

# THE ROLE OF DISMISSAL IN THE PURSUIT OF TEACHER QUALITY

While policymakers are interested in the use of stepped-up measures to improve the quality of the teaching force, principals and superintendents often assert that there are debilitating limits on their abilities to dismiss low-performing teachers. Many principals and superintendents believe that the dismissal of a teacher will confront so many legal barriers that it is probably not worth pursuing. Anecdotal reports indicate that administrators feel it is impossible in the face of legal constraints, as well as prohibitively expensive, to terminate a teacher (Walsh-Sarnecki, 2007). There is a reported perception that it would take a principal in a big city school system two years to fire a tenured teacher given the extensive hearings and appeals process (Honawar, 2007). According to one report, in an effort to fire two tenured teachers accused of verbal abuse of students or others over one four-year period, Dearborn, Michigan, spent $178,308 (including the costs of lawyers, paid leave for the teachers pending outcome of the cases, and substitute teachers); at the same time, it spent $233,181 to buy out two teachers accused of substance abuse and two others accused of sexual misconduct (Walsh-Sarnecki, 2007).

But other evidence suggests that some districts have become more willing than they were in the past to consider teacher dismissal. The New York City public schools, in an effort to address issues of teacher quality, reportedly hired a team of five lawyers headed by a former prosecutor to help principals prepare cases to dismiss teachers who fail to raise student test scores or perform poorly in the principal's evaluation (Honawar, 2007). In Washington, D.C., a new plan was announced for implementation of individual ninety-day improvement plans for low-performing teachers followed by dismissal if they showed no improvement. The district also dismissed seventy teachers who failed to attain the "highly qualified teacher" status required by the No Child Left Behind Act (NCLB). A lawsuit has been filed against the school district by the teachers' union challenging the dismissals (Sawchuk, 2008b).

Overall, however, the number of teachers terminated as a result of performance evaluation has been described as negligible (Zirkel, 2003). In the 2003-2004 school year, there were about 33.3 million public school teachers in the nation (U.S. Department of Education, 2003–2004). According to the U.S. Department of Education, on average across the nation that year, a school district dismissed or did not renew the contracts of 3.1 teachers. The federal data do not include the reasons for those actions, but they do show that a slight majority of these teachers had more than three years of experience. The average years of experience of a dismissed teacher ranged from 0.5 in Michigan to 38.6 in Rhode Island, where 94 percent of those dismissed or not renewed had more than three years of experience (U.S. Department of Education, 2003–2004). In New York City public schools, only one one-hundredth of 1 percent of teachers are fired for incompetence in a typical year, or about ten teachers out of the eighty thousand in the district (Honawar, 2007).

During the 2003–2004 school year, Massachusetts had approximately 84,500 full and part-time teachers employed in its 371 school districts (U.S. Department of Education, 2003–2004). That same year, the average number of teachers in a Massachusetts district who were dismissed or did not have their contracts renewed was 4.2, although that number is somewhat misleading given the wide range in size of districts within the state (U.S. Department of Education, 2003–2004). The majority of these teachers had three or fewer years of experience, which is not surprising given that state law allows teachers with three years of continuous experience in one district to attain "professional teacher status" (Massachusetts Education Reform Act, 1993), which operates somewhat like tenure and makes dismissal procedures for more experienced teachers more complicated, including the right to use arbitration to challenge a dismissal.

Between 1994 and 2007 in Massachusetts, fifty-eight teacher dismissal disputes were decided by independent outside arbitrators, and twenty-six of these were upheld by the arbitrators, with an increasing proportion of the cases won by the school districts beginning around 2002 (Massachusetts Department of Education, 2008a). Michigan between 2004 and 2008, with approximately 100,000 teachers (U.S. Department of Education, 2003–2004), had seventy-nine dismissal hearings. The school districts won an estimated 90 percent of the cases (Walsh-Sarnecki, 2007).

Dismissal of a teacher is the most dramatic and painful approach to dealing with problems of teacher quality. In some schools, principals report a practice some call ''dance of the lemons'' or ''passing the trash,'' in which ineffective teachers are not dismissed but are instead offered incentives to leave a school. In one report from Michigan, dozens of tenured teachers who were determined to be incompetent or to have committed acts of impropriety were paid to leave, with no notations of low performance on their records; about a quarter of these apparently went on to teach in other districts (Walsh-Sarnecki, 2007).

The very small proportion of teachers dismissed from public schools may reflect several factors. It could be that teacher education programs work better than their critics claim. Traditionally the quality of candidates entering the teaching force was determined by teacher education programs conducted by colleges and universities operating under state regulation and, sometimes, voluntarily accredited by professional associations. These state-approved programs led to certification of eligibility to teach in the public schools, and criticism has been lodged that these institutions did not play an effective role in weeding out those who did not hold promise for being successful teachers. Only in rare cases would a state remove a credential for cause. In recent years, these cases usually have been limited to the most egregious misconduct or failure to meet state credential requirements. Teacher hiring, supervision, evaluation, professional development, and teacher termination rested in the hands of local administrators and school boards. Local districts would rarely remove a teacher for cause, and when these terminations did occur, they were generally for serious misconduct, often unrelated to the effectiveness of the individual's classroom teaching.

Most teachers are in fact competent and diligent in their work. And local systems of teacher assessment and evaluation may create the conditions for effective and continuous professional development for teachers that effectively foster student learning. Nevertheless, administrators may be uncertain or ineffective in their evaluative practices. There may be no real relationship between teacher evaluation practices and teacher quality. (See Chapters Eight and Nine, this volume.) Local administrators may be unwilling or unable to impose harsh sanctions like dismissal for unsatisfactory teachers. Many times the desire to remove a teacher may have little to do with ineffective instructional practice but may relate to such factors as financial exigencies within a school district. Or a teacher's relationship with an administrator or the local community may deteriorate so much that dismissal is initiated regardless of otherwise successful teaching performance by that teacher.

It is not clear what the statistics on teacher dismissal really represent. What we do know is that teacher dismissal has not happened often. And even when a teacher's dismissal is contemplated, it does not appear that local school officials know much about the legal parameters of dismissal. The evidence is that many school administrators have limited knowledge about the legal standards governing teacher evaluation and teacher accountability (Zirkel, 2003). In fact, few teacher dismissal cases end up being resolved by courts, and when teacher dismissals are challenged in court, judges most often uphold the dismissals. There may be a gap between practitioners' understanding of the law of teacher dismissals and the reality of those requirements. At the same time, schools may give insufficient attention to the clarity of the criteria for defining competent teacher performance and the appropriate processes to use to evaluate teachers and address teacher shortcomings, even dismissal.

There is some interesting variability in teacher dismissal cases, as well as some trends to note. Certainly hard-working educators and public officials try to do the right thing for students and schools, but there are also some stories that reflect failure to act professionally on the part of educators. There are legal standards that apply in assessing challenges to dismissal but also many ways for courts to avoid intruding into local decision making about teacher dismissal. There are also some rather fragile grounds for making determinations about teacher quality represented in the cases that are decided by courts.

We turn now to the legal standards for dismissal, the role of courts and legislatures in relation to local education officials, and some of the stories of teacher dismissal depicted in court cases. These narratives offer some of the most important insights into local educational practice, as well as the role of the law in resolving disputes (Brooks & Gewirtz, 1996).

## LEGAL STANDARDS GOVERNING TEACHER DISMISSAL

The law governing teacher dismissals is based on standards arising from federal and state constitutions, state statutes and regulations, state and federal civil rights laws, and the provisions of the individual teacher's employment contract, as well as local school district collective bargaining agreements negotiated between a district and its teacher union. Collectively these provisions govern both the processes for termination and the criteria for determining that a teacher is suitable for dismissal. The criteria and processes of teacher evaluation are often both relevant in dismissal decisions.

Contract law governs all teachers. The contract law provisions governing teacher dismissal are stated in a teacher's individual contract, as well as in provisions negotiated in a collective bargaining agreement (*Whitfield* v. *Little Rock Public Schools*, 1988). These contractual provisions, which often describe the processes for evaluating or sanctioning a teacher, can provide more protections that state law requires, but at a minimum, state law procedural protections must be followed. Few or no state law provisions govern the teaching force in private schools or public charter schools, consistent with the public policy goal of limiting state regulation of these types of schools. Since contract law may be the only legal provisions that apply, most of the discussion in this chapter is not applicable to private and charter schools.

Almost 75 percent of the teachers in the United States are unionized (Moe, 2006), and a local school district's collective bargaining agreement with a teachers' union will almost always have provisions concerning teacher evaluations and dismissals (Pullin & Melnick, 2008). Many contracts also include provisions on the standards for teacher performance (Johnson & Donaldson, 2006). Johnson and Donaldson have concluded that there is no consistent evidence that collective bargaining has either improved or diminished the quality of the teaching force.

The role of teacher unions in grievances, arbitrations, and litigation concerning teacher quality issues has been considerable (Pullin & Melnick, 2008). Johnson and Donaldson (2006) point out that local teacher unions vary in the extent of detailed requirements negotiated into their contracts for evaluation procedures or the criteria for evaluation. One primary function of the union is advocacy on behalf of dismissed teachers, including the provision of legal services. Local unions may vary in the extent to which they aggressively defend members who have received negative evaluations or face dismissal, with some districts operating with highly contentious relationships between the union and district administrators over these types of issues.

# PROCESSES FOR TEACHER DISMISSAL

Several types of procedural protections apply to teacher dismissal. For one, individual teacher contracts, the provisions of a district collective bargaining agreement, statutes, and state or federal constitutions govern the processes that must be followed to terminate a teacher. For another, in some situations, the opportunity to remediate deficiencies is an additional, and more substantive, process that must be followed.

The time lines to be followed and notifications to be given concerning evaluations and dismissals or other sanctions are generally spelled out in a fairly straightforward manner in state statutes and regulations or the contract or collective bargaining agreement. Yet many dismissal efforts are derailed by simple failure to follow the mandated process. The most common type of court cases arising from teacher dismissals involve procedural defects in the school district or the state's handling of the procedures for the dismissal or an evaluation. In addition to these matters governed by state statute, broad standards for fairness in the way a teacher is treated arise under state or federal constitutional provisions.

## Statutory Procedures

The procedures for teacher dismissals are set out in state statutes and regulations. These provisions are designed to ensure that teachers are treated fairly and that government decision making is based on appropriate reasons. State statutes governing teacher tenure and dismissal are often regarded by legislatures as necessary to regulate the otherwise unfettered powers of local school officials. One court, for example, noted "legislative recognition that, compared to other professionals, teachers receive little in the way of material rewards and need the protection of job security," and therefore protections against arbitrary treatment were needed (*Wheeler* v. *Yuma School District,* 1988, p. 867). Yet when courts apply these statutes, judges most often decide cases in favor of school districts.

More procedural protections generally are required for more experienced teachers. For example, all teachers in Massachusetts who have taught in a school for more than ninety days are entitled to receive before they are dismissed written notice that they face dismissal, an explanation of the grounds on which they could be dismissed along with enough documentation to allow them to respond to the charges against them, and, if desired, an informal meeting to review the issue, at which the teacher may be accompanied by legal counsel. Moreover, teachers who have obtained professional teacher status (PTS) by serving in the public schools of a school district for the three previous consecutive school years can be dismissed for only one of seven reasons listed in the statute: "inefficiency, incompetency, incapacity, conduct unbecoming a teacher, insubordination or failure . . . to satisfy teacher performance standards . . . or other just cause" (Massachusetts Education Reform Act, 1993). For these PTS teachers, the reasons to justify dismissal must be explicit, and the procedural protections are much more significant than those for other teachers. PTS teachers have access to independent arbitration. At an arbitration hearing, the school district has the burden of proving the grounds for dismissal. In determining whether the school district has satisfied its burden of proof, the arbitrator must consider the best interests of the pupils in the district and the need to elevate standards of performance. The arbitrator is required to issue a "detailed statement of the reasons for his or her decision," which is subject to judicial review (Massachusetts Education Reform Act, 1993, para. 6). Ultimately, the district or PTS teacher who loses in front of the arbitrator has the right to appeal to the state courts.

The role of the Massachusetts state courts in reviewing an arbitrator's decision is limited to consideration of whether the arbitrator exceeded his or her authority (*School Committee of Lowell* v. *Oung*, 2008; *School District of Beverly* v. *Geller*, 2001). Strong state public policy favoring arbitration even allows a grossly erroneous, but not fraudulent, decision to stand as long as the arbitrator does not exceed his or her authority. Sometimes, though, an arbitrator is found to have exceeded his authority, even when he thought he was improving schools for the greater good for children. In the first state court case reviewing an arbitration decision under the Massachusetts Education Reform Act of 1993, the arbitrator's decision was overturned (*School District of Beverly* v. *Geller*, 2001). In the *Geller* case, a twenty-year veteran teacher in public school who had PTS was dismissed for conduct unbecoming a teacher after it was found that he had used physical force against three sixth-grade students on three different occasions (pushing students against wall and yelling in their faces). The arbitrator found that the teacher had done those things and that they were indeed inappropriate, unacceptable, and could not be condoned, but he nevertheless reinstated the teacher because he felt it was in the best interest of the students that such a teacher, with such a good record of experience and no prior disciplinary problems, should be retained. The state's highest court overturned the arbitrator's decision on grounds that once it was determined that the teacher had done the things for which he was charged, which amounted to conduct unbecoming of a teacher, the arbitrator did not have authority to reinstate the teacher.

Initially Massachusetts teachers tended to be more successful in decisions made by arbitrators than they had been in courts; arbitrators regularly issued decisions that seemed to contravene the intent of the legislature to make it less difficult to dismiss a veteran teacher when it passed the state's Education Reform Act (Stewart & Adams, 1998). After the decision in *Geller*, school districts began winning a greater proportion of the arbitration cases (Massachusetts Department of Education, 2008a).

There are variations in how states have written into statute their requirements on the processes for handling teacher dismissal cases, involving ultimately either or both independent arbitration and judicial review. For example, in Florida, state administrative hearing officers conduct hearings and review evidence about a dismissal and then issue determinations to school districts (West's Florida Statutes Annotated, 2008). In one dispute, a hearing officer held hearings and reviewed detailed testimony and documentary evidence before issuing a twenty-seven-page, single-spaced decision in a case overturning a school district's dismissal of a special education teacher (*Leon County School Board* v. *Waters,* 2007).

# Constitutional Protections

In addition to the procedures spelled out in state statutes, some overriding constitutional protections apply to teacher dismissals. These arise from the protections of due process of law and equal protection of the law under the federal and state constitutions. The extent of requirements on public officials under these constitutional provisions depends on the nature of the teacher's employment status prior to dismissal and the basis on which a school seeks to terminate a teacher.

Unless a teacher faces the loss of tenure or termination of a contract during the period covered by the contract (what courts would refer to as a property interest in continued employment), constitutional due process protections are required, but requirements are minimal. Teachers with tenure or the equivalent of tenure, like the PTS teachers in Massachusetts, have greater legitimate expectations for retaining their job and are, under the federal and most state constitutions, entitled to more due process protections when they face dismissal. When a public school teacher has a property interest in continued employment because of an individual contract, a collective bargaining agreement, or the traditions of past employment practices in a school district, dismissal requires a notification of the basis for the proposed dismissal, a description of the evidence that will be used to support the dismissal, and the opportunity to respond to the charges. If a state statute or an interpretation of state constitutional provisions requires more procedural protections than the federal or a state constitution would require, those must also be provided.

Federal constitutional law recognizes that a significant harm to one's professional reputation coupled with damage to future prospects for obtaining professional employment constitutes a ''liberty interest'' protected by due process requirements (*Paul* v. *Davis,* 1976; *Board of Regents* v. *Roth*, 1972; *Perry* v. *Sinderman,* 1972). Despite these constitutional principles concerning teachers' reputational interests, Zirkel (2003) concludes, based on his review of the court cases, that judges are generally unwilling to recognize a liberty interest when a teacher is terminated for incompetence.

Another due process issue arises under the principle of substantive due process, which focuses on whether the result of a decision is fair when an important individual interest is at stake. Government action can violate substantive due process if it is arbitrary and capricious or is fundamentally unfair. When a state or school district decision has no conceivable rational relationship to a legitimate state objective, a decision can violate the substantive due process guarantee. One court described the rather minimal judicial review of school district action here as a check to see whether school officials acted reasonably and had evidence to substantiate their termination of a teacher (*Gwathmey* v. *Atkinson*, 1976).

Under the principles of equal protection guarantees, public officials must not sort people into groups and treat them differently without appropriate reasons and means for doing so. Thus, where a local board failed to articulate "sound educationally based reasons" for retaining a nontenured teaching staff member over a tenured one, the decision of the local school board dismissing the tenured teacher was overturned (*Ellicott* v. *Board of Education of Township of Frankford, Sussex County*, 1991). Districts found to have based dismissal decisions on racial, ethnic, or gender grounds can also be found to have violated equal protection guarantees.

## The Duty to Provide Remediation Opportunities

One form of protection extended to teachers in some states is the requirement, set forth in collective bargaining agreements, school district policy, or state law or by the application of constitutional principles of due process, that teachers facing dismissal be given an opportunity to remediate their weaknesses (Dagley & Veir, 2002). State laws vary in their specific provisions concerning the opportunity to remediate, with many of these requirements specifically linked to obligatory school district evaluations of teachers. Presumably the evaluation feedback to the teacher would need to be sufficient to allow the teacher to know what needed to be done to improve performance. When sufficient remediation has been offered and the teacher fails to improve, termination is usually supported (*Hicks* v. *Gayville-Volin School District*, 2003).

Courts have found that some teacher performance is simply not remediable, such as instances involving sexual impropriety with students (*Board of Education . . .* v. *Hunt*, 1985, involving a male physical education teacher who pinched little girls' buttocks), cheating on standardized student tests (*Scoggins* v. *Board of Education*, 1988), or corporal punishment of students. Sometimes a teacher's problems are regarded as so dangerous that remediation should not be attempted. Often these involve disciplinary issues where the school district has a special need to ensure that students are protected and learning can occur (*Russell* v. *Special School District No. 6*, 1985; *Carter* v. *State Board of Education*, 1980).

One set of commentators has pointed out the recent proliferation of state laws increasing the requirements for local districts to provide remedial opportunities for teachers facing dismissal. These commentators argue that such requirements will make it more difficult to terminate teachers by placing more procedural and substantive hurdles in front of local officials (Dagley & Veir, 2002).

## Court Review of Dismissal Decisions

Whether applying statutory or constitutional provisions, courts are very deferential to the decisions of public school officials. They extend great deference to arbitrators as well. One court offered this typical description of what judges look for to support a teacher dismissal: "substantial evidence...such relevant evidence as a reasonable mind might accept as adequate to support a conclusion" because substantial deference should be given to local decision makers (*Whaley* v. *Anoka-Hennepin Independent School District No. 11*, 1982, p. 130).

These acts of deference are part of a long tradition of court cases of all types involving education in which judges specifically chose to defer to local or state education officials on grounds that second-guessing educational decision making is not an appropriate role for courts (Zirkel, 2003; Dagley & Veir, 2002). In part, this deference, or judicial abstention as it is sometimes called, is based on a presumption that local school administrators are competent to make qualitative judgments about teachers because they are licensed or certified by the state on the basis of their professional training and experience (Dagley & Veir, 2002).

Generally the role of courts includes the responsibility to enforce the provisions of the statutes passed by the legislature and ensure that the intent of the legislature is met. Sometimes, though, judges may be persuaded that there are good public policy reasons to overturn a decision concerning a teacher. So, for example, a decision might be overturned if it was found to conflict with the goals of the legislature when it wrote a statute regulating the teaching profession (*School District of Beverly* v. *Geller*, 2001).

As is the situation in other types of litigation, depending on the relevant state laws, courts have established standards for how to weigh the evidence in making a decision about a teacher (*McGuinn* v. *Douglas County School District No. 66*, 2000). These standards vary from state to state. Some states require "substantial evidence," others a "preponderance of the competent evidence," and others "clear and convincing evidence" before disciplinary action may be taken against a teacher.

Under the general principles of administrative law that apply to court reviews of all types of government decision making, not just teacher dismissals, the original decision must not have been "arbitrary and capricious" (*Von Gizycki* v. *Levy*, 2004). *Black's Law Dictionary* defines "arbitrary and capricious" as "willful and unreasonable action without consideration or in disregard of facts or law or without determining principle" (1990, p. 105). When courts review decisions by administrative agencies, they commonly follow the definition adopted in the seminal U.S. Supreme Court case discussing the arbitrary and capricious standard (*Citizens to Preserve Overton Park, Inc.* v. *Volpe*, 1971). In that case, the Supreme Court determined that a reviewing court must conduct a more thorough review than merely looking for substantial supporting evidence for the decision; the reviewing court must determine whether (1) the action was within the agency's statutory authority; (2) the action was arbitrary, capricious, an abuse of discretion, or otherwise contrary to law; and (3) the agency followed procedural requirements. In defining what was "arbitrary, capricious, an abuse of discretion, or otherwise not in accordance with law," the Court held that the reviewing court "must consider whether the decision was based on consideration of the relevant factors and whether there has been a clear error of judgment.... Although this inquiry into facts is to be searching and careful, the ultimate standard of review is a narrow one. The court is not empowered to substitute its judgment for that of the agency" (p. 416; see also Breyer, Steward, Sunstein, & Spitzer, 1998, 2002). As a result, courts have not frequently been willing to overrule a particular agency decision in the education context or in most other situations involving the administration of any public agency.

In the thousands of court decisions annually reviewing state or federal administrative action in all sorts of decisions in public education and other government activities, a relative few invalidate an action on grounds it was arbitrary and capricious. "Litigants attempting to persuade a reviewing court that the balance struck by an agency among relevant factors is arbitrary and capricious must be prepared to persuade the court that the agency's decision has no reasonable basis. Given the artfulness of agency opinion writers, the skills of government lawyers, and the plausibility of agency claims of 'expertise,' this is a difficult burden to carry" (Breyer et al., 2002, p. 437). Some commentators argue "the intensity of judicial review unquestionably varies in practice. Courts look more searchingly at decisions by agencies that they think least competent or most biased, and they are most deferential to those agencies having a reputation for competence and impartiality. Thus the notion of arbitrary or capricious review embodies a range of standards; it is not applied uniformly" (p. 439). It is interesting to speculate whether in this era of NCLB accountability, contemporary judges will view education officials as generally highly competent.

In teacher dismissal cases, the "arbitrary and capricious" standard has been used consistently for almost a century (*McKinnon* v. *State*, 1916). For a court to be satisfied that a teacher's dismissal is not arbitrary or capricious, the decision maker's statement of reasons for the dismissal must provide sufficient information to allow a determination of a rational basis for the school district's exercise of its discretion. In *Lewis Central Education Association* v. *Iowa Board of Education Examiners* (2001) and *Arrocha* v. *Board of Education of City of New York* (1999), the courts found that dismissal decisions were not arbitrary or capricious where decision makers considered all factors in the state statute and all the evidence, and weighed the evidence properly. In *Feldman* v. *Board of Education of City School District of City of New York* (1999), the courts upheld a board of education's termination of teachers' city teaching licenses and dismissals, finding that the action was not arbitrary and capricious where the teachers failed to achieve passing grade on National Teacher Examination within five years of issuance of their licenses. But in one

Iowa case, a long-term veteran fourth-grade teacher successfully challenged as arbitrary a school district's termination of him for alleged incompetence when two parents complained that he responded in too much detail to student questions about homosexuality after showing a sex education video selected by the school nurse (*Collins* v. *Faith School District No. 46-2*, 1998). Parent complaints are obviously behind the initiation of many dismissals, and these cases present particular challenges for school officials who are attempting to balance community demands against the imperative to avoid unlawful terminations.

Despite the fears of many education officials that they may be successfully sued for a teacher dismissal, the role of the courts in these matters is quite limited. In fact, judicial review of school officials' decisions is so constrained that sometimes courts uphold a local decision to dismiss a teacher even when the judges are thoroughly uncomfortable with the result. (See the discussion below of the "immorality" case: *Fiscus* v. *Board of School Trustees*..., 1987.)

## THE ROLE OF EVALUATIONS IN TEACHER DISMISSALS

Unless a teacher is to be considered for dismissal or termination based on out-of-class conduct like criminal activity or an inappropriate relationship with a student, dismissals on grounds of incompetence are based on some type of evaluation of teacher performance, although many of the evaluations were by no means formal or structured.

Legal standards and professional standards often address the same goals and require the same approaches. For example, the late Jay Millman (1997), a respected testing expert, described four criteria for teacher accountability systems: fairness, comprehensiveness, competitiveness with other means of evaluation, and consequential validity. Millman's criteria in many ways are the same types that the legal system would pose (see Beckham, 1997). And at least one commentator has suggested that many of these professional and legal issues are also issues of professional ethics (Strike, 1990). Strike's ethical principles for evaluation are due process, privacy, equality, public perspicuity, humaneness, client benefit, academic freedom, and respect for autonomy. He suggests a bill of rights for teacher evaluation that also includes four rights for educational institutions that seem equally germane for the discussion here: the right to exercise supervision and make personnel decisions intended to improve the quality of the education they provide; the right to collect information relevant to their supervisory and evaluative roles; the right to act on such relevant information in the best interest of the students whom they seek to educate; and the right to the cooperation of the teaching staff in implementing and executing a fair and effective system of evaluation.

The Joint Committee on Standards for Educational Evaluation (2008), a committee of representatives of the eighteen major national education associations and organizations, has promulgated standards on the evaluation of educators known as the Personnel Evaluation Standards (see Chapter Twelve, this volume). These standards address four categories of concern in personnel evaluation. Propriety standards are intended to ensure that evaluations are conducted legally, ethically, and with due regard for the welfare of those involved in the evaluation, as well as those affected by its results. Utility standards are "intended to guide evaluations so that they will be informative, timely, and influential" and serve the information needs of intended users. Feasibility standards are intended to ensure that evaluation systems are as easy to implement as possible, efficient in their use of time and resources, adequately funded, and viable. Accuracy standards are intended to ensure that the information obtained is technically accurate and that conclusions are linked logically to the data. These standards also parallel the legal standards under the constitution and many statutes. Zirkel (2003) notes, however, that these standards have been for the most part ignored by courts, state legislatures, and local policymakers.

A 2002 survey found that forty-three states had laws requiring teacher evaluation by local districts (Dagley & Veir, 2002). By one recent estimate, only sixteen states have specific guidelines on how to conduct teacher evaluations. Recently states have begun to pay more attention to the criteria for teacher evaluation and the desirability of uniformity, at least to some extent, in state guidelines or criteria for the process and content of teacher evaluations (Sawchuk, 2008a). These are seen as an effort to clarify the descriptions of what constitutes effective teaching, reduce the arbitrariness of individual evaluations, and enhance certainty about decisions on teacher performance.

Massachusetts laws and regulations illustrate one state's approach to teacher evaluations. The law and regulations set out descriptions of the processes and criteria for evaluations that local school districts should implement under the leadership of the school superintendent and in cooperation with the teacher union. The regulations from the state board of education set out seventeen principles of effective teaching, with approximately four descriptors of characteristics of effective teaching for each principle. The principles address currency in curriculum content, effective curricular and instructional planning and assessment, classroom management, effective instruction, promotion of high standards and expectations for student achievement, promotion of equity and appreciation of diversity, and fulfillment of professional responsibilities, including professional collaboration, relations with parents, and participation in ongoing professional development (Massachusetts Department of Education, 2008b).

Some states articulate their criteria in a mandated or suggested evaluation form for local districts to use. Even in situations where a state establishes a written evaluation form, failure to strictly adhere to the form does not necessarily invalidate an evaluation and subsequent dismissal if anecdotal evidence backs up the conclusion to dismiss reached by a school district (*Hamburg* v. *North Penn School District*, 1984).

Some court cases focus specifically on evaluations themselves, independent of dismissal. In one West Virginia case, a teacher filed a grievance over his principal's determination that he did not meet performance standards concerning student grading because such a large proportion of his students received grades of D or F in his science classes. The teacher argued that his principal's evaluation of his grading practice did not meet state board of education requirements that teacher evaluations be "open and honest" and based on "performance standards." The state appellate court decided that state evaluation requirements for West Virginia were met because the local school district had the discretion to set the performance standards and the authority to describe some performance standards fairly generally rather than expressly and to set explicit standards for a particular employee. Where the school district was not acting arbitrarily and the teacher was given multiple warnings about his grading practices and was given a chance to improve, but did not do so, the court found that he was treated fairly and that the state's evaluation requirements were met (*Brown* v. *Wood County Board of Education*, 1990).

If a teacher faces termination on the basis of evaluations and his or her previous evaluations were satisfactory, the odds of a school district's winning a court case challenging a dismissal for cause based on classroom performance go down significantly (Zirkel, 2003).

## LEGAL GROUNDS FOR TEACHER DISMISSAL

Whether or not state statutes or regulations include standards for how teachers should be evaluated, most of the grounds for teacher dismissal are outlined in state laws. Some grounds for dismissal relate to individual performance of a teacher. These arise in most dismissals challenged in court and are often associated with the concept of "just cause" or "good cause" to justify a termination, terminology that can on occasion challenge notions of what constitutes acceptable teaching practice.

When a state authority removes an individual's certification, this can be grounds for dismissal from employment in a district within that state, as can the failure to attain Highly Qualified Teacher status as required by the No Child Left Behind Act. In some states, the consequences of dismissal in addition to loss of employment might include revocation or suspension of certification, referral for review to consider loss of certification, or at least a mandatory report to the state credentialing body that a dismissal or failure to renew a contract occurred (*Burton* v. *Town of Littleton*, 2005).

Many states have provisions to describe more general circumstances for dismissal of groups of teachers such as for financial exigencies or reductions in enrollment. For example, Massachusetts statutes address the right of a superintendent to lay off teachers for reductions in force or reorganization resulting from declining enrollment or other budgetary reasons. However, the same law also sets limits on these dismissals: no teacher with professional teacher status can be laid off in a reduction in force or reorganization if there is another teaching position for which the teacher is certified and out of which that teacher could bump another teacher who did not have PTS status (Massachusetts Education Reform Act, 1993). The Massachusetts 1993 Education Reform Act also allows the state to create an expedited system to dismiss teachers in chronically underperforming schools as part of the state's reform and accountability system; here PTS teachers can be dismissed for good cause on five days' notice, but they are also given access to an expedited arbitration review if they seek it.

The most challenging legal issues concern the application of the criteria for teacher dismissal for reasons related to a teacher's performance. Several types of teacher dismissal might occur: dismissal for legitimate cause that concerns classroom instruction, dismissal for legitimate cause that is not directly related to classroom performance, and dismissal that would be unacceptable because it would violate civil rights or constitutional guarantees. For this discussion concerning teacher quality issues, the focus will be on the more provocative grounds for dismissal beyond financial exigency or schoolwide accountability: situations involving individual determinations of incompetence, insubordination, immorality, or unacceptable activity outside school.

## Criteria in State Laws for Dismissal of a Teacher

State laws show a good bit of consistency as well as some idiosyncratic variation in the stated grounds for teacher dismissal. For example, the Massachusetts statute sets out seven acceptable reasons for teacher dismissal: inefficiency, incompetence, incapacity, conduct unbecoming a teacher, insubordination, failure to satisfy teacher performance standards, or other just cause (Massachusetts Education Reform Act, 1993).

Missouri's state law allows termination based on physical or mental condition unfitting a teacher to instruct or associate with children; immoral conduct; incompetence, inefficiency, or insubordination in the line of duty; willful or persistent violation of, or failure to obey, the school laws of the state or the published regulations of the board of education of the employing school district; excessive or unreasonable absence from performance of duties; or conviction of a felony or a crime involving moral turpitude (Missouri Revised Statutes, 1969).

Nevada law sets out nineteen reasons, including "advocating overthrow of the Government of the United States or of the State of Nevada by force, violence or other unlawful means, or the advocating or teaching of communism with the intent to indoctrinate pupils to subscribe to communistic philosophy." Nevada also allows termination for "breaches in the security or confidentiality of the questions and answers of the [state student] achievement and proficiency examinations...or...intentional failure to observe and carry out the requirements of a plan to ensure the security of [those] examinations" (Nevada Revised Statutes, 2001).

The first of these Nevada criteria seems oddly old-fashioned as a type of requirement initiated in many states in the early 1950s as part of the McCarthy era, but it may have gained new traction as a result of the terrorist attacks of 9/11. The latter requirement seems quite contemporary and a matter that many states are just starting to address in the face of recent problems with high-stakes accountability testing.

A consideration of some of the teacher dismissal cases initiated under the various state statutes illustrates how education officials and judges grapple with the issues. The stories of the teachers in these cases also provide a vivid narrative of the role of dismissal in the pursuit of teacher quality.

## Incompetence

A determination that a teacher should be dismissed on grounds of incompetence or poor performance would seem to be at the heart of the pursuit of teacher quality. Most of the cases do in fact represent just such an approach, although a few notable variations were found. And many of the cases represent a fairly superficial take on what constitutes minimally acceptable teaching practice. The dismissal cases related to teacher competence do not often reflect a deep understanding of what teachers need to know and be able to do as reflected in the social science literature or in other chapters in this book. This may or may not reflect the practice of local educators or the level of comprehension of judges who are deciding these cases.

The notion of a teacher's competence or quality is embedded in state laws, and the criteria for competence can vary from state to state. These criteria can also vary from district to district within a state, based on the degree to which the state sets out detailed requirements for local districts concerning teacher quality and teacher evaluation standards. The capability or willingness of local education officials can also determine how competence is defined and approaches to teacher quality are implemented.

The grounds for determining teacher incompetence can be seen in the stories told in some of the court cases. In some cases, it was the little things that did in the teacher, regardless of what was going on in the classroom. Incompetence is sometimes measured by excessive absences or tardiness. Failure to make or follow lesson plans or to follow mandated curriculum are other common grounds for teacher dismissal (Ey, 2008).

Some of teacher dismissals concern personality factors or what one might label "dispositional" attributes or capabilities to interact successfully with other educators. In one Pennsylvania case, a teacher was found to be "a disruptive influence at her school; who demonstrated an inability to control her pupils or events in her classroom; who continually failed to maintain poise and composure in front of her students and in dealings with other professional employees and parents; and who made repeated unfounded complaints, accusations, and threats against other professional employees, administrators, custodians, and clerical staff" (*Hamburg* v. *North Penn School District*, 1984, pp. 377–378).

Failure to maintain student discipline is a frequent basis for teacher dismissal. Incompetence was demonstrated when a teacher "did not maintain the required and standard degree of control of her class, lacked teaching skills in that she did not use her voice properly, demonstrated emotionality in correcting students, used incorrect and substandard English and grammar, and used an inadequate variety of materials and individualized instruction" (*Eshom* v. *Board of Education . . .* , 1985, p. 472). Failure to maintain order in a classroom is seen as evidence of incompetence; in *Conward* v. *Cambridge School Committee* (1999), the shoving of a student by a teacher was seen as inappropriate for the scholastic environment. There are many similar cases (see, for example, *Gwathmey* v. *Atkinson*, 1976; *Whaley* v. *Anoka-Hennepin Independent School District No. 11*, 1982; *Mongitore* v. *Regan*, 1987; *Artherton* v. *Board . . .* , 1988; see also Ey, 2008).

Other cases, albeit a minority of them, represent a somewhat more comprehensive understanding of teacher quality. Some of the incompetence cases go more to the heart of issues concerning effective instructional practice. In one Iowa dismissal case, for example, school officials based the termination of a junior high teacher's contract on fourteen specific reasons for incompetence that could be divided into four groups: inadequate maintenance of discipline during class, excessive and ineffective use of films, ineffective classroom teaching, and failure to improve and cooperate with school administrators. The state's highest court upheld the dismissal (*Board of Directors of Sioux City Community School District* v. *Mroz*, 1980). The dismissal of a Louisiana teacher was upheld on grounds that she could not adapt to current instructional procedures, was incapable of organizing and carrying on a constructive instructional program, maintained a chaotic classroom, and displayed a lack of knowledge of ordinary English grammar (*Jennings* v. *Caddo Parish School Board*, 1973).

One teacher's dismissal was upheld on grounds of her inability to compute grade averages for students and to improve teaching practice as evidenced by the fact that she "did not teach the students, never gave any input to the students, and never supplied the students with new information designed to lend meaning to the material assigned to the students and did not follow the assigned lesson plan. She presented no new information to the students, no modeling, no demonstrative explanation, and no monitoring of the students relative to the subject lesson. [The principal] also observed appellant's lack of classroom discipline and a lack of any method or practice to insure the students were understanding the materials" (*Artherton* v. *Board* ... , 1988, pp. 522–523).

One teacher's excessive use of worksheets, lack of rapport with students, lack of appropriate student discipline, and lack of student progress was adequate grounds for dismissal (*Whaley* v. *Anoka-Hennepin Independent School District No, 11*, 1982). According to the court, the excessive use of worksheets alone would have been sufficient basis to justify the dismissal. Yet lack of student progress was based in part on testimony by staff and other faculty members who observed his students in class and measured their progress by the speed at which they moved through the skills tests and worksheets used in the district.

One court focused on trying to articulate a standard for how to determine that a teacher is unfit to teach. The court concluded, "Because the essential function of a teacher is the imparting of knowledge and of learning ability, the focus of this evidence must be the effect of the teacher's questioned activity on the students ... [an] 'adverse-effect doctrine'" (*Hagerty* v. *State Tenure Commission* 1989, pp. 116–117). Here, the court found that the teacher's directions to students were unclear, her enthusiasm was low, student participation was limited and unencouraged, and her students were unattentive and unmotivated. Many of her former students were having difficulty in the subject area later in high school. In addition, Hagerty's inability to communicate with and motivate her students adversely affected their educational process.

In a recent Massachusetts case, a school district was sued over its assessments of some of its teachers' fluency in the English language. As a result of a voter referendum, the state had passed a statute requiring that all children, no matter their language background, be placed in English language classrooms and that all teachers be fluent and literate in English. School districts were required to certify the English language proficiency of their teachers based on classroom observations or interviews by administrators or by passage of a test or some other method approved by the state. When three long-term teachers whose first language was not English were dismissed by their school district on grounds of lack of fluency, they filed a legal challenge. Each of the teachers had always received satisfactory evaluations by the district, but each was subject to a language proficiency test required by the district (but not a test that had been approved by the state). An arbitrator overturned the dismissals, ordering reinstatement of the teachers and the award of back pay. A state appellate court upheld the arbitrator's decision (*School Committee of Lowell* v. *Oung*, 2008). The district, it was determined, had impermissibly based its fluency determinations solely on a test not approved by the state. Furthermore, the district and the testing company had not made evidence or test scorers available for review at the arbitration hearing, unfairly denying the teachers a chance to contest the test-based determinations on language proficiency.

Sometimes a teacher is dismissed for deficiencies that should have been addressed in a teacher education program or the initial hiring process (*Eshom* v. *Board of Education...*, 1985). Under a South Carolina statute allowing dismissal for "evident unfitness to teach," Mr. Adams was a teacher who was dismissed on grounds that the school principal found a low basic level of English proficiency and incorrect use of English, misspelled words, misuse of words, wrong tenses, and other errors in comments written on report cards sent to parents. Adams had written notes or tests on the board with misspellings and grammatical errors so notable that the teacher who followed him the following period into the classroom where they both taught stated that she always hurried into the room after Adams left so that she could erase his writing before students came in for the next class (*Adams* v. *Clarendon County School District*, 1978; see also *Jennings* v. *Caddo Parish*, 1973).

Poor relationships when working with parents can be acceptable grounds for dismissal in some states. For example, in *Wheeler* v. *Yuma School District*, 1988, a court determined that the Arizona legislature, in allowing teacher dismissal for incompetence, intended to include related factors like relations with parents in addition to a teacher's classroom performance.

On rare occasions, a teacher dismissal on grounds of incompetence is overturned because the allegations of incompetence were in fact a pretext for other reasons that an administrator or a district wanted to dismiss a teacher. In *Leon County School Board* v. *Waters* (2007), a state administrative hearing officer found substantial evidence that a school principal was "out to get" (p. 20) a teacher and had engaged in a series of efforts over several years to try to demonstrate the teacher's incompetence. The principal, Huckaby, began to have conflicts with the teacher, Waters, four years prior to the attempted dismissal. At that time, Huckaby was assistant principal of the school and complained that Waters went over her head to the principal in a dispute over student discipline. Following that episode, Huckaby engaged in numerous efforts over the years, first as assistant principal and then as principal, to try to demonstrate that Waters was incompetent. Ultimately the school board accepted her recommendation of dismissal of Waters. However, the hearing officer reviewing the case offered unusually detailed analysis of considerable testimony and evidence and concluded that the dismissal should be overturned because Huckaby was biased and inequitable in her treatment of Waters in comparison to the way she treated other teachers. The hearing officer also refused to accept the principal's efforts to wrap her conduct in the mantle of "research-based justifications," finding that her testimony was peppered with jargon and that she was entitled to little credibility on this or any other matter (p. 24).

## The Use of Student Test Scores to Determine Competence

The use of student test scores to determine teacher competence has drawn increased interest in the policy literature and among state and local policy-makers. *Editor's note*: See Chapter Nine for more on how these test scores are analyzed for teacher evaluation purposes. State statutory efforts here are fairly recent and can lead to unintended consequences.

Only a handful of reported cases have been decided to date concerning the use of student test results to make judgments about teachers. These provide some guidance on how courts might assess these types of programs in the future. They also illustrate how judges' reviews of a new type of teacher assessment strategy are conducted under the same types of legal standards applied to other types of school decisions about teacher quality. And they demonstrate how judges can be influenced by the same types of policy momentum that influence education officials and other policymakers.

In *St. Louis Teachers Union, Local 420, American Federation of Teachers, AFL-CIO* v. *Board of Education of the City of St. Louis* (1987), the St. Louis, Missouri, Board of Education implemented a new method for evaluating English language, communications, and mathematics teachers on the basis of student achievement on the standardized California Achievement Test (CAT). A teacher in one of these subject areas who received an "unsatisfactory" evaluation would be sporadically reviewed in other areas. This additional review led to several teachers' receiving overall unsatisfactory reviews that could result in salary losses and possible termination. The teachers and their union sued the state board of education, arguing that the district violated the equal protection and due process clauses of the U.S. Constitution by acting "arbitrarily, capriciously, and irrationally" in evaluating teachers on the basis of student CAT scores since the CAT was not designed for use as a teacher evaluation instrument.

The federal district court judge found that ensuring the competency of teachers and improving the quality of education are legitimate state objectives and that the district did not violate equal protection by choosing to review only some teachers since the CAT itself evaluated only reading, language, and math, and the defendant board evaluated a teacher only on the CAT indexes that correspond to the subjects that teacher teaches. The court went on to find that classifying teachers on the basis of student test results is rational rather than arbitrary, discriminatory, and capricious and that holding these "unsatisfactory" teachers to further evaluation is also rationally related to state interests and does not deny teachers the equal protection of the law. The case was later settled out of court.

A 1973 federal appellate court decision upheld a teacher dismissal based on student scores (*Scheelhaase* v. *Woodbury Central Community School District*). In the face of accreditation problems in a school district, a new school superintendent was given a mandate to improve a school within one year; as a result, he decided to terminate teachers. The specific reason he gave for the termination of Mrs. Scheelhaase, a longtime teacher in the district, was the "below average scholastic accomplishment [on two basic skills tests] of [her] students" (p. 239). Scheelhaase and her witnesses claimed that this use of student test scores was inappropriate and that the superintendent misinterpreted the test score statistics. The teacher argued that the district acted arbitrarily and that her substantive due process rights were violated as a result. Although the trial court had determined that a teacher's professional competence could not be determined solely on the basis of her student's achievements and the teacher should be reinstated, the appellate court disagreed. The federal appeals court said that state laws set the standards for how teachers are to be hired and fired. When state law empowers a local board of education to act with its best discretion, even when others might conclude that it acted unwisely or wrongly, a district may terminate a teacher so long as it is furthering the best interests of the state educational system, although this goal has to be balanced against the teacher's claim that the superintendent acted arbitrarily and capriciously. The only requirement is that superintendents act in "good faith and in the line of what they think is honestly their duty" (p. 241). The court emphasized that "such matters as the competence of teachers and the standards of its measurement are not, without more, matters of constitutional dimensions. They are peculiarly appropriate to state and local administration" (p. 244). The teacher's dismissal was allowed.

In *Massachusetts Federation of Teachers, AFT, AFL-CIO* v. *Board of Education* (2002), the two state teacher unions sued the Massachusetts State Board of Education to try to stop implementing a new state regulation requiring diagnostic testing of math teachers before their contracts could be renewed in certain low-performing schools (defined on the basis of student performance on the MCAS, the state's large-scale accountability testing program). The state's highest court reviewed the case in the context of the purposes of the Education Reform Act of 1993 and concluded that the "Board has broad authority to establish such policies as are necessary to fulfill the purposes of the Act and to promulgate regulations that encourage innovation, flexibility, and accountability in schools and school districts" (p. 766). This gives the state board considerable discretion, the court said, specifically in the area of mathematics, where the state's students had historically lagged. Because the board also has discretion in granting certification, it may use this discretion to ensure that teachers are qualified. Since the standard for judicial review of the implementation of a state regulation is "highly deferential" (p. 771) to the determinations of the government agency, the court decided that the regulation was entirely within the board's authority and the regulation was fully consistent with the state education reform act's accountability provisions and focused exactly on what the act attempted to correct. In response to the teachers' assertions that the rule violated their equal protection rights, treating math teachers in low-performing schools differently from math teachers in other schools, the court said the regulations will be upheld as long as they are

> rationally related to the furtherance of a legitimate State interest . . [and] the challenged regulations are rationally related to the furtherance of a legitimate State interest in providing a high quality public education to every child of this Commonwealth. Assessment of the subject matter knowledge of mathematics teachers is a means for evaluating one possible underlying reason for poor student performance on the math MCAS test. . . . It is permissible for the Legislature and, by extension, the board, to focus its initial efforts aimed at scholastic improvement in one area of perceived academic weakness, namely math skills [pp. 777–779].

The Massachusetts teachers had also asserted violations of their substantive due process rights, arguing that there is no rational connection between poor student performance on the math MCAS test and the subject matter knowledge of selected teachers since student MCAS scores are driven to an overwhelming degree by socioeconomic factors and funding inequities rather than by deficiencies in teacher subject matter knowledge. But the court found that even if the teachers did present such evidence, it would not invalidate the rational basis for assessment of teacher competency unless the teachers could prove that teacher subject matter knowledge is never a reason for poor student performance on the MCAS.

Given the increasing attention to the use of student test scores to determine teacher quality, it is perhaps not surprising that these initiatives have led to some inappropriate teacher behavior. States have acted accordingly, and it is not surprising that courts tend to support education officials in their actions. So a Georgia appellate court found that it was appropriate for the state to temporarily suspend the license of a kindergarten teacher who changed some of her student's incorrect answers on the Iowa Tests of Basic Skills (*Professional Standards Commission* v. *Denham*, 2001).

Sometimes in policymakers' zeal to use student test scores, unanticipated consequences can ensue. A Florida state statute requires that each district establish a teacher assessment system and that the "assessment procedure for instructional personnel and school administrators must be primarily based on the performance of students assigned to their classrooms or schools ... [and] may include other criteria approved to assess instructional personnel and school administrators' performance, or any combination of student performance and other approved criteria'' (Florida Revised Statutes, 2008). Under a prior version of this statute, some teacher dismissals were overturned by state court judges when administrator evaluations determined a teacher was incompetent but there was not primary consideration of student performance data in making the decision to dismiss a teacher. This was, as one commentator noted, an "ironic twist" in the pursuit of teacher quality when the teachers were reinstated, with back pay, as a result of the court decisions (DeNardo, 2008). There are now several Florida state court and administrative hearing officer decisions affirming the legislature's mandate to give significant consideration to student performance results in determining teacher competence in light of the state statute (see *Leon County School Board* v. *Waters*, 1986; *Sherrod* v. *Palm Beach County School Board*, 2006; *Young* v. *Palm Beach County School Board*, 2006). The legislature has now clarified the power of local districts to consider additional performance criteria.

## Insubordination

Many teacher dismissal cases represent the challenges of working relationships in any workplace. Teachers who talk back to the principal or fail to follow directives may face dismissal. A few of the cases represent situations in which dismissal seems to have been the end result of what were simply very abrasive relations between a teacher and an administrator. Other cases represent instances in which the teacher might have been legitimately dismissed on grounds of poor teaching practice, but it was the act of insubordination that led to the more easily established grounds for dismissal.

The commonly understood definition of *insubordination* is willful failure or refusal to obey reasonable orders of a superior. For example, one teacher was legitimately dismissed for use of profanity to students after having received a written warning to stop doing this (*Ware* v. *Morgan County School District* 1985). There can be a link between an evaluation process and an insubordination charge. In one case, in evaluations over a three-year period, a principal had requested that a teacher submit class discipline rules, seek help from other teachers, and make other efforts to improve his teaching effectiveness. When the teacher failed to follow those suggestions, there were sufficient grounds to support dismissal on the basis of insubordination (*Thompson* v. *Board of Education*, 1983).

Failure to comply with school rules regarding teaching responsibilities is a common ground for dismissal on the basis of insubordination. One teacher was dismissed for failure to turn student grades in on time, coupled with outbursts after being warned about grading policies (*Bellairs* v. *Beaverton School District*,

2006). Failure to follow school grading policies or submit lesson plans are common types of insubordination (*Dolega* v. *School Board of Miami-Dade County*, 2003). In one case, the teacher failed to take attendance in accordance with school policy, failed to prepare weekly written lesson plans, failed to record grades in a grade book, violated the school district's conflict-of-interest policies, and failed to teach the entire curriculum required by the district (*Harvey* v. *Jefferson County School District*, 1985). Another teacher was found insubordinate for failing to provide her principal with lesson plans, providing disorganized and confusing lesson plans, and refusing to teach the curriculum adopted by the school (*School District No. 1, City and County of Denver* v. *Cornish*, 2002). In another case, a dismissal for insubordination was upheld when a tenured teacher received both instructions and a warning letter not to do so but continued to have grading done by students or teacher aides, failed or refused to notify the superior as to the times of major testing for evaluation purposes, and failed or refused to contact designated staff members to discuss discipline problems (*Rafael* v. *Meramec Valley R-III Board of Education*, 1978).

Some insubordination cases go to the heart of teaching performance. One court upheld a refusal on grounds of insubordination to renew the contract of a teacher who took a confrontational approach to supervisors and insisted that she, rather than her supervisors, controlled her curriculum and classroom methods (*Barnes* v. *Spearfish School District No. 40-2*, 2006). Professional development, or refusal to pursue it, has also been the focus of insubordination cases. One teacher was dismissed when she refused her principal's direction to attend an enrichment program intended to improve her skills in classroom management (*Howell* v. *Alabama State Tenure Commission*, 1981). Another teacher was dismissed for insubordination when she was absent from school three days to attend a reading conference after her school board had denied her request for leave to attend (*Christopherson* v. *Spring Valley Elementary School District*, 1980).

Some of the insubordination cases focus on duties ancillary to classroom teaching. In a Mississippi case (*Jackson* v. *Hazlehurst Municipal Separate School District*, 1983), sufficient grounds for dismissal on the basis of insubordination were found by a court when a teacher had been directed in writing by the principal to assist in supervising students at a junior high school football game; the teacher, unwilling to do so, responded by crumpling the paper on which the assignment was written, throwing it on floor, and telling the principal that he would not comply with assignment. Previously this teacher had directly refused to comply with the principal's directive that he oversee student behavior on the junior high campus during a midmorning break in examinations. In another case from Colorado, a court upheld the dismissal for insubordination of a high school teacher who refused to participate in any hall supervision duties after being ordered to do so by his principal (*Lockhart* v. *Board of Education*, 1986).

Overall, accusations of insubordination are generally fairly effective grounds for teacher dismissal. One commentator found that in court decisions in which teachers were accused of insubordination, nearly twice as many cases resulted in a finding that the teacher was insubordinate rather than not (Ghent, 2007).

## Immorality, Unfitness, and Neglect of Responsibilities

Another group of dismissal cases rests on issues of teacher morality and neglect of duty. For readers who remember the 1970s, we might describe these as the cases involving sex, drugs, and rock and roll. This is a difficult realm, involving some cases with teacher (mis)conduct that relate to appropriate teaching practice and some that perhaps do not. Notable here are the changing social norms over time concerning morality, as well as what might best be described as regional variations in what is considered acceptable conduct. Also notable are issues concerning the relationship between ''morality'' and ''fitness to teach.''

It was not too long ago that female teachers could be summarily dismissed for pregnancy, in or out of wedlock (Pullin & Melnick, 2008). Some of these cases involved perceptions of morality, and others were the result of perceptions about the role of women in the workplace. More contemporary cases reflect a variety of perspectives about individual conduct and the role of teachers in our society. And, sadly, some represent sheer stupidity on the part of teachers who ought to know more about how to behave as responsible adults, whether they were educators or not.

Consistent with most of the recent court decisions, one court stated, ''We do not believe that the legislature [in its criteria for teacher dismissal] intended to potentially subject every teacher to discipline, even dismissal, for private peccadillos or personal shortcomings that might come to the attention of the board of education, but yet have little or no relation to the teacher's relationship with his students, his fellow teachers, or with the school community'' (*Weissman* v. *Board of Education* . . . , 1976, p. 1274). In general, the cases from the 1970s on require some evidence of a relationship between a teacher's misconduct and his or her ''fitness'' to teach effectively, with no clear rules on how to measure this relationship, other than a broad principle that students, schools, and communities need to be protected from harm and that teachers need to be able to work effectively in schools.

The case law portrays several different ways in which unfitness to teach was demonstrated. In *MacKenzie* v. *School Committee of Ipswich* (1961), a teacher's profane utterance was found to be improper and unbecoming conduct. In another Massachusetts case, a teacher's behavior, much of it in front of students, was ''insolent, abusive, loud and out of control,'' and thus supported a charge of unbecoming conduct (*Kurlander* v. *School Committee of Williamstown*, 1983, p. 357). Another teacher who pushed students, behaved in an "argumentative and overbearing manner," and pushed a fellow teacher was found to have engaged in conduct unbecoming a teacher (*Springgate* v. *School Committee of Mattapoisett*, 1981).

Some cases involve sexual misconduct. A Washington State court case (*Wright* v. *Mead School District No. 354*, 1997) involved a high school music teacher who over the course of five years had a series of sexual relationships with his students and also consumed alcohol with students on school trips while he was employed in a previous school district. When a second school district that later employed him found out about these incidents almost ten years later, the teacher was dismissed for what school officials characterized as his prior "unprofessional, unacceptable, and immoral conduct" (p. 627). The court upheld the dismissal, untroubled by the time lapse between misconduct and the dismissal, and described the grounds for determining how a teacher's conduct affects his teaching performance, including consideration of the age and maturity of the students, the likelihood the teacher's conduct had an adverse impact on students, the likelihood the conduct might be repeated, and the negative impact of the teacher's conduct on other teachers.

On some occasions, dismissal for teacher misconduct is grounded on "neglect of duty" in failing to enforce school policies. Some courts regard "neglect of duty" to relate directly to "fitness to teach." In a Colorado case, a teacher dismissal was upheld when a teacher who was sponsor for the student group was found to have been drinking beer with the cheerleaders at an out-of-town basketball tournament in violation of school rules against drinking (*Blaine* v. *Moffat County School District*, 1988).

Some court decisions do not fit so readily into these analytical approaches. In an Indiana case, *Fiscus* v. *Board of School Trustees . . .* (1987), a state appellate court upheld the dismissal in midyear for "immorality" of a long-term and tenured teacher with an unblemished record. Fiscus was dismissed for a single incident in which she allegedly uttered the phrase "f**k you" in her classroom when the sole evidence of the incident was the testimony of several fifth-grade boys with whom the teacher had been having disciplinary problems both in and out of school for an extended period of time.

## Out-of-School Activities

Sometimes dismissals are based on state statutes allowing dismissal when a teacher is found guilty of criminal or other inappropriate out-of-school conduct. Check forgery and swindling his partners in a part-time computer business resulted in one district's determination that the teacher's continued presence in the small school district would result in faculty disorder and an unsatisfactory learning environment. It was determined that this constituted an appropriate ground for dismissal under the Minnesota statute (*Matter of Shelton*, 1987).

## Unacceptable Grounds for Dismissal

Situations that might involve a teacher's constitutional or civil rights are unacceptable grounds for dismissal. As citizens and as public employees, teachers are entitled to the protections of state, local, and federal civil rights statutes, as well as state and federal constitutions. As a result, teachers who feel that their dismissal was the result of discrimination on the basis of race, ethnicity, gender, religion, or disability have a basis for bringing a legal challenge against a dismissal under federal laws. Titles VI and VII of the Civil Rights Act of 1964 bar discrimination on the basis of race or ethnicity. Title VII also bars discrimination on the basis of gender, as does Title IX of the Education Amendments of 1973. Both the Americans with Disabilities Act and Section 504 of the Rehabilitation Act of 1973 bar discrimination on the basis of disability; many states have similar, or even more expansive protections for individuals with disabilities.

When a teacher challenges a dismissal on grounds that the decision was unlawfully tainted by discrimination on the basis of race, gender, or disability, a court scrutinizes these claims by first establishing whether a teacher falls into a category of protected individuals. It determines whether discrimination occurred and then examines education officials' reasons for their decisions and whether they are educationally defensible.

Discrimination on the basis of race is barred under Title VII of the federal Civil Rights Act of 1964. However, if there is a legitimate reason for dismissing a teacher, the race discrimination claim will not prevail. When an African American teacher argued that she was treated differently from white teachers, the district was successful in overcoming that claim when it established that she had leaked to her students in advance the questions from an Advanced Placement English exam they would be taking (*Richardson* v. *Newburgh Enlarged City School District*, 1997).

Courts are still trying to understand how to apply laws barring discrimination on the basis of disability in many contexts, including the evaluation and dismissal of teachers. It is clear that these nondiscrimination statutes apply. Under a Washington State law, a school district cannot refuse to hire or discharge a teacher with a disability simply because of the disability, but no such prohibition exists if the disability prevents performance of the essential functions of the job that cannot be accommodated or remediated. As a result, a court upheld the dismissal of a long-time special education teacher with a degenerative eye disease after his vision deteriorated so much that he could no longer implement pedagogical approaches or ensure the safety of his students (*Clarke* v. *Shoreline School District,* 1986).

Over a period of time, the U.S. Supreme Court substantially limited the number of individuals who were entitled to protections under the federal disability rights laws, but in September 2008, the Americans with Disabilities Amendment Act of 2008 was signed to make these laws applicable to a broader range of individuals. What will probably not change, however, is enforcement of state or local requirements for holding a teaching position and courts' frequent confirmation of the power of government to impose credential, testing, job responsibility, or other requirements on teachers as minimum qualifications for employment that will not be waived in the face of an existing disability. In one case, an experienced but uncertified teacher with dyslexia asserted that her dismissal for failure to obtain permanent certification unlawfully discriminated against her on the basis of her disability. The teacher argued she was not given an accommodation for her disability in the state examination required for teacher certification and her continued employment. The court deciding the case readily upheld the right of the local district and the state to make a standardized exam a necessary qualification for continued employment as a certified teacher (*Falchenberg* v. *New York City Department of Education*, 2005).

For individuals with disabilities, a significant issue often is whether an individual can perform teaching responsibilities with the provision of reasonable accommodations by schools. When a long-term teacher with chronic kidney disease and associated fatigue asked to be allowed to teach a shortened school day, a federal court of appeals supported the school district's refusal to accommodate this request. It concluded that a minimum $7\frac{3}{4}$-hour day was an essential function of a teacher's job, based in part on the fact that this was a component of the collective bargaining agreement with the district teacher union (*Kurek* v. *North Allegheny School District*, 2007). However, in another case, a court recognized that the job of teaching can take many forms and that districts should take into account different assignments for teachers, including tutoring or administrative responsibilities, that might afford a teacher with a disability a reasonable accommodation that would allow continued employment (*Mustafa* v. *Clark County School District*, 1998).

In several cases, educators have alleged that the schools in which they worked afforded a hostile environment or that their supervisors or coworkers harassed or retaliated against them on the basis of their membership in a protected group, as a result of which bad teaching evaluations or dismissal or an involuntary resignation occurred. Although courts do recognize these claims, they set a high bar for proof from teachers that they were the targets of discriminatory treatment (*Trepka* v. *Board of Education of the Cleveland City School District*, 2002; *Engel* v. *Rapid City School District*, 2007).

Some teacher dismissal cases have addressed teachers' rights to freedom of expression and freedom of religion. Teachers have protected First Amendment rights to religious beliefs and freedom of expression, but these rights as public employees have been found to be more limited than the rights of a general citizen if the government has an appropriate educational reason for doing so. In past cases, courts have held that a teacher can be terminated if he or she refuses on religious grounds to teach the mandatory curriculum, given the overriding interest a school district has in mandating the curriculum (*Palmer* v. *Board of Education* . . . , 1979). Out-of-class conduct is treated similarly, as in the case where a guidance counselor with an otherwise exemplary performance record was not rehired because she prayed with students, advocated abstinence, and stated her disapproval of contraception. The court concluded that she was not rehired because of her conduct in her work, not her Christian beliefs, and that this was an acceptable practice by the school district given its obligation to ensure the constitutionally required separation of church and state (*Grossman* v. *South Shore Public School District*, 2007).

In another case, a student teacher who expressed his views against abortion by showing pictures of fetuses and engaging in other notable behavior based on his religious beliefs at his student teaching site was confronted by the principal. When confronted, the student teacher informed the principal that he was more interested in pleasing God than in pleasing the principal, stating that he thought the principal was "the devil" and the school faculty her disciples and that it was wrong to allow religion to be denigrated in the public schools. The student teacher's constitutional claims were treated by a federal court of appeals under the same standards as would apply to an employed teacher in that school. When the student claimed that constitutional rights to free speech and due process protected him from being dismissed from the program, the court concluded that the school district's right to set and control its curriculum outweighed the interests of the student teacher (*Hennessy* v. *City of Melrose*, 1999).

There were cases in the 1970s overturning teacher dismissals on grounds that teachers had freedom of expression under the First Amendment of the U.S. Constitution to choose, for example, which books they wanted to use to teach an English course (*Parducci* v. *Rutland*, 1970). In more recent years, however, courts seem to give more latitude to school officials seeking to control their curriculum. The momentum of the current standardization movement can be expected to increase this.

Also relevant to teacher dismissals beyond issues of the curriculum are the expressive rights of teachers and other public employees about all sorts of matters associated with the educational institutions in which they work and other matters of public concern and debate. Here, the rights of teachers are clearly not viewed as broadly as the rights of ordinary citizens, with a balance struck between individual rights and the authority of public schools to regulate their employees (*Pickering* v. *Board of Education*, 1968). An educator can be dismissed if a public expression of opinion was made as part of conducting the teacher's official duties and the value of a teacher's speech does not outweigh the school district's interest in maintaining the effective and efficient function of the schools. However, a teacher cannot be dismissed if the dismissal was substantially motivated by the teacher's expression of an unpopular view about issues of broad public concern (*Mount Healthy City School District* v. *Doyle,* 1977; *Connick* v. *Meyers,* 1983). In one case, a nontenured middle school physical and health teacher who was not rehired claimed that the decision related to his concerns about the safety of his students. The teacher had been assigned to team-teach with a more senior teacher, and when she consistently was tardy or absent from classes they were supposed to teach together, he began entering information about this in a journal, discussed his concerns with two more experienced teachers in the school, and reported his concerns to his superiors. When he refused to tell school administrators which teachers had been advising him and when the derelict coteacher accused him of sexual remarks, his contract was not renewed. A state labor department investigator determined that the teacher was disciplined and terminated in a discriminatory manner. The federal court judge deciding the case agreed and determined that the effort to communicate about the coteacher's absence and the need to protect student safety were important matters of public concern that involved constitutionally protected expression and should not have been used against him by the district (*Wilcoxon* v. *Red Clay Consolidated School District Board of Education,* 2006).

# DISCUSSION

State laws have set the criteria and procedures for teacher termination, and these reflect our societal norms about fair treatment of individuals and appropriate approaches to government decision making. State laws and regulations also reflect basic expectations about teacher quality and teacher evaluation. There is some indication, such as in the Massachusetts statute setting out criteria for evaluating teachers, that state laws can reflect the social science research on effective teaching. There is also indication that state statutes can reflect popular policy ideas, no matter the shortage of social science to support the concept, such as the Florida statutes embracing the use of student test scores to evaluate individual teachers.

The state statutes and the court cases, although the cases are a small number on which to base conclusions, reflect both current practices in teacher evaluation and also how far these practices need to go. The cases demonstrate a powerful deference given to local education officials and legislatures by judges. In addition to extending considerable deference to state and local officials in pursuing efforts to improve teacher quality, courts have imposed to date two primary types of standards in assessing these programs. They have asked whether there is any rational link between the government's goals and the means of achieving those goals and whether a program is operated in a rational, rather than an arbitrary and capricious, manner. Courts have not necessarily probed, or been given, social science evidence concerning the rationality of many teacher evaluation approaches, although such evidence relates to both these legal questions.

For the future, intriguing considerations arise from the potential for improvement in teacher evaluation practices. Will these evaluations increase the formation and development of good teachers, resulting in the need to dismiss fewer teachers? Or will teacher dismissals increase and be based on grounds more clearly associated with good pedagogical practice? As policymakers call for more use of social science evidence in educational programs, such as the provisions of NCLB calling for more evidence-based approaches, will the calls for better evidence influence teacher evaluation practice and judges' and legislators' reactions to that practice? Or will research-based claims be seen as jargon, as they were (and might have been) when presented by principal Huckaby in an effort to justify her long campaign to fire Mr. Waters?

Administrators' and teacher colleagues' individual judgments are the most important judgments about teachers that are made in schools. But teachers deserve fair and professional treatment, and communities and parents deserve to know that the best efforts are being made to ensure the quality of schools. Will practices in local schools and teacher education programs improve, and what future role will laws and judges play? In too many instances, a teacher dismissal reflects failures of our system as much as failures on part of the teacher. Mr. Adams, the teacher who did not know the basic conventions of spelling and grammar, should not have been allowed to complete a teacher education program or probably even begin one. When Ms. Fiscus had a bad day and swore in her classroom, did she display sufficient evidence of immorality to be dismissed? Was she an incompetent teacher for whom an evaluation system had failed either to identify or remediate problems? Or was she a competent teacher who should have been allowed to retain her job when she had a bad moment in dealing with a bunch of constantly misbehaving prepubescent boys?

One legal commentator has concluded that many of the steps that need to be taken to improve teacher dismissal rely more on "enlightened human relations" practices and professional norms and ethical standards rather than legal requirements (Zirkel, 2003, p. 4). As this book and others demonstrate, meaningful approaches to improving teacher quality through evaluation require more attention to factors such as teachers' pedagogical content knowledge and classroom practice. These matters have been paid relatively little in-depth attention in the case law, although legislators and other public officials are now taking more steps to define the indicators of teaching quality and mechanisms for evaluating these.

In no type of case, as one commentator concludes, does a teacher going to court face odds that clearly favor an outcome on the teacher's behalf (Zirkel, 2003). When it comes to judging teachers, courts prefer to leave this work to educators and local public officials. At the same time, the procedural requirements involved in legal proceedings are a considerable cost (time, money, distraction from the business at hand, anguish) to the district, so no one really wins here. As a result, this chapter is as much about the role of courts and the relationship among the different branches of government as it is about teacher quality. Yet the cases and statutes discussed here reflect the struggle to define and promote good teaching practice. In the end, few teachers are formally terminated or dismissed for cause. State laws set forth a number of grounds for teacher dismissal on factors such as incompetence or insubordination. And many of the cases discussed here reflect what most of us might agree meets those standards. Yet when teachers are dismissed, as the collective stories in the cases indicate, most dismissals do not reflect efforts to ensure outstanding pedagogy as it is being defined in the professional and social science literature. A teacher dismissal is more likely to be for something clearly wrong and uncontroversial like drinking beer with the cheerleaders, serious sexual misconduct, changing student responses on a test, or failing to adhere to the fundamental requirements of a teaching job like following through on assignments to supervise students than for some rich component, high-quality pedagogical practice.

*Diana Pullin expresses her sincere gratitude to the Spencer Foundation in Chicago for a generous Resident Fellowship, which allowed for the completion of this work.*

# REFERENCES

*Adams* v. *Clarendon County School District*, 241 S.E.2d 897 (Sup. Ct. S.C. 1978).

Americans with Disabilities Act. (1990). 42 U.S.C. §§ 12101 et seq.

*Arrocha* v. *Board of Education of City of New York*, 712 N.E.2d 669 (N.Y. 1999).

*Artherton* v. *Board of Education of School District of St. Joseph.* 744 S.W.2d 518 (Mo. App. 1988).

Ballou, D., & Podgursky, M. (1997). *Teacher pay and teacher quality*. Kalamazoo, MI: W. E. Upjohn Institute for Employment Research.

*Barnes* v. *Spearfish School District No. 40-2*, 725 N.W.2d 226 (S.D. 2006).

Beckham, J. (1997). Ten judicial commandments for legally sound teacher evaluation. *Education Law Reporter, 117,* 435–442.

*Bellairs* v. *Beaverton School District,* 136 P.3d 93 (Ore. App. 2006).

*Black's Law Dictionary.* (1990). St. Paul, MN: West.

*Blaine* v. *Moffat County School District.* 748 P.2d 1280, (Sup. Ct. Colo. 1988).

*Board of Directors of Sioux City Community School District* v. *Mroz,* 295 N.W.2d 447, 448-49 (Iowa 1980).

*Board of Education of Argo-Summit School District No. 104, Cook County* v. *Hunt.* 487 N.E.2d 24 (Ill. App. 1985).

*Board of Regents* v. *Roth,* 408 U.S. 564 (1972).

Braun, H. I. (2005). *Using student progress to evaluate teachers: A primer on value-added models.* Princeton, NJ: Educational Testing Service.

Breyer, S. G., Steward, R. B., Sunstein, C., & Spitzer, M. (1998). *Administrative law and regulatory policy: Problems, text, and cases* (4th ed.). New York: Aspen.

Breyer, S. G., Steward, R. B., Sunstein, C., & Spitzer, M. (2002). *Administrative law and regulatory policy: Problems, text and cases* (5th ed.). New York: Aspen Law and Business.

Brooks, P., & Gewirtz, P. (Eds). (1996). *Law's stories: Narrative and rhetoric in the law.* New Haven, CT: Yale University Press.

*Brown* v. *Wood County Board of Education,* 400 S.E.2d 213 (W. Va. 1990).

*Burton* v. *Town of Littleton,* 426 F.3d 9 (1st Cir. 2005).

*Carter* v. *State Board of Education,* 414 N.E.2d 153 (Ill. App. 1980).

*Christopherson* v. *Spring Valley Elementary School District,* 413 N.E.2d 199 (Ill. App. 1980).

*Citizens to Preserve Overton Park, Inc.* v. *Volpe,* 401 U.S. 402 (1971).

Civil Rights Act of 1964. 42 U.S.C. 2000d, 2000e.

*Clarke* v. *Shoreline School District,* 720 P.2d 793 (Sup. Ct. Wash. 1986).

*Collins* v. *Faith School District No. 46-2,* 574 N.W.2d 889 (S.D. 1998).

*Connick* v. *Meyers,* 461 U.S. 138 (1983).

*Conward* v. *Cambridge School Committee,* 171 F.3d 12 (1st Cir. 1999).

Dagley, D. L., & Veir, C. A. (2002). Subverting the academic abstention doctrine in teacher evaluation: How school reform legislation defeats itself. *Brigham Young University Education and Law Journal, 2002,* 123–140.

DeNardo, C. (2008, February 11). FCAT tosses teachers lifeline. *Palm Beach Post.* Retrieved February 18, 2008, from http://palmbeachpost.com.

*Dolega* v. *School Board of Miami-Dade County,* 840 So. 2d 445 (Fla. District Ct. App. 3d District, 2003).

*Ellicott* v. *Board of Education of Township of Frankford, Sussex County,* 598 A.2d 237 (N.J. Super. App. Div. 1991).

*Engel* v. *Rapid City School District,* 506 F.3d 1118 (8th Cir. 2007).

*Eshom* v. *Board of Education of School District No. 54,* 364 N.W.2d 7 (Neb. 1985).

Ey, R. M. (2008). Cause of action to challenge discharge of public school teacher on grounds of incompetence. *Causes of Action (1st ser.), 21,*423. Retrieved September 16, 2008, from www.westlaw.com.

*Falchenberg* v. *New York City Department of Education*, 375 F. Supp. 2d 344 (S.D.N.Y. 2005).

*Feldman* v. *Board of Education of City School District of City of New York*, 686 N.Y.S.2d 842 (N.Y. App. Div., 1999).

*Fiscus* v. *Board of School Trustees of Central School District*, 509 N.E.2d 1137 (Ind. App. 1987).

Florida Revised Statutes. 1012.34(3). (2008).

Ghent, J. (2007). What constitutes "insubordination" as ground for dismissal of public school teacher? *American Law Reports 3d*, 78, 83–126.

*Grossman* v. *South Shore Public School District*, 507 F.3d. 1097 (7th Cir. 2007).

*Gwathmey* v. *Atkinson*, 447 F. Supp. 1113 (D. Va. 1976).

*Hagerty* v. *State Tenure Commission*, 445 N.W.2d 178 (Mich. App. 1989).

*Hamburg* v. *North Penn School District*, 484 A.2d 867 (Penn. 1984).

*Harvey* v. *Jefferson County School District*, 710 P.2d 1103 (Sup. Ct. Colo. 1985).

*Hennessy* v. *City of Melrose*, 194 F.3d 237 (1st Cir. Mass.) (1999).

*Hicks* v. *Gayville-Volin School District*, 668 N.W.2d 69 (S.D. 2003).

Honawar, V. (2007, December 5). New York City taps lawyers to weed out bad teachers. *Education Week*, p. 13.

*Howell* v. *Alabama State Tenure Commission*, 402 So. 2d 1041 (Ala. App. 1981).

*Jackson* v. *Hazlehurst Municipal Separate School District*, 427 So. 2d 134 (Miss. 1983).

*Jennings* v. *Caddo Parish School Board*, 276 So. 2d 386 (La App. 1973).

Johnson, S. M., & Donaldson, M. (2006). The effects of collective bargaining on teacher quality. In J. Hannaway & A. Rotherham (Eds.), *Collective bargaining in education: Negotiating change in today's schools*. Cambridge, MA: Harvard Education Press.

Joint Committee on Standards for Educational Evaluation. (2008). *The personnel evaluation standards: How to assess systems for evaluating educators* (2nd ed.). Thousand Oaks, CA: Corwin Press.

*Kurek* v. *North Allegheny School District*, 233 Fed. Appx. 154 (3rd Cir. 2007).

*Kurlander* v. *School Committee of Williamstown*, 16 Mass. App. Ct. 350 (1983).

*Leon County School Board* v. *Waters*, 2007 WL 2200601 (Fla. Div. Admin. Hearings, 2007).

*Lewis Central Education Association* v. *Iowa Board of Education Examiners*, 625 N.W.2d 687 (Iowa 2001).

*Lockhart* v. *Board of Education*, 735 P.2d 913 (Colo. App. 1986).

*MacKenzie* v. *School Committee of Ipswich*, 342 Mass. 612 (1961).

Massachusetts Department of Education. (2008a, August 5). *Summary of arbitration awards*. Retrieved September 5, 2008, from www.doe.mass.edu/lawsregs /arbitration.

Massachusetts Department of Education. (2008b, October 16). *Evaluation of teachers and administrators*. 603 C.M.R. 35. Retrieved October 20, 2008, from www.doe.mass.edu.lawsregs.

Massachusetts Education Reform Act. (1993). Massachusetts General Laws, Chapter 69 Section IJ, Chapter 71, Sections 41, 42.

*Massachusetts Federation of Teachers, AFT, AFL-CIO* v. *Board of Education*, 436 Mass. 763 (2002).

*Matter of Shelton*, 408 N.W.2d 594 (Ct. App. Minn. 1987).

*McGuinn* v. *Douglas County School District No. 66*, 612 N.W.2d 198, 203 (Neb. 2000).

*McKinnon* v. *State*, 72 So. 676 (Fla. 1916).

Millman, J. (1997). How do I judge thee? Let me count the ways. In J. Millman (Ed.), *Grading teachers, grading schools: Is student achievement a valid evaluation measure?* (pp. 243–247). Thousand Oaks, CA: Corwin Press.

Missouri Revised Statutes. (1969). § 168.114 (1).

Moe, T. (2006). Union power and the education of children. In J. Hannaway & A. Rotherham (Eds.), *Collective bargaining in education: Negotiating change in today's schools*. Cambridge, MA: Harvard Education Press.

*Mongitore* v. *Regan*, 520 N.Y.S.2d 194 (1987).

*Mount Healthy City School District* v. *Doyle*, 429 U.S. 274 (1977).

*Mustafa* v. *Clark County School District*, 157 F.3d 1169 (9th Cir. 1998).

Nevada Revised Statutes. (2001). § 391.312.

No Child Left Behind Act. (2001). 20 U.S.C. 6301 et seq.

Odden, A., & Kelley, C. (2002). *Paying teachers for what they know and do: New and smarter compensation strategies to improve schools*. Thousand Oaks, CA: Corwin Press.

*Palmer* v. *Board of Education of City of Chicago*, 466 F. Supp. 600 (D. Ill., 1979), aff'd 603 F.2d 1271 (7th Cir. 1979), cert. den. 444 U.S. 1026 (1980).

*Parducci* v. *Rutland*, 316 F. Supp. 352 (D. Ala., 1970).

*Paul* v. *Davis*, 424 U.S. 693 (1976).

*Perry* v. *Sinderman*, 408 U.S. 593 (1972).

*Pickering* v. *Board of Education*, 391 U.S. 563 (1968).

*Professional Standards Commission* v. *Denham*, 556 S.E.2d 920 (Ga. App., 2001).

Pullin, D. (2004, September–October). Accountability, autonomy, and academic freedom in educator preparation programs. *Journal of Teacher Education, 55*, 300–312.

Pullin, D., & Melnick, S. (2008). Teachers unions. In T. Good (Ed.), *Twenty-first century education*. Thousand Oaks, CA: Sage.

*Rafael* v. *Meramec Valley R-III Board of Education*, 569 S.W.2d 309 (Mo. App. 1978).

Rehabilitation Act. (1973). 29 U.S.C. 794.

*Richardson* v. *Newburgh Enlarged City School District*, 984 F. Supp. 735 (S.D.N.Y. 1997).

*Russell* v. *Special School District No. 6*, 366 N.W.2d 700 (Minn. App. 1985).

Sawchuk, S. (2008a, October 1). Standards for teacher evaluation mulled. *Education Week*, pp. 18, 21.

Sawchuk, S. (2008b, October 15). D.C. set to impose teacher-dismissal plan. *Education Week*, p. 6.

*Scheelhaase* v. *Woodbury Central Community School District*, 488 F. 2d 237 (8th Cir. 1973), cert. den. 417 U.S. 969 (1974).

*School Committee of Lowell* v. *Oung*, 893 N.E.2d 1246 (App. Ct. Mass. 2008), review denied 452 Mass. 1110 (2008).

*School District of Beverly* v. *Geller*, 755 N.E. 2d 1241 (Mass. 2001).

*School District No. 1, City and County of Denver* v. *Cornish*, 58 P. 3d 1091 (Colo. Ct. App. 2002; cert. denied, 2002).

*Scoggins* v. *Board of Education*, 853 F.2d 1472 (8th Cir. Ark. 1988).

*Sherrod* v. *Palm Beach County School Board*, 963 So. 2d 251 (Fla. Ct. App. 2006).

*Springgate* v. *School Committee of Mattapoisett*, 11 Mass. Ct. App. 304 (1981).

*St. Louis Teachers Union, Local 420, American Federation of Teachers, AFL-CIO* v. *Board of Education of the City of St. Louis*, 652 F. Supp. 425 (E.D. Mo. 1987).

Stewart, H., & Adams, S. (1998, Summer). Arbitration of teacher dismissals and other discipline under the Education Reform Act. *Massachusetts Law Review*, 18–31.

Strike, K. (1990). The ethics of educational evaluation. In J. Millman & L. Darling-Hammond (Eds.), *The new handbook of teacher evaluation: Assessing elementary and secondary school teachers* (pp. 356–373). Thousand Oaks, CA: Corwin Press.

*Thompson* v. *Board of Education*, 668 P.2d 954 (Colo. App. 1983).

*Trepka* v. *Board of Education of the Cleveland City School District*, 28 Fed. App. 455 (6th Cir., 2002).

U.S. Department of Education, National Center for Education Statistics. (2003–2004). *Schools and staffing survey, public school, public school teacher, public school principal, public school library media center, and district data files, 2003-04.* Retrieved September 9, 2008, from http://nces.ed.gov/surveys/sass.

*Von Gizycki* v. *Levy*, 771 N.Y.S.2d 174 (N.Y. App. 2004).

Walsh-Sarnecki, P. (2007, December 30). In metro Detroit, bad teachers can go on teaching. *Detroit Free Press*.

*Ware* v. *Morgan County School District*, 719 P.2d 351 (Colo. App. 1985).

*Weissman* v. *Board of Education of Jefferson County School District No. R-1*, 547 P.2d 1267 (Colo. 1976).

West's Florida Statutes Annotated. (2008). § 1012.34.

*Whaley* v. *Anoka-Hennepin Independent School District* No. 11, 325 N.W.2d 128 (Sup. Ct. Minn. 1982).

*Wheeler* v. *Yuma School District*, 750 P.2d 860 (Sup. Ct. Ariz. 1988).

*Whitfield* v. *Little Rock Public Schools*, 756 S.W.2d 125 (Ark. App. 1988).

*Wilcoxon* v. *Red Clay Consolidated School District Board of Education*, 437 F. Supp. 2d 235 (D. Del. 2006).

*Wright* v. *Mead School District No. 354*, 944 P 2d 1 (Wash. App. Div. 1997).

*Young* v. *Palm Beach County School Board*, 968 So. 2d 38 (Fla. Ct. App. 2006).

Zirkel, P. A. (2003). Legal boundaries for performance evaluation of public school professional personnel. *Education Law Reporter, 172*, 1–15.

# PART FOUR

# BROADER ASSESSMENT ISSUES

**Chapter Twelve:** Setting Standards for Teacher Evaluation
*Barbara B. Howard, Arlen L. Gullickson*

**Chapter Thirteen:** Thinking Systemically About Assessment Practice
*Pamela A. Moss*

**Chapter Fourteen:** Teacher Quality: An American Educational Dilemma
*David K. Cohen*

CHAPTER TWELVE

# Setting Standards for Teacher Evaluation

Barbara B. Howard, Arlen R. Gullickson

*Appalachian State University; Western Michigan University*

With the growing emphasis on accountability, standards-based reform seems to have captured public interest only in the past decade or so. However, standards in education have a long history of guiding best practices to garner public trust in the quality and integrity of educational endeavors, including teacher evaluation. Recognizing the need to establish guiding principles for best practices to promote sound teacher evaluation, the Joint Committee on Standards for Educational Evaluation, led by Daniel Stufflebeam, published the first edition of the *Personnel Evaluation Standards* in 1988. Since then, teacher evaluation has continued to evolve as greater and greater emphasis is placed on higher levels of student achievement, quality of the classroom teacher, and the principal's instructional leadership skills. Teacher evaluation in a school or district should not only provide its users with information that will ensure the quality of teachers but guide principals in making critical decisions concerning school improvement as well (Howard & Sanders, 2006).

Sound teacher evaluations are defined as those that meet standards by addressing four generally accepted attributes of educational evaluation: propriety, utility, feasibility, and accuracy (Joint Committee . . . , 1988, 2008). Sadly, teacher evaluations may not play as critical a role in school improvement in many schools for a variety of reasons. Many times, such deficiencies are as much the result of system design as implementation by principals as evaluators or district administrators as supervisors of principals. In the absence of sound teacher evaluation at the building level, teachers and principals are often left without the credibility necessary to fully identify and reward those teachers who exemplify strong professional practice while supporting through improvement strategies those who have not yet achieved such high levels of quality performance (Howard & Harman, 2007).

The second edition of *The Personnel Evaluation Standards,* issued in 2008 under the leadership of Arlen Gullickson, updates the principles and standards of sound teacher evaluation following major shifts in research and thinking in the field since the mid-1980s. Since teacher evaluation policies and practices are greatly influenced by the culture of the state and district of implementation, neither the standards nor this chapter attempts to promote one specific method over another. It is more helpful to examine issues surrounding teacher quality that might be addressed by teacher evaluations aligned with the generally accepted principles and guidelines for sound evaluations.

## ESTABLISHING SOUND TEACHER EVALUATION TO SUPPORT TEACHER QUALITY

There has been long-held support for the idea that the quality of teacher performance in the classroom supersedes all other elements in its significant effect on student learning, usually measured through student achievement on standardized tests. The quality of a student's educational experience is a direct result of the classroom teacher's ability to exercise sound professional judgment and skill in creating an engaging learning environment. Without question, such complex practices also reflect in-depth knowledge of curriculum, student development, and research-based strategies. However, the bottom line remains that no curricula, programs, or initiatives rely on the quality of an individual teacher's ability to implement it with fidelity (Kyriakides, Demetriou, & Charalambous, 2006; Danielson, 2001; Stronge, 2002; Sanders, 2000; Wright, Horn, & Sanders, 1997; Sanders & Rivers, 1996; Rowan, Chiang, & Miller, 1996).

Schools and districts embrace professional development programs as the primary means of increasing teacher quality by improving knowledge and skill in specific areas. In the push for higher teacher quality, professional development is also viewed as a key component, but Danielson (2001) cautions that to be effective, such initiatives must be structured around the goals of the district and school rather than the inclinations of the individual provider. Some programs go beyond the traditional informational sessions by including more long-term support through establishment of professional learning teams or communities. Such learning teams offer a critical formative peer feedback process that supports adult learning (Jolly, 2008). Regardless of the professional development program in place, effectiveness still rests on the individual teacher's ability to deliver quality instruction. Formative teacher evaluation through peer feedback and review is helpful in promoting improved understanding and implementation of a program, but it lacks the additional accountability of formal or summative evaluation of teacher performance. Sound teacher evaluations provide a feedback loop directly linked to major school goals so that explicit criteria express expectations of teacher performance, and specific professional development activities address any identifiable deficiencies of performance (Joint Committee..., 2008). Thus, teacher evaluation, a long-neglected process required in most schools, may offer a direct link to school reform through improvement of teacher quality if the evaluation is conducted in a sound, meaningful manner (Joint Committee..., 2008; Danielson, 2001; Howard & McColskey, 2001).

Most states and school districts have policies regarding teacher evaluation that embrace the idea that such supervisor evaluations improve teacher quality in the classroom. However, over the years, there has been little, if any, evidence that teacher evaluation has had any impact on teacher performance (Davis, Ellett, & Annunziata, 2002; Ellett & Teddlie, 2003; Toch & Rothman, 2008). Many traditional forms of teacher evaluation tend to rely heavily on teacher behaviors or specific teacher styles requiring the evaluator to check whether such behaviors were observed during one or two classroom visits. These methods tend to limit the scope of teaching to a list of minimally competent skills. There is usually little, if any, differentiation in criteria between the novice of one year and the veteran of twenty years other than that the novice is typically observed more times by more people (Howard and McColskey, 2001). When principals were considered managers, this style of evaluation was acceptable. However, Sinnema and Robinson (2007) argue that the time has passed when the major expectations for outputs of teacher practice were rote memorization of concrete facts and orderly conduct of students. Within the past decade or so, policymakers, educators, and the public have clamored for educational leadership to have a stronger focus on teaching and learning that reflects ambitious goals for student learning. These 21st Century goals embrace critical thinking, inquiry, problem solving, collaboration, and deep understanding of complex issues to prepare students for jobs in a changing society (Leithwood, Seashore Louis, Anderson, & Wahlstrom, 2004; Prestine & Nelson, 2005). To meet the challenges of these goals, all educators must have a deep understanding of both content and pedagogy, coupled with the ability to meet the demands of a rapidly growing diverse population of students. No longer are school leaders being judged on their ability to effectively manage budgets, buildings, and organizational structures to set the stage for learning. Now they are being held accountable for the actual performance of those under their supervision: the classroom teachers.

Syntheses of research in the area of educational leadership support the correlation between strong leadership and student achievement (Hallinger, 2005; Witziers, Bosker, & Kruger, 2003; Hallinger & Heck, 1998). Sinnema and

Robinson (2007) present the compelling argument that the school leader is responsible for ensuring that all organizational structures, including teacher evaluation, should work not only to set the stage for learning but to align, support, and improve the instructional practice of the individual teacher. If the overriding purpose of teacher evaluation is to improve instruction, then the policies and practices in this area should be viewed as potentially powerful tools for instructional improvement when conducted in a meaningful way.

While it is difficult to argue this point, teacher evaluation has not met its potential in many schools and districts for several reasons. One is that summative and formative evaluations are often fraught with political and legal complexities that hamper the ability and desire of supervisors to honestly assess teachers. These same complexities often put teachers on the defensive, thus significantly decreasing the impact of evaluations designed to improve practice. Another may be the narrow scope of teacher evaluations that rely too heavily on one style or philosophy of teaching that conflicts with current research-based programs being adopted within a school. In this case, either the evaluation or the initiative loses credibility with the teachers, creating a tension that serves neither teachers nor students (Davis et al., 2002; Ellett & Teddlie, 2003; Kleinhenz & Ingvarson, 2004).

Other threats to the potential of teacher evaluation to improve teaching may include the following common missteps: insufficient evaluator training and support; inadequate resources to carry out the evaluation; lack of follow-up, including professional development to address the deficiencies found through evaluation; misalignment to district or school goals; teachers' misunderstanding of the evaluation procedures; and misuse of the evaluation results by the administrators, the public, or the teacher (Howard & Harman, 2007).

Ingvarson and Rowe (2008) address the lack of understanding surrounding the issue of teacher quality and teacher evaluation. In arguing for strong teacher performance standards (what a teacher should know and be able to do) that offer explicit criteria for a teacher's performance, they further support the need for valid methods of evaluating teacher quality by operationalizing such performance standards. The focus of their argument is the need to build capacity among teachers in terms of professionalism and its evaluation. They argue that in the absence of credible teacher evaluation, increasing teacher quality aligned with performance standards is difficult, if not impossible.

Given that the most valuable resource in any school is the teaching force, it stands to reason that continuing investigation into the links among teaching practices, student performance, and school reform efforts is a crucial need. One such link continues to be that between teacher performance and merit pay as a reform effort for improving schools. Hart and Teeter (2002) found that public opinion in the United States favored reforms that might result in increases in teacher salaries, but only if these reforms guarantee higher teacher quality linked directly to measurable student outcomes. However, the dearth of sound teacher evaluation systems able to accurately identify such high-quality teaching has stymied the progression of merit pay initiatives across the country for decades (Ramirez, 2001; Toch & Rothman, 2008).

Issues surrounding the links among teacher quality, student achievement, and evaluation are not new. School leaders have long struggled with the need to promote high student achievement through increased teacher performance, but the current political and educational climate provides even greater urgency. While teacher evaluation should not be viewed as the silver bullet or panacea to school reform efforts, it should not be ignored as a crucial part of such efforts. When teacher evaluation in both its design and implementation aligns with the generally accepted principles of sound evaluations, school leaders, teachers, policymakers, and the public may realize the powerful potential of this often underused tool of instructional leadership. This alignment should take place at all levels of policymaking and implementation—from the state to the district to the school. Careful consideration of all the complexities of conducting teacher evaluations should include alignment of practices with the principles and guidelines for sound personnel evaluations. The link between teacher evaluation and teacher quality can be better forged and understood with adherence to such standards.

## DEVELOPMENT OF THE PERSONNEL EVALUATION STANDARDS

The Joint Committee on Standards for Educational Evaluation (2008) defines personnel evaluation as "the systematic assessment of a person's performance and/or qualifications in relation to a professional role and some specified and defensible institutional purpose" (p. 27). The second edition of *Personnel Evaluation Standards* (Joint Committee..., 2008) reflects best practices and principles for all aspects of teacher evaluation. Although the standards apply to the evaluation systems for all personnel engaged in the performance of educational activities, this chapter discusses the standards only in light of their use for classroom teachers in prekindergarten through twelfth-grade settings.

The Joint Committee on Standards for Educational Evaluation (JCSEE) is composed of representatives of professional organizations that include the following: American Association of School Administrators; American Counseling Association; American Educational Research Association; American Evaluation Association; American Indian Higher Education Consortium; American Psychological Association; Canadian Evaluation Society; Canadian Society for the Study of Education; Consortium for Research on Educational Accountability and Teacher Evaluation; Council of Chief State School Officers; National Association of Elementary School Principals; National Association of Secondary

School Principals; National Council on Measurement in Education; National Education Association; National Legislative Program Evaluation Society; and the National Rural Education Association. Its mission is to issue and support the implementation of three sets of standards for educational evaluation: program, personnel, and student. Each set of standards addresses the unique processes associated with its field while maintaining a common bond through development, revision, and organization of each edition. The standards are regularly reviewed and revised by the Joint Committee.

Certified by the American National Standards Institute (ANSI), the standards for personnel evaluation represent generally accepted principles of sound evaluation practices that range from the development or selection of a model of teacher evaluation to the implementation of one. The ANSI process is one of rigorous review and revision requiring documented efforts to solicit input from an international mix of researchers, developers, and practitioners who are generally acknowledged as experts in the field of personnel evaluation. A panel or task force of writers responsible for incorporating valid reviews into the revisions reports directly to the Joint Committee, which oversees the work. The standards are far from being the work of one individual, one group of individuals, or even one organization. The Joint Committee representatives offer opportunities to their memberships to participate in reviews, national hearings, and field trials through listservs, Web sites, conferences, and printed brochures.

These standards differ significantly from those established by such organizations as the National Board for Professional Teaching Standards and the Interstate New Teacher Assessment and Support Consortium (INTASC) in terms of purpose. Standards established by these organizations are performance standards: they define what teachers should know and be able to do. Like state standards for teacher performance, such standards are concerned with the knowledge, skill, and criteria by which teachers are judged. In contrast, the Joint Committee issued the Personnel Evaluation Standards to provide standards for the performance standards themselves: guidelines for making sound judgments on the quality of teacher practice that should be used regardless of the particular teacher performance standards one wishes to evaluate. In the case of the classroom teacher, personnel evaluation provides an assessment in direct relation to the duties, including the knowledge and skills, required of the classroom teacher.

Since the Joint Committee does not support or endorse any one system or type of teacher evaluation, the principles of sound evaluation apply to all systems regardless of philosophy. A system that is totally observation-based with a checklist of teacher behaviors and a performance-based process with multiple sources of data and a multifaceted rubric should meet the same standards of sound personnel evaluation. The Joint Committee is more concerned with promoting the practice of conducting personnel evaluations that ensure performance reviews resulting in attainment of institutional goals and missions directly related to improved educator quality and student learning.

# ASSUMPTIONS UNDERLYING THE DEVELOPMENT OF THE STANDARDS

Six major assumptions undergird the development of the Personnel Evaluation Standards, which evolved in direct support of these assumptions. The first assumption is that personnel evaluation must be an integral part of any educational organization's attempt to provide effective services to students. In other words, the criteria must be linked directly to the goals of the educational organization.

The second assumption demands that all personnel evaluations be constructive in nature, causing no undue harm or demoralization of the person being evaluated. Procedures must be in place to prohibit unfair treatment of any educator by an evaluator. There are standards in place to help safeguard the professional nature of evaluations so that the integrity of both the teacher and the evaluator is not compromised. These standards address a range of activities, from protection of confidentiality to the nature of interactions between teacher and evaluator.

The third assumption underscores the need for any personnel evaluation to consider the diversity of educators. This includes all forms of diversity, such as race, culture, gender, age, disability, and other differences, that may prejudice the evaluator and wrongly influence the outcome of an evaluation. The system in place must ensure that evaluators are trained and supported through oversight to prevent bias from unduly influencing judgment. A clear statement on the issue of diversity is a valued part of the Personnel Evaluation Standards. Standards that support this assumption include those that safeguard against bias and unreliable reports by promoting explicit criteria, accurate data collection, and reliable reporting.

The fourth assumption is that personnel evaluations will be used to guide professional development. This integrates personnel evaluation with professional growth, thus preventing the bureaucratic nature of systems reduced to meeting deadlines and filing paperwork. This assumption is critical to the linkage between teacher quality and evaluation. By establishing standards for balanced evaluations with follow-up, the potential for increased teacher quality through meaningful feedback is enhanced. Feedback is an important step, but the administrator must provide specific avenues for improvement through professional development that targets the documented deficiency of performance. This provides a caution against using teacher evaluation merely as a means of removing incompetent teachers. Deficiencies in performance must first be addressed in a reasonable and responsible way.

The fifth assumption recognizes that many theories, approaches, and philosophies of teaching and learning underlie specific criteria of performance expectations. In this pluralistic society, the Joint Committee does not presume to enforce one philosophy over another. The standards should support the user's philosophy by providing guidance on how to evaluate, not what to evaluate. The standards provide specific guidance in service orientation and explicit criteria.

Finally, in the sixth assumption, the Joint Committee recognizes the various and complex natures of systems for personnel evaluations in the area of education that spans birth through graduate school. The assumption is that not all users will need all twenty-seven standards at any given time to accomplish any given task. To better serve the users, the Joint Committee settled on a functional table of contents that allows users to select the purpose of the evaluation (for example, training of evaluators, tenure, promotion, and dismissal) and focus on the most relevant of the twenty-seven standards given the need (Joint Committee . . . , 2008).

## ATTRIBUTES OF SOUND SYSTEMS OF EVALUATION

The Joint Committee organized the second edition of *The Personnel Evaluation Standards* (2008) so that the twenty-seven standards are categorized according to the appropriate attribute. Each standard has a name and an alpha-number identifying its attribute and location within the attribute section of the book. For example, the first propriety standard is identified as P1, the sixth utility standard is listed as U6, and so on. Twenty-seven standard chapters explore the meaning and application of each standard.

The four attributes of sound personnel evaluations are propriety, utility, feasibility, and accuracy. Specific standards within each attribute address issues that may confront users of the evaluations. Each standard in its own way contributes to the credibility of the outcomes of the evaluation process. There is some overlap among the standards necessary for achieving the full breadth of the process. However, each standard addresses unique considerations. Each standard chapter explores not only the rationale and guidelines but the common errors or missteps that prevent teacher evaluations from being useful to either the teacher or the evaluator. By paying attention to these nuances of the standards, evaluators and policymakers may avoid numerous mistakes in design and implementation. For a full understanding of these standards, users must be familiar with the complete standard chapter and avoid a cursory look at the standard statements, which may appear deceptively simplistic.

## Propriety Standards

The seven propriety standards assist evaluators in confronting issues of a legal or ethical nature. For example, since most employment decisions may involve the constitutional right to property (employment) guaranteed by the Fourteenth Amendment, great care must be taken that any decision resulting in possible loss of that employment follows due process under law (Standard P2–Appropriate Policies and Procedures).

The first propriety standard, P1–Service Orientation, addresses the practice of orienting teachers to the nature of the evaluation in terms of how the evaluation supports the institutional goals of the school or district. It is imperative that job descriptions or criteria not only be aligned with goals but be fully explained to teachers. Thorough exploration of the meaning of the criterion as it relates to job expectations can align the daily efforts of the classroom with the overall efforts of the school and district in meeting students' need. If teachers are expected to address student learning through a philosophy or approach to teaching, it makes no sense to evaluate them in isolation of this expectation. The likelihood that all teachers, not just the most motivated or dedicated, will embrace, let alone implement, district goals is decreased when there is no accountability through a performance review. Leaving the performance review out of the picture is just another way to close the door on the classroom, allowing teachers to continue teaching in their preferred manner, even if that manner is totally out of alignment with district goals.

Additional legal issues confronting an evaluator may include those surrounding access to personnel records. The confidential nature of personnel records requires that the system put into place safeguards to prevent unauthorized access and use of these records. It is up to the district as well as the individual principal to ensure that teacher evaluation records are kept in secure locations at all times. To prevent possible damage to the professional reputation of the teacher and credibility of the report itself, no one without a legally justified need should be able to access personnel records. Users of teacher evaluations must be able to rest assured that the data collected, analyzed, and reported are complete, unaltered, and authorized by the evaluator. Oversight of any system of evaluation should provide these assurances. *Editor's note*: Chapter Eleven describes court rulings regarding teacher evaluations that lead to dismissals.

The legal issues within the propriety standards overlap with the ethics of teacher evaluation. How teachers are treated throughout the evaluation process requires a certain sense of fairness among evaluators. In determining the quality of teacher practice within the classroom, evaluators must balance their judgment not only with areas in need of improvement but also areas of strength in order to build a common understanding of high-quality performance among all teachers. This sense of balance between areas of need and areas of strength provides a more comprehensive approach to evaluation addressed by the fifth standard of propriety, P5–Comprehensive Evaluation.

Additional issues of ethics involve interactions between evaluators and teachers. Both conflict of interest and bias on the part of the evaluator can influence the judgment of the evaluator in a way totally unrelated to the actual performance of the teacher, thus damaging the integrity of the evaluation findings. It is important that safeguards such as oversight, training of the evaluator, and procedures for contesting an evaluation report be put into place. If a conflict of interest exists, for example, a procedure should be available to remedy the situation, such as the replacement of one evaluator for another.

The propriety standards further address interactions between the evaluator and teacher that may be unprofessional, and therefore unfair or illegal. Both written and verbal communications between an evaluator and teacher must be professional and constructive in nature. The credibility of the evaluator and the worth of the report will be seriously damaged by an evaluator who is callous, sarcastic, unprofessional, or untrustworthy. Even callousness through omission should be carefully avoided. If an evaluator collects data concerning a teacher's performance through observation, survey, or review of documentation and fails to provide immediate and fair feedback, trust in the evaluation process is seriously damaged, rendering it useless as a means of improvement.

The final propriety standard, P7–Legal Viability, is one that must be followed by every system of evaluation and the evaluators who use it. This concerns the need for all aspects of an evaluation to meet federal, state, and local laws in terms of employment and constitutional rights. In states with collective bargaining, it is essential that the system of evaluation be included in the master agreements reached between teacher associations and school districts. Those involved, whether administrators, union representatives, or teachers, must agree that all procedures are fair, equitable, and in line with relevant laws.

## Utility Standards

The six standards that address utility define how evaluation reports will be used and by whom. Throughout the utility standards is the underlying theme that the primary use of any teacher evaluation should be to promote teacher professional growth in practices that support institutional goals.

The first, U1–Constructive Orientation, supports P1–Service Orientation by adding the specificity that evaluation procedures should be aligned not only with district and school goals but with the level of professional development offered to support these goals. If the process is to be used for merit pay, tenure, dismissal, or promotion, this must be defined from the outset. It is not fair to collect and analyze data on teacher performance for the purpose of tenure and then use the same data to determine merit pay without having first specified that intent. Teachers must be aware of all uses of evaluation data prior to collection and analysis.

The users as well as uses must be clearly defined by the system in its procedural documentation and written policies. The users of evaluation reports include not only teachers and principals but school board members, district-level administrators, and anyone else who has a vested interest in promoting teacher quality within the school and district. Transparency of both use and users provides a critical level of assurance to those being evaluated.

Training of the evaluator ensures credibility in the system and its outcomes. If judgments are to be made, those making the judgment must be skilled and knowledgeable about both the data collection and procedures for analysis. Reliance on evaluator instinct or experience in other areas can be a dangerous step toward subjectivity and unreliable outcomes. No administrator should ever be placed in the position of using a teacher evaluation instrument without receiving adequate training prior to its use. Lack of appropriate training jeopardizes the reputation of the evaluator and the meaningfulness of the report. It leads to the impression that teacher evaluation is a bureaucratic paper trail with little or no influence on teacher quality in the classroom and beyond. This is one of the common missteps associated with lack of power of teacher evaluation in the area of school reform and improvement of teacher performance in the classroom.

If the quality of reports is never questioned or reviewed by anyone at the district level, the functional reporting of the evaluation results will have little or no impact on the quality of teachers. Frequently district office human resource administrators are charged with collecting and checking evaluation reports. If these reports follow a schedule of due dates, with principals dropping off stacks of completed folders at the same time, the chances of a careful review of individual folders become nil because time and personnel are not available. Generally a cursory glance for signatures, appropriate dates, completion of scoring, and number of completed observations within the parameters of due dates is all the beleaguered human resource director can provide. In this case, very little, if any, effort is given to seeking whether the information provided in the folders is useful to the school, the evaluator, or the teacher. Unless there is an issue of dismissal, tenure, or promotion, the evaluation report is checked off as a legal requirement.

This common practice negates the value that teacher evaluation could have contributed to a district's professional development program. Without a systematic method for categorizing areas of strength and areas in need of improvement, districts tend to paint faculties with a broad brush of improvement through schoolwide or districtwide staff development opportunities, wasting even more resources. With the technology now available to create useful databases of evaluation results, districts can provide more targeted professional development by making truly data-driven decisions as to who should attend specific trainings. Advances in electronic storage of evaluation reports provide secure means of data organization and retrieval through efficient systems of query, allowing districts to make broader use of personnel evaluation results.

A sixth standard under utility was added in the second edition of the standards to emphasize this link between evaluation results and professional development. If an evaluation is not followed up with specific individualized opportunities for professional development, the effort and resources devoted to preparing the evaluation report may be wasted. The need for credible feedback based on explicit criteria is essential to making this link. This sixth standard, U6–Follow-Up and Professional Development, guides the users of teacher evaluation to ask the question, "So what?" It is not enough to identify areas of weakness if nothing is done to address it. It is also unnecessary and impractical to begin immediate dismissal procedures for every teacher who falls short of district expectations if those shortcomings can be appropriately addressed through systematic development. Weeding out marginal or poor teachers should not be the primary function of any system of teacher evaluation.

## Feasibility Standards

Three specific standards address the need for a system of teacher evaluation to be practical and feasible in terms of implementation. A system that requires excessive time, effort, and expense on the part of the evaluator and district will have an adverse effect on implementation. A model system of evaluation on paper must also be a model system in practice to be of any use to the teacher, school, or district.

The first standard, F1–Practical Procedures, cautions users not to adopt and attempt to implement systems that cause an undue burden to the evaluators, who are often principals with many other job responsibilities. The collection of data should be as unobtrusive and job-embedded as possible so that it is not burdensome to the teacher or the evaluator. There have been instances, for example, when teachers have changed classrooms and teaching styles to accommodate the demands of the teacher evaluation data collection procedures with little or no regard for possible interruptions to student learning. In one case, a technology teacher was forced each year to leave his hands-on interactive lab to deliver a lecture in another classroom to accommodate an instrument that required an observation of very proscriptive teacher behaviors not observable in a lab setting facilitated, rather than directed, by a teacher. This teacher and his students lost at least one class period each semester in order to accommodate the teacher evaluation process. Cases such as this seriously damage the integrity of the teacher evaluation system and its ability to influence teacher growth within the school. In addition, it is not usually feasible as a matter of practical procedures for a teacher to move students around to accommodate an evaluation process.

For their part, teachers should not do anything for evaluation purposes that they would not do for their students in the regular course of their jobs. Otherwise why are they doing it, and why is it being evaluated?

Political feasibility (F2) refers to the inclusion of a process to allow questioning by diverse populations of stakeholders. When a system is developed, all stakeholders should be considered as potential users. The system should anticipate questions and put into place a procedure for addressing such questions. This may be through public forums, orientations to new faculty, or inclusion of a grievance form in each evaluation packet.

If the district cannot afford the necessary resources to implement a system of evaluation effectively, its effectiveness is seriously compromised. Fiscal feasibility (F3) should be one of the key standards considered in developing or selecting a model of teacher evaluation for a district.

## Accuracy Standards

If the data collected and analyzed throughout the process are less than accurate, the judgments rendered as a result will not be valid and credible. Numerous safeguards must be put into place to ensure that data reflect the performance level of the individual. The eleven accuracy standards outline the principles for putting into place these safeguards.

The first accuracy standard addresses the issues confronting evaluators in making valid judgments (A1). The tenets of this standard guide evaluators as they collect accurate data from a variety of sources based on the criteria set forth by the evaluation system. Although there is no substitute for training the evaluator in implementing the system, the system must provide safeguards to ensure that the data sources and means of analyses are fully aligned with job expectations as defined by the explicit criteria set forth in written policies.

The written policies of the evaluation system should define expectations of job performance (A2–Defined Expectations). The procedures for administration of the evaluation system should include verbal and written opportunities for these definitions to be clarified for both evaluators and teachers to ensure understanding. Such definitions must be relevant and pertinent to the job of the teacher.

All personnel evaluation systems must have safeguards against unusual or extenuating circumstances that may unduly influence the judgment of the evaluator. Such circumstances may arise unexpectedly through a sudden change in school routine. A fire drill during an observation must be fully noted by the evaluator so that the data collected are placed in context. Anything that could not be predicted or controlled by the teacher that may have an adverse effect on the outcome of the evaluation could potentially harm the level of accuracy of the report. Evaluation systems should have procedures in place that require evaluators to note such circumstances on data collection forms.

The remaining accuracy standards address issues that may confront evaluators, resulting in threats to the validity of the judgments such as bias on the part of the evaluator or conflict of interest between the evaluator and teacher. Additional issues affecting the accuracy of the evaluation reports may include unreliable data, lack of oversight, or obvious bias of evaluators leading to challenges of the reports.

The accuracy of the data collected and their analyses affect the validity of the judgment made. Although a system may put into place procedures to safeguard the collection of inaccurate data, a great deal more depends on evaluators who are trained in all aspects of evaluation with appropriate oversight to ensure that evaluations are fair, useful, feasible, and accurate.

## APPLYING THE PERSONNEL EVALUATION STANDARDS

The Joint Committee included tools for understanding and applying the standards in the standards book. A functional table of contents identifies common tasks associated with personnel evaluation, such as training evaluators and lists standards most relevant to the task. This information allows users to target specific standards first. In addition, a list of key questions helps users through a preliminary check of their evaluation practices. This begins a process of meta-evaluation in which users can identify the strengths of their system while targeting areas of need (Howard & Sanders, 2006; Howard & Harman, 2007).

Each standard chapter is organized to assist users in fully comprehending the nature and implication of the standard. An explanation is followed by a rationale, both supported by current literature pertaining specifically to the principles of the standard. Guidelines for use provide the user with a sense of how the standard directly affects practical application. Common errors alert users to those pitfalls that are likely to occur when the standard is ignored. At least two illustrative cases with analyses provide brief case studies from the field to exemplify application of the standard. At the end of each chapter is a list of supporting literature.

Included in the publication is a case study outlining the meta-evaluation of a district's system of teacher evaluation. This case study provides the methodology for analyzing a district's system against the context of the twenty-seven standards. While time-consuming, a meta-evaluation is advisable for any district wishing to increase its effectiveness.

# SUGGESTED STEPS FOR APPLICATION OF THE STANDARDS

The Joint Committee recommends a series of steps designed to provide guidance in applying the standards based on over twenty years of work in the development and implementation of standards in evaluation. By following these steps, the user can more effectively and efficiently determine if a system of personnel evaluation is aligned with the standards.

The steps are as follows:

1. Become familiar with each standard by examining each standard chapter. Discussions among various stakeholders or users on the meanings of the standards within context can deepen understanding.

2. Clarify your purpose for applying the standards. For example, a district wishing to adopt a new model may approach the application quite differently from one wishing to strengthen an existing model.

3. After selecting an appropriate set of standards, focus discussion on these standards in light of the purpose.

4. Apply the standards selected to the existing or proposed model of teacher evaluation. Using the key questions can assist users greatly in doing this effectively. For example, if a district wishes to examine oversight procedures, the user would examine standards such as P2 and P3 to determine if there are appropriate written policies easily accessible to all users and if, once completed, there is access to records only by those with authority. This may entail an examination of handbooks, storage facilities, and so forth.

5. Decide on a course of action based on review. This step is based on the review and provides an outcome of the process.

# DISCUSSION

The performance of educators within the context of their jobs determines the outcomes of student learning. Ineffective or marginal teachers do not provide the level of engagement, motivation, and learning experience necessary to improve student learning, regardless of the age of the student. Without a system for performance appraisal that provides constructive, credible feedback for improvement or movement out of the profession, the hope for the hapless student subjected to the lackluster performance of a marginal teacher must be pinned on having more effective teachers in future years, and even with that, recovery may be doubtful (Wright et al., 1997; Sanders & Rivers, 1996). Facing the many global economic and political challenges of this century, our students deserve better, and our communities demand better.

# REFERENCES

Danielson, C. (2001). New trends in teacher evaluation. *Educational Leadership*, *58*(5), 12–15.

Davis, D. R., Ellett, C. D., & Annunziata, J. (2002). Teacher evaluation, leadership, and learning organizations. *Journal of Personnel Evaluation in Education*, *16*(4), 287–301.

Ellett, C. D., & Teddlie, C. (2003). Teacher evaluation, teacher effectiveness and school effectiveness: Perspectives from the USA. *Journal of Personnel Evaluation in Education*, *17*(1), 101–128.

Hallinger, P. (2005). Instructional leadership and the school principal: A passing fancy that refuses to fade away. *Leadership and Policy in Schools*, *4*(3), 221–239.

Hallinger, P., & Heck, R. H. (1998). Exploring the principal's contribution to school effectiveness: 1980–1995. *School Effectiveness and School Improvement*, *9*, 157–191.

Hart, P. D., & Teeter, M. (2002). *A national priority: Americans speak out on teacher quality*. Princeton, NJ: Educational Testing Service.

Howard, B. B., & Harman, S. S. (2007). An application of the Personnel Evaluation Standards to determine the effectiveness of a system of teacher evaluation. *ERS Spectrum: Journal of Research and Information*, *25*(2), 45–55.

Howard, B. B., & McColskey, W. H. (2001, February). Evaluating experienced teachers. *Educational Leadership*, *58*(5), 48–51.

Howard, B. B., & Sanders, J. R. (2006). Applying the personnel evaluation standards to teacher evaluation. In J. H. Stronge (Ed.), *Evaluating teachers: A guide to current thinking and best practice* (2nd ed., pp. 54–68). Thousand Oaks, CA: Corwin Press.

Ingvarson, L., & Rowe, K. (2008). Conceptualising and evaluating teacher quality: Substantive and methodological issues. *Australian Journal of Education*, *52*(1), 5–35.

Joint Committee on Standards for Educational Evaluation. (1988). *The personnel evaluation standards: How to assess systems for evaluating educators*. Thousand Oaks, CA: Corwin Press.

Joint Committee on Standards for Educational Evaluation. (2008). *The personnel evaluation standards: How to assess systems for evaluating educators* (2nd ed.). Thousand Oaks, CA: Corwin Press.

Jolly, A. B. (2008). *Team to teach: A facilitator's guide to professional learning teams*. Dallas: National Staff Development Council.

Kleinhenz, E., & Ingvarson, L. C. (2004). Teacher accountability in Australia: Current policies and practices and their relation to the improvement of teaching and learning. *Research Papers in Education*, *19*(1), 31–39.

Kyriakides, L., Demetriou, D., & Charalambous, C. (2006). Generating criteria for evaluating teachers through teacher effectiveness research. *Educational Research*, *48*(1), 1–20.

Leithwood, K., Seashore Louis, K., Anderson, S., & Wahlstrom, K. (2004, September). *How leadership influences student learning.* Retrieved March 9, 2009, from http://www.wallacefoundation.org/KnowledgeCenter/KnowledgeTopics/CurrentAreas ofFocus/EducationLeadership/Pages/HowLeadershipInfluencesStudentLearning .aspx.

Prestine, N. A., & Nelson, B. S. (2005). How can educational leaders support and promote teaching and learning? In W. A. Firestone & C. Riehl (Eds.), *A new agenda: Directions for research on educational leadership* (pp. 44–60). New York: Teachers College Press.

Ramirez, A. (2001, February). How merit pay undermines education. *Educational Leadership*, *58*(5), 16–20.

Rowan, B., Chiang, F. S., & Miller, R. J. (1996). Using research on employee performance to study the effects of teachers on students' achievement. *Sociology of Education*, *70*, 256–284.

Sanders, W. L. (2000). *Value-added assessment from student achievement data.* Paper presented at the Annual National Evaluation Institute, San Jose, CA.

Sanders, W. L., & Rivers, J. C. (1996). *Cumulative and residual effects of teachers on future student academic achievement.* Knoxville: University of Tennessee Value-Added Research and Assessment Center.

Sinnema, C.E.L., & Robinson, V.M.J. (2007). The leadership of teaching and learning: Implications for teacher evaluation. *Leadership and Policy in Schools*, *6*, 319–343.

Stronge, J. H. (2002). *Qualities of effective teachers.* Alexandria, VA: Association for Supervision and Curriculum Development.

Toch, T., & Rothman, R. (2008). *Rush to judgment: Teacher evaluation in public education.* Washington, DC: Education Sector.

Witziers, B., Bosker, R. J., & Kruger, M. I. (2003). Educational leadership and student achievement: The elusive search for an association. *Educational Administration Quarterly*, *39*(3), 398–425.

Wright, S. P., Horn, S. P., & Sanders, W. L. (1997). Teacher and classroom context effects on student achievement: Implications for teacher evaluation. *Journal of Personnel Evaluation in Education*, *11*, 57–67.

# CHAPTER THIRTEEN

# Thinking Systemically About Assessment Practice

Pamela A. Moss

*University of Michigan*

A s the previous chapters in this book illustrate, assessment is needed for a number of purposes in teaching and teacher education across stakeholders and institutional contexts: to support teachers' learning from initial preparation throughout their careers; for routine performance review and the decisions that accompany it; to enable consequential individual decisions about licensure, certification, hiring, tenure, and dismissal; and for program evaluation and accountability. Looking across the chapters, however, one comes away with a sense of a patchwork quilt in the ways these purposes are served with few discernable themes or patterns to support a coherent career trajectory or reform strategy. Given the range of institutional entities that play a role in serving these purposes—including teacher education programs, both college-based and alternative; P–12 schools; district, state, and federal education agencies and related policy and legislative bodies; intermediate units; organizations engaged in assessment research and development work; and professional organizations—and the varied formal and informal relationships among them, this is not surprising. In Chapter Fourteen, David Cohen outlines some of the historical and political factors that help explain these circumstances.

In educational measurement, the focus of our work has traditionally been on the development and evaluation of particular assessments, and their underlying constructs, to serve particular purposes. Indeed, much of this book is organized in terms of particular purposes or types of assessment. Proximal purposes reflect the interpretations, decisions, and actions that assessment is intended to support; distal purposes often reflect the intended effects of its use more broadly on some aspect of the educational system. While this focus on particular assessments and purposes is both useful and necessary, it is insufficient to bring coherence across institutional contexts and purposes. We need to think more systemically in our assessment development work (Moss, Girard, & Haniford, 2006).

The most prominent attempt to bring coherent guidance to professional practice, and the learning opportunities and assessments that address it, has been the development of standards for professional teaching practice (like those of the National Board for Professional Teaching Standards, the Interstate New Teacher Assessment and Support Consortium, or other professional organizations) alongside standards for student learning. However, as Cohen points out, such standards have provided a relatively weak intervention in part because they are "not focused in sufficient detail to discriminate acceptable from unacceptable work" and in part because the system lacks the necessary infrastructure to support a coherent career trajectory or reform effort. He notes that these problems are political and educational as well as technical.

Furthermore, the questions implied in the purposes described often require more evidence than a single assessment can provide. For instance, it is important to illuminate the distinction between warranting the validity of the interpretation of a score from an assessment and warranting the validity of a consequential decision about an individual (which may be informed by a valid score but should typically rely on other or additional kinds of evidence and judgments). That these two sorts of warrant can be different is not a radical suggestion, even within the discourse of educational and psychological measurement. As the Standards for Educational and Psychological Testing assert: "In educational settings, a decision or characterization that will have major impact . . . should not be made on the basis of a single test score. Other relevant information should be taken into account if it will enhance the overall validity of the decision" (American Educational Research Association, American Psychological Association, & National Council on Measurement in Education, 1999, p. 146). And so we need ways of supporting interpretations, decisions, and actions that draw on and integrate multiple forms of evidence over time. Again, this has implications for the infrastructure that needs to be put in place.

In this chapter, I provide readers with resources—theory and practical examples—to help in conceptualizing a more coherent system of assessment practices across purposes and institutional contexts. By institutional contexts, I mean different contexts within a single institution, as well as those in different institutions. Consistent with Cohen's argument but with a somewhat different focus, this involves far more than a set of assessments keyed to the same standards or general conceptions of good practice. Thinking systemically requires the design of an infrastructure that takes multiple elements of the social system into account—including conceptual and material tools that characterize sound practice, but also knowledgeable people to understand and use them, social structures (norms, routines, roles, and opportunities for interaction) through which they are put to work, concrete examples of what it means to use them well, and careful consideration of which elements should cross institutional boundaries to enable coherent professional and organizational learning and accountability, but not constrain practice in ways that are counterproductive (Wenger, 1998; Bowker & Star, 1999). To illustrate some of these possibilities for building a coherent assessment system, I offer an example of one in-progress approach to systemic assessment development we are exploring as part of the Teacher Education Initiative in the School of Education at the University of Michigan (Moss, Boerst, & Ball, 2008).

The type of infrastructure I describe differs from the one described by Cohen in a number of respects, although the two may well be considered complementary. The infrastructure Cohen calls for—reverse "common" curricula or curriculum frameworks, common examinations that are tied to the curricula, teacher education that is grounded in learning to teach the curricula that students are to learn, and a teaching force whose members succeeded in those curricula and exams as students among other things"—focuses initially on K–12 students' curricula and, ideally, operates at the national level (although he notes there are subsystems that enact it). The one we are designing focuses on student teachers who must be prepared to work across different K–12 curricula and has a more local ambit. It begins within an institution—in our case, a teacher education program—and works outward to create viable partnerships and learning communities in collaborating contexts. While we anticipate that elements of the system we are developing can inform design work at the state and national levels, we are developing it so that it can build coherence locally within existing policy structures.

An important issue for any infrastructure is how to manage the tension between what elements of the design are specified in advance and what are allowed to vary in ways that are consistent with sound teaching practice. In other words, following Wenger (1998), "Inherent in the process of design is the question of how the power to define, adapt, or interpret the design is distributed" (p. 235) and consideration of "what forms of participation can be designed that do not require reification of the subject matter [in our case, teacher education] beyond what is already part of the practice" (p. 266).

# INTERPRETIVE ISSUES IN THE ASSESSMENT OF TEACHING PRACTICE

I begin with a characterization of the nature of teaching practice and then turn to examples of the sorts of issues teaching practice raises for assessment. By teaching practice, I mean doing the complex work of teaching. While this certainly draws on the knowledge of subject matter that is the focus of many states' licensure assessments (National Research Council, 2001; Goldhaber, Chapter Four, this volume), it entails putting that knowledge to work in circumstances that are complex, relational, interactive, and contingent.

In their call for new directions in research on teaching and teacher education, Grossman and McDonald (2008) note that teaching practice—and that of other professions that share the goal of human improvement (Cohen, 2005)—depends heavily on the relationship between the professional and clients. "Teachers must ensure the cooperation of their students if they are to teach" (Grossman, Compton, Igra, Ronfeldt, Shahan, & Williamson, 2009). Moreover, Grossman and colleagues (2009) note, "Teachers face particular challenges then in developing educative relationships with students; they must accept all students who enter the classroom and figure out how to connect with them." Thus, Grossman and McDonald argue that we need to prepare "novices for the relational as well as the intellectual demands of teaching" (p. 185).

Cohen, Raudenbush, and Ball (2003) depict the dynamics of instruction as a set of evolving interactions among teachers, students, content, and the environments in which they work (Figure 13.1). "What we casually call teaching," they argue, "is not what teachers do, say, or think, though that is what many researchers have studied and many innovators have tried to change.... [Rather]teaching is what teachers do, say, and think with learners, concerning content, in particular organizations and other environments, in time" (p. 124).

By interactions, explain Ball and Forzani (2007), "we mean active processes of interpretation that constitute teaching and learning. Teachers interpret and represent subject matter to students, who interpret their teachers, the content, and their classmates and then respond and act. In turn, teachers interpret their students, all of this in overlapping contexts and over time (Lampert, 2001)" (p. 531). Thus the arrows "represent the dynamic process of interpretation and mutual adjustment that shapes student learning, instructional practice, and policy implementation" (p. 531). To support and assess teaching, we need to look "inside these educational transactions" (p. 529).

The focus on interactions highlights the dynamic and contingent nature of teaching practice. As Kazemi, Lampert, and Ghousseini (2007) note, "Ambitious teaching is a complex performance requiring not only skills, knowledge and disposition, but also the capacity to judge when, where, and how to

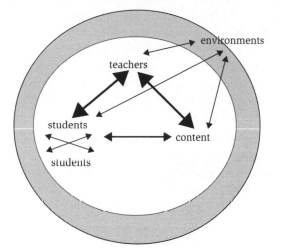

**Figure 13.1** The Instructional Triangle

*Source*: Cohen, Raudenbush, and Ball (2003, p. 124).

use skills and knowledge in direct interaction with learners to further their teaching. Large parts of ambitious teaching practice are contingent—that is, dependent on teacher/student interactions'' (p. 1). Similarly, Hammerness, Darling-Hammond, and Bransford (2005) argue, ''The information needed to make effective teaching decisions emerges in the context of practice'' (p. 374): ''For example, information about what ideas students have developed about a topic, how they are understanding or misunderstanding the material being taught, and how different students learn best emerges in the actual work of teaching—and guides future planning and instruction. How different strategies work with this or that group of students, as well as individuals, also emerges in the course of enacting plans, and cannot be fully known ahead of time in the abstract'' (p. 374). Thus, as Grossman and colleagues (2009) conclude, ''Teaching involves complex practice under conditions of uncertainty.''

The research agenda my colleagues and I have undertaken with high-stakes portfolio assessment illuminates the kinds of problems readers have in consistently evaluating complex evidence of teaching practice and the issues involved in generalizing from samples of teaching practice in particular contexts to judgments about a teacher's readiness to teach. In conventional measurement terms, these would be framed as problems of generalizability across readers and contexts of teaching. With generalizability, the key question is, ''How likely is it that this finding would be reversed or substantially altered if a second independent assessment of the same kind were made?'' (Cronbach, Linn, Brennan, & Haertel, 1997, p. 1). For instance, we illuminate instances where multiple interpretations can be justifiably inferred from the same body of evidence (Moss, Schutz, & Collins, 1998; Schutz & Moss, 2004; Moss, Coggshall, & Schutz, 2006), echoing the problems of meaning to which Kennedy (in Chapter Eight, this volume) referred, and where a teacher's practice can look quite different in different classroom contexts (Moss et al., 2004), raising serious questions of generalizability relevant to many purposes of assessment. Our goal was not to estimate the frequency with which these problems occur; rather, the goal was to illuminate issues for assessment developers and users to take into account and consider the challenges these issues raise for validity theory more generally.

I focus here on the second of these issues, generalizability across contexts of teaching. In a series of case studies reported in Moss et al. (2004), we draw primarily on two kinds of evidence typically unavailable in portfolio assessment literature: comparisons of two portfolios completed by the same teacher in the same year and comparisons between a portfolio and a three- to five-day case study (observation and interview completed shortly after portfolio submission) intended to parallel the evidence called for in the portfolio assessment. For each comparison, we asked the teacher to choose a class that differed from the original portfolio class but was part of their routine teaching assignment. We compared the two data sources in terms of the criteria used by the state.

While in the majority of the twenty-nine comparisons we examined, we found that the two data sources (portfolio-portfolio or case-portfolio) led to consistent or, at the least, coherent portraits with respect to the assessment criteria, we noted a number of instances in which the second portrait (case or portfolio) differed substantially. In the differences in performance we found, it is clear that context matters. We found differences in a teacher's performance across classes that differ in perceived or institutionally designated ability level of students, subject matter taught, and cultural background of students. In the paper (Moss et al., 2004), we explore seven comparisons in detail. For instance, in one case, we saw differences in performance across two subject matter domains: statistics and algebra. Is it easier for novice teachers to develop ''rich and challenging'' tasks that foster ''connections'' and ''reflect students' interests, styles and experiences'' in some domains than in others? We found multiple cases of differences in performance across classes that differ in perceived ability level of students. While it is not surprising that teachers tailor their practices to their perceptions of students' needs, when these differences support different judgments about performance with respect to the criteria on which the teachers are assessed, they illuminate important issues for developers and users to consider. Portfolio-based evidence of student learning, and teachers' reflections on their choices, were typically insufficient for readers to make judgments about whether these practices were reasonable or a manifestation of inappropriately low expectations. Through the case studies, we have also come to understand features of the local context that help us better understand the choices a teacher made in the portfolio: to what extent these factors should be illuminated in the portfolio and considered in the scoring are issues for the assessment developers to consider. While the domain implied in a license to teach is quite broad, the domain to which a typical portfolio assessment can be generalized may be considerably smaller. (The extent to which these findings generalize to other types of assessments of teaching practice is, of course, an open empirical question.)

Thus, the nature of teaching practice—complex, relational, interactive, and contingent—presents a number of special challenges for assessment development. Among these are how to meaningfully, usefully, and fairly evaluate teachers' practice when multiple aspects of context vary in ways that cannot be fixed in school contexts. These include variations in the content being taught; the prior learning experiences of the teacher's students; the school, classroom, and home cultures of the students; the resources and policies of the schools and districts in which teachers are working; and so on. Thus, teaching practice and its assessment necessarily involve multiple types of interactions that must be understood and addressed in developing interpretations about quality and putting them to work to improve teaching and learning. Taken together with the need to address multiple purposes within and across institutional contexts, these technical issues suggest the importance of thinking outside the bounds of conventional measurement practice to build a coherent (assessment) infrastructure.

## DESIGNING INFRASTRUCTURE TO SUPPORT COHERENCE ACROSS PURPOSES AND INSTITUTIONAL CONTEXTS

A coherent assessment system needs to serve the multiple purposes of multiple stakeholders working in different institutional contexts. To illustrate one approach for designing a coherent system, I describe a developing assessment system designed initially for use within a university-based teacher education program and its partnering institutions. Table 13.1 provides a working list of purposes (represented as questions) and stakeholders across the time span most directly relevant to the teacher education program. The time span ranges from admissions, through learning and field experiences, to the first years of teaching (although the illustration here focuses only on the methods class and related field instruction and the student teaching semester). Stakeholders include student teachers, university-based methods and field instructors, school-based cooperating teachers, program leaders and instructors in their programmatic roles, along with various stakeholders outside the teacher education institution who have a stake in its decisions. The purposes span what are commonly understood as formative and summative purposes and focus

**Table 13.1. Purposes an Integrated Assessment System Might Serve for Stakeholders in Different Roles**

| | Stakeholders | | | | |
|---|---|---|---|---|---|
| *Learning and Decision Contexts over Time* | *Student Teachers* | *Instructors (in their teaching roles in particular courses and field experiences)* | *Cooperating Teachers* | *Program Leaders and Instructors (in their program development roles)* | *Outside Stakeholders* |
| Admissions | What do I want to learn? Where am I starting in my professional development? | What capabilities do students bring to the program? | | Who should we admit? What are the qualifications of an entering cohort? | What are the qualifications of an entering cohort? |
| Courses or other learning experiences and related field instruction | What have I learned? What can I do to enhance my practice? | What do I do next (coaching)? Have students learned what I hoped they would learn? What learning opportunities should I provide or recommend next? What grade should I assign? How can I improve this learning experience and my practice? | What do I do next (coaching)? Has my student learned what I hoped she or he would learn? What learning opportunities would I recommend next? How can I improve this learning experience and my practice? | Are and how are students making progress? What are typical learning trajectories? How do students evaluate their learning experiences? How can we improve the curriculum? How can we better support university instructors and cooperating teachers? | What and how are students learning? Is there demonstrable evidence of progress in learning to teach over time? |

| | | | | | |
|---|---|---|---|---|---|
| Culminating teaching experience, lead teaching | In addition to above: Am I ready to take responsibility for my own classroom? How can I demonstrate my teaching to prospective employers? | In addition to above: Is this student ready to assume responsibility for his or her own classroom? What should my letter of recommendation say? | In addition to above: Is this student ready to assume responsibility for his or her own classroom? What should my letter of recommendation say? | In addition to above: Are students ready to assume responsibility for their own classrooms? What qualities of teaching practice do students demonstrate just prior to graduation? Do students feel well prepared? | In addition to above: What evidence is there that students from the teacher education program are ready to assume responsibility for their own classrooms? What are the qualities of teaching practice for students who graduate from the program? |
| Postgraduate | What have I learned? What can I do to enhance my practice? | | In addition to the above: What is the validity of our graduation decisions? How can we support our graduates? | | In addition to the above: What is the validity of the graduation decisions they have made? |

sometimes on individuals and sometimes on groups of individuals. These purposes address questions at various levels of scale, from those focused on a particular action or interaction, to a particular activity or kind of activity, to the set of activities that shape learners' experiences over time. Furthermore, because many of the questions are about what does and does not work to support learning and because much of the evidence of teaching practice is relational and contingent, evidence is often required of the interaction between student teachers and the various elements of the environment in which they are studying and working. Certainly good stand-alone assessments provide evidence relevant to important questions like these, but few questions or problems educators face can be addressed with a single source of evidence. Different questions and problems require different kinds and configurations of evidence. And yet in order for the system to be coherent across these purposes, a common infrastructure is needed (Moss, Girard, & Haniford, 2006).

## Different Assessment Practices Serving Different Purposes

Not all of the assessment purposes described in Table 13.1 can or should be addressed by a formal assessment or set of assessments. An analysis of assessment practice by anthropologists Jordan and Putz (2004) helps expand conventional conceptions of assessment to serve these various purposes. Based on a series of studies in different workplace and other learning contexts, they developed a three-part framework for characterizing assessment practice. Briefly, they identify *"inherent assessments* as happening informally and nonverbally in all social situations (when actors choose what to do next); *discursive assessments* as occurring when members of a social group talk about what they are doing in an evaluative way; and *documentary assessments* as coming about when activities are evaluated according to a scheme that produces numbers and symbols" (p. 346). Although it is documentary assessment that we typically think about when we use the term *assessment,* and most of the assessment discussed in this book would fit within that category, I argue (with Jordan and Putz) that inherent and discursive assessment are at least equally significant in monitoring and supporting (or constraining) practice. I focus primarily on discursive forms of assessment and distinguish them from more documentary forms of assessment.

Discursive assessments, write Jordan and Putz (2004), "make issues public, propose common standards, suggest and enforce divisions of labor, and monitor group behavior such that the work will get done" (p. 350). They note that routine work is filled with such assessments, and they are often crucial for the smooth flow of activities: "A work group may begin to talk about how it is doing, how much more remains to be done, that a particular worker is lagging and why, the impact of defective parts on the speed of an assembly line, or the effect of a plane delay on activities in an airport" (p. 350). Discursive assessments, they continue, become social objects: "They can be referred to, doubted, agreed with, or revised by people who are part of the group" (p. 350). Jordan and Putz argue that discursive assessments are central to learning. They create

> a shared understanding of individual roles and responsibilities and thereby work out a division of labor. At the same time, these informal assessments create a public verbal representation of the capabilities, resources, and issues for a group that enable them to consider implications of the current state, as they understand it, for behaving more effectively [p. 350].

Documentary assessment "occurs when an enduring record of some kind is produced . . . that is reflective and evaluative of some activity" (p. 351). Thus, documentary assessments can be taken out of the context in which they were produced and used across institutional contexts to "evaluate the extent to which pre-established performance targets have been achieved and [when appropriately designed] to establish cross-group comparability" (p. 351). Drawing on their own research in multiple institutional contexts, Jordan and Putz (2004) argue for the importance of research that illuminates how documentary assessment actually functions, including how it shapes practice (like discursive assessment) in both the local context where the information is produced and the external contexts where it is used; and, equally important, how endogenous forms of inherent and discursive assessment function in the local context and how the design of the environment might enhance their use. They see these questions as crucial for leaders in local contexts to address.

This emphasis on discursive as well as documentary assessment can be located as well in the work of teacher education researchers. In their case studies of practice in professional education with teachers, clergy, and clinical psychologists, Grossman et al. (2009) note that "one of the well-documented problems of learning from experience is knowing what to look for, or how to interpret what is observed." This requires "the existence of a language and structure for describing practice. . . . Without such a language, it is difficult to name the part or to provide targeted feedback on students' efforts to enact the components of practice." Their research suggests the value of engaging a pedagogy of practice in teacher education that begins with "decompositions"—breaking practice into its constituent parts—and "approximations" of practice in the university classroom to prepare students for the challenge of integrating these components in fieldwork and induction where they face the full complexity of teaching. What is needed, say Grossman and McDonald (2008), are "powerful ways of parsing teaching that provide us with the analytic tools to describe, analyze, and improve teaching practice" (p. 185). The project described here draws on these important ideas. Teacher education programs need to provide student teachers with regular opportunities to practice—to use their knowledge in teaching (Hammerness et al., 2005) and to reflect on that practice with skills and language of close analysis (Darling-Hammond, Pacheco, Michelli, LePage, & Hamerness, 2005, p. 441). This is what Ball and Cohen (1999) describe as opportunities for "learning in and from practice" (p. 10).

Thus, we need to recognize that not all assessments should or can be subjected to an explicit documentation. Much that might be called assessment is simply a routine part of social interaction in a learning environment. Given this, we need a set of conceptual tools and routines that can be applied explicitly when needed, but can also provide actors with adequate information and rules of thumb to shape their daily practice. Thus, we need to consider the meta-issue of how learning environments are resourced—with knowledgeable people, material and conceptual tools, norms and routines, and evolving information about learning—to support sound, evidence-based interpretations, decisions, and actions when explicit inquiry is not possible (Moss, Girard, & Haniford, 2006). We also need to consider the issues of how assessment, both discursive and documentary, is supporting the professionals' learning to support students' learning and one another's learning (Moss, Girard, & Greeno, 2008).

Echoing Wenger's question (1998) about how the power to adapt the design is distributed, it is important to consider what material elements of the assessment system should cross contextual boundaries, what administrative expectations should accompany their use (for instance, whether they are examples or requirements), and how these materials and expectations should and do shape practice in the contexts in which they are used. The multiple stakeholders and contexts engaged in assessment practice in teacher education include, for instance, multiple classes taught by different instructors or teachers in the teacher education program as well as in the schools and districts where student teachers are placed, and communities of administrators and teachers at the program and institutional levels. Given these multiple contexts, how do we maintain coherence without constraining practice in ways that are counterproductive—without, as Wenger (1998) puts it, requiring "reification . . . beyond what is already part of the practice" (p. 266). The concepts of "boundary object" and "boundary infrastructure," developed by Star and colleagues (Bowker & Star 1999; Star & Griesemer, 1989), provide additional theoretical resources to address this question in the design and evaluation of assessment systems. A boundary object is an object that inhabits multiple heterogeneous social worlds—for us, the multiple contexts through which student teachers move—and enables communication and cooperation across these worlds. "Boundary infrastructures" involve "objects that cross larger levels of scale than boundary objects" (Bowker & Star, 1999, p. 287). As Bowker and Star (1999) note, participants from different social worlds each answer "to a different set of audiences and [pursue] a different set of tasks" (p. 388), and "because . . . objects and methods mean different things in different worlds, actors are faced with the task of reconciling these meanings if they wish to cooperate" (p. 388). Furthermore, "unless they use coercion, each translator must maintain the integrity of the interests of the other audiences in order to retain them as allies" (Star & Griesemer 1989, p. 389).

Thus, a boundary object is a particular kind of cultural tool that not only crosses boundaries but is also plastic enough to adapt to local needs while maintaining a common identity across sites (Star & Griesemer, 1989, p. 393). It enables translation and therefore cooperation, but without coercion: "The creation and management of boundary objects is a key process in developing and maintaining coherence across intersecting social worlds" (Star & Griesemer, 1989, p. 393). How boundary objects function, of course, depends on how people take them up in local contexts and what opportunities there are for interaction and multiple memberships for the same individuals across contexts (Bowker & Star, 1999, p. 298).[1] To what extent do the elements of an assessment system function like boundary objects, supporting cooperation without constraining local practice beyond what is consistent with sound practice?

In the following section, I provide a working example of the infrastructure being designed to support an assessment system in teacher education, and I use it to illustrate the theoretical resources described above.

## A Working Example in Teacher Education

The assessment development effort sketched here is one component of a comprehensive reform project—the Teacher Education Initiative (TEI), directed by Deborah Loewenberg Ball—to redesign how teachers are prepared for practice at the University of Michigan and to build knowledge and tools that will inform teacher education more broadly (http://www.soe.umich.edu/tei).[2] Our goals for the assessment component of the TEI, which I coordinate, are to develop an integrated assessment system that:

- Focuses on teaching practice grounded in professional and disciplinary knowledge as it develops over time

- Addresses multiple purposes of a broad array of stakeholders

- Creates the foundation for programmatic coherence and professional development of those who work with beginning teachers (Moss, Boerst, and Ball, 2008)

Following the work of Ball, Grossman, Lampert, and colleagues cited above, we are developing core components for the assessment system that provide an infrastructure that can then be usefully deployed for different purposes (both discursive and documentary forms of assessment). We intend these core components and their various representations to serve as boundary objects, connecting school and university classrooms and program-level administrative communities over time. The program infrastructure has six elements, which I describe and illustrate with examples from our work in elementary mathematics education. (This builds on the work of Deborah Ball, Hyman Bass, Timothy Boerst, and Laurie Sleep, among others, in the Mathematics Methods Planning Group and on our collaboration with Mark Wilson and his colleagues at the University of California, Berkeley.) The focus of the example is on elements of teaching practice and does not emphasize the equally important content and foundational knowledge needed for teaching or the sorts of assessments that might support and evaluate that knowledge.

First, we are identifying *high-leverage practices* that can be articulated, unpacked, studied, scaffolded, rehearsed, and then reintegrated into teaching. By *high leverage,* we mean practices that occur frequently in teaching, are core across approaches to teaching, are crucial to improving the learning and achievement of all students, and can be articulated and taught (Boerst, Sleep, Cole, & Ball, 2008). Examples of high-leverage practices we are working on in elementary mathematics education, for instance, are leading a discussion, planning a sequence of lessons, assessing within and between lessons, explaining mathematical ideas, and using mathematical tools and representations.

Second, for each high-leverage practice, we are developing *learning and assessment activities, staged over time,* such that they become increasingly complex and integrated into the routine of teaching, along with guidelines for creating multimedia records that provide sufficient evidence of that practice for serving different purposes. With leading a discussion in elementary mathematics, for instance, following multiple opportunities to observe and analyze the practice, an early task has student teachers leading a fifteen-minute discussion around a single mathematical problem; a second task has them leading a whole class discussion as part of a regular lesson; and later tasks provide opportunities to lead discussions through a sequences of lessons that build on their pupils' earlier work. We intend these activities both to serve as examples of activities instructors might undertake to support more discursive forms of assessment and to provide more formal opportunities for documentary assessment that would allow us to monitor progress at the program level.

Third, we are developing a *shared language for guiding and analyzing that practice* that points to its essential components and describes increasing levels of sophistication. This shared analytical language provides a palette of language that can be put to different purposes in different representations. Consistent with Jordan and Putz's (2004) description of discursive assessment, we intend the language to be of use in routine interaction, as well as for more formal assessment opportunities. With leading a discussion, the analytical language is divided into four areas, each with multiple aspects that unpack a (student) teacher's practice: initiating, taking up, and coordinating participation; making contributions; recording and representing mathematics; and designing for and appraising discussion. Area 1 (initiating, taking up, and coordinating participation), for instance, includes launching the discussion, eliciting responses, following up on responses, and facilitating mathematical connections. We are experimenting with different tools that represent these areas and aspects in different ways to serve different stakeholders' needs, from guiding questions to support field instructors and cooperating teachers in giving feedback to student teachers, to rubric-like representations that allow us to monitor group performance over time.

Fourth, in conjunction with the shared language, we are also developing *questions about the general and immediate contexts* that shape the practice and need to be taken into account in any interpretation or evaluation of the practice. In the example of leading a discussion in mathematics, these include questions about the mathematical task selected for discussion (including its affordances for discussion), the general and immediate classroom context (such as the pupils' familiarity with the norms of mathematical discussion), and opportunities for student teachers' learning, including feedback and support while the activity was unfolding and about the sufficiency and quality of multimedia records to support interpretation. How these factors are brought into play in assessment depends, of course, on the purpose of the assessment.

Fifth, to bring the analytical language into educative contact with records of practice, we are developing *annotated exemplars of practice* that illustrate practice in the domain in terms of the analytical language. The annotated exemplars provide crucial means of developing a shared practice across university and school contexts. In Grossman and colleagues' (2009) terms, they provide *representations* of teaching practice and illustrate "what to look for," and "how to interpret what is observed" (p. 21). The very act of creating exemplars—of routinely engaging stakeholders from different institutional contexts in dialogue about actual cases of practice—is relevant to the development of a coherent infrastructure. These exemplars can be used for preparation of methods and field instructors, cooperating teachers, and student teachers themselves in supporting and assessing student teachers' practice. Exemplars can also be used to help in developing standards of practice to support consequential decisions.

Finally, as sufficient records of practice accumulate across time for individuals, within and across high-leverage domains, we plan to develop general *descriptions of learning trajectories within those domains,* along which students' and beginning teachers' progress can be located, recognizing that such learning trajectories are necessarily situated within the institutional contexts and learning opportunities in which they were produced. (See Mislevy, Moss,

& Gee, 2009, and Wilson, 2005, 2009, for discussions of the nature of learning trajectories or progressions.)

It is useful to distinguish two major sets of purposes for assessment activities: assessment activities that support teaching and learning within a course or other learning opportunity and that are the responsibility of the instructors; and those collaboratively developed culminating assessment activities—records of practice plus evaluations—that are also intended to be shared and incorporated into the program-level assessment system. Both will be informed by the components described above. The program-level component of the assessment system will require a database that houses multimedia records of practice for student teachers collected over time from admission through the first years of teaching and analyses of those records, including narrative analyses, scores reflecting the qualities of the teaching observed, and codes reflecting contextual factors that shape that performance. These databases can be used for making and warranting consequential decisions about readiness to teach, program development and evaluation, inquiry into the validity of the assessment system for different purposes, accountability to outside stakeholders, and research into the development of beginning teachers.

A crucial element of the design of the assessment system is the design of the social structures through which it works—the opportunities for student teachers and for those who support and assess their work to develop common understandings and language about what constitutes good practice. Opportunities for instructors to meet together across courses and other learning experiences and across school and university contexts are crucial. Central to these meetings is the opportunity to observe common examples of practice—live or through multimedia records—and to talk together (and with expert practitioners) about the quality of the practice using the common language for unpacking it.

Under the leadership of Tim Boerst, who coordinates settings for the TEI, we are experimenting with various staffing configurations. We are experimenting with configurations that entail teaching methods courses in school settings so that cooperating teachers can participate and learning and assessment activities for student teachers can be better coordinated with the ongoing teaching and learning of pupils in the school; offering routine professional development opportunities for cooperating teachers and field instructors where they have opportunities to work on their own practice as teachers as well as their work as teacher educators with student teachers; and bringing cooperating teachers and field instructors together for more formal opportunities to score records of practice for program level purposes. These relationships will, we hope, begin to provide opportunities for more systematic study of the relationship between teaching practice and pupil learning that Cohen calls for. While these activities are still very much at the pilot stage, it will be important for the teacher education program to find ways to routinize opportunities like these for collaborative work to help maintain coherence across the system and allow the infrastructure to evolve as our understanding of teaching practice evolves.

Our goal is an integrated assessment system, drawing on mixed methods, that can serve the multiple purposes described in the opening paragraphs and can evolve as our understanding of teaching practice evolves. These purposes include methods that support clinical and deliberative judgment of designed and naturally occurring teaching activities to facilitate student teachers' learning and methods that support aggregation, comparison, and modeling to serve program-level assessment purposes. Questions of validity for different purposes at different levels of scale are taken up by structuring multiple opportunities for corroboration and challenge across multiple observers and sources of evidence over time. (See Moss, Girard, & Haniford, 2006, and Mislevy, Moss, & Gee, 2009, for discussions of validity relevant to this sort of multimethod assessment practice.)

# DISCUSSION

An infrastructure is needed to support coherent assessment across the multiple purposes and institutional contexts in teaching and teacher education. The theoretical resources discussed here illuminate a number of issues and elements of social systems that might productively be considered in designing an infrastructure. Designing a productive infrastructure requires attention to both conceptual and material tools that work across institutional contexts ("boundary objects," in Star and colleagues' terms) as well as social structures through which actors working in local contexts can cooperate in putting the tools to work. Furthermore, it requires attention to informal discursive types of assessment that support routine interaction about the work of teaching, as well as more formal types of documentary assessment that enable shared information across boundaries, organizational learning and accountability, and consequential decision making.

The example in this chapter points to particular ways of resolving the issues raised, but the issues are equally relevant to analyzing and comparing alternative approaches. Delandshere and Petrosky in Chapter One in this book and Wei and Pecheone in Chapter Three describe approaches to assessment in teacher education that differ in instructive ways in terms of the issues described here. We see, for instance, potential boundary objects of different sorts, with different levels of specificity, and administrative expectations about their use that result in different roles and opportunities for agency by different stakeholders. The contrasts illuminate productive questions for empirical study. Other chapters in this book focusing on other sectors of the educational system could be analyzed and contrasted in terms of the same sets of issues. An overarching consideration will be how to manage the balance among expert knowledge, administrative authority, and professional autonomy (Gamson,

2007; Moss & Piety, 2007): what elements of local practice can be productively designed from afar and what elements left to local agency. How do different answers to these questions shape the capacities, commitments, and cultures of educators and the organizations in which they work? And, ultimately, how do they enhance or impede equity in students' opportunities to learn?

*Acknowledgments: This chapter describes work from two distinct assessment projects involving multiple collaborators and funders. Work on the validity of large-scale portfolio assessments was undertaken in collaboration with Laura Haniford, Raymond Pecheone, Aaron Schutz, and Mark Wilson, among others, at the University of Michigan and University of California, Berkeley, with grants from the Spencer Foundation and the Institute for Education Sciences. The development of the assessment system for the Teacher Education Initiative (TEI) at the University of Michigan is being undertaken in collaboration with Deborah Loewenberg Ball, Timothy Boerst, Francesca Forzani, Donald Freeman, Annemarie Palincsar, and multiple colleagues at the University of Michigan, with Mark Wilson and colleagues at Berkeley. TEI assessment development work in elementary mathematics education is supported by a grant from the National Science Foundation. Any opinions, findings, or conclusions expressed here are my own and do not necessarily reflect the views of the NSF. My conceptualization of assessment has also benefited from conversations with colleagues participating in the Spencer Foundation's Idea of Testing Project, especially Jim Gee, Jim Greeno, and Bob Mislevy. I am also grateful to Deborah Ball, Timothy Boerst, and Mary Kennedy for helpful comments on an earlier draft of this chapter.*

## Notes

1. Bowker and Star (1999) draw a cautionary distinction between engineered and organic boundary objects, the former being designed from afar and the latter growing naturally in the interaction between members of different social worlds. The illustration below, arguably, has engineered as well as organic elements. And yet for Bowker and Star, boundary infrastructures entail "stable regimes" (p. 313) of boundary objects, which require, it seems, a judicious use of engineering with "sufficient play to allow for local variation together with sufficient consistent structure to allow for the full array of bureaucratic tools (forms, statistics, and so forth) to be applied" (p. 314).

2. The extended example of assessment in teacher education has involved substantive contributions at the University of Michigan from Deborah Ball, Hyman Bass, Merrie Blunk, Timothy Boerst, Monica Candal, Sara Constant, Francesca Forzani, Donald Freeman, Jennifer Lewis, Annemarie Palincsar, Cathy Reischl, Laurie Sleep, and Meri Tenney-Muirhead; and at the Berkeley Evaluation and Assessment Research Center from Mark Wilson, Amy Dray, Brent Duckor, Xiaoting Huang, and Heeju Jang.

# REFERENCES

American Educational Research Association, American Psychological Association, & National Council on Measurement in Education. (1999). *Standards for educational and psychological testing*. Washington, DC: American Educational Research Association.

Ball, D. L., & Cohen, D. K. (1999). Developing practice, developing practitioners: Toward a practice-based theory of professional education. In L. Darling-Hammond & G. Sykes (Eds.), *Teaching as the learning profession: Handbook of policy and practice* (pp. 3–32). San Francisco: Jossey-Bass.

Ball, D. L., & Forzani, F. M. (2007). What makes education research "educational"? *Educational Researcher*, *36*(9), 529–540.

Boerst, T., Sleep, L., Cole, Y., & Ball, D. L. (2008, January 25). *Practice as evidence of learning: Using performance assessments in a methods course*. Presentation at the annual meeting of the Association of Mathematics Teacher Educators, Tulsa, OK.

Bowker, G. C., & Star, S. L. (1999). *Sorting things out: Classification and its consequences*. Cambridge, MA: MIT Press.

Cohen, D. (2005). Professions of human improvement: Predicaments of teaching. In M. Nisan & O. Schremer (Eds.), *Educational deliberations* (pp. 278–294). Jerusalem: Keter.

Cohen, D. K., Raudenbush, S. W., & Ball, D. L. (2003). Resources, instruction, and research. *Educational Evaluation and Policy Analysis*, *25*(2), 119–142.

Cronbach, L. J., Linn, R. L., Brennan, R. L., & Haertel, E. H. (1997). Generalizability analysis for performance assessments of student achievement or school effectiveness. *Educational and Psychological Measurement*, *3*(57), 373–399.

Darling-Hammond, L., Pacheco, A., Michelli, N., LePage, P., & Hamerness, K. (2005). Implementing curriculum renew in teacher education: Managing organizational and policy change. In L. Darling-Hammond & J. Bransford (Eds.), *Preparing teachers for a changing world* (pp. 442–479). San Francisco: Jossey-Bass.

Gamson, D. (2007). Historical perspectives on democratic decision making in education: Paradigms, paradoxes, and promises. In P. A. Moss (Ed.), *Evidence and decision making: The 106th Yearbook of the National Society for the Study of Education, Part I* (pp. 15–45). Malden, MA: Blackwell.

Grossman, P., Compton, C., Igra, D., Ronfeldt, M., Shahan, E., & Williamson, P. (2009). Teaching practice: A cross-professional perspective. *Teachers College Record*, *111*(9). Retrieved January 19, 2009, from http://www.tcrecord.org/content.asp?contentid=15018.

Grossman, P., & McDonald, M. (2008). Back to the future: Directions for research in teaching and teacher education. *American Educational Research Journal*, *45*(1), 184–205.

Hammerness, K., Darling-Hammond, L., & Bransford, J. (2005). How teachers learn and develop. In L. Darling-Hammond & J. Bransford (Eds.), *Preparing teachers for a changing world: What teachers should learn and be able to do* (pp. 358–389). San Francisco: Jossey-Bass.

Jordan, B., & Putz, P. (2004). Assessment as practice: Notes on measures, tests, and targets. *Human Organization, 63*(3), 346–358.

Kazemi, E., Lampert, M., & Ghousseini, H. (2007). *Conceptualizing and using routines of practice in mathematics teaching to advance professional education.* Chicago: Spencer Foundation.

Lampert, M. (2001). *Teaching problems and the problems of teaching.* New Haven, CT: Yale University Press.

Mislevy, R. M., Moss, P. A., & Gee, J. P. (2009). On qualitative and quantitative reasoning in validity. In K. Erican & M. Wolff-Roth (Eds.), *Generalizing from educational research: Beyond the quantitative-qualitative opposition.* Mahwah, NJ: Erlbaum.

Moss, P. A., Boerst, T., & Ball, D. L. (2008). *A vision of an integrated assessment system for teacher education.* Unpublished manuscript, University of Michigan.

Moss, P. A., Coggshall, J., & Schutz, A. M. (2006). *Reaching ethical decisions in portfolio assessment of teaching.* Paper presented at the Annual Meeting of the American Educational Research Association, San Francisco.

Moss, P. A., Girard, B. J., & Greeno, J. G. (2008). Sociocultural implications for the practice of assessment II: Professional learning, evaluation, and accountability. In P. A. Moss, D. Pullin, J. P. Gee, E. H. Haertel, & L. J. Young (Eds.), *Assessment, equity, and opportunity to learn.* Cambridge: Cambridge University Press.

Moss, P., Girard, B., & Haniford, L. (2006). Validity in educational assessment. *Review of Research in Education, 30*(1), 109–162.

Moss, P. A., & Piety, P. J. (2007). Introduction: Evidence and decision making. In P. A. Moss (Ed.), *Evidence and decision making: The 106th Yearbook of the National Society for the Study of Education, Part I.* Malden, MA: Blackwell.

Moss, P. A., Schutz, A. M., & Collins, K. M. (1998). An integrative approach to portfolio evaluation for teacher licensure. *Journal of Personnel Evaluation in Education, 12*(2), 139–161.

Moss, P. A., Sutherland, L. M., Haniford, L., Miller, R., Johnson, D., Geist, P. K., et al. (2004, July 20). Interrogating the generalizability of portfolio assessments of beginning teachers: A qualitative study. *Education Policy Analysis Archives, 12*(32). Retrieved May 28, 2005, from http://epaa.asu.edu/epaa/v12n32/.

National Research Council. (2001). *Knowing what students know.* Washington, DC: National Academy Press.

Schutz, A. M., & Moss, P. A. (2004). "Reasonable" decisions in portfolio assessment: Evaluating complex evidence of teaching. *Educational Policy Analysis Archives, 12*(33). Retrieved May 31, 2009 from http://epaa.asu.edu/epaa/v12n33.

Star, S. L., & Griesemer, J. R. (1989). Institutional ecology, "translations" and boundary objects: Amateurs and professionals in Berkeley's Museum of Vertebrate Zoology, 1907–39. *Social Studies of Science, 19*(3), 387–420.

Wenger, E. (1998). *Communities of practice: Learning, meaning, and identity.* Cambridge: Cambridge University Press.

Wilson, M. R. (2005). *Constructing measures: An item response theory approach.* Mahwah, NJ: Erlbaum.

Wilson, M. R. (2009). Measuring progressions: Assessment structures underlying a learning progression. *Journal of Research in Science Teaching, 46*(6), 716–730.

# CHAPTER FOURTEEN

# Teacher Quality

## *An American Educational Dilemma*

David K. Cohen

*University of Michigan*

When inspectors visit a construction site to assess the quality of work, they do so against the building code; it typically is written out in detail and used to guide work and teach apprentices. When head residents or attending physicians supervise interns as they take patients' histories or check their blood pressure, they compare the interns' work with established procedures, many of which are written down, and are used to guide work and teach novices. In these cases and many others, the assessment of quality in workers' performance is framed by and conducted in light of occupational standards.

That is not the case for teaching in U.S. K–12 schools. There have been no common standards against which teachers' performance could be judged and no inspections of their performance in light of such standards. There have been standards of a sort, but they have not focused on performance, or focused in sufficient detail to discriminate acceptable from unacceptable work. If we want to understand teacher assessment in the United States, we must explain this unusual situation.

## THE UNIQUENESS OF U.S. SCHOOLS

Because local control and weak government were the foundations of U.S. public education, it never developed the common instruments that are found in many national school systems and in a few U.S. subsystems. These include common curricula or curriculum frameworks, common examinations that are tied to the curricula, teacher education that is grounded in learning to teach the curricula that students are to learn, and a teaching force whose members succeeded in those curricula and exams as students, among other things. Teachers who work with such infrastructure have instruments that they can use to set academic tasks tied to curriculum and assessment. The framework can help them to define quality in students' work and valid evidence of quality. They have a common vocabulary with which they can work with each other to identify, investigate, discuss, and solve problems of teaching and learning. Hence they can have professional knowledge and skill, held in common. School systems with such infrastructure also have means with which the system might influence instruction, at scale.

The existence of such infrastructure does not ensure excellent or effective education; that depends on how well it is designed and how educators use it. Use can be influenced by agencies that oversee practice and shape quality; the chief example is inspectorates, whose staff visit schools and classrooms, assess quality, offer advice, and help to improve practice. Use also can be influenced by standards for entry to the occupation, requirements for education and training, and criteria for promotion. In some national systems, promotion and tenure depend on the demonstration of competent practice in the classroom.

There are no mechanisms of these sorts in the U.S. educational mainstream, but some elements are found in some subsystems. One example is the Advanced Placement (AP) program in secondary schools. AP courses have common curriculum frameworks and common examinations, and students' AP exam scores can make a difference for college admission and course placement for newly admitted students. But the AP program has never moved to use these elements for teacher assessment. Several of the Comprehensive School Reform Designs (CSRD) also have common curricula or curriculum frameworks, and at least a handful educate supervisory staff to observe and evaluate teachers' performance, with an eye mostly to improving that performance. There is no evidence that they use these observations to make up-or-down decisions about teachers' continued work, nor could they very well, since the CSRD organizations work in public schools in which those decisions are made, if they are made at all, by the school authorities. The National Board for Professional Teaching Standards (NBPTS) is the only national organization that has created occupational standards for teaching; I discuss it later in this chapter.

One other salient feature of such infrastructure is that it can inform assessment of teaching. For given common curricula and teacher education grounded in the curricula, it would be possible to devise standards of teaching quality that are referenced to teaching those curricula. It would be possible to devise standards that specify which elements of the subject should be taught, when or in what order they might most fruitfully be taught, and even how they can be taught more or less well. It also would be possible to create standards for students' performance that were grounded in the curriculum.

Because there was no common infrastructure for U.S. public education, it developed several anomalous features. One of the most important concerned testing: because there was no common curriculum, it was impossible to devise tests that assessed the extent of students' mastery of that curriculum. When E. L. Thorndike and his colleagues and students invented tests of students' academic performance, they devised tests of students' performance in no particular curriculum. In part, they intended to develop tests of students' academic abilities or aptitudes, which Thorndike and many other psychologists then thought were largely genetic in origin. There is no evidence that Thorndike and others consciously entertained and then rejected curriculum-referenced tests. How could they have, since even the idea of common curriculum was completely foreign to American thought? The result, however, was tests that were designed to be independent of particular curriculum and are used to assess students' progress in learning. That has to rank as one of the strangest creations in the history of education.[1]

Teacher education was a second anomaly: absent a common curriculum, teachers could not learn how to teach it, let alone how to teach it well. Hence teacher education consisted of efforts to teach teachers to teach no particular curriculum. This was very strange, since to teach is always to teach something, but the governance structure of U.S. education forbade the specification of what that something would be. Teacher education was accommodating: teachers would be taught how to teach no particular version of their subjects. That arrangement created no incentives for intending teachers to learn, relatively deeply, what they would teach, nor did it create incentives for teacher educators to learn how to help intending teachers to learn how to teach a particular curriculum well. Instead it offered incentives for them to teach novices whatever the teacher educators thought was interesting or important (which often was not what happened in schools) or to offer a generic sort of teacher education. Most teachers reported that they arrived in schools with little or no capability to teach particular subjects.

Textbooks developed along similar lines. Absent much guidance from an established curriculum, or even, until very recently, curriculum frameworks, publishers had incentives to produce texts that covered anything that might be taught in that subject in that grade. As knowledge accumulated and conceptions of how it might be taught grew more diverse, textbooks grew as well; some now far exceed what could be dealt with seriously in a year.

Many efforts to write academic standards followed this pattern; standards grew to include such a range of topics that no teacher or school system could possibly deal with all or even most of what was offered, to guide academic quality. Two agencies have studied standards. The Thomas B. Fordham Foundation reported:

> The average grade has risen to "C-Minus." States are writing stronger standards with more detail and content and fewer digressions into pedagogical matters. We've identified eight states (and the District of Columbia) that now have solid enough standards to earn an "honors grade" when averaged across the subjects.
> (That compares with just three states in the previous [1998] round.) . . . . This means that 42 states still hold mediocre or inferior expectations for their K-12 students, at least in most subjects. Hence it must be said, 17 years after *A Nation at Risk,* 11 years after the Charlottesville Summit, and in the same year that our "National Education Goals" were to be met: most states still have not successfully completed the *first step* of standards-based reform [Finn & Petrill, 2000, p. vii].

The American Federation of Teachers (AFT) (2001) report a year later began with a slightly more positive view: "29 states and the District of Columbia, up from just 13 states six years ago, have clear and specific standards in the core subject areas of English, mathematics, social studies, and science at three educational levels—elementary, middle, and high school" (AFT, 2001, p. 5). But the report had little good to say thereafter:

Progress on standards-based reform falls short. Unaligned tests are driving the reform:

- Almost a third of the states' tests are based on weak standards;
- Forty-four percent of those tests are not aligned to the standards;
- Fewer than one-third of the tests are supported by adequate curriculum [p. 6].

Both Fordham and the AFT strongly support standards-based reform, so these reports do not reflect hostility to the policies. They do reflect the fact that absent a common curriculum or curriculum standards, which would be guides to what would be taught and learned, educators, publishers, and interested others have no incentive to limit themselves to what was usable in common; rather, they had incentives to include what might be used somewhere by some significant segment of the profession or market.

One result of these developments, evident in several cross-national assessments, has been a distinctive U.S. approach to education: it is a mile wide and an inch deep. Many topics are "covered," but quickly and superficially. Students' knowledge and academic skills are thin compared with students from other nations that have common curriculum and do not organize schooling around generic teaching, learning, and testing (Schmidt, 2002).

# STANDARDS OF TEACHING QUALITY

Teacher assessment has developed in ways that parallel these features of U.S. education: standards for the schools and departments of education that educate teachers also have been generic. The National Council for Accreditation of Teacher Education (NCATE) is the chief organization that sets standards to accredit education schools and departments, and so it tried to set standards of teaching. But absent educational infrastructure, those standards have been generic. For instance, the NCATE standard for reading, writing, and oral language in programs of elementary education is: "Elementary teachers demonstrate a high level of competence in use of English language arts, and they know, understand, and use concepts from reading, language, and child development to teach reading, writing, speaking, viewing, listening, and thinking skills and to help students successfully apply their developing skills to many different situations, materials, and ideas" (NCATE, 2008, p. 53).

That is what NCATE describes, curiously, as "what an elementary teacher must know and be able to do": every term in that one-sentence standard requires definition in order to be useful for any purpose, including mere understanding, but no definitions are offered. NCATE does, however, refer readers who seek explanation to the Elementary Education Standards and Supporting Explanation, which were devised and published by the Association for Childhood Education International (ACEI) (2007). Although ACEI offers a "supporting explanation" of the NCATE standard for reading, writing, and oral language, it is only a little less generic. It said, for example, of intending teachers that

> candidates are adept at teaching the fundamentals of the English Language Arts. They model effective use of English, including its syntax, lexicon, history, varieties, literature, and oral and written composing processes. Candidates understand how elementary children develop and learn to read, write, speak, view, and listen effectively. They use their knowledge and understanding of language, first and second language development, and the language arts to design instructional programs and strategies that build on students' experiences and existing language skills and result in their students becoming competent, effective users of language [p. 5].

True, but how could one know if an intending teacher had mastered the teaching practices to which this paragraph so generally refers, unless one knew her performance in a particular curriculum? The ACEI standard continues, a little more specifically:

> They teach students to read competently and encourage students' enjoyment of reading through multiple instructional strategies, technologies, and a variety of language activities. Candidates teach children to read with a balanced instructional program that includes an emphasis on use of letter/sound relationships (phonics),

context (semantic and syntactic), and text that has meaning for students. In addition, candidates teach students a variety of strategies to monitor their own reading comprehension [p. x].

The standard continues in the same vein for a few more paragraphs. It nicely exemplifies the American educational dilemma: how to set standards for teaching, when the essential element, the curriculum to be taught, is nowhere to be found. The result is a generic recitation of processes and topics, with references to "competence" and "balance," which lack any educational content. One cannot say that it is wrong, for it is too generic to be right or wrong. But one also cannot say that it offers more than the most vapid guidance for quality in teaching reading, writing, and oral language in elementary schools. Such standards offer little that might inform teacher assessment. They do, however, prompt the key question for teacher assessment in the United States: How can teaching quality be assessed when there is no agreement on what should be taught, no common curriculum, and no common standards for what should be taught? How can the quality of teaching be validly assessed when there is no agreement on what teachers should teach? These are the educational equivalent of asking how the quality of plumbing could be judged absent building codes that set out standards for the quality of materials and operations.

For most of our history, those responsible for schools and school systems answered these questions in ways that were more political than educational: states and localities set their own standards for teaching quality, using methods and measures they deemed appropriate. That was consistent with the systems that Americans invented to govern public education, and with the absence of any educational infrastructure that could inform standards of quality. Teaching quality was determined by what the governing authorities, the states, decided. Since states also controlled the public normal schools and universities in which most teachers were educated, and since educators were public employees, not members of an independent occupation, there were no independent professional standards of teaching quality. Standards were whatever suited elected local and state politicians and the administrators who worked for them. Since in the absence of an educational infrastructure, there was neither agreement on what should be taught nor the capability for systematic inspection of teaching, the standards would not be based on teaching performance in a particular curriculum.

The standards that developed were independent of teaching performance.[2] They applied in the first instance to candidates for teaching and consisted chiefly of lists of required undergraduate courses. They were criteria not of teaching quality but of teacher quality; the tacit assumption was that the latter was a proxy for the former. Students who satisfactorily completed the courses and their undergraduate degree were said to be qualified to teach, but apart from a bit of student teaching, these evaluations had little to do with teaching performance. The course structure and content in teacher education were not the result of mapping backward from evidence of good teaching to the teacher education that would lead to good teaching. If a candidate was hired and then was able to keep decent order in class, he or she usually was awarded tenure in three to five years. If teachers took more courses and earned an advanced degree, their quality as teachers was assumed to increase, and they were rewarded with more salary.

These arrangements worked in several senses. They helped to create the impression that the quality of teaching was regulated in ways that were consistent with the local control of schools, and they helped to ensure that the supply of teachers to those schools was not hampered by undue regulation. If more teachers were needed during an era of enrollment growth, local authorities could hire them without much regard to whether they met even very modest criteria of quality. The arrangements also worked in the sense that they helped to keep the cost of schooling in check, for modest criteria of quality required only modest teacher preparation; that reduced the opportunity costs to teachers, and thus the cost to districts, in which teachers' salaries would have to take account of the costs of much more extensive professional education and income forgone.

## RESEARCH ON TEACHING QUALITY

But if the criteria of teacher quality worked in all of these senses, they did not work in the sense that they were a valid proxy for teaching quality. Researchers took an active interest in the assessment of teaching quality, beginning at the start of public education in Massachusetts and continuing to the present. Beginning early in the twentieth century, they tried to determine whether criteria of teacher quality, which were widely in use among states and localities, were educationally valid; that is, were they also criteria of teaching quality? Since there was no common curriculum, educational validity could not be decided by determining either the extent to which teachers taught the intended curriculum or the quality of their teaching of that curriculum. That left what students learned. Many studies in many locations found no relationship between the criteria of teacher quality and students' scores on standardized, norm-referenced tests. Teachers' experience was modestly related to students' scores: the students of teachers who had three to five years of experience had higher scores than the scores of students of inexperienced teachers, but after five years, experience yielded no added average gain for students.

Research on teacher quality continued, but the dismal results encouraged researchers to turn their attention to quality in teaching, not teachers. The unusual conditions of U.S. education still were a problem, for absent a common curriculum, criteria of quality could not be grounded in what teachers taught. That left principals' evaluations and other measures of students' learning, and researchers did many studies of both. They especially tried to relate a great variety of possible criteria of teaching quality to students' scores on standardized, norm-referenced tests. But those tests were designed to screen out any particular curriculum, so their validity as a criterion for the influence of teaching on learning was doubtful. This was especially so when studies were conducted in more than a single school district or a single state, for every teacher taught a particular set of topics with a particular conception of what it meant to learn them—and that variation likely increased as teachers in more districts and states were included. Hence the criterion measures in these studies were unlikely to capture much of the variation in what teachers actually taught, and thus in the quality of that work. That there was such variation, even among teachers who used the same texts in the same subject, was demonstrated by a series of studies done at Michigan State University (Schwille et al., 1983; Freeman et al., 1983). To the extent that tests did not pick up that variation, which they were designed to not do, could they be a valid measure of teaching quality? To the extent that teachers teach different topics and tests do not reflect that variance, the ratio of measurement error to valid scores increases.

With a few exceptions, much of the research turned up disappointing results. The studies that did turn up consistent relationships between teaching and learning, and thus were stable indicators of teaching quality, focused on process measures of interaction between teachers and students rather than the content taught and learned. Process conceptions of teaching quality is another curious feature of the U.S. nonsystem. For example, William Cooley and Gaea Leinhardt (1978) reported, in a congressionally mandated study, that more time alone did not boost students' scores but that time spent on "academic tasks" did matter. Teachers who spent more time on instruction, set tasks more clearly, and attended to students' task performance had students with higher test scores.

Jere Brophy (1986, 1986b) summarized the results of other investigations, which then were referred to as process-product studies, that also used process measures of teacher quality. Teachers who did more to boost students' test scores planned lessons carefully, selected appropriate materials, made their goals clear to students, maintained a brisk pace, checked students' work regularly, and retaught material when students seemed to have trouble. They also spent more time on instruction, had coherent strategies, deployed lessons and other resources in ways that fit with the strategies, and believed that students could learn and that they had a responsibility to help. Although the lessons were traditional, they reportedly were well organized and paced.

Teachers who did not use such practices deployed resources in scattered and inconsistent ways, and they had vague objectives and disorganized lessons. Classroom work was not well paced, and teachers either did not regularly check to see how students were doing, or, if they did, they made few midcourse corrections. They did not try to make educationally fruitful connections with students, and when they worked with disadvantaged children, they watered down their instruction (Brophy, 1986a; Brophy & Good, 1986).

The process-product studies had a brief shelf life despite being mostly quite well designed. One problem was that some critics argued that they embodied a rather rudimentary conception of teaching, in which routine mastery of routine material was central (Shulman, 1986). Another critique, a cousin of the first, was that the tests that were the criterion of quality focused much more on basic skills than what came to be called "higher-order thinking" or "understanding." When, shortly after Brophy's pieces were published, conceptions of teaching moved toward such "higher-order" work, the process-product studies were thought to be inconsistent with the new view of teaching. They faded from view, despite the absence of any evidence that the process criteria that Brophy and others identified were not also valid for more ambitious assessments that reflected more ambitious and less routine conceptions of teaching.

Given the absence of a common curriculum and linked assessments, and the consequent lack of stability in any working definition of teaching, the quick reversal is not surprising. But that calls attention to another difficulty that arises from the American educational dilemma: to lack the infrastructure that supports a common view of what is to be taught and learned is also to lack a source of stability, over time and through change, in the aims and methods of teaching. It also is to lack stability in the reference frame for research on teaching, learning, and the quality of teaching and learning.

## CREATE A SYSTEM IN THE NONSYSTEM?

Both of those problems of teacher improvement came into sharp focus in connection with the movement for educational reform that began with publication of *A Nation at Risk* in the early 1980s (National Commission on Excellence in Education, 1983). One early response to the pressure for reform was the Carnegie Commission's 1986 report, *A Nation Prepared: Teachers for the 21st Century* (Carnegie Task Force on Teaching, Carnegie Corporation, 1986) which led to the creation of the National Board for Professional Teaching Standards. NBPTS was founded in 1987, developed standards and assessments for "accomplished teaching," and began operations in 1994. It aimed to create high and rigorous standards for what teachers should know and be able to do and to certify teachers who met those standards. The board created standards in twenty-five K–12 subspecialties and devised assessments that are specific to each specialty. The assessment consists partly of a computer-based activity in which teachers respond to several questions that tap their subject matter knowledge and partly of a portfolio that teachers assemble to document their classroom performance in videotapes and in written reflections on their teaching. *Editor's note*: See Chapter Ten for more on the National Board.

The NBPTS aims not only to create a large cadre of teachers of advanced quality, but also, in the process, to create an organization that is the creature of the occupation and, as in other occupations, can set standards of occupational quality and determine how performance is assessed. That is a very ambitious agenda, in large part because of the absence of an educational infrastructure. For instance, because there is no common curriculum, the board's standards and assessments would amount, by intent or default, to something akin to a proto-national curriculum and to operate in a way that could be valid across varied state and local curricula. Absent such an effort, how could it decide what content and pedagogical knowledge to establish and assess, at what grades? In addition, since each state certifies and licenses its own teachers, NBPTS has had to solicit states to offer incentives for teachers to prepare for and go through the board's procedures.

In effect, NBPTS has had to try to create a system-within-the-nonsystem and to persuade the nonsystem to support a sort of work that it had never done. That is not a mission impossible, but it has been difficult. I discuss it here in part because it illustrates the manifold difficulties of trying to devise a valid and usable system of teacher assessment within a nonsystem of schooling that contains none of the educational infrastructure that could support such an assessment scheme.

Those difficulties arise from two chief sources. One is that the larger systems were in many ways at cross-purposes with NBPTS; the new organization was, after all, a remedy for the failings of the established systems, so the creation and operation of NBPTS was a sort of organ transplant, subject in many different ways to an immune response and rejection. Another is that when the commission urged the creation of NBPTS, it did so as part of a set of related recommendations for change in U.S. education. These included creating a board of professional teaching standards, restructuring schools to prove a professional environment for teaching, restructuring the teaching force, creating a new category of lead teacher, and making teachers' salaries competitive with those of other professions. The Carnegie task force envisioned NBPTS as part of sweeping, fundamental changes in teaching, school organization, the finance of teaching, the structure of the occupation, the content and quality of teacher education to make it more knowledge intensive, the creation of new preprofessional curriculum in teacher education to prepare people for practice, and several other things. NBPTS exists, but few of the other changes have been made. The Carnegie Corporation of New York, which sponsored the commission from which NBPTS originated, later cautiously observed, "Some of the Task Force's recommendations are still working their way into America's vastly complex and generally unruly educational system" (Carnegie Corporation of New York, 2003, p. 2).

Hence, when a National Academy of Sciences panel studied the nature and effects of NBPTS, its report was a study in careful qualification. For example, in discussing participation in NBPTS, it wrote, "From the committee's examination of participation patterns, it is not clear whether the board should be judged successful at creating a significant cadre of advanced certified teachers" (National Research Council, 2008, p. 152). In discussing the quality of the assessments, the panel found

> the lack of technical documentation about the assessment to be of concern. It is customary for high-stakes assessment programs to undergo regular evaluations and to make their procedures and technical operations open for external scrutiny. It was difficult to obtain basic information about the design and development of the NBPTS assessments that was sufficiently detailed to allow independent evaluation. We also found it difficult to get a reasonable picture of what is actually assessed through the assessment exercises and portfolios [p. 116].

In one of the most fascinating aspects of its report, the panel discussed the criteria for assessing the NBPTS system and the validity of the assessments: "Validity requires both relevance to the construct of interest (in this case, accomplished teaching) and reliability. The NBPTS assessments seem to exhibit a high degree of relevance" (p. 117). Yet the panel did not attempt to analyze the validity of the board's standards, which are the operational definition of accomplished teaching, and the basis for the assessments. It discussed the standards briefly and did not explain why it did not attempt to analyze their validity. I assume that at least part of the explanation is that the validity of standards is an educational rather than a psychometric matter. In the absence of agreement among educators and others in the United States about the nature of accomplished teaching and well-established traditions of professional practice that exemplified such teaching, it would be impossible to investigate the validity of the standards.[3] Hence only a few examples of the many standards were even discussed, and the panel attended much more to the assessments and their reliability, which could be dealt with as a psychometric matter. On that heading, it wrote of the assessments, "Their reliability (with its consequences for decision consistency) could use improvement.... The reliability estimates for the assessments tend to be reasonable for these assessment methods, although they do not reach the levels we would expect of more traditional assessment methods. The question is whether they are good enough in an absolute sense, and our answer is a weak yes" (p. 117).

In its discussion of the effects of board certification on teachers' practice, perhaps the most central point for the NBPTS process considered in its own right, the panel wrote:

> It is difficult to draw any firm conclusions from the research....The survey results and our own discussions with teachers suggest that teachers learn from the process, but we cannot ignore the fact that this information is entirely subjective.... We also hesitate to draw firm conclusions about the effects of the certification process on teachers' practices.... We cannot say whether any learning that teachers acquire from the process translates into higher achievement test scores for their students. The findings from existing studies are contradictory. Despite the fact that the most recent Clotfelter, Ladd, and Vigdor (2007b) paper found improvement in teachers' effectiveness, we note that the improvement is not large, and it is likely that any positive effects reported in future studies will also show only small effects [pp. 194–195].

From my perspective, however, perhaps the most revealing discussion in the panel's report was its comment on all of the effects that the task force had envisioned:

> The Carnegie Task Force envisioned that the Board's influence would reach well beyond any impact that individual board-certified teachers might have on their students. However, there is very little basis for conclusions about whether or not the board has had impacts on the education system, such as improved working conditions for all teachers, influence on the practice of nonboard-certified teachers, or changes in teacher preparation or professional development. Results from qualitative studies indicate that school systems are not making the best uses of their board-certified teachers. Principals and other school administrators sometimes discourage board-certified teachers from assuming responsibilities outside the classroom. Principals worry about showing favoritism toward board-certified teachers and downplay the significance of the credential. Some board-certified teachers report that they conceal their credential so as not to seem to be showing off. These kinds of findings indicate that board certification is simply not widely accepted as a signal of excellence or as an expected way for a teacher to progress professionally.... Despite these negative reports, there are isolated cases in which board certified teachers are rewarded, used effectively, and offered new opportunities [p. 357].

My point in this discussion is not to suggest that the NBPTS failed, because I do not think that it failed. Rather, I want to probe what success entails, and the many difficulties that attended success, as this remarkable organization attempted to build a new system of teaching standards and assessment within a nonsystem that contained none of the infrastructure that could support such an enterprise.

# TEACHING QUALITY AND STUDENTS' LEARNING

Although at first the reform movement was diffuse, it came to focus increasingly on standards. These state and federal policies offered a new orientation for education: schools and teachers were to focus on school outcomes—students' test scores—and they would be accountable for producing them. If they did not, schools and teachers would suffer. This new policy frame created incentives for school systems and researchers to see teaching quality in terms of outcomes, and improved measurement techniques made it possible to describe those outcomes in more detail than before. The outcome-oriented policies also created intense interest among researchers and those who managed school systems in finding ways to identify teachers who were more effective in boosting students' test scores. Several researchers, working in the new environment, found very large differences among teachers' effects on students' learning; some students gained a good deal more on tests than their otherwise similarly situated peers, and the teachers in those classrooms often repeated the effect year after year. That strongly suggested differential effectiveness in teaching, but researchers were unable to explain its cause; the attributes of teachers that were conventionally observed in surveys were unrelated to the observed differences in teachers' effectiveness (Rivkin, Hanushek, & Kain, 1998).

The growing interest in identifying teachers who boost students' test scores collided with research, discussed earlier in this chapter, reporting few effects of teacher attributes, and teacher education and certification, on student performance. That led to a set of new proposals and state and local schemes for teacher assessment. Three schemes center on efforts to create what might be regarded as behavioral measures of teaching quality. In two of these schemes, researchers tried to use or devise measures of teaching competence and assess their relation to value-added measures (VAMs) of student achievement, while in the third, the VAM is used as the prime measure of teaching quality. In all three cases, the guiding idea is that some behavioral measures of teaching competence, tied to VAMs, should become the central feature of teacher assessment, teacher pay, and teacher tenure. There are important differences among the schemes, and I discuss them because they illuminate the appeal of such schemes and the problems they present. *Editor's note*: VAMs are discussed in further detail in Chapter Nine.

One set of studies centers on efforts to analyze what the authors refer to as knowledge and skill-based teacher evaluation and pay schemes (see Milanowski, Kimball, & White, 2004). In these studies, the researchers investigated whether teachers whose performance was more consistent with some set of standards of competence in teaching had students who scored higher on standardized tests. They identified four districts that used versions of the Danielson Framework, which identifies four large domains of teaching competence: planning and preparation, the classroom environment, instruction, and professional responsibilities (Danielson, 1996). The Danielson Framework is, as the four domains suggest, oriented to a great variety of processes, including everything from the clarity of speech to details of classroom management and reflection on practice; the academic content of instruction appears to play a part, but not a major part, in the framework. The authors of the studies made it clear that they also would be interested in other frameworks that set standards of competence in teaching; though they found the Danielson Framework useful, it is one among several that would be worth considering.

Their studies in the four districts that used versions of this framework centered on whether assessment of teachers' performance, in the terms that the framework specified, was related to value-added measures (VAMs) of student achievement:

> We assessed the relationship between teachers' performance evaluation scores and student achievement by correlating teachers' overall evaluation scores with estimates of the value-added academic achievement of the teachers' students. Our value-added measure was estimated controlling for prior student achievement and other student characteristics, such as socioeconomic status, that influence student learning. At each site, we have analyzed multiple years of data [Heneman et al., 2006, p. 4].

The researchers collected data for several years at each of the sites, and the average correlations between teachers' overall average scores on the Danielson Framework and their students' value-added reading scores ranged from a high of .37 in one district to a low of .23 in another; the range of correlations in math was between .32 and .11 (Heneman et al., 2006, pp. 4–5).

One virtue of these exploratory studies is that the measure of teaching competence is relatively complex. Unlike one of the plans discussed below, it is not chiefly a value-added model of teacher effects but a carefully thought-out analysis of teaching. One problem is that, as would be expected in the United States, there is no obvious association with any curriculum, there being none, and another, similar in nature, is that there is no obvious association with the tests used for students. So as with my discussion of NBPTS, although the absence of an educational infrastructure creates the opportunity for devising schemes like the Danielson Framework, it also creates several large, likely sources of error in efforts to discern the relationship between teaching behavior and students' test scores. Another problem, which I discuss below, concerns the validity and the reliability of VAMs.

A somewhat different approach to devising measures of teaching competence, and relating them to students' performance, was devised by John

Schacter and Yeow Meng Thum (2004), who sought to use research to identify effectiveness in teaching. They reviewed research, including the work that Brophy and his colleagues did, on the effects that teaching practices had on students' performance, and they used it to create standards of teaching quality that the research suggested were likely to predict student achievement gains. They devised twelve standards of teaching performance: "Teacher Content Knowledge, Lesson Objectives, Presentation, Lesson Structure and Pacing, Activities, Feedback, Questions, Thinking, Grouping Students, Motivating Students, Classroom Environment, and Teacher Knowledge of Students."[4]

Schacter and Thum asked, "Do our measures of teaching quality predict student achievement gains against a methodologically rigorous value-added assessment model?" (p. 14). To answer the question they studied fifty-two elementary school teachers from five schools in Arizona. They devised observational measures of the teaching quality standards, trained graduate students to do eight observations for each teacher during one school year, and collected pre- and postscores on the Stanford 9 test. The analysis showed that "teachers who implement effective teaching as measured by our 12 teaching standards and performance rubrics produce students who make considerable achievement gains.... The standardized regression coefficient of 0.91 represents a very large effect" (p. 19). It does indeed. The authors note that their measures of teaching quality account for more than 80 percent of the variance among teachers in students' achievement gains, an unprecedented result in social research.

Based on this study, Schacter and Thum (2004) propose that

> the cornerstone of any teacher accountability system, should be clearly delineated teaching standards and rubrics that explicate and focus every teacher in the school on effective teaching. Before schools adopt teaching standards and rubrics they should take care to ensure that the teaching strategies and behaviors endorsed by the standards increase student achievement as measured through comprehensive validation studies. When these criteria are met, both training to increase inter-rater reliability and coaching strategies to improve teaching performance should be put into place [p. 420].

Several evaluators would assess each teacher, to ensure reliability in estimates of teaching quality, and there would be professional education to ensure opportunities to improve. Both collective and individual effort and effectiveness would be rewarded: 50 percent of a teacher's salary reward would be for teaching that was based on the criteria of teaching quality, which the authors describe as an input standard; 20 percent would be for each teacher's students' test gains; 15 percent would be for average grade-level gains; and another 15 percent for average schoolwide achievement gains.

One strength of these ideas is the careful attention to previous studies of teaching quality. Another is the recognition that trained observers of teaching quality could help not only to identify existing quality differences, but also to help to improve weak teaching. The evaluators could become an inspectorate. The weaknesses of the study include its small size, local sites, the inclusion only of teachers who volunteered to be studied and thus were not likely to be very weak, the cost to educate and maintain evaluators for each district, and the authors' confidence in the validity and reliability of student achievement tests. Were all but the last two problems remedied, it is quite likely that the huge coefficients and variance explained would shrink; what we cannot know until a replication that corrects these weaknesses is done is how much the effects would be reduced. The more they shrank, the less useful this approach to discerning teaching quality would be. The last problem, achievement tests that are weak for these purposes, would be more difficult to remedy (more on that shortly).

Robert Gordon, Thomas Kane, and Douglas Staiger (2006) take a different approach to performance rewards, though their premise is little different from that of Schacter and Thum (2004):

> Certification of teachers bears little relationship to teacher effectiveness (measured by impacts on student achievement). There are effective certified teachers and there are ineffective certified teachers; similarly, there are effective uncertified teachers, and ineffective uncertified teachers. The differences between the stronger and the weaker teachers only become clear once teachers have been in the classrooms for a couple of years. In response to this evidence, our proposal aims to improve teacher effectiveness by increasing the inflow of new teachers and requiring minimum demonstrated competency on the job [p. 5].

There is an entry-level problem with all three efforts: studies of the relation between teacher education and certification and students' performance were rather crudely done, for researchers had no detailed evidence on teacher education or student performance. In the past several years, a strong group of researchers, with access to unprecedented data and research funds, has done a series of careful studies of teaching quality. In part of the work, they investigate differences in the quality of teacher education in several dozen programs in New York City, and the programs' effects on the quality of teachers' education and on value-added measures of student performance (Boyd, Grossman, Lankford, Loeb, & Wyckoff, 2008a).

Their results do not support the assertion, common in the research literature and reflected in these two proposals, that teacher education has no effect on student performance. The researchers report significant differences in teacher education quality, even in the constrained regulatory environment of New York State and City. Some programs give appreciably more attention to teaching practice than others, and some give more attention to academic content than others. The researchers also report that teachers' education does affect their students' learning: some programs graduate teachers whose students learn a good deal more than the students whose teachers graduate from other programs. This finding is robust even when the entering characteristics of students and teachers, which might reflect selectivity, are controlled: "Features of teacher preparation can make a difference in outcomes for students. One factor stands out. Teacher preparation that focuses more on the work of the classroom and provides opportunities for teachers to study what they will be doing produces teachers who are more effective" (p. 26).

The effect is consequential: "The estimated effects of many of the measures of teacher preparation are educationally important, about the same size as the effect of the first year of teaching experience" (p. 27). By the second year of teaching, those New York City teachers who had attended less effective teacher education programs had learned enough on the job to improve their students' work to levels that were comparable to those of teachers from more effective programs. But that comparability seems to depend on results that are not corrected for measurement error. When that is corrected, the effects size of teacher education programs on student performance increases "by a factor of four" (p. 26): graduates of more effective programs were several times more effective in boosting students' performance than graduates of the less effective programs.

The researchers are suitably cautious in their interpretation of the results, and they point out that detailed study of these relationships is just beginning. The study does not establish the magnitude of effects of teacher education or close the door on assertions that teacher education is ineffective. It shows that careful study of the relationship between teacher education and student achievement yields empirically grounded reasons to suppose that some teacher education has educationally consequential effects; if this is the case, assertions that it is ineffective are not defensible. The researchers point out in another paper that the variability among the programs they studied was quite constrained: a more varied sample of programs could reveal more substantial effects (Boyd et al., 2008b).

This was published after the two proposals discussed here and should provoke serious reconsideration of both conventional teacher education that is weakly oriented to practice and proposals for test-based assessment of teaching quality. Since both seem unlikely, it is useful to consider the Gordon et al. (2006) proposal, for it differs in several respects from that of Schacter and Thum (2004). Gordon et al. aim to reduce reliance on conventional measures of teacher quality, increase reliance on measures of teaching performance, tie performance measures to student achievement, and improve the assessment of teachers' contribution to students' performance. They propose to drop barriers to entry into teaching for those without traditional certification to open the way for potentially effective teachers, and make it much more difficult to tenure those who turn out to be less effective in boosting students' scores. They organize their proposal around five recommendations.

The first two recommendations are linked: reduce barriers to entry into teaching for those without traditional teacher certification and make it harder to tenure the least effective teachers. The weak effects of certification and the coming need for many new teachers as baby boomers retire are offered to justify the first proposal. The second is framed as a modification to existing tenure laws and practices: given the existence of relatively good evidence on the relation between teachers' performance and students' achievement, states should establish a presumption that "teachers in the bottom quartile of effectiveness after two years of teaching do not qualify for tenure and are not allowed to continue teaching" (Gordon et al., 2006, p. 13). The focus on the bottom quartile reflects two things: a sensible wish to weed out the weakest teachers, who disproportionately wind up in schools that poor children attend, and the authors' view that existing tests of student achievement are better suited to discern extremes than to make fine distinctions elsewhere in the distribution. Denial of tenure to the bottom quartile would not be a requirement and would apply only to new teachers, not those already tenured. Yet rapid expected turnover in the teaching force due to retirements led Gordon and his colleagues to expect that the majority of teachers would soon be covered by the scheme. They also argue that new teachers should be given comments on how they are doing and opportunities to improve.

The third recommendation is to provide salary bonuses to teachers who are highly effective at boosting student performance and work in high-poverty schools. The aims are to link teachers' compensation more closely to classroom performance and less to experience and academic degrees, and to get more of the highly effective teachers to the schools in which they are most needed. Although the authors assert no fixed view on the size of such bonuses, they propose fifteen thousand dollars, which would be between half and one-third of the average starting salary for teachers in the United States. Teachers would be reassessed every five years to determine if bonuses were still warranted.

The fourth and fifth recommendations address the instruments that would enable the first three to work: devise ways to evaluate teachers using a variety of performance measures and build state data systems that would enable such performance evaluations. These are the heart of the matter, and where the main problems begin, for without valid and defensible measures of teaching quality, none of the other steps could work. Gordon et al. (2006) insist that evaluation center on the effect of teaching on students' learning and envision value-added assessment, which requires longitudinal data on students' performance. This means that states would have to develop data systems that enabled them to track student achievement and link students and teachers. They urge federal support for such systems, but they recognize that "no single measure of performance is a perfect measure of what students should be learning, and statistical evidence from student scores should not be the only measure by which teachers are evaluated" (p. 18). One reason the authors offer this caution is poor alignment between tests and state standards; another is that many tests focus on basic skills rather than more ambitious work; still another is growing evidence of cheating, narrowed curriculum, and test coaching, all in response to accountability. These are not problems that Schacter and Thum noticed.

In light of these considerations, Gordon et al. (2006) suggest that teacher assessment also include what they term "subjective" evaluations; these might be anything from classroom observations done by principals or outside evaluators to the NBPTS teacher assessment system. In principle, they might include Schacter and Thum's (2004) twelve criteria and trained evaluators. Since there is no scientific or professional agreement on teacher assessment, they propose that the federal government fund states to develop their own systems of teacher evaluation, subject to three conditions. States could use student achievement tests but could not use conventional measures, such as degrees or courses taken, of teacher performance. Between one-third and two-thirds of teachers' evaluation must be tied to students' test scores, the rest consisting of subjective evidence of teaching quality. And the evidence would have to cover "a period of time," not just a few months or a year (p. 19). Gordon and his colleagues conclude by proposing that up to ten states serve as volunteers and take three years to develop the data systems and implement the other features of the proposal. They would be federally funded and selected in a grants competition. Evaluation of the effects would be done, and if the results were broadly positive, all states that accept funds under Title II of NCLB, the teacher quality provisions, would be required to implement the system. Federal funds would pay for everything.

Both proposals arise from the outcome-oriented policy frame that standards-based reform brought: student outcomes are what count, and teachers are the key influence on student outcomes, so teacher assessment should focus on deciding which teachers produce better results. If states or localities measure the results that teachers produce, they can select those whose students consistently do better. There would be no need to invest in teacher education, which in most studies had little or no effect on students' performance.

The appeal of these ideas arises in the promise of large improvement in schools and student performance, without fundamental redesign of the system or huge investment. But one's view of the proposals should depend on whether the assessment technology is strong enough to support such approaches to the assessment of teaching; there is no evidence that the assessment technology could support what these authors propose. My doubts arise partly from the assessment schemes and partly from the political and legal tests that the schemes would have to pass to endure. The key question is whether tests of achievement are sufficiently valid and reliable measures of teaching quality to make them the sole or chief criterion, and thus for teachers' continued employment.

One reason for a negative answer is that in most studies, save Schacter and Thum, there are significant differences between expert observers' evaluation of teaching and test results. There are only modest correlations between the value that teachers add to students' scores and how observers rank teaching quality. In the largest and most systematic study of these issues in elementary schools, Pianta, Belsky, Vandergrift, Houts, and Morrison (2008) report that based on the work of expert raters, "observed classroom experiences . . . matter somewhat when it comes to producing gains in children's performance" (p. 388). With the exception of Schacter and Thum, other studies report only modest correlations between test-based and observational measures of teaching quality. In a careful review of the evidence, Hill (2009) concluded, "The weight of the evidence . . . suggests that observational and value-added indicators of teacher effectiveness do converge, but the extent of convergence is unknown. If Schacter and Thum (2004) is replicated, this is strong evidence for the validity of scores in identifying high-quality teaching. If other studies are more typical, however, there is cause for concern. Even validity coefficients of 0.5 (the lower bound in Schacter & Thum) imply many VAM-based [i.e., value-added] accountability systems would be rewarding teachers with mediocre instruction as 'high-performing.'" Hill writes that "more research in this arena is certainly needed; in the meantime, caution seems wise" (p. 9).

But maybe the observational measures are erroneous. If that were the case, different tests of the same academic domains of student performance would yield the same or very similar results. But Hill notes that there are only two studies of how closely related different tests are in valued-added analyses of student gains. The first study compared scores on two math subscales from the Stanford 9 and found correlations of value-added gains of between .01 and .46, depending on model specification. This means that there is "a strong sensitivity of value-added estimate to the domain of mathematics sampled" (p. 10), which varies among tests. The other study used scores on three reading tests, and correlations among the value-added scores among the tests ranged between .17 and .51. This also means that there are very large differences in how teachers would be rated in value-added accountability schemes, depending on the test used. Hill writes that "if this district had been using a pay-for-performance plan similar to the one in place in Houston, Texas, swapping outcome measures would affect the performance bonuses of nearly half of all teachers" (p. 10).

The moral of this story is that the validity of value-added measures of teaching quality is highly sensitive to the tests used, and many teachers would be incorrectly identified as effective or ineffective as a result. Schacter and Thum (2004) never mention this problem, but it may be one reason that

Gordon and his colleagues restrict themselves to removing the lowest quartile of teachers and argue for test development. One trouble, however, is that the problems noted also would incorrectly place some teachers in that quartile.

If teacher evaluation were done at the state level and if states required that only the same statewide test be used for student and teacher evaluation, the problem of variation among tests could be obviated within states. But it would not be obviated among states, which certainly would use different tests; teachers in some states would be rated as ineffective when they would have been rated as effective in another state that used a different test. It could be politically and perhaps legally difficult for states to sustain their teacher rating schemes in the face of such irrationality.

But hold that problem aside for a moment: forget variation of tests among states; assume the political and legal primacy of state decisions; and ask, Would not using the same test in value-added formats yield usable and defensible scores within a state? The answer depends on the tests' reliability: how much error there is in measurement of gains in students' achievement. One can think about this as the ratio between "true score variance" and "observed variance," when the latter includes the former and measurement error. One also can think about it as the consistency between scores on the same test, given to the same students, at two closely related times. Researchers persistently find test-retest reliability to be low, bouncing between .3 and .5 (.5 means that scores contain roughly equal amounts of true score and error variance, and .3 means that error greatly outweighs true scores). These reliabilities are in the same range as those derived in more complex statistical measures of reliability. Thus, even if a state used one test, there would be extensive error in decisions about what teaching was effective. Hill (2009) wrote that there would be "an inability to accurately distinguish between two teachers unless they are very far apart in effectiveness. This renders accountability systems with specific cut-points—for instance, to pay or not pay a bonus—problematic. Two individuals on either side of the cut-point may be indistinguishable in score, from a statistical perspective, because each score lies within the confidence interval of the other. Yet these teachers would have very different outcomes."

There are several other reasons to doubt that the measurement technology these two groups of researchers propose could bear the educational, political, and judicial weight of implementation. One is that students in high-poverty schools and poorer districts often have fewer educational resources than their peers in more advantaged schools and districts: larger classes, weaker leadership, more student and teacher mobility, and so on. That inequality could reduce the value that teachers add to students' scores, penalize teachers for conditions beyond their control, erroneously reduce their "quality" scores, and erode the schemes' legitimacy and political and legal standing. Schacter and Thum (2004) fail to mention this, while Gordon and his colleagues (2006) try to explain it away.

Another problem returns us to the validity of the assessments: How truthful are their reports of teachers' effects on students' learning? Several economists and measurement experts roughly agree that the VAMs are at least somewhat invalid measures of teachers' contribution to students' learning because students are not randomly assigned to teachers; some teachers systematically get more or less able students. Merit pay schemes that used such VAMs would reward some teachers for being assigned to or having recruited more able students and penalize others for working with less able students.[5]

Still another difficulty, which Gordon et al. (2006) take more seriously, is the effect that accountability often has on behavior. They note that existing tests are vulnerable to invalidity because, with NCLB and related state policies, they have been designed to focus on basic work to make scores seem strong. They also note the frequent lack of alignment between tests and curriculum or between tests and standards. In such situations, tests tend to become a proto-curriculum, especially when high or moderate stakes for educators are attached to them; teachers teach to the tests, help students to do well, or alter scores. Although they note this problem in connection with NCLB and existing tests, they do not mention that it would be endemic for the scheme they propose. The high stakes for teachers that would attach to students' test scores in both schemes would create incentives for teachers to cheat, teach to the tests, and work with students whose scores were just below the class average and could relatively easily be improved, rather than weaker students whose improvement would require more work, skill, time, and determination.

Teachers, after all, cannot produce learning without the learners' active engagement; teaching is a practice of human improvement in which the people to be improved play a central role. Contrary to nineteenth-century usage, teachers cannot ''learn'' students; only students can do the learning, with teachers' assistance. If students are not accountable for their learning and if many of them resist or have difficulty, teachers would have strong incentives to work with students whose scores can most easily be boosted, not with weaker students who would require more time, skill, and effort from teachers. NCLB's accountability provisions already create such effects. A recent RAND study of the classroom effects of NCLB quoted an elementary school teacher in California:

> The high-basic child that's almost proficient...[is] our target group.... Every teacher got a printout of their target group. Every teacher has about four to five kids in their class. We went over strategies on how to make sure you involve them and you get them involved. We talked about seating. These children should be closer up to you. Whenever another child answers a question, refer back to that student and make sure, ''Can you tell me what the answer was?'' or, ''What did

Johnny say?'' and always keep those four to five kids questioning and making sure they're their target. They're the kids that we need to push up to proficient [Hamilton et al., 2007, p. 106].

Each of these proposals has strengths. Heneman and his colleagues (2006) use a carefully developed framework that attempts to identify a complex and far-ranging set of teaching behavior that can identify competent performance. Schacter and Thum (2004) use earlier research on teaching quality to advantage, and devising research-based measures of teaching quality strengthens the approach to what Gordon et al. (2006) refer to as ''subjective'' measures of teaching quality. They also offer an intelligent and defensible system of rewards. It is especially noteworthy that they offer appreciable rewards for what teachers do—the quality of teaching—as well as for student scores, and the former well outweighs the latter. Their scheme could help to create incentives for quality classroom work and reduce the likely damaging consequences of a scheme oriented chiefly to results, as the Gordon et al. proposal is. The system of trained evaluators also is thoughtfully done.

But the several weaknesses in their study are so serious that it would have to be replicated before it could be taken seriously as a guide to action, and even if the results did replicate with some strength, there would be large problems of implementation. Perhaps the most significant is that their proposal for district-by-district implementation would mean that each district would have to educate and maintain a crew of evaluators. That would create substantial diseconomies of scale, would add substantial costs, and could introduce differences among evaluation criteria or their use. One solution could be statewide action, but that could encounter serious opposition from many localities. Another solution—a familiar response to the cost of serious teacher evaluation—is a checklist; that would greatly reduce the validity and reliability of quality ratings and invite litigation. This penny-wise and pound-foolish approach turned some earlier proposals into caricatures of themselves. The most recent case in point is the transformation of the original proposals for systemic reform into simplistic test-based accountability.

Gordon and his colleagues' proposal is less careful with respect to the evaluation scheme but more careful about the weaknesses of the outcome measures; the former leads them to vague proposals for ''subjective'' evaluation, while the latter leads them to focus only on the lowest quartile of teachers. Their proposal to mount a definitive implementation and evaluation of a system in three years, given all the problems that would have to be solved, seems more fanciful than careful. It also seems likely that there would be serious state and federal budgetary impediments to the creation and implementation of such schemes, but these were not clear when they wrote.

These considerations lead me to a few conclusions. One is that the measures of teaching competence used by Heneman et al. (2006) and Schacter and

Thum (2004) have the advantage of being based on research and professional knowledge, which are more complex than a simple VAM, the key to Gordon et al.'s (2006) proposal. But they all have the disadvantage of operating in an educational system in which there is no educational infrastructure, which almost certainly increased the error in all of their estimates. And they all are open to the weaknesses of VAMs. It seems unlikely, given these considerations, that value-added measures of student performance would work well enough to ensure that weak and strong teaching were reliably identified. It is difficult to see how they could survive legal, educational, or political challenges if it could not be shown that the technology was valid and reliable enough to avoid many errors in the identification of quality teaching.

My argument does not arise from hostility to teacher assessment; it is badly needed. It does arise from my analysis of the barriers to a coherent assessment of teaching quality in a system of schooling that was carefully designed to impede coherent government action. The existing system of educating teachers and assessing their quality was well adapted to that system of schooling because the entire system sought to regulate educational quality based on crude measures of school inputs. Recent efforts to graft outcome-oriented approaches to the assessment of teaching quality onto that crude system are a mismatch. Among other things, they rely on tests that were designed to serve other purposes than the assessment of educational interventions, to assess the quality of the educational intervention that we call teaching.

There would be serious technical problems to improved assessment of quality in teaching, but the central problems are not technical. They are political and educational. Public education in the United States lacks the elements of a viable system with which to assess the quality of teaching, including common curricula, common criteria of performance in teaching, tied to the curricula, and the capability to inspect and improve teaching. There would be serious technical problems in the construction of such a system, but the chief barriers would be making the educational decisions, mobilizing political support for such an approach, and agreeing on its educational content. The infrastructure to which I refer is not radical or unfamiliar for education throughout the world, only in the United States.

The political and educational barriers are not trivial, yet absent common curricula, common assessments, common measures of performance, and teacher education tied to these things, it will be terrifically difficult to devise technically valid and educationally usable means to judge and act on teaching performance. The proposals that I discussed are correct to argue that any educationally useful assessment must attend to teaching performance. They are not correct to assume that existing tests of student achievement, devised for other purposes, would be fruitful criteria of teaching quality. The approach that I urge would be a large task, but not nearly as daunting as the effects of continuing not to solve the problem. For without standards and measures of quality practice, grounded in linked curriculum, assessments, and teacher education, it will be impossible to build a knowledgeable occupation of teaching, and a knowledgeable occupation is the only durable solution to the problem of quality in teaching.

*David K. Cohen thanks Heather Hill, Fritz Mosher, Seneca Rosenberg, and Magdalene Lampert for comments on an earlier draft.*

## Notes

1. For a recent discussion of the consequences of such tests, see Stroup (2009).

2. For a comprehensive discussion of the research, see Rosenberg (2008).

3. A hint that I think supports my interpretation can be found in this passage from the concluding chapter of the report: ''We found this deficiency to be particularly troublesome as we explored the content-related validity evidence for the national board assessment. Ordinarily, the primary focus in an evaluation of a credentialing assessment is content-related validity evidence—that is, the evidence that the assessment measures the knowledge and skills it is intended to measure, based on the content standards that guide the development of the assessment. Content-related validity evidence, such as documentation of how the content standards were established, who participated in the process, what the process involved, and how the content standards were translated into test items, was the most difficult for us to obtain from the NBPTS (National Research Council, 2008, p. 249).

4. After the teaching standards and rubrics were drafted, they were intensively reviewed and revised based on the suggestions of five curriculum specialists, eight principals, and fifty-five teachers (Schacter & Thum, 2004).

5. For more on these issues, see Rothstein (2009), Koedel and Betts (2009), and McCaffrey, Lockwood, Sass, and Mihaly (n.d.).

## REFERENCES

American Federation of Teachers (AFT).(2001). *Making standards matter 2001*. Washington, DC: Author.

Association for Childhood Education International (ACEI). (2007). *Elementary education standards and supporting explanation*. Olney, MD: Author.

Boyd, D., Grossman, P., Lankford, H., Loeb, S., & Wycoff, J. (2008a). *Teacher preparation and student achievement*. Retrieved July 12, 2009, from http://www.caldercenter.org/publications.cfm.

Boyd, D. J., Grossman, P. L., Lankford, H., Loeb, S., & Wyckoff, J. H. (2008b). *Overview of measuring effect sizes: The effect of measurement error*. Retrieved July 12, 2009, from http://www.caldercenter.org/publications.cfm.

Brophy, J. (1986a). Research linking teacher behavior to student achievement: Potential implications for instruction of Chapter 1 students. In B. I. Williams, P. A. Richmond, & B. J. Mason (Eds.), *Design for compensatory education: Conference proceedings and papers*. Washington, DC: Research and Evaluation Associates.

Brophy, J. (1986b, October). Teacher influences on student achievement. *American Psychologist, 41*, 1069–1077.

Brophy, J., & Good, T. (1986). Teacher behavior and student achievement. In M. C. Witrock (Ed.), *Handbook of research and teaching* (3rd ed.). New York: Macmillan.

Carnegie Corporation of New York. (2003). *Carnegie results*. Retrieved July 2009 from http://www.carnegie.org/results/03/pagetwo.html.

Carnegie Task Force on Teaching, Carnegie Corporation. (1986). *A nation prepared: Teachers for the 21st century*. New York: Author.

Cooley, W., & Leinhardt, G. (1978). *Instructional dimensions study: The search for effective classroom processes*. Pittsburgh: Learning Research and Development Center.

Danielson, C. (1996). *Enhancing professional practice: A framework for teaching*. Alexandria, VA: Association for Supervision and Curriculum Development.

Finn, C., & Petrill, M. (Eds.). (2000). *The state of state standards*. Washington, DC: Thomas B. Fordham Foundation.

Freeman, D. J., Belli, G. M., Porter, A. C., Floden, R. E., Schmidt, W. H., & Schwille, J. R. (1983). The influence of different styles of textbook use on instructional validity of standardized tests. *Journal of Educational Measurement, 20*, 259–271.

Gordon, R., Kane, T., & Staiger, D. (2006). *Identifying effective teachers using performance on the job*. Washington, DC: Brookings.

Hamilton, L. S., Stecher, B. M., Marsh, J. A., McCombs, J. S., Robyn, A., Russell, J. L., et al. (2007). *Standards-based accountability under No Child Left Behind: Experiences of teachers and administrators in three states*. Santa Monica, CA: RAND.

Heneman, H. G., III, Milanowski, A., Kimball, S. M., & Odden, A., (2006). *Standards-based teacher evaluation as a foundation for knowledge- and skill-based pay*. Philadelphia: Center for Policy Research in Education.

Hill, H. C. (2009). Evaluating value-added models: A measurement perspective. *Journal of Policy Analysis and Management, 28*, 702–709.

Koedel, C., & Betts, J. R. (2009). V*alue-added to what? How a ceiling in the testing instrument influences value-added estimation* (Working Paper no. 14778). Cambridge, MA: National Bureau of Economic Research

McCaffrey, D., Lockwood, J. R., Sass, T. R., & Mihaly, K. (n.d). *The inter-temporal variability of teacher effect estimates*. Unpublished paper.

Milanowski, A., Kimball, S. M., & White, B. (2004). *The relationship between standards-based teacher evaluation scores and student achievement: Replication and extensions at three sites*. Madison: Wisconsin Center for Educational Research Consortium for Policy Research in Education.

National Commission on Excellence in Education. (1983). *A nation at risk: The imperative for educational reform*. Washington, DC: Author.

National Research Council. (2008). *Assessing accomplished teaching: Advanced-level certification programs*. Washington, DC: National Academies Press.

NCATE (National Council for Accreditation of Teacher Education). (2008). *Professional standards accreditation of teacher preparation institutions*. Washington, DC: Author.

Pianta, R., Belsky, L., Vandergrift, N., Houts, R., & Morrison, F. (2008). Classroom effects on children's achievement trajectories in elementary school. *American Educational Research Journal, 45*(2), 365–397.

Rivkin, S. G., Hanushek, E. A., & Kain, J. F. (1998, August). *Teachers, schools, and academic achievement* (NBER Working Paper no. W6691). Cambridge, MA: National Bureau of Economic Research. Retrieved May 2009 from http://ssrn.com/abstract=122569.

Rosenberg, S. (2008). *What makes a good teacher? Pursuing the holy grail of education research*. Unpublished paper, School of Education, University of Michigan.

Rothstein, J. (2009). *Teacher quality in educational production: Tracking, decay, and student achievement* (Working Paper no. 14442). Cambridge, MA: National Bureau of Economic Research.

Schacter, J., & Thum, Y. M. (2004). Paying for high- and low-quality teaching. *Economics of Education Review, 23*, 411–430.

Schmidt, W. H. (2002). Too little too late: American high schools in an international context. In D. Ravitch (Ed.), *Brookings papers on education policy 2002*. Washington, DC: Brookings Institution Press.

Schwille, J. R., Porter, A. C., Belli, G. M., Floden, R. E., Freeman, D. J., Knappen, L. B., et al. (1983). Teachers as policy brokers in the content of elementary school mathematics. In L. S. Shulman & G. Sykes (Eds.), *Handbook on teaching and policy*. New York: Longman.

Shulman, L. (1986). Paradigms and research programs in the study of teaching: A contemporary perspective. In M. C. Wittrock (Ed.), *Handbook of research on teaching* (3rd ed.). New York: Macmillan.

Stroup, W. M. (2009, March 18). What Bernie Madoff can teach us about accountability in education. *Education Week*. http://www.edweek.org/ew/articles/2009/03/18/25.

# DISCUSSION QUESTIONS

**Part One: Assessment of Teacher Candidates**

1. How could teacher education programs avoid the portfolio problems that Delandshere and Petrosky describe in Chapter One?

2. What is the proper role of dispositions in selecting, preparing, and assessing teacher candidates?

**Part Two: Assessment for Transition into Teaching**

1. Should local districts be free to hire someone who has not achieved the state's required cut score?

2. Should states establish different rules regarding the consequences of failure for their tests than they establish for their performance assessments?

3. Wei and Pecheone in Chapter Three evaluate performance appraisals against a set of criteria. Are some of these criteria more important than others? Did they miss some important criteria?

4. Wei and Pecheone sort performance appraisals into four broad categories. Considering these broad categories as a whole, are some more generally useful than others?

5. In Chapter Two, Hines argues against the assessment of teachers' dispositions. But in Chapter Five, Delli advocates the use of hiring interviews that focus on teachers' attitudes and values. Would Hines approve of these interviews? What is the difference between a disposition and an

attitude or value system? How would each be relevant to teaching quality?

6. How could schools augment their hiring interviews to strengthen their hiring processes?

## Part Three: Assessment of Practicing Teachers

1. How well do the induction systems described by Youngs, Pogodzinksi, and Low in Chapter Six meet the criteria advocated by Wei and Pecheone for educative performance assessments?

2. If a district devised a tenure assessment system like the one advocated by Sykes and Winchell in Chapter Seven, would it reduce the likelihood that the district would ever need to fire a teacher?

3. Is it possible to have the kind of formative assessments advocated by Youngs, Pogodzinksi, and Low and also have a summative assessment of the sort advocated by Sykes and Winchell?

4. How well would the annual performance assessments described in Chapter Eight help districts prepare for a dismissal, given the record on teacher dismissals described in Chapter Eleven?

## Part Four: Broader Assessment Issues

1. Can a local district solve the infrastructure problems outlined by Cohen in Chapter Fourteen? If not, what governing agencies should do this work?

2. Examine the personnel systems used in a district near you. Does it meet the standards Howard and Gullickson describe in Chapter Twelve?

3. How can districts reconcile, on one side, the need for assessments that are meaningful to teachers, and on the other side, the need for assessments that stand up to legal and policy scrutiny?

# INDEX

## A

Aaronson, D., 133, 253, 274

Academics, and teacher preparation, 55

Accountability, xv–xvi, 74, 97, 188, 275, 283–284; and behavior, 396; external systems, and survey information, 270; new, 251–254, 275; outcome-based, 252; value-added for, 264–265

Accountability portfolio, 38–39

Accuracy standards, 349–350; defined expectations, 349; evaluation report accuracy, 350; issues confronting evaluators in making valid judgments, 349; safeguards against undue influence on the judgment of an evaluator, 349–350; threats to the validity of evaluator judgments, 350

Activation theme, teacher perceiver interviews (TPIs), 155

Adams, S., 304

*Adams v. Clarendon County School District*, 316

*Adolescence* (Hall), 46

Aguerrebere, Joe, 285, 293

Aguirre, J. M., 114

Algina, J., 215

American Board for Certification of Teacher Excellence (ABCTE), 289, 290

American Education Research Association, 341, 356

American Federation of Teachers (AFT), 378

American Federation of Teachers (AFT)/National Education Association (NEA), 205, 219

American Psychological Association, 341, 356

Americans with Disabilities Act, 324

Amrein-Beardsley, A., 215, 288

Anderson, G. L., 53

Anderson, J. A., 14

Anderson, L., 194

Anderson, M. C., 254

Anderson, R. S., 71, 95

Anderson, S., 339

Andress, J. M., 46

Angoff, W. H., 135

Angrist, J. D., 142–143

Annual performance assessment, 224–249, *See also* Performance-based assessments; aspects of teaching currently evaluated, 241–243; central principles, 239–240; criteria for defining teaching quality, 226; early evaluations, 228–230; Early High-Inference Form (Oakland Public Schools, circa 1945), 231–232; essential qualities of a good teacher, 227–228; *Handbook of Research on Teaching* (Brophy/Good), 235–236, 246; Low-Inference Form (Florida Performance Measurement System, circa 1990), 233–234; objective evaluation forms, 230–231; objectivity/ meaningfulness, balancing, 230–236; organizing information presented, 236; performance rubrics, 244–245; public values, accommodating, 227–230; quantity and pacing of instruction, 235; questioning students, 236; research-based teacher evaluation (RBTE), 236–239; *Second Handbook of Research on Teaching* (Rosenshine/Furst), 234–235; standards solution, 239–245; teaching events, capturing on a form, 226–227

Annunziata, J., 339, 340

Anthony, E., 286, 287, 288

Archer, C. P., 51, 57

Arends, R. I., 73, 84, 85, 99

Arens, S., 14, 19, 20, 22, 26, 27, 35

Argyris, C., xx

Armour-Thomas, E., 176

*Arrocha v. Board of Education of City of New York*, 308

*Artherton v. Board of Education of School District of St. Joseph*, 314, 315

Arvey, R., 151

Asher, C., 194

Ashton, J., 288

Assessment, *See* Teacher assessment

Assessment practice, *See also* Teacher Education Initiative (TEI); assessment activities, purposes for, 370; boundary infrastructures, 366–367; boundary object, defined, 367; coherent assessment system, 356, 361; different practices serving different purposes, 364–367; discursive assessments, 364–365; documentary assessment, 365–366; infrastructure, 357; infrastructure design supporting coherence across purposes/institutional contexts, 361–371; interpretive issues in, 358–361; social structures as support for assessment system, 370; Teacher Education Initiative (TEI), 367–371; thinking systematically about, 355–374

Association for Childhood Education International (ACEI), 379

Assumption tests, 266–271

Athanases, S. Z., 71

Automated Teacher Screener, 154

Ayers, R. R., 102

**B**

Baker, W., 240

Ball, D. L., 272, 357, 358, 359, 366–368

Ballou, D., 144, 215, 260, 268, 274, 276, 298

Bangert, A. W., 103

Bank Street College child study, 89–90; candidate learning, impact on, 90; defined, 89; technical quality, 89

Banks-Santilli, L., 90, 91

Baratz-Snowden, J., 215

Barbarin, O., 80, 81

*Barnes v. Spearfish School District No. 40-2*, 321

Baron, J. B., 176

Barr, A. S., 48, 231

Barrow, L., 133, 253, 274

Bartell, C. A., 170

Barton, J., 13, 14, 17, 23, 38

Baruch, D. W., 55

Bassett, K., 69, 99, 360

Becker, B. J., 150

Beckham, J., 309

Beers, C. S., 93, 95

Beginning Teacher Support and Assessment programs (California), 170, 178–179, 184

Beijaard, D., 14, 38

Belanoff, P., 11

Bell, C., 176, 209

Bell, C. R., 51

*Bellairs v. Beaverton School District*, 320

Belli, G. M., 382, 401

Belsky, L., 394

Bembry, K. L., 254

Berk, D., 3

Berlin, I. N., 55–56

Berliner, D., 221, 288

Bernard, V. W., 56, 58

Berry, B., 100, 101, 182

Bestor, Albert, 54

Betts, J. R., 274, 399

Biddle, B. J., 234, 337

Bird, T., 15

Bischoff, K., 284

*Black's Law Dictionary*, 307

*Blaine v. Moffat County School District*, 323

Blair, G. M., 53

Bleeker, M., 188, 189, 190, 196

Bloom, G., 194

Blount, J. M., 45

*Board of Directors of Sioux City Community School District v. Mroz*, 314

*Board of Education of Argo-Summit School District No. 104, Cook County v. Hunt*, 330

*Board of Education v. Hunt*, 306

*Board of Regents v. Roth*, 305

Boardman, A. E., 262

Boerst, T., 357, 367–368

Bolton, D. L., 153

Bond, L., 240

Borko, H., 14, 17, 18, 19, 20, 21

Borman, G., 174, 219, 241

Bosker, R. J., 339

Boston, M., 82

Boston, M. B., 82

Boundary infrastructures, 366–367

Boundary object, defined, 367

Bower, D., 18, 20, 22, 39, 95, 97–98

Bowker, G. C., 357, 366, 367, 372

Boyce, A. C., 228–229, 230

Boyd, D., 136, 139, 204–205, 390

Boyd, D. J., 391

Boyd, William L., 283fn

Boyer, F. G., 234, 235

Bransford, J., 359

Braun, H. I., 298

Brennan, R. L., 359

Brewer, D., 201

Brewer, D. J., 139, 252

Breyer, S. G., 308

Bridges, E., 203, 205

Briggs, D., 268

Briggs, T., 54

Brooks, P., 301

Brophy, J., 150, 166, 171, 218, 235, 383, 389

Brown, B., 150, 154

*Brown v. Wood County Board of Education*, 311

Bryant, D., 80, 81, 272

Bryk, A. S., 171, 258

Buchmann, M., 245

Budzinsky, F., 101

Bullock, A. A., 14

Bunch, G. C., 114

Burant, T. J., 43, 60

Burchinal, M., 80, 272

Burge, F., 123

Burkham, D. T., 255

Burns, S., 92

*Burton v. Town of Littleton*, 312

Butsch, R.L.C., 229

## C

Cable, D. M., 153

California Commission on Teacher Credentialing (CCTC), 105, 106, 107, 110

California Department of Education & Commission on Teacher Credentialing, 170, 171, 175, 176, 194, 195

California Formative Assessment and Support System (CFASST), 167, 173, 177, 179–180; and teacher quality, 188–189

*California Standards for the Teaching Profession* (California Department of Education & Commission on Teacher Credentialing), 194

California Teacher Portfolio, 170–173, 175, 194

California Teaching Performance Assessment (TPA), 105–108; culminating teaching experience, 106; designing instruction, 106; learning assessment, 106; statewide teaching performance assessment,

costs of implementing, 107; subject-specific pedagogy, 105–106; tasks, 105–106; technical quality, 106–107; tensions in the formative and summative purposes of, 107–108

California Teaching Performance Expectations (TPEs), 105, 110

California Teaching Standards, 175–176, 182–183

Campbell, D. M., 14

Campion, J., 151

Campion, M., 150, 154

Candidate stimuli for screening decisions, 152

Cantrell, S., 254, 289, 290

Capie, W., 236

Capraro, M. M., 14

Cardinal Selection Interview, 154

Carey, R. D., 57

Carnegie Corporation of New York, 385

Carnegie Forum on Education and the Economy, 284

Carnegie Foundation Task Force on Teaching as a Profession, 10, 284

Carnegie Task Force on Teaching, Carnegie Corporation, 386

Carter, R. L., 215

*Carter v. State Board of Education*, 306

Castle, S., 69, 92

Causal effects: defined, 254; and value-added, 254–255

Causal inferences, 254

Cavalluzzo, L., 288

Center on Education Policy, 216

Central Connecticut State University Mid-Point Assessment Task (MAT): candidate learning, impact on, 85–86; technical quality, 85

Chait, R., 202, 205

Chapter guide, 4

Charalambous, C., 338

Charters, W. W., 228

Chiang, F. S., 338

Child and the Curriculum, The (Dewey), 46

Child case studies, 88–93; Bank Street College child study, 89–90; discussion of, 92–93; George Mason University Reading, Writing, Spelling Analysis Task, 91–92; Wheelock College Focus Child Assessment Project, 90–91

Christopherson v. Spring Valley Elementary School District, 321

Chubb, J., 210

Chubbuck, S. M., 43, 60

Chung, R. R., 69, 110, 111, 112, 114, 117, 125

Chung Wei, R., xiii–xiv, xix

Cignetti, P. B., 14

Citizens to Preserve Overton Park, Inc. v. Volpe, 307

Civil Rights Act of 1964, 324

Clarke v. Shoreline School District, 324

Classroom Assessment Scoring System (CLASS), 80–81, 218, 272; teacher learning, impact on, 80–81; technical quality, 80

Clifford, G. J., 45, 54

Clifford, R., 80, 272

Clotfelter, C. T., 139

Clover, W. H., 151, 152

Cochran-Smith, M., vii, xvii, xx

Coggshall, J., 69, 99, 360

Cohen, D., 358

Cohen, D. K., vii–viii, 358, 359, 366

Cohen, S., 45–46

Coherent assessment system, 356, 361

Coix, J., 123

Coker, H., 235, 257, 271

Coker, J. G., 235

Cole, D. J., 14

Cole, Y., 368

Coleman, J. S., 255

Coleman Report (1966), 255

Collins, A., 13, 14, 17, 23, 38

Collins, K. M., 99, 100, 360

Collins v. Faith School District No. 46–2, 309

Commercially designed teacher selection interviews, 153–155; defined, 154; interview objectivity, perception of, 154

Common Core of Teaching (Connecticut), 176–177

Common Sense School Reform (Hess), 289

Compton, C., 369

Conant, J. B., 54

Connecticut BEST Portfolios, 100, 173, 176, 181–184, 187–188; implementation of, 101; local evaluation systems based on, 169, 191

Connecticut Competency Instrument (CCI), 169, 191

Connecticut Teaching Competencies, 176

Connick v. Meyers, 327

Consulting teachers, 180

Conward v. Cambridge School Committee, 314

Cook School District Simulation (Western Oregon University Cook School District Simulation), 86–87; candidate learning, impact on, 87; technical quality, 87

Cooley, W., 382

Cooper, D. H., 229

Cooper, M., 3

Corcoran, S. P., 3

Corey, S. M., 52

Correnti, R., 253

Corrigan, D., 14, 16, 19

Council of Chief School State Officers, 13

Crocker, L., 103

Cronbach, L. J., 359

Crosson, A.,, 81, 82

Cuban, L., xv, 50, 59

Culp, V. H., 57

Curriculum-embedded assessments, 69

Cussler, M. T., 62

Cut scores, 134; setting, 135–140

**D**

Dagley, D. L., 306, 307, 310

Danielson, C., 79, 93, 94, 175, 176, 195, 217–219, 218, 219, 240, 240–241, 246, 275, 338, 339, 388

Danielson C., 275

Danielson Framework, 388, *See* Pathwise/Danielson Framework for Teaching

Darling Farr, L., 14, 18, 19, 22

Darling-Hammond, L., 21, 23, 37, 71, 95, 100, 101, 150, 166, 170, 182, 211, 359, 366

Daugherty, S., 144

Davis, C. L., 71, 95

Davis, D. R., 339, 340

de Forest, J., 47, 49, 50, 54

DeAngelis, K., 144

DeArmond, M., 144

Dee, T. S., 145

Delandshere, G., viii, xviii, xix, 9, 14, 19, 20, 22, 26, 27, 35

Delli, D. A., xix, 149, 149–162, 150, 151, 152, 153, 155, 156, 158

Delli, Dane A., viii

Delli, L. M., 150

Demetriou, D., 338

DeMeulle, L., 71, 95

DeNardo, C., 320

Denner, P. R., 93, 101, 104, 105

Derham, C., 14

Desimone, L. M., 3

Dewey, J., 21, 46, 235

Dietz, M., 14, 16, 38

DiMichael, S. G., 55

Diperna, J., 14

Discursive assessments, 364–365

Disposition assessment, 43–65; and community norms, 56–57; "good" dispositions, defining, 44–47; good teachers, qualities of, 48–51; hiring practice criticisms, 57; mental pathology, fear of, 55–56; negative feelings toward children, 55; personality adjustment, 52–54; personality, history of the science and psychology of, 43–44; pressures against use of, 51–52; scientific assessment of teacher dispositions/personality, 48–51; selecting teachers based on personality, 56–59; and teacher preparation/teacher quality improvements, 51–56; weeding out potential candidates based on personality, 58–59

Dixon, M., 58

Documentary assessment, 365–366

Doherty, M. E., 151, 152

*Dolega v. School Board of Miami-Dade County*, 321

Dolfin, S., 188, 189, 190, 196

Donaldson, M., 302

Donnelly, A. M., 14

Downer, J. T., 80, 81

Downie, N. M., 51

Du Mez, J., 14

Duffett, A., 204, 205

Dwyer, C. A., 79, 94, 234

**E**

Early Adolescent/English Language Arts Assessment Development Laboratory (ADL), 11

Early, D., 80, 272

Early evaluations, 228–230

Early High-Inference Form (Oakland Public Schools, circa 1945), 231–232

*Education of American Teachers, The* (Conant), 54

Educational Testing Service, 135, 142, 172–173, 178, 185, 195, 218

*Educational Wastelands* (Bestor), 54

Edwards, M. N., 150

Effective teaching, defined, 171–172

Ehrenberg, P., 69

Ehrenberg, R., 201

Ehrenberg, R. G., 139

Elbow, P., 11

Elementary and Secondary School Act (2001), *See* No Child Left Behind Act (NCLB)

Eliassen, R. H., 51

Ellena, W. J., 234

Ellett, C. D., 236, 339, 340

*Ellicott v. Board of Education of Township of Frankford, Sussex County*, 306

Embedded Signature Assessments (ESAs), 109, 118–119, 120, 123

Empathy theme, teacher perceiver interviews (TPIs), 155

Employment interview, 149, 151–154; candidate stimuli for screening decisions, 152–153; commercially designed teacher selection interviews, 153–154; interview objectivity and commercial interview products, 154; organizational research on, 151; preemployment decisions of school administrators, research addressing, 152–153; role-playing, 151–152; screening decisions and interviewing decisions, differentiating between, 153; structured, 150, 153; teacher

perceiver interviews (TPIs), 155–158; unstructured, 150

*Engel v. Rapid City School District*, 325

*Enhancing Professional Practice, Framework for Teaching* (Danielson), 246

Erickson, F., 171

*Eshom v. Board of Education of School District No. 54*, 314, 316

Estabrooks, C., 123

Evans, W. N., 3

Evertson, C., 150, 234

Experienced teachers, portfolio assessments of, 24–27

Ey, R. M., 314

**F**

*Falchenberg v. New York City Department of Education*, 325

Fallon, D., 123

Farkas, S., 204

Feasibility standards, 348–349; F1–Practical Procedures, 348; F2–Political Feasibility, 349; F3-Fiscal Feasibility, 349

Feiman-Nemser, S., 193

*Feldman v. Board of Education of City School District of City of New York*, 308

Feng, L., 267

Fenstermacher, G., xviii, 208, 272

Fenstermacher, G. D., 171, 172

Fenstermacher, V., 287

Ferguson, R. F., 139

Fickel, L., 95–96

Finn, C., 378

*Fiscus v. Board of School Trustees of Central School District*, 309, 323

Fixed student contribution, use of term, 261

Flanders, N. A., 234, 235

Floden, R. E., 170, 382

Florida Performance Measurement System, 166–172, 176, 237

Florida Revised Statutes, 320

Focus Child Assessment Project (Wheelock College): candidate learning, impact on, 91; components of, 90; weekly assignments/feedback, 90–91

Focus theme, teacher perceiver interviews (TPIs), 155

Ford Foundation's Fund for the Advancement of Education, 54

Forienza-Bailey, A., 21

Formative assessment: and unstructured portfolios, 94–98

Formative Assessment System (FAS) (New Teacher Center), 168, 173, 177, 183–184, 187–190, 192–196; and teacher quality, 189–190

Formative assessments in induction: assessors and support providers, selection/training of, 184–188; California Formative Assessment and Support System (CFASST), 167, 173, 177, 179–180; decisions associated with the use of, 172–188; Florida Performance Measurement System, 166; Georgia Teacher Performance Assessment Instruments, 166; history of and conceptions of, 166–172; local assessment systems (based on Connecticut BEST Portfolios), 169; local assessment systems (based on Connecticut Competency Instrument), 169; and new teacher assessment, 165–199; New Teacher Center's Formative Assessment System (FAS), 168; Pathwise/Danielson Framework for Teaching, 167, 173, 177, 179; peer assistance and review (PAR) programs, 168; rubrics, 182–184; teacher quality, potential impacts on, 188–191; teaching standards, 174–177; Texas Appraisal System, 166

Forzani, F. M., 358

Fowlkes, J., 194

Framework for Teaching Observation Survey, 218

Freeman, D. J., 382, 401

Freeman, F. S., 53

French, R., 166

Fritzen, A., 3

Fuhrman, S., 251

Fuller, W. E., 57

Fullerton, J., 254, 289, 290

Furst, N., 234, 235

Futrell, M. H., 95

G

Gage, N. L., 150

Gallagher, H. A., 235

Gallagher, J. J., 194

Gallimore, R., 246

Gallucci, C., 118

Gallup Organization, 153, 156

Gamson, D., 372

Gareis, C. R., 93, 95

Garnier, H., 82

Gee, J. P., 370–371

Geist, P. K, 360, 374

George Mason University Reading, Writing, Spelling Analysis Task, 91–92; candidate learning, impact on, 92; technical quality, 92

Georgia Teacher Performance Assessment Instruments, 166–172, 176

Gergen, K. J., 226

Gestalt theme, teacher perceiver interviews (TPIs), 155

Getzels, Jacob Warren, 47, 50

Gewirtz, P., 301

Ghent, J., 322

Ghousseini, H., 358

Gill, J. H., 22

Gilovich T., 153

Girard, B., 356, 364, 366, 371

Girard, B. J., 356, 366

Girod, G., 77, 86, 87, 101, 102

Girod, M., 77, 86, 87, 102

Gitomer, D. H., 3, 142, 144

Gladstone, R., 51

Glazerman, S., 178, 179, 180, 183, 185, 188, 189, 190, 191, 192, 196

Goe, L., 177, 178, 192, 195, 196, 209, 216

Gold, Y., 193

Goldhaber, D., viii–ix, 144, 145, 205, 213, 214, 217, 286, 287, 288

Goldhaber, D. D., 136, 139, 140, 141, 252

Goldstein, J., 176, 191, 194

Gomez, E., 254

"Good" dispositions, defining, 44–47

Good, T., 166, 218, 389

Good, T. L., 235

Good teachers, qualities of, 48–51, 227–228

Gordon, R., 212, 213, 216, 217, 219, 252, 390, 391, 392, 393, 395, 396, 397, 398

Gorman, C. D., 151, 152

Gowan, J. C., 57

Gowan, W. N., 49

Grant, G., 17

Green, J., 234

Greeno, J. G., 356, 366

Greenwald, R., 3

Griesemer, J. R., 366, 367

Gropper, N., 89, 90

Gross, B., 144, 205

Grossman, P., 204–205, 365, 369, 390

Grossman, P. L., 391

*Grossman v. South Shore Public School District*, 326

Groth, L., 92

Groth, L. A., 92

Guilford-Zimmerman Temperament Survey, 48

Gullickson, A. R., ix, 337–338

Guryan, J., 142–143

Guthrie, J. W., 45, 54

*Gwathmey v. Atkinson*, 305, 314

**H**

Haberman Star Teacher Selection Interview Tool, 154

Habib, L., 14, 15, 38

Haertel, E. H., 359

*Hagerty v. State Tenure Commission*, 315

Haggerty, H. R., 55

Hale, N., 52

Hall, G. Stanley, 46

Hall, M. W., 81

Hallam, P. J., 100, 101

Hallinger, P., 339

Hallman, H. L., 14

*Hamburg v. North Penn School District*, 311, 314

Hamerness, K., 366

Hamilton, L., 257, 259, 267, 275

Hamilton, L. S., 397

Hammerness, K., 359

Hamre, B., 218

Hamre, B. K., 80, 81

Han, B., 260, 272

*Handbook of Research on Teaching* (Brophy/Good), 235–236, 246

Haniford, L., 356, 360, 364, 366, 371, 374

Hannaway, J., 284, 331

Hansen, M., 144, 145, 213, 214, 217

Hanushek, E., 253, 273

Hanushek, E. A., xvii–xviii, 133, 142, 201, 205, 215, 387

Harman, S. S., 338, 340, 350

Harris, D., 276

Harris, D. N., xviii, ix, 144, 251, 252, 253, 267, 269, 270–271, 274, 275, 278

Harris, L. B., 88, 93, 101, 104
Harris, M., 151
Hart, P. D., 340
Hartmann, C., 14
*Harvey v. Jefferson County School District*, 321
Haskew, L. D., 51, 55, 57
Hattie, J. A., 240
Hauge, T. E., 14
Hawk, P. P., 14
Haycock, K., 3
Hayden, F. S., 57
Haynes, D., 71
Heck, R. H., 339
Hedges, L. V., 3, 5, 253
Helm, C., 43
Helm, C. M., 43
*Hennessy v. City of Melrose*, 326
Herrick, V. E., 52
Hess, F., 290
Hibpshman, T., 135
*Hicks v. Gayville-Volin School District*, 306
Hiebert, J., 3, 246
Hill, C. W., 231
Hill, H., 394, 395
Hill, H. C., 272
Hines, L. M., ix, 43, 44
Hiring decisions, 149, 158–160; cost implications, 159–160; employment interview, 149, 151; legal considerations, addressing, 159; methodology/ instrumentation, examining, 159; published research, reviewing, 158–159; rationale, developing, 158; recommendations to districts, 158–160; simulated interviews, 151–152; structured interviews, 150; teacher applicants, as paper people, 149; teacher selection and hiring practices, 150–153; teacher selection research base, 151; unstructured interviews, 150

Hoffman, N. J., 44
Holdzkom, D., 166
Holland, P.W., 254
Holland, R., 290
Holmstedt, R., 202
Honan, E., 71, 95
Honawar, V., 297, 298, 299
Horn, B., 257
Horn, S. P., 253, 273, 338, 351
Houang, R. T., 267
Hough, H. J., 290
Houts, R., 394
*How Gertrude Teaches Her Children* (Pestalozzi), 44–45
Howard, B. B., 337, 338, 339, 340, 350
Howard, Barbara B., x
*Howell v. Alabama State Tenure Commission*, 321
Howes, C., 80, 272
Huebner, T., 17
Hugo-Gil, J., 188, 189, 190, 196
Humphrey, D. C., 290
Hundersmarck, S., 150
Hunt, J., (governor, N.C.), 285, 287
Hunt, J. T., 49–50

I
Igra, D., 358, 369
Individualized perception theme: teacher perceiver interviews (TPIs), 155
Ingersoll, R. M., 3
Ingle, W. K., 144
Ingvarson, L., 340
Ingvarson, L. C., 340
Innovation theme, teacher perceiver interviews (TPIs), 155
Input drive theme, teacher perceiver interviews (TPIs), 155
Institute for Learning, 71, 81
Instructional Quality Assessment (IQA), 81–82; candidate learning, impact on, 82; technical quality, 81–82

INTASC Teaching Portfolio, 99–101; creation of, 99; design of, 99; practicality/feasibility, 101; required teacher submissions, 99; scoring of, 99; teacher learning, impact on, 100–101; technical quality, 100

Interstate New Teacher Assessment and Support Consortium (INTASC), 11, 12, 13, 15, 16, 19, 25, 29, 71, 76, 84, 88, 172–173, 239, 384

Interviews: employment, 149, 151–154; simulated, 151–152; teacher perceiver interviews (TPIs), 155–158; videotaped, 152

Investment theme, teacher perceiver interviews (TPIs), 155

Isenberg, E., 188, 189, 190, 196

Iwaszkiewicz, K., 254

J

Jackson, L., 123

Jackson, P. W., 47, 50

*Jackson v. Hazlehurst Municipal Separate School District*, 321

Jacob, B. A., 213, 271, 273

Jacobsen, R., 216

Jansen, A., 3

*Jennings v. Caddo Parish School Board*, 314, 316

Johnson, A., 178, 179, 180, 183, 185, 188, 189, 190, 192, 196

Johnson, C. E., 236

Johnson, D., 360

Johnson, S. M., 302

Johnson, W. R., 54, 60

Joint Committee on Standards for Educational Evaluation, 310, 337–338, 339, 341, 344, 350–351

Jolly, A. B., 338

Jones, M. L., 49

Jordan, B., 364, 365, 368

Jordan, H. R., 254

Jorgenson, D. W., 215

Junker, B., 81, 82, 246

Justice, L., 81

K

Kaboolian, L., 174, 176, 196

Kaestle, C. F., 59

Kain, J. F., 133, 201, 253, 273, 387

Kane, T., 289, 290, 390, 391, 392, 393, 395, 396, 397, 398

Kane, T. J., 201, 212, 213, 216, 217, 219, 252, 254, 272, 278

Kazemi, E., 358

Kearney, N. C., 53

Keeling, D., 203

Kelley, C., 298

Kellor, E. M., 100, 101

Kelly, J., 285, 286

Kemple, J. J., 204

Kennedy, M. M., x, xvii, xviii–xix, 1, 150, 220, 241

Kerchner, C., 194

Kerchner, C. T., 191, 194, 208

Kick, F., 14

Kimball, S., 100, 101

Kimball, S. M., 174, 219, 241, 387

KimWolf, M., 81, 82

King, L. A., 230

Kirk, P. L., 57

Klein, S. P., 71, 166

Kleiner, M. M., 142

Kleinhenz, E., 340

Klinzing, H. G., 170

Knappen, L. B., 382

Knowles, K., 136

Knowles, K. T., 121

Koedel, C., 274, 399

Koerner, James, 54

Kolodziejczyk, S., 254

Konstantopoulos, S., 5, 253

Koppich, J., 194

Koppich, J. E., 191, 194, 208, 219, 290

Koretz, D., 216, 257, 259, 267, 275

Krieg, J. M., 3

Kristof, N. D., 291, 294

Kromrey, J., 236, 237

Kruger, M. I., 339
Kuligowski, B., 166
*Kurek v. North Allegheny School District*, 325
*Kurlander v. School Committee of Williamstown*, 323, 325
Kuzniewski, M. L., 154
Kyriakides, L., 338

L

La Paro, K. M., 80
Labaree, D., 52, 207
LaBue, A. C., 49
Ladd, H. F., 139
Lagemann, E. C., 48, 50
Laine, R. D., 3
Lamke, T. A., 49
Lampert, M., 358
Lang, W. S., 94
Langholz, J., 194
Lanier, P., 194
Lankford, H., 136, 139, 204–205, 390, 391
Latham, A. S., 3, 142, 144
Lave, J., 22
Lavely, C., 205
Lawrence, D., 185
Lee, V. E., 255
Lefgren, L., 213, 271, 273
Leibbrand, J., 69
Leinhardt, G., 382
Leipold, L. E., 47
Leithwood, K., 339
*Leon County School Board v. Waters*, 304, 316, 320
LePage, P., 366
*Let's Talk Sense About Our Schools* (Woodring), 59
Levin, J. A., 203
Levison, A., 81, 82
*Lewis Central Education Association v. Iowa Board of Education Examiners*, 308

Licensure tests, 1, 4, 133–147; basic types of, 135; history and cut score setting, 135–136; idea behind, 133–134; imperfection in predicting teaching effectiveness, 137; performance of prospective teachers on, 134; scores, and teacher quality, 139; states' emphasis on, variations in, 135; and teacher quality, 137–138; teacher tests and student achievement, 136–141; and the teacher workforce, 141–143
Lieberman, J. M., 95
Liggitt, W. A., 58
Lin, S., 104, 105
Linn, R. L., 359
Lippincott, A., 18, 20, 22, 39, 95, 97–98, 118
Listening theme, teacher perceiver interviews (TPIs), 155
Liston, 21
Little, O., 209, 216
Local assessment systems: based on Connecticut BEST Portfolios, 169, 191; based on Connecticut Competency Instrument (CCI), 169, 191
*Lockhart v. Board of Education*, 322
Lockwood, J. R., 257, 258–259, 260, 267, 268, 270, 272, 273, 274, 275, 399
Loeb, S., 139, 204–205, 390, 391
Lomask, M., 101
Long, C., 71
Looper, S., 14
Lorentz, J. L., 235
Lortie, D. C., 51, 56, 216
Loughran, J., 14, 16, 19
Louis, T., 257, 259, 275
Low-Inference Form (Florida Performance Measurement System, circa 1990), 233–234
Low, M., xi, 165

Lucas, M. E., 215
Lundeberg, M., 3
Lynch, J. M., 57
Lyons, N., 14, 22, 23
Lyons, N. P., 71, 95, 96

**M**

Ma, C. X., 215
Macdonald, M. B., 95
*MacKenzie v. School Committee of Ipswich*, 322
Madigan, Kathy, 290
Mansvelder-Longayroux, D., 14, 38
Mariano, L. T., 257, 273
Marsh, J. A., 397
Marshall, R., 208, 218
Martin, L. M., 51
Martineau, J., 267
Mashburn, A. J., 80, 81
Massachusetts Department of Education, 300, 304, 310
Massachusetts Education Reform Act, 299, 303, 312
*Massachusetts Federation of Teachers, AFT, AFL-CIO v. Board of Education*, 318
Mata, S., 71
Mathematica Policy Research, 179
Mathies, B. K., 14
Matsumara, L. C., 81, 82, 246
*Matter of Shelton*, 324
Max, J., 69, 99, 360
Mayfield, E. C., 150
McCaffrey, D., 267, 399
McCaffrey, D. F., xi, xviii, 251, 257, 258–259, 260, 267, 268, 270, 272, 273, 274, 275
McColskey, W. H., 339
McCombs, J. S., 397
McConney, A. A., 78, 101, 102
McDaniel, R., 210
McDiarmid, B., 123
McDiarmid, G. W., 75

McDonald, M., 365
McDonnell, L., 207
McGreal, T., 93, 94, 175, 176, 275
McGreal, T. L., 275
*McGuinn v. Douglas County School District No. 66*, 307
McIntyre, K. E., 57
McKibbens, D. E., 90, 91
*McKinnon v. State*, 308
McKnight, C. C., 267
McSwain, 55
Medicalization of education, 45–46
Medley, D. M., 235, 257, 271
Melenyzer, B. J., 14
Melnick, S., 302, 322
Mencken, H. L., 160
Mendro, R. L., 254
Menuey, B. P., 205
Metzger, S. A., 154, 155, 157–158
Meux, M., 234
Meyer, D. K., 14, 16, 23
Micerri, T., 236, 237
Michalec, P., 14, 17, 18, 19, 20, 21
Michelli, N., 366
Mid-Point Assessment Task (MAT) (Central Connecticut State University), 84–86; candidate learning, impact on, 85–86; technical quality, 85
Mihaly, K., 399
Milanowski, A., 241, 271, 387
Milanowski, A. T., 174, 219, 241
Miller, R. J., 253, 338
Miller-Smith, K., 151
Millman, J., 309
Milman, N. B., 14
Minnesota Multi-Phasic Personality Inventory, 48
Minnesota Teacher Attitude Inventory, 48
*Miseducation of American Teachers, The* (Koerner), 54

Mislevy, R. M., 370–371

Mission theme: teacher perceiver interviews (TPIs), 155

Missouri Revised Statutes, 313

Mitchell, D. E., 178, 192

Mitchell, K., 136

Mitchell, K. J., 121

Mixed-purposes portfolio, 27–29

Moe, T., 210, 302

Mones, L., 53–54

*Mongitore v. Regan*, 314

Monk, D. H., 269

Morine-Dershimer, G., 236

Morris, A. K., 3

Morrison, F., 394

Moss, P., 100, 101, 356

Moss, P. A., xi, 99, 100, 355, 356, 357, 360, 366, 370–371, 372

*Mount Healthy City School District v. Doyle*, 327

Moyer, P. S., 92

Mulhern, J., 203

Murnane, R. J., 204, 262, 271

Murphy, P. K., 150

*Mustafa v. Clark County School District*, 325

MyTeachingPartner (MTP), 80

**N**

Nagle, J. F., 116

*Nation at Risk, A*, 10, 378, 383

*Nation Prepared, A: Teachers for the 21st Century, A* (Carnegie Commission report), 10, 383

National Association of State Directors of Teacher Education and Certification Knowledge Base Portal, 135

National Board for Professional Teaching Standards (NBPTS), 1, 10, 12, 13, 15, 172–173, 239–240, 283, 283–296, 284, 287, 293–294; assessments, 286; birth of, 284–286; certification standards, 285–286;

core propositions of, 286; creation of, 383–384; education reform, 286–287; founding board, 284–285; national voluntary certification, 286–287; scoring, objectivity in, 243–245; system-within-the-nonsystem, creation of, 384; teacher/learning, advancing the quality of, 287

National Commission on Excellence in Education, 10, 383

National Council for Accreditation of Teacher Education (NCATE), 12, 15, 43, 70, 99, 379

National Research Council, 358, 385, 399

Naumberg, Margaret, 52

Nelson, B. S., 339

Nettles, D. H., 14

Nevada Revised Statutes, 313

New accountability, 251–254, 275

New teacher accountability policies, 252

New teacher assessments, 165–199; nature/frequency/timing of, 177–182; purposes of, 173–174

New Teacher Center, 168, 173–177, 179, 180, 195, 196; Continuum of Teacher Development, 74; Formative Assessment System (FAS), 168, 173, 177, 182–185, 187–190, 192–194

Newman, F. M. & Associates, 246

Neyman, J., 254

Nichols, S., 221

No Child Left Behind Act (NCLB), 124, 135, 165, 251, 294, 297, 299, 396; public accountability requirements for, 297, 308

Norman, A. D., 104

Nye, B., 5, 253

**O**

Objective evaluation forms, 230–231

Objectivity theme, teacher perceiver interviews (TPIs), 155

Observation-based assessment, 73–83; assessor training, 74; discussion of, 82–83; indispensable nature of, 74

Observation-based research tools, 79–82; Classroom Assessment Scoring System (CLASS), 80–81; Instructional Quality Assessment (IQA), 81–82

Observation-based teacher education tools, 75–79; Praxis III (Educational Testing Service), 78–79; Teacher Work Sample Methodology (TWSM) observation component, 77–79; Washington Performance-Based Pedagogy Assessment (PPA), 75–77

Odden, A., 166, 170, 171, 172, 174, 178, 179, 195, 298, 387

Office of the Superintendent of Public Instruction, 75

Ohio Legislative Service Commission, 79

Olafson, L., 3

Olsen, R. J., 204

Omaha Teacher Interview, 154

On-demand performance tasks, 83–88; Central Connecticut State University's Mid-Point Assessment Task, 84–86; discussion of, 88; Western Oregon University Cook School District Simulation, 86–87

Orland-Barak, L., 14, 16

Osguthorpe, R. D., 3

Outcome-based accountability, 252

Ownby, L., 170

**P**

Pace, R. R., 142

Pacheco, A., 366

PACT, *See* Performance Assessment for California Teachers (PACT)

Paek, P., 177, 178, 192, 195, 196

Palmer, D., 150, 154

*Palmer v. Board of Education of City of Chicago*, 326

Pankratz, R., 103, 104

Pankratz, R. S., 103

Paper people: teacher applicants as, 149; use of term, 151

PAR, *See* Peer assistance and review (PAR) programs

Pardieck, S. C., 14

*Parducci v. Rutland*, 326

Pathwise/Danielson Framework for Teaching, 167, 173–175, 177–180, 179–180, 182–183, 185, 187, 192–195; assessment activities, 178; and teacher quality, 189–190

Patry, F. L., 58

*Paul v. Davis*, 305

Paxton, S., 194

Pearson, G.H.J., 56

Pease, S. R., 211

Pecheone, R., 100, 101, 110, 117

Pecheone, R. L., xii, xix, 69, 166, 181

Pecheone, R. R., 110, 111, 125

Pcck, C., 118, 123

Peer assistance and review (PAR) programs, 168, 173, 177, 180–181, 194, 206, 208, 218–219; and teacher quality, 190–191

Pelletier, L., 194

Performance Assessment for California Teachers (PACT), 108–119, 122–123; bias reviews and analysis, 110–111; defined, 108; design, 109; development of, 108–109; funding of, 108–109; PACT Embedded Signature Assessments (ESAs), 109, 118–119, 120; PACT Teaching Event, formative potential of, 111–118,

120; scoring system, 109–110; technical quality, 110

Performance-based assessments, 69–132; current state of the field, 72–73; observation-based assessment, 73–83; on-demand performance tasks, 83–88; purpose of, 70–72

Performance rubrics, 244–245

Perry, D., 286, 288

*Perry v. Sinderman*, 305

Personal assessments, 72

Personality: scientific assessment of, 48–51; selecting teachers based on, 56–59

Personality assessment, 48–51; history of the science and psychology of, 43–44; maladjusted personality traits, 46–47; and teacher preparation/teacher quality improvements, 51–56

Personality development research, 48

Personnel evaluation standards, 310: applying, 350–351; development of, 341–344

*Personnel Evaluation Standards* (Joint Committee on Standards for Educational Evaluation), 337–339

Peske, H. G., 3

Pestalozzi, Johnann, 44–45

Peter, M. G., 14

Peterson, D., 236, 237, 271

Peterson, K. D., 205

Peterson, M., 82

Petrill, M., 378

Petrina, S., 53

Petrosky, A. R., xii, xviii, xix, 9

Pianta, R., 80, 81, 218, 272, 394

Pianta, R. C., 80

*Pickering v. Board of Education*, 326

Piety, P. J., 372

Plake, B. S., 121, 136

Plan-teach-reflect-act process, 170

Player, D., 205

Podgursky, M., 298

Pogodzinski, B., xii, 165, 192

Pohland, P. A., 230

Ponte, E., 177, 178, 192, 195, 196

Porter, A. C., 166, 170–172, 174, 178, 179, 184, 382

Portfolio assessments, 93–121; of experienced teachers, 24–27

Portfolios, 9–42, 92–93; adoption recommendations, 37; advocacy for the use of, 11–12; as basis for awarding national certification, 26; case examples of portfolio practice, 27–36; claims made about, 20–21; common features of, 93; differences in, 93–94; extensive use of, 9; future of, in preservice teacher education, 36–39; learning from the cases, 33–36; legal and psychometric issues in using, 94–95; mixed-purposes portfolio, 27–29; personalization of, 24; philosophy statements in, 34; portfolio assessments of experienced teachers, 24–27; portfolio literature, learning from, 13–24; practices, differences in, 15–20; proliferation of, 11; and reflection focused on content and pedagogy, 37–38; retrospective on, 10–13; single-purpose learning portfolio, 29–33; structured, 94, 98–121; as summative evaluation tools, 94; support/guidance, 34–35; unstructured, 94–98; use in teacher education programs, 12

Pounder, D. G., 152

Praxis III (Educational Testing Service), 78–79, 140–142; analytical rubrics, 78; teacher learning, impact on, 79; teacher performance assessment criteria, 78; technical quality, 79

Preemployment decisions of school administrators, 152–153

Preservice teacher education: future of portfolios in, 36–39; portfolio assessments of experienced teachers, 24–27; portfolios, 9–42

Prestine, N. A., 339

*Principles and Procedures for Teacher Selection* (American Association of Examiners and Administrators of Educational Personnel), 57

*Process-product studies*, 382

*Professional Standards Commission v. Denham*, 319

Propriety standards, 345–346; legal issues within, 345; P1–Service Orientation, 345; P2–Appropriate Policies and Procedures, 345; P5–Comprehensive Evaluation, 346; P7–Legal Viability, 346

Public values, accommodating, 227–230

Published research, reviewing, 158–159

Pullin, D., xii–xiii, xix, 297, 302, 322

Putnam, W., 123

Putz, P., 364, 365, 368

## Q

Quality control device: teacher assessment as, 1–2

## R

*Rafael v. Meramec Valley R-III Board of Education*, 321

Ramirez, A., 341

Rapport drive theme, teacher perceiver interviews (TPIs), 155

Raths, L., 53

Raudenbush, S. W., 258, 358, 359

Ravitch, D., 45, 49, 50, 59

Reading, Writing, Spelling Analysis Task (George Mason University), 91–92; candidate learning, impact on, 92; technical quality, 92

Reavis, W. C., 229

Reckase, M., 267

Recruitment: and teacher quality, 3

Reese, J. P., xiii, 283

Reese, W. J., 50

Rehabilitation Act of 1973, 324

Renaissance Teacher Work Sample (RTWS), 103–105; candidate learning, impact on, 104–105; development of, 103; teaching dimensions for assessment, 103; technical quality, 103–104

Research-based teacher evaluation (RBTE), 236–239, 236–240; criticisms of, 236–237

Resnick, L., 246

Resnick, L. B., 81

Reynolds, E. J., 57

Rice, J. M., 203

Richardson, V., xviii, 171, 172, 208, 272, 287

*Richardson v. Newburgh Enlarged City School District*, 324

Richert, A. E., 19, 23, 38, 95

Rike, C. J., 43

Rivers, J. C., 201, 253, 338, 351

Rivkin, S. G., 133, 139, 205, 253, 273, 387

Rivlin, H., 54

Robinson, B., 46

Robinson, D. Z., 121, 136

Robinson, V.M.J., 339, 340

Robyn, A., 397

Rocchio, P. D., 53

Rockoff, J. E., 133, 139, 201

Rogers, D., 47

Role-playing, employment interviews, 151–152

Ronfeldt, M., 369

Rorschach test, 48

Rosaen, C., 3

Rosenberg, S., 399

Rosenshine, B., 234, 235, 238–239, 245
Rossi, R., 144
Rotberg, I. C., 95
Roth, J., 215
Rothertham, A. J., 204, 291
Rothman, R., 217, 218, 219, 339, 341
Rothstein, J., 215, 266, 269–270, 274, 399
Rothstein, R., 216, 255
Rowan, B., 253, 272, 338
Rowe, K., 340
Roy, A. D., 254
RTWS, *See* Renaissance Teacher Work Sample (RTWS)
Rubenstein, B. O., 56
Rubin, D. B., 254
Ruscoe, G., 95–96
Russell, J. L., 397
*Russell v. Special School District No. 6*, 306
Rutledge, S. A., 144
Ryan, C. W., 14
Ryans, D. G., 57, 229, 234

## S

Salzman, S. A., 93, 101, 104
Sander, W., 133, 253, 274
Sanders, J. R., 337, 350
Sanders, W., 257, 276, 288
Sanders, W. L., 201, 253, 273, 338, 351
Sass, T., 252, 267, 269, 270–271, 278
Sass, T. R., 257, 259, 267, 272, 274, 399
Sawchuk, S., 299, 310
Sawyer, E. A., 139
Saxton, A., 257
Scates, D. E., 53
Schacter J., 389–390
Schafer, W. D., 267
Schalock, H. D., 78, 101, 102
Schalock, M., 101, 102

Schalock, M. D., 78, 101, 102
*Scheelhaase v. Woodbury Central Community School District*, 318
Schellhammer, F. M., 52
Schilling, S. G., 272
Schlechty, P. C., 204
Schmidt, W. D., 157
Schmidt, W. H., 267, 378, 382
Schmitt, N., 150
Schneider, B., 171
Schön, D., xx
Schön, D. A., 21
*School Committee of Lowell v. Oung*, 304, 316
*School District No. 1, City and County of Denver v. Cornish*, 321
*School District of Beverly v. Geller*, 304, 307
*School Executive*, 58
Schools and Staffing Survey, 142
Schraw, G., 3
Schunck, J., 203
Schutz, A. M., 99, 100, 360
Schwab, R. S., 3
Schwille, J. R., 382
*Scoggins v. Board of Education*, 306
Scott, C. W., 202
Scott-Hendrick, L., 178, 192
Seashore Louis, K., 339
*Second Handbook of Research on Teaching* (Rosenshine/Furst), 234–235
Sedlak, M., 45, 57
Sefotr, N., 178, 179, 180, 183, 185, 192
Selection Research Incorporated, 155
Senesky, S., 178, 179, 180, 183, 185, 192
Sentner, S., 21
Seroussi, M., 101
Setodji, C., 257, 273
Sexton, S., 203
Shahan, E., 369

Shainker, S., 90, 91

Shaklee, B. D., 69

Shanker, A., 284

Sharp, L. K., 43

Shavelson, R. J., 103, 125

Shaw, P., 93

Shepard, L. A., 171

*Sherrod v. Palm Beach County School Board*, 320

Shulman, L., 95, 218, 383

Shulman, L. S., 10, 12, 21, 245, 246

Siddle, J., 14, 17, 18, 19, 20, 21

Sienty, S., 71

Silva, E., 204

Simmons, J. E., 156

Simon, A., 234, 235

Simulated interviews, 151–152

Singer, J. D., 204

Sinnema, C.E.L., 339, 340

Sixteen Factor Personality Test (Cattell), 48

Sklar, K. K., 44

Slater, S. C., 82

Sleep, L., 368

Sloan, T., 118

Smith, B. O., 234, 236, 237

Smith, K., 14

Smith, T., 3, 240

Snyder, J., 18, 21, 22, 23, 37, 39, 95, 97–98

Snyder, Lippincott, and Bower, 18

Soar, R. S., 235

Sound systems of evaluation, attributes, 344–350

Southeast Center for Teaching Quality, 293

Spaulding, R. L., 235

Spencer, D., 46, 55

Spitzer, M., 308

*Springgate v. School Committee of Mattapoisett*, 323

*St. Louis Teachers Union, Local 420, American Federation of Teachers,*

*AFL-CIO v. Board of Education of the City of St. Louis*, 317

St. Maurice, H., 93

Staiger, D., 289, 290, 390, 391, 392, 393, 396, 397, 398

Staiger, D. O., 201, 212, 213, 216, 217, 219, 252, 254, 272, 278

Standards for Educational and Psychological Testing, 356

Stansbury, K., 71, 166

Star, S. L., 357, 366, 367, 372

State testing systems, 134

Stecher, B. M., 397

Stedman, P., 194

Steele, M., 82

Steffes, L., 194

Stein, M. K., 82

Steward, R. B., 308

Stewart, H., 304

Stewart, H. A., 52

Stigler, J. W., 246

Stone, B. A., 95

Stone, J. E., 288

Stout, R. A., 51

Strauss, R. P., 139

Strike, K., 309

Strong Vocational Interest Blank, 48

Stronge, J. H., 93, 95, 338

Stroot, S., 194

Stroup, W. M., 399

Structured interviews, 150

Structured portfolios, 98–121; California Teaching Performance Assessment, 105–108; defined, 94; discussion of, 119–121; examples, 98; INTASC Teaching Portfolio, 99–101; Performance Assessment for California Teachers (PACT), 108–119; Renaissance Teacher Work Sample (RTWS), 103–105; teacher work sampling, 101–103

Student achievement, *See* and IEP team: assessing teachers' contributions to, 251–282; new teacher accountability policies, 252; outcome-based accountability, 252; and standardized and outcome-based incentives, 251–252; Teacher Incentive Fund program, 252; teacher value-added (VA) measures, 252

Stufflebeam, D., 79, 234, 337

Sullivan, J. H., 14

Summers, A. A., 139

Sunstein, C., 308

Sutherland, L. M., 360

Sutherland, P., 174, 176, 196

Sykes, G., xiii, xix, 201, 211

Sykes, Gary, 10

Symonds, P. M., 52, 53, 55, 57

Szczesiul, E., 176

**T**

Tanner, William, 51

Taylor, L. L., 139

Teacher applicants, as paper people, 149

Teacher assessment, xvi; annual performance, 224–249; contribution to improvements in the quality, 1–2; contributions of, to quality of workforce, 1–2; disposition, 43–65; evaluation at the preservice level, approaches to, 70; fostering change in, 122; National Board for Professional Teaching Standards (NBPTS), 286; performance-based, 69–132; and students' role in learning, 2; and teacher quality, 5–6; and teaching task, understanding of, 2; uncertain relationship between teacher quality and, 1–6; university-based approaches to, strength of, 69–70; volume of, 1

Teacher Assessment Project (TAP) (Stanford University), 10–11

Teacher education: curriculum-embedded assessments, 69; perspectives for promoting organizational change in, 122; programs, 1

Teacher Education Initiative (TEI), 367–371; annotated exemplars of practice, development of, 369; goals for assessment component of, 367; high-leverage practices, identification of, 368; learning and assessment activities, staged over time, development of, 368; learning trajectories descriptions within high-leverage domains, 369–370; questions about general/immediate contexts, development of, 369; shared language for guiding and analyzing a practice, development of, 368–369

Teacher educators, 4–5

Teacher effectiveness: use of term, 220

Teacher evaluation: accuracy standards, 349–350; establishing, to support teacher quality, 338–341; feasibility standards, 348–349; personnel evaluation standards, applying, 350–351; personnel evaluation standards, development of, 341–344; propriety standards, 345–346; setting standards for, 337–353; sound, defined, 337–338; sound systems of evaluation, attributes of, 344–350; utility standards, 346–348

Teacher Incentive Fund program, 252

Teacher induction: formative assessments, role of, 165–199

Teacher perceiver interviews (TPIs), 153, 155–158; Teacher FIT interview, 158; TeacherInsight System, 157–158; themes, 155

Teacher preparation: and academics, 55

Teacher quality, xvi, xviii, 375–401, *See also* Tenure; and California Formative Assessment and Support System (CFASST), 188–189; correlation between teacher test performance and, 138; and credentials, 3; definitions of, 3; and Formative Assessment System (FAS) (New Teacher Center), 189–190; and formative assessments in induction, 188–191; increasing using licensure tests, 133–147; meaning of, 3–4; National Board for Professional Teaching Standards (NBPTS), creation of, 383–384; and Pathwise/Danielson Framework for Teaching, 189–190; and peer assistance and review (PAR) programs, 190–191; performance rewards, 389–390; research on, 381–383; standards of, 379–381; and student learning, 5, 387–399; subjective measures of, 397; system-within-the-nonsystem, creation of, 384–386; and teacher evaluation, 338–341; U.S. schools, uniqueness of, 375–378; use of, 3; and variation among tests, 394–395

Teacher selection: science and psychology of, 43–65

Teacher tenure, *See* Tenure

Teacher tests: and accountability, xv–xvi; idea behind, 133–134; state levels of emphasis on, 135; and student achievement, 136–141; theory behind, 136

Teacher value-added (VA) measures, 252, 252–282; background on, 253–254; defined, 252; value-added for accountability (VAM-A), 253; value-added modeling for program evaluation (VAM-P), 253–254

Teacher Work Sample Methodology (TWSM) observation component, 77–79; candidate learning, impact on, 78; instruction, basis of, 77–78; technical quality, 78

Teacher work sampling, 101–103; basis of teacher evaluations, 101–102; teacher profile, 102; technical quality, 102–103

Teacher workforce: and licensure tests, 141–143

TeacherInsight, 154, 157–158

Teachers' classroom practices: and teacher quality, 3

Teachers for a New Era project, 124

Teaching events, capturing on a form, 226–227

Teaching performance assessments (TPAs), 70–72: California TPA, 105–108; defined, 105

Teaching portfolios, *See* Portfolios

Teddlie, C., 339, 340

Teeter, M., 340

TEI, *See* Teacher Education Initiative (TEI)

Tekwe, C. D., 215

Tellez, K., 114

Tenure, 201; assessing, 201–224; brief history of, 202–204; as "complaint driven" system, 203; criticisms about incompetent teachers, history of, 203; current status of, 204–206; first state teacher tenure legislation (1909), 202; and the formation of a teaching profession, 207–210; framework for the appraisal of, 206–214; natural deselection, 205–206; as an organizational process, 210–212; perspectives on, 206; principals' escape hatches, 203; reform recommendations, 214–220; states' adoption of, 202–203; for

teacher quality control, 212–214;
unease provoked by, 204;
value-added models (VAMs),
213–214; widget effect, 203–204
Tenure-granting process: and teacher
assessment, 1
Terpstra, M., 3
Texas Appraisal System, 166–172, 176
Thompson, C. C., 144
Thompson, M., 177, 178, 192, 195,
196
Thompson v. Board of Education, 320
Thum, Y. M., 389–390
Thurstone Temperament Schedule, 48
Tillema, H., 14
Timmons, M., 14, 17, 18, 19, 20, 21
Tisadondilok, S., 76
Toch, T., 217, 218, 219, 276, 339, 341
Todd, P. E., 262
Toledo Plan, 218
Tracz, S. M., 71
Trepka v. Board of Education of the
Cleveland City School District,
325
Trow, W. C., 53
Trumbo, D., 150
Tucker, P. D., 93, 95, 205
Turner, R. L., 234
Tusin, L. F., 14, 16, 23
Twohig, P., 123
Tyack, D., 50, 59
Tyack, D. B., 45, 50, 57, 58
Tyler, F., 49–50

U
Ueno, K., 3
Ulrich, L., 150
University of Southern Maine, 96
Unstructured interviews, 150
Unstructured portfolios: defined, 94;
and formative assessment, 94–98
Urban Teacher Selection Interview,
154
Urban, W. J., 202

U.S. Department of Education,
National Center for Education
Statistics, 299, 300
U.S. Equal Employment Opportunity
Commission Uniform Guidelines for
Employee Selection, 158–159
Utility standards, 346–348; evaluator
training, 347; quality of reports,
347; constructive orientation,
346–347; follow-up and
professional development, 348;
underlying theme, 346

V
Value-added, See also Teacher
value-added (VA) measures: ad hoc
methods, 256; assumption tests,
259–260, 266–271; and causal
effects, 254–255; economic models,
260–264; economic vs. statistical
models, 265–266; estimates of
individual teacher effects, statistical
properties of, 271–274; estimating
causal effects in statistical models
for, 258–259; models and
assumptions, 255–274; statistical
methods, 256–258; for teacher
accountability, 264–265; tenure,
213–215
Value-added models (VAMs),
213–214, 387–388, 396, 398
Vance, V. S., 204
Vandergrift, N., 394
Vandervoort, L., 288
Veenman, S., 193
Veir, C. A., 306, 307, 310
Ventures for Excellence, 154
Vera, E. M., 149, 150, 151, 152, 153
Verloop, N., 14, 38
Vermunt, J., 14, 38
Videotaped interviews, 152
Vigdor, J. L., 139
Villegas, A. M., 43, 60
Von Gizycki v. Levy, 307

**W**

Wade, R. C., 14, 16, 21, 23

Wagner, R., 151

Wahlstrom, K., 339

Waller, W., 228

Walsh-Sarnecki, P., 298, 300

Waples, D., 228

*Ware v. Morgan County School District*, 320

Washington Performance-Based Pedagogy Assessment (PPA), 75–77; candidate learning/program improvement, impact on, 76–77; preservice teacher evaluation, 75; technical quality, 76

Wasley, P. A., 75

Watson, G., 52

Weaver, W. T., 3

Webb, N. M., 103, 125

Week, J., 268

Weeres, J. G., 191, 194, 208

Weick, K. E., 210, 212

Weinstein, C., 171

Weisberg, D., 203

Weisberg, Y., 81, 82

*Weissman v. Board of Education of Jefferson County School District No. R-1*, 322

Wenger, E., 22, 357, 366

WestEd, 270

Western Oregon University Cook School District Simulation, 86–87; candidate learning, impact on, 87; technical quality, 87

West's Florida Statutes Ann. § 1012.34, 304

*Whaley v. Anoka-Hennepin Independent School District. No.* 11, 307, 314, 315

*Wheeler v. Yuma School District*, 303, 316

Wheelock College Focus Child Assessment Project, 90–91; candidate learning, impact on, 91; components of, 90; weekly assignments/feedback, 90–91

Whipp, J. L., 43, 60

White, B., 100, 101, 174, 219, 241

*Whitfield v. Little Rock Public Schools*, 302

Whitford, B. L., 95–96

Whittaker, A., 114

Wiggins, G., 124

*Wilcoxon v. Red Clay Consolidated School District Board of Education*, 327

Wilder, T., 216

Wiley, E., 268

Wilkerson, J. R., 94

Willett, J. B., 204

Williams, C. O., 57, 58

Williamson, P., 358, 369

Wilson, L. A., 47

Wilson, M., 100, 101

Wilson, M. R., 368, 370

Wilson, S., xv, 275

Wilson, S. M., 182

Wilson, S. W., 100, 101

Winchell, S., xiv, xix, 201

Wineburg, M., 72

Wise, A. E., 69, 71, 166, 211

Wittek, L., 14, 15, 38

Wittrock, M. C., 246

Witty, P., 47

Witziers, B., 339

Wolf, K., 12, 14, 16, 21, 26, 38

Wolfe, B. L., 139

Wolpin, K. I., 262

Wood, C. J., 230

Woodring, Paul, 59

Wray, 14, 16, 21

Wray, S., 14, 93

Wright, O., 151

Wright, P., 276

Wright, S. P., 253, 273, 288, 338, 351

*Wright v. Mead School District No.* 354, 323

Wu, M.-J., 154, 155, 157–158

Wyatt, R. L., 14
Wyckoff, J., 139, 204–205
Wyckoff, J. H., 136, 391
Wycoff, J., 390
Wyman, R. M., 14

### Y
Yarbrough, D. B., 14, 16, 21, 23
Yost, D. S., 21
Young, I. P., 149, 152, 153, 154, 155, 156
*Young v. Palm Beach County School Board*, 320

Youngs, P., xiv, xv, 150, 165, 166, 170, 171, 172, 174, 176, 178, 179, 192, 195
Yusko, B., 193

### Z
Zeichner, K., 14, 16, 21, 93
Zeichner, K. M., 21
Zimiles, 52
Zirkel, P. A., 299, 305, 307, 310, 311, 328, 329
Zorbaugh, H., 46, 58